gilbert
LAW SUMMARIES

PROPERTY

Twelfth Edition — 1985

Jesse Dukeminier
Professor of Law
University of California,
Los Angeles

HBJ **HARCOURT BRACE JOVANOVICH LEGAL AND PROFESSIONAL PUBLICATIONS, INC.**

EDITORIAL OFFICES: 176 W. Adams, Suite 2100, Chicago, IL 60603

gilbert
LAW SUMMARIES

REGIONAL OFFICES: Chicago, Los Angeles, New York, Washington, D.C.

Distributed by: **LAW DISTRIBUTORS**   14415 S. Main Street, Gardena, CA 90248 (213) 321-3275

SERIES EDITOR
Elizabeth L. Snyder, B.A., J.D.
Attorney At Law

QUALITY CONTROL EDITOR
Ann R. Kerns, B.A.

SUMMARY OF CONTENTS

gilbert
capsule summary
property

appropriate form of action to obtain a remedy. These highly technical actions have been abolished or reformed, although their impact remains in today's concept of possession . . . . [37]

    a. **Actions to recover damages**

      (1) **Trespass:** Trespass required a showing that defendant intentionally or negligently acted to inflict a direct forcible injury to the plaintiff's property or person. The basis for a trespass action is *injury to possession*. This action included *trespass to chattels* and *trespass to land* . . . . [38]

      (2) **Trespass on the case:** Such an action would lie where one of the elements of a trespass action was missing (*e.g.,* indirect or consequential injury rather than an immediate injury) . . . . [42]

      (3) **Trover:** A suit in trover was used to recover the value of the plaintiff's *chattel* that the *defendant had converted*. Trover did not apply to trespass to land . . . . [43]

    b. **Actions to recover possession:** *Replevin* was used to recover possession of a *chattel*. *Ejectment* was used to recover possession of land . . . [45]

    c. **Modern law:** The basic difference in remedies afforded by these common law actions—the return of the thing as opposed to damages—exists today in modern codes of civil procedure . . . . [48]

2. **Defense of Jus Tertii:** The majority rule is that a defense of jus tertii (*i.e.,* only a true owner may bring suit) is not allowed. The fact that a possessor recovers *damages* from a defendant does not bar a second recovery by the true owner . . . . [49]

3. **Law and Equity:** In most jurisdictions today, law and equity courts have been merged and *legal* remedies (damages) and *equitable* remedies (*e.g.,* injunction) may be sought and applied in the same action . . . . [59]

E. BAILMENTS

1. **Definition:** A bailment is the *rightful possession* of goods by one who is *not the owner*. The true owner is a *bailor*; the person in possession is a *bailee*. A bailee must assume *actual physical control* with the *intent to possess* . . [62]

2. **Rights and Duties of Bailee**

    a. **Rights against third parties:** A bailee may collect full damages resulting from a third party's wrongdoing; the bailee is then liable to the bailor for the recovered amount. The bailor *cannot* recover from both the bailee and the third party . . . . [74]

    b. **Duty of bailee to exercise care:** The standard of care varies with the type of bailment and usually is commensurate with who gets the *benefit* of the bailment: . . . . [76]

      (1) **Sole benefit of bailee**—*extraordinary* care

      (2) **Mutual benefit of bailor and bailee**—*ordinary care* and liable for *ordinary negligence*

      (3) **Sole benefit of bailor**—only *slight care* and liable only for *gross negligence*

      (4) **Modern trend**—a standard of *ordinary care under the circumstances*

    c. **Duty to redeliver:** A bailee is held to *strict liability* for redelivery. However, an *involuntary bailee* is liable only if *negligent* in delivering the goods to the wrong person . . . . [84]

3. **Contractual Modification of Liability:** Most courts permit bailees to limit their liability by contract provisions *if the bailor consents*. However, such provisions will not relieve the bailee from *gross or willful negligence* . . . . [87]

F. ACCESSION

Accession is the improvement or augmentation of personal property of another by *labor* or *labor and new materials*. A person may lose title by the accessions of another, but is entitled to the unimproved value of property lost . . . . [89]

G. ADVERSE POSSESSION

1. **Overview**

If a landowner does not bring an action to eject an adverse possessor within the statutory period, the owner is thereafter **barred** from bringing an ejectment action .... [94]

a. **Effect:** The running of the statute of limitations not only **bars the owner's claim** to possession, but also **creates a new title** in the adverse possessor .... [95]

b. **Purpose of doctrine:** The doctrine of adverse possession protects title, bars stale claims, rewards productive use of land, and gives effect to expectations (a basic policy of property law) .... [96]

c. **Possessor's rights before acquiring title:** Before the statute of limitations runs, the adverse possessor has all the rights of a possessor, but he has **no** interest in the property valid against the true owner .... [102]

2. **Requirements of Adverse Possession:** An adverse possessor must show: . [103]

a. **Actual entry giving exclusive possession:** The community must reasonably consider the adverse possessor the owner. Constructive possession is not sufficient; actual entry on some part of the land is required . [104]

b. **Open and notorious:** The possessor must occupy the property in an open, notorious, and **visible** manner so as to give **reasonable notice** to the owner that the possessor is claiming dominion adverse to the owner's rights .... [109]

c. **Adverse and under a claim of right:** A claim of right means that the adverse possessor is acting **adversely** to the owner .... [117]

(1) **Objective test:** The state of mind of the possessor is not controlling. The possessor's **actions** must appear to the community to be acts of an owner. This test is similar to open and notorious possession . . [118]

(2) **Subjective test:** Some jurisdictions interpret claim of right to mean the possessor has a **good faith belief** that he has title .... [120]

(3) **Color of title:** A few states require an adverse possessor to have color of title (an instrument that, unknown to the possessor, is defective; *e.g.,* forged deed) .... [124]

(4) **Boundary disputes:** If a neighbor occupies adjacent land, **mistakenly** believing it to be his, the **majority** holds that he is an adverse possessor. Actual intent is not determinative (**objective test**). However, recent cases suggest that **good faith** is still relevant. The **minority** view holds that there is no adverse possession unless the neighbor has an **actual hostile intent** to claim the land .... [128]

(a) **Agreement on boundaries:** An oral agreement may fix a boundary line, and if one party acts in reliance thereon, the other party is **estopped** from denying the boundary. **Acquiescence** in a boundary over a long period is evidence of an agreement between the parties .... [134]

(5) **Special situations concerning adversity**

(a) **Landlord-tenant:** Entry made with permission cannot become adverse until the possessor (tenant) **clearly repudiates** the lease so as to give the landlord notice that she is holding adversely .... [140]

(b) **Cotenants:** A cotenant in possession does not become an adverse possessor until she ousts the other tenants and claims sole ownership .... [141]

d. **Continuous, uninterrupted possession:** Continuous possession requires only the **degree of occupancy** and use that the **average owner** would make of the property. An adverse use is continuous when it is made without a break in the essential **attitude of mind** required for adverse use. [142]

(1) **Seasonal use:** A person can be in continuous possession when she takes possession only during a particular season, if seasonal possession is how the average owner would use the property (*e.g.,*

members have vested. Thus, if the gift to one member of the class might vest too remotely, the whole class gift is void (all-or-nothing rule) . . . . [616]

6. **Remote Possibilities:** An interest is void, under the Rule, if there is *any possibility* the interest might vest beyond the permitted period (*e.g.*, the fertile octogenarian, the unborn widow) . . . . [626]

7. **Wait-and-See Doctrine:** About half the states have reformed the Rule. Under the wait-and-see doctrine, the interests are judged by *actual events*, not by possible events . . . . [632]

8. **Equitable Reformation Doctrine:** This rule, also called the cy pres doctrine, reforms an invalid interest, within the Rule's limitations, to approximate most closely the intention of the creator of the interest . . . . [639]

V. CONCURRENT OWNERSHIP

A. TENANCY IN COMMON

1. **Nature of the Tenancy:** Each tenant has an *undivided interest* in the property, including the *right to possession* of the whole. When one co-tenant dies, the remaining tenants in common have *no survivorship rights*. Equal shares are not necessary for tenants in common, and the co-tenants can own different types of estates in the same property . . . . [642]

2. **Alienability:** Each co-tenant can transfer his interest in the same manner as if he were the sole owner . . . . [647]

3. **Presumption:** Today, a tenancy in common is presumed whenever a conveyance is made to two or more persons who are not husband and wife . . [648]

B. JOINT TENANCY

1. **Nature of the Tenancy:** Joint tenants own an *undivided share* of the property and the surviving co-tenant has the right to the whole estate. The *right of survivorship* is the distinctive feature of a joint tenancy . . . . [649]

2. **Four Unities Requirement:** To be joint tenants, the tenants must take their interests (i) at the *same time*, (ii) by the *same instrument* (*title*), (iii) with *identical interests*, and (iv) with an *equal right to possess* the whole property . [654]

3. **Creation:** A joint tenancy can be created only by *express words* in an instrument . . . . [664]

4. **Severance of Joint Tenancy:** Modern law generally holds that severance of one of the four unities severs the joint tenancy and destroys the right of survivorship. It destroys the joint tenancy and creates a tenancy in common . [678]

   a. **Conveyance by joint tenant:** A joint tenant has the right to convey his interest, but by doing so he severs the joint tenancy with respect to that share . . . . [679]

   b. **Mortgage by joint tenant:** In *title theory states*, a mortgage usually conveys legal title and thus severs the tenancy. In *lien theory states* (the majority), a security interest, rather than legal title, is conveyed and a mortgage does *not* sever a joint tenancy . . . . [682]

   c. **Lease by joint tenant:** Depending upon the jurisdiction, a lease by one joint tenant *may* sever a joint tenancy, *may not* sever, or may *temporarily* sever for the duration of the lease . . . . [685]

   d. **Agreement among joint tenants:** Joint tenants can agree that one tenant has the right to exclusive possession without severance . . . . [688]

   e. **Other situations:** *Divorce* usually terminates a joint tenancy as does *simultaneous death*. Where one joint tenant *murders* the other, a severance occurs in some states. Other jurisdictions hold that no severance occurs; rather, courts award the victim's heirs everything except the murderer's life interest in half the estate . . . . [689]

5. **Avoidance of Probate:** Joint tenancy avoids probate since there is no need to change title at a joint tenant's death . . . . [692]

6. **Abolition of Joint Tenancy:** A few states have abolished joint tenancy . . [693]

VII. TRUSTS, CONDOMINIUMS, COOPERATIVES

A. THE TRUST

B. CONDOMINIUMS

of one unit in a development, with the **common areas** (e.g., halls, elevators) owned by all of the unit owners as **tenants in common** . . . . [838]

3. **Creation of a Condominium:** A condominium is usually created by a **declaration or master deed** which in many states must be recorded. All unit owners are members of an unincorporated **membership association** run by an elected board of directors, empowered to promulgate condominium rules. The board or a professional manager runs the condominium. Each purchaser of an **individual unit** is given a **deed** transferring title to him or her . . . . [846]

4. **Administration of Common Area:** Unit owners are liable for their shares of common **maintenance** expenses. **Improvements and renovation** costs are usually assessed as provided in the declaration or bylaws. Unit owners are jointly liable for injuries occurring in the common areas . . . . [853]

5. **Restrictions on Transfer:** Restrictions on transfer of the fee simple might be invalid unless carefully worded and reasonable (e.g., no racial discrimination) . . [858]

C. COOPERATIVES

1. **Introduction:** A cooperative apartment house is owned by a corporation whose stock is owned by the tenants. Thus, the residents are **both tenants** (under leases from the corporation) **and owners** of the cooperative corporation. The building has **one mortgage**; if one tenant defaults, the others must pay that share or face foreclosure. Taxes, maintenance, and repairs of the common areas are usually the responsibility of the corporation . . . . [866]

2. **Restrictions on Transfer:** Generally, both the lease and stock interest are subject to restrictions on transfer (e.g., consent of board of directors to transfer, right of first refusal by board). Racial restrictions are **not** valid . . [870]

3. **Termination of Lease:** A tenant's lease may be terminated by the corporation if the tenant fails to pay his assessed share or violates rules of conduct established by the corporation . . . . [875]

4. **Advantages:** Tenants **control** standards of maintenance and conduct. And if the value of the land rises, the **capital gain** accrues to the tenant-owners in the form of a rise in stock value. Furthermore, property taxes and mortgage interest are proportionately deductible on **income taxes** . . . . [880]

VIII. LANDLORD AND TENANT

A. INTRODUCTION

1. **Background:** Landlord-tenant law developed out of the feudal relationship between a landlord and his tenant farmer, and thus imposed few duties on the landlord. The modern trend is to adapt the law to the needs of the urban tenant. Today, a lease creates an estate in land (i.e., a **chattel real**). It is **both** a conveyance of an estate in land and a contract containing promises, which until recent times were independent; if one party breached, the other was still required to perform. Traditionally, property law was dominant; upon buying an estate in land, a tenant assumed the risks of caring for the land. During recent years, contract principles have become more important . . . . [884]

2. **Lease Distinguished From Other Relationships:** A tenant has the right to **possession**; this distinguishes the lease from other relationships . . . . [890]

   a. **Oil and gas lease:** Such a lease grants a profit or ownership of minerals in place and does not create a leasehold . . . . [896]

   b. **Billboard lease:** A billboard lease creates an easement which gives the lessee a right to **use** . . . . [897]

   c. **Lodging agreements:** These may create a license (e.g., hotel guest) or a lease (e.g., when lodger furnishes the place) . . . . [898]

B. TYPES OF TENANCIES AND THEIR CREATION

1. **Tenancy for Years:** A tenancy for years is an estate with a beginning and end **fixed** from the outset. Usually a **calendar period** is used (e.g., one year; two months). A tenancy for years differs from all other tenancies in that it has a

a. **Advertising:** Discriminatory advertising is prohibited .... [963]

b. **Exemptions:** There are certain specified exemptions from the Act: a single-family dwelling rented by the owner; four units or less where one is occupied by the owner ("Mrs. Murphy" exception); private clubs; and religious organizations .... [964]

c. **Enforcement:** Several remedies are provided including suit in federal court .... [970]

4. **Proving Discrimination:** Proof of discriminatory intent is not necessary; *discriminatory impact* is sufficient .... [974]

5. **State Statutes:** Many states also have statutes prohibiting discrimination in the sale or rental of housing on the basis of race and other grounds ... [977]

D. LANDLORD'S DUTY TO DELIVER POSSESSION

1. **Legal Right to Possession:** A landlord has the duty of delivering to the tenant the legal right to possession. If another person has *paramount title*, the landlord is in default and the tenant can terminate the lease, recover damages, or receive rent abatement .... [979]

2. **Actual Possession:** In most states, the landlord has the duty to deliver actual possession at the beginning of the lease. If a previous tenant does not get out in time, the landlord is in default. The minority hold that there is no duty to deliver actual possession; rather, the tenant has the burden of ejecting the hold-over tenant .... [983]

E. LANDLORD'S DUTY NOT TO INTERFERE WITH TENANT'S QUIET ENJOYMENT

1. **Covenant of Quiet Enjoyment:** A tenant has a right of quiet enjoyment of the premises without interference by the landlord. If not expressed in the lease, such a covenant is always implied .... [991]

2. **Actual Eviction:** If a tenant is evicted from the *entire* premises by anyone, the tenant's rent obligation terminates .... [994]

a. **Partial eviction:** If the tenant is evicted from all or *any* portion of the leased premises by the *landlord*, his rent obligation *abates entirely* until possession is restored to him. (Tenant may stay in possession without paying rent.) If the tenant is partially evicted by a third party with *paramount title*, tenant can terminate the lease, recover damages, or receive a proportionate rent abatement .... [995]

3. **Constructive Eviction:** If a landlord *substantially* interferes with a tenant's *enjoyment* of the premises without actually evicting the tenant, the tenant can claim constructive eviction and *vacate* the premises (*e.g.*, where water floods basement office) .... [999]

a. **Remedy:** A tenant's only remedy is to *move out* within a *reasonable time* and claim damages .... [1007]

b. **Acts of other tenants:** A tenant cannot claim a constructive eviction because of wrongful acts of a third person. However, a developing trend holds a landlord responsible for other tenants' acts if the landlord has the legal ability to correct the conditions and fails to do so .... [1012]

F. LANDLORD'S DUTY TO PROVIDE HABITABLE PREMISES

1. **Landlord's Duty at the Inception of the Lease**

a. **Common Law:** At common law, there is no implied covenant by the landlord that the premises are habitable or are fit for the purposes intended (caveat lessee) .... [1019]

(1) **Exceptions:** The three recognized exceptions to the above rule are: a *furnished house for a short term* (*e.g.*, summer cottage); *hidden defects known* to the landlord; and a building under *construction* .. [1020]

b. **Modern trend—implied covenant of habitability:** Many recent cases imply a *covenant of initial habitability* and fitness in leases of urban buildings, including apartments. This covenant may not apply to *commercial leases* [1025]

(1) **Remedies:** For the breach of the covenant, a tenant has contract

remedies of damages, restitution, and rescission. And a tenant may be able to use the rent for repairs or may withhold rent ...... [1032]

    c. **Statutory duties:** By statute, many states have imposed a duty of habitability before landlord leases the premises .... [1037]

    d. **Illegal lease:** A lease of premises which the *landlord knows* are in substantial violation of the housing code is illegal *if* the code prohibits rental of property in violation of the code. If the lease is illegal, the covenant to pay rent cannot be enforced .... [1038]

  2. **Landlord's Duty to Repair After Entry by Tenant**

    a. **Common law:** At common law, the landlord has *no duty* to maintain and repair the premises. If such a duty is expressed in the lease, the covenant to repair is *independent* of the tenant's covenant to pay rent. Upon the landlord's breach, the tenant must continue to pay rent and can sue for damages or specific performance .... [1041]

    b. **Modern trend—implied covenant of habitability:** Many recent cases have *implied* a *continuing covenant of habitability* and repair in urban leases. Contrary to common law, a tenant's covenant to pay rent is dependent upon the landlord's performance of his covenant .... [1044]

      (1) **Commercial leases:** A few cases have implied the covenant where it appears the commercial tenant has bargained for continuing maintenance (more likely for a single office than the entire building) [1047]

      (2) **Remedies for breach:** The tenant may *terminate* and recover *damages; repair and deduct* the repair costs; or receive a *rent abatement* .... [1052]

      (3) **Defense to landlord's rent action:** Since these are dependent covenants, a tenant can use a landlord's failure to repair as a defense in an action by the landlord for rent or eviction for nonpayment of rent, but not in any other eviction action ..... [1064]

      (4) **Waiver by tenant:** Clauses in a lease waiving the landlord's obligations under the implied covenant of habitability are generally not permitted .... [1066]

    c. **Statutory duties of landlord:** In some states, landlords have statutory duties of repair and maintenance, and tenants are given various remedies for breach (*e.g.*, repairing and deducting costs, rent withholding) ... [1069]

    d. **Retaliatory eviction:** Some recent cases hold that a landlord cannot evict a tenant in retaliation for an exercise of statutory rights that depend upon private initiative for their enforcement .... [1078]

G. LANDLORD'S TORT LIABILITY

  1. **Introduction:** At common law, with a few recognized exceptions, a landlord had no duty to make the premises safe. The tenant took the premises as is, and after taking possession the tenant was responsible for tort injuries . . [1092]

  2. **Dangerous Condition Existing at Time of Lease:** Modern courts have tailored several exceptions to avoid the harshness of the common law rule of no landlord tort liability .... [1094]

    a. **Concealed dangerous condition (latent defect):** If a landlord *knows or should have known* of a dangerous condition and has reason to believe the tenant will not discover it, she is liable for injuries caused by the condition if she did not *disclose* it to the tenant. No liability attaches *after* disclosure to the tenant .... [1095]

    b. **Public use:** A majority of courts holds a landlord liable for injuries even when only two or three members of the public will be on the premises at one time (*e.g.*, doctor's office) *if* (i) the landlord knew or should have known of the dangerous condition; (ii) had reason to believe the tenant would not correct it; and (iii) failed to exercise reasonable care to remedy the condition. For landlord liability, the defect must have existed at the *beginning* of the lease .... [1099]

  3. **Defects Arising After Tenant Takes Possession:** Generally, a landlord has no

c. **Destruction of premises:** At common law, a tenant was still obligated to pay rent for destroyed premises. Today, most states have statutes that provide that, absent a provision to the contrary in a lease, the tenant may terminate the lease if the premises are destroyed . . . . [1165]

d. **Eminent domain**

(1) **Effect on lease:** A permanent taking of *all lease property* by condemnation *extinguishes* the leasehold, and the lessee is entitled to compensation. A *temporary* taking does *not terminate* the lease. The tenant must continue to pay rent but can recover from the government the value of the occupancy taken. If there is a *partial* taking, the lease continues and rent is *not* proportionately abated, but lessee may recover from the government . . . . [1167]

(2) **Condemnation award:** Usually, a lump sum award is given for the entire fee simple. Of this sum, the tenant receives the fair market value of the unexpired lease term; the landlord receives the rest . . . [1170]

5. **Rights and Duties Relating to Fixtures:** At common law, fixtures cannot be removed by a tenant at the end of the lease. Courts look to the nature of the article, how it is attached, and the amount of damage that would be caused by removal to determine a tenant's intention as to whether an article is a fixture . . . . [1173]

a. **Exception:** A tenant is permitted to remove *trade fixtures*, *i.e.*, those installed for the purpose of carrying on a business or trade . . . . . . [1176]

b. **Modern trend:** The modern trend is to be very liberal in permitting a tenant to remove *any* installed chattel, as long as *no substantial damage* occurs. The tenant must remove fixtures *before* the end of the lease term . [1177]

I. LANDLORD'S REMEDIES

1. **Means of Assuring Performance**

a. **Distress:** At common law, if a tenant were in arrears in rent, the landlord could enter and *seize the tenant's chattels* as security for the rent. Many states have substituted a statutory right which usually eliminates the self-help feature or requires a peaceable entry. The constitutionality of some of these distress statutes is questionable . . . . [1180]

b. **Statutory liens:** Many states have enacted a landlord's lien on a tenant's goods, giving a landlord priority over other creditors or a right to enter peaceably with a *court order* and seize tenant's goods . . . . [1184]

c. **Security deposits:** Under lease provisions, a landlord may require a security deposit from a tenant which must be returned to the tenant at the end of the lease minus any *actual damages*. Some states require the landlord to pay a tenant interest on the security deposit . . . . [1185]

d. **Rent acceleration clause:** Such a clause in the lease may, upon a tenant's default, accelerate all rents due. Thus, a landlord can sue for all rent to the end of the term and leave a tenant in possession . . . . . [1193]

e. **Waiver of service and confession of judgment:** A clause waiving a tenant's rights *without notice* is usually invalid . . . . [1196]

2. **Eviction of Tenant**

a. **For breach of covenant:** Leases usually provide that a landlord can terminate the lease upon a tenant's breach of *any* covenant. This right to terminate may be *waived* if the landlord consents to the breach (*e.g.*, acceptance of rent with knowledge of breach). For a landlord to terminate for *nonpayment of rent*, he must first make a *demand* for the rent and then give *notice* of termination . . . . [1198]

b. **Through judicial process:** Every state has a summary procedure, known as forcible entry and detainer or unlawful detainer, to evict a tenant quickly and at low cost. Usually *notice* to quit must be given, although notice may be very short (*e.g.*, three days). Generally, the only issue raised is whether the landlord or tenant has the right to possession . . . . [1205]

(1) **Defenses:** A tenant may only assert those defenses which would

entitle her to possession or which would preclude the landlord from recovering possession (*e.g.*, illegal lease, landlord refused rent). Recently, some courts have held that no rent is due where the landlord has breached a statutory duty to repair or an implied covenant of habitability . . . . [1210]

    c. **Self-help:** The majority rule is that the landlord may use ***reasonable force*** to evict a tenant without any court process, although a growing trend is to prohibit self-help . . . . [1217]

3. **Abandonment by Tenant:** A landlord has several options when a tenant wrongfully vacates the property: . . . . [1224]

    a. **Landlord terminates lease:** If a landlord accepts possession from a tenant, with intent of effecting a ***surrender***, the lease is terminated, and the tenant is liable only for rent accrued and any damages . . . . . . [1225]

    b. **Nonaction by landlord:** The landlord may leave the premises vacant and sue for rent as it comes due. The majority holds that the landlord has ***no duty to mitigate damages*** by finding another tenant. (The modern trend is contra) . . . . [1228]

    c. **Repossession and relet:** A landlord can repossess and relet, but some courts hold that this ***effects a surrender***. Other views hold that ***no surrender*** occurs if the landlord gives the tenant ***notice*** of reletting, or if the landlord otherwise shows ***intent*** not to effect a surrender . . . . . [1232]

J. ASSIGNMENT AND SUBLETTING

1. **Assignment:** Unless the lease prohibits, a tenant can assign her interest in the leasehold. Thus, the assignee comes into ***privity of estate*** with the landlord and each can sue the other on lease covenants which run with the land . . . . . [1238]

2. **Sublease Distinguished From Assignment:** Unless the lease prohibits, a tenant can sublease and thus become the landlord of the sublessee. There is ***no privity of estate*** between the sublessee and the original landlord . . . . [1241]

    a. **Reversion retained:** At common law, a sublease occurs if the tenant retains a ***reversion***; *i.e.*, the tenant is entitled to possession again before the tenant's lease expires . . . . [1242]

    b. **Right of entry retained:** If a tenant retains a ***right of entry*** upon default in rent, some cases hold that the transfer is a sublease. This is contrary to the common law rule that holds it is an assignment since no reversion was retained. Recently, a few cases have held that the ***intent*** of the parties determines whether a transfer is a sublease or assignment . . . . [1243]

3. **Duty to Pay Rent:** Generally, a landlord can sue for rent any person who is either in ***privity of contract or privity of estate*** with him . . . . [1249]

    a. **Assignment:** If there is an assignment, the landlord can sue the tenant (privity of contract) or the assignee (privity of estate). The assignee's liability ends when he reassigns to a third party . . . . [1250]

    b. **Sublease:** A sublessee is ***not*** liable to the landlord for rent . . . . [1259]

    c. **Third party beneficiary suits:** If an assignee or sublessee expressly assumes the covenants of the master lease, he is directly liable to the landlord as a third party beneficiary of the contract between the tenant and the assignee or sublessee . . . . [1261]

4. **Covenants Running to Assignees:** To run to assignees, (i) the parties must so ***intend***; (ii) must be in ***privity of estate***; and (iii) the covenant must ***touch and concern*** the interest assigned (*i.e.*, leasehold or reversion) . . . . [1263]

    a. **Covenant to do or not to do act:** A covenant by the tenant ***or*** landlord to do or not to do a physical act ***on the leased*** premises touches and concerns the ***leasehold*** and runs with it (*e.g.*, to furnish heat) . . . . [1272]

    b. **Covenant to pay money:** Such a covenant touches and concerns the land if the payment is for property improvements or if it protects the property to make it more valuable (*e.g.*, to pay taxes) . . . . [1275]

    c. **Covenant to insure:** A covenant by the ***tenant*** to insure the property touches and concerns ***if*** the landlord is required to use the proceeds for

X. RIGHTS IN THE LAND OF ANOTHER ARISING BY OPERATION OF LAW

A. NUISANCE

the invader's conduct, the **suitability** of conduct to the locality, and the **impracticability** of preventing the harm .... [1537]

    (3) **Fault:** Fault of the defendant is not controlling, but his failure to use reasonable avoidance devices is important .... [1538]

  b. **Unintentional act:** Here, unreasonableness refers to the **actor's conduct** as well as the gravity of the harm. Utility of conduct is seldom a defense [1540]

  c. **Types of unreasonable interference:** To determine whether there is a nuisance courts consider: the character of the harm, the character of the neighborhood, the social value of the conflicting uses, and priority (whether the plaintiff has come to the nuisance) .... [1541]

  d. **Compare—trespass:** Trespass is invasion of **possession;** nuisance is invasion of **use and enjoyment.** Trespass requires an **intentional entry,** whereas nuisance requires unreasonable conduct, substantial injury, and usually a balancing of the equities in plaintiff's favor. Additionally, the remedies for nuisance are more flexible than for trespass .... [1551]

  e. **Economic analysis:** Modern economic analysis considers neither party the sole cause of harm; both are responsible due to conflicting land uses. [1553]

    (1) **Coase theorem:** This provides that the **market** will move the right to act to the person who values it the most if the transaction costs are low. Transaction costs include obtaining **information** about persons with whom one must deal, **negotiations, coming to terms** with the parties, and **enforcing** the bargains .... [1557]

      (a) **Note:** If many neighbors are damaged, transaction costs will be high because of problems caused by holdouts, free riders, and strategies used by certain of the neighbors. In these cases, the right will likely stay where it was initially allocated .... [1559]

    (2) **Initial allocation:** The initial allocation of the right (*i.e.,* the entitlement) can be based on economic arguments (*e.g.,* give to **highest valued user,** thus increasing society's total wealth; **first in time prevails** because of the greater investment), or on a moral basis (*e.g.,* **wealth redistribution**; **healthy environment**) .... [1563]

  f. **Remedies:** Whether a court grants an **injunction or damages** may depend on whether transaction costs are high. If so, a court may be more likely to grant damages (*i.e.,* a forced sale of plaintiff's right to sue for nuisance at an objectively determined price) .... [1569]

3. **Public Nuisance:** A public nuisance affects the **general public.** The test for determining a public nuisance is the same as for private nuisance. Usually only public officials have the right to stop a public nuisance .... [1576]

  a. **Enforcement by private persons:** A private individual may act against a public nuisance only if he can show **special injury, different in kind** from that suffered by the public .... [1577]

B. RIGHT TO SUPPORT

1. **In General:** The right to support of one's land from the adjoining lands is an incident of ownership .... [1580]

2. **Right to Lateral Support:** The right to lateral support of land is absolute and one who violates it is **strictly** liable. The majority view does **not** extend the absolute right of lateral support to **buildings**. (But an excavator is liable for his negligence.) .... [1581]

3. **Right to Subjacent Support:** The right to subjacent support (*i.e.,* underlying support) extends to land **and** buildings .... [1587]

C. RIGHTS IN WATER

1. **Streams and Lakes**

  a. **Riparian rights:** A large majority gives an owner of land adjacent to a stream or lake riparian rights in the **quantity, quality,** *and* **velocity** of the water. However, most **pollution** problems are treated as nuisances . [1589]

    (1) **Public rights:** A riparian owner may not infringe on public rights in

cross airspace). The height at which the servitude begins is usually set by the government. The real test is whether the use of airspace **harms the surface owner** . . . . [1618]

    b.   **Noisy flights as inverse condemnation:** A continuous interference with a surface owner's use of his land may result in **inverse condemnation** . . . [1619]

    c.   **Noisy flights as a nuisance:** In other cases, noise pollution from aircraft is classified as a nuisance for which **damages** will lie; an **injunction** is **not** applicable. Under a nuisance theory, neighboring landowners may recover and nongovernmental entities (*e.g.,* airlines) may be sued . . [1623]

  2. **Solar Enjoyment:** Jurisdictions are split as to whether a cause of action will lie for a blocking of sunlight. Courts would probably give more protection to solar collectors than swimming pools . . . . [1627]

  3. **Weather Modification:** A landowner can enjoin weather modification (*e.g.,* cloud seeding) in airspace over his land . . . . [1629]

XI. PUBLIC LAND USE CONTROLS

A. ZONING

  1. **Theory of Zoning:** Zoning purports to prevent harm from incompatible uses by dividing a city into zones. Modern zoning also regulates uses to achieve public benefits or to maximize the tax base . . . . [1630]

    a.   **Separation of uses:** Single family homes are deemed the **highest use** (least harmful), and are to be protected from lower uses such as apartments, commercial, or industrial. The principle of **cumulative uses** allows higher but not lower uses in a district. Any classification **reasonably related** to the legitimate purpose of segregating residential and commercial uses will be upheld . . . . [1631]

    b.   **Density controls:** These indirectly control the number of people using an area (*e.g.,* height limitations, lot sizes, etc.) . . . . [1636]

  2. **Source of Zoning Power:** State statutes called **enabling acts** grant authority to local governmental units (city or county) to regulate land use . . . . [1637]

  3. **Constitutional Limitations:** Zoning is a valid exercise of the police power. But it must be constitutional as applied to **each individual lot** . . . . [1639]

    a.   **Due Process Clause:** Zoning regulations are subject to the requirements of due process, both procedural and substantive . . . . [1640]

       (1) **Procedural:** **Legislative** zoning actions (enactment of ordinance for entire city) do not require notice to each landowner. **Administrative** actions (*e.g.,* variances) require individual notice . . . . [1641]

       (2) **Substantive:** A zoning regulation must bear a **rational relationship** to a permissible state objective (*i.e.,* public health, safety, and general welfare). The only time a zoning ordinance is subject to strict scrutiny is when it infringes on a fundamental right (*e.g.,* free speech). Note that housing is **not** a fundamental right . . . . [1642]

       (3) **State due process:** Unlike federal courts, state courts continue to recognize that state due process clauses have **considerable substantive content**. Thus, state courts strike down zoning regulations that are "arbitrary" or "unreasonable," even though *a* rational means of achieving the objective. State courts also require that an ordinance permit a landowner an **adequate return on his investment** [1644]

    b.   **Equal Protection Clause:** Plaintiff must prove a **discriminatory purpose or intent** (discriminatory effect is **not** enough). The rational relation test is used unless a suspect classification (*e.g.,* race) is involved . . . . [1646]

    c.   **Taking Clause:** A zoning regulation that takes property without compensation is void . . . . [1649]

    d.   **Note:** Zoning actions may also be challenged on the following bases: ultra vires, improper delegation, and possibly under the Civil Rights Act of 1871 and antitrust laws . . . . [1650]

  4. **Purposes of Zoning:** Recent litigation concerns zoning for purposes other than protecting the public health or safety . . . . [1658]

the comprehensive plan is *spot zoning* and is unlawful. Amendments are *presumptively valid*, but some recent cases shift the burden to the proponent of the amendment to show a *mistake* in the original ordinance or a *substantial change* in conditions . . . . [1693]

    b. **Variances:** A variance may be granted where ordinance restrictions cause an owner *practical difficulty* or *unnecessary hardship*. Many courts require written findings that can be scrutinized to determine whether the board abused its discretion . . . . [1698]

    c. **Special exception:** A special exception (special use) is allowed when certain conditions specified in the ordinance are met. Courts usually uphold special exceptions even where standards are unclear . . . . . . [1702]

    d. **Discretionary or non-Euclidean zoning**

       (1) **Contract zoning:** Rezoning a particular tract of land on the condition that the owner sign a contract with the city restricting the land's use has sometimes been upheld, sometimes struck down. Objections are that a city does not have the power to bargain with individual landowners, and that in effect this practice is spot zoning . . . . [1705]

       (2) **Density zoning:** Density or cluster zoning provides developers with an option to use spaces in various ways, provided a specified overall density is maintained. This use has often been upheld . . [1706]

       (3) **Floating zones:** A floating zone is a zone provided in the ordinance to which no land is assigned on the map until a landowner requests and is granted that classification. Floating zones are usually upheld [1707]

       (4) **Planned unit development:** In a PUD district (usually a large tract of land), a developer can mix uses. The test as to validity is whether such rezoning is in accordance with a comprehensive plan . . . . [1708]

    e. **Zoning by referendum:** Recently, some zoning ordinances provide that an amendment can be made only by public referendum. Even where the effect has been exclusionary, mandatory referenda have been upheld [1709]

B. SUBDIVISION CONTROL AND MAPS

  1. **Subdivision Regulations:** Unlike zoning ordinances, which regulate land use, subdivision regulations lay down *conditions for approval of a subdivision plan*. More discretion is permitted in determining whether the subdivision plans are satisfactory . . . . [1710]

    a. **Application:** Regulations that require a developer to put in paved streets, sewers, etc. are valid if reasonable. Requiring dedication for parks and schools is upheld in some states, but struck down in others on the ground that the need is not *specifically and uniquely attributable* to the developer's activity . . . . [1711]

  2. **Official Maps:** An official map, prohibiting building on land to be acquired by the city in the future, is *not* a taking unless the *owner applies for and is denied a building permit* and is thereby substantially damaged . . . . [1715]

C. EMINENT DOMAIN

  1. **In General:** Governments have the power to take title to property against the owner's will. The fifth amendment requires just compensation for a taking [1717]

  2. **What Is a "Taking"?**

    a. **Taking title:** If the government takes title to the land, it must pay for it . . [1718]

    b. **Physical invasion:** A physical invasion by the government is a *de facto taking* or *inverse condemnation* and must be paid for . . . . [1719]

    c. **Regulatory takings:** If a land use regulation is declared a taking, the regulation is *void* and enforcement is *enjoined*. Sometimes an owner sues for *damages* on a theory that an *inverse condemnation* has occurred. Courts have usually rejected this theory for regulatory takings, but recent developments indicate that damages may be allowed in the future . [1722]

       (1) **Tests of taking**

          (a) **Harm test:** Police power is validly exercised to *prevent harm* and thus no compensation need be given. But where the purpose is for a *public benefit*, a taking has occurred. The harm test is illusory unless a *neutral rule* or legislative preference is established to distinguish harm from benefit . [1728]

(b) **Test of severe economic loss:** The imposition of severe economic loss may show a taking. However, the loss can be very severe (seventy-five percent *not* a taking) before a taking is found. This test may mean that an owner must be left with *some reasonable economic value* in the property . . . . [1732]

(c) **Reciprocity test:** Regulations that involve reciprocal advantages (each of the regulated owners receives *some* advantage although not necessarily equal) are *not* a taking . . . . [1738]

(d) **Balancing test:** This test balances private loss against public gain. The trend is to look at both the *utility* of the action (economic efficiency) and its *fairness* . . . . [1739]

3. **What is Public Use?** The fifth amendment prohibits a taking of land ''. . . for public use . . .'' without just compensation. The Supreme Court has interpreted ''public use'' to mean a *public purpose* (*i.e.*, it must *benefit* the public) . . . . [1743]

a. **Urban renewal:** In urban renewal, the government exercises eminent domain and then transfers title to a private redeveloper to develop according to an urban renewal plan. It has been upheld as being for a public purpose . . . . [1745]

4. **What Is Just Compensation?**

a. **Market value:** Usually, just compensation means the market value—*i.e.*, price a willing buyer would pay a willing seller. Market value includes the value of possible *future expectations* as well as existing uses (including the value of an expected renewal of a lease) . . . . [1750]

(1) **Exception:** Where there is no relevant market such as for *special purpose property*, any just and equitable method may be used . [1752]

b. **Condemnation blight:** Value of property may decline because of the threat of condemnation before official action is actually taken. Compensation must be paid as if the value-depressing acts of the government had not occurred. If announcement of a project *increases* land values, the owner is not entitled to the increase . . . . [1756]

c. **Loss of business and goodwill:** Generally, a business on condemned land is, in itself, not taken and no compensation is necessary. The same is true as to a loss of business goodwill . . . . [1758]

d. **Partial taking:** If only part of a tract is taken, the owner is entitled to severance damages. In some states, this is difference in the value of the *entire tract* before taking and the value of the *remainder* after taking (before and after rule). Another method is to give an owner the *sum of the value* of the part taken and any *net damages* to the remainder after offsetting benefits (value plus damage rule) . . . . [1760]

XII. THE SALE OF LAND

A. THE CONTRACT FOR SALE OF LAND

1. **Broker's Role:** A broker's contract gives him the exclusive right to sell the property at the price or terms in the contract *or at any other price or terms agreed upon by the parties*. A broker earns a commission only *when the buyer pays the purchase price*. However, the seller is liable for the commission if she defaults . . . . [1764]

2. **Statute of Frauds:** The Statute requires that a contract for the sale of land be *in writing* and *signed by the party to be charged*. The writing can be informal, and may consist of several documents. It must, however, contain all the *essential terms*: *i.e.*, parties' identification; property description; and terms and conditions of the sale, including price (the *price* must be in the writing if it

and principal which are spread out over many years (*e.g.*, thirty-year mortgage). A *second mortgage* is a mortgage on the same tract of land, given after and with notice of the original mortgage. The second mortgagee's rights are *subject to* the rights of the first mortgagee; thus, since the risks are greater, second mortgages have a higher interest rate .... [1834]

    a. **Deed of trust:** In many states, the borrower transfers title to a third person *as trustee* for the lender to secure the debt. The major difference concerns the power to sell the land upon default. However, in many states, modern statutes have largely eliminated this difference ..... [1838]

    b. **Installment land contract:** A buyer may agree to pay for a land purchase over a period of years. The buyer receives possession and the seller keeps title until the last payment. Modern courts have alleviated the harshness of the rule that permitted the seller to keep both the land and all payments made upon default .... [1839]

4. **History of the Mortgage:** Originally, if the borrower did not pay *on the agreed date*, the land belonged to the lender. Equity intervened to give borrowers a right to redeem *at any time* after the agreed date. This created difficulties for the sale of the land upon default so equity then gave the lender the right to *foreclose the right of redemption*. Today, foreclosing the mortgage is a judicial proceeding involving a public sale; the equity of redemption is barred, the debt is paid, and excess proceeds are given to the borrower ...... [1840]

    a. **Equitable mortgage:** Today, some lenders use several devices to obtain a fee simple as security. Courts look to the *substance* of the transaction, and where the intent was to use land as security for a debt, a court will declare an equitable mortgage; *i.e.*, it will be *treated as a mortgage* [1841]

    b. **Statutory period of redemption:** Many states give borrowers a statutory period (*e.g.*, two years) *after judicial foreclosure* during which they can redeem the land from the foreclosure purchaser .... [1842]

5. **Theory of the Mortgage:** *Title theory* states treat legal *title* as being in the mortgagee. *Lien theory* states consider that legal title remains in the mortgagor and the mortgagee merely has a *lien* on the property ...... [1843]

6. **Transfer of the Mortgagor's Interest**

    a. **Sale subject to the mortgage:** The new buyer takes the land subject to the lien but is *not personally liable* on the debt. The original mortgagor remains personally liable. If the debt is not paid, the mortgagee may sue the mortgagor or proceed against the land by foreclosure and sale ..... [1845]

    b. **Sale with assumption of the mortgage:** If the new buyer assumes the mortgage, she becomes *personally liable* on the debt although the original mortgagor remains secondarily liable. Thus, the mortgagee can sue either person on the debt; if he sues the original mortgagor, the mortgagor can then sue the new buyer or foreclose .... [1847]

    c. **Due-on-sale clauses:** A due-on-sale clause in a mortgage provides that, at the mortgagee's election, the *entire mortgage debt* is due upon sale of the mortgagor's interest. Although controversial, most such clauses are legally enforceable .... [1849]

7. **Transfer by the Mortgagee:** A mortgagee can transfer the note *and* the mortgage (together, not separately) to another person .... [1851]

8. **Default by the Mortgagor:** Upon default, the mortgagee can sue on the debt or foreclose. A minority of states requires the mortgagee to foreclose and exhaust the security before suing on the debt. Either way, after a foreclosure sale, the mortgagee can get a *deficiency judgment* against the mortgagor for the difference between the sale proceeds and the debt amount .... [1853]

    a. **Legislation:** To protect a mortgagor in default, some states have enacted certain provisions such as fair market value requirements, no deficiency judgments on purchase money mortgages, and the statutory right of redemption .... [1854]

C. THE DEED
1. Formalities

a. **Statute of Frauds:** To transfer an interest in land, the Statute of Frauds requires a writing signed by the *grantor*. Acknowledgment is unnecessary but is required for *recordation* of the deed. A *spouse's signature* is necessary only to release certain rights in the property (*e.g.,* dower rights) . . . . [1859]

b. **Words of grant:** Technical words used at common law are not now necessary; any words indicating an intent to transfer are sufficient . [1868]

c. **Consideration:** This is *not* necessary to transfer; one may *give* land away [1870]

d. **Parts of the deed:** The usual deed sets forth the parties, consideration, words of grant, land description, the habendum clause, any exceptions or reservations, covenants, the grantor's signature, and acknowledgement . . . . [1871]

e. **Description of the grantee:** A grantee need not be actually named but must be sufficiently described so it can be determined who is intended . [1879]

   (1) **Grantee's name left blank:** Older cases would hold the deed a nullity. A majority of modern cases holds that the intended grantee is the agent of the grantor with *implied authority* to fill in the blank . [1882]

2. Description of Land Conveyed

a. **Admission of extrinsic evidence:** If the description in the deed furnishes any means of identification, the description is sufficient. Extrinsic evidence is usually admissible to clear up ambiguities but may not contradict the deed. Contradictory evidence is only admissible in a suit to reform because of mutual mistake . . . . [1884]

b. **Canons of construction:** When there is a conflicting description, preference is given in the following order: original survey monuments, natural monuments, artificial monuments, maps, courses, distances, name, and lastly, quantity . . . . [1887]

c. **Streets and railways:** Where streets or railways are used as boundaries, there is a rebuttable presumption that the *grantee's title extends to the center* of the right of way (or to the full width if the grantor owns it). The presumption is *not applicable* where a city is the grantor or if the side of the street is described as the boundary . . . . [1894]

d. **Water boundaries:** Here, a deed is usually construed to give a grantee the land under the water so as to permit access to the water . . . . [1896]

D. DELIVERY OF THE DEED

1. In General: Delivery requires words or conduct by grantor that show an *intent* to make an immediate transfer. Usually, this means a *manual transfer* of the deed, but manual transfer is unnecessary if other acts sufficiently show intent [1897]

a. **Presumptions:** Delivery is presumed: (i) if the deed is *handed* to the grantee; (ii) if it is *acknowledged* by the grantor before a notary; or (iii) if it is *recorded* . . . . [1900]

   (1) **Deeds effective at death:** If a grantor executes a deed and puts it away someplace, and it can be shown the grantor intended the deed to be legally effective *before* death, it is a validly delivered deed. If not effective until death, the deed is invalid for lack of delivery . . . . [1901]

b. **Cancellation of delivery:** After effective delivery, *title has passed* to the grantee and it cannot be revoked or passed back to the grantor without delivery of a new deed . . . . [1902]

2. Conditional Delivery to Grantee

a. **Written condition:** A deed containing a provision that it is only to take effect on the happening of a certain event may be interpreted to mean that there is *no delivery until the condition happens* (a nullity); or it may be interpreted to mean that the grantor intends the deed to be *immediately effective, but it is passing only an interest subject to a condition* *precedent* (grantee receives a *springing executory interest*). The words of condition are crucial if the deed is not to be held invalid as a will substitute on the basis of no delivery .... [1903]

    (1) **Power to revoke:** If the grantor retains the power to revoke the deed, the courts are split as to whether effective delivery has occurred .... [1907]

  b. **Oral condition:** If delivery is made to the grantee upon an oral condition, the delivery is good and the *condition is void* .... [1909]

3. **Deed in Escrow:** A deed delivered in escrow with oral conditions attached is valid and the oral condition is also valid. However, if the instructions retain a *power to revoke* in the grantor, the escrow is invalid and no delivery occurs since the agent is then considered to be solely the agent of the grantor ..... [1912]

  a. **Commercial escrow:** A commercial escrow agent is a fiduciary for *both* parties. Therefore, written instructions are binding on the grantor. But where the instructions are *oral,* the grantor may recall the deed while still in the agent's hands, *unless* there is a *written contract of sale* ... [1918]

  b. **Relation-back doctrine:** When there is a valid delivery in escrow, upon subsequent delivery to the grantee by the escrow agent ("second delivery"), the *title relates back to the first delivery* if "equity and justice require" .... [1923]

4. **Estoppel of Grantor:** When the grantor voluntarily gives possession of a deed to the grantee (*e.g.,* to examine it), and the grantee conveys to a BFP, the grantor may be *estopped* to deny delivery on a theory of negligent entrustment. Where a grantor puts a deed into escrow and a grantee wrongfully obtains possession of the deed and then conveys to a BFP, the cases are evenly split as to whether grantor is or is not estopped ..... [1930]

E. SELLER'S WARRANTIES

1. **Covenants of Title:** Covenants of title in the deed govern the scope of a seller's liability; *no* covenants of title are implied .... [1935]

  a. **Types of deeds**

    (1) **General warranty deed:** This usually contains all six of the usual covenants (*see* below) and warrants title against defects arising *before* as well as *during* the time the grantor has title. A *special warranty deed* contains all six of the covenants, but covers only defects arising *during* the grantor's tenure .... [1937]

    (2) **Quitclaim deed:** A quitclaim deed contains no warranties ...... [1939]

  b. **Covenants for title in warranty deeds:** The six usual covenants are: [1941]

    (1) Covenant of *seisin* (grantor is owner);

    (2) Covenant of *right to convey*;

    (3) Covenant *against encumbrances*;

    (4) Covenant of *quiet enjoyment*;

    (5) Covenant of *warranty* (*i.e.,* grantor will defend grantee against any lawful claims existing at time of transfer); and

    (6) Covenant of *further assurances* (grantor will perfect grantee's title, if necessary).

  c. **Merger of contract into deed:** Once the buyer accepts a deed, the contract merges into the deed, and the buyer can sue only on the warranties in the deed .... [1948]

  d. **Breach of covenants**

    (1) **Present covenants:** These are breached *when made,* if at all, and include the covenants of *seisin, right to convey, and against encumbrances.* The majority rule is that the covenants of seisin and against encumbrances are breached even if the *grantee knew* of the defect. Present covenants *do not run with the land* and cannot be enforced by a remote grantee .... [1949]

    (2) **Future covenants:** Covenants of *quiet enjoyment, warranty, and further assurances* are breached when the grantee is actually or

constructively **evicted.** Knowledge of the defect by the grantee is **no defense.** A future covenant **runs with the land** if there is **privity of estate** between the original grantor-covenantor and the remote grantee. This means the covenantor conveyed either **title or possession** to his grantee, who conveyed it to the remote grantee . [1956]

    (3) **Damages for breach:** The grantee cannot recover more than the covenantor received as consideration. If the land is a **gift,** some courts allow no recovery for breach; other courts allow the grantee to recover the market value at the time the covenant is made . [1965]

        (a) **Covenant of seisin:** If title to the entire tract fails, the grantee may recover the full purchase price. If there is a **partial breach,** the grantee may recover damages proportionate to that part of land to which title fails. Or, if the grantee receives good title to a part that is not usable, he can rescind and recover the entire purchase price . . . . [1969]

        (b) **Covenant against encumbrances:** If the encumbrance is not removable, damages are the difference in value of the land with and without the encumbrance. If the grantee can remove the encumbrance, damages are the cost of removal. If the grantee does not remove a removable encumbrance, he is entitled to only nominal damages unless he can prove actual loss . . . [1971]

        (c) **Future covenants:** For breach of a future covenant, a grantee receives his purchase price back, not the actual market loss. Courts are split on damages for a **remote grantee:** Some give a remote grantee out-of-pocket losses; others give what the covenantor received if it is more than his out-of-pocket loss . . [1972]

  e. **Estoppel by deed:** Where a grantor purports to convey land he does not then own, and subsequently he acquires title, title passes to the grantee **under the earlier deed** . . . . [1974]

2. **Liabilities for Defects in Houses**

  a. **Builder's liability:** Contrary to common law, most jurisdictions now imply a **warranty of habitability** in the sale of **new homes;** i.e., the builder warrants the building is free from defective materials and is properly constructed. Some courts apply this warranty on a tort theory, and it runs to **all persons** who buy the product. Liability cannot be waived and runs from the time the defect is discovered. Other courts use a contract theory wherein the warranty runs only to those in privity of contract to the builder, and it begins to run from the date of conveyance. The implied warranty of habitability has **not** yet been extended to the sale of commercial buildings . . . . [1977]

  b. **Lender's liability:** Lenders may be liable for defective housing where the lender exercises substantial control over the builder . . . . [1982]

  c. **Seller's liability:** A seller of a used house who is not a builder has **no liability** based on the warranty of habitability. However, she may be liable for **misrepresentation or fraud.** Modern cases hold that a seller must disclose known defects not readily discoverable by the buyer . . . . . [1983]

XIII. METHODS OF TITLE ASSURANCE

A. RECORDING SYSTEM

1. **Common Law Rule—Prior in Time:** A grantee who was **prior in time** prevailed over one subsequent in time . . . . [1984]

2. **Recording Acts:** To discourage the fraudulent acts by a grantor that the prior in time rule permitted, all states eventually enacted statutes providing for deed recordation in each county to protect a grantee from subsequent purchasers [1986]

3. **Mechanics of Recording:** Any instrument affecting title to land (e.g., mortgage) can be recorded. The grantee first files a copy with the county recorder. The recorder indexes the deed; the index book is used to find the deed in

subsequent title searches. Separate index volumes are kept for **grantors and grantees** (some urban areas index by tract, *i.e.,* blocks and lots) . . . . . . [1987]

4. **Types of Recording Acts:** There are three major types of recording acts . . . . [1999]

   a. **Race statutes:** As between two claimants, whoever **records first** wins; actual notice of prior claims is irrelevant . . . . [2000]

   b. **Notice statutes:** A subsequent purchaser is protected against a prior unrecorded instrument if he has **no actual or constructive notice** of a prior claim . . . . [2001]

   c. **Race-notice statutes:** A subsequent purchaser **without notice** is protected against a prior unrecorded instrument **only** if he records **before** the prior instrument is recorded . . . . [2002]

5. **Effect of Recordation:** Recordation protects a grantee by giving notice to all the world of the contents of the recorded instrument. It raises a **presumption** of delivery that can be rebutted, but it will **not** validate an invalid deed. Recordation also does **not** protect a grantee against interests arising by **operation of law** (*e.g.,* implied easement) . . . . [2003]

   a. **Effect of failure to record:** If a person does not record, the common law rule of *"prior in time, prior in effect"* is applicable . . . . [2007]

6. **Requirements for Recordation:** Nearly any instrument or decree affecting an interest in land can be recorded. Most states require an **acknowledgement** (some also require witnesses) for recordation . . . . [2010]

   a. **"Recordation":** To be recorded, the document must be entered in the recorder's books in accordance with the applicable statute or judicial decisions . . . . [2012]

      (1) **Recording unacknowledged instrument:** If an unacknowledged instrument is mistakenly recorded, it does **not** give constructive notice to subsequent purchasers. Where the acknowledgement is **defective** but the defect is not apparent on the face of the instrument, recordation gives constructive notice, but there is authority to the contrary . . . . [2015]

7. **Who is Protected by Recording Acts**

   a. **Purchasers:** All **purchasers** who are **without notice** and **give valuable consideration** (BFPs) are within the protection of the recording system (under race statutes, notice is irrelevant). Purchasers include **mortgagees** [2018]

      (1) **"Shelter rule":** A person who takes from a protected BFP stands in his shoes and is protected even though the person has notice of a prior unrecorded interest . . . . [2019]

      (2) **Donees:** Generally, donees are not protected . . . . [2020]

      (3) **Creditors:** There is considerable variation in the protection afforded creditors. Some acts protect creditors once they become judgment or lien creditors; other creditors gain protection only by purchasing the debtor-owner's interest at a judicial sale . . . . [2021]

   b. **Without notice:** The purchaser must be without **actual, record,** or **inquiry** notice of the prior claim **at the time he paid consideration** . . . . [2025]

      (1) **Inquiry notice**

         (a) **Quitclaim deed:** A majority of states do not require inquiry on a quitclaim deed; others are contra . . . . [2029]

         (b) **Possession:** In most states, a person is required to make inquiry of a person in possession of the land; however, some states impose a lesser inquiry burden . . . . [2031]

         (c) **Neighborhood:** In some states, a person is put on inquiry as to possible implied negative restrictions on use of the land by the looks of the neighborhood (especially subdivisions) . . . . . . [2033]

         (d) **Unrecorded instruments:** If a recorded instrument **expressly** refers to an unrecorded instrument, most states require inquiry. [2034]

   c. **Valuable consideration:** A person is not a BFP unless he gives valuable consideration. It must be more than nominal consideration but does not have to equal the market value; love and affection are **not** enough. A

TEXT CORRELATION CHART

Gilbert Law Summary Property	Browder, Cunningham, Smith **Basic Property Law** 1984 (4th ed.)	Casner, Leach **Property** 1984 (3rd ed.)	Cribbet, Johnson **Property** 1984 (5th ed.)	Donahue, Kauper Martin **Property** 1983 (2nd ed.)	Dukeminier, Krier **Property** 1981
I. POSSESSION					
A. General	24-110	29-52			
B. Acquiring Possession of Wild Animals	28-29	9-28	96-97	1-6, 18-19, 48-51	34-38, 40-41
C. Acquiring Possession by Finding Articles	29-35	29-35	92-126	77	1-34
D. Remedies of a Possessor	21-45	65-88			5-8
E. Bailments	96-110	39-43	127-135	81-86	6-11
F. Accession		178	168-177	353	80-81, 110-111
G. Adverse Possession	45-96	52-64	151-167, 554-573	108-162	82-129
H. Right to Exclude					
II. GIFTS AND SALES OF PERSONAL PROPERTY	697-756	89-135	178-228		711-726
A. Gifts of Personal Property				420-462	
1. Definition	697-698	89-91	55-59		
2. Intent		93-100	178-228		
3. Delivery	698-714, 722-729	93-108	178-228	420-427, 430-448, 455-456	711-726
4. Acceptance	729	100		454-455	
5. Bank Accounts	729-742, 746-756	114-125	201-220	456-462	
B. Bona Fide Purchasers of Personal Property	845-846	163-181	136-147	69-71	118, 128-129
III. FREEHOLD POSSESSORY ESTATES	220-244	205-219	242-289	506-528	350-396
A. Introduction	220-226	205-207	242-245	506-509	131-132, 350-362
B. The Fee Simple	226-239	208-212	245-257	509-511	362-380
C. The Fee Tail	239-241	213-218	285-289	511-514	380-384
D. The Life Estate	241-244	218-219	257-269	520-528	384-396
E. The Rule Against Restraints on Alienation	269-270	973-987		553-554, 569-616	372-385
F. Summary of Possessory Estates					
IV. FUTURE INTERESTS	244-277	290-351	290-336		409-484
A. Introduction	244-245	290	290		409-410
B. Reversion	245	290	290, 336	511-514, 520-550	410-411
C. Possibility of Reverter	245-246	212	275, 290, 336	514-520, 611-616	368, 411-413
D. Right of Entry	246-247	212, 291-293	275, 290	114-115, 514-520, 611-616	369, 412-414
E. Remainder	247-259, 262-265	293-335	290-320	133-134, 511-512, 520-554	358-359, 422-430, 434-436, 450-455
F. Executory Interests	259-262	297-299	308-336	514-515, 542-551,	430-437
G. The Rule Against Perpetuities	266-269	335-351	330-336	550-551, 594-616	458-484
H. Summary of Future Interests	244-245				
V. CONCURRENT OWNERSHIP	301-330	255-283	337-439	559-565, 621-653	485-530
A. Tenancy in Common	306, 313-315, 317-320	255-280	337-338	561	486
B. Joint Tenancy	301-304, 307-315	255-280	338-342	560, 621-628	486-515
C. Tenancy by the Entirety	304-306, 324-330	255-280	342-347, 416-423	560-561, 644-653	487-489, 533-540
D. Rights and Duties of Co-Tenants	316-330	260-280	359-430	628-644, 651-653	502-530
VI. MARITAL PROPERTY	288-300, 330-333	219-243	347-358		530-586
A. Common Law Marital Estates	288-294	219-237	347-352	558-561, 664-666	530-556, 561-562
B. Modern Statutory Rights	294-300	241-243	354-358	644-663	541-542, 562-575
C. Community Property	330-333	238-243	352-354	564, 676-682	556-586
VII. TRUSTS, CONDOMINIUMS, AND COOPERATIVES					
A. The Trust	6-7, 703	90, 127-135, 254		565-567	393-394, 438-439, 445-449, 688-690
B. Condominiums	176, 271, 681-686	282-283, 939-947	430-439	564-565, 587-591	148-165, 396-408
C. Cooperatives	680-681	282, 353, 940		564-565, 587-591	193, 402

TEXT CORRELATION CHART—continued

Gilbert Law Summary Property	Browder, Cunningham, Smith **Basic Property Law** 1984 (4th ed.)	Casner, Leach **Property** 1984 (3rd ed.)	Cribbet, Johnson **Property** 1984 (5th ed.)	Donahue, Kauper, Martin **Property** 1983 (2nd ed.)	Dukeminier, Krier **Property** 1981
VIII. LANDLORD AND TENANT	334-511	353-662	440-603	787-1035	133-349
A. Introduction	334-335	353-358	440-443	787-810	133
B. Types of Tenancies and Their Creation	335-345		441-459	810-827	133-148
C. Selection of Tenants			460-471	871-881	148-169
D. Landlord's Duty to Deliver Possession	359-365	359-368	471-477	924, 927, 931-936	169-175, 253-254
E. Landlord's Duty Not to Interfere with Tenant's Quiet Enjoyment	359-365	368-375, 492-501	477-481	852-864, 1007-1008	266-286
F. Landlord's Duty to Provide Habitable Premises	365-448	443-458, 501-552	481-521	864-879, 936-971, 1001-1003	254-266, 286-326
G. Landlord's Tort Liability	454-479	375-396, 521-522	521-536	941-942	254, 257-266, 304-305, 307-309, 325-326, 340-341
H. Tenant's Duties	604-605, 617-618	396-422	537-543, 566-574	925, 953-954, 961-963, 1022-1026	194-252
I. Landlord's Remedies	345-359, 441-454	423-443, 465-492, 587-605	589-603	827-908	214-252
J. Assignment and Subletting	494-511	553-585	574-589	1017-1021	175-194
K. Public Housing			543-566	1028-1035	326-349
IX. EASEMENTS AND COVENANTS					
A. Easements	512-597	1056-1114	604-669	1080-1143	969-1024, 1052-1092
B. Real Covenants	626-686	987-1030	669-684, 709-735	1143-1221	1024-1030
C. Equitable Servitudes	630-633, 642-680, 683-686	1030-1039	685-738	1167-1170	1004-1008, 1030-1051
X. RIGHTS IN THE LAND OF ANOTHER ARISING BY OPERATION OF LAW					
A. Nuisance	111-141	1144-1145	738-754	1040-1071	917-958
B. Right to Support	141-149	1195-1206	755-766	317-322	928-930
C. Rights in Water	176-219	1206-1226	766-829	322-359	64-82
D. Rights in Airspace	150-176	1227-1242	830-855	375-395	
XI. PUBLIC LAND USE CONTROLS					
A. Zoning	1204-1268	1116-1166	856-869, 905-965	1221-1309	1212-1422
B. Subdivision Controls and Maps	1269-1419		869-876		
C. Eminent Domain	1068-1203	1115, 1166-1192	884-904, 966-1002	1309-1341	1093-1211
XII. THE SALE OF LAND					
A. The Contract for the Sale of Land	971-1066	663-691	1135-1284	699-712	589-680
B. The Mortgage	989-992	739-754	1191-1197	714-727	619-641
C. The Deed	757-842	755-799	1292-1365	463-506	727-766
D. Delivery of the Deed	812-835	762-775	1316-1337	488-490, 498-501, 545-549, 771-772	680-707
E. Seller's Warranties	892-917	716-717, 755-761, 781-799	144-151	471-474, 705-706	727-766
XIII. METHODS OF TITLE ASSURANCE					
A. Recording System	843-891	801-899	1366-1442	490-505, 728-744	786-914
B. Title Registration	964-970	901-917	1529-1540	764-769	727, 890-914
C. Title Insurance	917-942	672, 688, 919-936	1540-1554	727-728, 751-764	766-785

approach to exams

Property is basic to the social welfare. People seek it, nations war over it, and no one can do without it. The function of property law is to determine **who** among the competing claimants gets **what when** and under **what conditions**. Given the complexity of the world today, that is a tall order. Just try to imagine all the resources in this country that might be claimed. There is land, there are watches, there are cars, and cows, and coins, and so on. Indeed, there is around us a whole "supermarket" of things. But property is not limited to things you can see or feel. Property can include a copyright, a promise, airspace, a right to fish, a right to continued employment, a right to be free of racial discrimination. All these the law may call property, deeming it useful to do so in the scheme of things. The law of property is complex because it is possible and desirable to have an enormous variety of arrangements for utilizing all the resources in society.

But because the law of property is complex, a law school course in property can cover a wide range of topics. Thus, it is difficult (if not impossible) to give a general approach to answering all property questions. However, some of the general concepts that run throughout this area of law are discussed below and may help you analyze property issues. Also, at the beginning of each chapter, a chapter approach targets the more specific considerations for topics covered in the particular chapter.

1. **What is Property?** In legal discourse, **property is what the law defines as property**. If a claim to a resource is not recognized by law, it is not property in a legal sense. Once recognized by law, a claim becomes a legal **right**. For example, if a judge declares that A can walk across Blackacre, free of O's interference, A has a property right; but if a judge declares that O can exclude A, O—and not A—has a property right. Hence, a central question in the law of property is:

   — What claims **should** the courts and the legislatures recognize as property? This depends, of course, on the applicable policies, on what the lawgivers want to accomplish. Two considerations are especially important in property law and run through most of it: **fairness** and **economic efficiency**. The lawgivers want to be fair, but at the same time, they want to keep costs of operating the system low so that society as a whole is richer. But these are not the only policies in view. Life, and the distribution of the world's goods, is not so simple.

2. **What is Property Law?** Property law has been largely formulated in each state by **courts** (deciding **cases**) and **legislatures** (enacting **statutes**). (Very little property law has been developed by the federal government.) Each state is free to develop its property law as it desires, provided it does not contravene the United States Constitution. Even so, because of a common heritage (the common law inherited from the English), there are far more similarities than differences in property law among the various states; property law in Florida is likely to be based on the same principles as property law in Massachusetts. Of course, the legislature may modify the common law (subject to the constraints of the state and federal constitutions), and if so, statutes prevail over earlier case law.

3. **How Do You Analyze "Property"?** The word "property" can be used to denote the thing or resource (even the intangible object) being discussed (for example, "the property was de-

stroyed by fire"). In this sense, all property can be divided into two types, **real** and **personal**. Generally speaking, **real property** is land and any structures built on it. **Personal property**, which is everything else, consists of **tangible** items (things that can be seen or felt, such as a watch or a book) and **intangible** items (property that cannot be seen, such as a bank account or the right not to be unfairly kicked out of law school).

In legal analysis, the word property often is used in another way. It denotes the **legal relationships among people** in regard to a thing. The thing may be real or personal, tangible or intangible; according to this usage, it is the legal relationship that is important. For example, if a lawyer says, "This watch is Joe's property" or "Joe owns this watch," the words "property" and "owns" do not refer directly to the watch but to the legal relationship Joe has with other persons in regard to the watch. Assume Suzy is sitting next to Joe. The statement that "Joe owns this watch" means that Joe can wear it—even smash it—without Suzy's consent; that Suzy is under a legal duty not to interfere with Joe's use, and Joe can recover damages from her if she takes it and smashes it; that Joe can recover the watch from a thief; that if Joe gives the watch to a repair shop, he is entitled to get it back. Observe that each of the foregoing statements describes a relationship between Joe and another person with respect to the watch (specifically, Joe's rights and others' duties). All these relationships can be collected together in a bundle, and thus what Joe has is "a bundle of rights."

In other words, "property," for lawyers, is conceived of as "a bundle of rights." You will become familiar with the peculiar conceptualizations inherent in the study of property (*e.g.*, a "bundle of rights") and will begin to view commonplace items with a different perspective.

4. **What is the Rationale for the Law?** This Summary attempts to describe in brief form all the various ways that lawyers have worked out for talking about property. One thing you will soon realize in the study of property is that property law is a highly analytical subject, but if you understand the terminology and the basic principles before going on to the meticulous details, this subject is not too difficult. However, understanding requires an **examination of reasons** for things. As the first Justice Harlan said in the *Civil Rights Cases*, 109 U.S. 3 (1883): "The letter of the law is the body; the sense and reason of the law is the soul." If you try to learn property law by rote—by memorization and drill—weeks, even months, may pass without you ever getting the feel of what you are doing. In this Summary, as each new term is introduced—and there are a lot of them—the term is defined. As each rule is set forth, illustrations of it are given so that it can be more easily understood, **and its underlying reasons are presented**.

It is impossible to overemphasize the importance of ascertaining and **understanding the purposes behind rules**. If you do not understand the purposes, you do not really understand the rules. At the end of your course in Property, most likely your exam will contain questions asking for the application of rules to new situations not discussed in class. (This is, in essence, what the lawyer does.) But you cannot properly apply rules to new fact situations without understanding that rules are construed to give effect to, and are limited by, their purposes. Hence always seek the reasons for a rule. If you understand the reasons, you can appropriately apply the rule to new or different fact situations.

Author's Note: This Summary cites almost all the principal cases in the leading casebooks used in first-year property courses. To find out about the rules of law discussed in the case, and how the case fits within those rules, look up the name of the case in the Table of Cases at the back of this Summary. Then turn to the section in the Summary where the case is cited.

Also note that the organization of this Summary more or less follows the organization of leading casebooks. But since no two casebooks follow exactly the same order, you should look up the topic you are studying in the Table of Contents and/or Text Correlation Chart to find where it is covered in this Summary.

I. POSSESSION

chapter approach

Possession is one of the most important concepts in the law of property. Possession differs from ownership, and to understand ownership, you must get a grasp on the slippery concept of possession.

This chapter covers all the traditional doctrinal areas associated with possession, including:

1. **Capture of wild animals:** The important issue is whether the pursuer has gained control over the animal (by capturing or mortally wounding).

2. **Finding property:** The important issues are basically two: (i) **why** does a prior possessor win? and (ii) when is a person **in possession** of objects found on his land of which he was unaware? The latter question may turn on whether the property was lost, mislaid, abandoned, or treasure trove—or found in a public or private place. These distinctions are usually tested on in a question concerning finders.

3. **Bailments:** The major issues are whether a bailment has been **created** (in which control and intent to control are important) and the **duties** of the bailee (especially the type of care required).

4. **Adverse possession:** Adverse possession of land is a basic idea which secures ownership. Look for all the elements: actual entry giving exclusive possession; open and notorious; adverse and under claim of right; and continuous for the statutory period. Also watch for issues on tacking and disability of the owner.

This chapter also discusses accession and the mistaken improver situation, the right to exclude, and the remedies of a possessor. Note that this chapter covers a wide range of possession issues. Property courses usually begin with problems in possession, but most teachers elect to teach some, and not all, of the topics covered in this chapter. Whether you will see any of these topics on your exam depends on your particular course and professor.

A. GENERAL

1. **Possession Defined:** [§1] Possession is difficult to define. A person is in possession of objects he physically controls (such as an apple held in his hand). But he also may be in possession of objects not in his presence, such as the chair left in the backyard when he left for work. He may even be in possession of objects in his house, or under the soil of his house, of which he is unaware. Hence possession has a number of meanings, depending on the context involved and the purposes in view.

   a. **Facts or legal conclusion:** [§2] The word possession may refer either to **facts** indicating physical control and intent to exclude others from control **or** to a **conclusion** by a court that a person is "in possession" and ought to be protected. In reading judicial opinions, try to determine which way the word is being used. Sometimes courts unconsciously slip from one meaning to the other.

(1) **Example:** Owner (hereafter in this Summary, "O") comes home from work to find that A has pitched a tent on O's front lawn and is inside it. The rule is that a person who is in *possession* of property can be ousted only by a court order, but a *trespasser* may be ousted by the owner using reasonable self-help. The question, then, is whether A is in possession of the space occupied by the tent or is a trespasser. A is not in possession of the space occupied by the tent. O is in possession and may use self-help in ousting A. If the law were that A is in possession, then O could not use self-help in ousting A but rather would be required to go to court to recover possession. This would be both expensive and unfair to O, and because of court delays might take a long time. Therefore, the law holds that O remains in possession even though A has physically occupied the space. "Possession" then is a key word in a legal rule ("a possessor can be ousted only by going to court") and is defined to carry out the purposes of that rule.

b. **Possession distinguished from ownership:** [§3]   Possession is not the same as ownership. *Ownership* is "title," and is usually proved by showing documents signed by the previous owner transferring title to the present titleholder. *Possession* is proved by showing facts relating to physical control and the intent to exclude. (The landlord, for example, owns the land and building; the tenant has possession of an apartment.)

(1) **Example:** A buys a watch from a jeweler, who bought it from the manufacturer. B steals the watch from A. To recover the watch, A must prove ownership *or* prior possession of the watch. To prove ownership, A must produce the sales slip from the jeweler or other indicia of title, which A has probably lost. To prove prior possession, A only has to prove that the watch was in A's physical possession before the theft. That may be much easier to prove than ownership.

c. **Constructive possession:** [§4]   A person is in "constructive possession" when the law treats him *as if* he is in possession although, in fact, he is not. It is a convenient fiction which permits judges to reach a desired result. For example, at common law a possessor who was dispossessed was given swift judicial remedies for the recovery of possession—remedies not available to owners of property, who had to prove ownership in a foot-dragging lawsuit. To permit owners of land who never went into possession to use these swift remedies, the courts held that an owner of land is in constructive possession of the land even though not in actual possession, provided the land is not in the actual possession of another. [Gillespie v. Dew, 1 Stew. 229 (Ala. 1827)]

2. **Why the Law Protects Possessors:** [§5]   An old saw says "possession is nine-tenths of the law." There is much truth in that statement because the law does emphatically protect possessors. Some of the reasons are:

a. ***Protecting possession is an efficient way to protect ownership*** since ownership may be difficult to prove. (*See supra,* §3.)

b. ***Protecting possession prevents*** a stronger person from ousting a possessor, thus disturbing the ***public peace and order.***

c. ***Protecting possession facilitates trade*** in the possessed object because the buyer to some extent can rely upon the seller's possession when the seller cannot prove ownership. (This is further discussed in the section on bona fide purchasers of personal property, *infra,* §§236-249.)

d. ***Protecting possession gives effect to the expectations*** of a person who has asserted a right in a thing until another person comes along with a better right.

e. ***In the cases of persons capturing wild animals or finding lost property,*** protection of possession rewards them for making a useful item ***available to society.***

f. ***Protecting possession is an easy and efficient way*** of allocating resources, even if that allocation is arbitrary.

B. ACQUIRING POSSESSION OF WILD ANIMALS

1. **Rule of Capture:** [§6]   If wild animals (sometimes called animals ***ferae naturae***) are captured, they belong to the captor. But ***capture is required***; merely chasing the animal is not enough. Thus, if A is on a horse pursuing a fox, and B spots the fox and shoots it, killing it, B is entitled to the fox. [Pierson v. Post, 3 Cai. R. 175 (N.Y. 1805)]

    a. **Rationale:** Various reasons can be found for this rule:

       (1) **Competition:** Society's object is to capture foxes (to destroy them) or ducks (to put them on the table). To foster competition, resulting in more wild animals being captured, society does not reward the pursuer, only the captor. It is assumed that this brings more persons into pursuit, resulting in more capture.

       (2) **Ease of administration:** Rewarding capture, an objective act, is an easier rule to administer than protecting pursuit, which is hard to define and can take many forms. Thus the rule of capture promotes certainty and efficient administration in a situation where the stakes (a fox, some ducks, some fish) are not high and not worth a lot of judicial time.

       (3) **But note:** The rule of capture—designed to destroy wild animals—was laid down in the 19th century when it was desirable to destroy wild animals. Today, the rule of capture, promoting pursuit and killing, leads to overcapture of fish and overinvestment in capture technology (Save The Whale!). Similarly, other species have become endangered by a rule that treats wild animals as common property until reduced to possession.

b. **Wounded or trapped animals:** [§7]   If an animal has been *mortally wounded* or *trapped* so that capture is virtually certain, the animal is treated as captured. But if the animal is only in the process of being entrapped, and the door *has not snapped shut,* it has not been captured. Thus, if A has driven a school of fish into a net and is in the process of encircling them but they could still turn tail and escape, A has not captured the fish. Until the net has closed, another person (B) can sweep in and take the fish. [Young v. Hichens, 6 Q.B. 606 (1844)]

(1) **Unfair competition:** [§8]   Although the law wants competition to promote capture, it also wants competition to be fair so as to attract into the pursuit more persons. Protecting against unfair competition also protects against monopolies (with resulting high prices). Thus, B in *Young v. Hichens,* above, could not sink A's boat. In fact, the actual action of B in dashing in with a smaller net to take the fish before the big net closed comes close to being unfair competition and might be so deemed today.

(2) **Cage not escape-proof:** [§9]   In order to trap or net a wild animal, the animal must be confined in an enclosure, but it is not necessary that there be absolutely no possibility of escape. The captor acquires possession if he uses *reasonable precautions against escape.* Thus fish in A's net, which has a series of smaller and smaller entrances from which escape is possible but unlikely, are possessed by A. B, who removes the fish from the net, is guilty of larceny. [State v. Shaw, 65 N.E. 875 (Ohio 1902)]

c. **Interference by noncompetitor:** [§10]   If a person is in the process of entrapping animals, a competitor who also wants to capture the animals can interfere with the other person's activity and try to capture the animals. But a *person who does not want to capture the animal cannot interfere. (Remember:* Society wants the animal caught.) Thus if A puts out decoys on his pond to attract ducks and sets nets to catch them, B, a neighbor, cannot shoot off guns to scare the ducks away. But B can shoot to kill the ducks while flying over his land. [Keeble v. Hickeringill, 103 Eng. Rep. 1127 (1707)]

(1) **Conservation:** This rule promotes killing; it does not promote conservation of wildlife, which may be a goal of society today. But observe how, in these wild animal cases, the rules are designed to achieve ends. They show the *instrumental nature of the law* (which is perhaps why many teachers like to begin Property with the wild animal cases).

d. **Custom:** [§11]   While the general rule is that the captor must acquire physical control over the animal, in some hunting trades, *custom,* which is more effective in getting animals killed, *may dictate a different result.* Among American whalers, *e.g.,* the custom was to award the whale to the ship which first killed the whale—even though the whale sank and was discovered several days later floating on the surface by another whaler. This custom advanced the killing of whales (society's object), because the killer ship could be off looking for other whales without waiting around for the whale to rise. This custom was recognized by the courts as giving possession. [Ghen v. Rich, 8 F. 159 (D. Mass. 1881)]

2. **Wild Animals with Animus Revertendi:** [§12]   Captured wild animals that develop an *animus revertendi* (habit of return) continue to belong to the captor when they roam at large. Thus if deer are captured, then tamed, and return home after grazing, they are not available for capture by another. The *reason* behind this rule is that domesticated animals are valuable to society and this effort to tame wild animals is rewarded.

3. **Escaped Wild Animals:** [§13]   If a captured wild animal that has *no animus revertendi* escapes, the captor loses possession, and the animal is again subject to capture by another. However, if the animal is not native to the area, but unusual (*e.g.,* an elephant in the Pennsylvania woods), a hunter may be put on notice that the animal has escaped and some other person has prior possession. In that case, the hunter cannot capture the animal for himself. [E.A. Stephens & Co. v. Albers, 256 P. 15 (Colo. 1927); Conti v. ASPCA, 77 Misc. 2d 61 (1974)]

4. **Regulation by State:** [§14]   States can and do regulate hunting and fishing by game laws. These laws have the purpose of preventing overkill and preserving natural resources. It has sometimes been argued that the reason why these protective laws are valid is that the state owns wild game, and therefore prevails over a person who takes possession of it. But this argument is entirely fictional. The better reason is that the state has the power to regulate the taking of game under its *police power,* by which it prevents conduct harmful to the public. [Commonwealth v. Agway, Inc., 232 A.2d 69 (Pa. 1967)] (For more on the police power, *see* zoning, *infra,* §§1630 *et seq.*)

C. ACQUIRING POSSESSION BY FINDING ARTICLES

1. **General Rule:** [§15]   An owner of property does not lose title by losing the property. O's rights persist even though the article has been lost or mislaid. As a general rule, however, *a finder has rights superior to everyone but the true owner*—but there are important exceptions to this rule.

    a. **Example:** A finds a jewel and takes it to a jeweler to have it appraised. The jeweler refuses to give the jewel back to A saying that A does not own it. A is entitled to recover from the jeweler either the jewel or the full money value of the jewel. As between A and the jeweler, *the prior possessor has the superior right.* [Armory v. Delamirie, 1 Strange 505 (1722)]

    b. **Prior possessor wins:** [§16]   The rule that a prior possessor wins over a subsequent possessor is an important and fundamental one. It applies to *both personal property* and *real property.* The reasons for the rule include:

        (1) Protecting prior possession also *protects an owner* who has no indicia of ownership (title papers, etc.).

        (2) Entrusting goods to another—as A entrusted the jeweler in the above example—is an efficient practice, facilitating all kinds of purposes, that ought to be encouraged. The jeweler is a *bailee,* who must surrender the goods to a prior possessor. Imagine O's not getting clothes back from the laundry, or a neighbor not having to return a lawnmower—unless O could prove ownership.

(3) Prior possessors *expect* to prevail over subsequent possessors. By giving them their expectations, the law reinforces the popular belief that the law is just.

(4) The protection of **peaceable possession** is an ancient policy in law, aimed at deterring disruptions in the public order.

c. **Relativity of title:** [§17] Note that title to the jewel in the above example is relative to who the claimants are. The owner of the jewel prevails over A, the finder. A, the finder, prevails over a subsequent possessor. Suppose that A, after finding the jewel, lost it and B thereafter found it. Would B prevail over A? No. A, the prior possessor, prevails over B, a subsequent possessor. A's rights are not lost by losing the article. [Clark v. Maloney, 3 Har. 68 (Del. 1840)]

d. **Prior possessor a trespasser:** [§18] The "prior possessor wins" rule applies to objects acquired through theft or trespass. Thus if A steals a jewel and hands it to B, who refuses to return it, B is liable to A. B cannot question A's title or rightful prior possession if B is merely a subsequent possessor. *Rationale:* To rule in favor of B would not likely deter crime, but it would likely immerse owners and prior possessors in costly litigation with subsequent possessors to prove they are not thieves. [Anderson v. Gouldberg, 53 N.W. 636 (Minn. 1892)—"Any other rule would lead to an endless series of unlawful seizures and reprisals in every case where property had once passed out of possession of the rightful owner"]

e. **What constitutes possession:** [§19] For the finder to become a prior possessor, the finder must—like the captor of wild animals—acquire **physical control** over the object **and** have an **intent** to assume dominion over it.

(1) **Example:** A discovers a shipwreck at the bottom of the Mississippi River. The ship sank some twenty-seven years before and was abandoned by the owners. A attaches a temporary buoy to the wreck, intending to return the next day, but A does not return. Nine months later, B finds the wreck and salvages it. B prevails over A because A has shown only an intent to take possession and has not shown sufficient acts of physical control. A must place his boat over the wreck, **with the means to raise it**, to give notice to subsequent searchers of his prior possession. [Eads v. Brazelton, 22 Ark. 499 (1861)]

(2) **Rationale:** The court defines the acts necessary to constitute possession in such a way as to encourage salvage of shipwrecks. Note that the court says that nothing short of placing a salvage boat over the wreck, capable of salvaging it, will constitute possession.

f. **Unconscious possession:** [§20] A person may constructively possess something of which she is unaware if she is in possession of the premises where the article rests. If so, she is entitled to the benefit of the "prior possessor wins" rule.

(1) **Example:** A landowner is in constructive possession of the objects located under the surface of her land even though she is unaware of the objects. If A hires B to clean out her pool—or cesspool—and B finds a ring at the bottom of the

pool, the ring belongs to A, not B, even though A was unaware that the ring was there. [South Staffordshire Water Co. v. Sharman, [1896] 2 Q.B. 44]

(2) **Caution:** Whether a person who is unaware of an object is in "constructive possession" involves the courts in resolving conflicting policies. Since "constructive" means "in the eyes of the law," courts have to decide which of the claimants has the better claim. This matter is discussed further in the exceptions to the general rule, below.

2. **Finder Versus Owner of Premises:** [§21]   Often the finder will claim an object; so will the owner of the premises where the object is found. (This assumes that the owner of the premises *does not own the object*; if she did, she would prevail over the finder.) The owner of the premises claims to be in either actual or, more usually, constructive prior possession. Some of the cases are in conflict; many are confused in their reasoning or make no attempt to relate "constructive possession" to the policies at issue.

   a. **Finder is trespasser:** [§22]   If the finder is a trespasser, the owner of the premises where the object is found always prevails over the finder. This rule discourages trespass and unauthorized entries on property. [Favorite v. Miller, 407 A.2d 974 (Conn. 1978)]

   b. **Finder is employee:** [§23]   If the finder is an employee of the owner of the premises, some cases hold the employee cannot keep the object. Some courts reason that an employee is *"acting for"* an employer in the course of his or her duties (a question-begging line of thought). Others emphasize that the employee has a *contractual duty* to report the object to the employer. This duty is usually imposed, for instance, by hotel owners on the people who clean the rooms in order to facilitate the return of the object to the hotel guest who left it. But if the guest never claims it, why should the duty to report preclude the finder from getting it? *Remember:* Rewarding honesty is a social good, and rewarding the report of the find may encourage reports, which are the first steps toward getting objects back to their owners.

   c. **Finder is on premises for a limited purpose:** [§24]   If the finder is on the premises for a limited purpose (*e.g.,* cleaning out a stopped sewer drain), it may be said that the owner gave permission to enter only for a limited purpose of cleaning, under the direction of the owner, and the owner of the premises is entitled to objects found. [South Staffordshire Water Co. v. Sharman, *supra,* §20]

   d. **Object found under the soil:** [§25]   If the object is found under or embedded in the soil, it is awarded to the owner of the premises, not to the finder. [Goddard v. Winchell, 52 N.W. 1124 (Iowa 1892); Elwes v. Brigg Gas Co., [1886] 33 Ch. D 562] *Rationale:* Owners of land *expect* that objects found underneath the soil belong to them; they think of these objects as part of the land itself.

      (1) **Exception—treasure trove:** [§26]   Treasure trove is found gold, silver, or money *intentionally buried* or concealed in the soil *with the intent of returning to claim it.* Under English law, treasure trove belongs to the crown (the state). [Attorney General v. Overton Farms, Ltd., [1980] 3 All E.R. 503] American

courts have generally rejected giving treasure trove to the state. Some give it to the finder; others give it to the landowner. [*See, e.g.,* Schley v. Couch, 284 S.W.2d 333 (Tex. 1955)—holding that currency buried in the ground was "mislaid" property and belonged to the landowner]

e. **Object found in private home:** [§27]   Objects found inside a private home are usually awarded to the owner of the home. *Rationale:* The homeowner has an intent to exclude everyone and to admit persons only for specific limited purposes (to deliver laundry, to eat dinner, etc.) that do not include finding property. Also, the homeowner has strong expectations that all objects inside the home of which he is unaware are "his."

(1) **Example:** A, a guest at a party in B's home, finds a diamond ring under the sofa which no one claims to own. B is in constructive prior possession of the ring and can keep it until the true owner reclaims it.

(2) **Owner not in possession:** [§28]   If the owner of the house has not moved into the house (has not made it his "personal space"), it has been held that the owner of the house is not in constructive possession of articles therein of which he is unaware. [Hannah v. Peel, [1945] 1 K.B 509]

(a) **Example:** O owns a large house requisitioned by the government to quarter soldiers. O bought the house two years earlier and never moved in. A soldier finds in the house a brooch hidden on a window ledge. After a couple of months, the soldier's conscience begins to work and he reports the find. The soldier prevails over O because O never moved into the house and took physical possession of it. (The fact that the house was involuntarily taken from O by the state for the limited purpose of quartering soldiers, thus depriving O of the possibility of physical possession, was ignored by the court in *Hannah v. Peel.* But perhaps the motivating factor was rewarding honesty.)

f. **Object found in public place:** [§29]   In dealing with objects found in a public place, courts have generally resolved the issue by resorting to the "lost-mislaid" distinction or to the "public part-private part" distinction.

(1) **Lost-mislaid distinction:** [§30]   *Lost* property is property which the owner accidentally and casually lost (*e.g.,* a ring slips through a hole in a pocket). *Mislaid* property is property **intentionally placed** somewhere and then forgotten (*e.g.,* a purse placed on a table and forgotten).

(a) **Lost property goes to the finder:** [§31]   Lost property goes to the *finder* rather than the owner of the premises.

(b) **Mislaid property does not go to finder:** [§32]   Mislaid property goes to the *owner of the premises.*

1) **Example:** A finds a wallet on the floor of a beauty shop and a ring on the counter in the same shop. The *wallet* is *lost* property because it is

assumed that it was not intentionally placed on the floor. A, the finder, prevails over the owner of the shop, and can take the wallet home to keep for the true owner (if the true owner shows up). [Bridges v. Hawkesworth, 21 L.J.Q.B. (n.s.) 75 (1851)] The *ring* is *mislaid* property because, from its position, it is assumed it was intentionally placed on the counter and forgotten. The ring goes to the owner of the shop to keep until the true owner claims it. The finder has no rights in the ring. [McAvoy v. Medina, 93 Mass. (11 Allen) 548 (1866)]

(c) **Rationale:** The purpose of classifying property as mislaid is to facilitate the return of the object to the true owner: Since it is assumed the object was intentionally placed where it is found, it is likely that the *true owner will remember* where she placed it and will return to the shop to claim it. In addition, it is sometimes said that a mislaid object is voluntarily left in the *custody* of the owner of the shop (even though she is unaware of it), and therefore she has prior possession. (Possession is thus defined to include a fictional involuntary custody.) [Foulke v. New York Consolidated Railroad, 228 N.Y. 269 (1920)]

(d) **Criticism:** [§33]   The lost-mislaid distinction has been roundly criticized.

1)   From the findings of fact, the court must infer whether the owner casually dropped the object or placed it there intentionally and forgot it. This is often a guess. In the preceding example, was the wallet casually dropped on the floor? Or was it placed on the counter and accidentally brushed to the floor by another customer? Or was it (like many purses nowadays) intentionally placed on the floor?

2)   It is assumed that the true owner will retrace her steps only if the property is mislaid (and not if it is lost); therefore awarding *lost* property to the finder—who may disappear in the crowd—does not lessen the chances of return to the true owner. Experience indicates that when a person misses something, she retraces her steps whether the object was casually lost or mislaid.

(2) **Private portion of public place:** [§34]   If an object is found in a private portion of a public place, the owner of the premises is likely to be said to have possession prior to a finder. The classic case is finding money or notes in a safe deposit vault in a bank. The standard result is that the bank prevails over the finder, either on the ground that the bank has been entrusted with *custody* by the true owner or that the vault is a *private place.* However, a recent Illinois case, *Paset v. Old Orchard Bank & Trust Co.,* 378 N.E.2d 1264 (Ill. 1978), held that property found in a bank safety deposit vault area should remain with the bank *for one year,* and then, if unclaimed, go to the finder. Although the reasoning of this case rests on analogy to an Illinois estray statute, the principle announced seems sound enough to be applied by other courts to property found in any business establishment. It makes sense in terms of the purposes of the law:

(i) to facilitate return of the object to the true owner, and (ii) to reward the finder for honesty and for returning a useful item to the marketplace.

3. **Abandoned Property:** [§35] Abandoned property is property intentionally abandoned by the true owner, who no longer claims any right to it (*e.g.,* items left in a garbage can). Abandoned property is awarded to the finder. However, by federal statute, property abandoned in a combat zone belongs to the federal government and not to the soldier who finds it. The purpose of this statute is to discourage looting. [United States v. Morrison, 492 F.2d 1219 (Ct. Cl. 1974)]

4. **Statutory Changes:** [§36] In some states, statutes have been enacted abolishing the distinctions developed by the courts in finders cases. New York, for example, has abolished the distinctions between lost, mislaid, and abandoned property and treasure trove. All such property is treated as lost property and goes to the finder. The statute also abolishes the distinction between finding an article in a public or in a private place. Again, the finder wins over the owner of the premises. Thus under the New York statute, in *Hurley v. City of Niagara Falls,* 30 App. Div. 89 (1968), a contractor hired to build a recreation room in a basement was held entitled to $4,900 he found under a sink in the basement. Any claim that the homeowner might have had under the common law concepts of mislaid property and private place were swept away by the statutory reform.

D. REMEDIES OF A POSSESSOR

1. **Forms of Action:** [§37] At common law, a plaintiff had to bring suit in an appropriate *form of action* to obtain the particular remedy desired. If the plaintiff brought the wrong form of action, he would be thrown out of court. The forms of action were unbelievably technical and have been abolished or reformed in almost all jurisdictions. However, because for so long they were an important part of our laws, and because some of them *required an allegation of prior possession,* they had an impact on what the law deems to be possession. The courts sometimes defined "possession" in such a way as to enable the plaintiff to bring a lawsuit, or to prevent him from doing so. Thus the concept of possession occupied a central place in the procedural system. A brief sketch is in order. (*See also* Civil Procedure Summary.)

a. **Actions to recover damages:** [§38] There were several actions permissible where the plaintiff wanted to recover damages for injury to himself or the property, including the following:

(1) **Trespass:** [§39] A suit in trespass required the plaintiff to show that the defendant intentionally or negligently acted so as to inflict a direct, forcible injury to the plaintiff's person or to property in his possession. Plaintiff had to allege his prior possession or right to possession. The gist of a trespass action is *injury to possession.* If no substantial harm could be shown, nominal damages were given. There were two kinds of trespass actions:

(a) **Trespass to chattels:** [§40] This action was for any *forcible carrying away* of or injury to plaintiff's chattels, or for excluding the plaintiff from possession of his chattels. The Latin name of this action was **trespass de bonis asportatis,** meaning injury "by carrying away goods."

1) **Example:** O is in possession of a cow. A seizes the cow, and gives it to her friend, B. O can sue A in trespass for damages. The measure of damages is not the value of the cow, but the injury done to O by having his possession disturbed. If O recovered the cow from B, *e.g.,* A would be liable only for the value of the cow (milk) from the time of A's seizure to the time of O's recovery.

(b) **Trespass to land:** [§41]   This action was for any forcible interference with plaintiff's possession of land. The Latin name was **trespass quare clausum fregit** ("trespass q.c.f."), meaning "because he broke the close."

1) **Example:** O, owner of Blackacre, finds A has cut trees on Blackacre, and in doing so has damaged O's corn crop. O can sue A for money damages to his possessory interest (*i.e.,* the loss in value of Blackacre by having the trees cut and damage to the corn).

(2) **Trespass on the case (known as "case"):** [§42]   Trespass on the case developed as an action where one of the elements of a trespass action was missing. Trespass on the case would lie when the defendant's acts were not immediately injurious but injury was indirect or consequent (*e.g.,* if A drove a nail through the hoof of O's cow, which did no immediate injury, but later caused a crippling infection, case would lie). Or case would lie when the defendant had a duty to act but failed to do so (from which the modern law of unintentional torts stems). Or case would lie where the injury was to property not in the plaintiff's possession (remember, the gist of trespass is injury to **possession**). To sue in case, the plaintiff did **not** have to allege prior possession—only that the defendant had a **duty,** that the defendant **breached** the duty, and that the breach **resulted in substantial harm to the plaintiff.** Substantial harm, not possession, is the gist of trespass on the case.

(a) **Example:** Consider the facts of *Pierson v. Post, supra,* §6. A, on a horse, is pursuing a fox. B sees the fox running in front of A. B shoots and kills the fox. Should A sue B in trespass or in case? A sued in case, which does not require an allegation of injury to something in A's possession (the fox), but merely alleges a tortious interference with A's pursuit of the fox. For unknown reasons, the court treated the action as one in trespass, where the crucial issue is whether A had possession of the fox.

(3) **Trover:** [§43]   A suit in trover was a suit to recover the value of the plaintiff's chattel which **the defendant had converted** (usually by selling it to a party unknown). Originally the action lay only by an owner or prior possessor **against a person who had found the plaintiff's chattel** and refused to give it up, but in time the action was permitted against anyone who refused to deliver up the plaintiff's chattel. (Nonetheless, to bring the action, the plaintiff still had to allege that "plaintiff had casually lost and defendant had found" the chattel—a pure-

ly fictional allegation that the defendant could not deny.) In trover, the plaintiff was entitled to **full value** of the chattel at the time the conversion took place. In effect, the plaintiff waives the right to the return of the chattel and insists that the defendant be subjected to a forced purchase of it.

    (a) **Example:** A finds a jewel belonging to O. A takes the jewel to a goldsmith to have it appraised. The goldsmith refuses to return it. A can sue the goldsmith in trover and recover the full value of the jewel. [Armory v. Delamirie, *supra*, §15]

    (b) **Trover distinguished from trespass:** [§44] Trover did not apply to damage to land, only to chattels, whereas trespass q.c.f. applied to land. Trespass, not trover, applied in cases where the chattel was damaged but not converted. However, there was a good deal of overlap between these forms of action, and the plaintiff might elect the one which gave the larger recovery. Recall that the measure of damages differed (trespass—injury to possession; trover—value of chattel at time of conversion).

  b. **Actions to recover possession:** [§45] If the plaintiff did not want damages but wanted to recover possession, the plaintiff could bring one of the following actions:

    (1) **Replevin of chattels:** [§46] Plaintiff could bring **replevin** to recover possession of a **chattel** from the defendant which defendant had wrongfully distrained. (An earlier form of action, **detinue,** was absorbed by the development of replevin.) Plaintiff had to allege either that he was in prior possession or owned the chattel.

      (a) **Example:** Plaintiff cuts logs on land belonging to O, without O's consent. Defendant takes the logs away from the plaintiff. Plaintiff's **prior possession gained as a trespasser** is sufficient to enable him to bring replevin against defendant. [Anderson v. Gouldberg, *supra*, §18]

    (2) **Ejectment:** [§47] Plaintiff could bring **ejectment** to recover possession of **land.** Although this was originally an action by a possessor (not an owner) to recover possession, it was a more expeditious remedy than that available to owners, and owners came to use this remedy to recover possession. Ultimately it became the most common method of **trying title** to land (in such case sometimes called "ejectment to try title"). Plaintiff had to allege either prior possession or title to the land.

  c. **Modern law:** [§48] The common law actions of trespass, case, trover, replevin, and ejectment have in most states been simplified and in many renamed. But the essential difference in remedies afforded by these actions—the return of the thing as opposed to damages—is preserved in modern codes of civil procedure.

  2. **Defense of Jus Tertii:** [§49] A defense of jus tertii is the defense that neither the plaintiff nor the defendant, **but a third party,** is the true owner, and only the true owner can bring the lawsuit. Is this defense permitted in suits by A (a prior possessor) against

B? Distinguish between suits to recover possession (replevin and ejectment) and suits to recover damages (trespass, case, and trover).

a. **Actions to recover possession:** [§50]   In actions to recover possession, the jus tertii defense is not allowed.

   (1) **Example:** O owns Blackacre. A takes possession of Blackacre for a few years and then moves away. B takes possession of Blackacre. A sues B in ejectment. B defends that A is not entitled to prevail because O owns Blackacre. A prevails over B because all A has to show is prior possession. [Tapscott v. Cobbs, 52 Va. 172 (1855)]

b. **Actions for damages:** [§51]   If A sues B for *damages* rather than possession, and B has to pay A damages, B might be liable later to O (the true owner) for damages. (A recovery by A does not bar a second recovery by the true owner unless A is a bailee. *See infra,* §75.) Nonetheless, the majority rule is that B *cannot* assert the defense of jus tertii and must pay A damages, thus taking the risk that B will later have to pay O as well. *Rationale:* Because title is so difficult to prove, the plaintiff is not put to such proof if the plaintiff can prove prior possession. (Other reasons for protecting prior possessors are given *supra,* §5.) [Jeffries v. Great Western Railway, 119 Eng. Rep. 680 (1856); Holden v. Lynn, 120 P. 246 (Okla. 1911)]

   (1) **Minority rule:** [§52]   A minority of courts deems the possibility of double liability to be unfair to B and does not permit A, a prior possessor, to recover *damages* from B where B shows that O is the true owner. [Barwick v. Barwick, 33 N.C. 80 (1850); Russell v. Hill, 34 S.E. 640 (N.C. 1900)] But in jurisdictions following this minority rule, A can recover *possession* from B. Recovery of possession does not subject B to the risk of double liability.

   (2) **Allegation of ownership:** [§53]   If A alleges in his complaint that he *owns the property,* but is able to prove only prior possession, it has been held that A's suit against B for damages must fail because A has failed to prove ownership. [Winchester v. City of Stevens Point, 17 N.W. 3 (Wis. 1883)] This holding makes little sense, since prior possession should be sufficient for the recovery of damages. *Tactic:* Do not allege more than what must be proven or the judges may be distracted from the fundamental issue.

   (3) **Interpleader:** [§54]   Under modern statutes, B can interplead O in a suit by A against B. This will bring O into the lawsuit and avoid double recovery against B. But B, the wrongdoer, has the burden of locating O and subjecting O to the jurisdiction of the court. This may be difficult to do if O is living in Montana and the suit is brought in Florida, and O does not want to enter the lawsuit. As a practical matter, however, B can negotiate with O and buy her superior claim, thus defeating A. Thus in modern times the possibility of double recovery is often unrealistic, especially in suits over land where owners can be ascertained by searching the public land records.

3. **Measure of Damages:** [§55]   Where a prior possessor is permitted to sue a subsequent possessor for damages, what is the measure of damages? Is the prior possessor entitled to **permanent damages** to the entire property **or** only to **damage to date** to his possessory interest? *Remember:* The prior possessor's interest may end when the true owner asserts her rights, so the prior possessor may not be the "permanent owner." The issue is best understood by an example.

   a. **Example:** O owns Blackacre. A takes possession of Blackacre. B, a neighbor, erects a dam which floods Blackacre. Can A recover from B the permanent loss in value of Blackacre or only the loss that A has suffered to date by not being able to farm the land? The cases are split. Some courts say A can have permanent damages, leaving B with the risk of double liability if O later sues B. [Illinois & St. Louis Railroad & Coal Co. v. Cobb, 94 Ill. 55 (1879)] Other courts give A only damages for being deprived of possession to date. [LaSalle County Carbon Coal Co. v. Sanitary District of Chicago, 103 N.E. 175 (Ill. 1913)]

   b. **Life tenant as plaintiff:** [§56]   A similar problem of measuring damages arises when a life tenant sues a third party in tort for damage to the property. What amount can a life tenant recover in tort from a third party who damages the property?

      (1) **Majority view:** [§57]   The prevailing view is that since the life tenant is not responsible to the owners of the remainder for damages to the property which are not the life tenant's fault, the life tenant is entitled to recover only damages to her interest as life tenant. The owner of the remainder can bring a separate suit for damages to the remainder. [Zimmerman v. Shreeve, 59 Md. 357 (1882)] *Criticism:* The wrongdoer may escape some liability when the owners of the remainder are unborn or unascertained and cannot sue. It is hard to assess separately the damages sustained by the life estate. This view requires multiplicity of actions.

      (2) **Minority view:** [§58]   Since the life tenant has possessory title, she, like an adverse possessor, is able to recover for all damages to the property. She holds the amount recovered as trustee for the owners of the remainder who must then sue the life tenant, not the tortfeasor. [Rogers v. Atlantic, Gulf & Pacific Co., 213 N.Y. 246 (1915)] *Criticism:* This limits the owners of the remainder to the amount recovered by the life tenant (who might have hired a stupid lawyer), and requires them to rely upon the solvency of the life tenant.

4. **Law and Equity**

   a. **History:** [§59]   In addition to courts of law, England had a separate court of equity in which the chancellor sat. In medieval times, the courts of common law, adhering to their ancient customs and formulas, left many wrongs without redress. The chancellor, a cleric and keeper of the king's conscience, intervened to give relief. Gradually there developed a court of chancery (later known as a court of equity, meaning "fairness" or "justice"). Chancery imparted a much needed element of elasticity into the remedies available from the law courts. In America, separate courts of chancery exist in some states, but in most states, law and equity have been merged, and *legal* and *equitable remedies* may be sought and applied in the same action.

b. **Remedies:** [§60]   The law courts offered the remedy of *damages* to an aggrieved party. Thus if B refused to return A's cow, A could sue B at law for the value of the cow. Equity, enforcing personal duties, offered an *injunction* as a remedy. The chancellor would order B *to do* something (such as to let A into possession) or *not to do* something (such as forbidding B from interfering with A's use of the land).

(1) **Modern importance:** [§61]   It remains important to know whether a remedy is legal or equitable because the legal rules for granting *damages* or the equitable rules for granting an *injunction* may differ. (*See* the discussion of real covenants and equitable servitudes, *infra,* §§1418 *et seq.*)

E. BAILMENTS

1. **Definition:** [§62]   A bailment is the *rightful possession* of goods by one who is *not the owner.* The true owner is a *bailor,* the person in possession a *bailee.* The bailee has the duty to care for the goods and deliver them to the owner as agreed.

a. **Examples:** A bailment arises when O leaves an appliance with an electrician for repair, checks a coat, has furniture moved by a moving company, or deposits mail in the post office. In each case O is a bailor. These bailments arise out of consensual arrangements of the two parties. But bailments can also arise from *involuntary* possession (*see infra,* §73).

2. **Creation:** [§63]   To create a bailment, the alleged bailee must assume *actual physical control* with the *intent to possess.* Since a bailee has duties and liabilities, courts define "physical control" and "intent" in such a way as to carry out the expectations of the parties and to be fair. If a court thinks that liability would be unexpected or unfair, it can usually find that the defendant did not have "physical control" or "intent to possess."

a. **Actual physical control:** [§64]   To have a bailment, the bailee must take actual physical control of the object.

(1) **Parking lot cases:** [§65]   A frequently litigated situation involving creation of a bailment involves A leaving his car in a parking lot owned by B. Is B a bailee for A (and subject to a bailee's liability for loss or damage)? Distinguish two types of cases:

(a) **Park and lock:** If A parks his own car in a lot, retains the keys, and does not deliver the car to the attendant, *no bailment* is created. *Example:* Parking on the common airport parking lot, where A pays when he leaves, does not create a bailment. Most courts hold parking in a park-and-lock lot does not create a bailment because B has not assumed control over the car. [Wall v. Airport Parking Co. of Chicago, 244 N.E.2d 190 (Ill. 1969); *but see*

McGlynn v. Newark Parking Authority, 432 A.2d 99 (N.J. 1981)—park-and-lock garage has duty to use reasonable care to protect cars (this may represent a new trend)]

    (b) **Attended lots:** If A leaves the keys with an attendant, who gives A a ticket identifying the car for redelivery, a **bailment is created.** If A does not leave the keys, but B has attendants present parking other cars and able to exercise surveillance—thus **creating expectations** in A that B has accepted a duty of reasonable care—a bailment may be found even though the attendant has no physical control of the car. [Parking Management, Inc. v. Gilder, 343 A.2d 51 (D.C. 1975)]

  (2) **Coat cases:** [§66] Another ambiguous bailment situation often arising is where a customer hangs a coat on a coat rack provided for customers in a commercial establishment. If the customer merely put her coat on the seat beside her **without the knowledge of the proprietor,** there is no bailment. When a coat rack is provided—and used—the proprietor has **not** undertaken a duty to watch it. Unless the proprietor **knows** that the coat is put on the rack and in some way **indicates** that it will be cared for, the risk of loss remains with the owner of the coat. [Theobald v. Satterthwaite, 190 P.2d 714 (Wash. 1948)]

  (3) **Custody distinguished:** [§67] Another method of avoiding bailee rights and liabilities is to find that a person had **custody** rather than possession. Possession is required for a bailment. Custody is where goods are handed over but the owner does not intend to relinquish the right of dominion over them. A common example is where a department store clerk hands goods to a customer for examination. The **customer has custody,** not possession, and is not a bailee.

    (a) **Servants:** [§68] A servant entrusted with goods by his master is **not a bailee,** but a custodian. The distinction is important in criminal law. A person who feloniously takes goods from the **possession** of an owner is guilty of common law **larceny.** A person who fraudulently converts goods in his possession that belong to another is guilty of the statutory crime of **embezzlement.** Thus, if the accused **had possession** of the goods he **cannot be convicted of larceny.** By saying that a servant has only custody, the law permits servants to be convicted of larceny of their master's chattels. [State v. Schingen, 20 Wis. 79 (1865)]

b. **Intent:** [§69] The bailee must have an **intent** to exercise physical control, and in consensual arrangements the bailor must intend to give up the right to possess the object. In some cases, intent can be tricky because it is defined in accordance with the purposes of some rule based upon "possession."

  (1) **Mistake as to identity of object:** [§70] At common law, larceny required a taking of **possession** with a **contemporaneous intent** to steal. Thus, if a person took possession and **later** decided to steal the goods, he was not guilty of larceny—but might be guilty of embezzlement.

(a) **Example:** In the celebrated case of *Queen v. Ashwell,* 16 Q.B.D. 190 (1885), A asked B to lend him a shilling. B unknowingly pulled a sovereign (worth twenty times as much) out of his pocket and handed it to A. A soon thereafter discovered the coin was a sovereign, took it to a pub, and spent some of it. A was prosecuted for larceny. To prove larceny, the crown had to show that A got possession at the moment (and not before) he discovered the coin was a sovereign and decided to keep the coin with its additional value. Thus the issue was whether A got possession at the moment B handed him the coin (not larceny), or later upon its conversion (larceny). The court was evenly divided. Although A had physical control when B handed him the coin, half the judges thought A had *an intent* to control the coin even though he was under a mistaken belief that it was a shilling, and therefore he took possession at the handing over, and was not guilty of larceny. The other half thought A had, at the handing over, only an intent to control the coin *if it were a shilling*—and that he formed the intent to control the sovereign only when he realized the truth. Under the latter view, A would be guilty of larceny.

(b) **Note:** The distinction above seems extremely subtle because A actually had possession of the coin when he received it from the owner, but it illustrates how judges hide their policy differences over the propriety of convicting A of larceny in a debate over the meaning of "possession." "Possession" is a workhorse word of the law—used in many contexts to do many chores and defined accordingly.

(2) **Mistake as to contents:** [§71]   If a person is mistaken as to the contents of a parcel, he may not be deemed in possession of the contents of the parcel, even though he is in possession of the parcel. Thus, suppose a statute **forbids the possession** of marijuana. O gives A a parcel which, unknown to A, is filled with marijuana. A is to deliver the parcel to B. Enroute to B's home, A is arrested. A has not violated the statute. The court will read into the statute the requirement of **intent** to possess marijuana because it seems unfair to convict an innocent and unknowing person. [State v. Cox, 179 P. 575 (Or. 1919)]

(3) **Value undisclosed to bailee:** [§72]   If a bailor gives an article to a bailee but does not disclose the exceptional value of the article, a bailment is created. The risk of caring for the article in its true value is put upon the bailee when he accepts possession of the article.

(a) **Example:** O owns a ring set with a very valuable cabochon sapphire. O hands it to A, asking A to deliver it to B. A agrees to do so, not knowing that the ring is very valuable. A negligently loses the ring. A bailment has been created. [Peet v. The Roth Hotel Co., 253 N.W. 546 (Minn. 1934)]

(4) **Involuntary bailment:** [§73]   The normal bailment is consensual. In a few situations, however, a bailment arises even though the bailor and bailee have not consented to the bailee's possession. In a sense, the legal consequence of a bailment is imposed on the person without his consent. Such a situation may in-

volve a **finder,** a person who pens up **stray cattle,** or a **landlord** who resumes possession of leased premises after the tenant has vacated the premises leaving some goods behind. These are called **constructive** or **involuntary bailments.** The basic issue is whether it is reasonable to impose liability upon such persons, and if so, to what extent. (*See infra,* §§81-86.)

3. **Rights and Duties of Bailee**

a. **Rights against third parties:** [§74]   As against a third party, a bailee is entitled to full damages resulting from wrongdoing by the third party. The third party **cannot** assert a **jus tertii** defense (*see supra,* §49). As against a third party, possession is as good as ownership.

   (1) **Rights of bailor:** [§75]   If the bailee recovers from the third party wrongdoer, the bailee is liable to the bailor for the amount recovered—even though the bailee was not originally liable to the bailor. Once the **third party pays the bailee,** the bailor **cannot** recover from the third party. [The Winkfield, [1902] P. 42]

b. **Duty of bailee to exercise care:** [§76]   Generally, all bailees are under a duty to exercise care over the bailed goods, but the standard of care varies with the type of bailment. Traditionally, the degree of care has been commensurate with **who gets the benefit** of the bailment.

   (1) **Bailment for the sole benefit of bailee:** [§77]   If the bailment is for the sole benefit of the bailee (as when a person borrows a lawnmower), the bailee is required to use **extraordinary care.** The bailee is liable for even slight neglect that results in the goods being lost, damaged, or destroyed.

   (2) **Bailment for mutual benefit of bailor and bailee:** [§78]   If the bailment benefits both the bailor and bailee (as when O leaves a clock at the repair shop), the bailee must **exercise ordinary care** and is liable for **ordinary negligence.**

      (a) **"Mutual benefit":** [§79]   A mutual benefit is clear where the bailee charges for the service. In other cases, courts have stretched the facts to find some benefit to both parties from the service rendered. Thus, if a hotel cashier accepts a ring for delivery to a guest in the hotel, the hotel gets a benefit from rendering a service to a guest (goodwill if nothing else). [Peet v. The Roth Hotel Co., *supra,* §72]

   (3) **Bailment for sole benefit of bailor:** [§80]   Where the bailment is for the sole benefit of the bailor (as when O asks B to keep his silver while he is on holiday), it is a "gratuitous" bailment. A gratuitous bailee must use **only slight care** and is liable only for **gross negligence.** *But note:* Some courts, while giving lip service to the rule, in effect reject it by defining "gross negligence" as lack of reasonable care under the circumstances. [Preston v. Prather, 137 U.S. 604 (1890)]

(a) **Compare—involuntary bailment:** [§81] Where the bailment is not consensual, but the bailee has the goods thrust upon her, so to speak, the bailee *does not have to take affirmative steps* to protect the property. For example, the finder can ignore the find, or the farmer can drive the cattle off her property. But if she does take possession, she is usually held to the same standard as a bailee for the sole benefit of the bailor. She must use *slight care.* A landlord cannot throw the departed tenant's goods on the street, for instance, but must put them in some fairly safe place.

(4) **Modern trend:** [§82] This system of classification by benefits is not very satisfactory. In almost all bailments *some* benefit results to both parties. If B borrows neighbor O's lawnmower, for example, O benefits by goodwill. Similarly, a finder or farmer who pens stray cattle benefits at least by goodwill, maybe by a reward, and perhaps by ultimate ownership if the true owner does not show up. Nor are the distinctions between gross, ordinary, and slight negligence always easy to apply to facts. In view of this, modern courts may well be moving away from this system to a *standard of ordinary care under the circumstances.* [*See* Shamrock Hilton Hotel v. Caranas, 488 S.W.2d 151 (Tex. 1972)—*discussed infra,* §86]

(5) **Burden of proof:** [§83] The old rule assigned the bailor the burden of proving that the bailee acted negligently. However, because the bailor may have no knowledge of the facts concerning the loss of the bailed goods, modern courts have rejected the old rule as inequitable and have placed the burden on the *bailee* to prove due care. [Knowles v. Gilchrist Co., 289 N.E.2d 881 (Mass. 1972)] Similarly, if a contract provision sets a dollar limitation on the bailee's liability for negligence, the burden of proof is on the bailee to show that the goods were negligently lost (with resulting limited liability) rather than converted to the bailee's own use (liability for full value of goods converted). Otherwise, the bailee could steal the goods and then claim they mysteriously disappeared and be liable only for negligence because the bailor could not prove how the goods were lost. [Joseph H. Reinfeld, Inc. v. Griswold & Bateman, 458 A.2d 1341 (N.J. 1983)]

c. **Duty to redeliver:** [§84] Regardless of the standard of care required of a bailee while the goods are in his custody, a bailee is held to *strict liability* when it comes to redelivery. If the bailee misdelivers the goods to the wrong person, he is stuck with liability even though he used reasonable care. Thus if the bailee delivers the goods to A on a forged order from the bailor, the bailee is liable. This is a *harsh rule,* and one of doubtful soundness inherited from past times.

(1) **Exception:** [§85] An *involuntary bailee* is liable only if the bailee was *negligent* in delivering the goods to the wrong person. The courts impose strict liability on the ordinary bailee because he is in breach of contract when he misdelivers. But an involuntary bailee has no contract and has a lesser liability.

(a) **Example:** A and B are investment brokers. A's agent brings a bearer bond to B's office, and drops it through a letter slot in a door. B picks it up, sees it is the wrong bond ordered, opens the door and calls for A's agent. C, who is not A's agent, responds promptly and B, not knowing A's agent, hands the faker the bond. As an involuntary bailee B can be liable only if negligence is shown. [Cowen v. Pressprich, 202 App. Div. 796 (1922)]

(b) **Negligence by involuntary bailee:** [§86]   If negligence is shown in misdelivery, an involuntary bailee is liable. Thus in *Shamrock Hilton Hotel v. Caranas, supra,* §82, the plaintiff, a hotel guest, left her purse containing valuable jewelry in the hotel restaurant. A busboy found it and delivered it to the cashier, who misdelivered it to another person. The court held that the hotel was a constructive bailee and was negligent in misdelivering the purse. It also held that there was *mutual benefit* to the hotel and the guest, and therefore the hotel was liable for ordinary negligence in caring for the item. This is an example of a case applying an ordinary negligence standard to an involuntary bailee.

4. **Contractual Modification of Liability:** [§87]   Bailees often attempt to limit their liability by provision in the contract. Most courts permit such contractual limitations provided they do not relieve the bailee from *gross or willful negligence.*

   a. **Bailor must consent:** [§88]   A contractual limitation on liability requires the *consent of the bailor.* (A contract requires assent of both parties.) Posting a sign is not enough unless the bailee can show the bailor saw and accepted the sign. Putting a limited liability provision on a claim check will not work either unless the bailee can show that the bailor was, or should have been, aware of it. If the bailor thought the claim check was merely for identification purposes, no contract limiting liability results. [Kergald v. Armstrong Transfer Express Co., 113 N.E.2d 53 (Mass. 1953)]

F. ACCESSION

1. **Doctrine of Accession:** [§89]   The doctrine of accession comes into play when one person adds to the property of another either *labor* or *labor and new materials.* A person whose property is taken and used by another is always entitled to the value of the property taken, but that person may lose title by the accessions ("additions") of the other. If the improver is denied title by accession, the original owner is entitled to the value added by the taker.

   a. **Labor added:** [§90]   Where A adds labor to B's raw material, the courts usually award the final product to the owner of the raw material (B), *unless* A's efforts have *sufficiently increased* its value to make it unfair to award the final product to B. Just how much is "sufficient" is difficult to determine. In addition, most states require that for A to recover, he must show that he acted *in good faith* and not willfully.

      (1) **Example:** A, relying on a permission that he supposes came from B, enters B's land, cuts timber, and makes hoops from the timber. The standing timber was worth $25; the hoops are worth $700. The hoops belong to A, though B can sue

A for $25 damage for trespass. [Wetherbee v. Green, 22 Mich. 311 (1871)] But if the timber was worth $2.87 and the value of A's labor is worth $1.87, A has not sufficiently increased the value of the timber to have his labor rewarded. [Isle Royale Mining Co. v. Hertin, 37 Mich. 332 (1877)]

(2) **Compare—trespass:** A's act in the preceding example is a trespass, regardless of his good faith. Nonetheless, where it would be *grossly unjust* for B to appropriate A's labor to himself, A will get compensation for his labor and B damages for A's trespass.

b. **Labor and materials added:** [§91]   Where A adds labor and materials to raw material owned by B, the final product is generally awarded to the *owner of the principal material,* even if that person happens to be the one who willfully and wrongfully took the other's material and transformed it by adding her own.

(1) **Example:** A, a starving artist, steals a canvas from B and, using her own oils, A paints a valuable painting. If the painting is more valuable than the canvas, A will get it—but, of course, she must pay B the value of the canvas.

2. **Mistaken Improver:** [§92]   The doctrine of *mistaken improver* is similar to the doctrine of accession applicable to *real estate.* Suppose that A builds a house on land owned by B. If A acted willfully, with knowledge that he was building on B's land, A has no remedy; the house belongs to B. Courts give A a remedy *only* if the improvement is *in good faith.* The usual remedy is that the landowner (B) has the option of paying A the value of the house or of selling A the land at fair market value. [Hardy v. Burroughs, 232 N.W. 200 (Mich. 1930); Somerville v. Jacobs, 170 S.E.2d 805 (W. Va. 1969)]

3. **Confusion:** [§93]   Confusion involves an intermingling of fungible goods of different owners which can no longer be separately identified. *Example:* A *negligently* mixes his wheat with B's wheat. The general rule is that each receives a proportionate part of the wheat. If A *intentionally* mixes his wheat with B's, knowing B's wheat is better, A runs a risk of being punished by losing all his wheat. The cases are split.

G. ADVERSE POSSESSION

1. **Overview**

a. **Theory of adverse possession:** [§94]   The basic theory of adverse possession is simple: If, within the number of years specified in the state *statute of limitations,* the owner of land does not take legal action to eject a possessor who claims adversely to the owner, the *owner is thereafter barred* from bringing an action in ejectment. Once the owner is barred from suing in ejectment, the adverse possessor has title to the land.

(1) **Example:** O owns Blackacre. A, a squatter, enters Blackacre in 1975 and possesses the land adversely to O for ten years. O does nothing during the ten-year period. The state statute of limitations provides that if an owner of land does not bring an action to recover possession within ten years after the cause of

action first arises, the owner is forever barred from bringing such an action. In 1985, O's action in ejectment is barred and A owns Blackacre.

b. **Effect of adverse possession:** [§95]   Adverse possession is a means of acquiring **title** to property by long, uninterrupted possession. The running of the statute of limitations on the owner's action in ejectment **not only bars** the owner's claim to possession, it also strips the owner of title and **creates a new title** in the adverse possessor.

c. **Purpose of doctrine:** [§96]   Acquiring title by adverse possession might look at first glance like acquiring title by theft, but the doctrine serves several important purposes:

(1) **To protect title:** [§97]   Protection of possession in fact protects ownership because title may be difficult to prove (*see supra,* §3). The same policy underlies adverse possession. [Simis v. McElroy, 160 N.Y. 156 (1899)]

(a) **Example:** O owns Blackacre in 1930. A deeds Blackacre to B in 1940, and in 1975, B deeds Blackacre to C. B is in possession from 1940 to 1975, and C is in possession after 1975. In 1985, C contracts to sell Blackacre to D. Upon searching the records, D finds no deed from O to A and alleges that C does not have title. It is possible that O gave A a deed to the property before 1940 and the deed was lost and not recorded, but in any event B and C thought they were the owners after 1940 and acted as such by taking possession. O is now barred by the statute of limitations and C can convey to D a good title based on adverse possession. [Rehoboth Heights Development Co. v. Marshall, 137 A. 83 (Del. 1927)]

(b) **Land records:** Land title records are kept in each county courthouse, but these records are deficient in many respects. The doctrine of adverse possession makes these records more reliable by protecting possessors whose record title is deficient in some way. It also tends to limit record searches of title to land to a reasonable period of time and not back to a sovereign, which would be very costly.

(2) **To bar stale claims:** [§98]   A and B both may be claiming Blackacre, and B goes into possession. As time passes, witnesses die or their memories grow dim, and the evidence of the respective claims of A and B becomes less and less reliable. Thus, another purpose of the statute of limitations is to require a lawsuit to be brought to oust a possessor while the witnesses' memories are still fresh.

(3) **To reward those who use land productively:** [§99]   Society likes to have land used for farming or housing or other productive enterprises. By rewarding the possessor who is productive, and penalizing the owner who would let the land lie unproductive, the doctrine of adverse possession encourages productivity.

(4) **To honor expectations:** [§100]   Persons in possession of property quite naturally, after a long time, acquire attachments to land and expectations that they

can continue to use the property as they have long done, however they came by it. ***Giving effect to expectations*** is a policy running all through the law of property.

d. **Length of time required:** [§101]   The statutory period for adverse possession varies from state to state—from five to twenty-one years. The modern trend is to shorten the period of adverse possession.

e. **Possessor's rights before acquiring title:** [§102]   Before the statute of limitations bars the true owner, the adverse possessor has all the rights of a possessor described above: He can evict a subsequent possessor who takes possession away from him ("prior possessor wins," *supra,* §16). [Brumagin v. Bradshaw, 39 Cal. 24 (1870)] He can sue a third party for damages to the property, recovering either permanent damages or damage to the possessory interest (*see supra,* §§37-48). He has an interest—"possession"—which he can transfer to another (*see* "tacking," *infra,* §148). [Howard v. Kunto, 477 P.2d 210 (Wash. 1970)] ***But,*** before the expiration of the statutory period, an adverse possessor has **no interest in the property valid against the true owner.** The true owner may retake possession at any time. (This is another example of relativity of title discussed *supra,* §17.)

2. **Requirements of Adverse Possession:** [§103]   In order to establish title by adverse possession, the possessor must show (i) an ***actual entry*** giving ***exclusive*** possession that is (ii) ***open and notorious,*** (iii) ***adverse and under a claim of right,*** and (iv) ***continuous*** for the statutory period. Even if the statute of limitations does not specify these requirements, courts have, on their own, added them. Hence, adverse possession law is a blend of statutes and judicial decisions.

a. **Actual entry giving exclusive possession:** [§104]   The word "actual" merely signifies that possession must be of such a character that the community would reasonably regard the adverse possessor as the owner. It cannot be "constructive" possession—*i.e.,* possession that the law fictionally imputes to someone for some purpose. This possession must be seen. Hence, the requirement of actual possession differs little from the requirement of open and notorious possession.

(1) **Jury function:** [§105]   It is for the jury to decide whether the acts constitute an actual, open and notorious ***possession*** (*i.e.,* acts that usually accompany the ownership of lands similarly situated) and not merely a series of ***trespasses.*** *Rationale:* Since the acts required are acts that "look like ownership" to the community, a jury is the best judge of that. [Brumagin v. Bradshaw, *supra*]

(2) **Purpose of entry requirement:** [§106]   The primary purpose of the entry requirement is to ***trigger the cause of action,*** which starts the statute of limitations running. It also shows the extent of the adverse possessor's claim. (*See also* "constructive adverse possession," *infra,* §§165 *et seq.*)

(3) **Constructive possession of part:** [§107]   If there is an actual entry on ***part*** of the land described in a deed, the possessor may be deemed in constructive pos-

session of the rest (*see* "constructive adverse possession," *infra,* §§165 *et seq.*). But an actual entry on some part of the land is required.

(4) **Exclusive possession:** [§108]   The requirement that the adverse possessor be in exclusive possession means that she not be sharing possession with the **owner** nor with the **public generally.** If the adverse possessor were so sharing possession, the owner would probably not realize the adverse possessor was claiming ownership against him. However, it is possible for two or more persons, acting in concert and sharing only among themselves, to acquire title by adverse possession as tenants in common.

b. **Open and notorious possession**

(1) **Definition:** [§109]   The adverse possessor must occupy the property in an **open, notorious,** and **visible** manner. Her acts must be such as will constitute **reasonable notice** to the owner that she is claiming dominion, so that the owner can defend his rights. Generally, open and notorious acts are those that look like typical acts of an owner of property; they are acts from which the community, observing them, would infer the actor to be claiming ownership. Obviously what types of acts are required turns on the type of land involved. The acts must be **appropriate** to the condition, size, and locality of the land.

(a) **Possession of farmland:** [§110]   Fencing, cultivating, and erecting a building on farm land are usually deemed open and notorious acts. [Cheek v. Wainwright, 269 S.E.2d 443 (Ga. 1980)] Similarly, using land for cattle pasturage can be an open and notorious act, but, in a state like Texas, where unenclosed land is open for grazing by anyone's cattle, the adverse possessor must fence the land in order to acquire title by adverse possession. [McDonnold v. Weinacht, 465 S.W.2d 136 (Tex. 1971)]

(b) **Possession of wild, undeveloped land:** [§111]   Wild, undeveloped land not suitable for farming but suitable for hunting and fishing can be adversely possessed by acts indicating a claim of dominion.

1) **Example:** O owns Blackacre, wild and undeveloped land, suitable only for hunting and fishing. A erects a **hunting cabin** on the land, and uses it about six times a year, including each hunting season. A **pays taxes** on the land. A **sells the timber on Blackacre** to B, and **executes a number of oil leases.** These acts are sufficient to constitute adverse possession. Fencing the land or living on it are not necessary. [Monroe v. Rawlings, 49 N.W.2d 55 (Mich. 1951)]

(c) **Possession of city land:** [§112]   The erection of a fence or a building may constitute adverse possession. But the totality of the acts must give a picture of a person claiming dominion. For example, the Supreme Court held that where the adverse possessor took sand and gravel from a city lot principally valuable for sand and gravel, **and granted permission** to others to take sand and gravel, **and sued in trespass** those who took sand and gravel without permission, **and paid taxes,** these acts constituted adverse possession of a lot within a city. [Ewing v. Burnet, 36 U.S. 39 (1837); *but see* Madson v. Cohn, 22 Cal. App. 704 (1932)—clearing weeds, planting six bushes and trees, and paying taxes were held to be insufficient acts]

(d) **Statutory requirements:** [§113]   Some states have statutes that require specific kinds of acts for adverse possession. New York statutes, for example, provide that if the claimant does not enter with color of title (*see infra,* §§124-127), adverse possession can be claimed only where the land "has been protected by a substantial inclosure" or has been "usually cultivated or improved." Hence in New York, a person **without color of title** would have to show—in the preceding examples—that a hunting cabin is a "usual improvement" and that taking sand and gravel was a "usual cultivation" in order to win. The other acts (paying taxes, giving leases, suing persons for trespass) are not relevant. [Van Valkenburgh v. Lutz, 304 N.Y. 95 (1952)]

(2) **Possession of property underground:** [§114]   Because of the requirement of actual, open and notorious possession, is it possible to possess what lies under the surface of the earth?

(a) **Minerals:** [§115]   If the minerals have **not** been severed from the surface estate prior to entry of the adverse possessor upon the surface, **possession of the surface is possession of the minerals.** They are treated as part of the land. On the other hand, **if the minerals have been severed,** possession of the surface does not carry possession of the minerals. To start adverse possession running against the owner of the minerals, the adverse possessor must start removing them. Possession of the surface does not give a cause of action to the separate owner of the minerals until the minerals are disturbed. The minerals have **never been actually possessed** by the surface possessor.

   1)   **Example:** O owns Blackacre. O sells the mineral rights to X. A enters Blackacre and adversely possesses the surface for thirty years, but does not disturb the minerals. A now owns Blackacre, but X still owns the minerals under Blackacre. [Failoni v. Chicago & North Western Railway, 195 N.E.2d 619 (Ill. 1964)]

(b) **Caves:** [§116]   Possession of a cave under the surface owner's land, of which the surface owner is unaware, does not establish adverse possession because it is **not open and notorious.** [Marengo Cave Co. v. Ross, 10 N.E.2d 917 (Ind. 1937)]

c.   **Adverse and under a claim of right:** [§117]   To be an adverse possessor, a person must hold **adversely** to the owner and **under a claim of right.** Sometimes the word **hostile** is inserted as an element of adverse possession. It does not mean animosity but only that the possession is **without the owner's consent—it is not subordinate to the owner.** One purpose of the claim of right requirement is to help assure that the true owner is not lulled into believing an occupant will make no claim against him. The key question in determining whether a person is adverse and under a claim of right is: Does the court apply an **objective** or **subjective** test? This question has been the subject of much litigation and dispute.

(1) **Objective test:** [§118]   Under the objective test, the state of mind of the possessor is not very important; what is important are the **actions of the possessor.** The possessor's actions, including statements, must **look like** they are claims of ownership. If they look that way to the community, the claim is adverse and **under a claim of right.** Under the objective test, a person can be an adverse possessor even though **he is not actually claiming title** against the true owner. The important thing is that **he is not occupying** the land **with permission** of the owner. Permission negates a claim of right. [Ottavia v. Savarese, 155 N.E.2d 432 (Mass. 1959)]

    (a) **Example:** A enters land owned by O and occupies it for over twenty years. A uses the land as the average owner would, but frequently asserts that he is making no claim of title, but will surrender the land to the true owner when he appears. **Legally, A is making a claim of right** and is an adverse possessor. He is not occupying with the permission of the owner, and the owner **has a cause of action** in ejectment upon which the statute is running. Regardless of A's state of mind, his occupation of the land is **prima facie evidence** that he does so under a claim of title. The very nature of the act of entry and possession is the assertion of a claim of right, and triggers the owner's cause of action. [Patterson v. Reigle, 4 Pa. 201 (1846)]

    (b) **Actions inducing owner not to bring suit:** [§119]   If the adverse possessor's actions are such as to induce the owner not to bring suit, the adverse possessor ceases to be adverse. (*Rationale:* Fairness to the owner.) The most common action raising this issue occurs when the adverse possessor **offers to purchase** the land from the owner. If this offer is a **disclaimer** of ownership, inducing reliance by the owner, the statute of limitations stops running (if it has started). On the other hand, if the offer to purchase is an attempt by the possessor who claims title **to avoid litigation,** adversity continues. It is for the jury to decide on the facts whether the offer is a disclaimer inducing nonaction, or an attempt by a claimant of title to avoid litigation. [Warren v. Bowdran, 31 N.E. 300 (Mass. 1892)]

(2) **Subjective test:** [§120]   Under the subjective test, a claim of right means that the adverse possessor must have a **bona fide or good faith belief** that he has title. If the possessor knows he has no title, and that someone else has title, his possession is not adverse. Under this view, a mere squatter (a person who enters into possession knowing it belongs to another) cannot be an adverse possessor. As one court said, "This idea of acquiring title by larceny does not go in this country." [Jasperson v. Scharnikow, 150 F. 571 (9th Cir. 1907)]

    (a) **Example:** O tells A, "Blackacre is yours. Go and farm it." A enters Blackacre and farms it. A did not actually have title because the Statute of

Frauds requires that title to land be transferred by a written instrument. However, A has a bona fide claim of title and is an adverse possessor. [Newells v. Carter, 119 A. 62 (Me. 1922)]

(b) **Mistaken belief:** [§121]   Within the group of states requiring a bona fide claim of title, a subgroup holds—at least in boundary disputes—that if the possessor *mistakenly believes* that he has title but, *if he knew the truth, would not claim title,* he is not occupying adversely. This view is treated more fully in connection with boundary disputes (*see infra,* §§128 *et seq.*).

(c) **Criticism of subjective test:** [§122]   There are problems with the requirement of a bona fide claim of title: (i) It ignores the fact that the owner can bring an action in ejectment against the possessor, upon which the statute of limitations should run. (ii) It does not take into account the attachment a possessor acquires through time. As Holmes put it, "A thing which you have enjoyed and used as your own for a long time, whether property or an opinion, takes root in your being and cannot be torn away without your resenting the act and trying to defend yourself, however you came by it." [10 Harv. L. Rev. 457, 477 (1897)] (iii) It does not reward the occupant who has used the land in a productive way. (For other criticisms in connection with boundary disputes, *see infra,* §132.)

(d) **Recent cases:** [§123]   Although the objective test is recommended by all the commentators (Am. Law Prop., Powell, Restatement) and said by some to be the majority rule, a recent study of cases since 1966 shows that courts require the possessor to act in good faith. A possessor acting under an honest mistake is holding adversely, but a person who knows the land does not belong to him is not holding under a claim of right. Thus, willful trespassers and squatters have not prevailed unless they have strong equities in their favor. [Helmholz, 61 Wash. U.L.Q. 331 (1983)]

(3) **Color of title:** [§124]   Do not confuse *claim of title* with *color of title.* Claim of right (or claim of title) expresses the necessary adversity, discussed *supra.* Color of title refers to a claim founded on a *written instrument* (a deed, a will) or a judgment or decree which is for some reason defective and invalid. *Examples:* The grantor's name is forged to the deed; the grantor does not own the land deeded; the grantor was mentally incompetent; the deed is improperly executed; the deed is a tax deed void because the owner was not given notice of the tax sale. In all these cases, the grantee takes possession *under color of title.* Where a person enters with color of title, no further claim of title or proof of adversity is required.

(a) **Color of title not required:** [§125]   In most states, color of title is *not* required to be an adverse possessor. Even where a bona fide claim of title is required, color of title is not necessary. In the example (*supra,* §120) where O orally gives Blackacre to A, A has no color of title, but A—believing the oral transfer was valid—possesses under a claim of title.

1) **Minority views:** [§126] In a few states, entry under color of title is required for adverse possession. In a few others, the requirements for adverse possession are more lenient, or the statutory period shorter, for claimants under color of title.

2) **Constructive adverse possession:** [§127] Entry under color of title is an advantage in all states under the doctrine of constructive adverse possession (*infra,* §165).

(4) **Boundary disputes:** [§128] Claim of right issues often arise between adjoining landowners where one of the parties (A) has been in open and notorious possession of a strip of land along his boundary, ***mistakenly believing it to be his.*** In fact, it belongs to his neighbor B. There are several views taken of adverse possession in this context.

(a) **Objective test—majority view:** [§129] The majority of courts apply the objective test of claim of right (*supra,* §118) to boundary disputes. Thus, the possessor's mistake is not determinative; the possessor is necessarily holding under a claim of right if his actions appear to the community to be a claim of ownership and if he is not holding with permission of the owner. Under this test, if A fences in the land, or otherwise indicates the boundaries and maintains the strip, A acquires title by adverse possession when the statutory period expires. [Joiner v. Janssen, 421 N.E.2d 170 (Ill. 1981); West v. Tilley, 33 App. Div. 2d 228 (1970)]

1) **Note—good faith:** Although the majority of courts have embraced the objective test in boundary disputes, recent cases suggest that good faith is still relevant and that trespassers in bad faith will not prevail. Encroachment by an honest mistake is not in bad faith.

(b) **The Maine doctrine:** [§130] A minority of jurisdictions hold that if the possessor is ***mistaken*** as to the boundary and would ***not*** have occupied or claimed the land ***if he had known the mistake,*** the possessor has ***no intention*** to claim title and adversity is missing. This is called the "Maine doctrine." [Preble v. Maine Central Railroad, 27 A. 149 (Me. 1893)]

1) **Example:** A, ***intending*** to claim only to the true boundary line, erects a fence on what A ***mistakenly*** believes to be the correct boundary line dividing his land from that of his neighbor B. In fact, the fence is ten feet over onto B's land, giving A possession of ten feet of B's land. The fence remains for the period of limitations. Under the majority view, A owns the ten feet by adverse possession. Under the Maine doctrine, A's actual state of mind is relevant. If A would not have claimed title to the ten feet had he known it belonged to B, A does ***not*** possess under a ***claim of right,*** and hence there is no adverse possession.

2) **Distinguish bona fide claim of title:** [§131] The Maine doctrine and the view that the adverse possessor must have a bona fide claim of title

are similar but not quite the same. Suppose that A, a greedy neighbor, has an intent to claim title to the ten feet whether or not he is mistaken. Under the Maine doctrine, A would get title by adverse possession, but A would not get title if the court requires a bona fide claim of title for adverse possession.

3) **Criticism:** [§132]   The Maine doctrine has been criticized on the following grounds: (i) An *action in ejectment* lies against the possessor regardless of his actual intent, and the statute bars the action after a specified period. (ii) If actual intent is determinative, the intentional *wrongdoer wins* when the good neighbor would not. (iii) The Maine doctrine *encourages* honest neighbors to *lie* on the witness stand ("I wanted it as mine in any case"). (iv) The objective test of adverse possession—evidenced by the possessor's acts and conduct—is more reliable and *cheaper to administer* than a subjective test of what was actually in the possessor's mind.

(c) **The New Jersey view:** [§133]   New Jersey for a long time adhered to the Maine doctrine, but New Jersey has now joined the majority and applies the objective test with this qualification: "When the encroachment of an adjoining owner *is of a small area* and the fact of an intrusion is not clearly and self-evidently apparent to the naked eye but requires an on-site survey for certain disclosure," the encroachment is *not open and notorious.* In that case, the statute of limitations will run against the owner only if the owner has *actual knowledge* of the encroachment. [Mannillo v. Gorski, 255 A.2d 258 (N.J. 1969)]

(d) **Agreement on boundaries:** [§134]   Apart from adverse possession, boundary disputes can be resolved by other doctrines that assume an agreement between the neighboring parties. An oral agreement is unenforceable because the Statute of Frauds requires a written instrument for the conveyance of land, and in the example *supra,* an agreement by A and B would in effect be conveying ten feet of B's land to A. Nonetheless, courts have found ways of enforcing oral agreements.

1) **Agreed boundaries:** [§135]   The doctrine of agreed boundaries provides that if there is uncertainty between neighbors as to the true boundary line, an *oral agreement* to settle such uncertainty is enforceable—*not* as a *conveyance,* which would violate the Statute of Frauds, but as a *way of locating the boundary described in the deeds.* [Joaquin v. Shiloh Orchards, 84 Cal. App. 3d 192 (1978)]

2) **Acquiescence:** [§136]   The doctrine of acquiescence provides that long acquiescence—but perhaps for a shorter period of time than the statute of limitations—is evidence of an agreement between the parties fixing the boundary line.

3) **Estoppel:** [§137]   Estoppel applies where neighbor B makes positive representations about, or conducts himself so as to indicate, the loca-

tion of a common boundary, and neighbor A substantially changes his position in reliance on such representations or conduct. Neighbor B is estopped to deny the validity of his statements or acts. Estoppel has also occasionally been applied when neighbor B remains silent in the face of substantial expenditures by neighbor A.

(5) **Special situations concerning adversity:** [§138] Whether the possessor is holding *adversely* or *permissively* arises in a few situations that recur frequently enough to deserve special mention.

(a) **Oral transfers of land:** [§139] Suppose that O, owner of Blackacre, tells his son A that Blackacre is his. A agrees to make necessary repairs and pay taxes and to let his father O remain in possession. (This purported oral transfer violates the Statute of Frauds and is void.) O remains in possession. A pays taxes and upkeep. Is O A's tenant, holding adversely to himself? Yes, the courts attribute O's possession as tenant to A, and A will acquire title by adverse possession when the statutory period runs. Technically this is odd since O, being both owner and tenant in possession, never had a cause of action in ejectment against himself which was barred by the statute. To carry out an oral agreement where evidence of that agreement is very clear and reliable, courts have overlooked the technical problem and held that O's possession is A's possession. [Newells v. Carter, *supra,* §120]

(b) **Landlord—tenant:** [§140] A tenant who enters into possession with the permission of the landlord obviously holds permissively and not adversely. However, if the tenant subsequently *clearly repudiates* the lease in such a manner as to give notice to the landlord that she is now holding adversely, the tenant can become an adverse possessor. Tenants rarely win as adverse possessors because the repudiation is rarely of the requisite clarity.

(c) **Co-tenants:** [§141] The possession of a tenant in common or a joint tenant is not ordinarily adverse to her co-tenant(s), *since each co-tenant has the right to occupy or to rent the property.* To claim adversely, one co-tenant in possession must *oust* her co-tenant physically, deny him his share of the rents and profits, or *exclude* him *under a claim of sole ownership.* The acts must be so openly and notoriously hostile that the co-tenant will reasonably know that the possessory co-tenant is claiming exclusive ownership of the property.

1) **Note:** Taking possession or collecting rents from the property, growing and cutting crops, taking minerals, and paying taxes are *not enough* by themselves, singly or collectively, to establish adversity, since they do not necessarily imply that the party in possession is claiming sole ownership. Any co-tenant has the right as a co-owner to do these things (*see infra,* §§718-744), and other co-tenants have no cause of action to prevent them being done. [Mercer v. Wayman, 137 N.E.2d 815 (Ill. 1956)]

d. **Continuous, uninterrupted possession: [§142]** The fourth requirement for adverse possession is that the possession continue uninterrupted throughout the statutory period.

(1) **Continuous possession: [§143]** Continuous possession requires only the *degree of occupancy* and use that the *average owner* would make of the particular type of property. An adverse use is continuous when it is made without a break in the essential *attitude of mind* required for adverse use. A person can be in continuous possession even though there are considerable intervals during which the property is not used.

(a) **Purpose: [§144]** The purpose of the continuity requirement is to give the owner notice that the possessor is claiming ownership, and that the entries are not just a series of trespasses.

(b) **Seasonal use: [§145]** Use of a summer home only during the summer for the statutory period is continuous use. [Howard v. Kunto, *supra*, §102] Similarly, seasonal use of a hunting cabin during the hunting seasons, or the grazing of cattle on range lands in summer, may be sufficiently continuous possession, if such lands are normally used this way. [Monroe v. Rawlings, *supra*, §111]

1) **Compare—easements: [§146]** Intermittent use may give rise to a prescriptive easement if it does not suffice to gain title by adverse possession. For example, if a house is built on the property line, going into a neighbor's yard to put up storm windows in the fall and take them down in the spring results in a prescriptive easement. (*See infra,* §§1358 *et seq.*)

(c) **Abandonment: [§147]** Abandonment is the *intentional relinquishment* of possession. If the possessor abandons the property for *any period* of time, without intent to return, continuity of adverse possession is lost. The adverse possession comes to an end, and possession returns constructively to the true owner. If the adverse possessor later returns, the statute of limitations begins to run anew.

(2) **Tacking by successive adverse possessors: [§148]** To establish continuous possession for the statutory period, an adverse possessor can tack onto her own period of adverse possession any period of adverse possession by *predecessors in interest.* Thus, separate periods of actual possession by those holding hostilely to the owner can be tacked together, provided there is *privity of estate* between the adverse possessors (*see below*).

(a) **Example:** O owns Blackacre. In 1965, A enters adversely. In 1978, A sells her interest to B, who continues to hold adversely to O. In 1982, B dies and his interest is inherited by C, who takes possession and continues to hold adversely to O. The statutory period is twenty years. In 1985, C acquires title by adverse possession—thirteen years of A's possession and four years of B's possession are tacked on to three years of C's own possession.

(b) **Privity of estate:** [§149]   To tack on to a preceding possession, there must be privity of estate between the two possessors. Privity of estate in this context means that a possessor **voluntarily** transferred to a subsequent possessor either an **estate in land** (*see infra*, §§270 *et seq.*) or **physical possession.** Where the transfer is not voluntary, as in the case of someone **ousting** the prior possessor, there is no privity of estate. [Brand v. Prince, 35 N.Y.2d 634 (1974)]

1) **Rationale:** Why is privity required? In England, it is not required. The statute of limitations runs against the true owner from the time adverse possession began, and as long as adverse possession continues unbroken, it makes no difference who continues it. The English simply penalize the owner who sleeps on his rights. In this country, courts require privity because they view title by adverse possession as something **to be gained by meritorious conduct**—an involuntary transfer by ouster or seizure is not regarded as meritorious.

2) **Example:** A owns lot 1, but by mistake builds his house on the adjoining lot 2 owned by O. Five years later, A sells "his house" to B, giving B a deed describing lot 1 and transferring to B physical possession of lot 2 (where the house is). B can tack A's possession of lot 2 on to his own. [Howard v. Kunto, *supra*]

(c) **Ouster by third party:** [§150]   When an adverse possessor (A) is ousted by a third party (X), X **cannot tack** on A's period of prior possession because of lack of privity. Privity of estate requires a **voluntary** transfer for tacking.

1) **Reentry by A:** [§151]   Suppose that six months after A is ousted by X, A manages to reenter the property and resume possession. What effect does the ouster by X have on A's adverse possession rights? There are three views:

a) **The statute of limitations starts running anew** on A. This view is generally rejected by courts as unfair to A, especially where A has acted promptly in recovering possession.

b) **The statute of limitations continues uninterrupted** from A's earlier possession. The difficulty with this position is A is tacking X's possession onto her own, and there is no privity between them. Nonetheless, it seems fair to A, and can be reached by treating X as a "trespasser" and not a "possessor." This is, of course, merely a manipulation of terms to reach a desired result. Most courts reach this result when A has acted promptly to regain possession.

c) **A can tack her prior possession onto her later possession, but the statute is tolled during the period** of X's possession, because in that period O had no cause of action against A (who was out of possession). Under this view, A has to stay in possession the statutory period plus six months (when X was in possession). This view apparently has little case support but is favored by 3 Am. Law Prop. §15.10.

(d) **Abandonment:** [§152]   Tacking is ***not permitted*** where one adverse possessor ***abandons*** the property, even though another enters immediately. The statute of limitations starts running anew on the new entry. For tacking, there must be privity of estate—a voluntary transfer between possessors. (Of course, there is no forced entry here, and the reason for requiring privity of estate does not apply. Nonetheless, courts, having required privity of estate and having defined it as a voluntary transfer, are caught in their conceptual web and do not permit tacking upon abandonment. The English courts do. *See supra*, §149.)

(e) **Tacking on the owner's side:** [§153]   Once adverse possession has begun to run against O, it runs against O and all of O's successors in interest. Hence, if A enters against O in 1970, and O conveys to C in 1975, the statute continues to run against C—from 1970. Thus, successive ownerships are tacked on the owner's side as well as on the adverse possessor's side.

(3) **Interruption by true owner:** [§154]   If the true owner reenters the land openly and notoriously for the ***purpose of regaining possession,*** an interruption has occurred. Interruption of possession by the true owner stops the statute of limitations from running.

(a) **Objective test:** [§155]   In most states, interruption can occur without an actual intent to oust the possessor. Courts use the same sort of objective test for interruption as they use for establishing possession under a claim of right. If the owner's acts are ordinary acts of ownership and would give notice of claim to the average person, they are an interruption. There is a ***presumption*** that the use of land by the owner is the exercise of his ***right*** to use it, and therefore when the owner uses land such use presumptively asserts ownership. [Mendonca v. Cities Service Oil Co., 237 N.E.2d 16 (Mass. 1968)]

e. **Payment of property taxes:** [§156]   In several states, principally in the west, the adverse possessor must pay taxes on the land in order to prevail. [*See, e.g.,* Cal. Civ. Proc. Code §325] This requirement is traceable to the influence of land-rich railroad companies in the western states in the 19th century. With vast tracts of land, the owners found it virtually impossible to discover potential adverse possessors by visual inspection, but the payment of taxes is recorded in the courthouse, giving notice to the owner. In all states, payment of taxes is good evidence of a claim of right.

3. **Disabilities of Owner:** [§157]   Most legislatures think it unfair for a statute of limitations to run upon a person who is unable to bring a lawsuit (under a legal disability). Therefore, most statutes give an ***additional period*** of time to bring an action if the

owner is under a disability. However, disability provisions are strictly limited in two ways: (i) only the disabilities **specified** in the statute (*e.g.,* insanity, infancy) can be considered; and (ii) usually only disabilities of the owner **at the time adverse possession begins** count. The best way to understand disability provisions, and how they work, is to look at a typical statute.

a. **Typical statute:** [§158]   The following statute contains a typical disabilities provision: "An action to recover the title to or possession of real property shall be brought within twenty-one years after the cause thereof accrued, but if a person entitled to bring such action, **at the time the cause thereof accrues**, is within the **age of minority**, of **unsound mind**, or **imprisoned**, such person, after the expiration of twenty-one years from the time the cause of action accrues, may bring such action **within ten years after such disability is removed**." [Ohio Rev. Code Ann. §2305.04 (Baldwin 1975), *applied in* Ewing v. Burnet, *supra,* §112]

b. **Read statute carefully:** [§159]   Observe that only three disabilities count (minority, insanity, imprisonment); that they must be disabilities at the time the adverse possessor first enters; and that in case such disabilities exist, the owner or her successor in interest has twenty-one years **or** ten years after the removal of the disability (whichever period is longer) to bring an action.

(1) **Example:** A enters Blackacre in 1960 when the owner (O) is two years old. The age of majority is eighteen. The statute of limitations is twenty-one years or ten years after the disability (minority) is removed, whichever is longer. The twenty-one year period expires in 1981, but if O reaches her majority in 1976, she has until 1986 to bring suit. The alternative period will expire earlier if O dies under age eighteen; it will expire ten years after O's death. Thus, if O dies at age twelve (1970), O's heir has until 1980 to bring suit under the alternative period—but since the period will not expire in any event until 1981, the alternative period, expiring before 1981, is not used.

(2) **Suit by guardian:** [§160]   A guardian of O can bring suit while O is a minor or insane. Thus a person under a disability may not be without legal representation.

c. **Only disabilities at time of initial entry count:** [§161]   Like the Ohio statute, the large majority of statutes provides that only a disability of the owner **existing at the time the cause of action arose** is considered. Subsequent disabilities of the owner or of any successor in interest have no effect on the operation of the statute of limitations. Also, **no tacking of disabilities is allowed.**

(1) **Example:** (Under the Ohio statute) O is two years old in 1960 when A goes into adverse possession of Blackacre. O becomes insane in 1970, at age twelve. If O lives to attain majority, the statute will run in 1986, ten years after O comes of age. The statute is not extended by O's insanity.

(2) **Example:** Suppose O dies in 1974 and O's heir, H, is insane. The initial disability, O's infancy, is terminated and the statute runs in ten years—in 1984. The heir's insanity does not affect the operation of the statute.

d. **Maximum period of disabilities:** [§162]   Some statutes provide a maximum period by which the statute of limitations can be tolled by reason of disability. For example, the Massachusetts statute limits the maximum time to twenty-five years after the cause of action accrues, whether or not disabilities have been removed. [Mass. Gen. Laws, ch. 260 §25]

4. **Extent of Land Acquired by Adverse Possession:** [§163]   Assuming all requirements for adverse possession are satisfied, to what physical area does the adverse possessor's claim extend? There are two basic rules, depending upon whether the possessor entered with or without color of title. (For explanation of "color of title," *see supra,* §124.)

a. **Without color of title:** [§164]   If the adverse possessor did not enter under color of title, his claim extends only to such part of the land as he *actually occupied or controlled* in a manner consistent with ownership of such premises.

b. **With color of title—doctrine of constructive adverse possession:** [§165]   If the claimant goes into actual possession of some portion of the property under color of title (*e.g.,* defective deed), he is deemed to be in adverse possession of the entire property described in the instrument. On the theory that he intends to control all the land described in the instrument, the adverse possessor is in *constructive adverse possession* of the part of the tract he does not actually possess. [New York-Kentucky Oil & Gas Co. v. Miller, 220 S.W. 535 (Ky. 1920)]

(1) **Requirements:** [§166]   The doctrine of constructive adverse possession *under color of title* applies only where (i) the adverse possessor enters in *good faith* (believing his paper title to the whole property is valid); (ii) he occupies a *significant* portion of the property compared to the whole; and (iii) the tract described in the deed is recognized in the community as *one defined parcel* of land. If the described tract consists of *two or more lots* regarded by the community as separate parcels, possession of one lot is *not* considered constructive possession of the other lots. *Rationale:* Possession of a portion of the tract described in the deed regarded by the community as a separate lot will not give notice to the owner of the separate other lots of the extent of the claim.

(a) **Example:** X forges O's name to a deed from O to A. A believes the signature is genuine. The deed describes Blackacre (owned by O) and Whiteacre (owned by B). A moves into the farmhouse on Blackacre, but does not go onto Whiteacre. A has *actual possession* of the farmhouse of Blackacre and *constructive possession* of all the rest of Blackacre, for the farmhouse is a significant part. Unless the community regards Blackacre and Whiteacre as one farm (unlikely on these facts), A does not have constructive adverse possession of Whiteacre. A has done no act to put B on notice of the claim to Whiteacre.

(2) **Someone else is in possession at time of entry:** [§167]   The doctrine of constructive adverse possession does not apply if someone else is in actual possession of any portion of the land at the time of the adverse possessor's entry. If the owner is actually occupying some portion, his prior constructive possession

of the whole prevents constructive possession by an adverse possessor; the adverse possessor is limited to the portion he actually occupies. Similarly, if a prior adverse possessor with color of title to the whole is occupying some portion, his prior constructive possession of the whole will prevent constructive possession by the second adverse possessor.

    (a) **Example:** A enters onto Blackacre under a forged deed (A does not know of the forgery), taking actual possession of two acres in the woods. At the time of A's entry, O is living in the farmhouse on Blackacre and has constructive possession of Blackacre. Therefore, A's possession consists only of the two acres A actually occupies. A cannot have constructive possession of land already in constructive possession of another.

    (3) **Advantage of doctrine:** [§168]   Even though color of title is required for adverse possession in only a few states (*supra,* §126), entry under color of title is of advantage in all states, because it permits the adverse possessor to claim constructive possession beyond his actual possession.

5. **Nature of Title Acquired by Adverse Possessor:** [§169]   Although the statute of limitations is usually couched only in terms of barring the true owner from suing for possession, once the statute of limitations has run, a **new title** arises in the adverse possessor. The adverse possessor's right to possession, heretofore good against all the world except the rightful owner, is now good against the rightful owner as well.

a. **New title:** [§170]   The adverse possessor does not receive the old owner's title by operation of law. Old title is **extinguished,** and a new title is created in the adverse possessor.

b. **Relation back:** [§171]   Once the adverse possessor is vested with title, it relates back to the date of initial entry so as to bar any other claims by the old owner. Suits by the former owner for trespass or mesne profits (annual rental value of the land), on which separate statutes of limitation have not yet run, are barred.

    (1) **Example:** If A enters adversely in 1965 and acquires title by adverse possession in 1985, O cannot thereafter sue A for damages for cutting timber in 1984 (on which a six-year statute of limitation runs). [Counce v. Yount-Lee Oil Co., 87 F.2d 572 (5th Cir. 1927)]

c. **Limitations on title:** [§172]   The adverse possessor's title may be subject to liens, easements, covenants, or mineral interests in another. If the adverse possessor has never interfered with these interests, no statute has barred them.

d. **Transferability:** [§173]   Once the adverse possessor has title, it can be transferred in the same manner as any other title to land. And, it can be lost through adverse possession by another.

    (1) **Writing required:** [§174]   The Statute of Frauds requires a written instrument for transfer of an interest in land (except for transfers by intestate succes-

sion or operation of law). Hence, the adverse possessor's title cannot be transferred orally, cannot be abandoned, and is not lost by failure to remain in possession.

    (a) **Example:** A erects a building on a neighboring lot owned by O and acquires title to the lot by adverse possession. O thereafter asks A to remove the building and leave the land. A does so. Title remains in A. A deed is required to transfer title back from A to O.

  (2) **Recordation of title acquired by adverse possession:** [§175] Title acquired by adverse possession *cannot be recorded* because it does not arise from recordable documents. If the adverse possessor wishes to make his title appear on the public records, he must file a *quiet title action* against the former owner. [46 A.L.R.2d 539 (1956)]

6. **Interests Not Affected by Adverse Possession:** [§176] Recall that the basic principle of adverse possession is that a statute of limitations is running on a person who has a cause of action and does not bring a suit. If a person has *no cause of action,* she is not barred by the statute running. Thus persons who have no cause of action are not barred by adverse possession. The application of this principle can become rather tricky, particularly to future interests.

  a. **Future interests:** [§177] A future interest is a present right to possession of the property in the future (*see infra,* §§415 *et seq.*). The most common example is where O transfers land to B for life, and on B's death to C. B has a *life estate*, and C has a future interest called a *remainder*. Only the life tenant, B, has the right to possession while B is alive. Until B dies, C has no right to possession. Hence, the statute of limitations does not run against a remainder *existing at the time of entry* by the adverse possessor, A, because C, the holder of the remainder, has no right to eject A from possession.

    (1) **Example:** O owns Whiteacre. In 1959, O conveys Whiteacre to B for life, remainder to C. In 1960, A enters adversely. The statute of limitations is twenty years. In 1985, B dies. C is now entitled to possession and has until 2005 (twenty years from 1985) to eject A. (In 1980, A acquired title to B's life estate by adverse possession, but this interest terminated on B's death.) [Harper v. Paradise, 210 S.E.2d 710 (Ga. 1974)]

    (2) **Compare—entry prior to O's transfer:** If, in the above example, A had entered Whiteacre in 1958, *before O created the remainder*, the statute would begin to run *against O and his succesors in interest* in 1958, and A would acquire title in 1978. Although C never had a chance to evict A, C is barred because she is a *successor in interest to O* in whom the cause of action originally arose. In the preceding example, the adverse possessor entered against B, who had a cause of action, and the statute of limitations runs against B and his successors in interest. But C is *not* a successor in interest to B; she is a successor in possession. "Successor in interest" means one party takes her interest from the other,

and C acquired her remainder interest from O, not from B. B gave C nothing. (For more on successors in interest, *see supra,* §153.)

b. **Liens, easements, equitable servitudes:** [§178]   If the land is subject to outstanding liens, easements, or equitable servitudes when the adverse possessor enters, any title acquired by the adverse possessor *remains subject to such interests.* The owner of such interests is not affected by adverse possession until he has a cause of action against the possessor. [*In re* Nisbett & Potts' Contract, [1905] 1 Ch. 391]

   (1) **Example:** O owns Greenacre, which is subject to a covenant benefitting B's land restricting Greenacre's use to residential purposes. It is also subject to an easement of way benefitting C's land. A enters adversely, does not violate the covenant, does not interfere with C's passage, and occupies the land for twenty years. O is barred, but B and C are not barred, for they have never had a cause of action against A.

c. **Government land:** [§179]   Except where a statute is construed to provide otherwise, a governmental entity (federal, state, or municipal) is *exempt* from operation of statutes of limitation. Public policy forbids a private individual from acquiring title to government land by adverse possession. *But note:* There are exceptions to the general rule. In some states, adverse possession of streets and roadways is permitted. In some states, land held by a county or city in its private capacity, and not for public use, is subject to adverse possession. [Hinckley v. State of New York, 234 N.Y. 309 (1922)]

7. **Adverse Possession of Chattels:** [§180]   A person can acquire title to chattels by adverse possession just as he can acquire title to land. Once the remedy is barred, the adverse possessor has title. [Chapin v. Freeland, 8 N.E. 128 (Mass. 1886)] Generally the requirements for adverse possession of chattels are the same as for land, except the period of limitations is shorter. There is, however, *one great difference* between adversely possessing land and adversely possessing chattels: Adverse possession of land is open and notorious whereas adverse possession of chattels seldom is. How should this difference be handled?

   a. **Old rule:** [§181]   The old rule is that adverse possession starts running only when the possessor satisfies the standard requirements of open and notorious possession. Accordingly, what the possessor has done in the way of openly displaying the object—so as to give notice to the true owner—is crucial.

   b. **Modern trend—discovery rule:** [§182]   A recent case, *O'Keeffe v. Snyder,* 416 A.2d 862 (N.J. 1980), rejected this view and held that the cause of action accrues at the time of theft, absent fraud or concealment, unless the owner is entitled to the benefit of the *discovery rule* (applicable in medical and legal malpractice actions). Under the discovery rule, the conduct of the *owner,* not the possessor is controlling. Under this rule, the cause accrues when the owner first knows, or reasonably should know through the exercise of a reasonable diligence, of the cause of action, including the identity of the possessor.

(1) **Example:** A steals a valuable painting belonging to O. A hangs it in his home, and occasionally lends it to a local charitable show. Under the old rule, adverse possession runs when A's actions can be called "open." Under *O'Keeffe,* adverse possession runs from the time of the theft unless O can show that she used due diligence and failed to locate the painting; if O can show due diligence, adverse possession begins to run when O locates the painting. Under the discovery rule the key is, of course, whether the owner used due diligence.

H. RIGHT TO EXCLUDE

1. **Essence of Private Property:** [§183]   It is generally accepted that the essence of private property is the right to exclude others, the right to exclusive possession over whatever things the law of property assigns to a person. Courts have traditionally granted great protection to this right. The *use* of property may be restricted by zoning laws, and the *transfer* may be curtailed by a lawful restraint on alienation, but the courts seldom permit another person to enter the property of the possessor. However, the right to exclude has certain exceptions, for there are few, if any, absolute rights in our legal system (*e.g.,* in the law of mistaken improver, *supra,* §92 and nuisance, *infra,* §1533). Recently, the right to exclude has come into conflict with civil rights and first amendment rights.

   a. **Civil rights:** [§184]   Where a legislature has acted by passing legislation to protect civil rights, ensuring equal admittance to public accommodations or housing, the courts have upheld such legislation as a constitutional exercise of the police power. [Heart of Atlanta Motel, Inc. v. United States, 379 U.S. 241 (1964); *and see* the Fair Housing Act, *infra,* §862]

   b. **Freedom of speech:** [§185]   The right to exclude and the first amendment right to free speech have principally come in conflict where one or more persons wish to exercise free speech within a shopping center. The persons may want to pass out religious tracts, protest a war or some government action, or solicit votes for a candidate or ballot proposition. Supreme Court decisions originally limited the right to exclude in favor of free speech. [Marsh v. Alabama, 326 U.S. 501 (1946); Amalgamated Food Employees Union Local 590 v. Logan Valley Plaza, Inc., 391 U.S. 308 (1968)] But later, the Court withdrew its protection of free speech in these cases, holding that the first amendment did not require the owner to allow access to the property for such purposes. [Hudgens v. NLRB, 424 U.S. 507 (1976)—overruling Logan Valley] However, the Supreme Court has held that a state may broaden a *state* constititutional right of expression on private property beyond the protection offered by the Federal Constitution. [Pruneyard Shopping Center v. Robins, 447 U.S. 74 (1980)]

II. GIFTS AND SALES OF PERSONAL PROPERTY

chapter approach

Gifts and sales of personal property are traditionally taught after possession because they involve issues related to possession. For questions on gifts, remember to look for all three elements: (i) intent, (ii) delivery, and (iii) acceptance of the gift. But note that the second element is the one you are most likely to be tested on: Has the donor *delivered possession* to the donee? Be sure to consider all the possibilities—including constructive or symbolic delivery, delivery to third persons, etc.

In a sales question, the central issue is whether a purchaser can acquire title to personal property from a *possessor* who does not own the property. The general rule says no, but there are limited exceptions for a *bona fide purchaser*. (Note that you probably won't find a sale of personal property question on your property exam because such issues are covered by the U.C.C. and taught in a course on Commercial Law.)

A. GIFTS OF PERSONAL PROPERTY

1. **Definition:** [§186]   A *gift* is a *voluntary* transfer of property *without any consideration*. There are three requirements for a gift of chattels: (i) the donor must *intend* to make a gift; (ii) the donor must *deliver* the chattel to the donee (there are some acceptable substitutes for manual delivery); and (iii) the donee must *accept* the chattel. Almost all the litigation concerning gifts occurs over the second requirement, *delivery*—i.e., what it means and what substitutes are acceptable in place of manual delivery.

   a. **Gift inter vivos:** [§187]   An inter vivos gift is a gift made during the donor's life when the donor is not under any threat of impending death. The ordinary gift is an inter vivos ("during life") gift. An inter vivos gift, once made, is *irrevocable*. The donor cannot get the object back. (Of course the donee could, if she wished, give it back.)

   b. **Gift causa mortis:** [§188]   A gift causa mortis is a gift made in *contemplation of immediately approaching death*. The requirements for making an inter vivos gift and a gift causa mortis are substantially the same, though a court may be more strict in the case of a gift causa mortis, because there may be greater danger of fraudulent claims since the donor is dead and cannot speak. A gift causa mortis is *revoked* if the donor recovers from the illness that prompts the gift. In practical effect, a gift causa mortis is a substitute for a will—*i.e.*, a deathbed will where the donor, instead of making a written will, delivers the object to the donee.

      (1) **Example:** O, having suffered a cerebral hemorrhage, and critically ill, hands over some stock certificates to A, saying, "If anything happens to me, these stocks are yours." O dies shortly thereafter. This is a valid gift causa mortis. The words implying "if I die" do not state a condition precedent, but are mere-

ly the expression of the condition attached by law to every gift causa mortis—
that it does not become irrevocable until the donor dies. [Titusville Trust Co. v.
Johnson, 100 A.2d 93 (Pa. 1953); *In re* Nols' Estate, 28 N.W.2d 360 (Wis.
1947)]

    (2) **Donor must die of contemplated peril:** [§189]   If the donor does not die of the
peril comtemplated when she hands over the chattel, but dies a short time later
of some other cause, the gift causa mortis is revoked. The donee cannot keep
the chattel.

        (a) **Example:** O, contemplating an operation for removal of a tumor, delivers
jewelry to A, saying, "If I die as a result of this operation, this jewelry is
yours." O is opened by the surgeon, who finds a cancerous, inoperable
tumor, and sews O up. O recovers from the operation, and shortly thereafter dies of cancer. O did not say, "If I die from cancer," but said, "If I die
from this operation." The operation was the peril prompting the gift. The
gift is revoked by O's recovery from the operation. [Brind v. International
Trust Co., 179 P. 148 (Colo. 1919)]

    (3) **Ambiguous intent:** [§190]   The fact that the donor is under apprehension of
death does not necessarily mean that a gift causa mortis is involved. Evidence
may be introduced to show that the donor intends the gift to stand whether she
lives or dies. If the evidence shows such intent, the gift is ***not revoked*** by the
donor's recovery. The gift stands as an inter vivos gift.

        (a) **Example:** O, seriously ill with pneumonia and expecting to die, sends for A
and hands A a diamond ring. O recovers from the illness and lives for four
more years. After O's recovery, A hands the ring back to O to wear. O
takes it, under protest, saying, "I gave A this ring and I want A to have it,
but A insists that I wear it, and I want it understood that the ring belongs
to A." This evidence shows O's intent when she handed the ring over during her illness, and the gift to A is a valid inter vivos gift. [Newell v. National Bank of Norwich, 214 App. Div. 331 (1925)]

2. **Intent:** [§191]   The donor must intend to ***pass title presently***, and not merely to transfer possession. In the absence of a deed of gift, intent will always have to be shown by
extrinsic evidence. The requirement of delivery sustains intent by requiring an objective
act—but ***intent*** and ***delivery*** are ***separate requirements***.

    a. **Promise compared:** [§192]   A promise to give property ***in the future*** is ***not*** a gift. A
gift transfers title to the donee right now. A gratuitous promise (*i.e.,* a promise
without consideration) is enforceable neither as a gift nor under the law of
contracts.

3. **Delivery**

    a. **In general:** [§193]   In the leading case of *Cochrane v. Moore,* 25 Q.B.D. 57
(1890), affirming *Irons v. Smallpiece,* 106 Eng. Rep. 467 (1819), the English

court laid down a requirement that, in a parol gift, *delivery* of the chattel is required. This has been the law ever since. The facts of *Cochrane* are interesting. One Benzon made an oral gift to Moore of a one-fourth interest in a horse. Later Benzon sold the horse to Cochrane. Moore claimed a one-fourth undivided interest in the horse. The court held this was not a valid gift because Benzon had not delivered the horse to Moore. Of course, physical delivery of an undivided one-fourth interest in a horse is difficult, but there are some substitutes for physical delivery that could have been used by Benzon. (*See infra,* §196—"sealed instrument," §200—"symbolic delivery," and §201—"constructive delivery.") (The court went on to hold, however, that Cochrane, who upon being told by Benzon of Moore's interest in the horse said that was "all right," had declared himself a trustee for Moore. Thus Moore did end up with a one-fourth undivided equitable interest in the horse. *See infra,* §217—"oral trusts.")

(1) **Reasons for requirement:** [§194] The requirement of delivery owes a lot to the medieval requirement of livery of seisin (*see infra,* §278). In medieval times, when many people could not read and write, land was conveyed by the parties going on the land, and before witnesses, the grantor handed a clod of dirt to the grantee. This symbolic act made vivid the change of ownership. But medieval days are gone, and people now transfer land by a written instrument. Why has the delivery requirement for chattels persisted? Three functions of delivery have been suggested:

(a) **Ritual:** Delivery of the chattel impresses the grantor with the *legal significance* and *finality* of the act. Once she hands over the object, she realizes it belongs to another. Or, as the common phrase goes, the grantor "must feel the wrench of delivery."

(b) **Evidentiary:** Delivery of the chattel is reliable, *objective* evidence of the grantor's intent to give. There is no need to rely upon oral testimony; reliance is placed upon the objective act of delivery. Moreover, the presence of the object in the grantee's hands substantiates his claim of a gift.

(c) **Protective:** Requiring delivery protects the unwary or barely competent donor from making improvident oral statements.

(2) **Manual transfer not necessary:** [§195] The requirement of delivery does not necessarily mean that the object must be "handed over." It means that the donor must do an *act* that evinces an intent to be immediately bound. Several types of acts are acceptable as substitutes for "handing over." These are called *symbolic* or *constructive* deliveries. However, if symbolic and constructive deliveries are broadly defined, the delivery requirement becomes basically a question of *intent*, and delivery as a separate requirement is in effect abolished. Judges differ in their attitudes on this. Some believe the delivery requirement serves valid purposes and pay great attention to physical movement or control of the chattel. Others, emphasizing the carrying out of intent, resort to "constructive delivery" when they believe the donor intended the gift. This latter approach is best summed up in a New Jersey case, *Scherer v. Hyland,* 380

A.2d 698 (N.J. 1977): "This approach would find a constructive delivery adequate to support the gift **when the evidence of donative intent is concrete and undisputed**, when there is every indication that the donor **intended to make a present transfer** of the subject matter of the gift, and when the **steps taken** by the donor to effect such a transfer must have been **deemed by the donor as sufficient** to pass the donor's interest to the donee." Because of this split in judicial philosophy, gift cases are often decided by a divided court and may be difficult to reconcile one with another.

(3) **Transfer by written instrument**

    (a) **Sealed instrument:** [§196]   Title to a chattel could be transferred at common law by a **deed**, as well as by delivery of the chattel, but the word "deed" referred only to a sealed instrument. At modern law, the distinction between sealed and unsealed instruments has been abolished, but it is probable that a sealed instrument may still be used for transferring a chattel without delivery of the chattel. [Grymes v. Hone, 49 N.Y. 17 (1872)]

    (b) **Unsealed instrument:** [§197]   Whether an unsealed instrument is effective today to make a gift without delivering the chattel is debatable. The cases are conflicting. Some hold that a gift can be made by an ordinary writing, but a significant number of courts still follow the old rule that a gift by an unsealed writing is ineffectual without delivery of the chattel.

        1) **Example:** O, in a hospital about to undergo serious surgery, writes a note to her husband and puts it on a table by her bed: "In my bedroom closet you will find $75 and my savings bank book. I give these to you. Your kissing, loving wife." O's husband finds the note when he comes to the hospital. O dies in the operation. *Held:* 4 to 3, that no gift has been made. Although the informal writing establishes O's desire to make a gift, it does not satisfy the separate and distinct requirement of delivery because the donor was not by the writing deprived of her control over the property. [Foster v. Reiss, 112 A.2d 533 (N.J. 1955); *but see* the later New Jersey case of Scherer v. Hyland, *supra,* §195—seemingly disapproves of Foster v. Reiss]

        2) **Distinguish impracticality of manual delivery:** [§198]   If manual delivery is **impracticable**, some courts may give effect to an informal writing as a symbolic delivery, although they would not permit a writing to suffice if manual delivery were practicable.

            a) **Example:** O writes out and hands to A a memorandum reading: "I give my watch and my grand piano to A as a birthday present." O is wearing the watch, and the grand piano is in the room where O and A are. If the court permits symbolic delivery only where physical delivery is impracticable, O has made a gift of the piano but not of the watch, which she could easily hand over. If the court permits a gift by delivery of a writing whether or not manual delivery is impracticable, then O has made a gift of the piano and the watch.

3) **Exception—certain choses in action:** [§199] A chose in action not evidenced by a written instrument can be transferred by a written assignment. (For further explanation, *see infra,* §215.)

b. **Symbolic delivery:** [§200] Where actual manual delivery is *impracticable* because the chattel is too large, or the situation of the parties will not permit it, *symbolic delivery* is permitted. A symbolic delivery is the handing over of some object which is symbolic of the thing given. The most common example of symbolic delivery is where the donor hands over an *instrument in writing* under circumstances where manual delivery is difficult or impracticable.

(1) **Example:** Leopold Cohn, in the presence of his entire family, in New Jersey, on his wife's birthday, writes out and hands to his wife the following: "I give this day to my wife Sara as a birthday present 500 shares of Sumatra Tobacco Company stock. [signed] Leopold Cohn." Cohn owns the stock, but it is in the name of his partnership and is in the firm's safe deposit box in New York. The partnership has been dissolved but the shares have not yet been reregistered in Cohn's name. Because it is impracticable to deliver the stock, the writing is a sufficient symbolic delivery and the gift is good. [*In re* Cohn, 187 App. Div. 392 (1919); Matter of Mills, 219 N.Y. 642 (1916)—change in account books is sufficient symbolic delivery]

c. **Constructive delivery:** [§201] Where actual manual delivery is *impracticable, constructive delivery* is permitted. A constructive delivery is the handing over of the *means* of obtaining possession and control (usually a key), or in some other way *relinquishing dominion and control* over the property.

(1) **Handing over of a key:** [§202] The typical constructive delivery case involves the handing over of a key to a locked receptacle (box, trunk, room). If it is *impracticable* to manually transfer the receptacle or the articles in the receptacle, handing over the key is constructive delivery of the contents. *But remember:* Delivery of the object of the gift must be impracticable.

(a) **Example:** O, lying on his deathbed, calls in his housekeeper Julia, hands her the keys to all the furniture in the house, and says she is to have everything in the house. In his bedroom bureau, which one of the keys unlocks, is an insurance policy. O has not made a gift of the insurance policy because it is in the room where O lies dying and is capable of manual delivery. Julia does, however, receive as a gift all the furniture unlocked by the keys (either a constructive or symbolic delivery) because it is impractical to hand the furniture over manually. [Newman v. Bost, 29 S.E. 848 (N.C. 1898)]

(b) **Note:** If O, *while on his deathbed,* had delivered the key to his safe deposit box in the bank to Julia, Julia would take the contents by constructive delivery. But if O were ambulatory and able to go to the bank, take out the contents, and hand them over to Julia, the cases are in conflict over whether handing over a key would be constructive delivery. [Estate of Evans, 356 A.2d 778 (Pa. 1976)—no delivery; *In re* Stevenson's Estate, 69 N.E.2d 426 (Ohio 1946)—constructive delivery]

(2) **Surrender of dominion and control:** [§203] Sometimes constructive delivery is said to take place whenever the donor has surrendered dominion and control. But beware of this statement. "Dominion and control" refers *both* to the *actual control* retained and *to the court's conclusion* that such control is either too great (in which case there is no gift) or insignificant (in which case there is a gift). But it does not tell much about why the court so concludes. A court that finds a constructive delivery because of a surrender of control is probably satisfied that the donor's intent is obvious and clear, and finds some act to be a substitute for delivery.

   (a) **Example:** Hettie Young, owning 150 shares of stock in Sun Oil Co., delivers the stock certificate to Sun Oil to reissue the stock in the name of her nephew, Maynard, and return the new certificate to her. Soon after Hettie receives the new certificate naming Maynard as owner, Maynard is killed. Hettie delivers the new stock certificate to Sun Oil and directs that the certificate be cancelled and a new certificate issued in her name. What should Sun Oil do? Hettie argues that she has "never given up possession and control"—that until she hands the stock to the donee she has made no gift. Maynard's widow argues that the gift is complete as soon as the stock is reregistered in Maynard's name. *Held:* The transfer of stock registration on the company's books makes out a prima facie case that the donor has surrendered dominion and control over it, and has made a gift. [Owens v. Sun Oil Co., 482 F.2d 564 (10th Cir. 1973)]

(3) **Donor deems acts sufficient:** [§204] Constructive delivery can be broadly defined to include any acts that the donor deems sufficient to pass a present interest to the donee. This approach, deemphasizing delivery and emphasizing intent, is more concerned with whether, on the facts, the ritual and evidentiary purposes of delivery (*supra,* §194) are met.

   (a) **Example:** O, depressed from being crippled in an auto accident, receives a check for $17,400 from the insurance company. O endorses the check in blank and puts it with a suicide note to her lover, giving all her possessions to him. O leaves her apartment and commits suicide. This has been held a valid constructive delivery of a gift causa mortis. [Scherer v. Hyland, *supra,* §195]

d. **Delivery through third person:** [§205] A donor can deliver a chattel to a third party as agent to hold for the donee. If the third party is the *agent of the donor, no gift* takes place until the donor's agent delivers the chattel to the donee. *Rationale:* Since the donor can control her agent, she has not parted with dominion and control. On the other hand, if the third party is the *agent of the donee* or an *independent* *agent*, the gift is effective upon delivery to the donee's agent. This rule is easy to state, but it is often difficult to determine whose agent the third party is. This usually depends upon the intent of the donor, which may be unclear.

(1) **Example:** O sells Blackacre to A, taking back a promissory note by A to pay B $500 secured by a mortgage on Blackacre. O sends the note and mortgage to his lawyer, telling the lawyer to record the mortgage and mail the note and mortgage to B, as a gift from O. The lawyer records the mortgage, but fails to mail the note and mortgage to B. O tells B he has given her $500. A year later the lawyer returns the note and mortgage to O. The cases are in conflict over whose agent the lawyer is. [Bickford v. Mattocks, 50 A. 894 (Me. 1901)—holding lawyer is donor's agent and no delivery; Meyers v. Meyers, 134 A. 95 (N.J. 1926)—holding lawyer in gift causa mortis is donee's agent and delivery good]

(2) **Gift to be delivered on death:** [§206] Often property will be handed to a third party with directions by the donor to deliver the property to the donee upon the donor's death. This is a will substitute, and some courts formerly held it to be *testamentary* and *void*, because it was not in accordance with the requirements of the Statute of Wills (a written instrument signed in front of two witnesses, who also must sign, is required for a valid will in most jurisdictions). This is rather silly, because if the event were anything other than donor's death, the gift would be good—provided, of course, that the agent is the *agent of the donee*. Most modern cases uphold a gift where the property is delivered to a third party to be delivered to the donee on the donor's death. [Innes v. Potter, 153 N.W. 604 (Minn. 1915)]

(a) **Other contingencies:** [§207] A direction to the third party to deliver to the donee *if the donee survives* the donor is usually held a valid delivery. The contingency can be any event, so long as it is one over which the donor has no control. If the donor can *control* the event, or if the donor can *get the property back* from the third party on demand (*i.e.*, revoke the gift), the attempted gift is not good. The donor has not surrendered dominion and control.

e. **Revocable gifts:** [§208] Although there are a few cases to the contrary, the general rule is that no gift is made when the donor retains the right to revoke the gift. It does not matter whether delivery has been made to the donee or to a third person for the donee. Retaining the power to revoke is said to be inconsistent with surrendering dominion and control (necessary for a gift) and also inconsistent with transferring a present interest.

(1) **Example:** O deposits money in a bank account in the name of his two minor daughters, subject to his own order. O retains the passbook and makes deposits and withdrawals as he pleases in the names of his daughters. O has no intention to vest control in his daughters until his death, and no gift has been made. [Tygard v. McComb, 54 Mo. App. 85 (1893)]

(2) **Gifts causa mortis:** [§209] There is an exception in case of a gift causa mortis, which is revoked by law upon the donor's recovery (*supra,* §189). If the donor, fearing impending death, delivers property to a third party to deliver to the donee upon the donor's death, and **expressly retains** the right to get the property back upon recovery, this adds nothing to the donor's rights at law and does not prevent a valid gift causa mortis. [Grymes v. Hone, *supra,* §196]

(3) **Compare—revocable trust:** [§210] A donor can transfer property to X in **trust** for a donee and retain the power to revoke the trust (*see infra,* §811). Revocable trusts are in wide use today. If a trust can be made revocable, why cannot a gift? Permitting the donor to retain **orally** the power to revoke a delivered gift would of course stir up much litigation if the donor changed her mind and wanted the object back. It would be conducive to fraud. But if the terms of the gift, including the power of revocation, are in a **written instrument** which accompanies delivery, it is not easy to say why a revocable gift should not be permitted—provided the object is still in the hands of the donee when the donor revokes the gift. There is no danger of fraud, and the ritual and evidentiary purposes of delivery are satisfied. Perhaps the explanation is that the law of gifts still pays obeisance to the shibboleth that the donor must surrender dominion and control to make an effective transfer, whereas the law of trusts is more concerned with carrying out intent and less concerned with dogma.

f. **Goods in possession of donee:** [§211] If the goods are in the possession of the donee (usually as bailee), it is not necessary that they be redelivered to the donor and then delivered again from the donor to the donee. In this case, delivery is dispensed with; proving the intent of the donor by clear and convincing evidence is all that is necessary.

(1) **Example:** O keeps his securities in a vault. O transfers the vault to the name of his son, who now has possession of the securities. At Christmas, O tells his son and daughter he is making a gift to them, and directs his son to transfer 8,000 shares of Santa Fe railroad stock to himself and 8,000 to his sister. Before the son does so, O dies. The son's gift is good, because the donee (son) is already in possession of the subject matter of the gift. The daughter's gift is also good because the son, being in possession, is regarded as holding the daughter's stock in trust for her until he, the trustee, can deliver it to her. [Matter of Mills, *supra,* §200]

(2) **Gifts causa mortis:** [§212] With respect to gifts causa mortis, a substantial number of cases require the donee in possession of the goods to redeliver them to the donor, who in turn must hand them back to the donee. The courts here are worried about the substantial danger of fraud; also, where there is no physical delivery, the transaction resembles very closely an invalid oral will. There is no objective act, only oral testimony on which to rely. Nonetheless, a minority of courts do hold a gift causa mortis valid without redelivery when the donee is already in possession.

g. **Choses in action:** [§213]   A chose in action (a right to sue somebody) is ***intangible personal property***. How is it delivered? There are two types of choses in action, and the delivery rules vary according to type.

(1) **Evidenced by written instrument:** [§214]   A chose in action may be evidenced by a written instrument—*e.g.*, a bond, a life insurance policy, a savings account book, a promissory note. The legally important thing, of course, is the ***underlying debt***, a chose in action which is not destroyed if the evidence of the debt is destroyed. If someone loses his savings account book, the bank still owes him money. Gifts of choses in action evidenced by a written instrument are treated more or less like gifts of tangible property: The donor ***must deliver the instrument evidencing the debt*** or have a new instrument issued to the donee.

(2) **Not evidenced by written instrument:** [§215]   A chose in action may not be evidenced by a written instrument—*e.g.*, a debt without a promissory note, a suit for personal injury. Such a chose can be transferred ***by the written assignment of the donor.***

h. **Engagement rings:** [§216]   An engagement ring is in the nature of a pledge for the contract of marriage, and if the recipient breaks the engagement, she is required, upon demand, to return the ring. The transfer is treated as a conditional gift. If the donor breaks off the engagement, preventing the condition from happening, the donor is not entitled to the ring back. [De Cicco v. Barker, 159 N.E.2d 534 (Mass. 1959)] However, if one of the parties is already married when the engagement ring is given, the ring does not have to be returned if they do not marry. An agreement to marry under such circumstances is void as against public policy. The gift is good, and the condition of marriage is struck down. [Lowe v. Quinn, 27 N.Y.2d 397 (1971)]

i. **Oral trusts:** [§217]   An oral trust of real property is forbidden by the Statute of Frauds, which requires a written instrument for the creation of an interest in land. The Statute of Frauds does not apply to personal property, and an oral trust of personal property can be created. There are two kinds of oral trusts—one where a third party is trustee and the other where the settlor is trustee.

(1) **Transfer in trust:** [§218]   If O transfers property to X in trust for A, O must deliver the property to X. The ordinary rules of delivery (discussed above) apply.

(2) **Declaration of trust:** [§219]   If O orally declares himself trustee of goods for the benefit of A, ***no delivery is required***. It would be stupid to require O to deliver (hand over) goods to himself as trustee. This is a major loophole in the requirement of delivery. It is not necessary for O to use the words "declare myself trustee" if the evidence shows that O intended to declare himself trustee.

(a) **Example:** Thomas Smith buys some bearer bonds and puts them in his safe deposit box in an envelope reading: "13 P & A railroad bonds, $1,000 each, held for Tom Smith Kelly. [signed] Thomas Smith." Smith keeps an account book in which he credits the interest from the bonds to Tom, but does not give Tom any interest from the bonds before his death. The evidence is sufficient to hold that Smith declared himself trustee of the bonds for Tom. No delivery is required. The transfer in trust is valid. [Smith's Estate, 22 A. 916 (Pa. 1891)]

(b) **Imperfect gift as a trust:** [§220]   In some cases beneficiaries attempt to sustain as a declaration of trust a gift that is invalid for want of delivery. Courts have generally resisted these attempts unless there is evidence of *intent to transfer in trust* and acceptance of a trustee's duties. In the preceding example, the fact that Smith acted as if he were a trustee, keeping the bond interest separate from his own and crediting it on his books to the donee was very important in finding a trust.

4. **Acceptance:** [§221]   Acceptance by the donee is required for a gift. The donee can reject the gift if he wants. But the law *presumes acceptance* when the gift is beneficial to the donee. Sometimes this is stated this way: The gift takes effect immediately upon delivery, subject to the right of the donee to repudiate the gift. [Miller v. Herzfeld, 4 F.2d 355 (3d Cir. 1925)]

5. **Bank Accounts:** [§222]   Bank accounts raise special problems and are given separate treatment here. There are four types of bank accounts where two or more persons have an interest in the account: (i) payable on death account; (ii) Totten trust; (iii) power of attorney account; and (iv) joint and survivor account. Each of these is discussed below.

   a. **Payable on death account:** [§223]   A payable on death account ("P-O-D account") is one in which O (depositor) deposits money in a bank with the right to withdraw any sums as she pleases, and if any amount remains on deposit at O's death, it is to be paid to A. This is a *substitute for a will*, and a large majority of courts have held it invalid because it is testamentary and not executed with the formalities required for a will (two witnesses, declaration that instrument is a will, etc.). Thus a P-O-D account is void in most states. The designated beneficiary takes nothing. Because of this, persons desiring a survivor designation on a bank account have used the joint and survivor bank account as a practical substitute for the banned P-O-D account.

      (1) **Uniform Probate Code:** [§224]   Uniform Probate Code section 6-104, enacted in more than a dozen states, provides that a P-O-D account is valid. The Uniform Probate Code reasons that there is no more room for fraud in a P-O-D account than in a joint account, and less room than in other will substitutes acceptable today, such as life insurance, death designees on U.S. bonds, pension plans, etc.

      (2) **Totten trust:** [§225]   A Totten trust is a P-O-D savings account held in trust by O for the benefit of A. O has the right to withdraw all the money on deposit if she wishes. This differs from the P-O-D account only in that the depositor deposits *not* in the name of "O, payable on O's death to A" (void), but in the

name of "O *as trustee for A*, with the right in O to withdraw all sums deposited." This is a "poor person's will" validated in *Matter of Totten*, 179 N.Y. 112 (1904). Since it is in trust form, it can be revocable. (*Note:* Gifts cannot be revocable, but a trust can be.) And it is not testamentary because O intends to make a **present transfer in trust** (even though A has no enforceable claim during O's life). The real reasons for recognizing the Totten trust are that the possibility of fraud is slim, and there has been substantial compliance with the functions of the Statute of Wills. Once the Totten trust was recognized, however, any policy reason for banning the P-O-D account ceased to exist—because the difference between a P-O-D account and a Totten trust is purely a matter of form, not of substance.

b. **Power of attorney account: [§226]** A power of attorney account is one in which O deposits money in her own name, giving A a power of attorney to draw on the account. A's power expires on O's death or upon its prior revocation by O. Banks do not like power of attorney accounts, because the bank may not learn of O's death (and the expiration of A's power) until after A has illegally withdrawn the money after O's death. A bank has a possible liability in such a case. Because the P-O-D account is legally banned, and the power of attorney account is discouraged by banks, the joint and survivor account has become the "all purpose" account.

c. **Joint and survivor account: [§227]** A joint and survivor account is one in which O deposits money, with the right in either O or A to draw on the account; in the event of death of one, the survivor takes what remains in the account. This is the common "joint tenancy account." It is not deemed testamentary (though A does take the remaining funds at O's death) because A receives the **present right to withdraw** the funds. [Dyste v. Farmers & Mechanics Savings Bank, 229 N.W. 865 (Minn. 1930)]

(1) **If joint account is a P-O-D account in disguise: [§228]** The **presumption** is that by signing the joint tenancy card O intends to make a gift to A, but the presumption can be overcome by clear and convincing evidence. If extrinsic evidence shows that O did not intend anyone but herself to have the right to make withdrawals, O has not made a gift to A because A is given no present right to withdraw. The account is treated as if it were a P-O-D account, and A takes nothing at O's death.

(a) **Example:** Helen Michaels opens a joint and survivor savings account in the name of herself and her son, Harry. Harry does not learn of this until after Helen's death. Unless there is clear and convincing evidence that Helen opened the account solely for its survivorship feature, Harry takes on Helen's death. [Estate of Michaels, 132 N.W.2d 557 (Wis. 1965); Malone v. Walsh, 53 N.E.2d 126 (Mass. 1944)]

(b) **Other joint assets: [§229]** The principle discussed above applies to other personal property held in joint tenancy as well as to joint bank accounts. Thus, in *Blanchette v. Blanchette*, 287 N.E.2d 459 (Mass. 1972), a husband purchased stock in the name of himself and his wife. Upon divorce, the evidence showed that the husband put title in joint names to give the wife survivorship rights only, that he retained all control of the stock certificates and dividends, and that he had no intention of giving the wife any present interest. The court held that no gift took place, and the stock belonged to the husband.

1) **Criticism:** [§230] The *Blanchette* case indicates vividly what is wrong with the law here. Having ruled that the donor cannot use an informal written instrument giving only survivorship rights (a P-O-D designation), the courts then proceed to admit extrinsic evidence to show that a written instrument creating a joint account is really intended to be a P-O-D account. The policy of the law preferring written instruments over oral testimony is thus turned on its head.

(2) **If joint account is a convenience (power of attorney) account in disguise:** [§231] If *extrinsic evidence* shows that O opened the account for the purpose and *convenience* of permitting A to pay O's bills, with no intention of creating survivorship rights, O has not made a gift to A and A takes nothing on O's death. The **presumption** is that by signing the joint tenancy card O intends to make a gift to A, but the presumption can be overcome by clear and convincing evidence. In other words, if extrinsic evidence shows that the joint account was really intended as a *power of attorney account*, it will be treated as such by the court. But in resolving what is clear and convincing evidence, much litigation has resulted.

(a) **Example:** Josephine, living alone and aging, needs someone to pay her bills and look after her bank account. She opens a joint bank account with her son Frank. This presumptively is a gift to Frank of sums remaining on deposit at Josephine's death. But if it is shown that Josephine intended only a convenience account, Frank does not take on Josephine's death.

(3) **Contract theory:** [§232] A few courts have held that the issues raised above respecting joint accounts are not to be resolved by the law of gifts but by the law of contracts. The deposit agreement signed by the depositors and the bank creates a contract, and the bank is obliged to pay out the money in accordance with the contract. Under contract theory, it should not matter whether the passbook is retained by the depositor or the account is merely for convenience of the depositor—but when the cases are examined the same issues somehow arise under contract theory. However the matter is viewed, a gratuitous transfer of funds on deposit is at stake, and gift law must intrude itself.

(4) **Rights during lifetime:** [§233] During the lifetime of O and A, questions may arise as to what rights O and A have over a joint account. Can O withdraw all the money? Can A? The general rule is that a joint account belongs, during the lifetime of all parties, to the parties *in equal shares* (not in proportion to the net contributions by each to the sums on deposit). If one of two joint tenants withdraws more than one-half, the other joint tenant can recover the excess from

the withdrawing tenant. If one joint tenant knows of the other's withdrawal in excess of one-half, he is deemed to make a gift of it unless he objects within a reasonable time.

(a) **Example:** O deposits $5,000 in a joint account with A. Subsequently, while A is dying and "to avoid problems," O withdraws all the money from the account and puts it into O's sole account. Upon A's death, A's administrator is entitled to recover $2,500 from O. [Bricker v. Krimer, 13 N.Y.2d 22 (1963); *In re* Estate of Kohn, 168 N.W.2d 812 (Wis. 1969)] Note that O's withdrawal penalizes O, because had O waited until A died, O would be entitled to all the money as survivor.

(b) **Creditors' rights:** [§234]   As a general rule, creditors can reach what the debtor can alienate. Thus, the creditor of a joint tenant on a bank account can reach the tenant's proportionate interest. If the joint tenants have so mixed the account that the separate contributions of each cannot be ascertained, the creditor of each can reach the whole. [Park Enterprises, Inc. v. Trach, 47 N.W.2d 194 (Minn. 1951)]

(c) **Uniform Probate Code:** [§235]   The Uniform Probate Code provides that, during the lifetime of the parties, the parties own the joint account in proportion to the net contribution of each. [U.P.C. §6-103] Thus if O makes the entire deposit, O can withdraw all without A's consent, and O's creditors can reach all. On the other hand, the Uniform Probate Code does not say what the parties' rights are if A withdraws more than he is entitled to. Presumably, unless O ratifies it by words or conduct, O can require A to return to the account the amount withdrawn. [*In re* Estate of Thompson, 423 N.E.2d 90 (Ohio 1981)]

B. BONA FIDE PURCHASERS OF PERSONAL PROPERTY

1. **Nature of Problem:** [§236]   With land, title records are kept in a county courthouse, and a purchaser can learn whether his seller has title to the land he wants to buy by searching the public records. With regard to personal property generally, there is no comparable system of recorded titles. (Imagine what kind of system would be required to document title to autos, television sets, watches, art, clothes, jewelry, books, cows, etc. It might, of course, be more feasible in these days of computer storage, but it still would have to contain a staggering amount of information all indexed so that the information about each item would be retrievable. Since personal property—unlike land—can be moved from state to state, or outside the country, it might have to include all personal property in the United States—or, for completeness, in the world!) Since the purchaser of personal property cannot easily ascertain that the seller has title, can the purchaser rely upon the ***possession*** of the seller as transferring title to him? If the seller is in wrongful possession (*e.g.,* by theft or fraud), will the buyer win over the true owner? The rules discussed below apply to this situation.

2. **General Rule:** [§237]   The general rule is that the seller can transfer ***no better title than he has.*** If the seller does not own the object or lawfully represent the owner, the buyer

does not get title. [Hessen v. Iowa Automobile Mutual Insurance Co., 190 N.W. 150 (Iowa 1922)] This is a harsh rule that has been mitigated to some extent by exceptions in favor of a **bona fide purchaser** in a **few situations**. First, consider the exceptions and then who is a bona fide purchaser. The Uniform Commercial Code, enacted in all states, has changed the common law in some respects.

3. **Exceptions**

a. **Negotiable instruments:** [§238]   A major exception to the general rule is that title to money or negotiable instruments (such as bank checks or promissory notes) passes to a bona fide purchaser ("BFP"). The reason for this exception is to facilitate trade by permitting bills to be paid by paper that freely circulates from hand to hand without the recipient having to ascertain who has title to the paper. [Miller v. Race, 1 Burr. 452 (1758)]

b. **Seller has voidable title:** [§239]   If the seller has a "voidable" title, he can transfer a good title to a bona fide purchaser. This exception is included in Uniform Commercial Code section 2-403(1) (enacted in all states): "A person with voidable title has power to transfer a good title to a good faith purchaser for value." A voidable title is one the **owner can void** (*e.g.,* where the title is acquired by fraud or by a check which bounces). [Sheridan Suzuki, Inc. v. Caruso Auto Sales, 110 Misc. 2d 823 (1981)]

(1) **Example:** Walter Gwynne falsely represents to O that he is Baldwin Gwynne, a man of financial responsibility. In reliance on this representation, O delivers a quantity of jewelry to Walter. Walter in turn sells it to A, a bona fide purchaser. A wins over O. Why? O intended to transfer title to Walter, even though mistaken as to his identity. O could have voided the title in Walter before Walter sold to A, a bona fide purchaser, but, after A relies on Walter's possession, it would now be unfair for O to void the title. [Phelps v. McQuade, 220 N.Y. 232 (1917)]

(a) **Common law:** [§240]   The common law drew a trifling distinction here. If Walter **personally** appears before O, (voidable) title passes to Walter because O **intends** to transfer title to that person standing in front of him, whom he mistakenly believes is someone else. If Walter makes the misrepresentation in a **letter**, (voidable) title does not pass to Walter, because O intends to deal only with the person whose name is signed to the letter (Baldwin Gwynne). U.C.C. section 2-403(1) apparently renders this distinction obsolete, but it is not entirely clear that it does.

(2) **Reason for exception:** [§241]   There is a general equitable principle—which appears in various guises in the law—that where one of two innocent persons must suffer by the fraudulent act of a third person, the one who could have prevented the harm to the other should suffer the loss. Applied here, that principle means that O, rather than the BFP, should suffer the loss, because O could have prevented the loss to the BFP (by not delivering the goods to the imposter), whereas there is nothing the BFP could do to prevent loss to O.

(3) **Compare—void title:** [§242]   A *voidable* title is one where the owner intends to pass title, but can void the transaction because of fraud, misrepresentation, or duress. A *void* title is one where the owner does not intend to pass title or has no capacity to do so. The best example is a title acquired by theft. A *bona fide purchaser from a thief takes no title.* *Rationale:* If a purchaser from a thief were protected, owners would spend a larger amount of resources in securing their property from theft. Such "defense expenditures" are not socially productive. Also persons whose property is stolen have done nothing to cause a third person (a BFP) to be harmed.

c. **Estoppel:** [§243]   If the owner of goods by words or conduct *expressly or impliedly represents* that the possessor is the owner or is authorized to pass title, *inducing reliance* by the purchaser, the owner is estopped to deny the truth of the representation. *Estoppel* is a general principle running through the law.

(1) **Example:** O, a piano mover, delivers possession of a wagon to George Tracy, a new employee of O. In order to retain the business Tracy has built up for himself as a piano mover, O paints on the wagon the words, "George Tracy, Piano Mover." Tracy sells the wagon to B, a bona fide purchaser. O is estopped to deny that Tracy is the owner. [O'Connor v. Clark, 32 A. 1029 (Pa. 1895)]

d. **Entrusting goods to a merchant**

(1) **Common law rule:** [§244]   The common law principle of estoppel might apply to the situation where an owner entrusted goods to a merchant in the business of selling goods. But mere delivery of possession to the merchant was not enough to estop the owner. The owner must do more, such as *stand by* while the merchant displays the goods with goods for sale, or clothe the merchant with *apparent authority* to dispose of the article (*e.g.,* giving the merchant a bill of sale or letting the merchant put his name on the item). [Porter v. Wertz, 68 App. Div. 141 (1979)]

(2) **Uniform Commercial Code:** [§245]   The Uniform Commercial Code, enacted in all states, provides for statutory estoppel as applied to entrusting goods to a merchant. This statutory estoppel does not replace but supplements the common law; if the facts come within *either* the requirements of a common law estoppel *or* the requirements of the U.C.C., the owner is estopped. The U.C.C. provides that the *mere act of entrusting* is sufficient to protect the bona fide purchaser; additional acts giving the merchant apparent authority to dispose of the article are not necessary. Section 2-403(2) and (3) provide:

(2) Any entrusting of possession of goods to a merchant who deals in goods of that kind gives him power to transfer all rights of the entruster to a buyer in ordinary course of business.

(3) "Entrusting" includes any delivery and any acquiescence in retention of possession regardless of any condition expressed between the parties to the delivery or acquiescence and regardless

of whether the procurement of the entrusting or the possessor's disposition of the goods have been such as to be larcenous under the criminal law.

(a) **Example:** O entrusts a painting to A, an art dealer, for examination. A gives the painting to a friend, B, a delicatessen employee. B, representing that he owns the painting, sells it to C, a bona fide purchaser. If C had purchased the painting from A, a merchant, C would prevail over O. But since C bought the painting from B, O prevails over C for three distinct reasons: (i) B is not the merchant entrusted by O; (ii) B is not an art merchant; and (iii) the sale was not in "the ordinary course of B's business" because B did not deal in paintings. [Porter v. Wertz, 53 N.Y.2d 696 (1981)]

4. **Bona Fide Purchaser:** [§246]   A bona fide purchaser is one who **does not know** of the seller's wrongful possession but has a **good faith belief** that seller has title, and, in addition, pays a **valuable consideration**. A bona fide purchaser is protected under the above exceptions to the general rule, but a buyer who is **not** a bona fide purchaser is **never protected**.

   a. **Example:** A obtains possession of O's watch by fraudulent representation, giving A a voidable title. A sells the watch to B, a bona fide purchaser. B prevails over O. If A had **given** the watch to B, or if B had **known** of the fraud, B would not be a bona fide purchaser and would not prevail over O.

   b. **Rationale:** A bona fide purchaser has a strong appeal to the conscience of a court, whereas a person who knows of the wrong or is not financially damaged has no such appeal to equity.

   c. **Preexisting debt:** [§247]   At common law, some courts held that a person is not a purchaser for a valuable consideration if he takes title only in exchange for a preexisting debt. The idea was that to be a bona fide purchaser the purchaser must give **new consideration** at the time of the purchase.

      (1) **Example:** O transfers his horse to A, who pays for it with a bad check. A thus takes voidable title. A owes B $100. A transfers the horse to B, and B discharges A's debt. B is not a bona fide purchaser. B must give up the horse to O, and A's debt is revived. [Hurd v. Bickford, 27 A. 107 (Me. 1892)]

      (2) **Uniform Commercial Code:** [§248]   The U.C.C. states that a person gives "value" for rights if he acquires them in partial or total satisfaction of a preexisting claim. [U.C.C. §1-201(44)] This reverses the common law rule (referred to above) applied by some courts.

   d. **Inquiry notice:** [§249]   In order to be a bona fide purchaser, a purchaser must have **no actual** notice of the seller's wrongful title **nor any inquiry notice**. "Inquiry notice" is notice the purchaser is deemed to have when the facts and circumstances should lead a reasonable person to make inquiries. From these inquiries, the purchaser would have learned of the defect in the seller's title.

(1) **Example:** A, a poor man, acquires a very expensive oil painting from O on credit when he has no reasonable expectations of paying for it and no intention of paying for it. (This is fraud, and A has a voidable title.) A sells the painting to B. If the circumstances should make B suspicious (*e.g.*, A is dressed in rags, and B has earlier seen the painting hanging in O's shop), B must make inquiry of O to see if O has passed title to A. [Higgins v. Lodge, 11 A. 846 (Md. 1888)]

III. FREEHOLD POSSESSORY ESTATES

chapter approach

This chapter and the two following acquaint you with the historic "law of estates." The estate system originated in feudal times but still underlies our present property law. It is an entirely artificial way of thinking about ownership, known only to Anglo-American law, but something you must master. If it seems strange at first, be assured that it will become more familiar in time. The core ideas are essential tools of analysis for your property exam and for everyday property problems.

This chapter begins with the historical background of the law of estates. Although few exam questions test your knowledge of English history, comprehension of this material will make it easier to understand the estates that grew out of it.

The chapter covers three of the four possessory estates in land: (i) the *fee simple*; (ii) the *fee tail*; and (iii) the *life estate*. (The fourth, the *leasehold*, is discussed in chapter VIII.) Estates are classified by *duration*. Remember that there are only four possessory estates, and any present possessory interest must be classified as one of these. To identify an estate:

1. Look for the *technical language* that creates the estate (*e.g.*, "and his heirs," "and the heirs of his body," etc.). Although this language may no longer be necessary to make a valid conveyance, lawyers use it, and it is often found on exams.

2. Consider how long the estate can *endure* (*e.g.*, forever, for someone's life, until the happening of some event, etc.).

And be sure to review the summary of possessory estates *infra*, §414.

A. INTRODUCTION

1. **The Feudal Background: [§250]** In 1066, William of Normandy crossed the English channel, defeated King Harold at the battle of Hastings, and claimed England as his own. William—called the Conqueror by history—imposed on England a feudal system that was more strictly organized than the previous system, and it is from this system that the law of real property developed. The key features of the feudal system are briefly noted below.

   a. **The feudal ladder: [§251]** William, claiming all England as his, parcelled out great tracts of land to his chief supporters who became William's *tenants-in-chief*. In exchange for land each tenant-in-chief agreed to render the king specified *services*, such as providing forty knights each year to fight for the king, or sounding a horn when the king's enemies approached from Scotland, or furnishing the king with ten fat geese or other foodstuffs for his household. The services provided the king with military and economic support to govern England. Each tenant-in-chief, holding an immense acreage, parcelled out portions of the land to subtenants, extracting from each **subtenant** a promise to render services. These services might support the tenant-in-chief in running his household or they might provide the tenant-in-chief with knights to fight for the king, thus meeting the tenant-in-chief's obligation to the king. The subtenant in turn might **subinfeudate** to another tenant, extracting services from him. In this way, a feudal ladder was built up, with the possessor of land at the bottom and the lords above him entitled to various services.

(1) **Feudal relationships:** [§252]   Under the feudal system, each man, save the king, was made inferior to someone else. Each **tenant** was the **vassal** of some **lord**, and all were under the sovereign lord, the king. Each tenant swore an oath of loyalty to his lord, an oath which made the tenant "the lord's man," and bound the parties together for life.

(2) **Subinfeudation:** [§253]   The process of creating another rung in the feudal ladder below the particular tenant was called **subinfeudation.** Any tenant had a right to subinfeudate, creating a vassal beneath him. When he did so, he became a **mesne lord**, meaning he had a lord above him and a tenant below him.

(a) **Substitution:** [§254]   A tenant who did not want to remain in the feudal ladder could **substitute** another tenant in his place with his lord's consent. Substitution was different from subinfeudation in that with substitution the tenant substituted another tenant in his place in the feudal ladder, whereas with subinfeudation the tenant created a new tenant beneath him.

b. **Feudal services:** [§255]   Services reserved by the contract of subinfeudation were the feudal equivalent of taxes. As history would have it, the man at the bottom of the feudal ladder—**the man in possession**—was the big winner. Possession, which rose in value with inflation, maintained its value while the value of services (fixed obligations) declined. A modern analogue to this aspect of the feudal system occurred before the 1970s, when home buyers purchased homes and took possession; the real cost of fixed mortgage payments declined with inflation, but the value of the homes rose. So it was in feudal times. Inflation has a wealth redistribution effect favorable to the possessor, and unfavorable to owners of fixed obligations.

c. **Feudal incidents:** [§256]   Feudal incidents were, like services, a form of taxes. They fell due on a number of occasions but principally when the tenant below died. The great difference between services and incidents was that **services were fixed rents** (e.g., ten fat hens), but when incidents fell due, the lord got **possession** of the land back. With inflation, services grew less and less valuable, while possession kept pace with inflation. Hence the lords jealously guarded the incidents, while letting services fall into ceremonial payments. The feudal incidents included the following:

(1) **Escheat:** [§257]   If a tenant died **without heirs**, the tenant's position in the feudal ladder was eliminated, and **possession** of the land or whatever rights the tenant had **reverted to the lord**.

(a) **Example:** The king conveys Blackacre to A in fee simple. In turn, A conveys Blackacre to B in fee simple. A holds of the king, and B holds of A. If B dies without heirs, possession of the land returns to A by escheat. If B is alive and A dies without heirs, A's position in the feudal ladder drops out and B now holds of the king. If B thereafter dies without heirs, the land escheats to the king.

(2) **Forfeiture:** [§258]   If a tenant were convicted of breaching his oath to his lord or of a felony, he forfeited his tenure to his lord. The lord retook *possession* or the tenant's rights.

(3) **Wardship and marriage:** [§259]   These affected only minor heirs. If a tenant (T) died leaving a minor heir (H), the lord (L) was entitled to manage the tenant's lands for his own profit until H came of age (an incident called *wardship*), and was entitled to sell the minor heir in *marriage*. (In those days, marriage was a highly commercial arrangement, priced in accordance with the expected inheritance.) Wardship gave L whatever T was entitled to receive from the land, and marriage of a minor heir with the prospect of great wealth was obviously valuable.

(4) **Devaluation by subinfeudation:** [§260]   Subinfeudation devalued these feudal incidents, and was opposed by the top lords who had all to gain by the incidents imposed on tenants below. Why did subinfeudation make the incidents less valuable? Because by interposing another tenant between the lord and the tenant in possession, when the incidents fell due the lord did not get possession (which was the valuable thing) but *only the mesne lord's rights against the tenant in possession*. To illustrate, suppose T, in possession, holds of L. When T dies with a minor heir, L gets possession of the land back until the heir comes of age. Possession is a valuable right. Now suppose that T subinfeudates to his daughter D, for a rose at midsummer. T is now a mesne lord with only a right to the service of one rose. Then T dies, leaving a minor heir. L is not entitled to possession, but only to that to which T was entitled—a rose at midsummer.

d. **Statute Quia Emptores (1290):** [§261]   To put a stop to subinfeudation, and eliminate the creation of new mesne lords, the top lords had Parliament enact the Statute Quia Emptores in 1290. This statute *prohibited* further *subinfeudation in fee simple*; afterwards, the network of tenures could only contract, not grow. Over time, with escheats and forfeitures, the mesne lords dropped out of the feudal ladder, and by the sixteenth century almost all land had come to be held directly from the king. As the price for prohibiting further subinfeudation, the top lords had to concede to all free tenants the right to *alienate their land* (substitute another tenant in the feudal ladder) without the lord's consent. The Statute Quia Emptores thus established the principle that *land should be freely alienable*, one of the most important principles of English and American property law. Quia Emptores also provided that if a new tenant were substituted only with respect to a portion of the land, the feudal services were apportioned accordingly.

(1) **Example:** T holds Blackacre of L with a service of ten bushels of wheat annually. T desires to give one-half of Blackacre to his daughter at a nominal service ("a rose at midsummer") because he can furnish the ten bushels of wheat from the half retained. *Before Quia Emptores*, T can subinfeudate one-half of Blackacre to his daughter for a nominal service. When T dies, L is entitled to feudal incidents in the land given T's daughter, measured by T's rights in such land ("a rose at midsummer"). *After Quia Emptores*, T can freely substitute his daughter as the tenant of one-half his fief. She becomes the tenant of L, and owes L one-half the services due (five bushels of wheat annually). But T cannot subinfeudate in fee simple to his daughter and reserve services to himself. T cannot create any new relationship of lord and tenant. [*Cf.* Van Rensselaer v. Hays, 19 N.Y. 68 (1859)]

(2) **Only subinfeudation in fee simple banned:** [§262] The Statute Quia Emptores only forbade subinfeudations in fee simple. It did not forbid the creation of new tenurial relationships by granting estates *less* than a fee simple. Hence, in the example above, T could convey to his daughter a fee tail, a life estate, or a term of years with reversion in T. The hierarchy of estates is discussed *infra*, §287, but it should be noted at this point that Quia Emptores did not prevent the development of estates less than a fee simple, with a reversionary interest in the grantor.

e. **Decline of feudalism:** [§263] English feudalism reached highest flower in the thirteenth century, of which the Statute Quia Emptores marked the end. Thereafter feudalism went into a gradual decline stretching over a long period. The Renaissance, which had emerged in Italy in the fifteenth century, reached England a hundred years later, during the reigns of those powerful Tudor monarchs, Henry VIII (1509-1547), and his daughter, Elizabeth I (1558-1603). This was the age of exploration and discoveries, which was followed by the commercial revolution, the industrial revolution, and then the modern era. But feudalism did not sink without a trace. It has its continuations in the law.

f. **Tenure in the United States**

(1) **Land held tenurially:** [§264] A basic principal of the feudal system of land tenure was that all land was held either directly or indirectly from the crown. This theory is still followed in England, but it only matters for purposes of escheat. In the United States, some states still follow the theory of tenure—that all land is held from the state (substituted for the crown), but, as in England, this matters only in cases of *escheat*. If a person dies intestate (*i.e.,* without a will) and without heirs, his or her land escheats to the state in which the land is located.

(a) **Theory of tenurial escheat:** [§265] The theory of escheat in the tenurial system was that the lord had given the tenant a limited estate—one which expired when the tenant died without heirs. When the tenant died the land *reverted to the lord.* If the tenurial theory is followed today, escheat to the state takes place by way of *reversion* to the state.

(2) **Land owned allodially:** [§266]   In some states the notion of tenure has been discarded and land is owned *allodially*, *i.e.*, without any notion of holding from anyone, even the state. If a person dies intestate without heirs, his or her lands escheat to the state *as an intestate successor* by virtue of a state statute, and not by any theory of reversion to the state. The result—escheat to the state—is the same in all states where a person dies intestate without heirs. But the route may differ, depending upon whether the state follows the tenurial or the allodial theory.

(3) **The difference between "title reverting" and "title passing":** [§267]   The basic distinction between the tenurial and allodial theories of escheat is that under the tenurial theory land *reverts* or returns to the *original owner*, whereas under the allodial theory land *passes forward* to a new *owner*. This difference can best be illustrated by reference to inheritance taxes. Inheritance taxes are often levied on property which "*passes* by will or intestate succession." Under such a statute, if O, owner of Blackacre, dies intestate, leaving H as his heir, an inheritance tax is levied. Title *passes* from O to H. On the other hand, if the decedent, A, had merely a life estate in Blackacre, no tax is levied at A's death, because the life estate ends at A's death, and nothing *passes* from A. The land returns (or *reverts*) to the person who gave A the life estate, and no tax is levied on title reverting, only on title passing. This illustrates the difference between title *passing* forward and title *reverting* backward.

2.   The System of Estates

a. **Historic development:** [§268]   Out of feudalism developed the system of estates in land, which remains central to our modern law, both in theory and in practice. Although a nonlawyer talks about owning "property" or "land," what he holds legally is an *estate* in land. An estate is an interest in land which *is or may become possessory*. More important at the moment, in understanding the development of the law, an estate is an interest *measured by some period of time*. In feudal days, a tenant was granted land by his lord for some period of time—*e.g.*, for life, for ten years, for so long as he kept up the bridges. Gradually the law simplified and categorized these holdings by developing a system of estates. Dealing with standardized estates rather than with the hundreds of different tenurial arrangements as to duration made the law easier to administer. And so it came about that the judges recognized only three types of freehold estates and three types of leasehold estates. Lord and tenant had to fit their wishes into one of these six categories, although some variations within a category were permitted.

(1) **Compare—other meanings of estate:** [§269]   The word "estate" is often used in other senses, such as referring to an area of land, *e.g.*, "Jones has an estate in the country," or to property in general, *e.g.*, "Jones died with an estate worth $100,000." Such usage does not occur in this chapter.

b. **Types of estates:** [§270]   The common law developed the following estates, each indicating the period of time for which the land might be held.

(1) **Fee simple:** [§271] A fee simple is an estate that has the potential of *enduring forever*. It is created by O, the owner of Blackacre, granting the land "to A and his heirs." This estate resembles absolute ownership, and the holder of a fee simple is commonly called the owner of the land (*see infra*, §289).

(2) **Fee tail:** [§272] A fee tail is an estate that has the potential of enduring forever, but **will necessarily cease if and when the first fee tail tenant has no lineal descendants to succeed him in possession**. A fee tail is created by O granting the property "to A and the heirs of his body" (*see infra*, §340).

(3) **Life estate:** [§273] A life estate is an estate that will end necessarily **at the death of a person**. It is created by granting the property "to A for life" (*see infra*, §369).

(4) **Leasehold estate:** [§274] Leasehold estates include estates that endure: (i) for any fixed calendar period or any period of time computable by the calendar (called a "term of years" regardless of the length of the period); *or* (ii) from period to period until the landlord or tenant gives notice to terminate at the end of a period (called a "periodic tenancy"); *or* (iii) so long as both the landlord and tenant desire (called a "tenancy at will"). (Leasehold estates are dealt with in detail in Chapter VIII of this Summary.)

c. **Freehold and nonfreehold estates:** [§275] The fee simple, fee tail, and life estate are "freehold" estates. Freehold was the highest form of holding under feudal tenure. The leasehold interests are not freehold because in the early feudal system they were not considered to be estates at all but merely personal contracts. The important difference between freehold and nonfreehold estates is that a freeholder in possession has **"seisin,"** whereas a leaseholder has only **possession**.

(1) **Seisin:** [§276] "Seisin" was an important concept in feudal times, and remains important in understanding how the estates system developed. A person is seised if he holds an **estate of freehold** and either has **possession of the land** or a **tenant holds possession** from him. Except where the land is leased and the landlord holds the seisin, "possession by a freeholder" embodies the fundamental idea of seisin.

(a) **Example:** O, fee simple owner of Blackacre, grants Blackacre to A for life. By this grant, O conveys seisin (possession) to A. A is now seised. If O had conveyed Blackacre to A for ten years, O would retain seisin. A, a termor holding a term of years (a nonfreehold estate), could not be given seisin. Instead, A, a termor, was given possession. This illustrates the essential difference between freehold and nonfreehold estates. A termor could not hold seisin because seisin was considered too important a thing to be entrusted to a termor, who was looked upon by the early judges as a rascally fellow. (*See infra*, §450.)

(2) **Feudal services:** [§277] In the feudal system, the overlord collected feudal services and incidents from the person seised of land. To perpetuate the feudal

system and keep wealth flowing to the top of the ladder, some person always had to be responsible for the services. Hence the rule was: ***There could never be an abeyance of seisin.***

(3) **Livery of seisin:** [§278]   Seisin was endowed by the medieval mind with a real existence. It was a "thing" which passed from one person to another. In order to convey a freehold estate, the parties had to go on the land and perform a ceremony known as "***livery of seisin.***" This involved the grantor and grantee going on the land and the grantor, before witnesses, delivering seisin to the grantee by some symbolic act such as handing over a clod or twig. This visual ritual was important in a society in which few could read and write. It attested a change of ownership in the clearest possible way.

d.   **Reification of estates:** [§279]   The medieval mind had a philosophical tendency to reify abstract ideas, and the chief example of this in law is the ***reification of estates***. English lawyers thought of an estate as a thing and gave it qualities and characteristics of a thing. For example, consider a fee simple estate. During life, O can ***convey*** the fee simple to another, or on O's death, it ***passes*** to her heirs. Creditors can ***reach*** the fee simple and ***sell*** it to pay O's debts. Note how every verb in the preceding two sentences relates to the fee simple as a thing; ***it*** is conveyed, ***it*** passes, ***it*** is reached and sold. After talking this way for a while, estates become almost visible entities. And they were—to the medieval mind. The easiest way to learn the law of estates is to make that flight of imagination—***imagine estates as things, but never believe they really are***.

(1) **Bundle of rights:** [§280]   Bear in mind that modern analysis insists that an estate is a "bundle of rights"; *i.e.,* estate is a word denoting legal relations between persons with respect to a thing. (But even this modern metaphor cannot eliminate reification entirely; it refers to an estate as a "bundle.") What rights are in the bundle involves issues of public policy—not merely an analysis of qualities of imagined objects—and rights in the bundle have varied from century to century and from place to place.

3.   **Creation of Estates:** [§281]   Estates are created by using appropriate words in a deed or will. For example, a deed conveying Blackacre "to A for life" creates a life estate in A in Blackacre.

a.   **Words of limitation and words of purchase:** [§282]   "Words of limitation" in an instrument describe what ***type*** of estate is created. "Words of purchase" identify the person in ***whom*** the estate is created. Suppose that O conveys Blackacre by deed "to A and his heirs." The words "to A" are words of purchase. The words "and his heirs" are words of limitation, indicating a fee simple. ("Purchase" here has nothing to do with the modern meaning of the word; rather it signifies only that the person takes by deed or will, and not by intestate succession.)

(1) **Example:** In 1600, O conveys Blackacre "to A for life, remainder to the heirs of B." The words "to A" are words of purchase, the words "for life" are words of limitation explaining that A is getting a life estate. The words "the heirs of B"

are words of purchase, giving the remainder to the heirs of B, a person or persons who will be ascertained upon and not before B's death. (B is given no interest by this conveyance; his heirs are the takers.) The words "the heirs of B" are also words of limitation. Under the doctrine of primogeniture in effect in 1600, B had only one heir, his eldest son. Therefore the use of the plural "heirs of B" is read to mean "the heir of *B and his heirs*." The heir of B takes a fee simple.

4. **Possessory Estates and Future Interests:** [§283]   Every estate can be classified either as a possessory estate or as a future interest.

   a. **Possessory estate:** [§284]   A possessory estate gives the holder the right to immediate possession.

   b. **Future interest:** [§285]   A future interest does not entitle the owner to present possession, but it **will or may** become a possessory estate in the future. A future interest, like a possessory estate, is an existing "thing." The fact that it is nonpossessory does not preclude it from being treated as in existence. It is a "thing" waiting to become possessory.

      (1) **Example:** T, testator, devises land "to A for life, and on A's death, to B in fee simple." B has a future interest known as a remainder, which entitles the person who holds it to possession on A's death. B's remainder can be transferred by B. B's creditors can reach and sell the remainder. The value of the remainder (as determined by A's life expectancy) is taxed by the federal estate tax upon B's death during A's life. Thus, B has an *existing nonpossessory interest*.

5. **Estates in Personal Property:** [§286]   The law of estates developed at a time when land was the only property of substantial value, and it is sometimes called the law of estates in land. As personal property grew in amount and importance, the courts applied the system of estates to personal property. Because of the feudal origins of estates, there is technically a fee simple only in land ("fee" originally meant "fief"); the correlative estate in personal property is "absolute ownership." However, "fee simple" in land and "absolute ownership" of personal property are functional equivalents. "Absolute ownership," like the fee simple, can be divided into smaller possessory estates (such as a life estate), followed by future interests. Generally, the same types of possessory estates and future interests can be created in personal property as can be created in real property.

6. **Hierarchy of Estates:** [§287]   At common law, estates were ranked according to their potential duration. A *fee simple* was longer in potential duration than a *fee tail*, which was longer than a *life estate*. All freehold estates were presumed to be longer in duration than a leasehold.

   a. **Example:** O, owner of a fee simple, conveys a fee tail to A. (This leaves a reversion in O; the property will return to O when the fee tail expires.) A then conveys a life estate to B. (This leaves a reversion in A. The property will return to A at the death of B. If A's fee tail ends during B's life, the property will return to O.)

7. **No New Estates May Be Created:** [§288]   The fee simple, the fee tail, the life estate, and the leasehold estates are the only estates permissible. New types cannot be created. If an attempt is made to create a new type of estate, the language of the creating instrument will be construed to create an estate within *one of the existing* categories.

   a. **Example:** Royal Whiton devises land "to my granddaughter Sarah *and her heirs on her father's side*." The highlighted words do not fit into any of the categories of estates. Royal is trying to create an estate which will descend only to Sarah's agnate kin. The law knows no such an estate as this. The court will construe the highlighted words so that they fit within an accepted category of estate. The closest estate is a fee simple, created by a devise "to Sarah *and her heirs*." Hence Sarah has a fee simple, which she can dispose of by deed or will. If she does not transfer the fee simple, it will descend at her death to her heirs generally, enate as well as agnate. ("Enate" means heirs on her mother's side; "agnate" means heirs on her father's side.) [Johnson v. Whiton, 34 N.E. 542 (Mass. 1893)]

B. THE FEE SIMPLE

1. **Fee Simple Absolute:** [§289]   A fee simple absolute is absolute ownership, so far as absolute ownership is known to Anglo-American law. It is of *potentially infinite duration* (therefore called a "fee"). There are *no limitations on its inheritability* (therefore called "simple"). It *cannot be divested*, nor will it end upon the happening of *any* event (hence called "absolute").

   a. **Creation of fee simple:** [§290]   A fee simple, like all estates, is created by an instrument using words.

      (1) **Common law (applicable to deeds):** [§291]   At common law, it was necessary to use the technical words, "*and his heirs*," to create a fee simple by deed. "To A and his heirs," for example, created a fee simple. A's heirs, of course, take nothing by this deed. The words "and his heirs" are only words of limitation indicating that A takes a fee simple.

         (a) **Example:** O, owner in fee simple, conveys "to A in fee simple." At common law, A takes only a life estate. To create a fee simple, O should have conveyed "to A and his heirs."

         (b) **Historical development of fee simple:** [§292]   In early feudal times, land was held through a wholly personal and contractual relationship between the lord and the tenant swearing fealty (allegiance) to him. The tenant held the land only for his life, and the lord expected to dispose of the land as he pleased after the tenant's death. Through time, the tenants received the following additional rights:

            1) **Inheritability:** [§293]   Tenants first bargained for the inheritability of their holdings. It was natural for a tenant to wish to pass the holding, including any improvements by the tenant, to his heirs. The lord

would assent in advance to accept the tenant's heirs on the tenant's death by granting the land "to A and his heirs." The words "and his heirs" are thus called "words of inheritance." At common law, ***primogeniture*** (inheritance of all land by the eldest son) prevailed. Hence, a grant to "A and his heirs" permitted A, then his heir (eldest son), then his heir's heir (eldest son's eldest son) and so on, to succeed each other in possession. If the words "and his heirs" were omitted, the lord had not assented to inheritance, and the land was not inheritable. A had only a life estate.

2) **Alienability:** [§294]   Prior to the Statute Quia Emptores (1290 A.D.), land could be alienated during life only with the consent of the lord, who had a strong interest in making sure the succeeding tenant was not his enemy. Quia Emptores gave tenants the right to alienate their holdings without the lord's consent. Once the fee became alienable, the feudal realities behind a conveyance to "A and his heirs" became meaningless. If A conveyed to "B and his heirs," A and his heirs dropped out of the picture. The lord's assent to inheritance by A's heirs became irrelevant. B's heirs took on B's death, and the lord had never assented to that. The development of alienability perhaps caused the judges to think of A's holding as not resting on a contract between A and his lord but as being a fee simple ***estate*** with an existence all its own. In any event, the words "and his heirs" now became a pure formality, indicating a fee simple estate was granted—but they continued to be a necessary formality until modern times.

3) **Devisability:** [§295]   Land was not devisable at law until 1540, when the Statute of Wills was enacted. At that time, the fee simple took on the three characteristics today associated with it: it is freely alienable by the owner during life; it can be disposed of at death by the owner's will; and if not disposed of by will, it will pass to the owner's heirs. (If none of these things happens—if the owner of a fee simple dies intestate without heirs—the fee simple will escheat to the state.)

(2) **Common law (applicable to wills):** [§296]   The words "and his heirs" were never necessary to create a fee simple by will (first permitted in 1540; *see* above). Any words indicating that the testator intended to devise a fee simple would do. Therefore, a will devising Blackacre "to A, my entire estate," or "to A in fee simple" is sufficient to convey the entire fee simple.

(3) **Modern law:** [§297]   The ancient requirement of words of inheritance in a deed ("and his heirs") has been abolished in almost all states. Under modern law, either a deed or will is **presumed to pass the largest estate the grantor or testator owned.** A conveyance of Blackacre "to A" conveys a fee simple, if the grantor had a fee simple. But, in spite of the abolition of the necessity of using words of inheritance, lawyers, being creatures of centuries of habit, still use them in creating a fee simple.

(a) **States still mired in feudalism:** [§298]   A couple of states, South Carolina and perhaps Maine, still require the words "and his heirs" to be used in creating a fee simple by deed. In other states, the issue may not be clearly settled, and the title to land may be uncertain where the words of inheritance have been omitted.

  1) **Example:** In the jurisdiction it is not settled whether words of inheritance are necessary to create a fee simple. O conveys Blackacre "to A and assigns forever." Subsequently A contracts to sell a fee simple in Blackacre to B. After examining the records, B wants to back out of the contract because B is not sure A has a fee simple to sell. B sues A for return of the earnest money deposited upon signing the contract. In a suit between O and A, A might well win an argument that O gave A a fee simple. But since O is not a party to the lawsuit, and it might prejudice him to make a determination without his presence, there is a possible defect in A's title, and B is entitled to the return of the earnest money. [Cole v. Steinlauf, 136 A.2d 744 (Conn. 1957); *and see* Dennan v. Searle, 176 A.2d 561 (Conn. 1961)—court held that words of inheritance were not required under Connecticut law, but that the Cole case had been correctly decided because the issue there involved marketability of title and the case law was then unclear]

b. **Inheritability:** [§299]   If the owner of a fee simple dies intestate, the fee simple is inherited by the owner's heirs generally.

(1) **Heirs defined:** [§300]   The word "heirs" means in law those persons who succeed to the *real property* of an intestate decedent under the statute of intestate succession of the applicable state (sometimes called the *statute of descent*). For lawyers, it is *not* a synonym for children, though it is sometimes used that way by nonlawyers. Thus, if O dies leaving a husband and a child, and under the intestate succession law the husband and child succeed to title to O's land, O's heirs are O's husband and child.

(a) **Spouse at common law:** [§301]   At English common law a spouse could not be an heir; he or she was given only curtesy or dower in real property (*see infra*, §§761-775). If the decedent left no blood relatives at all, the land escheated to the overlord or the crown—subject to the spouse's dower or curtesy. This disqualification of the spouse as an heir has been abolished in all states. If the decedent leaves no blood kin, in all states the spouse will succeed to title—even in states that have retained dower and curtesy. In most states, dower and curtesy have been abolished, and the spouse is given a fractional share as heir of the decedent.

(b) **Ancestors at common law:** [§302]   At English law, an ancestor could not inherit title to land from a decedent. This peculiar disqualification of ancestors has been abolished in all American states. If a decedent leaves no children nor spouse, the decedent's parents usually take as heirs.

(c) **Next of kin:** [§303]   The term "next of kin" refers to those persons who succeed to the *personal property* of an intestate decedent under the applicable statute of intestate succession (sometimes called the *statute of distribution*). At English law, the successors to real and personal property were not necessarily the same. Land passed under the rule of primogeniture to the eldest son ("the heir," as he was commonly referred to in England). Personal property was divided equally among all children. Primogeniture was abolished in this country shortly after the American Revolution, and today all children—male and female—share equally. In almost all states today the same persons succeed to decedent's personal property as succeed to decedent's land. Hence, in most states, "next of kin" and "heirs" are synonymous.

(2) **Applicable statute:** [§304]   It should be obvious from the above discussion of the meaning of "heirs" that the word "heirs" cannot be given content without looking at some statute of intestate succession. These statutes vary considerably from state to state, but the following represents the general pattern of the Uniform Probate Code, adopted in many states:

(a) **Share of spouse:** [§305]   If the decedent leaves a spouse, the spouse takes one-half. The other one-half goes to decedent's issue, or, if none, to the decedent's parents, or, if none, to the spouse.

(b) **Share of issue**

1) **Issue defined:** [§306]   The word "issue" means children, grandchildren, great-grandchildren, and all further descendants. It is synonymous with "descendants," a term often used by nonlawyers for what lawyers call "issue."

2) **Children's share:** [§307]   If the decedent leaves a spouse and children, the spouse takes half, and the children divide half. If the decedent leaves no spouse, the children take all in equal shares.

a) **Representation:** [§308]   If a child *predeceases the decedent*, leaving issue, the issue *represent* the child and take the child's portion. This is called a *per stirpes* (by the roots) distribution. The principle of representation can get complicated when several issue predecease the decedent. (*See* Wills Summary.)

b) **Grandchildren's share:** [§309]   Grandchildren do not take if their parent is alive. Generally speaking—and subject to much variation if the decedent leaves no children but only grandchildren and more remote issue—grandchildren share only under the principle of representation.

c) **Example:** O dies intestate, leaving no spouse, a child A, and two sons of a child B who predeceased O. A and the two sons of B are

O's heirs. A takes one-half; the two sons of B, representing B, divide the other half.

3) **Adopted children:** [§310] An adopted child is treated as a child of the adoptive parent and not as a child of her natural parents.

4) **Illegitimate children:** [§311] An illegitimate child inherits as a child of her mother and, if paternity is established, as a child of her father. (On inheritance from the father there is great variation from state to state.)

5) **Stepchildren:** [§312] Stepchildren do not take. Except for the spouse and adopted children, *only blood relatives* of the decedent take as heirs.

(c) **Parents' share:** [§313] If the decedent leaves issue, parents do not take. If the decedent leaves a spouse and no issue, parents take one-half and the spouse one-half. If the decedent leaves no spouse and no issue, parents take all.

(d) **Collateral relatives:** [§314] The term "collateral relatives" includes all blood kin except ancestors and descendants. Hence it includes brothers, sisters, nephews, nieces, uncles, aunts, and cousins. If the decedent leaves no spouse, issue, or parent, the collateral relatives take. The common law developed a complicated system for determining which collateral relatives took, and the rules for making this determination remain complicated today. (*See* Wills Summary.)

1) **Ancestral property:** [§315] At common law, property passing to collaterals went only to those who were "of the blood of the first purchaser." This meant generally that the collateral had to be related by blood to the ancestor from whence the property came. Thus, if O died owning Blackacre, which O had inherited from his mother, only O's enate collaterals (collaterals related by blood to his mother) could inherit Blackacre. If O left surviving two aunts—his mother's sister and his father's sister—O's mother's sister took Blackacre. The doctrine of ancestral property has been abolished in most states.

(3) **Devisee and legatee defined:** [§316] If a decedent leaves a will, the persons who are *devised* land are called *devisees*. The persons who are *bequeathed* personal property are called *legatees*. The difference between heirs on the one hand and devisees and legatees on the other is that heirs take when decedent leaves no will; devisees and legatees take under a will.

2. **Defeasible Fees:** [§317] A fee simple can be created so that it is defeasible on the happening of some event, and the owner of the fee simple then loses, or may lose, the property. If the fee simple is defeasible, it is of course not absolute. The following are

the three different kinds of defeasible fees simple. *Note:* All of these are called fees simple because they have the **potential** of infinite duration, though not the certainty. Defeasible fees are most commonly encountered in deeds **restricting the use** of land, but they may be used for other purposes as well. Sometimes defeasible fees are called by another name, "qualified fees," but it is much easier to master the system of estates if **each estate is given only one name** and that name is consistently used. The names used in this Summary are the names most commonly used today.

a.　**Fee simple determinable**

(1)　**Definition:** [§318]　A fee simple determinable is a fee simple estate so limited that it will **automatically end** when some specified event happens.

(a)　**Example:** O conveys Blackacre "to School Board so long as the premises are used for school purposes." The words "so long . . . purposes" are **words of limitation**, limiting the duration of the fee simple given. The School Board has a fee simple determinable that will automatically end when Blackacre ceases to be used for school purposes. When that event happens, the fee simple automatically reverts to O.

(b)　**Automatic termination:** [§319]　A fee simple determinable is a fee simple because it **may** endure forever. But, if the contingency occurs (Blackacre is used for other than school purposes, as above), the estate **automatically** ends. The estate terminates immediately upon the occurrence of the event—nothing further is required—and the fee simple **automatically reverts** to the grantor. This is the distinguishing characteristic of the determinable fee.

(c)　**Other names for fee simple determinable:** [§320]　The fee simple determinable is sometimes called a "fee simple on a special limitation," "fee simple on a conditional limitation," or a "base fee," although these alternate names are now passing from usage. Whatever name is used, the same estate is meant.

(2)　**Creation of fee simple determinable:** [§321]　A determinable fee is created by language that connotes that the grantor is giving a fee simple only until a stated event happens. Traditional language to create this estate includes "to A **so long as** . . .," "to A **until** . . .," "to A **while** . . .," or language providing that upon the happening of a stated event the land is to **revert** to the grantor.

(a)　**Motive or purpose:** [§322]　Words in an instrument that state the motive or purpose of the grantor do not create a determinable fee. For a determinable fee, it is necessary to use words **limiting the duration** of the estate.

1)　**Example:** O conveys Blackacre "to Board of Education upon the understanding that the land is conveyed solely for the purpose of being used for the erection and maintenance of a public school." The Board erects a school. Thirty years later, the board ceases to use Blackacre for a school. The Board has a fee simple absolute, not a fee simple determinable, and can do with Blackacre as it wishes. The words in quotation marks merely state the grantor's motive. The grantor has retained no rights in Blackacre. [Roberts v. Rhodes, 643 P.2d 116 (Kan. 1982); Hagaman v. Board of Education, 285 A.2d 63 (N.J. 1971)]

(3) **Transferability:** [§323] A fee simple determinable may be transferred or inherited in the same manner as any other fee simple, as long as the stated event has not happened. But the *fee simple remains subject to the limitation* no matter who holds it.

(4) **Correlative future interest:** [§324] Since there is a possibility that the grantee's determinable fee may come to an end upon the happening of the stated event, the *grantor* has a future interest called a *possibility of reverter*. A possibility of reverter may be retained expressly or may arise by operation of law. (The possibility of reverter is discussed more extensively *infra*, §§434 *et seq.*)

   (a) **Example:** O conveys Blackacre "to the Library Board so long as used for library purposes." By operation of law, O retains a possibility of reverter, which will automatically become possessory if and when the Library Board ceases to use Blackacre for library purposes.

(5) **Abolition:** [§325] California and Kentucky have abolished the fee simple determinable. Language that would create a fee simple determinable at common law creates a fee simple subject to condition subsequent (below).

b. **Fee simple subject to condition subsequent**

   (1) **Definition:** [§326] A fee simple subject to condition subsequent is a fee simple that does not automatically terminate but may be *cut short* (divested) at the *grantor's election* when a stated condition happens.

      (a) **Example:** O conveys Blackacre "to A, but if liquor is ever sold on the premises, the grantor has a right to reenter the premises." The words "but if . . . premises" are *words of condition* setting forth the condition upon which the grantor can exercise her right of entry. They are not words limiting the fee simple granted A. A has a fee simple subject to condition subsequent. O has a right of entry. If O does not choose to exercise her right of entry when liquor is sold, the fee simple continues in A.

      (b) **Does not automatically end:** [§327] A fee simple subject to condition subsequent is a fee simple because it may endure forever. If the contingency occurs, O merely has the *power* to reenter and to terminate the estate. The fee simple subject to condition subsequent *does not automatically end* upon the happening of the condition. Rather, the estate continues in the grantee until the grantor *exercises* her power of reentry and terminates the estate. The grantor has the option of exercising the power or not.

(c) **Other names for the fee simple subject to condition subsequent:** [§328] Note that the "fee simple conditional" (discussed *infra*, §341) is an entirely different estate from the fee simple subject to condition subsequent. Substantial confusion is possible unless the estate here discussed is always referred to as "a fee simple subject to condition subsequent" or "fee simple on condition subsequent." Such usage is followed in this Summary.

(2) **Creation of fee simple subject to condition subsequent:** [§329] A fee simple subject to condition subsequent is created by first giving the grantee an unconditional fee simple and then providing that the fee simple may be divested by the grantor or her heirs if a specified condition happens. Traditional language to create such an estate includes: "to A, *but if* X event happens . . .," or "to A, *upon condition* that if X event happens . . .," or "to A, *provided, however*, that if X event happens . . .," the grantor retains a right of entry.

(3) **Transferability:** [§330] This estate may be transferred or inherited in the same manner as any other fee simple until the transferor is entitled to *and does exercise* the right of entry.

(4) **Correlative future interest:** [§331] If the grantor creates a fee simple subject to condition subsequent, the grantor retains a *right of entry*. This interest is sometimes called a "right to reenter," a "power of termination," or a "right of reacquisition." But regardless of which name is applied, the law is the same. The law does not require that a right of entry be expressly retained by the grantor. If the words of the instrument are reasonably susceptible to the interpretation that this type of forfeitable estate was contemplated by the parties, the court will imply a right of entry. [Gray v. Blanchard, 8 Pick. 284 (Mass. 1829); *but see* Storke v. Penn Mutual Insurance Co., 62 N.E.2d 552 (Ill. 1945)—court will not imply a right of entry where none is provided in a deed because equity will not aid a forfeiture] (The right of entry is discussed more extensively *infra*, §§440-445.)

(5) **Fee on condition subsequent distinguished from fee simple determinable**

(a) **Construction of ambiguous language:** [§332] These two estates are very similar and often the language in deeds can be classified either way. If the court has a choice, the *fee on condition subsequent is preferred* on the ground that the forfeiture is *optional* at the grantor's election and not automatic. The general policy of courts is to *avoid forfeiture* of estates ("equity abhors a forfeiture"). [Storke v. Penn Mutual Life Insurance Co., *supra*]

1) **Example:** O conveys "to A so long as intoxicating liquors are not sold on the premises, and if they are sold, O has a right to reenter." The words "so long as" point to a fee simple determinable. The retained right of entry points to a fee simple subject to condition subsequent. The court can classify the language to create either estate, but the fee simple subject to condition subsequent is preferred.

2) **Construction from extrinsic circumstances:** [§333] Sometimes a court goes to extraordinary lengths in construing an ambiguous instrument so as to reach a desirable result. *Oldfield v. Stoeco Homes, Inc.,* 139 A.2d 291 (N.J. 1958), is such an example. In that case, Ocean City, N.J., wanted to develop some swampy land it owned. The city sold the land to Stoeco by deed providing that "within one year from the date of the deed Stoeco shall fill the land," and further providing that a failure to do so "will automatically cause title to revert to the city." Stoeco ran into engineering trouble in filling the land, and eighteen months after the deed, the city, more interested in getting development than in resuming possession, passed a resolution extending the time for performance for several more years. Some taxpayers objected to this extension and sued, alleging that Stoeco's determinable fee automatically ended one year after the deed, title reverted to the city, and the city could not thereafter legally give away public land by a resolution. The issue was whether Stoeco took a determinable fee which automatically ended, or a fee on condition subsequent with a right of entry which could be waived. If the former, the city's resolution passed title back to Stoeco free (forbidden); if the latter, the resolution merely *left* title where it was, in Stoeco, and did not pass title to Stoeco. The court, sympathetic to the city's desire to further development, held that Stoeco had a fee on condition subsequent. It paid little attention to the words of the deed, but instead discovered intent in the entire circumstances surrounding the transaction.

(b) **Automatic vs. optional termination:** [§334] The distinction between automatic and optional termination governs the consequences in several contexts. In cases of automatic termination, the fee simple goes back to the grantor by operation of law. Where termination is optional, the grantor must act affirmatively to terminate the fee simple estate.

1) **Example—Statute of Frauds:** [§335] O conveys a fee simple to A, defeasible if liquor is sold, but it is unclear what kind of defeasible fee simple is created. After A sells liquor, O says to A, "You shouldn't have done that. But if you don't do it again, I won't disturb you." If A has a fee simple subject to condition subsequent, O has *waived* her right of entry, which was optional. If A has a fee simple determinable, the estate terminates upon sale of liquor and O has title to the land. Because of the Statute of Frauds, it will require a written instrument for O to retransfer title to A. [*Cf.* Oldfield v. Stoeco Homes, Inc., *supra*]

2) **Example—statute of limitations:** [§336] O conveys land "to School Board *so long as* used for a school, but if the Board ceases to use the land for a school, O retains *the right to reenter.*" In 1950, the Board ceases to use the land for a school but stays in possession. O does nothing. The statute of limitations is twenty years. If the Board has a fee

simple determinable, the fee simple reverts to O in 1950, and the Board is thereafter in adverse possession. In 1970, the Board takes title by adverse possession. If the Board has a fee simple subject to condition subsequent, O's right of action is subject to the condition precedent that she elect to declare a forfeiture; hence, her right of action has not yet arisen and the statute of limitations has not run on her. However, some modern cases do not follow this theory, and hold that where O retains a right of entry, the statute of limitations begins to run from the time the condition is broken. [*See* Johnson v. City of Wheat Ridge, 532 P.2d 985 (Colo. 1975)]

(c) **Restraints upon marriage:** [§337]   Restraints upon marriage are sometimes struck down as violations of public policy, particularly where the restraint is against a first marriage. (Section 426 of the Restatement of Property, comment d, provides that a restraint on marriage is valid when imposed by a person on his or her spouse, but that a restraint imposed on another is valid only if reasonable.)

1) **Limitation-condition distinction:** [§338]   Sometimes courts have resorted to a limitation-condition test to determine the validity of the restraint. A conveyance by O "to A and her heirs so long as she does not marry" (a fee simple determinable) is said not to be against public policy since O *intended* to give A *support* only until A's husband supported her. On the other hand, a conveyance by O "to A and her heirs, but if she marries, to B" is viewed as a penalty upon marriage. Supposedly the distinction turns upon O's intent. Does O intend to provide A with support while single or to penalize A for marriage? The former is acceptable; the latter is not. But this technical distinction permits O to escape the dictates of public policy by carefully choosing the words. [Lewis v. Searles, 452 S.W.2d 153 (Mo. 1970)]

c. **Fee simple subject to an executory limitation**

(1) **Definition:** [§339]   A fee simple subject to an executory limitation is a fee simple that, upon the happening of a stated event, is automatically *divested* in favor of a *third person*.

(a) **Example:** O conveys Blackacre "to School Board, but if within the next twenty years Blackacre is not used for school purposes, then to A." Observe that the forfeiture interest is in *another grantee*, A, and not in the grantor, O. A's future interest is called an *executory interest*.

(2) **Comment:** Do not worry too much about the fee simple subject to an executory limitation at this point. It will become much clearer in the next chapter (Future Interests), where the executory interest is explained in detail (§§560 *et seq.*). It must be mentioned here with the other types of defeasible fees for completeness, but the important thing to master at this point is the difference between the determinable fee which *automatically expires* and a fee on condition subsequent which is *cut short*.

C. THE FEE TAIL

1. **Historical Background:** [§340]   In feudal England, land was the basis of family power, status, and wealth. One of the chief objectives of landowners, particularly large land-owners, was to keep land in the family. The fee tail was invented for just that purpose—to keep the land safe for succeeding generations. The fee tail is more easily understood if the feudal social practices of holding land are kept in mind. Land was held in primogenitary dynasties, with the primogenitary heir (usually the eldest male) as current head. Some land might be given by the head of family to younger sons, even to daughters, but most of it—including the castle or great house—went to the eldest son. If a daughter was given any land, usually it was given to her husband (who had complete control of his wife's lands anyway). The fee tail was one device of reuniting land given a younger son or daughter with the patrimony when the issue of the younger son or daughter ran out.

   a. **The fee simple conditional:** [§341]   The first attempt of the landed lords to tie up land in the family was a *fee simple conditional*. This was created by a grant "to A and the heirs of his body." The judges held that A could convey a fee simple *if* a child were born to A. Thus, A's estate was thought of as a *fee simple conditional upon having issue*. If A had issue, A could convey a fee simple and transfer the land outside the family, cutting off the rights of A's issue and the reversioner.

   b. **Statute de Donis Conditionalibus (1285 A.D.):** [§342]   The landed lords were not happy with the judicial decisions that A could convey the land outside the family if A had a child. They sought relief in Parliament, which in those days was amenable to the wishes of the great lords. In 1285, Parliament enacted the Statute de Donis Conditionalibus. This statute abolished the fee simple conditional, and permitted the creation of a new estate in land, the fee tail. The name, fee tail, came from the French "tailler," meaning to carve, with the idea that the grantor was carving an estate just to suit himself (and keeping the land in the family).

2. **Nature of Estate:** [§343]   A fee tail has two principal characteristics: (i) *it lasts as long as the grantee or any of his descendants survives*, and (ii) *it is inheritable only by the grantee's descendants*. (*See infra*, §357.)

3. **Creation of Fee Tail:** [§344]   At common law, a fee tail was created by an instrument using words of inheritance and words confining succession to the issue of the grantee: "*to A and the heirs of his body*." The term "heirs of the body" refers to the grantee's *issue* or *lineal descendants*. It includes not only children, but grandchildren and more remote descendants as well. The fee tail goes to each succeeding generation in turn.

   a. **Variations in deed:** [§345]   At common law, to convey any kind of fee interest by deed, the technical word "heirs" had to be used (*supra*, §291). Thus, a deed "to A and his issue" or "to A and his children" created no more than a life estate in the grantee. Under modern law, the requirement of technical words ("heirs") to create a fee has generally been abolished. Therefore, a grant "to A and his issue" (or "descendants") may be treated as tantamount to a grant "to A and the heirs of his body"—sufficient to create a fee tail.

b. **Life estate in A, remainder to heirs of A's body:** [§346]   Distinguish carefully between the fee tail ("to A and the heirs of A's body") and a life estate in A with remainder to the heirs of A's body ("to A for life, remainder to A's bodily heirs"). In the latter case, A has only a life estate and cannot prevent his bodily heirs from taking on his death. If A has a fee tail, A can disentail, convey a fee simple to a buyer, and cut off the rights of issue. [Bauer v. Bauer, 360 P.2d 852 (Kan. 1961); on disentailing, *see infra*, §361]

4. **Future Interests Following Fee Tail:** [§347]   It was important to the landed aristocracy that when the fee tail expired, the land return to the family. Thus a father might convey a tract of land to his second son, A, upon his marriage—"to A and the heirs of his body"—and desire the land to return to the father or to the father's eldest son (the heir and head of the family) if A and his issue expired. A might have a child who had a child who died without having a child, upon which event A's blood line would become extinct and the fee tail end. Fortunately for the father, the Statute de Donis provided that the land would revert to him (the grantor) when the fee tail expired. It was also held that the father could direct that the land go to another upon the fee tail's expiration. Thus, the following future interests are possible to become possessory upon the expiration of the fee tail.

a. **Reversion:** [§348]   O conveys Blackacre "to A and the heirs of his body." A has a fee tail; O has a reversion in fee simple to become possessory upon expiration of the fee tail. [Long v. Long, 343 N.E.2d 100 (Ohio 1976)]

b. **Remainder:** [§349]   O conveys Whiteacre "to A and the heirs of his body, and if A die without issue, to B and her heirs." A has a fee tail; B has a vested remainder in fee simple to become possessory upon the expiration of the fee tail. B's interest is called a remainder, rather than a reversion, because a reversion can only be created in the grantor or testator's heirs. The analogous future interest in a grantee is called a remainder (*see infra*, §423).

c. **Meaning of "die without issue":** [§350]   A remainder after a fee tail was usually introduced, as in the preceding example, by the words "if A die without issue." What did this phrase "die without issue" mean? As is easily seen here, when it follows a grant of a fee tail, it means "when A and all A's descendants are dead." In other words, it means the event terminating the fee tail. This construction of "die without issue" was called **indefinite failure of issue** because the event awaited the indefinite future. Obviously it might happen hundreds of years from now.

(1) **Definite failure of issue:** [§351]   Another construction of "if A die without issue," not used in the context of a fee tail, is if A has no issue surviving him **at his death**. This is called a **definite failure of issue** construction because, for the holder of the remainder to take, A's issue must fail at a definite time, *i.e.*, at A's death. This construction would make no sense applied to a remainder following a fee tail because the grantor's intent is that B take the land whenever the fee tail expires—at A's death or at the death of A's children or grandchildren or more remote descendants if they die without issue.

(2) **Preference for indefinite failure construction:** [§352] The words "if A die without issue" were first used in the context of a gift over following a fee tail and, as explained above, the indefinite failure of issue construction made perfect sense. But English courts thought that once a phrase was defined by judges, it should have the same meaning in law thereafter regardless of whether the context was different. This assignment of arbitrary meaning to words does have the virtue of simplifying the classification system, but it gives short shrift to the grantor's intent. The grantor may have intended by the words something entirely different from the judges' meaning. In any case, English courts laid down a rule that whenever "if A die without issue" is used, it means *indefinite failure of issue* unless the grantor expressly states otherwise.

    (a) **A most peculiar rule of construction:** [§353] Following this preference for the indefinite failure of issue construction, English courts applied it to this conveyance: "to A and his heirs, but if A die without issue, to B and her heirs." This means when A and his descendants expire, B and her heirs get the land. That event is the same event that terminates a fee tail in A, and so the judges, looking through form to substance, held A had a fee tail, not a fee simple. Thus, there emerged a rule that if a remainder were limited to take effect on the death of the preceding (fee simple) tenant without issue, it converted the preceding fee simple into a fee tail. [Caccamo v. Banning, 75 A.2d 222 (Del. 1950)—applying rule of construction]

(3) **American law:** [§354] Almost all American states have abolished the preference for the indefinite failure construction. It makes no sense in contemporary American society where persons should not be presumed to intend gifts to take effect years in the future upon the expiration of a bloodline. If the grantor wants an indefinite failure construction, he must expressly say so in most states. Otherwise the instrument will be construed to mean definite failure of issue.

5. **Characteristics:** [§355] The fee tail originally had two important characteristics:

a. **During tenant's life:** [§356] The tenant in fee tail for the time being (either the original grantee or his descendant) can do nothing to defeat the rights of the tenant's lineal descendants. In practical effect, he has *only a life estate*. On the death of the tenant in fee tail, the land automatically goes to his lineal descendants. *Caveat:* After 1472, the fee tail tenant could defeat the rights of his lineal descendants by disentailing (*see infra*, §361).

b. **Upon tenant's death:** [§357] The fee tail can be inherited only by the issue (lineal descendants) of the original grantee, and not by his collateral kin. If the blood descendants of the original grantee run out, the property is returned to the original grantor (or his heirs), or to any holder of the remainder named in the grant creating the fee tail.

6. **Types of Fees Tail:** [§358] Unless otherwise specified in the grant, a fee tail was inheritable by any issue of the fee tail tenant. However the grantor could tailor the fee tail more specifically to his wishes.

a. **Fee tail male:** [§359]   A grantor could create a fee tail that limited succession to male descendants of the grantee. *Example:* "To A and the male heirs of his body." Likewise, a fee tail female could be created, but it was uncommon.

b. **Fee tail special:** [§360]   A grantor could create a fee tail special which was inheritable only by the issue of a grantee and a specific spouse. *Example:* O, the father of the bride, Joan, conveys Blackacre as a wedding gift to the groom "William and the heirs of his body by his wife Joan." A child of a previous or subsequent marriage of William could not take, nor could any issue of such child. If Joan died childless, it would no longer be possible for issue of William to take the fee tail, so William would have a *fee tail special with possibility of issue extinct*. In such an event, William would not be permitted to disentail, and be treated as having a life estate. This rule made sense, given the male-dominated family structure and the desire to keep land in the family.

7. **Disentailing:** [§361]   The judges perceived many mischiefs in the fee tail, keeping land in the family generation after generation. No relief was to be expected from Parliament, controlled by the landed barons, so the judges set their ingenuity to work and invented a *fictitious lawsuit*, known as a *common recovery*, whereby a tenant in tail in possession could go into court and —after paying court and lawyer's fees—walk out with a *fee simple absolute*. The details of the common recovery are unimportant for purposes of this Summary; the important thing is that a tenant in tail by indulging in this fictitious lawsuit could turn his fee tail into a fee simple absolute, barring all the rights of issue, reversioners, and owners of the remainder. [Taltarum's Case, Y.B. 12 Edw. 4, 19 (1472)—approving the common recovery]

a. **Disentailing by deed:** [§362]   In time other simpler methods of disentailing were evolved, until in the nineteenth century disentailing was permitted by a *deed* from the fee tail tenant to another.

(1) **Example:** O conveys Blackacre "to A and the heirs of his body, and if A die without issue, to B and her heirs." By this conveyance A takes a fee tail, and B a vested remainder in fee simple. Thereafter A conveys by deed "to C and his heirs." The deed to C, purporting to convey a fee simple, gives C a fee simple absolute, cutting off all rights in A's issue and in B. C can now, if he wishes, convey a fee simple back to A. Hence any fee tail tenant can by deed convert his fee tail into a fee simple in another or in himself.

8. **Status Under Modern Law**

a. **Fee tail still exists in a few states:** [§363]   The fee tail is permitted only in Delaware, Maine, Massachusetts, and Rhode Island. However, in these states, the fee tail tenant can at any time disentail and convey a fee simple absolute by deed, as explained above. Moreover, his creditors can reach the entire property just as if he had a fee simple. Therefore, there is no advantage in creating a fee tail; it merely excludes collateral kindred of the grantee from inheritance. (A, the fee tail tenant, can even get around this limitation by conveying a fee simple to a "straw person," who then conveys the fee simple back to A. A's collateral kindred can now inherit the fee simple.)

b. **Fee tail abolished in most states:** [§364]   The fee tail has been abolished in England and in all American jurisdictions except the four states mentioned above. The question then arises: What estates are created by a transfer "to A and the heirs of his body?" There are several statutory and judicial solutions.

(1) **A has a life estate:** [§365]   Some states hold that A has a life estate or, what amounts to the same thing, an unbarrable fee tail for A's life, with a remainder in fee simple to A's issue. [Morris v. Ulbright, 558 S.W.2d 660 (Mo. 1977)]

(2) **A has a fee simple:** [§366]   The large majority of states holds that A has a fee simple, but these states split on a subsidiary point. About half provide that A has a *fee simple absolute*; the justification for this view is that since A could disentail and convey a fee simple absolute, the law will treat A as having done so. The other half of states provide that A has a fee simple, but any remainder to become possessory on failure of issue is given effect if, and only if, *A leaves no descendants at his death*. The difference between the states can best be seen by an illustration.

(a) **Example:** O conveys Blackacre "to A and the heirs of his body, and if A die without issue, to B and her heirs." In half the states, A takes a fee simple absolute, and A's issue and B take nothing. In the other half, A takes a fee simple, and A's issue take nothing, but B takes a future interest which will become possessory if at A's death no issue of A are alive. If A leaves issue at A's death, B's interest then disappears (or, using the technical word, "fails"). In these latter states, "die without issue" is not construed as indefinite failure of issue (*see supra*, §350) but as *definite failure of issue*.

(3) **A has a fee simple conditional:** [§367]   In South Carolina and Iowa, which do not recognize the Statute de Donis, a conveyance "to A and the heirs of his body" gives A a fee simple conditional. If a child is born to A, A can convey a fee simple. If a child is not born, A's estate ends at A's death. (*See supra*, §341.)

c. **Drafting:** [§368]   No competent lawyer today uses the phrase "to A and the heirs of his body." Litigation may arise over its meaning. And the grantor's intent can be carried out far more specifically and clearly by creating a life estate in A followed by a remainder or remainders. Nonetheless, a transfer "to A and the heirs of his body" still occasionally crops up—usually in a home-made deed or will. Then the problems discussed above arise.

D. THE LIFE ESTATE

1. **Definition:** [§369]   A life estate is an estate that has the potential duration of one or more human lives. Life estates are very common today, particularly life estates in trust. When property is held by X in trust for A for life, A is entitled to all the rents and profits or other income from the property.

2. **Types of Life Estates**

a. **For life of grantee:** [§370]   The usual life estate is measured by the grantee's life. *Example:* O conveys Blackacre "to A for life." The grantee, A, gets an estate in the land for as long as A lives. On A's death, the land reverts to O, the grantor.

b. **Pur autre vie:** [§371]   Where the estate is measured by the *life of someone other than the owner of the life estate*, it is classified as a life estate pur autre vie (Law French term, meaning for the life of another). It comes to an end when the measuring life ends.

(1) **Creation of life estate pur autre vie:** [§372]   A life estate pur autre vie can be created in one of two ways: (i) A, a life tenant, conveys her life estate to B. B has a life estate pur autre vie. A remains the measuring life. Or (ii) O conveys Blackacre to B for the life of A. B is a life tenant pur autre vie. A is the measuring life. The estate will end on A's death.

(2) **If tenant predeceases measuring life:** [§373]   Suppose that B holds a life estate pur autre vie, with A as the measuring life. What happens if B dies leaving A surviving? The life estate does not end, of course, until A's death.

(a) **General occupant rule:** [§374]   At common law, the property was regarded as *without an owner*. A life estate was not an estate of inheritance, and thus could not go to B's heirs. Nor could it revert to O, because O had given away an estate to end at A's death. Nor could A take it, since she is merely the measuring life and has no interest in the property. When B died before A, the common law courts threw up their hands and awarded the land to the first person (even a complete stranger) who took possession of the land after B's death. That person was entitled to the estate until A's death and was known as the *general occupant*.

1) **Avoidance of common law treatment:** [§375]   To avoid this fortuity, conveyances of life estates pur autre vie at common law often contained words of inheritance—*i.e.*, A conveys "to B *and his heirs* for the life of A." In such a case, if B died before A, B's heirs take as *special occupants*, and a general occupant is excluded.

(b) **Modern law:** [§376]   The general occupant rule has been abolished everywhere. If B dies before A, the life estate pur autre vie descends to B's heirs.

c. **In a class:** [§377]   A life estate can be created in several persons, such as "to the children of A for their lives, remainder to B." Where a life estate is given to two or more persons, the principal question that arises is: What happens to the share of the first life tenant to die? Does this share go to the surviving life tenants or to those who hold the remainder? The usual construction is that it goes to the surviving life tenants and the remainder does not become possessory until *all* life tenants die. But if the instrument says "to the children of A for their lives, and *at their respective deaths* to B," the owner of the remainder, B, will take a share of the income upon the death of each life tenant. [Long v. Short, 553 S.W.2d 297 (Ky. 1977)]

d. **Defeasible life estates:** [§378]   Like a fee simple, a life estate can be created so as to be determinable, subject to condition subsequent, or subject to an executory limitation.

  (1) **Example:** O conveys "to A for life so long as A remains unmarried." A has a life estate terminable upon marriage. (The restraint on marriage *might* violate the rule against restraints on alienation. *See supra*, §337; *infra*, §§396 *et seq.*)

  (2) **Example:** O conveys "to A for life, but if A does not use the land for agricultural purposes, O retains the right to reenter." A has a life estate subject to a condition subsequent.

  (3) **Example:** O conveys "to A for life, but if B returns from Rome during A's life, to B." A has a life estate subject to an executory limitation.

e. **Construction problems:** [§379]   Sometimes it is not clear what estate is created by the language used. Courts must then construe the instrument to determine whether the estate conveyed is a fee simple, life estate, or leasehold estate. Each case depends on its own facts and the ***probable intent of the grantor***. The following are common examples of ambiguous language raising construction problems:

  (1) **Example:** "To my wife, W, so long as she remains unmarried." Does this create a fee simple determinable or a life estate determinable (on theory that the condition—marriage—could only happen during W's life)? *Majority view:* A ***fee simple determinable*** is created, even though the fee simple cannot be forfeited after W's death. [Lewis v. Searles, *supra*, §338; Dickson v. Alexandria Hospital, Inc., 177 F.2d 876 (4th Cir. 1949)]

  (2) **Example:** "To my wife, W, to be used as she shall see fit, for her maintenance and support." Does this give W a fee simple or a life estate with power to consume the principal? *Majority view:* A ***fee simple*** is created; the words "for her maintenance and support" merely state the reason for the gift. [White v. Brown, 559 S.W.2d 938 (Tenn. 1977)]

3. **Alienability of Life Estate:** [§380]   A life tenant ordinarily is free to transfer, lease, encumber, or otherwise alienate her estate inter vivos. Of course, the transferee gets no more than the life tenant had—an estate that ends at the expiration of the measuring life.

4. **Limited Utility of Legal Life Estate:** [§381]   A legal life estate is of limited utility because it is a very inflexible way of providing for successive ownership. Suppose that O dies, devising Blackacre to her husband, H, for life, and on his death, to their children. H may live a long time and various problems may arise which cannot be satisfactorily resolved except by going to court, and maybe not even then. Suppose that H wants to add a room on the house and needs to borrow money from a bank, giving the bank a mortgage. The bank will not lend money with only a life estate as security, for the bank's security ends at H's death. Or suppose that H wants to lease the land beyond his death, or wants to sell the land and move to a smaller place or more convenient location.

It is possible for H to do what he desires if *all the owners of the remainder are adult, competent, and consent*. But if one of them is a minor, or dies leaving a minor heir, consent cannot be given without a lawsuit and the appointment of a guardian ad litem to represent the minor. Then too, even if all are competent, securing agreement from them may be difficult to achieve. Thus H may be locked into a very inflexible position.

a. **Additional powers:** [§382] The instrument creating a life estate, in an attempt to provide flexibility, may give the life tenant powers to sell the property, lease it, mortgage it, etc. But this is seldom satisfactory. If the life tenant sells the property, for example, what is to be done with the proceeds?

b. **Equitable life estate:** [§383] Far more satisfactory than a legal life estate is an *equitable life estate*. To create such, O can devise Blackacre *to X in trust* for H for life, remainder to O's children. X, the trustee, owns the legal fee simple and has the usual powers of a fee simple owner to sell, mortgage, or lease. H has the right to receive all income from Blackacre or to take possession of it. X, the trustee, must *manage* the property *prudently*, and is held accountable for mismanagement. If desired, H can be named trustee by O. (For more on the trust, *see infra,* §§806 *et seq.*)

5. **Waste**

a. **Definition:** [§384] Waste is conduct by one in possession of land, who holds less than the fee ownership thereof (*e.g.*, a life tenant, lessee, mortgagor, etc.), which permanently impairs the value of the land or the interest of the person holding title or having some subsequent estate in the land (reversioner, remainderman, lessor, mortgagee, etc.). A common law form of action entitled "waste" lay against the life tenant, lessee, etc., for damages to the land. (Waste by a lessee is discussed in the landlord and tenant chapter, *infra,* §§1137 *et seq.*)

(1) **Rationale:** There are two ideas underlying the doctrine of waste, and the court may choose to emphasize one or the other in a particular case. The first is that the *grantor intends* that the life tenant shall have the general use of the land *in a reasonable manner*, but that the land shall pass to the owner of the remainder as nearly as practicable *unimpaired in its nature, character, and improvements*. The second is that where two or more persons own interests in land *fairness* requires that one shall not impose severe *economic damage* on the other.

b. **Types of waste:** [§385] Three different types of waste are recognized:

(1) **Affirmative (voluntary) waste:** [§386] This occurs when the life tenant destroys buildings, ornamental trees on the land, etc., or exploits the natural resources (minerals, timber, etc.) on the land, causing permanent injury. [Dorsey v. Speelman, 459 P.2d 416 (Wash. 1969)] However, cutting of trees in clearing woodland for conversion into more valuable cultivated farm land is not waste.

(2) **Permissive (involuntary) waste:** [§387]   This occurs when the land is allowed to fall into disrepair, or the tenant fails to take reasonable measures to protect the land from the elements. [Moore v. Phillips, 627 P.2d 831 (Kan. 1981)] Failing to pay the taxes and allowing the property to be sold at tax sale is treated as permissive waste. Nevertheless, merely failing to keep improvements on the property adequately insured is ordinarily **not** so treated. [Suydam v. Jackson, 54 N.Y. 450 (1873)]

(3) **Ameliorating waste:** [§388]   This occurs when the principal use of the land is substantially changed—usually by tearing down a building—**but the change increases the value of the land**. Ameliorating waste is actionable if the court finds that: (i) the grantor intended to pass the land with the specific buildings on it to the holder of the remainder; and (ii) the building can reasonably be used for the purposes built.

   (a) **Example:** In 1887, Isaac Brokaw erects a fine residence on Fifth Avenue and 79th Street in Manhattan. In 1913, Isaac dies, devising "my residence" to A for life, remainder to B. In 1929, A wants to take down the house (worth $300,000) and erect an apartment house (costing $900,000). This will increase A's income by $30,000 a year. A cannot take down the house because Isaac intended to pass **"my residence"** on to B, and the house is located in an area of fine houses and can reasonably be used as such. [Brokaw v. Fairchild, 135 Misc. 70 (1929)]

   (b) **Current use undesirable:** [§389]   If the house is located in an area that changes, perhaps by the location of factories and railroads nearby, so that it is no longer desirable as a residence, the life tenant can demolish the house, provided the value of the property is enhanced for business purposes. This result can be put on the ground that grantor's intent of passing the house on can no longer be carried out because changed conditions have made it impractical to do so. In that case, the house can be demolished if the parties will benefit economically. [Melms v. Pabst Brewing Co., 79 N.W. 738 (Wis. 1899)]

c. **Remedies for waste:** [§390]   The owners of the remainder may enjoin threatened waste by the life tenant or recover damages. If the ultimate future owner of the land is not now ascertained, damages may be impounded by the court pending determination of the ultimate takers.

6. **Sale of Property by a Court:** [§391]   If the life tenant and the owners of the remainder are all adults, competent, and agree, a fee simple in the land can be sold. If for some reason they cannot agree, can the life tenant get a court to sell the land, and order the proceeds reinvested in trust with the income paid to the life tenant?

a. **Holders of the remainder are able to consent:** [§392]   If the holders of the remainder are all ascertained, adult, and competent, they can consent to the sale and the general rule is that a court will **not** give the life tenant relief in this case. The parties can bargain among themselves about sale and division of the proceeds.

(1) **Equitable intervention:** [§393]   Equity may intervene and order sale of the property if the sale is necessary for the best interest of all the parties. This is a flexible remedy, which equity exercises sparingly, however, because of the underlying notion that the grantor wants *the land* (and not some economic value represented by other assets) passed on to the holders of the remainder. [Baker v. Weedon, 262 So. 2d 641 (Miss. 1972)]

b. **Holders of the remainder cannot consent:** [§394]   If the holders of the remainder cannot legally consent to the sale, because one or more is unascertained, under age, or incompetent, a court may order sale if it finds that sale is in the best interests of the holders of the remainder.

c. **Statutes:** [§395]   Statutes in many states authorize a court to sell a fee simple in land under specified conditions, upon petition of the life tenant. These statutes reflect a trend to loosen restrictions on a legal life estate, and to permit the life tenant to have the land sold and have the proceeds held in trust. Such statutes are more likely to appear in urbanized states with much development of land than in farm states where the notion of "family farm" still holds sway. The breadth of the judicial doctrine of sale may also differ accordingly.

E.   THE RULE AGAINST RESTRAINTS ON ALIENATION

1. **Introduction:** [§396]   The Statute Quia Emptores established, in the year 1290, a principle that land should be alienable. Working from that beginning, the courts laid down a number of rules designed to further the alienability of land. One of the most important is the rule *against direct restraints* on alienation. This rule invalidates certain types of restraints on certain types of estates.

2. **Types of Restraints:** [§397]   There are three types of direct restraints:

a. **Forfeiture restraint:** [§398]   A forfeiture restraint provides that if the grantee attempts to transfer his interest it is forfeited to another person. *Example:* O conveys Blackacre "to A and his heirs, but if A attempts to transfer the property by any means whatsoever, then to B and his heirs."

b. **Disabling restraint:** [§399]   A disabling restraint withholds from the grantee the power of transferring her interest. *Example:* O conveys Blackacre "to A and her heirs but any transfer hereafter in any manner of an interest in Blackacre shall be null and void."

c. **Promissory restraint:** [§400]   A promissory restraint provides that the grantee promises not to transfer his interest. *Example:* O conveys Blackacre "to A and his heirs, and A promises for himself, his heirs and successors in interest that Blackacre will not be transferred by any means."

3. **Restraints on a Fee Simple**

a. **Total restraints:** [§401] Any total restraint upon a fee simple—either forfeiture, disabling, or promissory—is *void.* The grantee may therefore alienate the estate and suffer no penalty. In the preceding examples, A, the grantee, has a fee simple absolute, alienable at will.

(1) **Rationale:** It is often said that one of the incidents of ownership is the right to sell property. A restraint upon alienation is repugnant to that principle and is therefore void. The repugnancy argument, however, begs the question: It merely defines a fee simple as including an inseverable right to alienate, and then finds the restraint inconsistent with that definition. The real reason for the rule lies in public policy. Restraints on alienation take property out of the market, making it unusable for the best use dictated by the market. They tend to make property unmortgageable and therefore unimprovable, to concentrate wealth in the class already rich, and to prevent creditors from reaching the property to pay the owner's debts.

b. **Partial restraints:** [§402] A partial restraint is one that purports to restrict the power to transfer to specific persons, or by a specific method, or until a specific time. The majority view is that partial restraints on alienation are to be treated like total restraints (*i.e., void*) [Hawkins v. Mathews, 425 S.W.2d 608 (Tenn. 1968)], but there are some established exceptions.

(1) **Sale with consent of another:** [§403] A deed may provide that the property may be sold only with the consent of another. Such a provision may be used in an attempt to control entry into a subdivision or neighborhood. Such provisions are usually held void.

(a) **Example:** Developer conveys lots in his subdivision by deeds containing the following provision: "And for the purpose of maintaining a high-class development, no owner of land hereby conveyed shall have the right to transfer the land without the written consent of the grantor." This covenant is void. The owners can sell to anyone without receiving the written consent of the grantor. [Northwest Real Estate Co. v. Serio, 144 A. 245 (Md. 1928)]

(2) **Sale to a member of the club:** [§404] A deed may provide that the property may be sold only to a member of a neighborhood association (*e.g.*, the Lake Watawga Association). Such a provision in effect gives the association power to veto a prospective buyer. If such a restriction on sale has no reasonable standards for admission to the association, giving the association members arbitrary power to deny membership, the provision in the deed is void. [Tuckerton Beach Club v. Bender, 219 A.2d 529 (N.J. 1966); Lauderbaugh v. Williams, 186 A.2d 39 (Pa. 1962)]

(3) **Sale of a cooperative apartment:** [§405] A provision in a cooperative apartment agreement restraining sale of stock ownership without the consent of the building's board of directors is usually held valid. *Rationale:* Tenants of a cooperative are liable for the entire mortgage on the building: the entire building

will be sold if one tenant defaults on mortgage payments and the other tenants do not make up the default. Because of the **financial interdependency** and living in close proximity to one another, cooperative apartment tenants need to assure themselves of the financial responsibility and desirability of the new lessees. A similar restriction on transferring a condominium unit may also be valid for more or less the same reasons. [Penthouse Properties, Inc. v. 1158 Fifth Ave., Inc., 256 App. Div. 685 (1939); Weisner v. 791 Park Avenue Corp., 6 N.Y.2d 426 (1959)]

(a) **Preemptive right:** [§406]   A preemptive right gives a person the right to first refusal if the owner desires to sell the property. This is a less onerous restriction than a flat prohibition of sale without the consent of the neighborhood association. A preemptive right given to a cooperative housing association is valid. *Example:* The cooperative association is given the right to purchase the unit at fair market value when the owner desires to sell. [Gale v. York Center Community Cooperative, 171 N.E.2d 30 (Ill. 1961)]

(4) **Racial restraints:** [§407]   Restraints prohibiting the transfer of the property to a person of a specified racial or ethnic group are not enforceable. Enforcement of a racially discriminatory restraint by the courts is discriminatory state action forbidden by the Equal Protection Clause of the fourteenth amendment of the United States Constitution. [Shelley v. Kraemer, *infra*, §444]

(5) **Reasonable restraints doctrine:** [§408]   In a few states, partial restraints on a fee simple are valid if reasonable. The restraint must have a **reasonable purpose** and be **limited in duration.**

c. **Co-tenants:** [§409]   An agreement by tenants in common or joint tenants that they will not partition the property (*see infra*, §756) is valid if reasonable in purpose and limited in time.

(1) **Example:** H and W own their home as tenants in common. After experiencing marital difficulties, H and W agree that neither shall transfer his or her interest to another, nor bring an action to partition the property. It is the intent of H and W to preserve the property as a home for the family. Since this restraint is limited to the life of H or W (whoever dies sooner), it is reasonably limited in time and is valid. [Michalski v. Michalski, 142 A.2d 645 (N.J. 1958)—holding agreement valid, but refusing to enforce it after nine years because of change in circumstances]

d. **Restraint on use:** [§410]   A restraint on the use of property makes the property less alienable by eliminating prospective purchasers who desire to make use of the property in a manner forbidden by the restraint. But restraints on the use of property have almost always been upheld. Even a restraint that the property can be used only by the grantee has been upheld. [Mountain Brow Lodge No. 82 v. Toscano, 257 Cal. App. 2d 22 (1967)]

e. **Restraints on remainders in fee simple:** [§411] A restraint on a remainder *in fee simple* is void if it would be void if imposed on a possessory fee simple. Courts do not usually distinguish between a restraint on a fee simple in possession and a restraint on a fee simple in remainder. They look merely to the type of estate that is restrained. Thus, any restraint on a remainder in fee simple is void.

4. **Restraints on a Life Estate**

a. **Legal life estate:** [§412] Since land owned for life is not marketable, as the life tenant may die at any time, a restraint on a life estate may add little practical inalienability—particularly where the holders of the remainder are unascertained and cannot join together with the life tenant in conveying a fee simple. Nonetheless, courts have struck down disabling restraints on a life estate, which have the effect of making the land legally inalienable. On the other hand, forfeiture and promissory restraints on a life estate (which can be released by the person holding the benefit of forfeiture or of the promise) have often been upheld.

b. **Equitable life estate:** [§413] A disabling restraint upon an equitable life estate in trust is known as a *spendthrift trust.* It is valid in most states. (*See infra*, §828.)

   (1) **Example:** O conveys Blackacre and some IBM stock "to X in trust to pay the income to A for life, then on A's death to convey the trust property to B." A spendthrift clause is inserted in the conveyance providing that A cannot alienate her life estate or income interest, and that A's creditors cannot reach them. The clause is valid.

   (2) **Rationale:** A restraint on an *equitable interest*, like the interest of A in this example, does not prevent alienation of specific property. The restraint here only prevents the alienation of a *quantum* of wealth represented by the trust assets as they are from time to time constituted.

F. SUMMARY OF POSSESSORY ESTATES [§414]

This bare-bones digest of the freehold possessory estates should serve as a review foundation for the law of future interests, which follows. After each of these estates, except the fee simple absolute, future interests will be created.

1. **Fee Simple**

a. **Fee simple absolute:** "To A and his heirs." No future interest is possible after a fee simple absolute.

b. **Fee simple determinable:** "To A and his heirs *so long as* used for a library." The grantor has a possibility of reverter, which becomes possessory *automatically* upon cessation of library use. If the conveyance provides that upon cessation of library use the property will go to another grantee (B), rather than return to the grantor, the grantee (B) has a future interest called an executory interest.

c. **Fee simple subject to condition subsequent:** "To A and his heirs, but if the land is not used for a library, O has a right to re-enter." The grantor has a right of entry, which he *may elect* to exercise or not.

d. **Fee simple subject to executory limitation:** "To A and his heirs, but if the land is not used for a library during the next twenty years, to B." B has an executory interest.

2. **Fee Tail:** "To A and the heirs of his body." The grantor has a reversion upon expiration of the fee tail. If the conveyance creates a future interest in a grantee following a fee tail (*e.g.*, "and if A die without issue, to B"), the future interest is a remainder.

3. **Life Estate:** "To A for life" or "to A for the life of B" (life estate pur autre vie). The future interest in the grantor following a life estate is a reversion. If the future interest is created in a grantee, it is ordinarily a remainder but can be an executory interest.

a. **Limited life estates:** A life estate may be made determinable, subject to condition subsequent, or subject to an executory limitation in the same manner as a fee simple may be so limited. For example, "to A for life or until remarriage" creates a life estate determinable.

IV. FUTURE INTERESTS

chapter approach

Now that you've mastered present possessory interests, you're ready to turn to future interests. The law of future interests has deep historical roots and an interdependent doctrinal structure that gives it a curious mathematical quality. More than any other field of law, it is law according to Euclid: It requires precision in analysis and rigor in doctrinal application. An approximate, rather than exact, understanding will not do. But don't despair, because the law of future interests is not difficult if approached correctly.

Your approach to future interests problems should follow two important rules:

1. Pay careful attention to the **exact language** used in the grant; and

2. Read and analyze the interests in a grant **in sequence**.

Besides these two rules, you should keep in mind these other helpful hints:

1. **Classify the present estate:** This may help you figure out the future interests, since some future interests can only follow a particular type of present interest (*e.g.*, a possibility of reverter can only follow a determinable estate, and a right of entry can only follow an estate subject to a condition subsequent).

2. **Look at who has the future interest:** If it is retained by the **grantor,** you've narrowed it down to a reversion, a possibility of reverter, or a right of entry. If it is given to someone **other** than the grantor, it must be a remainder or an executory interest.

3. **Think about how the future interest will become possessory:** For interests in a grantee, remember that a remainder waits patiently for the natural termination of the preceding estate, whereas an executory interest either divests the prior estate or springs out of the grantor's interest, in both cases cutting short the prior estate. For future interests remaining in the grantor, the reversion usually follows the natural termination of the prior estate (*e.g.*, after the life tenant dies). Similarly, the possibility of reverter does not cut short the preceding determinable estate, but succeeds it. On the other hand, the right of entry, like the executory interest, divests the preceding estate.

4. **Determine whether the interest is vested or contingent:** A contingent interest either is given to an **unascertained person** or is subject to a **condition precedent**. Classify each interest in sequence by looking at the "words between the commas" setting off the interests. And distinguish between a condition precedent, which comes "between the commas," and a condition subsequent, which divests a vested interest. (*Example—condition precedent*: "To A for life, then to B **if B survives A**, and if B does not survive, to C." *Example—condition subsequent*: "To A for life, then to B, **but if B does not survive A**, to C."

5. **Apply the following rules to contingent interests**
   (i) Destructibility of contingent remainders (applicable to contingent remainders only)

(ii) The Rule in Shelley's Case
(iii) The Doctrine of Worthier Title
(iv) The Rule Against Perpetuities
Of these rules, the last is the most important and the most likely to be examined upon in an examination.

With these hints in mind (and memorization of the identifying factors of the estate; *see infra*, §641), you should be able to answer future interests questions.

A. INTRODUCTION

1. **Future Interest Defined:** [§415]   A future interest is a nonpossessory interest capable of becoming possessory in the future. A future interest is a **present** interest in the sense that it is a presently **existing** interest. But it is **not** a presently **possessory** interest, and that is why it is called a future interest.

   a. **Example:** O conveys Blackacre "to A for life, and on A's death to B." A has a possessory life estate. B has a future interest called a remainder. It will become possessory on A's death. Before A's death, the remainder exists as a property interest in Blackacre. As with other property interests, B can transfer the remainder to C, and B's creditors can reach the remainder. It is an existing property interest, which will become possessory in the future.

2. **Categories Limited:** [§416]   Just as possessory estates are limited in number (fee simple, fee tail, life estate, leaseholds), so are future interests. There are only five categories of future interests: **reversion, possibility of reverter, right of entry, remainder**, and **executory interest**. (Remainders can be further divided into vested remainders and contingent remainders.) The language of each instrument creating a future interest must be construed so as to create one, and only one, of these future interests. Different rules apply to each future interest. This introduction contains a brief overview of the five future interests; then, each is discussed in detail later in the chapter.

3. **Future Interests in the Grantor:** [§417]   Future interests are divided into two basic groups: (i) future interests **retained by the grantor**; and (ii) future interests **created in a grantee**. If the future interest is retained by the **grantor** (or, if retained by a will, by the testator's heirs), the future interest **must be** either a **reversion, possibility of reverter**, or **right of entry**.

   a. **Reversion:** [§418]   A reversion is a future interest left in the **grantor** after the grantor conveys a vested estate of a lesser quantum than he has.

   (1) **Example:** O, owning Blackacre in fee simple, conveys Blackacre "to A for life." Since O did not convey a fee simple to anyone—but only a life estate, which is a lesser estate than a fee simple—O has a reversion. When A dies, Blackacre will revert to O.

b. **Possibility of reverter:** [§419] A possibility of reverter arises when a grantor carves out of her estate a *determinable* estate of the same quantum. In almost all cases it *follows a determinable fee*.

   (1) **Example:** O conveys Blackacre "to Board of Education so long as Blackacre is used for school purposes." The Board of Education has a determinable fee; O has a possibility of reverter. O's interest is not a reversion because O, owning a fee simple, has conveyed a fee simple determinable to the Board. All fees simple (absolute, determinable, subject to condition subsequent or executory limitation) are of the same quantum.

c. **Right of entry:** [§420] A right of entry is retained when the grantor creates an estate subject to condition subsequent and retains the power to cut short the estate.

   (1) **Example:** O conveys Blackacre "to Board of Education, but if the Board ceases to use Blackacre for school purposes, O retains a right to reenter." The Board has a fee simple subject to condition subsequent; O has a right of entry.

d. **Correlative estates:** [§421] From the explanations above, it is easy to see that possessory estates have correlative future interests in the grantor:
   (i) Life estate—reversion;
   (ii) Fee simple determinable—possibility of reverter;
   (iii) Fee simple on condition subsequent—right of entry.

4. **Future Interests in Grantees:** [§422] If a future interest is created in a grantee, it *must be* either a *remainder* or an *executory interest*.

   a. **Remainder:** [§423] A remainder is a future interest in a grantee that has the *capacity of becoming possessory* at the expiration of the prior estates, and *cannot divest* the prior estates.

      (1) **Example:** O conveys Blackacre "to A for life, and on A's death, to B and her heirs." A has a possessory life estate; B has a remainder in fee simple. B's interest is a remainder because it can become possessory upon A's death, and it will not divest A's life estate prior to A's death.

   b. **Executory interest:** [§424] Generally speaking, an executory interest is a future interest in a grantee that, in order to become possessory, *must divest* or cut short the prior estate, or *spring out* of the grantor at a future date. The basic difference between a remainder and an executory interest is that a *remainder never divests* the prior estate, whereas an executory interest almost *always does*. Legal executory interests were not permitted prior to 1536; they were authorized by the Statute of Uses (1536).

      (1) **Example—shifting executory interest:** O conveys Blackacre "to A and his heirs, but if B returns from Rome, to B and her heirs." A has a fee simple subject to executory limitation; B has a shifting executory interest. B's interest

can become possessory only by divesting A of the fee simple. A shifting interest is a useful device to shift title upon the happening of some uncertain event.

    (2) **Example—springing executory interest:** O conveys Blackacre "to my daughter A when she marries B." O retains the fee simple and creates an executory interest in A to spring out of O in the future when A marries B. A springing interest was, in early days, a useful device to give the groom assurances that the bride would come to the altar endowed with property.

  c. **Transfer after creation:** [§425] The name of an interest is given upon its creation. The name does not change if the interest is transferred to another person. Thus, interests initially retained by the grantor do not undergo a name change if subsequently transferred to a grantee. If O retains a reversion, and subsequently conveys his reversion to A, A has a reversion, not a remainder. Similarly, the name of a remainder does not change to a reversion if, after the remainder is created, it is transferred back to O.

    (1) **Example:** O conveys Blackacre "to A for life, remainder to B." Subsequently B conveys his remainder to O. The name of the future interest does not change. O has a remainder, not a reversion. Thus the name of a future interest depends upon whether the interest was initially retained by the grantor (and so a reversion, possibility of reverter, or right of entry) or created in a grantee (and so a remainder or executory interest).

5. **Legal or Equitable Interests:** [§426] Future interests can be *legal* future interests or *equitable* future interests. Legal future interests are created without the imposition of a trust. *Example:* O conveys Blackacre "to A for life, remainder to B and his heirs." *Equitable* future interests are created in a trust. (The trust is explained in more detail *infra*, §§806 *et seq.*)

  a. **Example:** O conveys property "to X in trust to pay the income to A for life, and on A's death to convey the trust assets to B." X is the trustee, owning a legal fee simple in the trust assets. A has an equitable life estate, and B has an equitable remainder. If X does not carry out his fiduciary duties, which include managing the property prudently and paying the income to A, A can sue X for misfeasance in office.

B. REVERSION

1. **Definition:** [§427] A reversion is a future interest left in the grantor after she conveys a vested estate *of a lesser quantum* than she has. A reversion may be expressly **retained**. *Example:* O conveys Blackacre "to A for life, reversion to O." Where it is not expressly retained, a reversion will arise **by operation of law** where no other disposition is made of the property after expiration of the lesser estate. *Example:* O conveys Whiteacre "to A for life." O has a reversion in fee simple by operation of law.

  a. **Quantum of estates:** [§428] As mentioned above, a reversion arises when the grantor transfers a vested estate of a **lesser quantum** than she has. The hierarchy of estates determines what is a lesser quantum: The fee simple is of longer duration than the fee tail; the fee tail is of longer duration than a life estate; the life estate is of longer duration than the leasehold estates.

(1) **Examples**

 (a) O, owner of a fee simple, conveys a fee tail or a life estate to A. In either case, O has conveyed a lesser estate than O's fee simple. Therefore, O has a reversion.

 (b) As above, O conveys "to A for A's life." A then conveys a life estate "to B for B's life." B has a life estate pur autre vie. A has a reversion because if B's life estate terminates at B's death, the property reverts to A for the rest of A's life. Thus, a *life estate pur autre vie carved out of a life estate* is a lesser estate than the life estate out of which it is carved.

 (c) C, aged 80, has a life estate in Blackacre. C grants a 99-year lease to D. C has a reversion, because a leasehold estate is a lesser estate than a life estate. The reversion may have no value, because C probably will not live for another 99 years; nevertheless, C has a reversion. D's leasehold interest will, of course, terminate upon C's death within 99 years. This example shows how *property without value* may be created, but it is not necessary for a thing to have value to be called property.

b. **Rule of reversions:** [§429] It is easy to ascertain in most cases when a grantor has a reversion if you keep in mind that O will retain a reversion if he has conveyed a *lesser estate* (or lesser estates) than the estate he originally had. "Lesser" refers to the hierarchy of estates above. Thus, if O, owner of a fee simple, carves from his estate anything less than a vested fee simple, it is possible for the land to return to O. But if O conveys a fee simple (either as a *present possessory interest* or as a *vested remainder*), O has conveyed an estate of the *same size* as he originally had, and possession cannot return to him.

(1) **Example:** O, owner of a fee simple, transfers a fee tail, life estate, or leasehold; O has a reversion because he has conveyed an estate of lesser quantum than the fee simple he originally had. But if O conveys a life estate *and* a vested remainder in fee simple, O has no reversion. By conveying the vested remainder in fee simple, O has conveyed an estate of equal size to his original estate.

c. **Reversions are vested interests:** [§430] All reversions are vested interests even though not all reversions will necessarily become possessory. Some reversions will certainly become possessory, *e.g.*, O conveys "to A for life, reversion to O." Other reversions may or may not become possessory (*see, e.g.*, example below). In order to create a reversion, it is only necessary that there be *a possibility* of the interest becoming possessory.

(1) **Example:** O conveys Blackacre "to A for life, remainder to B if B survives A." O has a reversion because O has not created a vested remainder in fee simple.

If B dies before A, Blackacre will return to O at A's death. If A dies before B, Blackacre will go to B at A's death. Note that O does not have a contingent reversion. By common law dogma, *all reversions are vested*. So O has a vested reversion which can be divested by B's interest becoming possessory at A's death.

(2) **Significance:** [§431] The significance of a reversion being vested is that it is *alienable, accelerates* into possession upon the termination of the preceding estate, and is *not subject to the Rule Against Perpetuities*.

2. **Alienability:** [§432] A reversion has always been regarded as fully transferable both inter vivos and by way of testate or intestate succession. The transferee, of course, gets only what the transferor had—an interest that cannot become possessory until the preceding estate terminates.

3. **Compared to Possibility of Reverter:** [§433] Do not confuse a reversion with a possibility of reverter (*infra*, §§434-439). Each is a distinct interest, with different characteristics. A possibility of reverter arises where the grantor carves out of his estate a *determinable estate of the same quantum*. Most often it arises where the grantor conveys a fee simple determinable. A reversion arises where the grantor conveys *a lesser estate* than he has and does not in the same conveyance create a vested remainder in fee simple. There is *no such interest as a "possibility of reversion."* Do not use the phrase as it is likely to confuse you.

C. POSSIBILITY OF REVERTER

1. **Definition:** [§434] A possibility of reverter arises when a grantor carves out of her estate a *determinable* estate of the same quantum. In almost all cases met in practice, a possibility of reverter follows a determinable *fee*, not some lesser determinable estate. Thus, for all practical purposes, a possibility of reverter is a future interest remaining *in the grantor* when a *fee simple determinable* is created. (On determinable fees, *see supra*, §§318 *et seq.*)

a. **Example:** O conveys Blackacre "to A and his heirs so long as liquor is not sold on the premises." A has a determinable fee; O has a possibility of reverter.

b. **Created only in grantor:** [§435] A possibility of reverter *cannot be created in a grantee*.

(1) **Example:** O conveys Blackacre "to First Baptist Church so long as used for church purposes, and when it shall cease to use Blackacre for church purposes, to the American Red Cross." The Red Cross does *not* have a possibility of reverter because that can only be retained by O. The Red Cross has an *executory interest* (for explanation, *see infra*, §584). If O had omitted the language "and when . . . to the . . . Red Cross," O would have a possibility of reverter.

2. **Alienability:** [§436] At common law, a possibility of reverter could not be transferred inter vivos. *Rationale:* A possibility of reverter was *not* viewed as an existing interest,

but as a *mere possibility* of becoming an interest. Hence it was not a "thing" that could be transferred. However, upon the death of the owner of a possibility of reverter, the possibility of reverter was treated as a thing; "it" descended to the owner's heirs.

    a. **Modern law:** [§437] In most jurisdictions, a possibility of reverter is freely alienable, both during life and by will. *Rationale:* The possibility of reverter is now viewed as a *property interest*, and alienability is an inherent characteristic of any property interest.

    b. **Releasable:** [§438] A possibility of reverter, though inalienable to a stranger at common law, was releasable to the owner of the determinable fee. A release made the land marketable.

3. **Termination and Unenforceability:** [§439] Termination and unenforceability of a possibility of reverter are discussed below in connection with a right of entry. (*See infra*, §§443-446.)

D. RIGHT OF ENTRY

1. **Definition:** [§440] When a grantor creates an estate subject to condition subsequent (*supra*, §§326-338) and retains the power to cut short or terminate the estate, the grantor has a right of entry. Like a possibility of reverter, a right of entry cannot be created in a grantee. The right of entry is sometimes called "a power of termination."

    a. **Example:** O conveys Blackacre "to A and his heirs, but if intoxicating liquor is ever sold on the premises, O has a right to reenter and retake Blackacre." A has a fee simple subject to condition subsequent; O has a right of entry for breach of the condition subsequent.

2. **Alienability:** [§441] At common law, a right of entry was inalienable inter vivos because it was treated as a chose in action, and choses were inalienable. It was not thought of as a property interest, but as a special right in the grantor to forfeit the grantee's estate if he wished. A right of entry could be released, however, to the owner of the fee simple, and it was inheritable by the heirs of the grantor.

    a. **Modern law:** [§442] In some states, the right of entry is now alienable; in others, the common law is followed. In still others, a particularly harsh rule is followed: The mere attempt to transfer a right of entry destroys it.

        (1) **Example:** O conveys Blackacre "to Railroad Company, but if it fails to maintain an overpass, O has the right to reenter and retake Blackacre." Subsequently O conveys the right of entry to his son. In the last group of states mentioned above, this attempt to convey the right destroys it, and the railroad has a fee simple absolute. [Rice v. Boston & Worcester Railroad, 94 Mass. 141 (1886); *abrogated by* Oak's Oil Service, Inc. v. Massachusetts Bay Transportation Authority, 447 N.E.2d 27 (Mass. 1983)—holding right of entry alienable]

3. **Termination:** [§443]   At common law, a right of entry or a possibility of reverter could endure indefinitely, and because it was inheritable, the grantor's heirs could exercise the right of entry or enforce the possibility of reverter hundreds of years after the grantor's death. These interests were not subject to the Rule Against Perpetuities, which generally prevented the creation of future interests to become possessory far in the future. (*See infra*, §§605 *et seq*.) This remains the law in the large majority of states. In some states, however, statutes have been enacted expressly limiting the period during which a possibility of reverter or right of entry can exist. The typical statute limits them to thirty years, after which the preceding fee simple becomes absolute. Some states have made the termination statute retroactive, applying it to existing possibilities of reverter and rights of entry. But the courts are divided on whether retroactive application is unconstitutional as a taking of property without compensation. [*See* Cline v. Johnson County Board of Education, 548 S.W.2d 507 (Ky. 1977), *and* Trustees of Schools v. Batdorf, 130 N.E.2d 111 (Ill. 1955)—holding retroactive application constitutional; *but see* Board of Education v. Miles, 15 N.Y.2d 364 (1965)—contra]

4. **Unenforceability of Racial Restrictions:** [§444]   The fourteenth amendment to the U.S. Constitution provides that **no state** may deny persons equal protection of the laws—meaning, among other things, that no state can discriminate in granting or protecting property rights on the basis of race. The Supreme Court held in *Shelley v. Kraemer*, 334 U.S. 1 (1948), that **judicial enforcement** of a racial covenant forbidding use of property by black persons was discriminatory **state action** forbidden by the Constitution.

   a. **Example:** O conveys Blackacre "to A and his heirs and A promises that Blackacre will never be used or occupied by nonwhite persons." Thereafter A sells to B, a black man, who moves onto Blackacre. O sues for an **injunction** prohibiting B from using Blackacre, and sues A for **damages** for having sold to B. Injunction and damages are the judicial remedies ordinarily available for breach of a covenant. The court cannot grant O either an injunction or damages, because such judicial action would be **state action** interfering with B's right to enjoy property free of racial discrimination.

   b. **Enforceability of right of entry:** [§445]   If O creates a racial restriction in the form of a condition subsequent, giving himself a right of entry to enforce the condition, the racial condition cannot be enforced by a court. It falls under the ban of *Shelley v. Kraemer* on judicial state action that is discriminatory.

      (1) **Example:** O conveys Whiteacre "to A and his heirs, but if Blackacre is sold or leased to a black person, O may re-enter and retake A's lot." A can sell or lease to a black person. O's right of entry cannot be enforced in court. [Capitol Federal Savings & Loan Association v. Smith, 316 P.2d 252 (Colo. 1957)]

   c. **Enforceability of possibility of reverter:** [§446]   The enforcement by a court of a possibility of reverter upon breach of a racial restriction has been held **not** to be forbidden state action. The theory is that a possibility of reverter becomes possessory **automatically**; no judicial action is necessary for the fee simple to revert. [Evans v. Abney, 396 U.S. 435 (1970)]

(1) **Example:** Barringer conveys Blackacre "to Charlotte Park Commission so long as used as a park for white persons only." Subsequently the Park Commission admits black persons in the park. The fee simple title reverts to Barringer by operation of law and not by any judicial action. [Charlotte Park & Recreation Commission v. Barringer, 88 S.E.2d 114 (N.C. 1955)]

(2) **Criticism:** This result has been criticized on several grounds. (i) "Title reverting" is a metaphor which means that the state's protection of a property owner has moved from the Park Commission to Barringer. When the court moves its protection from the Commission to Barringer, that is state action. (ii) The phrase "by operation of law" means state action, since all law is at bottom action by the state. (iii) Public policy against discrimination should not be avoidable by use of a technical property form indistinguishable in substance from a fee simple subject to condition subsequent.

E. REMAINDER

1. **Definition:** [§447]   A remainder is a future interest created in a *grantee* which is *capable of becoming a present possessory estate upon the expiration of a prior possessory estate* created in the same conveyance in which the remainder is created. It is called a remainder because upon the expiration of the preceding estate the land "remains away" instead of reverting to the grantor. A remainder never divests or cuts short the preceding estate but always waits patiently until the preceding estate expires.

   a. **Example:** O conveys Blackacre "to A for life, then to B if B is then living." B has a remainder because B's interest is capable of becoming possessory upon the termination of the life estate.

2. **Essential Characteristics:** [§448]   The essential chracteristics of every remainder are:

   a. **Must have preceding estate:** [§449]   A remainder can be created only by *express grant* in the *same instrument* in which the *preceding possessory estate* is created. Unlike a reversion, it *cannot* arise by operation of law. If no preceding possessory estate has been created in a transferee, the future interest is not a remainder. The old law said: "A remainder needs a preceding freehold to support it."

      (1) **Example:** O conveys "to A if A marries B." No preceding estate has been created by O in anyone; thus A does not have a remainder. A has instead a springing executory interest (*see infra*, §582).

   b. **Must follow a fee tail, life estate, or term of years:** [§450]   The estate preceding a remainder can be a fee tail, a life estate, or a term of years. A remainder can follow any of these estates. But a remainder cannot follow a fee simple (*see infra*, §453).

      (1) **Example—fee tail:** O conveys "to A and the heirs of his body, and if A dies without issue, to B and his heirs." If the fee tail has not been abolished (*supra*, §363), A has a fee tail, and B has a remainder in fee simple.

(2) **Example—term of years:** O conveys "to A for ten years, then to B and his heirs." A has a term of years. B has a vested remainder in fee simple. At early common law, B's interest was not called a remainder. Why not? Before the Statute of Uses (1536), O could convey a freehold only by going on the land and performing the formalities required for livery of seisin (*supra*, §278). When O conveyed "to A for ten years, then to B and his heirs," A, a termor, could not hold seisin because he did not have a freehold estate (*supra*, §276). In the eyes of the law, seisin moved immediately to B. Therefore, it was said that B held a fee simple subject to A's term of years. Since livery of seisin is not important today, it is common and correct in the above situation to say B has a remainder. It can also be said, as the ancients did say, that B has a fee simple subject to A's term of years.

c. **Must be capable of becoming possessory on natural termination of preceding estate:** [§451] A remainder cannot divest a preceding estate prior to its normal expiration. A divesting interest in a transferee is an *executory interest*, not a remainder.

(1) **Example:** O conveys "to A for life, but if B returns from Rome during the life of A, to B in fee simple." B does not have a remainder; B has a shifting executory interest.

(a) **Comparison with executory interests:** [§452] Executory interests are treated fully *infra* (§§560 *et seq.*), but a brief statement is required here to compare these interests with remainders. Prior to the Statute of Uses (1536), two types of future interests were void at law. First, the law decreed *that no freehold interest could spring out of the grantor at a future date*; the grantor either had to give the interest now or not at all. *Example:* O conveys "to A and her heirs when A marries B." This *springing* interest was prohibited. Second, the law decreed that *no stranger could be given the right to terminate an estate and shift seisin away from a grantee*. *Example:* O conveys "to A and his heirs, but if B returns from Rome, to B and his heirs." This *shifting* interest was prohibited. After the Statute of Uses was enacted in 1536, springing and shifting interests were permitted and were called executory interests. The essential difference between remainders and executory interests is this: *Remainders wait patiently until the preceding estate expires; executory interests cut short the preceding estate*. Remainders are polite; executory interests are greedy and grasping.

(2) **No remainder after a fee simple:** [§453] A logical consequence of a rule that a remainder is an estate which becomes possessory on the natural termination of the preceding estate is that *there can never be a remainder divesting a fee simple*, which has an infinite duration. Any interest divesting or following a fee simple *must be an executory interest*, not a remainder. This rule applies to all types of fees simple, including a fee simple determinable (*see supra*, §318).

(a) **Example:** O conveys "to A and his heirs, but if A dies without issue surviving him, to B." B has an executory interest, not a remainder.

3. **Estates in Remainder:** [§454]   An estate in remainder may be a fee simple, a life estate, a term of years, or, in those jurisdictions where such an estate is permitted, a fee tail.

   a. **Example:** O conveys "to A for life, then to B for ten years, then to C for life, then to D." B has a remainder for a term of years, C has a remainder for life, and D has a remainder in fee simple. (All of these remainders are vested; *see* below.)

4. **Classification of Remainders:** [§455]   Remainders are classified either as "vested" or "contingent." A vested remainder is a remainder that is *both* created in an ascertained person *and* is not subject to any condition precedent. A *contingent* remainder is a remainder that is *either created in an unascertained person or subject to a condition precedent*.

   a. **How to classify:** [§456]   An appropriate—and easy—way to classify remainders is as follows. Take each interest *in sequence* as it appears. Determine whether it is given to an ascertained person or is subject to a condition precedent. Classify it. Move on to the next interest and do the same thing. Classification of each interest *in sequence* is the key to correct classification.

      (1) **Example:** O conveys "to A for life, then to B and his heirs if B survives A, and if B does not survive A, to B's children and their heirs." Take each interest in sequence. First, "to A for life." This gives A a life estate. Second, "then to B and his heirs if B survives A." Stop at the comma, which ends B's interest, and classify it: B has a *remainder* because it is capable of becoming possessory upon the termination of the life estate, and will not cut the life estate short. It is a remainder *in fee simple* ("B and his heirs"). It is a *contingent* remainder because it is subject to the express condition precedent, "if B survives A." Third, move on to the next interest, "and if B does not survive A, to B's children and their heirs." Classify it: The interest is a *remainder* because it is capable of becoming possessory upon termination of the life estate, and cannot cut the life estate short. It is a remainder to a class, B's children, *in fee simple*. It is a *contingent* remainder because it is subject to the express condition precedent, "and if B does not survive A." If the words of an instrument are classified *in sequence*, as in this example, the classification of remainders is not too difficult a task (at least with textbook examples, which are likely to be clearly framed to illustrate the rules).

      (2) **Why classify?** [§457]   The common law drew—and still draws—a sharp distinction between vested and contingent remainders. Vested remainders were favored and contingent remainders disfavored. The judges thought contingent remainders were objectionable because they made land inalienable. Therefore, they laid down several rules designed to curtail contingent remainders: (i) the rule of destructibility of contingent remainders (*infra*, §493); (ii) the Rule in Shelley's Case (*infra*, §513); (iii) the Doctrine of Worthier Title (*infra*, §542); and (iv) the Rule Against Perpetuities (*infra*, §605). In addition, contingent remainders were not alienable, whereas vested remainders were alienable (*see infra*, §§471-472). Thus several legal consequences turn upon whether a remainder is vested or contingent.

b. **Vested remainders**

(1) **Definition:** [§458]   The most common definition of a vested remainder is the one given above: A remainder created **in an ascertained person** and **not subject to a condition precedent**. Gray, Rule Against Perpetuities §101 defines it somewhat differently: "A remainder is vested in A, when throughout its continuance, A, or A and his heirs, **have the right to immediate possession, whenever and however the preceding freehold estates may determine**." Gray's definition emphasizes that a vested remainder must follow hard on the heels of the preceding estates, however they end, but both definitions add up to the same thing—*i.e.*, a remainder in an unascertained person or subject to a condition precedent cannot follow hard on the heels of the preceding estates, however and whenever they expire, because it is not capable of doing so.

  (a) **Example:** O conveys "to A for life, then to B in fee simple." B (an ascertained person) has a remainder not subject to a condition precedent. The word "then" following a life estate is a word of art meaning "on the expiration of the life estate." Whenever and however the life estate terminates, B (or her representative) will be entitled to possession. B's remainder is vested.

  (b) **Condition precedent:** [§459]   A condition precedent is an **express condition** attached to the remainder, such as, "to B if B reaches age thirty" or "to B if B survives A." *Note:* The expiration of the preceding estate is **not** a condition precedent.

(2) **Subclassification of vested remainders:** [§460]   There are three different types of vested remainders: indefeasibly vested, vested subject to open, and vested subject to complete defeasance. These differences are explained *infra*. Generally speaking, however, the crucial distinction is between vested remainders on the one hand and contingent remainders on the other. For most purposes, all vested remainders have the same legal consequences (a principal exception is the treatment of remainders vested subject to open under the Rule Against Perpetuities, *infra*, §617). It is important to master these different types of vested remainders primarily because of the light they shed on how vested remainders are distinguished from contingent remainders.

  (a) **Indefeasibly vested remainder:** [§461]   When a remainder is indefeasibly vested, the holder of the remainder is **certain to acquire** a possessory estate at some time in the future, and is also certain to be entitled to **retain permanently** thereafter the possessory estate so acquired.

    1) **Example:** O conveys "to A for life, then to B and her heirs." B (or her representative) is certain to take possession on A's death. If B dies before A, B's heirs or devisees are entitled to possession. Thus, B's remainder is indefeasibly vested. (If B dies intestate and without heirs during A's life, B's remainder escheats to the state. At A's death, the state takes the property.)

(b) **Vested remainder subject to open:** [§462] When a remainder is vested subject to open, it is vested in a **class of persons**, at least one of whom is qualified to take possession, but the shares of the class members are not yet fixed because more persons can subsequently become members of the class.

1) **Example:** O conveys "to A for life, then to A's children." If A has no children, the remainder is contingent, because no person qualifies as a child. If A has a child, B, the remainder is vested in B subject to "open up" and let in other children. B's remainder is sometimes called "vested subject to partial divestment." (Once the remainder has vested in B, the interests of the unborn children are called executory interests because they may partially divest B.)

2) **Class gifts:** [§463] A class gift is a gift to a group of persons described as a class, *e.g.*, "children of A," "brothers and sisters of A," or "heirs of A." A class is either **open** or **closed**. It is open if it is possible for other persons to enter the class. **It is closed if it is not possible for others to enter the class.** In a gift to the "children of A," the class is closed if A is dead. In a gift to the "brothers and sisters of A," the class is closed if A's parents are dead.

3) **Class-closing rule:** [§464] When a vested remainder subject to open becomes possessory, the class closes and no one born after that date can share in the class gift. This is called "the rule of convenience," because it makes it possible to distribute the property without worrying about unborn class members. By cutting out unborn persons, it also makes the property alienable. (But from the viewpoint of the unborn, the rule is misnamed, for it is certainly inconvenient for them!) The rule of convenience is: **The class closes whenever any member of the class can demand possession**, if it has not already closed physiologically.

    a) **Example:** O conveys "to A for life, then to the children of B." A and B are alive. Then A dies, B has two children, C and D. The class closes at A's death, and the property is divided between C and D. Children of B conceived after A dies do not share in the gift.

        1/ **Person "in being":** [§465] For purposes of property law, a person is treated as "in being" from the time of conception if he or she is later born alive. Hence, a child of B in the womb at A's death would share with C and D if later born alive.

    b) **Transmissible at death:** [§466] If a person takes a vested remainder subject to open, his interest is not divested if he dies before the remainder becomes possessory. In the preceding example, if C were to die before A, C's share would go to C's heirs or devisees.

(c) **Vested remainder subject to complete defeasance:** [§467] When a remainder is vested subject to complete defeasance, it is either vested subject to being divested by the operation of a **condition subsequent** or vested subject to defeasance by an **inherent limitation** of the estate in remainder.

1) **Example—condition subsequent:** [§468] O conveys "to A for life, then to B, but if B does not survive A, to C." The vested remainder in B is subject to total divestment upon the occurrence of a **condition subsequent** (B dying, leaving A surviving). C's executory interest will divest B if the condition subsequent happens.

2) **Example—inherent limitation:** [§469] O conveys "to A for life, then to B for life, then to C and his heirs." B has a vested remainder for life subject to total defeasance if B fails to survive A. The defeasance occurs because of the **inherent limitation** in a remainder for life: It fails if it does not become possessory within the life tenant's life. C has an indefeasibly vested remainder in fee simple.

3) **Vested subject to open and to complete defeasance:** [§470] A remainder can be both vested subject to open and to complete defeasance. For example, O conveys "to A for life, then to the children of A, but if no child survives A, to B." A, who is living, has a child, C. C has a vested remainder subject to open up and let in her brothers and sisters; it is also subject to complete defeasance if A leaves no children surviving him (*i.e.*, if C and all other children of A die before A).

(3) **Alienability:** [§471] Vested remainders are alienable inter vivos and devisable by will. A vested remainder descends to heirs if not otherwise disposed of.

(a) **Where not transmissible:** [§472] A remainder is "transmissible" if the remainderman can pass it to another at his death. A vested remainder can be so limited that it is not transmissible but is divested on death. *Example:* O conveys "to A for life, then to B, but if B does not survive A, to C." B's vested remainder is not transmissible. If B dies during A's life, B can pass nothing upon B's death. In that case, C's executory interest would divest B at A's death and become a vested remainder.

c. **Contingent remainders**

(1) **Definition:** [§473] A remainder is contingent if it either is limited to an **unascertained person** or is subject to a **condition precedent**.

(a) **Certainty of possession:** [§474] There is no certainty that a contingent remainder will ever become possessory. But certainty of possession has nothing to do with the classification of remainders as vested or contingent. A vested remainder subject to complete defeasance, like a contingent remainder, is not certain of becoming possessory. **The distinction between vested and contingent remainders is not whether the remainder is certain to** *become possessory but whether the remainder is limited to an unascertained person or is subject to a condition precedent.*

(2) **Remainders in unascertained persons:** [§475]   A remainder in an "unascertained" person means the person is not yet born or cannot be determined until the happening of an event. Such a remainder is contingent.

    (a) **Example—unborn children:** [§476]   O conveys "to A for life, then to A's children." A has no children. The remainder is contingent because the takers are not ascertained at the time of the conveyance. If a child is born, the remainder vests in that child subject to open and let in other children born later.

    (b) **Example—heirs:** [§477]   O conveys "to A for life, then to B's heirs." B is alive. Since no one is an heir of the living (but only an heir apparent), the takers are not ascertained; therefore, the remainder is contingent. B's heirs will be ascertained only at his death. If B dies during A's life, the remainder will vest in B's heirs at B's death.

        1) **Meaning of "heirs":** [§478]   "Heirs" means those persons who succeed to B's property *if B dies intestate* (*see supra*, §293). They are set forth in each state's statute of descent and distribution. Children and descendants are everywhere preferred over parents and more remote kin. To be an heir of B, a person must survive B. Dead persons do not inherit property. If, for example, B has a son, C, who dies before B, C is not an heir of B.

    (c) **Reversion:** [§479]   In each of the above examples, there is a reversion in O. *Note:* **Whenever O creates a contingent remainder in fee simple, there is a reversion in O.** Whenever O creates a vested remainder in fee simple, there is never a reversion in fee simple in O.

(3) **Remainders subject to condition precedent:** [§480]   A remainder subject to a condition precedent is a contingent remainder. A condition precedent is an **express condition** set forth in the instrument (other than the termination of the preceding estate), which must occur before the remainder becomes possessory. This definition requires elaboration (*see* below).

    (a) **What is a condition precedent:** [§481]   A condition precedent is a condition expressly stated in the instrument. Suppose that O conveys "to A for life, then to B *if B marries C*." B has a remainder subject to an express condition precedent. The condition precedent is marrying C. If B marries C during A's life, the remainder vests indefeasibly in B.

    (b) **What is not a condition precedent**

        1) **The termination of the preceding estate is not a condition precedent:** [§482]   If it were, all remainders would be contingent, because no one is entitled to possession until the preceding estate has terminated.

2) **Surplusage:** [§483]   Language that merely refers to the termination of the preceding estate is surplusage and does not create a condition precedent.

   a) **Example:** O conveys "to A for life, and on A's death, to B." The words "on A's death" merely refer to the natural termination of the life estate and do not state a condition precedent. They are therefore surplusage and may be struck out. B's remainder is vested. [Kost v. Foster, 94 N.E.2d 302 (Ill. 1950)]

3) **Survivorship:** [§484]   A remainder subject to a condition precedent *other than* survivorship is not also subject to an implied condition precedent of survivorship. *Remember:* The condition precedent must be expressly stated. Thus if O conveys "to A for life, then to A's issue and if A dies without issue to B," B's remainder is contingent on A's dying without issue. It is *not* contingent on B's surviving A; if B dies before A, B's remainder passes to B's heirs or devisees, and if A subsequently dies without issue, B's heirs or devisees take the property. There are two or three cases to the contrary, holding that all contingent remainders are contingent on surviving to the time of possession [*see, e.g.* Fletcher v. Hurdle, 536 S.W.2d 109 (Ark. 1976)], but these cases are aberrational and are sharply criticized.

(4) **Conditions subsequent distinguished:** [§485]   Sometimes it is difficult to distinguish between a vested remainder subject to divestment (*i.e.*, subject to a condition subsequent) and a remainder subject to a condition precedent. Whether a condition is precedent or subsequent depends upon the words of the instrument. The words must be read *in sequence* and the interests classified *in sequence*. The test, according to Gray, Rule Against Perpetuities §108, is as follows: "Whether a remainder is vested or contingent depends upon the language employed. If the conditional element is incorporated into the description of, or into the gift to the person taking the remainder, then the remainder is contingent; but if, *after words giving a vested interest, a clause is added divesting it*, the remainder is vested."

   (a) **Example:** O conveys "to A for life, then to B, but if B does not survive A, to C." B has a vested remainder subject to divestment by C's executory interest. The words "then to B," give B a vested remainder; the clause following is a divesting clause, giving the property to C if B dies before A.

   (b) **Example:** O conveys "to A for life, then to B if B survives A, but if B does not survive A, to C." B and C have alternative contingent remainders. A condition precedent has been expressly attached to B's remainder. O intended exactly the same thing as in the preceding example, but her intention was phrased differently. Here, O stated the condition of survivorship twice, once in connection with each remainder.

1) **Reversion in O with alternative contingent remainders:** [§486] In the preceding example where alternative contingent remainders are created, there is a reversion in O. How is it possible for the property to revert to O? Inasmuch as B will take if B survives A, and if B does not survive A, C will take, it looks impossible for the property to revert to O. The answer? At common law *a life estate could terminate prior to the life tenant's death* by forfeiture or merger (*infra*, §§498-503). If this happened, neither B nor C would be ready to take on the termination of the life estate, and the property would revert to O. Or B and A can die simultaneously, so that neither survives the other and the conditions precedent on B's interest and C's interest can never be satisfied. However unrealistic these possibilities may appear today, *in classifying future interests one must assume that the life estate can terminate before the death of the life tenant.*

(c) **Preference for vested remainders:** [§487] If the instrument is ambiguous, the law favors a vested construction rather than a contingent one.

1) **Example:** O conveys "to A for life, and at his death to A's children, the child or children of any deceased child to receive its or their deceased parent's share." Under the standard rule of construction, A's children take a vested remainder subject to condition subsequent on birth. Each child's interest is subject to be divested by his children if he dies before A. [Kost v. Foster, *supra*, §483]

2) **Condition subsequent must be read carefully:** [§488] In the above instrument, the condition subsequent is not operative to divest a child of A who dies before A *without children*. It is operative only to divest a child of A who dies before A *with children*. Thus, suppose A had two children, B and C, and C had a child, D. Then B and C died before A. B's share would go under his will as he devised, or to his heirs. C's share would be divested in favor of D.

3) **Rationale—alienability and intent of grantor:** [§489] At common law, the law favored vested remainders for several reasons. They were alienable. They were more effective in carrying out the grantor's intent, because they were not destructible by a gap in seisin (*infra*, §589), and also were not subject to the Rule Against Perpetuities. Where contingent interests have been made alienable and indestructible, as is true in most states, it is harder to justify the common law preference for vested remainders. [Browning v. Sacrison, 518 P.2d 656 (Or. 1974)]

(5) **Alienability:** [§490] Contingent interests, including contingent remainders and executory interests, were not alienable inter vivos at common law, except in equity for a valuable consideration, by operation of the doctrine of estoppel, or where released to the owner of the possessory interest.

(a) **Modern law:** [§491]   In a large majority of jurisdictions today, contingent interests are alienable inter vivos or, when survivorship is not a condition precedent, devisable by will. Of course, if the remainder is contingent because the limitation is to an unborn person, there is no one to make the conveyance, so the interest is inalienable.

(b) **Creditor's rights:** [§492]   Generally, creditors can reach any alienable property interest the debtor has. The rule is: If the debtor can voluntarily transfer it, the creditor can reach it. Thus creditors can reach vested remainders; they can also reach contingent remainders if they are alienable in the particular jurisdiction. [Kost v. Foster, *supra*]

5. **Destructibility of Contingent Remainders:** [§493]   The rule of destructibility of contingent remainders was an important rule of the common law. This rule has been abolished in most states (*see infra*, §511), but because it apparently is still in effect in some, it is discussed here in the present tense.

a. **Statement of rule:** [§494]   English judges laid down a rule that a legal contingent remainder in **land** is **destroyed if it does not vest at or before the termination of the preceding freehold estate**. If the preceding freehold terminates before the remainder vests, the remainder is struck down and can never take effect.

(1) **Example:** O conveys Blackacre "to A for life, remainder to A's children who reach age 21." At A's death, his children are all under age 21. The remainder is destroyed. Blackacre reverts to the reversioner, O, who owns it in fee simple absolute.

(2) **Rationale for rule:** The common law abhorred an abeyance of seisin (*supra*, §276). Feudal incidents fell due upon the death of the person seised, and the location and continuity of seisin were important to the collection of feudal dues. Thus the courts laid down this rule: If, upon termination of the preceding freehold, the holder of the remainder **is not able to take seisin** because his remainder is still contingent, the remainder is wiped out.

(a) **Example:** O conveys Blackacre "to A for life, then to B for life, then to B's children who reach age 21." Subsequently B dies, leaving an eldest child of 19. The contingent remainder in B's children is not destroyed because B did not have seisin. A has seisin. If A dies after B dies, and before any child of B has reached 21, the contingent remainder in B's children is then destroyed.

b. **Elements of the rule**

(1) **Preceding freehold:** [§495]   The preceding freehold estate in possession can be a fee tail or a life estate, both of which are estates having seisin. Since the fee tail is largely obsolete, this discussion will assume the freehold is a life estate. **The rule does not apply if the preceding estate is a leasehold**, because the termor does not have seisin.

(a) **Example:** O conveys "to A for 100 years if A so long lives, then to A's children who reach age 21." Subsequently A dies, leaving an eldest child of 19. The destructibility rule has no application because A did not have a freehold. Another way of looking at this is to say A did not have seisin to offer to the next estate, and the next estate is not destroyed unless seisin is offered and cannot be accepted. At A's death, possession returns to O, where it is reunited with seisin. Then, when any child of A reaches 21, seisin will spring out to such child, who will take a vested fee simple subject to partial defeasance by other children reaching that age.

(2) **Termination of life estate:** [§496]   The life estate can terminate either upon the death of the life tenant *or before the life tenant's death*. It is this later proposition that makes the rule more difficult than it appears.

(a) **Natural termination of life estate:** [§497]   A contingent remainder that does not vest upon the *natural* termination of the life estate (*i.e.*, at the life tenant's death) is destroyed.

   1) **Example:** O conveys "to A for life, remainder to the heirs of B." B is alive. This conveyance creates a life estate in A, contingent remainder in the heirs of B, reversion in O. Subsequently A dies, survived by B. At A's death, B has no heirs, because no one can be an heir of the living. The contingent remainder in the heirs of B is destroyed, and O owns the land.

(b) **Artificial termination of life estate:** [§498]   A contingent remainder that does not vest upon the *artificial termination* of the life estate is destroyed. "Artificial termination" refers to the following methods of termination:

   1) **Forfeiture:** [§499]   At common law, a person forfeited his property by a tortious conveyance (*i.e.* a conveyance by which a life tenant or a tenant in tail conveyed a fee simple). Such a conveyance was treated as repudiating and destroying the old estate and claiming a new fee simple by disseisin, which was transferred. Any contingent remainders dependent on the grantor's old estate failed.

      a) **Example:** O conveys "to A for life, then to A's children who reach age 21." A makes a tortious conveyance in fee simple to B while A's children are under 21. The remainder is destroyed. The reversioner has a right of entry to eject B.

      b) **Modern status:** [§500]   Forfeiture for tortious conveyance is wholly obsolete in the United States. In the above example, B would merely receive a life estate pur autre vie. The remainder would not be affected.

   2) **Merger:** [§501]   If the life estate and a vested remainder or reversion in fee simple come into the hands of the same person, any intermediate

contingent remainders are destroyed. The lesser estate (life estate) is merged into the larger (fee simple) and ceases to exist as a separate estate. A life tenant and reversioner can thus conspire to destroy contingent remainders.

   a) **Example:** O conveys "to A for life, remainder to B if B survives A." While B is alive, A conveys her life estate to O. The life estate merges into the reversion, and B's contingent remainder is destroyed. O has a fee simple absolute.

   b) **Exception—fee tail:** [§502] Life estates merge into a fee simple, but fees tail do not. Thus, suppose a conveyance "to A and the heirs of his body, and if A dies without issue, to B and her heirs if B is then living." A conveys his fee tail to O, the reversioner. B's remainder is not destroyed. (However, A can destroy B's remainder by disentailing; *supra*, §361.)

   c) **Exception—simultaneous creation:** [§503] If a life estate and the next vested estate are created simultaneously, they do not merge *at that time* to destroy intervening contingent remainders. Thus, suppose that T devises Blackacre "to A for life, remainder to A's children who survive A." A is also T's heir and inherits the reversion. The life estate and reversion do not merge at that time; otherwise the intent of T in creating the remainder would be frustrated. But if *A subsequently conveys the life estate and reversion to B*, the estates then merge, destroying the contingent remainder.

c. **Interests not affected by destructibility rule:** [§504] The destructibility rule does not apply to the following interests in property.

  (1) **Vested remainders and executory interests:** [§505] Vested remainders and executory interests cannot be destroyed by a gap in seisin. The destructibility rule *applies only to contingent remainders*.

    (a) **Example—vested remainder:** O conveys "to A for life, then to B for life, then to A's children who survive A." A conveys his life estate to O. The life estate cannot merge into the reversion because the vested remainder in B blocks it. O takes a life estate pur autre vie (for A's life).

    (b) **Example—executory interest:** O conveys "to A for 100 years if A so long live, then to A's children who survive A." A has a term of years determinable. The children have an executory interest, because there can be no contingent remainder after a term of years (*infra*, §509). A conveys his term to O. Seisin does not move from A to O, since A, a termor, never had it (*supra*, §275). Therefore, the children's executory interest is not affected. O now has a fee simple subject to A's children's executory interest but no longer subject to A's term of years.

(c) **Another example—executory interest:** O conveys "to A, but if A dies leaving children, to A's children who survive A, and if A dies without children, title shall return to O." A has a fee simple, subject to divestment by an executory interest in A's children who survive A, and subject also to a possibility of reverter in O. Later O conveys his interest to A, the fee simple owner. This cannot affect the executory interest in A's children. They take the land on A's death. [Stoller v. Doyle, 100 N.E. 959 (Ill. 1913)]

(2) **Personal property:** [§506] The destructibility rule has no application to personal property. There is no seisin in personal property, only in land.

(a) **Example:** O conveys "to A for 999 years." Subsequently A conveys the term "to B for life, remainder to B's children who reach age 21." B then dies, leaving an eldest child of 19. The destructibility rule does not apply because a term of years is personal property (a "chattel real"). The termor does not hold seisin.

(3) **Interests in trust:** [§507] Interests in trust—*i.e.,* equitable estates—are not subject to the destructibility rule. The trustee, owning the legal fee simple, has seisin. Upon the expiration of the *equitable* life estate, seisin is not offered to the next estate—and therefore the destructibility rule, based on continuity of seisin, does not apply.

(a) **Example:** O conveys Blackacre "to X and his heirs in trust to pay the income to A for life, then in trust to convey Blackacre to the children of A who reach age 21." Subsequently A dies, and his eldest child is 19. The remainder is not destroyed. The trustee X has seisin. Such children as reach age 21 will take the land.

d. **Avoidance of rule:** [§508] The destructibility rule can be easily avoided by a competent lawyer. The two most common ways of avoiding the rule are as follows.

(1) **Term of years:** [§509] If a drafter creates a term of years rather than a life estate, the destructibility rule can be avoided. *Example:* O conveys "to A for 100 years if A so long lives, then to A's children who reach age 21." Seisin remains in O. A has a term of years determinable; A's children have an executory interest and not a contingent remainder. If A dies leaving all children under 21, seisin stays in O, and the executory interest is not destroyed. It springs out of O when a child reaches 21.

(2) **Trustees:** [§510] The destructibility rule can also be avoided by creating *trustees to preserve contingent remainders*. The device works this way. O conveys "to A for life, then to X, Y, and Z as trustees for the life of A and to preserve contingent remainders, remainder to A's children who survive A." The trustees have a *vested* remainder following A's life estate. If the life estate terminates in any way, prior to A's death, the trustees step up and take seisin and hold it until A's death, paying the income to A. The purpose of this device was to *prevent artificial destruction* of contingent remainders by the termina-

tion of the life estate prior to the life tenant's death. If the life estate terminated before the death of A, the trustees took seisin, and blocked its passage on to the reversioner. Thus A could not destroy the contingent remainders with the collusion of O.

e. **Abolition:** [§511] The destructibility rule has been abolished in the large majority of the states by judicial decision or statute. [Abo Petroleum Corp. v. Amstutz, 600 P.2d 278 (N.M. 1979)]

(1) **Effect of abolition:** [§512] Where destructibility is abolished, a contingent remainder takes effect if the contingency occurs *either before or after the termination of the life estate*. Thus, if O conveys "to A for life, remainder to A's children who reach age 21," and A dies leaving all children under 21, A's children take if and when they reach 21. Their interest takes effect in possession after A's death, and is called either an indestructible contingent remainder or an executory interest.

6. **Rule in Shelley's Case:** [§513] One of the great traps of common law conveyancing was the Rule in Shelley's Case. This rule has been abolished in most states (*infra*, §540), but because it still exists in some, it is discussed here in the present tense.

a. **Statement of Rule:** [§514] If (i) one instrument (ii) creates a freehold in land in A, and (iii) purports to create a remainder in A's heirs (or in the heirs of A's body), and (iv) the estates are both legal or both equitable, then the remainder becomes a remainder in fee simple (or fee tail) in A.

(1) **Example—remainder to A's heirs:** O conveys "to A for life, then to A's heirs." The Rule in Shelley's Case converts the remainder limited to A's heirs into a remainder in fee simple in A. *Then* the doctrine of *merger* steps in, and A's life estate and vested remainder merge, giving A a fee simple in possession.

(2) **Example—remainder to heirs of A's body:** O conveys "to A for life, then to the heirs of A's body." The Rule in Shelley's Case converts the remainder limited to "the heirs of A's body" into a remainder in fee tail in A. The fee tail is then changed into whatever estate is substituted for a fee tail under state law, probably a fee simple (*see supra*, §§364-367). Then the remainder in A merges with A's life estate.

(3) **Doctrine of merger:** [§515] The doctrine of merger is an entirely separate doctrine from the Rule in Shelley's Case. The doctrine of merger is that a life estate in A and a remainder in A will merge unless (i) there is an intervening estate *or* (ii) the remainder in A is subject to a condition precedent to which his life estate is not subject. The doctrine of merger may or may not apply after the Rule in Shelley's Case has operated on the instrument.

b. **Reasons for Rule**

(1) **Feudal tax evasion:** [§516] The origin of the Rule in Shelley's Case is obscure, but it is probable that it arose to prevent feudal tax evasion. The feudal

incidents (*supra*, §256) were due only if the new tenant acquired his interest by descent from the former tenant, rather than by purchase under the terms of the conveyance. Sometimes this distinction appears in modern guise in decisions asking whether the words granting "a remainder to A's heirs" are words of purchase (giving A's heirs an interest in their own right as purchasers) or words of limitation (being words giving a fee simple to A, which might ultimately descend to A's heirs). The Rule in Shelley's Case makes the remainder into words of limitation.

(2) **Alienability:** [§517]   The Rule makes land alienable one generation earlier. In the preceding example, a fee simple can be conveyed by A immediately after the conveyance from O. The land is not tied up during A's lifetime. If the Rule in Shelley's Case has any modern justification, this is it.

(3) **Does not apply to personal property:** [§518]   Since the original reasons for the Rule had no application to personal property, in which there were no feudal incidents, the Rule in Shelley's Case does not apply to personal property.

   (a) **Example:** T devises her farm "to X as trustee, to be sold, with the proceeds to be held in trust to pay A the income for life, and on A's death to pay the principal to A's heirs." Under the doctrine of equitable conversion (*infra*, §1811), since the land must be sold on T's death and converted into personal property, equity treats the interests of A and A's heirs as being interests in personal property from the beginning. The Rule in Shelley's Case does not apply. However, if T had devised her farm "to X as trustee to pay A the income for life, and **on A's death either to sell the farm** and distribute the proceeds to A's heirs **or** to convey the farm to A's heirs," the case would be different. Because the sale is **optional**, equitable conversion would not apply to change the remainder to a remainder in personal property. The life estate and the remainder are both in land, and the Rule in Shelley's Case applies, giving A a fee simple. [City Bank & Trust Co. v. Morrissey, 454 N.E.2d 1195 (Ill. 1983)]

(4) **Internal logic:** [§519]   Some of the rules within the Rule in Shelley's Case follow from the premises and are understandable. But many of the aspects of the Rule are irrational, arbitrary, and hard to figure out from the premises. It has been said of Shelley's Case, "as in the case of Goldsmith's village parson . . . those who came to scoff remain to pray." [29 L.R.A. (n.s.) 965 (1911)—a long annotation of the Rule in Shelley's Case] The treatment of the Rule in Shelley's Case here is based on 3 Restatement of Property section 312, but some courts—unable to follow the elusive reasoning of the Rule—have come to results contrary to the Restatement.

c. **Operation of the Rule:** [§520]   The Rule is more readily understood if each element of the Rule is separately analyzed.

   (1) **"If one instrument creates a freehold estate in A":** [§521]   Although in England the freehold could be a fee tail or a life estate, all American cases applying

the Rule in Shelley's Case have involved a **_life estate_**. Hence the discussion here assumes the freehold in A is a life estate. The life estate can be measured by A's life or it can be a life estate pur autre vie.

(a) **Example:** O conveys "to A for the life of B, remainder to A's heirs." The Rule in Shelley's Case applies and A has a fee simple. This makes sense. Inasmuch as the remainder in A becomes possessory whenever and however the life estate ends, a life estate in A (even measured by B's life), and a vested remainder in A comprise the totality of interests in the land. *But compare:* If O had conveyed "to A for the life of B, remainder to B's heirs," the Rule in Shelley's Case would not apply. The life estate must be given to the ancestor of the heirs given the remainder.

(b) **Life estate determinable:** [§522]   The life estate can be determinable or subject to condition subsequent.

1)   **Example:** T devises a farm "to my wife W during widowhood, and upon W's death or remarriage, remainder to W's heirs." The Rule in Shelley's Case applies, giving W the remainder. The remainder merges with W's life estate, giving W a fee simple.

(c) **Life estate is in remainder:** [§523]   The freehold can be a life estate in possession or a life estate in remainder. The Rule in Shelley's Case applies to a conveyance "to A for life, then to B for life, remainder to B's heirs." B has a remainder in fee simple.

1)   **Subject to condition precedent:** [§524]   If the life estate in A is subject to a condition precedent which is not also applicable to the remainder to A's heirs, the Rule in Shelley's Case does not apply. (The Rule might apply later, when the condition is met. *See infra*, §537.)

a)   **Example:** O conveys "to A for life, then, if B marries C, to B for life, remainder to the heirs of B (whether or not B marries C)." The life estate is subject to a condition precedent which is not also applicable to the remainder. The Rule in Shelley's Case does not apply. (*But note:* If B marries C during A's life, the Rule in Shelley's Case **then** applies. *See infra*, §537.)

b)   **Remainder subject to same condition precedent:** [§525]   If the remainder is subject to the same condition precedent as the life estate, then the Rule in Shelley's Case applies. Thus if, in the preceding example, the language in parentheses had been omitted and the condition precedent of B marrying C were construed to be a condition precedent on the remainder as well as on B's life estate, the Rule in Shelley's Case would have applied. B would have taken a remainder in fee simple subject to the condition precedent of marrying C.

(d) **Lapse of life estate:** [§526]   If A is given a life estate, with remainder to A's heirs, under the will of O, and *A predeceases O*, A's life estate lapses (or fails). The Rule in Shelley's Case should not be applied because the freehold was never created, but surprisingly there is some authority applying the Rule in Shelley's Case, causing the remainder to A's heirs to lapse or fail as well.

(e) **Joint life estate:** [§527]   Suppose that O conveys "to H and W as tenants in common for their lives, remainder to the heirs of W." Does the Rule in Shelley's Case apply? The authorities are divided. Some say that W has the entire remainder in fee simple because W, as a tenant in common with H, was seised of a life estate in the whole, meaning W could enjoy the entire property for life (as of course could H). [Bails v. Davis, 89 N.E. 706 (Ill. 1909)] The Restatement says W has a remainder in fee simple only as to an undivided half. There is a reversion as to the other half. [3 Rest. §312, comment r]

(2) **"And purports to create a remainder":** [§528]   The Rule applies to a remainder to the heirs of A, the life tenant, even though there is an intervening estate between the life estate and remainder. For example, the Rule applies to a conveyance "to A for life, then to B for life, then to A's heirs." A has a remainder in fee simple by the operation of the Rule. A's remainder does not, however, merge with his life estate: B's intervening remainder for life prevents merger.

(a) **Contingent remainder:** [§529]   The remainder may be a remainder contingent upon the happening of some condition precedent. Thus the Rule in Shelley's Case applies to a conveyance "to A for life, then to A's heirs if A survives B." A has a life estate and a contingent remainder, contingent upon A's surviving B. The life estate and contingent remainder do not merge.

1) **Compare:** It was noted above (§524, *supra*) that the rule did *not* apply if the life estate were subject to a condition precedent not also applicable to the remainder. But the Rule *does* apply in the converse situation, where there is a condition precedent on the remainder but not on the life estate. [3 Rest. §312, comments o and p] This is simply an arbitrary distinction, without any reason.

(b) **Executory interest:** [§530]   The Rule in Shelley's Case, as traditionally stated, applies only where a remainder, not an executory interest, has been created. But a few modern cases have applied the rule to executory interests. [*See* 43 Minn. L. Rev. 13, 21 (1958)]

1) **Executory limitation:** [§531]   If both the life estate and the remainder are part of an executory limitation, the Rule applies. For example, it applies to a conveyance "to A for life, remainder to B, but if B predeceases A, to C for life, remainder to C's heirs." The remainder within

the shifting executory limitation is a remainder to C under the Rule, which merges with C's life estate giving C a shifting executory interest in fee simple.

(3) **"In A's heirs (or the heirs of A's body)":** [§532] The remainder must be given to A's heirs or heirs of the body in "an indefinite line of succession rather than a specific class of takers. The remainder must be to the heirs of the first taker *by the name of heirs* as meaning a class of persons to succeed to the estate from generation to generation. Where to the word *heirs* other words are added which so limit its meaning that it does not include the whole line of inheritable succession but only designates the individuals who are at the death of the life tenant to succeed to the estate, . . . the Rule in Shelley's Case does not apply." [Arnold v. Baker, 185 N.E.2d 844 (Ill. 1962)]

(a) **Indefinite line of succession:** [§533] The distinction between "heirs" meaning those persons who take on A's death and "heirs" meaning an indefinite line of succession is hard to grasp. It is easier to understand in the English context of primogeniture, where the distinction originated. Under the doctrine of primogeniture, a person has only one heir, and therefore the word "heirs" can easily be taken to describe an indefinite succession of heirs. After primogeniture was abolished, the distinction became pretty ephemeral, and some courts have not grasped it—or have ignored it.

(b) **Words meaning indefinite line of succession:** [§534] The Rule in Shelley's Case does not apply to a remainder limited to "A's children" or "A's issue," because those words cannot be taken to mean heirs in an indefinite line of succession. The words "heirs" or "heirs of the body," however, are rather arbitrarily said to refer to heirs in an indefinite line of succession, unless the grantor shows he means something different.

1) **Example:** J. H. Sybert devises land "to Fred for life, and after his death to vest in fee simple in the heirs of his body." Fred dies childless, leaving his wife Eunice as his heir. Does the Rule in Shelley's Case apply so that Fred took a life estate and remainder in fee tail, which was converted by the fee tail statute into a remainder in fee simple, which merged with Fred's life estate, giving Fred a fee simple? If so, Fred's fee simple passes to his wife on Fred's death. If the Rule does not apply, the reversioner takes the land because Fred died without bodily heirs. The words "heirs of the body" are traditional words bringing the devise within Shelley's Case, and the Rule applies. [Sybert v. Sybert, 254 S.W.2d 999 (Tex. 1953)] If J. H. Sybert had said remainder "to Fred's issue," the Rule in Shelley's Case would not apply. Of course "heirs of the body" and "issue" describe exactly the same persons but "issue" is said not to be a technical word signifying an indefinite line of takers. Rather it signifies persons who take at Fred's death. What this adds up to is that a remainder "to A's heirs" or "the heirs of A's body" are simply *magic words* triggering the Rule in Shelley's Case.

(c) **Distinction rejected:** [§535]   The requirement that "heirs" refer to an indefinite line of succession has been ignored by some American courts which have applied the Rule in Shelley's Case to the following: "to A for life, then to such persons as will inherit real property from A at his death." The English courts would not apply the Rule in Shelley's Case to such a conveyance, but some American courts have. [People v. Emery, 145 N.E. 349 (Ill. 1924)]

(4) **"And the estates are both legal or both equitable":** [§536]   The life estate and remainder must be either both legal or both equitable. If one is legal and the other is equitable, the Rule in Shelley's Case does not apply.

(a) **Example:** O conveys Blackacre "to X in trust for the life of A to pay A the income and profits, remainder to the heirs of A." X has a legal life estate pur autre vie, A has an equitable life estate and A's heirs have a legal remainder in fee simple. Since A's life estate is equitable and the remainder to A's heirs is legal, the Rule in Shelley's Case does not apply. If X had been given a legal fee simple, the life estate and remainder would both be equitable, and the Rule in Shelley's Case would apply. [City Bank & Trust Co. v. Morrissey, *supra*, §518]

(5) **Application of the Rule on a delayed basis:** [§537]   If the requirements for application of the Rule are not initially met at the time of the conveyance, **but are met subsequently**, the Rule in Shelley's Case will apply subsequently when the requirements are met.

(a) **Example:** O conveys "to A for life, then, if B marries C, to B for life, remainder to the heirs of B (whether or not B marries C)." The Rule does not apply initially because the life estate in B is subject to a condition precedent not also applicable to the remainder to B's heirs (*see supra*, §524). But if B marries C during A's life, satisfying the condition, the Rule in Shelley's Case applies on B's marriage to C. (Thus, for a wedding gift B gets a remainder in fee simple.)

d. **The Rule is a rule of law:** [§538]   The Rule in Shelley's Case is a rule of law (not a rule of construction) that applies regardless of O's intent. It cannot be avoided by expressions of intent, such as, "I intend that the Rule in Shelley's Case not apply." O's intent is irrelevant. If the conveyance by O comes within its terms, the Rule in Shelley's Case applies regardless of what O wants.

e. **Avoidance of Rule:** [§539]   The Rule cannot be avoided by a direct expression of intent, but it can be avoided by failing to come within its requirements. A conveyance "to A for 100 years if A so long live, then to A's heirs" is the standard device used by skilled drafters to avoid the Rule. The Rule does not apply because A has a **leasehold**, not a freehold.

f. **Modern status:** [§540]   The Rule in Shelley's Case has been abolished by statute in the great majority of jurisdictions. The Rule apparently is still in effect in Arkansas, Delaware, Indiana, North Carolina, and possibly a few other states. In some states, the abolition of the Rule in Shelley's Case is fairly recent, so the old law, which remains applicable to conveyances made before abolition, will be of some concern for many years.

(1) **Effect where abolished:** [§541]   If the Rule in Shelley's Case is abolished, a conveyance "to A for life, then to A's heirs" creates a life estate in A, and a contingent remainder in A's heirs.

7. **Doctrine of Worthier Title:** [§542]   The Doctrine of Worthier Title is the third of the three rules restricting remainders dealt with here, the others being the destructibility rule and the Rule in Shelley's Case. The Doctrine of Worthier Title has an inter vivos branch and (perhaps) a testamentary branch.

   a. **Common law doctrine**

      (1) **Inter vivos branch of Doctrine:** [§543]   When an inter vivos conveyance purports to create a *future interest* in the *heirs of the grantor*, the future interest is *void* and the grantor has a reversion. This rule is sometimes known as a rule against a remainder in the grantor's heirs.

         (a) **Example:** O conveys "to A for life, then to O's heirs." The remainder to O's heirs is void, and O has a reversion.

         (b) **Original reason:** [§544]   The original reason for the Doctrine of Worthier Title is probably the same as for the Rule in Shelley's Case. Feudal incidents were due upon *descent* of land. In the above example, feudal incidents would be due upon O's death if he had a reversion passing to his heirs, but not if his heirs took by way of a remainder created during O's life. Hence the Doctrine prevented O from depriving his lord of feudal incidents by an inter vivos conveyance of this kind.

      (2) **Testamentary branch of Doctrine:** [§545]   If a person *devises* land to his *heirs*, the devise is void and the heirs take by *descent*. The simplest example of this is a devise by T "to A for life, then to T's heirs." The devise to T's heirs is void; T's heirs take the reversion after A's death by descent. The Restatement of Property section 314(2) says the testamentary branch of the Doctrine of Worthier Title does not exist in this country, but occasionally it crops up. A recent Iowa case is illustrative.

         (a) **Example:** T executes a will devising land to her son A, who is T's only child. After T executes her will, A dies without issue. T then dies without changing her will. *If there is a devise to A*, it lapses because A predeceased T. The state anti-lapse statute says that a lapsed gift goes to the devisee's collateral relatives, *i.e.*, A's kindred on his father's as well as his mother's side. On the other hand, if *there is not a devise to A*, T's property will go to her own blood kindred (her heirs). Under the Doctrine of Worthier Title, since A is T's sole heir, the devise is void, and the property goes as if the devise had never been made. Faced with such a conflict, the Iowa court recently abolished the testamentary branch of Worthier Title, and held that T's property would go under the anti-lapse statute to A's heirs. [Estate of Kern, 274 N.W.2d 325 (Iowa 1979)]

b. **Modern rule:** [§546]   In view of the fact that the testamentary branch of the Doctrine is moribund or nonexistent, further references in this Summary to the Doctrine refer only to the inter vivos branch. The common law Doctrine of Worthier Title was a **rule of law** applicable to **land** only. The modern Doctrine of Worthier Title applies to **personal property** as well as to land. It is a **rule of construction**, not a rule of law. It raises a **presumption** that no remainder has been created, but this presumption can be rebutted by evidence of a contrary intent of the grantor. [Doctor v. Hughes, 225 N.Y. 305 (1919)]

(1) **Justification:** [§547]   The Doctrine of Worthier Title can be justified as a rule designed to carry out the grantor's intent. It is assumed that grantors seldom intend to create a remainder in their heirs that they cannot change, and therefore, the Doctrine gives the grantor the right to change his mind by voiding the remainder and creating a reversion in the grantor. Another justification for the modern rule is that it makes property alienable earlier. In the above example, A and O can together convey a fee simple. If the Doctrine did not apply, a fee simple could not be conveyed until O's death, when O's heirs are ascertained.

c. **Operation of the Doctrine**

(1) **Limitation to heirs:** [§548]   For the Doctrine to apply, a future interest must be given to the grantor's "heirs" or "next of kin," or some equivalent term must be used. The Doctrine does **not** apply to a future interest limited to "O's children" or "O's issue," or to "O's heirs ascertained at the death of the life tenant A." [Braswell v. Braswell, 81 S.E.2d 560 (Va. 1954)] This requirement of the Doctrine is rather similar to the requirement of the Rule in Shelley's Case that the technical word "heirs" be used. (*See supra*, §534.)

(2) **Kind of future interest immaterial:** [§549]   The Doctrine applies to a **remainder** or an **executory interest** limited to O's heirs. The future interest may be **legal or equitable**, or subject to a condition precedent other than the ascertainment of heirs.

(3) **Preceding estate:** [§550]   The character of the estate preceding the future interest in O's heirs is immaterial. It may be a fee simple defeasible, fee tail, life estate, or term of years.

(4) **Typical applications**

(a) **Revocation of trust:** [§551]   Suppose that O conveys property "to X in trust to pay the income to O for life, and on O's death to convey the trust assets to O's heirs." O retains no power to revoke. Subsequently O wants to revoke the trust and get the property back. Under trust law, a trust can be terminated if **all owners** of the equitable interests consent. Hence, if O's heirs do not have a remainder, but O has a reversion, O owns all the equitable interests in the trust and can terminate it. Under the Doctrine of Worthier Title, O is presumed to have a reversion and can terminate the trust. (Of course, contrary evidence can show that O intended to create a remainder in O's heirs and there has been considerable litigation over what contrary evidence is sufficient to rebut the presumption of a reversion.)

(b) **Devise by O:** [§552] Suppose that O conveys Blackacre "to A for life, then to A's issue, and if A should die without issue, then the land shall go to O's heirs." Subsequently O dies, devising all his property to B. O's heir is C. Under the Doctrine, O is presumed to have a reversion (and his heirs nothing). Therefore, O devises his reversion to B. Later A dies without leaving issue. B and not C owns Blackacre at A's death. [Braswell v. Braswell, *supra*, §548; King v. Dunham, 31 Ga. 743 (1861)]

(5) **Effect of abolition of Rule in Shelley's Case:** [§553] The abolition of the Rule in Shelley's Case has no effect on the Doctrine of Worthier Title. Suppose that O conveys Blackacre "to X in trust to pay the income to O for life, remainder to O's heirs." Under the Rule in Shelley's Case, the remainder limited to O's heirs becomes a reversion in O, which merges with O's life estate, giving O an equitable fee simple. If the Rule in Shelley's Case has been abolished, what happens? The Doctrine of Worthier Title presumes that the remainder is void and O has a reversion. Thus, the result is the same as under the Rule in Shelley's Case.

d. **Abolition of Doctrine:** [§554] The Doctrine of Worthier Title, unlike the Rule in Shelley's Case, is still valid in most jurisdictions. It has been abolished in many states, including California, Massachusetts, and New York. Where it has been abolished, the heirs of O take the future interest limited to them under the instrument.

(1) **New York law:** [§555] New York has abolished the Doctrine of Worthier Title, but at the same time, New York has enacted a statute that permits the settlor of a trust to revoke the trust when he or she has created a remainder in his or her heirs but otherwise owns all the equitable interests in the trust. [N.Y. Est., Powers & Trusts Law §6-5.9] Thus, in the context of revocation of trusts (*see supra*, §551), New York law comes to the same result reached under the Doctrine of Worthier Title, even though the Doctrine has been abolished.

e. **Recapitulation and comparison:** [§556] The destructibility rule, the Rule in Shelley's Case, and the Doctrine of Worthier Title should be compared. A comparison is helpful in remembering how the rules apply.

(1) **Destructibility rule:** [§557] This rule applies only to **legal contingent remainders** in **land**. It does not apply to equitable interests, to interests in trust, nor to personal property. It is a **rule of law**, not a rule designed to carry out the grantor's intent.

(2) **Rule in Shelley's Case:** [§558]   This Rule applies to *legal and equitable remainders* in *land*. It does not apply to personal property. It is a *rule of law*, not a rule designed to carry out the grantor's intent.

(3) **Doctrine of Worthier Title:** [§559]   This Doctrine applies to *legal and equitable remainders* and *executory interests* in *real or personal property*. It is a *rule of construction* designed to carry out the grantor's intent, and can be overcome by contrary evidence of intent.

F. EXECUTORY INTERESTS

1. **Historical Background of Uses**

   a. **Origin of uses**

   (1) **Development of equity:** [§560]   After the Norman Conquest (A.D. 1066), the king imposed upon England a feudal system in which power was exercised by landowners. Royal judges were appointed to administer the system, but in time these law courts became formula-ridden, inflexible, and dominated by technical procedure. When persons failed to obtain a remedy at law, they turned to the king for relief. Their petitions were heard by the king's council, of which the chancellor was the most learned member. In time, the petitions came to be heard by the chancellor alone, and the chancellor gradually developed his own court—the court of chancery. In this court, which was independent of—and, indeed, was a rival of—the law courts, the chancellor administered a system of justice called equity. Chancery was a court of conscience, whereas the common law courts were courts of rules.

   (a) **Equitable remedies:** [§561]   The chancellor acted in personam (upon the person). His ultimate sanction was to imprison a person who disobeyed. He could not award damages, as the law courts could. His remedy was an injunction ordering a person to do or not to do an act.

   (b) **Conflict with law courts:** [§562]   The chancellor's decrees often conflicted with decrees of the law courts, particularly when he ordered a person not to execute a judgment obtained in the law courts. Ultimately, James I decided that in a dispute between equity and law, equity would prevail.

   (2) **Development of the "use":** [§563]   In feudal times, it was frequently found expedient to vest ownership of property in one person who would hold it for the use and benefit of another. One early example was where O, going off to fight a crusade, enfeoffed (*i.e.*, conveyed a freehold of land into the possession of) his brother, A, with the understanding that O's wife and children would have the *use* of the land. The common law courts refused to enforce uses, but the chancellor compelled the *feoffee to uses*, A, to hold the land in accordance with the understanding, on the ground that it was unconscionable to permit A to violate the confidence reposed in him.

(a) **Note on terminology:** [§564]   In the above example, A is the *feoffee to uses*, and O's wife and children are the *cestuis que use*. In a similar arrangement in modern times, one would say A is the *trustee* and O's wife and children are the *beneficiaries*.

(b) **Seisin:** [§565]   A, the feoffee to uses, was seised of the property by the feoffment from O. In enforcing the use in favor of O's wife and children, the chancellor did not move seisin from A. The chancellor merely directed A, holding seisin, to do certain things—or to go to jail.

(c) **Rights of cestui que use:** [§566]   The feoffee to uses was required by the chancellor to permit the cestui to take possession or the profits of the land, to dispose of the land as the cestui instructed, and to protect the land.

b. **Common law conveyancing before the Statute of Uses, and how the rules were bypassed in equity:** [§567]   The common law courts had a number of restrictive rules related to conveyancing, which could be circumvented in equity. Below, first are stated the restrictive rules applied by the law courts, and then under each rule is related how a clever equity lawyer could arrange matters to avoid the rule.

(1) **Livery of seisin required:** [§568]   At law, to pass title to land, the grantor must enfeoff the grantee in a ceremony called *livery of seisin*. The feoffment had to be performed on the land, by the parties going out on the land and O handing over a clod or twig to A (*see supra*, §278). This feoffment ceremony was useful evidence of a transfer of title in a society where few could read and write. But it was inconvenient to persons who might want to pass title in a London solicitor's office, rather than go on the land, perhaps many miles from London.

(a) **Bypass in equity:** [§569]   Equity offered a way to avoid the ceremony of livery. This was the *bargain and sale deed*. It worked this way: O executes a deed by which O *bargains and sells* Blackacre to A and his heirs *for a consideration* (say £100). At law, this was a nullity because seisin had not been manually conveyed on the land. But since A had paid money for the land, the chancellor thought it would be unconscionable for O to retain the land. Therefore, the chancellor required O to *stand seised for the use of A*.

(2) **No springing interests:** [§570]   At law, a grantor could not create a freehold estate to *spring out* in the future, because O could not create a freehold estate without conveying seisin. Seisin had to be handed over—it could not spring from O in the future. An attempt to make seisin spring out from the grantor in the future (a springing interest) was a nullity at law.

(a) **Example:** O conveys "to A and her heirs when she marries B." This attempt to make seisin spring out in the future was ineffective at law. Seisin remained in O.

(b) **Bypass in equity:** [§571]   Under the highly commercial marriage arrangements of the times, the bride with a rich father had to come with dowry. But O would not want his daughter, A, to have the property that comprised the dowry until she married B. On the other hand, the bridegroom, B, would want assurances that A would have property upon marriage. Law would not permit seisin to spring out of O, the grantor, in the future. But the chancellor offered relief. If O would "enfeoff X and his heirs to the use of O, and upon the marriage of A to B, to the use of A," the chancellor would enforce the use. X would be seised of the land, but O and his daughter were entitled to all the income and profits.

(3) **No shifting interest:** [§572] At law, a grantor could not create a future interest in a grantee that would cut short a freehold estate. This was known as a rule against shifting interests. The reasons for this rule were that O could not derogate from his grant to A, and O could not create a right of entry in a stranger, which a shifting interest resembled. (*Note:* A right of entry can be created only in the grantor; *see supra*, §440.)

   (a) **Example:** O has a son, B, who is studying for the priesthood in Rome, but he may return home. O conveys Blackacre "to A and his heirs, but if B returns from Rome, to B and his heirs." (There must have been a lot of going and coming from Rome in those days, because this is the standard example used in all the old texts.) By this conveyance, A takes a fee simple, and B has no interest recognized at law.

   (b) **Bypass in equity:** [§573] The chancellor, unconcerned with the logic of the law courts, saw no harm in shifting interests which permitted O to plan for contingent events. Therefore if O would "enfeoff X and his heirs to the use of A and his heirs, but if B returns from Rome to B and his heirs," the chancellor would enforce the uses against X. X was said to stand seised to the use of A and, if the condition happened, B.

(4) **Methods of creating a use:** [§574] In order to get into the chancellor's court, the instrument had to *raise a use*, which gave the chancellor jurisdiction. To raise a use, one of the following three methods of transfer had to be employed.

   (a) **Feoffment to uses:** [§575] If O "enfeoffed X and his heirs to the use of A and his heirs," O transferred seisin to X by the feoffment, and X held seisin to the use of A. Thus a *feoffment to uses* raised a use.

   (b) **Bargain and sale:** [§576] If O for a consideration executed a *bargain and sale deed* to A and his heirs, the deed raised a use in favor of A.

   (c) **Covenant to stand seised:** [§577] After the Statute of Uses (below), a new method of raising a use was recognized. If *O covenants under seal to stand seised* for the use of a *relative*, a use was raised, on the theory that natural love and affection sufficed as consideration for the use.

2. **The Statute of Uses (1536)**

a. **Background of Statute:** [§578] By the time of the Tudors, the greater part of English land was held in use. This happened because by raising a use, feudal incidents (death duties) could be avoided, and the rich then as now wanted to avoid taxes. How were feudal incidents avoided by raising a use? Recall that feudal incidents fell due when seisin of the land descended to heirs upon the death of a tenant (*supra*, §256). To avoid death duties, clever lawyers invented a device whereby seisin would almost never pass at the death of a person. O would enfeoff A, B, C, D, and E and their heirs as joint tenants to the use of O for life, then to the use of O's first son in fee tail, then to the use of O's second son in fee tail, etc. Under the theory of joint tenancy (*infra*, §§649 *et seq.*), no seisin passed to the surviving joint tenants when one died. When the number of joint tenants holding seisin grew dangerously low, some more persons could be enfeoffed jointly with them. It was principally this use of the use, which deprived the crown of its feudal revenues, that brought on the Statute of Uses. To restore his feudal revenues, Henry VIII, an extremely strong willed king, forced a reluctant Parliament to enact the Statute of Uses in 1535, to become effective in 1536.

b. **Purpose of Statute:** [§579] The purpose of the Statute was to abolish uses, turning them into legal estates which would be subject to all the usual feudal incidents upon death of the legal owner.

c. **What the Statute did:** [§580] The Statute provided in substance that, "[i]f any person be seised of land to the use of another, the person having the use shall henceforth be deemed in lawful seisin and possession of the same lands in such like estate as he had in use." The Statute is said, therefore, to have "executed" or "converted" the use into a legal estate.

  (1) **Example:** After 1536, O enfeoffs "X and his heirs to use of A and his heirs." The Statute "executes the use" and turns A's use into a legal fee simple in A. X gets nothing.

3. **Springing and Shifting Interests Made Possible:** [§581] By turning uses into legal estates, the Statute of Uses made possible legal shifting and springing future interests, recognized before 1536 in equity as uses. With the passage of the Statute of Uses, springing and shifting interests became possible at law, and they became known as *executory interests*.

  a. **Springing interest:** [§582] A springing executory interest is a future interest in a grantee that springs out of the grantor at a date subsequent to the granting of the interest, divesting the **grantor**. [Abbott v. Holway, 72 Me. 298 (1881)]

    (1) **Example:** O conveys "to A and her heirs when A marries." A has a springing executory interest. It will divest the fee simple of O, the transferor, if it becomes possessory.

    (2) **Example:** O conveys "to A for 100 years if A so long live, then to A's heirs." The attempted contingent future freehold in A's heirs was void at law prior to the Statue of Uses because it was impossible to transfer seisin either to A (a

termor) or to A's heirs (unascertained). After the Statute, the limitation to A's heirs was given effect as a springing executory interest. Seisin stays with O until the death of A, when it springs out to A's heirs.

(3) **Example:** O conveys "to A for life, and one day after A's death, to B and her heirs." B has a springing executory interest. The law assumes that at the death of A, the fee simple reverts to O and—one day later—springs out to B. Of course it is very strange to say that O has a reversion in fee simple, which will certainly end one day later. It is a general principle that the essence of a fee simple is that it has the possibility of infinite duration, and O's fee simple (in reversion) does not have that possibility. The explanation is: The Statute of Uses did not change the old estates valid at law; it only made possible new estates. Before the Statute, O had a reversion in fee simple and B's springing interest was void. After the Statute, O's reversion in fee simple stays the same, but B's interest is now valid. (On this point, as Holmes said of another, a page of history is worth a volume of logic!)

b. **Shifting interest:** [§583]   A shifting executory interest is a future interest in a grantee that divests a preceding estate in another grantee prior to its natural termination. The shifting interest, like the springing interest, divests a prior interest. The difference between them is that a **shifting** interest divests a **grantee**, whereas a **springing** interest divests the **grantor.**

(1) **Example:** O conveys "to A and his heirs, but if B returns from Rome, to B and his heirs." A has a fee simple subject to an executory interest. B has an executory interest. (B's interest **cannot** be a remainder, because it is a divesting interest and remainders never divest.)

(2) **Example:** O conveys "to A for life, and on A's death, to B and his heirs, but if B does not survive A, to C and his heirs." C has a shifting executory interest—it vests, if at all, by cutting off B's vested remainder. Why is B's remainder vested? Remember to classify interests **in sequence.** B's interest comes first, and therefore must be classified first. Once it is classified as a vested remainder in fee, any further future interest in a grantee is necessarily a divesting executory interest. A remainder cannot follow a vested fee simple, either in possession or in remainder, and therefore C's interest cannot be a remainder if B's prior estate is a vested remainder in fee.

c. **An oddity:** [§584]   An executory interest is always either a springing or a shifting interest—except in the case of a future interest in a grantee following a **fee simple determinable.** This executory interest is neither springing nor shifting because the fee simple determinable ends by its own special limitation. The executory interest does not divest it but **succeeds** it.

(1) **Example:** O conveys Blackacre "to Board of Education so long as used for school purposes, then to the Red Cross." The Red Cross has an executory interest. *Rationale:* For obscure historical reasons, there cannot be a remainder

after any type of fee simple. The only other permissible future interest in a grantee is an executory interest, so the interest in the Red Cross is called an executory interest.

d. **Necessity of raising a use:** [§585]   For some years after the Statute of Uses, the grantor had to **raise a use** upon which the Statute would operate—if the grantor wished to create these new springing and shifting interests. If the grantor did not raise a use, to be converted by the Statute, he was caught within the old common law conveyancing rules.

    (1) **Example:** O "enfeoffs X and his heirs to the use of A for 100 years if he so long live, then to A's heirs." The **feoffment to uses** raised uses which were executed by the Statute, converting A's equitable term of years into a legal term of years, and converting the equitable springing interest in A's heirs into a legal springing interest. This shows the proper way of raising a use. On the other hand, if O had not enfeoffed X to the use of A, etc., but instead had enfeoffed A directly (O "enfeoffs A for 100 years if A so long live, then to A's heirs"), no use would be raised, the Statute would not operate, and the interest in A's heirs would be void. In the years immediately after the Statute, what was void at law prior to the Statute remained void unless the grantor **raised a use** on which the Statute operated.

    (2) **Modern law:** [§586]   In time, courts held that a use on which the Statute could operate would be implied where necessary to carry out the intent of the parties. Today no special form of conveyance raising a use is necessary to the creation of executory interests. Springing and shifting interests can be created in any jurisdiction by an ordinary deed or by will.

    (3) **Executory devises:** [§587]   In the years immediately following the Statute of Uses, executory interests were divided into springing and shifting **uses,** created by deed, and executory **devises,** created by wills. The latter were permitted by the Statute of Wills, enacted in 1540. Today there is no difference between executory interests created by deed and those created by will, and this distinction in terminology has passed out of common speech. Whether created by deed or will, springing and shifting interests are called executory interests.

4. **Effect on Destructibility of Contingent Remainders:** [§588]   The recognition of executory interests had no effect on the rule of destructibility of contingent remainders (*supra,* §493). Contingent remainders continued to be destroyed if they did not vest at or before the termination of the preceding freehold.

    a. **Executory interests are indestructible:** [§589]   Executory interests are indestructible because no gap in seisin can ever precede these interests. In the case of a **shifting** executory interest, this interest shifts seisin away from a prior vested interest prior to its termination. By definition, no gap in seisin occurs; the executory interest simply grabs seisin from the preceding holder. *Example:* O conveys "to A and his heirs, but if B returns from Rome, to B and his heirs." In the case of a **springing** executory interest, it always shifts seisin out of the grantor in the future. *Example:* O conveys "to A and her heirs upon my death."

(1) **Example:** Lawrence Doyle conveys Blackacre "to Frank Doyle and his heirs, but if Frank dies leaving a widow and children, to his widow for life, remainder to Frank's children who survive him, and if none survive him title shall revert to the grantor." Subsequently Lawrence conveys all his interest in Blackacre to Frank. If Frank took a life estate with contingent remainders in his widow and children, the subsequent conveyance of the reversion by Lawrence would destroy the contingent remainders. But Frank did not take a life estate. Frank took a fee simple, and the interests of his widow and children are executory interests. They cannot be destroyed by any conveyance of Lawrence to Frank. [*Stoller v. Doyle, supra,* §505]

b. **Contingent remainders remain destructible:** [§590] Contingent remainders remained destructible after the Statute of Uses. Suppose that O conveys Blackacre "to A for life, remainder to A's children who reach age 21." Subsequently A dies leaving only minor children. Under the rule of destructibility of contingent remainders, the remainder is destroyed. Why not give it effect *after* A's death as a springing executory interest? The judges could have done so if they had disfavored the destructibility rule, but they favored the destructibility rule because it made land alienable. Therefore they held, in *Purefoy v. Rogers,* 35 Eng. Rep. 1181 (1670), that any limitation capable of taking effect as a remainder must be construed to be a remainder and could not take effect as an executory interest. This was simply another way of stating that the destructibility rule was still in effect. A remainder—once destroyed under the destructibility rule—could not rise again as an executory interest.

c. **Rule Against Perpetuities made necessary:** [§591] The fact that executory interests were indestructible made it necessary—or so the judges thought—to invent a Rule Against Perpetuities to curb them. Otherwise by a succession of shifting interests, land could be tied up in the family indefinitely, thus: O conveys Blackacre "to A and his heirs, but if A die leaving a son, to such son and his heirs, and if such son should thereafter die leaving a son, to such son's son and his heirs, and if . . . (etc.)." Once the Rule Against Perpetuities was developed, it was extended to contingent remainders. At that point the movement to abolish the destructibility rule caught fire in England and in the American states. Today most states have abolished the destructibility rule, and only one rule—the Rule Against Perpetuities—governs the duration of contingent future interests.

5. **Effect of Statute of Uses on Conveyancing**

a. **Feoffment:** [§592] The Statute of Uses, for the first time, permitted legal title to be conveyed by a bargain and sale deed. Although feoffment was not abolished by the Statute, the convenience of transferring title by deed doomed the practice of livery of seisin of land, especially when the land was many miles removed from London. In 1677, the ***Statute of Frauds*** was enacted, requiring a ***written instrument*** to transfer title to land. The Statute of Frauds made livery of seisin obsolete unless accompanied by a written charter of feoffment.

b. **Bargain and sale deed:** [§593]   After the Statute of Uses, a bargain and sale deed could be used to raise a use which the Statute converted into a legal estate. The bargain and sale deed avoided feoffment with livery of seisin, but the ***Statute of Enrollments*** (1535) imposed a tax on any bargain and sale of a ***freehold***. Thus the convenience of a bargain and sale deed came at a cost.

c. **Lease and release:** [§594]   To avoid both the tax on the bargain and sale deed of a freehold and the inconvenience of livery of seisin, lawyers invented the ***lease and release***. It worked this way: O bargains and sells to A for one year. The bargain and sale raises a use in A, which is executed by the Statute of Uses, giving A a legal term of years. No tax has to be paid because A does not take a freehold. O then releases his reversion to A. This operates as a common law release of a future interest, not as a bargain and sale deed. The term of years and reversion merge, giving A a fee simple. This complicated method of conveying A a legal fee simple, which avoided a public ceremony and taxation, became standard procedure. It was not finally abolished until the ninteenth century.

d. **Covenant to stand seised:** [§595]   The covenant to stand seised developed after the Statute of Uses to transfer legal title to a near relative (*supra*, §577), but it could not be employed to convey title to a stranger.

e. **Modern deeds:** [§596]   Under modern law, a single simple deed using the verbs "grant," or "bargain and sell," or "convey," or similar language, is sufficient to create or transfer any kind of possessory or nonpossessory interest.

6. **Equity After the Statute of Uses:** [§597]   The Statute of Uses revived the crown's feudal revenues considerably, but loopholes were ultimately discovered in the Statute, and lawyers exploited them. Both common law judges and chancellors held that the Statute was in derogation of the common law and was to be strictly construed. After feudal incidents were abolished in 1660, the crown had no pecuniary interest in the Statute of Uses, and the chancellors thereafter systematically developed the modern trust—which made it possible again to separate the beneficial interest from the legal title.

a. **How the Statute was avoided:** [§598]   The Statute of Uses did not abolish the practice of conveying to uses. It merely converted the equitable estate into a legal estate. In some cases the Statute was held not applicable. These were called cases of ***unexecuted uses,*** of which the two most important were the following.

(1) **Use-on-a-use not executed:** [§599]   The Statute did not operate on a **use-on-a-use**. The law courts held that the Statute of Uses executed only ***one use***; that is, it converted only the first equitable estate into a legal estate. [Tyrell's Case, 2 Dyer 155a (1557)] The Statute did not operate to execute the second use.

(a) **Example:** O enfeoffs "A and his heirs for the ***use*** of B and his heirs for the ***use*** of C and his heirs." The Statute executes the first use, giving B legal title. It does not execute the second use; therefore, C has equitable title.

The judges had a notion that the second use (C's use) was repugnant and contrary to the first use (B's use), so they held it void. Some years later the chancellor—having grown bold again—held that the second use might be void at law, but he would give it effect in equity. Thus, in a way, the early history of the rise of uses repeated itself—but this time around the chancellor held that he would enforce a **trust** against B for C's benefit. The language of trusts superseded the language of uses.

(b) **Use to grantee's own use:** [§600]   The doctrine that the Statute executed only one use was extended, in the nineteenth century, to a conveyance "to A and his heirs **for his own use** for the use of B and his heirs." The Statute executed the first use, giving A a legal fee simple, but it did not execute the second use (B's). Thus the Statute could be nullified by the insertion of four words in an instrument, "for his own use." By the time this happened, however, equity had developed the modern trust, and the Statute of Uses had declined in importance.

(2) **Active duties imposed:** [§601]   The second class of cases where the Statute of Uses did not execute a use was where the feoffee to uses had **active duties**. Before the Statute the feoffee to uses had two duties, namely to defend the property against third persons and to convey the property as the cestui que use directed. These were regarded as passive trusts. The courts held that the Statute converted passive trusts only, and had no application where the feoffee was given active duties. Enforcing a use where there were active duties was, at bottom, purely an invention to circumvent the Statute of Uses. [Symson v. Turner, 21 Eng. Rep. 1119 (1700)]

(a) **Example:** O conveys "to X and his heirs **to manage** the property and pay the net income to A for life, and on A's death **to convey** the property to A's children." With respect to A, X has active duties (managing the property), and, therefore, A has an equitable life estate not converted into a legal life estate by the Statute. With respect to A's children, there is a split of authority as to whether the **duty to convey** is an active duty. The majority holds it is, and A's children have an equitable remainder. The minority holds it is not an active duty, and the Statute converts the equitable remainder in A's children into a legal remainder.

(b) **The modern trust:** [§602]   Building on the idea that the Statute did not operate where the feoffee to uses was given active duties, the chancellors developed the modern trust. In a trust, the trustee owns the legal title and the beneficiaries have equitable title. The trustee manages the property for their benefit and has the active duties of management. Generally speaking, it is possible to divide the equitable title into the same possessory estates and future interests as are permitted at law. (The trust is discussed in detail *infra*, §§806 *et seq.*)

1) **Example:** O conveys "to X and his heirs in trust for the benefit of A for life, then for B, and if B does not survive A, for C." X has the legal fee

simple, A has an equitable life estate, B has an equitable vested remainder in fee, subject to being divested by C's equitable executory interest in fee.

b. **Personal property:** [§603]   As there is no seisin in personal property, the Statute of Uses did not operate on uses created in personal property. Hence, if O transferred an East India Company bond to A and his heirs for the use of B and her heirs, the Statute would not operate. B's interest remained equitable. Most modern trusts consist of assets comprised of stocks and bonds and cash. The Statute of Uses has no application to such property.

7. **The Statute of Uses Today:** [§604]   The Statute of Uses has been accepted as a common law statute in most states. But some states have not accepted it, and others have repealed it. All of this matters little, however, because in *all jurisdictions* the two basic reforms of the Statute are effective: (i) a conveyance can be made by deed; and (ii) springing and shifting interests can be created.

G. THE RULE AGAINST PERPETUITIES

1. **Historical Background:** [§605]   Beginning with the Statute Quia Emptores (1290) (*supra*, §261), the idea of free alienation of property was an important force in the development of English property law. From feudal times to the nineteenth century, judges and the landed aristocracy engaged in a continuing series of running battles, the lords trying to find means of keeping land in the family, the judges trying to curb the dynastic devices invented by lawyers for the lords. The judges defeated the early dynastic device of the fee tail by permitting a fee tail tenant to engage in a fictitious lawsuit (known as a common recovery) which resulted in a fee simple (*see supra*, §361). Afterwards lawyers for the landed aristocracy turned to the creation of life estates and remainders as dynastic devices, but the judges threw up new roadblocks or firmed up existing ones. The three main hindrances to the dynastic urge were the rule of destructibility of contingent remainders (*supra*, §493), the Rule in Shelley's Case (*supra*, §513), and the Doctrine of Worthier Title (*supra*, §542). But these rules only applied to remainders, and a century after the Statute of Uses (1536) it appeared that some new rule would be necessary to curb executory interests made possible by the Statute. No existing rule clearly prohibited the creation of an indefinite series of shifting executory interests. *Duke of Norfolk's Case*, 3 Ch. Cas. 1 (1682), laid the foundation for a new Rule Against Perpetuities. As finally agreed upon, the Rule applies to all contingent future interests, contingent remainders as well as executory interests. After the Rule developed fully, the older rules applicable to contingent remainders alone (destructibility and Shelley's Case) were abolished in most jurisdictions. Thus, the Rule Against Perpetuities stands today as the principal guardian against the control of the living by the dead hand. (For a detailed treatment of this Rule, *see* Future Interests Summary.)

2. **Statement of the Rule:** [§606]   The classic formulation of the Rule is by John Chipman Gray, one of the first great teachers of property law at Harvard: *No interest is good unless it must vest, if at all, not later than twenty-one years after some life in being*

at the creation of the interest. Although Gray put the Rule in this one sentence, it took him more than 800 pages to explain it in the fourth edition of his treatise on the Rule. This subject will be covered in considerably fewer words here.

3. **Interests Subject to the Rule:** [§607]   The Rule applies to **contingent remainders** and **executory interests**. It does **not** apply to vested remainders nor to future interests in the grantor (reversion, possibility of reverter, and right of entry), which are treated as vested upon creation.

   a. **Example:** O conveys "to A for life, then to A's children for their lives, then to B and his heirs," A has no children. The conveyance is entirely valid. The remainder for life given to A's children will vest at A's death. The remainder in fee simple in B is a vested remainder when created.

4. **What-Might-Happen Is Test:** [§608]   The Rule is directed at the creation of **contingent** interests that might vest in the distant future (the distant future being defined as more than twenty one years after lives in being at the creation of the interest). If there is **any possibility** that a contingent interest will vest too remotely, the contingent interest is **void** from the outset. The thing to look for is the possibility of remote vesting. Courts do not wait to see what happens, but look at the interest at the time of creation and determine then if the interest will necessarily **vest or fail** within the period set by the Rule. If it will not necessarily vest or fail within the period—if there is any possibility that it may vest beyond the period—is it void.

   a. **Example:** In 1985, O conveys "to the first child of A who becomes a lawyer." A has a daughter D in law school. The gift is void. It is possible for the first child of A who becomes a lawyer to be a child not alive in 1985. This is what **might happen**. D may die before becoming a lawyer. Then A, bereft at D's death and desiring a lawyer in the family, procreates another child—Hope—born in 1987. In 1988, A dies. Some twenty-five years later, in 2013, Hope becomes a lawyer and claims the gift—but this is more than twenty-one years after the death of A. Thus, the gift is void.

   b. **Rule is a rule of proof:** [§609]   The preceding example illustrates that the Rule is a **rule of proof.** The person claiming the gift is valid must prove without the shadow of a doubt that there is no possibility of it vesting too remotely. The person claiming the gift is void must prove the opposite—*i.e.,* that there is a possibility of remote vesting. Whoever can prove the case wins.

      (1) **Possibility of vesting in time not sufficient:** [§610]   The Rule strikes down an interest if there is **any possibility** of remote vesting. It will not save the gift to prove that the gift **might** vest within the period. To save it, it must **necessarily** vest or fail within the period. Hence, in the preceding example, D cannot save the gift by showing it might vest in her. She must prove that it cannot vest in anyone beyond the period, and that she cannot do.

5. **Who Are Lives in Being?** [§611]   This is a crucial question, and if the beginning student of perpetuities law understands the answer he or she will have gone a long way to

understanding the Rule. The answer is: The measuring lives are those that permit you to prove that the interest is valid. Hence, measuring lives are validating lives. To sustain the validity of a contingent interest, the claimant must prove that the interest will necessarily vest or fail within twenty-one years after the death of some person now alive, *whom the claimant must name*. If the claimant cannot prove that the contingency will necessarily be resolved within twenty-one years of some named person's death, the interest is void ab initio. The only persons you need consider in making the proof are the persons who can affect vesting (*i.e.*, who can affect the identity of the beneficiaries or any condition precedent involved). These persons are known as the *persons causally related to vesting*. If a validating life is found (*i.e.*, a person who enables you to prove that the interest will vest or fail during, or within twenty-one years of the expiration of, such person's life), it will necessarily be found among the causally-related lives. It is impossible for a person who is not causally related to vesting to validate the gift. For example, in a bequest "to A when A marries" or "to A's first child," the measuring life is A because the contingency (marriage or birth of a child) must happen, if at all, during A's life (or within a period of gestation thereafter). Similarly, if the bequest is "to A's first child to reach age 21" the two contingencies (*birth* of a child who *reaches age 21*) must happen, if at all, within A's lifetime plus a period of gestation and twenty-one years thereafter. Now take a more difficult example, where there are no measuring lives, no lives by which you can prove the gift valid.

a. **Example:** O conveys "to A for life, remainder to A's first child who reaches age 25." A has no child at the date of the conveyance. The remainder is void because you cannot prove that it will necessarily vest or fail within twenty-one years of A's death or the death of any other person you can name. Suppose that one year after the conveyance A has a child C born. Then A dies, and twenty-four years after A dies, C reaches age 25 and the remainder vests. This is more than twenty-one years after A's death. Hence, A is useless in making the necessary proof. No other lives can help in making the proof either. (If A had a child alive age 24, the gift would still be void for the same reason the gift above to the "first child of A to become a lawyer" is void. The existing child can die tomorrow and not be the taker.)

b. **Example:** Professor Jones gives $1,000 to be divided among all members of her property class who are admitted to the bar. This gift is good. The members of the property class are the measuring or validating lives. The gift must vest or fail within their lives. (One cannot be admitted to the bar after one is dead.) How does this differ from the example above of a gift "to the first child of A who becomes a lawyer"? Here all possible takers are persons in being, and all you have to prove is that the condition precedent (admission to the bar) must happen, if at all, during their lives. In the earlier example, the taker might be a child of A not now in being. Therefore you could not prove that admission to the bar would necessarily take place, if at all, within lives in being.

c. **Lives in being when?** [§612]   The lives in being must be persons alive *at the creation of the interest*. In the case of an interest created by will, the lives in being must be persons alive at testator's death. In the case of an irrevocable inter vivos transfer, lives in being must be persons alive at the date of the transfer. In the case of a revocable trust, the period begins to run when the right to revoke terminates.

d. **Periods of gestation:** [§613]   Any actual periods of gestation are included within the permissible perpetuities period. For purposes of the Rule (as for all property law purposes), a person is treated as in being from the time of conception if later born alive.

(1) **Example:** T devises property "to my children for their lives, then to my grand-children who reach age 21." At T's death, his wife is pregnant and four months later gives birth to a son A. A shares in the life estate. At the death of A, his wife is pregnant and three months later gives birth to B. The gift to T's grand-children is good, and B shares in it if B reaches age 21.

e. **Reasonable number of lives:** [§614]   The measuring lives must be reasonable in number. They must not be so difficult to trace as to make evidence of their deaths unreasonably difficult to obtain. A bequest "to A's issue after the death of the last person now alive" is void.

6. **The Twenty-One Year Period:** [§615]   Why was the period of lives in being plus twenty one years selected? The judges thought it reasonable for a person to be able to tie up property for the lives of persons he knows (and perhaps deems incompetent to manage property) and for actual minorities thereafter. As the Rule was worked out over time, the original actual minorities period was turned into a twenty one-year period in gross. This proved to be a useful addition. If there are no relevant measuring lives, an interest is valid if it will vest or fail within twenty one years.

7. **Meaning of "Vest":** [§616]   The four-letter word "vest" in the Rule has an uncommon ability to beget other four-letter words, for it is here that all the learning about vested and contingent remainders discussed earlier (*supra,* §§455 *et seq.*) becomes relevant—indeed, decisive. A vested interest is not subject to the Rule Against Perpetuities; a contingent interest is.

a. **Exception—class gift:** [§617]   There is one major exception to applying the learning about vested and contingent remainders under the Rule Against Perpetuities. A *gift to a class* is not vested *in any member of the class until the interests of all members have vested.* Or to put it differently, a class gift is not vested under the Rule Against Perpetuities until the *class has closed* and *all conditions precedent have been satisfied* for every member of the class. If the gift to one member of the class might vest too remotely, the whole class gift is void. This is known as the "all-or-nothing" rule.

(1) **Example:** O conveys "to A for life, remainder to A's children who reach age 25." At the time of conveyance A has a child, B, age 26. Under standard classification discussed earlier, the remainder is vested in B subject to open, but *it is not vested under the Rule Against Perpetuities.* The remainder is a class gift and is *entirely void.* It is not possible to prove that all of A's children will reach age 25 within twenty-one years of A's death. It is possible for B to die tomorrow, and then for A to die leaving a child, C, age one. The gift will not vest in the afterborn child, C, until twenty-four years after A's death. This is too remote. The possibility of the gift vesting too remotely in one child voids the entire class gift. [Hagemann v. National Bank & Trust Co., 237 S.E.2d 388 (Va. 1977)]

b. **Executory interest:** [§618] An executory interest following a fee simple determinable or divesting a fee simple cannot vest in interest before it vests in possession. An executory interest following a determinable fee or divesting a fee simple **vests only when the condition happens and it becomes a possessory estate**.

8. **Application to Defeasible Fees:** [§619] The Rule Against Perpetuities does **not** apply to possibilities of reverter and rights of entry, which are regarded as vested interests, but it does apply to executory interests. This exemption of possibilities of reverter and rights of entry from the Rule has led to some strange results.

a. **Determinable fee:** [§620] A possibility of reverter is exempt from the Rule. An executory interest is subject to it. Any executory interest following a determinable fee which violates the Rule Against Perpetuities is struck out, as with a blue pencil, leaving the determinable fee standing. Whatever is left after striking out the void interest is given effect as written.

(1) **Example:** O conveys Blackacre "to the School Board so long as used for school purposes, and if the land shall cease to be used for school purposes to A and his heirs." A's executory interest, if valid, would be transmissible to A's heirs, and their heirs, and so on through time. It might not become possessory for centuries, and certainly it will not necessarily become possessory within lives in being at the date of O's conveyance plus twenty-one years. (A cannot be a measuring life because A's death cannot cause the vesting or failure of the executory interest in any way—A is irrelevant to vesting.) A's executory interest is void. The language "and if the land shall cease to be used for school purposes to A and his heirs," which is the language giving A an executory interest, is struck out. This leaves standing, "to the School Board so long as used for school purposes." This language gives the Board a determinable fee, which is not increased by striking out A's interest. Since the Board has only a determinable fee which will automatically end when the land ceases to be used for school purposes, O has a **possibility of reverter**. [First Universalist Society v. Boland, 29 N.E. 524 (Mass. 1892); City of Klamath Falls v. Flitcraft, 490 P.2d 515 (Or. 1972)]

(a) **Criticism:** This result is absurd in terms of policy. The land is tied up for exactly the same amount of time whether the future interest is an executory interest in a grantee or a possibility of reverter in the grantor. The result follows only because the possibility of reverter is exempt from the Rule, whereas the executory interest is subject to it.

(b) **How O should do it:** [§621] The lawyer for O can accomplish O's desires in the preceding example by using two deeds instead of one. The lawyer calls O, A, and a representative of the School Board into her office. The lawyer has prepared a deed reading, "O conveys Blackacre to A and A's heirs." O hands this deed to A. A now owns Blackacre. The lawyer has also prepared a deed reading, "A conveys Blackacre to the School Board so long as used for school purposes." A hands this to the Board representative. This gives the Board a determinable fee, leaving a possibility of reverter in A exempt from the Rule Against Perpetuities. Thus two pieces of paper rather than one will do the trick—and the lawyer may be liable for malpractice if she does not use them.

(2) **Exception—gift over from one charity to another charity:** [§622]   If there is a gift to Charity A followed by a divesting gift to Charity B if a specified event happens, the executory interest in Charity B is ***exempt from the Rule Against Perpetuities***. Thus, in the above example, if O had conveyed "to the School Board so long as used for school purposes, then to the Red Cross," the conveyance would be entirely valid. The reason for this exception is as follows. Charities are favorites of the law. A charitable trust can last forever. There is no objection to shifting enjoyment from charity to charity through time. *But note:* This exception applies ***only*** if ***both*** the possessory estate and the future interest are in charitable organizations.

b.   **Fee simple subject to an executory limitation:** [§623]   The example of the determinable fee above should be compared with a fee simple subject to an executory limitation. The difference in language is very slight but the difference in results is startling. Suppose that O conveys Blackacre "to the School Board, but if Blackacre shall cease to be used for school purposes to A and his heirs." The executory interest in A is void under the Rule Against Perpetuities for the same reason A's executory interest in the preceding example is void. The language creating the executory interest—"but if Blackacre shall cease to be used for school purposes to A and his heirs"—is struck out. This leaves a conveyance "to the School Board," which of course gives the Board a fee simple absolute. [*Proprietors of the Church in Brattle Square v. Grant*, 69 Mass. 142 (1855)]

c.   **Fee simple determinable created by will:** [§624]   A possibility of reverter is an interest which is retained by the grantor. if the determinable fee is created by a deed, or is retained by the testator's heirs, if the determinable fee is created by a will. A possibility of reverter cannot be created in a grantee—nor in a devisee. Hence, if testator creates a determinable fee by will, followed by a void executory interest in a devisee, testator's heirs have a possibility of reverter.

(1) **Example:** T devises Blackacre "to the Baptist Church so long as used for church purposes, then to A. All the rest and remainder of my property I devise to B." A's executory interest violates the Rule Against Perpetuities and is struck out, leaving a determinable fee in the church. T's heirs— and ***not B***— have a possibility of reverter. If B, the residuary devisee, were given the future interest after the determinable fee, B's interest as a residuary devisee would be an executory interest (just as A's interest as a specific devisee was an executory interest), and B's interest would be void. [*In re* Pruner's Estate, 162 A.2d 626 (Pa. 1960)]

(2) **Minority view:** [§625]   There is a Massachusetts case analyzing the above example in a different way: T created a determinable fee in the Church. A's executory interest is void under the Rule. This leaves a possibility of reverter in

testator, which passes to B under the residuary clause. T's heirs take nothing. [Brown v. Independence Baptist Church of Woburn, 91 N.E.2d 922 (Mass. 1950)] This view is logically fallacious, and assumes T died twice. Observe that one crucial step in the reasoning is that "this leaves a possibility of reverter in testator." But this cannot be. Testator is dead! Property rights cannot be created in a dead person. The law substitutes testator's heirs for testator, and if the possibility of reverter is left in testator's heirs, it is their property and cannot be disposed of by the residuary clause. This Massachusetts view assumes that testator died once to create the determinable fee, leaving a possibility of reverter in the resurrected testator, who died a second time to pass the possibility of reverter to B. *Remember:* A possibility of reverter cannot be created in any transferee—neither a grantee in a deed nor a devisee in a will.

9. **Remote Possibilities:** [§626] An interest is void under the Rule Against Perpetuities if by *any possibility*—however remote—the interest might vest beyond the permitted period. If a situation can be *imagined* in which the interest might not vest or fail within lives in being plus twenty one years, the interest is void. The following cases illustrate the harsh and sometimes surprising consequences of a vivid judicial imagination. They are the classic "traps for the unwary" that have brought the remote possibilities test under fire in recent years.

a. **The fertile octogenarian:** [§627] The law conclusively presumes that a person can have children so long as the person is alive. Evidence that a person is 80 years of age or has had a hysterectomy or vasectomy is irrelevant. After all, a person of any age can adopt a child. This principle is frequently overlooked by lawyers who naturally assume that 80-year-old persons will not have any more children, and proceed to draw instruments in violation of the Rule Against Perpetuities.

(1) **Example:** T devises property "to Mary, and if Mary's line of descendants ever runs out, to the daughters then living of Elizabeth Jee (aged 80)." T is survived by Mary, Elizabeth, and four daughters of Elizabeth. The event upon which the executory interest is conditioned—expiration of Mary's line of descent—is an event which may happen centuries hence. Is the gift to the Jee daughters valid? No. There are no measuring lives by which the gift can be proved valid. The executory interest will not necessarily vest or fail in Mary's life, nor in Elizabeth's life. What about in the lifetimes of the Jee daughters living at T's death? It says to the Jee daughters "then living," which requires the Jee daughters *to be alive* when the event happens or the gift fails. Why will the gift not vest *or* fail within the lives of the presently living daughters? Because Elizabeth Jee, aged 80, can have another daughter (call her Hope) and the gift can vest in Hope and not in the daughters now living. Hope, being now unborn, is not a life in being. [Jee v. Audley, 29 Eng. Rep. 1186 (1787)]

b. **The unborn widow:** [§628] The law assumes that a person's surviving spouse might turn out to be a person not now alive. For example, a man's present wife may die or be divorced, and the man may in the future marry a woman not now alive. This assumption leads to the unborn widow case.

(1) **Example:** T devises property "to my son A for his life, then to my son's widow for her life, then to my son's issue who survive my son and his widow." The life estate in the son's widow is valid because it will necessarily vest or fail at the son's death. The remainder to the son's issue is void because it will not vest until the death of the son's widow, and she may be a person not now alive.

c. **The slothful executor:** [§629]   The law assumes that a will may not be probated, nor a dead person's property distributed, within lives in being plus twenty-one years. Indeed, a few wills have been probated forty, sixty, or eighty years after testator's death. But this is rare. Ordinarily a decedent's estate is closed within five years of death. Nonetheless, any administrative contingency regarding the settlement of a decedent's estate may cause a gift to violate the Rule Against Perpetuities.

(1) **Example:** T devises Blackacre "to W for life, then to A, B, and C if they survive W, and if any of them do not survive W that share of any of them who is deceased at W's death to go to his executor or administrator to be applied by such as if it formed a part of his estate." T devises the residue of his estate to D. The remainders to A, B, and C are valid. Their remainders will vest if at all during their own lives, when they survive W. The alternative contingent remainders in the executors or administrators of A, B, and C are void because no one might be appointed executor or administrator within twenty-one years of their deaths. Thus, if A dies before W, his one-third share of the remainder fails and falls into the residue which passes to D. [Ryan v. Beshk, 170 N.E. 699 (Ill. 1930)]

10. **Application to Options:** [§630]   An option creates in the optionee a specifically enforceable right to purchase the property on the terms provided in the option. Because specifically enforceable, this right is regarded as an equitable interest in property. An option is void if it can be exercised more than twenty-one years after some life in being at its creation. The policy reason for subjecting options to the Rule is that with an option outstanding the owner will not dare to improve the land, and no one else will likely purchase it. Thus, options tend to make land unimprovable and inalienable.

a. **Example:** O conveys "to Union Oil Co. an option to purchase Blackacre, which option must be exercised within 120 days after the city acquires the right of way for widening a street fronting Blackacre." (The purpose of this option is, if the city widens the street, Union Oil wants Blackacre for a service station.) The option is void. The city might acquire the right of way many, many years from now. Therefore, the option will not necessarily be exercised within the perpetuities period. [United Virginia Bank/Citizens & Marine v. Union Oil Co., 197 S.E.2d 174 (Va. 1973)]

b. **Preemptive options:** [§631]   A preemptive option gives the optionee the right of first refusal if the owner desires to sell. If the preemptive option can be exercised beyond the perpetuities period, the option is void. The policy reason for subjecting preemptive options to the Rule is that after a period of time ascertaining and locating the owners of the preemptive option—who may be heirs of heirs of the original optionee—would be an unreasonable task.

(1) **Example:** O buys Blackacre from A by a deed that provides "whenever O desires to sell Blackacre, A has the right to repurchase Blackacre upon the same terms and conditions as O might be willing to sell it to another person." The preemptive option in A is void. [Atchison v. City of Englewood, 463 P.2d 297 (Colo. 1969); Pace v. Culpepper, 347 So. 2d 1313 (Miss. 1977)]

11. **Wait-and-See Doctrine:** [§632]   Under the common law Rule Against Perpetuities any possibility of remote vesting voids the interest. The what-might-happen test has come under fire in the last thirty years (fueled by widespread resentment at the results in cases of the fertile octogenarian, the unborn widow, and the slothful executor, above). About half the states have reformed the Rule. One of the reforms adopted is the wait-and-see doctrine. Under the wait-and-see doctrine, the validity of interests is judged by *actual events* as they happen, and not by possible events that might happen. The validity of an interest is not determined at the time the interest is created. It is necessary to wait and see what actually happens.

a. **Example:** T devises property "to A for life, then to A's children, but if all of A's children shall die without issue surviving at the time of their deaths, to B and his heirs." At T's death, A has one daughter C alive. Under the orthodox common law rule, the gift to B is void because A can have a child born after T's death and B's executory interest can vest upon the death of that as-yet-unborn child without issue. Under the wait-and-see doctrine, the court waits until A is dead. If A does not have another child, B's executory interest will divest C's vested remainder on C's death, if at all. Since C was a life in being at T's death, B's executory interest is valid. On the other hand, if A has a child after T's death, there is a further wait to see if this child survives C by more than twenty-one years. In other words, B's executory interest will be valid if it in fact vests within twenty-one years after the death of A and C. [Merchants National Bank v. Curtis, 97 A.2d 207 (N.H. 1953)]

b. **Measuring lives:** [§633]   What lives do you wait out? Implicit in wait-and-see is that you wait out the lives causally related to vesting. The wait-and-see doctrine states that it is not fatal that you did not find a validating life among the lives causally related to vesting. You can wait out these lives and see if the interest vests within twenty-one years after their expiration. Some states have chosen to make these measuring lives for wait-and-see explicit. A few states have chosen other lives than causally-related lives as measuring lives for wait-and-see.

(1) **Life estates:** [§634]   Four states adopting wait-and-see wait out only preceding life estates, and then determine the validity of the future interest on the basis of facts then existing.

(2) **Lives causally related to vesting:** [§635]   Five states adopting the wait-and-see doctrine have provided that the measuring lives are those causally related to vesting. Any person who is related to the occurrence of events that lead to vesting, either in possession or in interest, has a causal relationship to vesting of the interest. For example, a remainder cannot vest in possession until the life tenant dies, and therefore a life tenant is causally related to vesting. What lives are causally related to vesting in interest? A future interest is not vested in

interest until it is in an *ascertainable person* and *not subject to a condition precedent* and, in the case of a class gift, *the class is closed* and *all conditions precedent are satisfied for every member* of the class so that the *size of the shares is fixed.* If a person can affect the identity of the beneficiaries, any condition precedent, the closing of the class, or the size of the shares of a class gift, the person is causally related to vesting.

(a) **Example:** O conveys Blackacre "to A for life, remainder to A's children who reach age 25." The causally related lives are A and all of A's children living at the testator's death. Those children of A under age 25 can affect both the identity of the class members and the size of the class members' shares (by dying under 25). Those children over age 25 at the testator's death affect the size of the class shares because their present existence as qualified members of the class necessarily diminishes the size of the shares of children of A not now qualified but who may qualify.

(3) **Restatement test:** [§636] The Restatement (Second) of Property has adopted the wait-and-see doctrine. It specifies the following as measuring lives under the wait-and-see doctrine: the transferor; those individuals alive when the period begins to run who have *beneficial interests* vested or contingent in the property; and *parents and grandparents* alive when the period begins to run of all the beneficiaries of the property. [Rest. 2d §1.3 (1983)]

(a) **Example:** O conveys Blackacre "to Town of Columbus so long as used for a library, then to B and his heirs." The measuring lives are O, B, any other persons who have beneficial interests in Blackacre (such as the right to take minerals or timber or an easement), and their parents and grandparents. If B's executory interest does not vest within twenty-one years after the death of the survivor of those persons, it is void. (Under the causal relationship test B's interest is valid if it vests within B's life plus twenty-one years. No persons are causally related to cessation of library use.)

c. **Adoption of wait-and-see:** [§637] The wait-and-see doctrine has been adopted in one form or another in twenty states by statute or judicial decision: Alaska, Connecticut, Florida, Illinois, Iowa, Kentucky, Maine, Massachusetts, Maryland, Mississippi, Nevada, New Hampshire, New Mexico, Ohio, Pennsylvania, Rhode Island, South Dakota, Vermont, Virginia, and Washington.

d. **Drafting:** [§638] The wait-and-see doctrine and the equitable approximation doctrine (below) are saving devices for the lawyer who drafts an instrument that violates the common law Rule Against Perpetuities. But no instrument is competently drafted if you must wait and see if it is valid or if it must be reformed by a court. Even in states adopting wait-and-see or equitable approximation, a careful lawyer drafts an instrument that is valid under the common law Rule. A lawyer who drafts an instrument violating the Rule may be liable in malpractice. [Millwright v. Romer, 322 N.W.2d 30 (Iowa 1982)]

12. **The Equitable Reformation Doctrine:** [§639]   The second reform of the Rule Against Perpetuities, urged in the last thirty years, is the equitable reformation or cy pres doctrine. Under the equitable reformation doctrine, an invalid interest is reformed, within the limits of the Rule, to approximate most closely the intention of the creator of the interest. Exercising the reformation power, a court can reduce age contingencies to 21 years or make some other appropriate change to reform the invalid interest.

   a. **Example:** O conveys "to A for life, remainder to A's children who reach age 25." The remainder to A's children is void, as explained *supra*, §617. Exercising the reformation power, a court will reduce the age contingency to twenty-one years, thus saving the gift.

   b. **Adoption of equitable approximation:** [§640]   The equitable reformation doctrine has been adopted by statute or judicial decision in about half the states, often in conjunction with wait-and-see. The Restatement also adopts the equitable reformation doctrine. [Rest. 2d §1.5 (1983)]

H. SUMMARY OF FUTURE INTERESTS [§641]

In reviewing future interests, you may find the following table useful. It sets forth all types of future interests following the various possessory estates. If you can classify the future interests correctly you should have no problem in classifying future interests on an examination.

1. **Future Interests in the Grantor (or in Testator's Heirs if Created by Will):** These arise by *operation of law* when the grantor does not transfer his entire estate, or they can be *expressly created*.

   a. **Reversion:** A reversion is an interest remaining in a grantor who transfers a *vested estate of a lesser quantum* than he has. A reversion can follow any kind of possessory estate except a fee simple. If O, owner of a fee simple, makes a conveyance of a fee tail, a life estate, or a term of years and does not create a vested remainder in fee simple, O has a reversion.

      (1) **Fee tail:** O conveys "to A and the heirs of his body." O has a reversion because a fee tail is an estate of a shorter duration than a fee simple.

      (2) **Life estate**

         — O conveys "to A for life." O has a reversion. If A subsequently conveys "to B for B's life" or "to C for ninety years," A (as well as O) has a reversion. By the hierarchy of estates, a life estate pur autre vie and a term of years are estates of shorter duration than a life estate.

         — O conveys "to A for life, remainder to B if B survives A." O has a reversion.

         — O conveys "to A for life, remainder to B if B survives A, but if B does not survive A, to O." O has a reversion because O has not transferred a vested remainder in fee.

         — O conveys "to A for life, remainder to B." O does *not* have a reversion.

(3) Terms of years

— O conveys "to A for ninety nine years." O has a reversion.

— O conveys "to A for ninety nine years, and then to A's heirs." O has a reversion.

b. **Possibility of reverter:** A possibility of reverter is a future interest remaining in the grantor when the grantor creates a determinable estate of the **same quantum** as the grantor had. Almost always a possibility of reverter follows a fee simple determinable. A possibility of reverter becomes possessory **automatically**.

— "To A and his heirs so long as used for a school." The grantor has a possibility of reverter, which arises by operation of law because only a determinable fee was granted.

c. **Right of entry:** A right of entry is a future interest retained by the grantor giving the grantor **power to terminate**, at his election, the estate granted. Usually it is retained when granting a fee simple subject to condition subsequent.

— "To A and his heirs, but if the land is not used for a school, O has a right to re-enter." O has a right of entry, which he can exercise or not when the condition is breached.

2. **Future Interests in Grantees (or Devisees in a Will):** These cannot arise by operation of law, but **must be expressly created**.

a. **Remainder:** A remainder is a future interest in a grantee that is capable of becoming possessory **upon the expiration of the preceding estate**. A remainder never divests the preceding estate. A remainder cannot follow a fee simple, but can follow any other kind of possessory estate. Remainders are vested or contingent. A **vested** remainder is created in an ascertained person and is not subject to a condition precedent. A **contingent** remainder either is created in an unascertained person or is subject to a condition precedent. (In every example below where a contingent remainder is created, O has a reversion.)

(1) Fee tail

— O conveys "to A and the heirs of her body, and if A die without issue, to B." B has a vested remainder. The words "if A die without issue" are surplusage, merely referring to the expiration of the fee tail, and do not state a condition precedent.

— O conveys "to A and the heirs of her body, and if A die without issue, to B if B is then alive." B has a contingent remainder, subject to the condition precedent of B surviving the expiration of the fee tail.

(2) Life estate

— O conveys "to A for life, then to B." B has a vested remainder.

—O conveys "to A for life, then to B's heirs." B is alive. B's heirs have a contingent remainder because the takers are unascertained.

—O conveys "to A for life, then to B if B reaches age twenty five." B is aged fifteen. B has a contingent remainder because it is subject to a condition precedent.

—O conveys "to A for life, then to B if B survives A, and if B does not survive A, to C." B and C have alternative contingent remainders; each is subject to a condition precedent.

—O conveys "to A for life, then to B, and if B does not survive A, to C." B has a vested remainder subject to divestment.

—O conveys "to A for life, then to A's children." If A has no child, the remainder is contingent because the taker is unascertained. If A has a child, B, the remainder is vested in B subject to open up and let in other children born to A. B's remainder is sometimes called a vested remainder subject to partial divestment.

(3) **Term of years:** O conveys "to A for ten years, then to B." B has a vested remainder.

b. **Executory interest:** An executory interest is a future interest in a grantee that may *divest another grantee* (a shifting executory interest) or may *spring out of the grantor* at a future date (a springing executory interest). An executory interest can divest any type of possessory estate or future interest.

(1) **Fee simple**

—O conveys "to A, but if B returns from Rome, to B." B has a shifting executory interest which will divest a fee simple if the condition happens.

—O conveys "to B if B marries A." B has a springing executory interest which will divest O's fee simple if B marries A.

—*Exception to rule:* O conveys "to A so long as used for a library during the next twenty years, and if not so used, to B." B has an executory interest even though it will not divest the preceding fee simple determinable. It is an executory interest because of the rule that a remainder cannot follow a fee simple.

(2) **Fee tail:** O conveys a cottage "to A and the heirs of his body, but if A inherits the family manor, to B." B has a shifting executory interest.

(3) **Life estate**

—O conveys "to A for life, but if B returns from Rome during A's life, to B." B has a shifting executory interest which may divest A's life estate.

—O conveys "to A for life, then to B, but if B does not survive A, to C." C has a shifting executory interest which may divest B's vested remainder.

— O conveys "to A for life, then one day after A's death to B." B has a springing executory interest which will divest O's fee simple one day after A's death.

(4) Term of years

— O conveys "to A for ten years, but if A does not keep up the fence, to B." B has a shifting executory interest which may divest the term of years.

— *Exception to rule:* O conveys "to A for 100 years if A so long live, then to A's heirs." A's heirs have an executory interest even though it will not divest the preceding term of years determinable. It is an executory interest because before the Statute of Uses one could not have a contingent remainder following a term of years. In modern times, the interest in A's heirs is sometimes called a contingent remainder.

V. CONCURRENT OWNERSHIP

chapter approach

The preceding two chapters dealt with **successive** ownership (*e.g.*, a life estate in A, followed by a remainder in B). Property can also be owned by two or more persons **concurrently**. For example, A and B can be **concurrent** owners of a possessory fee simple, of a life estate, or even a remainder.

Exam questions on concurrent ownership generally require you to determine from the facts what type of concurrent interest is involved. The common law recognized three forms of concurrent ownership: (i) the tenancy in common; (ii) the joint tenancy; and (iii) the tenancy by the entirety. The chief distinguishing features of each are:

1. *Tenancy in common*—two or more persons own the property with **no** right of survivorship between them; when one tenant in common dies, her interest passes to her heirs or devisees.

2. *Joint tenancy*—two or more persons own **with a right of survivorship**; when one joint tenant dies, the survivor(s) takes all. Remember that the common law required the four unities (time, title, interest, and possession) for a joint tenancy.

3. *Tenancy by the entirety*—exists only between **husband and wife**, with a **right of survivorship**, which **cannot be severed** without consent of both spouses.

Questions regarding concurrent ownership may also involve the rights and duties of the co-tenants. Recall that, with the exception of survivorship rights and certain rights under a tenancy by the entirety, the rights and duties of co-tenants are basically the same regardless of the type of co-tenancy.

A. TENANCY IN COMMON

1. **Nature of the Tenancy: [§642]** A tenancy in common is a form of concurrent ownership wherein each co-tenant is the owner of a separate and distinct share of the property, which has not been divided among the co-tenants. Each owner has a separate **undivided interest** in the whole. Tenancies in common can arise by an express conveyance or devise to persons as tenants in common or when persons inherit property from a decedent.

   a. **Right to possession: [§643]** Each tenant in common has the right to possess and enjoy the **entire property**, subject to the same right in each co-tenant. One co-tenant can go into possession of the whole unless another co-tenant objects. The co-tenants can come to any agreement about possession they desire. If they are in conflict over possession, a court may order partition of the property or give some other remedy, discussed below.

(1) **Example:** O dies, leaving a son S and a daughter D as her heirs. D has the right to, and does, move into the house. Unless S objects, there is no problem with respect to the right to possession.

b. **No right of survivorship:** [§644] When a tenant in common dies, her interest passes to her devisees or heirs. It does **not** go to the surviving tenant in common. There is no right of survivorship among tenants in common. This is the chief difference between a tenancy in common and a joint tenancy, in which there is a right of survivorship.

(1) **Example:** A and B are tenants in common. Subsequently A dies intestate, leaving H as her heir. H takes A's share, and B and H now are tenants in common.

c. **Equal shares not necessary:** [§645] Equal shares are not necessary for a tenancy in common. A and B can be tenants in common, with A holding a three-fourths interest and B holding a one-fourth interest. It is **presumed** that the shares of tenants in common are equal, but this presumption can be overcome by evidence that unequal shares were intended. If A and B, who are not related to each other, purchase property as tenants in common, and A puts up three-quarters of the purchase price and B one-quarter, it will likely be held that A did not intend to make a gift to B, and that the parties have undivided interests proportionate to the consideration each paid. If B is a natural object of A's bounty, a gift from A to B does not seem so unlikely. In this case, the unequal consideration paid by A and B may be insufficient by itself to overcome the presumption of equal shares.

d. **Same estates not necessary:** [§646] Tenants in common can have different types of estates. Suppose that A and B are tenants in common, and that A dies, devising his half interest to C for life, remainder to D. C now owns a life estate and D a remainder in a one-half interest held in a tenancy in common with B.

2. **Alienability:** [§647] A tenant in common can sell, give, devise, or otherwise dispose of his undivided share in the same manner as if he were the sole owner of the property. For example, in the preceding illustration, A died devising his one-half interest to C for life, remainder to D. Thus each share of a tenancy in common can be divided into a life estate and future interests, or among a new group of concurrent owners.

a. **Example:** A and B are tenants in common. Subsequently A conveys his one-half interest to C, D, and E as tenants in common. Thereafter B, C, D, and E are tenants in common, B owning a one-half undivided interest and C, D, and E each owning a one-sixth undivided interest.

3. **Presumption of Tenancy in Common:** [§648] Under modern law, whenever a conveyance is made to two or more persons who are not husband and wife, they are presumed to take as tenants in common and not as joint tenants. (As to conveyances to husband and wife, *see infra*, §§665, 698.) This presumption can be overcome by evidence that a joint tenancy is intended.

B. JOINT TENANCY

1. **Nature of the Tenancy:** [§649]   A joint tenancy is a form of concurrent ownership wherein each co-tenant owns an undivided share of property (as in tenancy in common), and the surviving co-tenant has the right to the whole estate. The *right of survivorship* is the distinctive feature of the joint tenancy. There is no limit on the number of persons who can hold together as joint tenants. On the death of each joint tenant, the property belongs to the surviving joint tenants, until only one is left. The tenant who lives longest takes the property by himself.

   a. **Conveyance or devise required:** [§650]   A joint tenancy can be created by deed or by will, or by a joint adverse possession. Joint tenancy does *not* arise where persons inherit property by intestate succession. Heirs always take as tenants in common.

   b. **Real or personal property:** [§651]   A joint tenancy can be created in either real or personal property.

   c. **Right of survivorship:** [§652]   The right of the surviving joint tenant to the whole takes precedence over any devisees under the will of the dead joint tenant. Thus a joint tenant cannot devise his share of joint tenancy property. Similarly the right of survivorship takes precedence over any creditors of the dead joint tenant. If the creditors of a joint tenant do not attach the property before the debtor's death, they cannot reach the property after the debtor joint tenant's death.

2. **The Four Unities Requirement**

   a. **Fiction of one entity:** [§653]   By a common law fiction, joint tenants are regarded as composing *one entity*. Each joint tenant is seised *per my et per tout* (by the share or moiety and by the whole). In theory, then, each *owns* the undivided *whole* of the property; this being so, when one joint tenant dies, *nothing passes* to the surviving joint tenant or tenants. Rather, the estate simply continues in survivors freed from the participation of the decedent, whose interest is extinguished. Thus the surviving joint tenant is entitled to the whole by the right of survivorship, but no interest has passed to the surviving joint tenant. The dying joint tenant simply drops out. This is a rather odd theory, but it can have important consequences.

      (1) **Example:** State Blue imposes an inheritance tax on all property passing from a decedent by devise, bequest, or intestate succession. A and B are joint tenants. A dies. No inheritance tax is imposed on B by a statute taxing the *passing* of property at death.

   b. **Four unities required:** [§654]   Since joint tenants are seised of the undivided property as one fictitious entity, the common law requires that their interests be *equal* in all respects. They must take their interests (i) at the *same time*, (ii) by the *same instrument*, (iii) with *identical interests*, and (iv) with an equal *right to possess* the whole property. If these four unities of time, title, interest, and possession were not present, a joint tenancy could not be created at common law. When a grantor failed to create a joint tenancy because one of the four entities was not present, a tenancy in common was created. This still remains the law in most states, though some states say a joint tenancy can be created "if the grantor intends it"—a position which may lessen the importance of the four unities requirement.

(1) **Unity of time:** [§655]   The interest of each joint tenant must vest at the same time. For example, suppose that O conveys Blackacre "to A for life, then to the heirs of A and the heirs of B as joint tenants." The heirs of A are ascertained at A's death, and the heirs of B are ascertained at B's death. Since the holders of the remainder are ascertained at different times, the heirs of A cannot take as joint tenants with the heirs of B. They take as tenants in common.

(2) **Unity of title:** [§656]   All joint tenants must acquire title by the same deed or will, or by a joint adverse possession. The unity of title requirement has been most frequently litigated in a situation involving a conveyance by a sole owner to himself and another as joint tenants. This most often occurs in a conveyance by a husband to himself and his wife as joint tenants.

   (a) **Conveyance by H to H and W:** [§657]   A conveyance by H "to H and W as joint tenants" violates the *unities of time* and *title*. Because of the common law rule that one person cannot convey to himself, the conveyance by H "to H and W as joint tenants" is viewed as in reality only a conveyance of a one-half interest by H to W. Since the unities of time and title are lacking, at common law H and W held as tenants in common.

      1) **Use of a strawperson:** [§658]   Where H wants to convey "to H and W as joint tenants," he can accomplish his wishes by conveying the property to a "strawperson." (A strawperson is a person not intended to have any beneficial interest in the property, who must convey as directed by the beneficially interested parties. A strawperson is usually a lawyer or the lawyer's secretary.) After H conveys to the strawperson, the strawperson conveys "to H and W as joint tenants." The second deed complies with the four unities rule.

   (b) **Modern law:** [§659]   The common law rule that a conveyance by a sole owner to himself and another as joint tenants created only a tenancy in common has been abolished by statute in many states, though these statutes sometimes only permit a direct conveyance from *one spouse* to both spouses as joint tenants. [Hass v. Hass, 21 N.W.2d 398 (Wis. 1945)] Courts have sometimes avoided the common law rule by saying that H is conveying to a different entity (H and W) of which H is only a part. Hence, in most states a conveyance by H "to H and W as joint tenants" will create a joint tenancy. [Miller v. Riegler, 419 S.W.2d 599 (Ark. 1967)]

(3) **Unity of interest:** [§660]   Since in theory joint tenants hold but one estate as a single entity, the interest of each joint tenant must be *equal in an estate of one duration*. It is not possible, for example, for O to create a joint tenancy by conveying "one-half to A and his heirs, and one-half to B for life, A and B to

hold as joint tenants." A and B would hold as tenants in common, which does not require unity of interest (*supra*, §646).

(a) **Equal shares:** [§661]   To create a joint tenancy, the shares of each joint tenant must be equal. One joint tenant cannot be given a one-third share and the other a two-thirds share, for example. However, after the joint tenancy is created, any joint tenant can petition a court to terminate the joint tenancy by a partition sale. Upon sale of the property in equity, the court—acting to achieve fairness—may divide the sale proceeds in accordance with the proportionate consideration paid. In other words, the creating instrument must give the joint tenants equal shares, but an equity court may choose to ignore this to do equity on partition sale (*see infra*, §§724, 755). (Similarly, in a divorce proceeding where property is to be equitably divided, the court may ignore how title is held.)

(b) **Another interest in same property:** [§662]   Property can be divided into fractional shares, one of which is owned by persons as joint tenants and the other owned by persons as tenants in common. This is best seen by an illustration.

   1) **Example:** O conveys Blackacre as follows: "a one-half undivided interest to H and W as joint tenants, and a one-half interest to A." As between themselves, H and W are joint tenants, and if H dies first, W will own the entire one-half interest relieved of H's participation. As between H and W on the one hand and A on the other, the parties are tenants in common. There are no survivorship rights between A and the joint tenants H and W.

(4) **Unity of possession:** [§663]   Unity of possession requires that each joint tenant have the right to possession of the whole. After a joint tenancy is created, the joint tenants can agree that one joint tenant has the exclusive right to possession. Such an agreement ***does not break the unity of possession***; the joint tenant out of possession is merely waiving his or her right to possession. Obviously any other rule would be very inconvenient. The law likes joint tenants to settle problems over possession by agreement between themselves, out of court, and such agreements would not likely take place if they caused the severance of the right of survivorship.

3.   Creation of Joint Tenancy

a.   Presumption

(1) **Common law:** [§664]   At common law, it was ***presumed*** that any ***conveyance*** or ***devise*** to two or more persons (other than husband and wife) created a joint tenancy, unless a contrary intent was clearly set forth. This presumption favored sole ownership over multiple ownership, and the reasons for it lie in the feudal system. Being able to look to one rather than to several owners for feu-

dal services and incidents was more convenient for the lord. Shared responsibility was more difficult to enforce. Joint tenancy was preferred by the tenant class too because it reduced the burdens due the lord. Although each tenant in common owed the services separately, in a joint tenancy, with its fiction of one entity, any number of joint tenants comprised only one tenant owing services.

    (a) **Husband and wife:** [§665] Husband and wife were presumed at common law to take as tenants by the *entirety*. (*See infra*, §§667, 697.)

(2) **American law:** [§666] In all American jurisdictions, the common law presumption of a joint tenancy has been abolished, either by statute or judicial decision. The presumption today is that a conveyance to two or more persons creates a *tenancy in common*. [*In re* Michael's Estate, 218 A.2d 338 (Pa. 1966)]

    (a) **Husband and wife:** [§667] Statutes abolishing the common law presumption sometimes do not apply to husband and wife, who were presumed at common law to take as tenants by the entirety. In some states, husband and wife are still presumed to take as tenants by the entirety. In a few states, husband and wife are presumed to take as joint tenants. (*See infra*, §698.)

    (b) **Executors and trustees:** [§668] The presumption of tenancy in common does not apply to executors and trustees, who are presumed to hold as joint tenants. Upon the death of one fiduciary, the surviving fiduciary continues to manage the estate or the trust property. It would be very inconvenient— and not what the testator or settlor intended—to have the heirs of the dead fiduciary come in and claim to be co-executors or co-trustees. Joint tenancy among executors and trustees remains even in states that have otherwise abolished joint tenancies.

b. **Overcoming presumption of tenancy in common:** [§669] A joint tenancy can be created only by *express words* in an instrument indicating an intent to create a joint tenancy. The clearest way to create a joint tenancy is to convey "to A and B as joint tenants with the right of survivorship, and not as tenants in common." These words will create a joint tenancy but anything less might not. Courts have been rather harsh in demanding clear expressions of intent. Compare the following conveyances, which may not create a joint tenancy.

(1) **"To A and B as joint tenants":** [§670] In some states, a joint tenancy can be created *only if survivorship is expressly provided for*. Hence a conveyance "to A and B as joint tenants" is insufficient to create a joint tenancy.

(2) **"To A and B jointly":** [§671] The decisions are divided over whether a conveyance "to A and B jointly" will create a joint tenancy. Some courts view the word "jointly" as equivocal because it is often used, by nonlawyers, to describe a tenancy in common as well as a joint tenancy.

(3) **"To A and B and to the survivor of them"**: [§672]   Although there is an express statement that the survivor should take, it has been held that this does not overcome the presumption of tenancy in common because the words "as joint tenants" were not used. [Gagnon v. Pronovost, 71 A.2d 747 (N.H. 1950); *but see* Zomisky v. Zamiska, 296 A.2d 722 (Pa. 1972)—"to A and B as joint tenants and as in common with the right of survivorship" created joint tenancy]

(4) **"To A and B as joint tenants, and to the survivor and his heirs"**: [§673]   This phraseology looks very similar to the phraseology given above for creating a joint tenancy, but there is one important difference. There is an express gift here "to the survivor and his heirs" (it does not say "to A and B with the right of survivorship"). Does this express gift mean that A and B take a co-tenancy for their joint lives with a contingent remainder to the survivor rather than a joint tenancy? The cases are divided. Some hold this language creates a tenancy in common in A and B for life, with remainder to the survivor. [Hass v. Hass, *supra*, §659; *and see* Hunter v. Hunter, 320 S.W.2d 529 (Mo. 1959)— "to A and B as joint tenants with right of survivorship" equivalent of "to A and B as joint tenants (for life), and to the survivor and his heirs"] Others hold this language creates a joint tenancy. [Palmer v. Flint, 161 A.2d 837 (Me. 1960)]

(a) **Difference in effect**: [§674]   If A and B hold a joint tenancy, either A or B can convey his interest to C, severing the unities of time and title and thus terminating the joint tenancy. B and C would then hold as tenants in common. Hence either joint tenant can destroy the right of survivorship. If A and B hold a co-tenancy for their joint lives, with remainder to the survivor, neither A nor B acting alone can destroy the contingent remainder in the survivor. If A conveys to C, C takes A's life estate and A's interest in the contingent remainder, but B's rights are not affected.

(b) **Where joint tenancy abolished**: [§675]   A few states, in an excess of zeal to clear away the remnants of feudalism, abolished the joint tenancy in the last century. In such states, a deed "to A and B as joint tenants with right of survivorship" is construed to create a tenancy in common in A and B for their joint lives, with remainder in fee in the survivor. As stated above, the chief difference between this construction and a joint tenancy is that the survivor's remainder in the whole cannot be destroyed without consent, whereas the joint tenant's right of survivorship can be. [Holbrook v. Holbrook, 403 P.2d 12 (Or. 1965)]

c. **Bank accounts**: [§676]   The creation of a joint tenancy in a checking or savings account raises special problems. *First*, does the depositor intend to make a gift in joint tenancy with right of survivorship or intend to open the account merely for the convenience of having someone pay the depositor's bills? If the latter, the surviving "joint tenant" does not take the sum remaining on deposit, because the depositor had no intention of making a gift of it. (This matter has been dealt with earlier in the discussion of gifts of personal property, *supra*, §227.) *Second*, can a depositor create a joint tenancy with another by depositing in a joint account his own funds? Since the depositor previously owned the money, this transfer appears to violate the unities of time and title (as discussed *supra*, §§655-659). The courts however have held that such a transfer does not violate the unities of time and title, and joint bank accounts are valid in all states. [Miller v. Riegler, *supra*, §659] ***Third***, either joint tenant of a bank account can withdraw the whole sum on deposit, whereas a joint tenant in land can convey only her share. Thus, can the right of one joint tenant to destroy the whole joint tenancy in a bank account be squared with the common law joint tenancy in land? Whether it can be squared or not, courts have held that a joint tenancy can be created in a bank account.

(1) **Withdrawal of more than share: [§677]**   If O deposits $5,000 in a joint savings account in the name of O and A, the deposit creates an undivided half interest in the sum on deposit in A. If A withdraws more than his share from a joint account, O can recover from A the excess over his share. O can consent to an excess withdrawal by words or conduct, or ratify the withdrawal after the fact. Consent or ratification can be shown by the surrounding circumstances. This rule penalizes a joint tenant who withdraws the sum on deposit just before the other joint tenant dies. If he had waited until after death, he would have had the entire sum by survivorship. [Kleinberg v. Heller, 38 N.Y.2d 836 (1976); Estate of Kohn, 168 N.W.2d 812 (Wis. 1969)] Compare Uniform Probate Code section 6-103, adopted in many states, which provides that the parties own the joint bank account during their lifetimes "in proportion to the net contributions of each to the sums on deposit, unless there is clear and convincing evidence of a different intent."

4. **Severance of Joint Tenancy: [§678]**   Any joint tenant can at any time destroy the right of survivorship by severing the joint tenancy. Upon severance, the joint tenancy becomes a tenancy in common, and the right of survivorship is destroyed. At common law, severance occurred automatically when one or more of the four unities were severed. Modern law generally follows the proposition that severance of one of the four unities severs the joint tenancy. But inasmuch as one of the unities can be unknowingly severed, without intent to destroy the right of survivorship, in situations where a joint tenant conveys less than his entire share, some courts look to the intent of the parties in determining whether there is a severance.

a. **Conveyance by joint tenant: [§679]**   Each joint tenant has the right to convey his interest. A conveyance of the tenant's entire interest or share severs the joint tenancy with respect to that share. Either a conveyance to a third person or to another joint tenant severs the share conveyed from the joint tenancy.

(1) **Example:** A, B, and C are joint tenants. A conveys his share to D, thus destroying the unities of time and title between B and C and their new co-tenant, D. B and C remain joint tenants between themselves, but D holds her share as a tenant in common with them. If B subsequently dies, C owns a two-thirds interest and D a one-third interest as tenants in common. [Giles v. Sheridan, 137 N.W.2d 828 (Neb. 1965)] If A had conveyed his share to B, a co-tenant, rather than to a third party, D, the result would be similar. B would hold one-third as a tenant in common, and B and C would hold two-thirds as joint tenants. If

B subsequently died intestate, C would own a two-thirds interest and B's heirs a one-third interest as tenants in common. [Jackson v. O'Connell, 177 N.E.2d 194 (Ill. 1961)]

(2) **Contract to convey:** [§680]   A contract by one joint tenant to convey his interest in the property, which is specifically enforceable in equity, severs the joint tenancy. Under the doctrine of "equitable conversion" (*infra*, §§1811 *et seq.*), the execution of a contract gives the buyer equitable ownership and converts the seller's legal ownership into a contract right to receive the selling price. Thus the unity of interest is severed in equity.

(3) **Conveyance to self:** [§681]   Under old law a joint tenant who wished to convert the tenancy to a tenancy in common had to convey to a strawperson, who conveyed back to the joint tenant. The common law required that, in order to have a legal transfer, one person must convey to ***another*** person, and not to herself; hence the joint tenant could not convey directly to herself. Some recent cases have permitted a joint tenant to unilaterally sever the tenancy by conveying her interest to herself without using an intermediary. [Minonk State Bank v. Grassman, 447 N.E.2d 822 (Ill. 1983)]

b. **Mortgage by joint tenant:** [§682]   When one joint tenant gives a mortgage on the joint tenancy property, does this sever the joint tenancy because the unity of interest is destroyed? Jurisdictions are not in agreement on this question. Generally, courts divide between jurisdictions following the title theory of mortgages and those following the lien theory.

(1) **Title theory states:** [§683]   At common law, a mortgage had the effect of conveying the ***legal title*** to the mortgagee (money lender); the mortgagor (borrower) kept an ***equity of redemption*** entitling the mortgagor to get legal title back upon payment of the mortgage ("redeem the mortgage"). Since a mortgage by a joint tenant conveys the legal title of such joint tenant, the mortgage destroys the unity of interest and severs the joint tenancy. It cannot be revived by the mortgagor's paying off the mortgage. The title theory of mortgages is still followed in a number of states, but in some of them the consequences have been whittled away by the equitable idea that the mortgagee holds title only for security purposes and the courts reach the same results as in lien theory states.

(a) **Example:** A and B are joint tenants of Blackacre. A borrows $5,000 from Security Bank, and gives Security Bank a mortgage on A's interest in Blackacre. Under the title theory of mortgages, the joint tenancy is severed. A and B hold as tenants in common. Subsequently A pays off the debt and discharges the mortgage. Then A dies intestate. A's interest passes to his heirs. B has no right of survivorship.

(b) **Criticism:** Severance by one joint tenant giving a mortgage may not carry out the intent of the mortgagor, who may intend his interest to pass to the surviving joint tenant subject to the mortgage. He probably has no knowledge of the four unities requirement and the severance doctrine. Automatic application of the doctrine may lead to inadvertent severance.

(2) **Lien theory states:** [§684] Most states hold that the mortgagee does not have legal title, but a security interest called a lien. Legal title remains in the mortgagor. In lien theory states, a mortgage does not sever the joint tenancy but the states differ on whether the **surviving joint tenant takes one-half subject to the mortgage if the debt is not paid off before the debtor joint tenant dies.** This difference is best seen by an illustration.

  (a) **Example:** Suppose that A and B are joint tenants of Blackacre, located in a lien theory state. A gives a mortgage on her interest in Blackacre. This does not sever the joint tenancy. B still has a right of survivorship. Now suppose that A dies. Does B take A's interest subject to the mortgage or does B own the entire interest in Blackacre free of the mortgage? Jurisdictions split on this question. Some hold that B takes A's interest subject to the mortgage. This view seems illogical because the mortgage did not sever the joint tenancy, and the survivor should now have the whole. But it seems fair to the mortgagee, who would otherwise lose his security. Other courts hold that B has the right to A's half unencumbered by the mortgage. [People v. Nogarr, 164 Cal. App. 2d 591 (1958)] This latter position, though technically justified, has unfortunate consequences. A lender who knows of the rule will not give credit to one joint tenant; a lender who does not know of it loses his security if the debtor dies, and the survivor gets a windfall.

c. **Lease by joint tenant:** [§685] One joint tenant has the right to lease her interest in the property, even over the objection of the other joint tenant. [Swartzbaugh v. Sampson, 11 Cal. App. 2d 451 (1936)] Does the conveyance of a leasehold sever the joint tenancy? This question basically involves the same issues as severance by giving a mortgage, and not surprisingly the courts divide in the same ways.

  (1) **Common law—lease severs:** [§686] The classical common law was that the conveyance of a leasehold destroyed the unity of interest because the lessor joint tenant had only a reversion in the property whereas the other joint tenant had a fee simple. Their interests after the lease were different. This view makes logical sense and parallels the title theory of mortgages, but is subject to the same criticism that it results in unintentional severance.

  (2) **Modern view—lease does not sever:** [§687] The modern view is that there is no severance by one joint tenant giving a leasehold, and the surviving joint tenant takes the whole. But the cases split over **whether the surviving joint tenant takes one-half subject to the lease.** The split is similar to that over whether the surviving joint tenant takes subject to a mortgage given by the dead tenant. One view holds that the surviving joint tenant takes subject to the leasehold on a one-half interest. This view seems equitable. Another view is that the survivor holds the entire property not subject to the lease. Under this view, a lessee can protect himself against the risk of the lessor dying only by having all joint tenants sign the lease or by requiring the lessor to sever the joint tenancy beforehand. [Tenhet v. Boswell, 18 Cal. 3d 150 (1976)]

d. **Agreement among joint tenants:** [§688]   Joint tenants can agree among them-selves that one tenant has the right to exclusive possession (*supra,* §663). Such an agreement does not sever the joint tenancy. Joint tenants can make an agreement to hold as tenants in common. Such an agreement severs the joint tenancy even though none of the four unities is broken. In this situation **intention,** rather than the four unities, **controls**.

e. **Divorce:** [§689]   Divorce is usually held to terminate a joint tenancy between hus-band and wife, even though none of the four unities is broken. The reason is that converting a joint tenancy into a tenancy in common usually carries out the inten-tion of the parties upon divorce, who do not want the ex-spouse to have survivorship rights. An agreement between joint tenants to hold as tenants in common severs the joint tenancy, and courts sometimes infer such an agreement from the divorce proceedings.

   (1) **Example:** H and W own a family home as joint tenants. Upon divorce, H and W sign a property settlement agreement providing that W shall remain in the family home with the children, but that upon W's remarriage or upon the youngest child reaching twenty-one years of age, the home shall be sold and the proceeds divided equally between H and W (now ex-H and W). W dies soon thereafter and H claims the family home is still in joint tenancy. If it is held in tenancy in common, W's half interest will descend to her children and not go to H by right of survivorship. From these facts an agreement to hold as tenants in common will be inferred. [Mann v. Bradley, 535 P.2d 213 (Colo. 1975)]

f. **Murder of one joint tenant by another:** [§690]   If one joint tenant murders the other, some courts hold this effects a severance, converting the joint tenancy into a tenancy in common. The murderer thus cannot take the victim's share by right of survivorship. [Duncan v. Vassaur, 550 P.2d 929 (Okla. 1976)] This view is adopted by Uniform Probate Code section 2-803. Other courts penalize the murderer more severely. They hold that murder does not sever a joint tenancy and that the murder-er has the entire property, but they impose **constructive trust** on the murderer, awarding the victim's heirs everything except the murderer's life interest in half. The theory is that the murderer should not profit from his act, and the question of who would have survived in the normal course of events should be resolved against him. This solution is adopted by the Restatement of Restitution section 188.

g. **Simultaneous death:** [§691]   Suppose A and B, joint tenants, die simultaneously in a plane crash. Who takes the property? Half goes to A's estate and half goes to B's. The Uniform Simultaneous Death Act enacted in almost all states, provides: "Where there is no sufficient evidence that two joint tenants or tenants by the entirety have died otherwise than simultaneously the property so held shall be dis-tributed one half as if one had survived and one half as if the other survived. Where more than two joint tenants have died and there is no sufficient evidence that they died otherwise than simultaneously the property so held shall be divided into as many equal shares as there were joint tenants and the share allocable to each shall be distributed as if he had survived all the others." [Uniform Simultaneous Death Act §3]

5. **Avoidance of Probate:** [§692] The joint tenancy is a useful estate, particularly between husband and wife, because it *avoids probate*. When a person dies either intestate or testate, probate proceedings have to be opened in a local court in order to, among other things, change the title from the decedent to the new owner. Probate is time consuming and costly—executor's commissions, lawyer's fees, and court costs must be paid. With joint tenancy there is no need to change the title at a joint tenant's death, since the surviving joint tenant owns the whole by virtue of the right of survivorship. Hence joint tenancy avoids probate. It is very common for husband and wife to hold the family home in joint tenancy (or tenancy by the entirety).

6. **Abolition of Joint Tenancy:** [§693] A few states abolished the joint tenancy in the nineteenth century, considering it a legacy from feudalism with its four unities. In those days, a great many joint tenancies were created by the presumption in favor of joint tenancies (*e.g.,* a conveyance "to A's children" created a joint tenancy). Legislatures thought it unfair that the survivor should take the whole. Instead of abolishing the *presumption* of joint tenancy, as most legislatures did, a few went further and abolished the joint tenancy itself. In these states persons cannot avoid probate by creating a joint tenancy.

C. TENANCY BY THE ENTIRETY

1. **Nature of Tenancy:** [§694] A tenancy by the entirety is a form of concurrent ownership that can be created *only between husband and wife,* holding as *one person.* The tenancy by the entirety is like the joint tenancy in that the four unities (plus a fifth—the unity of marriage) are required for its creation, and the surviving spouse has the right of survivorship.

   a. **Fiction of one person:** [§695] It is of the essence of tenancy by the entirety that husband and wife are considered in law to be one person. As one person, they do not take the estate by the moieties or shares; rather both—holding as one—are seised *per tout et non per my.* The fiction that husband and wife are one person reflected the realities of English common law. A married woman was not a legal person; her husband represented her interests. Although today a married woman is a legal person and her husband's control of her property has been completely abrogated in all states, the peculiar legal fiction of unity of husband and wife still underlies the tenancy by the entirety and causes trouble.

   b. **Severance by one tenant impossible:** [§696] Although the tenancy by the entirety resembles the joint tenancy in that the same four unities are required for its creation, it is unlike the joint tenancy in that severance of the tenancy by one tenant is not possible. Neither tenant acting alone can sever the four unities and destroy the right of survivorship. This is the chief difference between a tenancy by the entirety and a joint tenancy.

2. **Creation of Tenancy by the Entirety**

   a. **English common law:** [§697] At English common law, husband and wife were legally one, and therefore it was impossible for husband and wife to hold with each other as tenants in common or as joint tenants. They were not considered separate entities and thus could not hold separate moieties (shares). Therefore a conveyance to H and W "as joint tenants" or "as tenants in common" created a tenancy by the entirety in H and W. This old rule has been abolished in all states. Modern law permits husband and wife to take as tenants in common or as joint tenants.

b. **Modern presumption:** [§698] Where the conveyance is unclear, most states that retain the tenancy by the entirety **presume** a conveyance to husband and wife creates a tenancy by the entirety. This presumption can be rebutted by evidence that some other estate was intended. To this extent, the old common law preference for a tenancy by the entirety is retained. In a few states that have the tenancy by the entirety, husband and wife, like others, are presumed to take as tenants in common. And in a few others, husband and wife are presumed to take as joint tenants (a middle position between the common law presumption and the presumption applicable to nonmarried persons).

c. **Conveyance to unmarried persons:** [§699] If a conveyance is made to two unmarried persons to hold as tenants by the entirety, it does not create tenancy by the entirety. Some courts hold such a conveyance creates a joint tenancy, on the theory that a joint tenancy is closer to the grantor's intent than a tenancy in common. Others apply the ordinary presumption of a tenancy in common. Still other courts construe a conveyance to unmarried persons as tenants by the entirety to create a tenancy in common for the tenants' joint lives, with remainder to the survivor. This construction perhaps comes closest of all to the grantor's intent because the remainder in the survivor cannot be destroyed by one party. [Knight v. Knight, 458 S.W.2d 803 (Tenn. 1970)]

3. **Rights of Tenants During Marriage**

   a. **English common law:** [§700] Because of the fiction that husband and wife were one, and the husband was that one, the tenancy by the entirety was heavily loaded in favor of the husband at common law.

      (1) **Husband's rights:** [§701] The husband had the following rights:

         (a) **Right to possession:** [§702] The husband had the right to exclusive possession and all the rents and profits while the tenancy endured. The husband could convey this right to a third party, giving the third party the right to possession—completely excluding the wife from possession. Inasmuch as creditors can reach what a person can voluntarily transfer, the husband's creditors could reach this right and sell it to pay the husband's debts.

         (b) **Right of survivorship:** [§703] The husband had the right to the entire property if he survived the wife. The husband could transfer this right to a third person, and the husband's creditors could reach it.

            1) **Example:** H's creditor seizes and sells H's interest in Blackacre, owned by H and W as tenants by the entirety. The purchaser at the creditor's

sale is entitled to possession and rents and profits. If W dies before H, the purchaser owns the entire interest in Blackacre at W's death, when her right of survivorship is extinguished. If H dies before W, W's right of survivorship gives her the entire interest in Blackacre at H's death.

(2) **Wife's right of survivorship:** [§704]   The wife had the right to the entire property if she survived the husband. This was the only right the wife had in a tenancy by the entirety. The right of survivorship could not be destroyed without the wife's consent, and it remained in the wife *even after the husband conveyed his entire interest* in the property. The wife's right of survivorship was not alienable by the wife without her husband's consent (recall that she was not a person sui juris). Therefore her creditors could not reach it.

(3) **No right to partition:** [§705]   Neither spouse has the right to a judicial partition of the property. Neither spouse acting alone can have the property sold since the other spouse's right of survivorship cannot be extinguished without his or her consent.

(4) **Not unconstitutional:** [§706]   Although the husband's rights in a common law tenancy by the entirety were much greater than those of the wife, this was held not to be a violation of the Equal Protection Clause of the Constitution. The tenancy by the entirety is an optional type of tenancy deliberately chosen by the grantor or by the husband and wife. [D'Ercole v. D'Ercole, 407 F. Supp. 1377 (D. Mass. 1976)] Fortunately this question cannot arise with respect to any *new* tenancies by the entirety since the rights of husband and wife now have been made equal by legislation in all states. (*Caveat:* Prior to 1980, Massachusetts was the principal state following the common law. In 1980, legislation in Massachusetts equalized the rights of the spouses, but it was not made retroactive. Tenancies by the entirety created before 1980 in Massachusetts are governed by old common law rules.)

b. **Modern law**

(1) **Married Women's Acts:** [§707]   In the nineteenth century, each American state enacted a Married Women's Act. These acts were passed to remove the common law disability of married women to control and dispose of their property. They provided, generally, that a married woman was able to receive, hold, manage, and dispose of real and personal property as if she were a single woman. (A single woman was under no disability at common law and could do with her property anything a man could.) Married Women's Acts did not specifically mention the wife's interest in a tenancy by the entirety, and hence it fell to the courts to apply the principle of the acts to entirety property. The position taken on the effect of the Married Women's Act on the tenancy by the entirety has important consequences for creditors, since a creditor can reach only such property as the debtor can voluntarily assign. The states can now generally be classified as taking one of two positions.

(2) **Act forbids either spouse to convey separately:** [§708]   The courts in the majority of states recognizing the tenancy by the entirety hold that the equality intended by the Married Women's Act can be achieved in this way: (i) give both husband and wife equal rights to possession during the marriage (thus, with respect to possession, putting the wife in the same position the husband had at common law), and (ii) forbid both husband and wife, acting alone, to convey his or her interest (thus, with respect to voluntary transfer and creditors, putting the husband in the same position the wife had at common law). Under this view, creditors of one spouse cannot reach the property because neither husband nor wife acting alone can transfer his or her interest. [Sawada v. Endo, 561 P.2d 1291 (Hawaii 1977)] Doubtless this exemption from creditors is one of the main reasons for the survival of the tenancy by the entirety. It serves to protect the family home from assignment by one spouse and from creditors of one spouse.

(3) **Act gives wife same rights husband had:** [§709]   Some courts hold that the Married Women's Act had the purpose of giving the wife the same rights as the husband had at common law. Thus, with respect to a tenancy by the entirety, the wife acquires the right to possession of one-half, and the right to convey her interest in the same manner as the husband could at common law. Neither spouse can destroy the right of survivorship of the other. (This view is taken in New York and New Jersey, among other states.)

(a) **Creditors' rights:** [§710]   Since each spouse can voluntarily convey his or her interest, a creditor of the husband can seize and sell his interest and a creditor of the wife can seize and sell her interest.

1) **Example:** H and W own Blackacre as tenants by the entirety. W's judgment creditor, A, levies execution upon W's interest, which is sold to B on execution sale. B is entitled equally to possession with H until H or W dies. If H dies first, B alone owns Blackacre. If W dies first, H alone owns Blackacre. [King v. Greene, 153 A.2d 49 (N.J. 1959)]

2) **Criticism:** The interest of one spouse, sold subject to survivorship rights in the other spouse, may not bring upon a creditors' sale a price commensurate with its economic value. An execution sale of an interest defeasible if the nondebtor spouse survives may result in a sacrificial sale of the interest.

3) **Partition after sale:** [§711]   A purchaser from H or W, including a purchaser at an execution sale, is a tenant in common with the other spouse during the lives of the spouses, but if the property is a family home, partition is not available to the purchaser. Equity refuses to grant partition in an attempt to protect the nondebtor spouse in the family home, but the nondebtor spouse must pay one-half the reasonable rental value to the purchaser. [Newman v. Chase, 359 A.2d 474 (N.J. 1976)]

4. **Divorce of Spouses:** [§712] In most states, a divorce terminates the unity of husband and wife and therefore the tenancy by the entirety. In some states, the tenancy by the entirety is converted into a joint tenancy, but in most it is converted into a tenancy in common on the theory that the spouses do not want survivorship rights after divorce.

   a. **Suit for partition:** [§713] At or after a divorce, one of the former spouses may sue for partition of the new tenancy in common or joint tenancy. A suit in partition is an equitable proceeding in which, before dividing the property, the court must determine the respective shares of the parties. Presumptively, tenants in common and joint tenants hold equal shares, but this presumption may be rebutted by evidence showing unequal contributions. Unequal contributions do not necessarily result in unequal shares, however, because one co-tenant may intend a gift to the other co-tenant. In partition suits after divorce, courts tend to divide the joint property into equal shares, even though the husband paid the consideration, on the theory that the wife has contributed homemaker services or performed her marriage vows. In effect, courts tend to apply the idea of community property (*infra,* §789) in partition proceedings between former spouses. [Sebold v. Sebold, 444 F.2d 864 (D.C. Cir. 1971)]

5. **Tenancy by the Entirety in Personal Property**

   a. **Common law rule:** [§714] Because at common law the husband was the owner of his wife's personal property, a tenancy by the entirety in personal property was a logical impossibility. Michigan, New Jersey, and New York are the chief states still prohibiting a tenancy by the entirety in personal property, although the reason for the prohibition has completely disappeared. In these states, an attempt to create a tenancy by the entirety in personal property will create either a joint tenancy (as the closest equivalent) or a tenancy in common.

      (1) **Conversion of real to personal property:** [§715] When real property held by the entirety is converted into personal property, problems arise in states not permitting a tenancy by the entirety in personal property. The conversion can be voluntary (as by sale) or involuntary (as where a building burns and is replaced by insurance proceeds, or land is condemned). Some lower New York courts held that proceeds from the voluntary sale of land held by the entirety may be regarded as realty, thus rendering the proceeds capable of being held by the entirety. [Empire State Federal Savings & Loan Association v. Wukowitz, 197 N.Y.S.2d 87 (1959)] But these cases seemingly have been overruled sub silentio by *Hawthorne v. Hawthorne,* 13 N.Y.2d 82 (1963), which held that insurance proceeds resulting from fire could not be held in tenancy by the entirety. If the parties can lose the inseverable right or survivorship by involuntary conversion, it would seem to necessarily follow that they can lose it by voluntary conversion.

   b. **Majority rule:** [§716] Most states recognizing the tenancy by the entirety permit it to be created in personal property (except possibly in a joint bank account; there, because either spouse can withdraw all funds, an inseverable right of survivorship is not possible). These states reason that the basis for the common law prohibition was destroyed by the Married Women's Act, which abolished the husband's ownership of the wife's personal property.

6. **Modern Status:** [§717]   The tenancy by the entirety is not recognized in about half the states. Some states have refused to recognize it because the common law unity of husband and wife, on which the estate is based, is repugnant to modern ideas of the marital relationship. Courts in other states have held that the tenancy by the entirety was abrogated by the Married Women's Act. In the eight community property states, the tenancy is not recognized because it is thought to be inconsistent with the equality principle underlying the community property system.

D. RIGHTS AND DUTIES OF CO-TENANTS

1. **Introduction:** [§718]   The rights and duties of co-tenants are more or less the same regardless of the type of co-tenancy. Of course, a joint tenant or a tenant by the entirety has a right of survivorship, and a tenant in common does not. And a tenant by the entirety may be legally unable to convey his or her interest without the consent of the spouse. And the common law unity of husband and wife may give tenants by the entirety different rights than other co-tenants. But these matters aside, the rights and duties of co-tenants are similar. Unless otherwise noted, the following discussion applies to all co-tenants.

2. **Possession by One Co-Tenant:** [§719]   Each co-tenant is equally entitled to the possession and enjoyment of the entire co-tenancy property. No co-tenant may exclude another co-tenant from any part of the property. Obviously these general rules are not very helpful when one co-tenant goes into exclusive possession. What rights has the co-tenant out of possession?

    a. **Agreement by parties:** [§720]   Co-tenants can agree among themselves that one co-tenant has the right to exclusive possession. The law encourages parties in conflict to resolve the conflict by private agreement rather than by a lawsuit. A private agreement is much cheaper than a lawsuit. A private agreement regarding possession does not sever the unity of possession nor does it sever a joint tenancy (*supra*, §§663, 688).

    b. **Accounting for reasonable rental value by co-tenant in possession:** [§721]   Must a co-tenant in possession pay a reasonable rental value to the co-tenant out of possession? Suppose that A and B are co-tenants. A goes into exclusive possession. B voluntarily remains out of possession. Must A pay B one-half the fair rental value of the property?

        (1) **Majority rule:** [§722]   If B is not excluded (ousted) by A, A is entitled to use and occupy every part of the property without paying any amount to B. B cannot recover a share of the rental value of the land unless B has been *ousted* by A, or A agreed to pay B, or A stands in a fiduciary relationship to B. [Pico v. Columbet, 12 Cal. 414 (1959)]

(a) **Rationale:** This rule promotes the productive use of property. It rewards the co-tenant who goes into possession and uses the property. It also follows logically from the premise that each co-tenant has the right to possession of all, and not merely a proportionate share, of the property.

(b) **Carrying charges:** [§723] Since A, in possession, does not have to pay rent to B, it is deemed fair that A must bear the ordinary expenses of upkeep (*e.g.*, taxes, mortgage interest, repairs). If taxes and mortgage interest exceed the fair rental value of the property, A has a right of contribution from the other co-tenants. Similarly, A will be credited for payment of more than his proportionate share in an accounting or partition action.

(c) **Equitable considerations:** [§724] Equitable considerations may cause a court to refuse to apply the general rule that the occupying co-tenant who is not liable for rent must pay expenses. For example, where a sister and a brother are co-tenants, and the sister cares for their mother in the co-tenancy property, the sister may be entitled, in a partition action, to contribution of one-half the cost of maintaining the property. Because of equitable considerations (caring for mother), the sister can occupy the property rent-free and require the brother to pay half of the maintenance. [Baird v. Moore, 141 A.2d 324 (N.J. 1958)]

(d) **Ouster:** [§725] In a jurisdiction following the majority rule, if one co-tenant ousts another co-tenant, she must pay the ousted co-tenant his share of the reasonable rental value of the property.

1) **Definition:** [§726] Ouster is an act by one co-tenant which **deprives another co-tenant of the right to possession.** There is an ouster when an occupying co-tenant refuses to admit another co-tenant into possession. Ouster also occurs if the occupying co-tenant denies the title of another co-tenant. It may occur if the occupying co-tenant refuses to pay an appropriate rental value demanded by a co-tenant out of possession. It may even occur where the occupying co-tenant does not reply to a letter making such a demand. It is a flexible definition by which a court tempers the majority rule, and makes it fairer to the tenant out of possession.

2) **Remedies:** [§727] An ousted co-tenant can bring a suit to collect his share of the reasonable rental value or a suit to partition the property. The former action is sometimes called a suit for mesne profits. Mesne profits are the reasonable value of the use of land, not the profits actually made.

(2) **Minority rule:** [§728] In a minority of states, A must account to B for B's share of the **reasonable rental value** of the premises. [McKnight v. Basilides, 143 P.2d 307 (Wash. 1943); *but see* Fulton v. Fulton, 357 P.2d 169 (Wash. 1960)—dismissing McKnight rule as dictum and shifting Washington back to majority rule]

(a) **Rationale:** This rule places the burden on the occupying co-tenant to show an agreement by the co-tenants that she was not to pay. By putting the burden on the person who will reap economic gain (the occupying co-tenant), and penalizing her if the parties act ambiguously, this rule induces co-tenants to come to an agreement as to the payment of rent. An agreement is desirable because it lessens litigation over the parties' rights.

(b) **Carrying charges:** [§729]   The occupying co-tenant is accountable for her share of the ***net reasonable rental value***, after deducting expenses of upkeep.

3. **Accounting for Rents Received from a Third Party:** [§730]   Any rents or other income collected by a co-tenant from a third party must be shared equally with the other co-tenants if the income exceeds the collecting co-tenant's proportionate share. The collecting co-tenant must account to the others for their proportionate shares. This rule was established by the Statute of Anne (1704). The collecting co-tenant must account for the net amount actually received, not for the reasonable rental value of the land.

   a. **Example:** A and B are co-tenants. A leases the land to C for $1,000 a year. A must pay B $500 out of each $1,000 payment A receives.

   b. **Time of accounting:** [§731]   When a co-tenant has a right to an accounting during the existence of the co-tenancy, he can bring a suit for accounting. Or he can wait and demand an accounting in a partition action, which separates the co-tenants and adjusts their rights in a final settlement. In a final accounting in a partition action, the court can require a tenant to account from the beginning of the tenancy. The statute of limitations does not begin to run until the termination of the co-tenancy, because a co-tenant is viewed as a fiduciary. (A statute of limitations does not run on a trustee from the time of breach, but only from the time the fiduciary relationship terminates.) [Goergen v. Maar, 2 App. Div. 2d 276 (1956)]

4. **Exploiting Natural Resources:** [§732]   A co-tenant is accountable for profits derived from a use of land that permanently reduces its value.

   a. **Minerals:** [§733]   If a co-tenant operates mines or oil wells, she is not entitled to take her fair share of the minerals in place, because of the difficulty in estimating the amount and value of the minerals. Instead, the co-tenant must pay a proportionate part of the net amount received for the extracted minerals to her co-tenants.

      (1) **Amount payable:** [§734]   The general rule is that the co-tenant must account for the net amount received for the minerals as they are extracted. But if the co-tenant is in the business of processing and selling minerals, it has been held that the extracting co-tenant is accountable for the net profits realized from her processing business. [White v. Smyth, 214 S.W.2d 967 (Tex. 1948)] The case is supportable on the rationale that requiring the extracting co-tenant to account for profits from her processing business induces her to come to an agreement with her co-tenants before extracting minerals. The same rationale

supports the minority rule regarding payment of rent to a co-tenant out of possession. It places the burden of reaching agreement on the active party, and hence is economically efficient.

(2) **Compare—farming:** [§735]   A co-tenant who excludes her co-tenants and farms the land is accountable for the fair rental value of the land, not the net profits received from her farming operation.

b.   **Timber:** [§736]   Unlike products underground, timber can be seen and a fractional share apportioned easily. For this reason, some courts hold that one co-tenant can cut her proportionate share of the timber without being liable to her co-tenants for its value. If she cuts more than her share, she must account. Other courts hold that, to prevent overcutting, no co-tenant can cut a share of the timber without the consent of the co-tenants. [Threatt v. Rushing, 361 So. 2d 329 (Miss. 1978)]

5.   **Actions by Co-Tenant to Protect Property:** [§737]   The general principle is that a co-tenant who pays money to keep up the property, which benefits all co-tenants, is entitled to reimbursement for more than his proportionate share of costs. But this is subject to exceptions and qualifications. The courts try to do what is just and equitable under the circumstances. The discussion below states the usual rule, but there are variations in particular jurisdictions.

a.   **Taxes:** [§738]   Each co-tenant has the duty to pay his share of taxes, in order to protect the property from a tax foreclosure sale. If one co-tenant pays more than his share of taxes, he can compel the other co-tenant to reimburse him immediately, or he can wait and present his claim in a suit for partition.

(1) **Exception—co-tenant in possession:** [§739]   If the paying co-tenant is in sole possession, he has the duty to pay the taxes and mortgage interest up to the amount of the reasonable rental value of the property. He can compel contribution only if taxes and other carrying charges exceed the reasonable rental value.

(2) **Rent received from third person:** [§740]   If the paying co-tenant receives rent from a third person, he must account to his co-tenant for the net rents received after deducting taxes and other carrying charges.

b.   **Interest on mortgage:** [§741]   Interest on a mortgage is treated the same way as taxes. These are "compulsory" carrying charges. A co-tenant who pays interest on the mortgage can compel contribution from nonpaying co-tenants who are personally liable on the mortgage. If the nonpaying co-tenant is not personally liable on the mortgage, the paying co-tenant can foreclose a lien on the other's interest.

(1) **Payment on principal:** [§742]   If a co-tenant pays off the **_principal_** of the mortgage, he is subrogated to the mortgagee and has whatever rights the mortgagee has. Paying off a mortgage gives the paying co-tenant a lien on the property, which the mortgagee had. If the other co-tenant does not pay his share of the principal when it falls due, the paying co-tenant can foreclose the lien by

having the property sold to pay the lien. In addition, if the mortgage is a joint obligation of the co-tenants, the paying co-tenant can get a ***personal judgment*** against the other co-tenant in the amount of his proportionate share. [Giles v. Sheridan, *supra*, §679]

c. **Repairs:** [§743]   Repairs are treated differently from taxes and interest on a mortgage. Repairs are voluntary. No person has a duty to repair his property. He may let it fall into decay if he chooses. This principle applies to co-tenants. A co-tenant who makes necessary repairs ***cannot compel contribution*** from his co-tenant. He must wait until an accounting or partition. In an accounting for rents received from a third person or for reasonable rental value, he can set off the amount spent on repairs. In a partition sale, he may be reimbursed for repairs before the sale proceeds are distributed.

d. **Improvements:** [§744]   Just as no co-tenant has a duty to repair, no co-tenant has a duty to improve. Thus, an improving co-tenant cannot compel contribution from his co-tenant. But in other respects, improvements are not treated like necessary repairs. There may be no reimbursement for them at all. The general principle applicable to improvements is that the improver should get the ***value added*** by the improvements, and if the improvements add no value, the improver is not reimbursed. The improver bears the risk. Thus in accounting for rents received or for fair rental value, the improver is credited only with the amount of increased rent or rental value attributable to the improvements. Similarly, in a partition action, where the property is physically partitioned, the court will give the improver the portion of the property containing the improvements if feasible. If a partition sale is ordered, the improving co-tenant receives the ***value added*** to the property by (not the cost of) the improvements. If the improvements add no value, the improver receives nothing for them.

(1) **Example:** A and B are co-tenants of land which cost $20,000. A erects a building thereon at a cost of $10,000. On partition sale the property is sold for $55,000, land being worth $30,000 and the building worth $25,000. From the proceeds A should receive one-half the value of the land ($15,000) and the whole value of the building ($25,000), for a total of $40,000. B should receive $15,000.

6. **Co-Tenants as Fiduciaries:** [§745]   A co-tenant is not, strictly speaking, a fiduciary. He does not hold his interest for the benefit of another. On the other hand, a co-tenancy is not a relationship between strangers where the parties can be expected to be guarding their respective interests. In view of this, courts sometimes treat one co-tenant as the fiduciary of another.

a. **When deemed fiduciaries**

(1) **Confidential relationship:** [§746]   If a confidential relationship exists among the co-tenants, any co-tenant who acquires an outstanding title or lien on the property is deemed to have acquired it on behalf of all the co-tenants. A confidential relationship may arise when two persons buy property together as co-tenants, each relying upon the good faith of the other.

(2) **Inherited title:** [§747]   Co-tenants who acquire their interests by will or intestate succession have usually been regarded as fiduciaries with respect to each other. Ordinarily such co-tenants are siblings or have some other family tie, and their expectations are that the other co-tenants will act in good faith toward them.

(a) **Example:** T devises land to W for life, remainder to W's children, A, B, and C. T's will gives W power to lease the land beyond her death. A buys a mineral lease from W for ninety-nine years, agreeing to pay a one-twelfth royalty of all minerals extracted. A is a fiduciary with respect to this lease. Subsequently, A subleases the minerals to D, who agrees to pay A a one-eighth royalty. W dies. B and C are entitled to share in the one-eighth royalty equally with A. [Givens v. Givens, 387 S.W.2d 851 (Ky. 1965)]

b. **Acquisition of outstanding title:** [§748]   The event that most commonly triggers fiduciary liability is the acquisition of an outstanding superior title. The most frequently litigated cases involve purchase by a co-tenant upon a tax sale or upon foreclosure of a mortgage. There is a great divergence of opinion in these cases. The following are the general rules, but the equities in a particular case may be controlling.

(1) **Tax sale:** [§749]   Each co-tenant has a duty to pay taxes on the property. If a co-tenant in a fiduciary relationship buys the property at a tax sale, or buys it from the purchaser within the period of redemption, she holds it for the benefit of all the co-tenants. The other co-tenants have the right to preserve their interests in the property by contributing their share of the sum expended to the purchasing co-tenant.

(2) **Foreclosure of mortgage:** [§750]   If all the co-tenants are liable on the debt securing the mortgage, and one co-tenant buys the property at the mortgage foreclosure sale, she is entitled to reimbursement from her co-tenants to the extent she paid their shares of the indebtedness. Conversely, the other co-tenants have the right to contribute to the purchase price within a reasonable time and reclaim their shares. [Laura v. Christian, 537 P.2d 1389 (N.M. 1975)]

7. **Adverse Possession:** [§751]   A co-tenant can adversely possess against another co-tenant, and if the adverse possession continues for the statutory period, it will ripen into title in the adverse possessor (*see supra,* §141). However, merely going into exclusive possession is insufficient to establish adverse possession. Similarly, refusing to admit a co-tenant into possession is not enough. To establish himself as an adverse possessor, a co-tenant must give the other co-tenants clear and unequivocal *notice of repudiation of the common title*. Any co-tenant has the right to be in possession of co-tenancy property. Hence, if the acts of the possessor are susceptible of explanation consistent with the existence of the common title, such acts do not give notice. [Mercer v. Wayman, *supra,* §141]

8. **Partition:** [§752]   Any tenant in common or joint tenant has the right to bring a suit in partition. This is an equitable proceeding in which the court either physically divides or

sells the common property, adjusts all claims of the parties, and separates them. When co-tenants are squabbling and cannot come to any agreement, the judicial remedy of partition terminates the co-tenancy and divides the common property. Partition is not available to tenants by the entirety because neither spouse can destroy the right of survivorship of the other spouse.

a. **Partition in kind:** [§753]   The court may order physical partition of the property into separate tracts if that is feasible. Once the land is physically partitioned, each party owns his tract alone in fee simple. If the separate tracts are not equal in value, the court will require one tenant to make a cash payment, called *owelty*, to the other tenant to equalize values.

   (1) **Example:** A court partitions land into two tracts: tract 1 worth $20,000, and tract 2 worth $18,000. The co-tenant who is assigned tract 1 will have to pay the other tenant $1,000 in cash, so that each ends up with property worth $19,000.

b. **Partition sale:** [§754]   If physical partition is not feasible or in the best interests of the parties, the court will order the property sold and the sale proceeds divided equally among the co-tenants. Houses, apartment houses, urban lots, and commercial property do not usually lend themselves to physical partition. Instead, sale is ordinarily ordered by the court. Rural land is the type most often physically partitioned, but even there the court will order the land sold if the total value of the land will be materially less if partitioned into separate tracts. [Johnson v. Hendrickson, 24 N.W.2d 914 (S.D. 1946)]

   (1) **Division of proceeds:** [§755]   The presumption is that upon partition of the property, each co-tenant is entitled to an equal share in the proceeds, subject to adjustments for payment of taxes, interest, repairs, and improvements (*supra,* §§738-744). This presumption is rebuttable by evidence that the co-tenants intended unequal shares. This most often occurs when there are unequal contributions to the purchase price. If no gift was intended by a co-tenant making a larger contribution, he is entitled to a proportionately larger share of the proceeds. [Beal v. Beal, 577 P.2d 507 (Or. 1978)]

c. **Agreement not to partition:** [§756]   Co-tenants may agree not to partition the land. If the agreement is for a reasonable purpose and for a reasonable length of time, such as the life of a co-tenant, it is not invalid as a restraint on alienation (*supra*, §409). But because partition is an equitable proceeding, if the court finds the agreement harsh or oppressive it will refuse to enforce the agreement and will grant partition. [Michalski v. Michalski, *supra*, §409]

d. **Partition by co-life tenant:** [§757]   One of two or more life tenants can maintain an action of physical partition against the other life tenants. Since the physical partition lasts only as long as the life estate endures, physical partition of a life estate does not affect the rights of the remainderman. If physical partition is impracticable, however, a co-life tenant may not be able to get a partition sale of the property in fee simple. A partition sale of the fee simple might adversely affect the remainderman, who might want to receive the land. The rights of a co-life tenant to partition sale are commonly governed by statute. [Penfield v. Jarvis, 399 A.2d 1280 (Conn. 1978)]

VI. MARITAL PROPERTY

chapter approach

Marital property is in the process of change in the United States. In this chapter are discussed common law marital estates and modern property rights of spouses, including rights in community property. Since these topics are but a small part of most property courses, the discussion here is brief, but it will provide you with the common law background necessary to understand many of today's laws.

A. COMMON LAW MARITAL ESTATES

1. **During Marriage:** [§758]   In feudal times, land was power, and the husband controlled this power. A wife was entitled to **support** from her husband, but all her property passed under the husband's control at marriage. Sometimes this is summed up by saying, "At common law, the husband and wife were one, and that one was the husband." There is much truth in that statement so far as property rights are concerned.

   a. **Jure uxoris of husband:** [§759]   During marriage, all the wife's personal property, except for her clothes and ornaments, but including her earnings, became the property of her husband. As for her real property, her husband had **jure uxoris** ("by the marital right"). This right gave the husband control and possession of the wife's lands for the duration of the marriage. All the rents and profits were his. The husband could, if he chose, convey his right to another. Jure uxoris was abolished in this country by the passage of Married Women's Acts in the nineteenth century. Today, married women have the same control over their property as do single women and men. A married woman's earnings belong to her, and not to her husband.

2. **Upon Divorce:** [§760]   The husband had the obligation of supporting his wife, and this obligation ordinarily continued after divorce. The court, upon divorce, would award the wife support (called **alimony**), unless the wife had been unfaithful or had otherwise forfeited her right to support.

3. **At Death of One Spouse:** [§761]   The common law developed a system of marital estates to protect the surviving spouse upon the death of the other spouse. At common law, a wife was given **dower**, and a husband **curtesy**. Dower and curtesy survive in a number of states and are referred to here in the present tense.

   a. **Dower:** [§762]   At her husband's death, a wife has dower in all freehold land (i) of which her husband is **seised during marriage** and (ii) which is **inheritable by issue** born of the marriage. Dower is a **life estate** in **one-third** of each parcel of qualifying land.

      (1) **Example:** H dies, owning Blackacre in fee simple. W is entitled to a life estate in one-third of Blackacre. H's heirs and devisees take Blackacre subject to W's dower.

(a) **Rationale:** In feudal times, dower was generous protection for the widow of a rich man. Upon the father's death, the eldest son and heir was entitled to move into the family mansion and take over the family lands. The widow might move into a dower cottage on the grounds, in which the eldest son might have been living with his family. The widow was entitled to one-third of the rents and profits from the land. For the widow of a poorer man, with small acreage or only a house, dower was not so generous. But the English courts fashioned marital rights on the model of a rich, landed gentleman. What was good for the landed class became the law for all.

(2) **In land seised during marriage:** [§763]   Dower attaches only to land of which the husband is seised during marriage. The husband has to be in possession and seised. Thus dower does **not** attach to any **leasehold** interest of the husband, nor to any **remainder** interest the husband has following a life estate in another. Nor does dower attach to the **personal property** of the husband, in which there is no seisin, nor to any **equitable interest** of the husband, where the trustee holds seisin. [Chaplin v. Chaplin, 24 Eng. Rep. 1040 (1733)]

(3) **In land inheritable by issue:** [§764]   For dower to attach, it must be **possible for issue** born of the marriage **to inherit** the land from the husband. Actual birth of issue is immaterial. Thus dower does not attach to land in which the husband has only a **life estate**. Nor does it attach to land which the husband owns with another person as **joint tenants** with the right of survivorship.

(4) **Examples of when dower attaches:** [§765]   H dies, owning some interest in the following tracts of land:
   —*Tract 1:* H owns in fee simple. (W has dower in Tract 1.)
   —*Tract 2:* H has a life estate, with remainder in A. (W does not have dower in Tract 2.)
   —*Tract 3:* H has a remainder interest following a life estate in B. (W does not have dower in Tract 3.)
   —*Tract 4:* H and A own as joint tenants with right of survivorship. The survivor owns the whole. (W does not have dower in Tract 4, since it is not inheritable by her issue.)
   —*Tract 5:* H has a 900-year term of years, and A has a remainder. (W has no dower in Tract 5.)
   —*Tract 6:* Owned by Ace Corporation; H owns all the shares in Ace Corporation. (W has no dower in Tract 6, because H's stock is personal property.)

(a) **Avoidance of dower:** [§766]   The above examples illustrate how easy it is for a husband to avoid dower if he decides to avoid it before taking title. Dower depends entirely on the husband taking title in some way that gives him **seisin, inheritable** by issue of the marriage. If he takes title in such a way as to prevent one of the conditions of dower from being satisfied, he has avoided dower. A husband in the real estate business, buying and developing land, might particularly want to avoid dower because his wife would have to sign every deed to release her dower (*see infra,* §768).

(5) **Rights during husband's life:** [§767]   Dower attaches to the land the moment the husband is seised during marriage. Until the husband dies, dower is *inchoate*—a word indicating that the wife has an interest that has not yet, but may become, possessory. (Sometimes inchoate dower is thought of as a mere expectancy, but when the wife is contending with persons who deal with her husband after inchoate dower attaches, it is treated and protected as an existing interest in her.) Once inchoate dower attaches, the wife prevails over any subsequent purchasers of the property and over any attaching creditors of the husband. They take the property subject to her dower.

(a) **Example:** H, married to W, purchases Blackacre, taking title in his own name. Upon purchase, W has inchoate dower in Blackacre. No subsequent person can cut out her dower if she survives H. Later H sells to a bona fide purchaser who has no notice of W's dower interest. H dies. W is entitled to a life estate in one-third of Blackacre. The purchaser takes the land subject to W's dower.

(b) **Release of dower:** [§768]   Because dower rights prevail over subsequent purchasers, a purchaser from a married man must have his wife release dower in order to take free of it. This means the wife must sign the deed, releasing her dower. If the purchaser does not know if the seller is married or not, the purchaser takes the risk. *The rule is:* Once inchoate dower has attached, a wife cannot lose dower without her consent.

(c) **Divorce:** [§769]   An absolute divorce puts an end to the marriage and to inchoate dower. A legal separation does not bar dower.

(6) **Rights on husband's death:** [§770]   On the husband's death, leaving his wife surviving, dower gives his wife the right to possession *for her life* of *one-third* of *each parcel* of land subject to dower. Unless the surviving wife and the heir or devisee agree otherwise, dower in each parcel is assigned to the wife by a court. When a parcel is divisible, one-third of the parcel is set off to the wife for her life. When a parcel is not capable of metes and bounds division, an assignment of one-third the rents and profits from the parcel is made. Note that the wife's dower is not terminated by remarriage after her husband's death.

(a) **Dower in defeasible estates:** [§771]   Suppose that the husband holds a defeasible fee which comes to an end after the husband's death. Does the widow's dower terminate too? Restatement of Property section 54 takes the position that dower is a derivative estate, giving the wife no greater rights than the husband had, and terminates when the deceased husband's fee simple terminates.

1) **Example:** O conveys Blackacre "to H and his heirs so long as intoxicating liquor is not sold on the premises." Subsequently H dies; W has dower in Blackacre. Under the Restatement, if liquor is sold on the premises, W's dower ends when the fee simple terminates. But there are cases permitting W's dower to continue.

(7) **Statutory abolition:** [§772]   Dower has been abolished in the majority of states. Dower exists only in Arkansas, the District of Columbia, Iowa, Kentucky, Michigan, Minnesota, Ohio, South Carolina, Virginia and West Virginia. In some of these jurisdictions, the spouse's dower share is increased from a life estate in one-third of realty to a fee simple in one-third or a fee simple in one-half. In some other states, the dower label is appended to the elective share, which means that common law dower has been abolished in fact although not in name. [*See, e.g.,* Mass. Gen. Laws ch. 189, §1]

   (a) **Constitutionality:** [§773]   The retroactive abolition of dower has been held constitutional and not a taking of the wife's property. For purposes of legislative revision of marital property interests, the wife's interest is viewed as a mere expectancy, and not a property interest. [Opinion of the Justices, 151 N.E.2d 475 (Mass. 1958)] In Michigan, dower is given to widows only, and not to widowers. This sex discrimination may be unconstitutional because it appears to deprive men of equal protection of the laws. [*See* Boan v. Watson, 316 S.E.2d 401 (S.C. 1984)—dower for widows only unconstitutional as gender based discrimination]

b. **Curtesy:** [§774]   At common law, upon his wife's death, a surviving husband had an estate somewhat comparable to dower, but it differed in several ways. First, the husband had curtesy *only if issue were born of the marriage* ("heard to cry within the four walls"). Thus the husband, but not the wife, was penalized if the couple proved barren. This gave the husband an incentive to produce issue—which was thought to be a very desirable state of affairs. Second, the husband received a life estate in *all his wife's lands*, and not merely in one-third, as in dower. This of course reflected the notion that males should control all the land, whereas a female needed only a certain amount for support. Third, the husband's curtesy extended to his wife's *equitable interests held in possession*. This came about because fathers set up trusts for their daughters to avoid jure uxoris of their husbands. Equity thought it fair to give a widower an estate at death in his wife's lands held in trust although the husband had no control of her lands in trust while she was living.

   (1) **Statutory abolition:** [§775]   By modern statutes, where dower has been retained, the husband has been given rights equal to dower rights, and common law curtesy has been abolished. Where dower has been abolished, so has curtesy. In every state except Michigan, the spouses are treated equally.

B. MODERN STATUTORY RIGHTS

1. **During Marriage:** [§776]   By statute, each spouse today has control over his or her property.

   a. **Antenuptial agreements:** [§777]   Prospective spouses may make an antenuptial agreement governing their property rights during marriage. If fair and reasonable or made with full disclosure, these contracts are probably enforceable, though they are as yet little litigated. [Stein-Sapir v. Stein-Sapir, 52 App. Div. 2d 115 (1976)]

b. **Uniform Marital Property Act:** [§778]   The Uniform Marital Property Act, promulgated in 1983, adopts the principles of community property although it avoids that term. The Act provides that all property acquired *during marriage other than by gift or inheritance is marital porperty.* This is the definition of community property in community property states (*see infra*, §789). All other property is *individual* property. Husband and wife have equal interests in marital property, and their rights in it during marriage and upon divorce or death are more or less the same as the rights of spouses in community property. In 1984, Wisconsin became the first state to adopt the Uniform Marital Property Act.

2. **Upon Divorce:** [§779]   Upon divorce, almost all common law states provide for an *equitable distribution* of the spouses' property. The equitable distribution statutes vary. Some authorize the court to divide all property of the spouses, regardless of the time and manner of acquisition. Others authorize division of all property acquired during marriage by any means. Still others authorize division only of property acquired during marriage from earnings. This last position adopts, in effect, a community property principle for equitable distribution. Equitable distribution requires the court to consider a broad range of factors. [*In re* Marriage of McManama, 399 N.E.2d 371 (Ind. 1980)]

a. **Antenuptial agreements:** [§780]   An antenuptial agreement providing for rights upon divorce may not be enforceable. Under older cases, an antenuptial agreement attempting to limit the husband's duty of support or providing for property division upon divorce was almost always held invalid. It was thought to give an incentive for divorce. However, some modern cases enforce the agreement if fair and reasonable *or* based upon full knowledge of each other's property. This is the same test used for enforcing an antenuptial agreement waiving the elective share at death (*see infra*, §786). [*In re* Marriage of Dawley, 17 Cal. 3d 342 (1976)]

3. **At Death—Elective Share:** [§781]   Almost all common law property states give the surviving spouse an elective share in the *decedent's property owned at death.* The share is usually one-half or one-third. Somes states retaining dower give the surviving spouse a choice of dower or an elective share.

a. **Differs from dower:** [§782]   An elective share applies to both *real and personal* property whereas dower applies only to land. The surviving spouse takes an interest in *fee simple*, not just for life. In these respects, the elective share is broader than dower. But in two important respects, the elective share gives the surviving spouse *less* protection than dower. First, when inchoate dower attaches, the wife is protected against subsequent purchasers from, and creditors of, the husband. The elective share, however, is *only in property owned by the decedent spouse at death.* The spouse may sell the property or creditors may attach it during life, thus depriving the surviving spouse of anything. Second, subject to certain exceptions noted below, the husband can give away the property during his lifetime without his wife's consent and eliminate her interest in the property.

    (1) **Example:** H dies survived by W and owning Blackacre, some stocks, and some cash. H also owned Whiteacre during marriage to W, but H gave Whiteacre

away to D five years before death. Under dower, W has a life estate in one-third of Blackacre and Whiteacre. Under a typical elective share statute, W can elect to take a one-third share of Blackacre, the stocks, and the cash.

b. **Election required:** [§783]   The surviving spouse has an option of taking an elective share *or* taking what the decedent left her by will. She cannot have both. If she elects her elective forced share, she must renounce the will benefits.

c. **Inter vivos transfers:** [§784]   Almost all states offer some protection to the surviving spouse against inter vivos gifts that defeat the spouse's elective share. In one state or another, the surviving spouse may be allowed to reach (take an elective share from) inter vivos gifts made with the *intent* to deprive her of her elective share, gifts in *fraud* of her elective share, *illusory transfers*, or *revocable transfers*. Inasmuch as these inter vivos transfers often take the form of a revocable trust, this matter is discussed *infra* at §§831-835, in connection with trusts.

(1) **Antenuptial transfers:** [§785]   Secret transfers made before marriage, when marriage is contemplated, may be deemed fraudulent as to the spouse. Fraudulent intent is ordinarily presumed when the gift is made without the knowledge of the prospective spouse. [Strong v. Wood, 306 N.W.2d 737 (Iowa 1981)]

d. **Antenuptial agreement:** [§786]   A spouse may waive his or her rights to an elective share in an antenuptial agreement. Such agreements have ordinarily been enforced if the agreement makes a fair and reasonable provision for the surviving spouse *or* the decedent spouse has made a full, accurate, and specific disclosure of his or her property.

C. COMMUNITY PROPERTY

1. **Introduction:** [§787]   Eight states (Arizona, California, Idaho, Louisiana, Nevada, New Mexico, Texas, and Washington) have community property between married couples. The system of community property is traceable to French or Spanish influence in the South and West. The summary below can only sketch the general idea of community property. Many variations exist in each of the eight states. (For a detailed discussion, *see* Community Property Summary.)

a. **Basic theory of community property:** [§788]   Community property rests upon a notion that husband and wife are a marital partnership (a "community"), that both contribute to the material success of the marriage, and that both should share equally in material acquisitions. Community property is owned in equal undivided shares by the spouses. Community property in one form or another exists throughout the continent of Europe, but it never crossed the English channel. Under the pressure of a militaristic feudalism, the English judges suppressed any tendencies toward community property. And by the time the feudal period had ended, the legal subjugation of the wife to the husband had become entrenched. Hence while husband and wife shared earnings equally on the continent, in England all earnings belonged to the wage earner who was, in the vast majority of cases, the husband. Community property recognizes and rewards the work of a spouse who stays at home and does housework. Common law property does not.

2. **What is Community Property:** [§789]   Community property consists of *earnings* of either spouse *during marriage* and property acquired through earnings. Property owned by either spouse *before marriage* or acquired after marriage by *gift, descent, or devise* is *separate property*. This division of property follows from the basic theory that husband and wife should share equally material acquisitions resulting from the labor of either during marriage.

   a. **Income from community property:** [§790]   Once property is characterized as community property, all income and proceeds of sale of the property are community property. If new assets are purchased with community funds, the new assets are community property. One spouse cannot, without the other's consent, change community property into separate property. Remember, community property belongs to both husband and wife.

      (1) **Example:** H earns $1,000 from his job at General Dynamics. H uses the $1,000 to buy ten shares of Beta stock in his own name. The Beta stock is community property, even though held in H's own name. H cannot change community property (earnings) to his separate property without W's consent. Thus, how title is held is not controlling; whether the asset is traceable to earnings is controlling.

   b. **Income from separate property:** [§791]   In Idaho, Louisiana, and Texas, the income from separate property is community property; in other states, the income from separate property retains its separate character. Where the characterization of the property is doubtful, there is a *strong presumption in favor of community property*.

   c. **Damages from personal injury:** [§792]   If the husband or wife recovers damages for personal injuries, the damages are community property. The theory is that the injury reduced the earning capacity of the spouse, and the damages should go to the community to compensate it for lost earnings.

   d. **Pensions:** [§793]   Pensions, which are earned, are treated as community property upon divorce if the pension rights are vested. Even if nonvested—because the employee spouse has not yet worked a sufficient number of years—pension rights may be treated as community property upon divorce. [Smith v. Lewis, 13 Cal. 3d 349 (1975)]

3. **Commingling of Community and Separate Property:** [§794]   If community and separate property have been commingled in such a manner that it is impossible to ascertain and identify each source, the commingled whole will be presumed to be community property.

   a. **Example:** H and W maintain a bank account depositing therein both earnings and income received from separate property. If no records are kept as to which deposits are separate property and which community, the commingled whole will be treated as community. The same result occurs when H and W buy a parcel of land using both separate and community funds to pay the purchase price and keep no records.

4. **Community Services Used To Enhance Separate Property:** [§795]   Where one spouse devotes time and effort in managing his or her separate property, thus increasing its value, the enhanced value is partly attributable to the spouse's separate investment and partly due to the spouse's skill and industry. The enhancement due to the spouse's skill and industry belongs to the community. How is this calculated? There are two principal rules applicable, and they are best seen by an illustration:

   a. **Example:** H at the time of marriage owns a business valued at $100,000. After marriage, H continues to manage the business. Profits of $80,000 have accumulated. What portion of the profits is community and what portion is separate property? First, the court must decide if the ***chief*** contributing factor in realizing profits is the capital investment of H or the personal efforts of H. If the court finds that the ***greater factor was H's efforts*** (a community asset), the court will allocate a fair return (say seven percent per annum) on the $100,000 investment to H as his separate property and allocate any excess to community property. [Pereira v. Pereira, 156 Cal. 1 (1909)] If the court finds that H's personal services were not the greater factor in creating profits, the court will allocate the reasonable value of H's services to community property (say a salary of $10,000 a year), and allocate the balance to separate property. [Van Camp v. Van Camp, 53 Cal. App. 17 (1921)] In determining which is the greater factor, subjective matters come into play, and the court tries to do substantial justice. If H is a person of special talents in the business, the court will probably follow the *Pereira* rule. On the other hand, if H's services could have been performed by another person of the same ability, the court will probably follow the *Van Camp* rule. [Beam v. Bank of America, 6 Cal. 3d 12 (1971)]

5. **Conveyance of Share:** [§796]   Neither spouse acting alone can convey ***his or her share*** of community property, except to the other spouse. However, ***by agreement of the parties***, community property may be converted into the separate property of either spouse, or conversely, separate property may be converted into community property.

   a. **Joint tenancy:** [§797]   Husbands and wives often buy property with community funds and take title in joint tenancy. In this case, there is, in most states, a rebuttable presumption that the parties desired to change the community property into a joint tenancy with rights of survivorship. In California, for purposes of dividing property upon divorce, all property acquired during marriage in joint tenancy form is presumed to be community property. The presumption can be rebutted only by a "clear statement in the deed" or other title document. [Cal. Civ. Code §4800.1—abrogating *In re* Marriage of Lucas, 27 Cal. 3d 808 (1980)]

6. **Management of Community Property:** [§798]   Either husband or wife, acting alone, can manage community property; either can sell it, lease it, invest it, etc. Thus, technically H has the right to manage W's earnings as well as his own, and W has the right to manage H's earnings as well as her own. Each is a fiduciary in exercising management powers. Each must use good faith in exercising authority and for breach of the fiduciary duty each is liable to the other spouse.

   a. **Example:** H and W own 100 shares of GM stock as community property. W decides the stock should be sold, and she sells the stock for its market price. She reinvests the proceeds in GE stock. Sale and reinvestment is within W's power.

b. **Real property:** [§799]   Usually land held as community property cannot be sold except with the consent of both husband and wife.

c. **Business interest:** [§800]   A spouse who is managing a business that is community property has the sole management and control of the business.

   (1) **Example:** W, a lawyer, operates a law practice. W maintains a bank account in her own name in connection with her law practice. W has sole management powers over the bank account and all the personal property used in her practice. H cannot sell the desks in W's office, nor draw on the business bank account.

d. **Gifts:** [§801]   The community property states follow different rules respecting gifts of community property by one spouse. In some states, a spouse may make reasonable gifts and, in others, gifts not in "fraud" of the other spouse. In still other states, the non-donor spouse may set aside the gift entirely.

7. **Rights at Dissolution of Marriage:** [§802]   When the marriage is dissolved by divorce, community property is usually divided equally. When the marriage is terminated by the death of one spouse, the decedent spouse has the right to transfer his or her one-half of the community property by will to anyone.

8. **Removal of Spouses to Common Law State:** [§803]   Rights in *personal property* are generally characterized by the law of the state where the married couple is domiciled when the property is acquired. Rights in *land* are characterized by the law of the state in which the land is located. Suppose that H and W are domiciled in California, and out of H's earnings the couple saves enough to buy Blackacre in Massachusetts and $100,000 in stocks and bonds. As far as the ownership of Blackacre is concerned, Massachusetts law controls, and Massachusetts does not recognize community property in Massachusetts land. However, the purchase money (community property) belongs half to W, and if W does not consent to how title is taken in Massachusets, a constructive trust will be imposed on Blackacre giving W a one-half interest. As for the stocks and bonds, they are community property, and if H and W thereafter move to New York, the stocks and bonds remain community property. The ownership of property, once given by the state where acquired, does not change when the property crosses state lines.

   a. **Removal to community property state:** [§804]   If H and W are domiciled in New York, they cannot have community property. If H and W move to California, the title to their existing assets remains the same. But after they move to California, all earnings *thereafter* while domiciled in that state are community property.

   b. **Migratory couples:** [§805]   If H and W move around a lot, among common law and community property states, their marital property may be completely entangled. If the marriage is terminated by divorce or death in a community property state, the problems are largely resolved by the strong presumption that all assets of H and W are community property. The spouse claiming that assets are separate property has the burden of proof. If the marriage is terminated in a common law property state, very difficult tracing problems may arise.

VII. TRUSTS, CONDOMINIUMS, AND COOPERATIVES

chapter approach

The three forms of ownership discussed in this chapter are all types of divided ownership. None fits easily into one of the prior chapters on divided ownership because each has features not covered under prior topics. The *trust* is a device whereby a trustee manages property for one or more beneficiaries. Title is divided into legal and equitable title, and the trust ordinarily has a life beneficiary and one or more remaindermen. The *condominium* and the *cooperative* are assemblies of various concepts to create new devices for sharing ownership and management of property. These recent arrivals on the property scene have proven popular in urban housing.

If you see these devices on your property exam, it will probably be in connection with other divided ownership issues (such as life estates and remainders) or, in the case of condominiums and cooperatives, in connection with landlord-tenant or easements and covenants problems.

A. THE TRUST

1. Introduction

a. **Trust defined:** [§806]   A trust is a fiduciary relationship with respect to property in which one person, the *trustee*, holds the legal title to property (called the res) subject to equitable rights in *beneficiaries* (sometimes called cestuis que trust). It is basically a device whereby one person manages property for the benefit of others. The person who creates a trust is called the settlor (or trustor).

b. **Intention to create an express trust:** [§807]   The most common kind of trust is an *express trust*, one created expressly by a settlor. The settlor must manifest an intent to create an express trust. To create an express trust of land, a written instrument is required (by the Statute of Frauds). The written instrument may be a deed or will. However, an express trust of personal property may be created inter vivos by written or spoken words or by conduct. It is not necessary to use the word "trust" if the evidence shows the settlor intended that relationship. An oral declaration of trust of personal property is valid in almost all jurisdictions.

   (1) **Declaration of trust:** [§808]   A declaration of trust is one where the *settlor* declares *herself* trustee for the benefit of another. *Example:* S orally declares before witnesses "I hold a one-quarter undivided interest in this horse in trust for the benefit of A." This is a valid declaration of trust. *No delivery* of the trust property is necessary for a declaration of trust. (Indeed, it is hard to deliver one-fourth of a live horse.) (*See* "Oral trusts," *supra*, §217.)

      (a) **Evidence:** [§809]   Since the settlor is the trustee under a declaration of trust, and notification of the beneficiary is not required, cases often arise over whether the settlor has sufficiently manifested an intent to create a trust. Usually the settlor must notify someone of the trust (*e.g.*, a third party, a corporation issuing stock to be held by the settlor in trust), and the settlor must segregate the trust property, identify it as such, and keep separate account books for the trust. [Farkas v. Williams, 125 N.E.2d 600 (Ill. 1955)]

(2) **Deed of trust:** [§810]   A deed of trust is an instrument *delivered* by the settlor to *another person* as trustee establishing the trust. *Delivery* is essential for a deed of trust, just as it is for a gift (*see supra*, §§193 *et seq.*).

(3) **Revocable trusts:** [§811]   Either a declaration of trust or a deed of trust may be made revocable by the settlor. The settlor may retain the power to revoke. (If the settlor revokes, the trust property is returned to the settlor.) Although a trust may be made revocable, a gift without a trust *cannot* be revocable. Hence, whenever a person wants to make a revocable transfer, a transfer in trust is almost always the desirable—perhaps the only—route.

c.   **Elements of an express trust:** [§812]   An express trust must have (i) a *trustee*, (ii) *property* for the trustee to manage, and (iii) *beneficiaries*.

(1) **Trustee:** [§813]   A trustee is necessary for a trust. The trustee can be one person, or two or more persons can act as co-trustees. If the office of trustee becomes *vacant*, a court will appoint a successor trustee if the trust instrument does not name a successor trustee.

(a) **Acceptance:** [§814]   The office of trusteeship carries onerous burdens and liabilities, as well as pecuniary gain in the form of trustee's fees. Because of the liabilities, a person must consent to be trustee. If a person named by the settlor's will as trustee refuses to serve, a court will appoint a trustee.

(b) **Who can be trustee:** [§815]   Any person of legal capacity can serve as trustee. The settlor can serve as trustee, a beneficiary can serve as trustee, or a third party can serve as trustee.

(c) **Must have active duties:** [§816]   The trustee must have *active duties* in order to have a trust. If the trustee does not have active duties, the trust is said to be *passive*, and the trust fails. The beneficiary takes legal title. (For the historical roots of this, *see supra*, §601, discussing the active trust as an unexecuted use.) However, modern courts are astute at finding some active duty whenever they are convinced the settlor intended a trust.

(2) **Res:** [§817]   To have a trust, there must be trust property (a *res*) for the trustee to manage. If there is no res, there is no trust. The trust property can be land, personal property (such as stocks and bonds), a future interest in property—it can be anything the law conceives of as "property."

(a) **Fractional interest:** [§818]   The trust res may be a fractional or undivided interest in specific property. For example, the trust res may be an undivided one-fourth interest in a race horse. [*See* Cochrane v. Moore, *supra,* §193]

(3) **Beneficiary:** [§819]   A trust cannot exist without someone to enforce fiduciary obligations against the trustee. Thus, a beneficiary is necessary to the validity of every trust. If there is no beneficiary, there is a **resulting trust** (or **equitable reversion**) in favor of the settlor.

(a) **Trustee as beneficiary:** [§820]   The trustee can be a beneficiary of the trust. But if the trustee is the **sole** beneficiary, there is no trust. Where one person holds **legal title and the entire equitable title**, the equitable title merges in the legal title. This makes sense; if A is the trustee and also sole beneficiary, it makes no sense to say that A is a trustee when the only person who can sue her is herself. A trust thus requires that someone **other than the trustee** be a **beneficiary** of some interest. The beneficiary's interest can be quite small, of little value, but it must be something the law calls an "interest." It must give rights to a beneficiary other than the trustee to sue the trustee.

1) **Example:** Albert Farkas buys stock and takes title in the name of "Albert Farkas, as trustee for Richard Williams." Farkas retains the right to receive the income from the stock, to amend the trust in any way, and to revoke the trust entirely, in which case the stock belongs to Farkas. If the trust has not been revoked, on the death of Farkas, the stock is to belong to Williams. This is a valid trust. Williams' contingent right to receive the stock on Farkas' death is an interest which gives Williams the right to sue Farkas for misfeasance in carrying out the trustee's duties. Williams' right may seem rather illusory, because if he sues Farkas during Farkas' lifetime, Farkas will revoke the trust, destroying Williams' interest. But nonetheless, until Farkas does revoke the trust, Williams has an interest. [Farkas v. Williams, *supra,* §809]

2. **Duties of a Trustee:** [§821]   In administering the trust, the trustee must exercise that degree of care, skill, and prudence as would be exercised by a **reasonably prudent person** in managing his or her own property. The trustee owes several duties to the beneficiaries, but the two duties most often resulting in litigation are the duty of making trust property **productive** and the duty of giving undivided **loyalty** to the beneficiaries. If the trustee breaches a fiduciary duty, the trustee is **personally liable**.

a. **Making property productive:** [§822]   The trustee has the duty to make the trust property productive, which includes the duty to invest the trust property in a prudent fashion and receive a reasonable return of income. In most states the trustee must **diversify** the trust investments. It is deemed imprudent to "keep all the eggs in one basket."

(1) **Example:** The trustees of the mine workers' pension fund keep $50,000,000 (or thirty percent of the fund's total resources) on deposit in a checking account in a bank, which pays no interest. This is a breach of the duty to make property productive. [Blankenship v. Boyle, 329 F. Supp. 1089 (D.D.C. 1971)]

b. **Undivided loyalty:** [§823]   The trustee owes the beneficiaries of the trust undivided loyalty. He must reap no personal advantage from his position and must not put himself in a position where a conflict of interest is possible. The trustee cannot borrow trust funds nor buy any of the trust assets. Self-dealing in any form is absolutely prohibited.

(1) **Example:** X, trustee, decides to sell 100 shares of Red Company, which has a market value of $50 per share. Instead of selling the shares on the New York Stock Exchange, X sells the shares to himself for $50 a share. This is absolutely forbidden, even though X pays the full market price. (Why? Because the dangers of improprieties—particularly in establishing market price—are too great in self-dealing.) Upon breach of duty, the beneficiaries can either set aside the transaction or affirm it. If Red Company stock rises to $75 per share, the beneficiaries will likely set aside the sale, and X will hold the stock in trust. If Red Company stock falls to $25 per share, the beneficiaries will likely affirm the transaction. The risk is on the self-dealing trustee.

(2) **Benefits to others:** [§824]   The trustee must manage the trust for the exclusive benefit of the beneficiaries, and not for the benefit of other persons or organizations. When trust investment activities have the purpose of benefiting others, the trustee is in breach of trust. [Blankenship v. Boyle, *supra*]

3. **Change in Circumstances:** [§825]   A trust instrument ordinarily contemplates that the trust assets will be tied up in trust for a substantial period of time. The settlor, however, cannot wholly foresee the future, and events may occur which require deviation from the terms of the trust instrument. Deviation may be possible by a court decree based on one of the following doctrines:

a. **Administrative deviation:** [§826]   A court may authorize a trustee to deviate from the *administrative terms* of a trust if compliance with the terms of the trust would *substantially impair* the accomplishment of the trust purposes **and** the settlor **did not anticipate** the changed circumstances.

(1) **Example:** Joseph Pulitzer dies in 1911, devising his *New York World* newspaper stock in trust for his family. Pulitzer's will directs the trustee not to sell the *World* stock, as he wants to perpetuate the newspaper in his descendants' hands. During the 1920s, the *World* begins to run losses every year and becomes entirely unprofitable. Upon application by the trustee, a court will authorize the trustee to sell the *World* stock. [*In re* Pulitzer's Estate, 139 Misc. 575 (1931)]

b. **Cy pres—applicable to charitable trusts:** [§827]   If the trust is a charitable trust, a court can apply the doctrine of *cy pres*. The cy pres doctrine states: When the settlor has a **general intent** to aid some form of **charity**, and the **particular** charitable purpose **becomes impracticable or impossible** to achieve, a court will reform the trust to carry out as nearly as possible under changed conditions the settlor's general charitable intent. *Note:* The settlor must have a **general** charitable intent. A desire to assist one specific charity alone will prevent the court from reforming the instrument to benefit other similar charities.

(1) **Example:** T bequeaths a fund in trust to grant scholarships to male members of the Salem Methodist Church to attend Harvard College. The Salem Church has only 236 members, mostly adults, and no one has applied for a scholarship. The church asks the court to reform the trust to enable it to give scholarships to male or female applicants for graduate or undergraduate study at Harvard, and to give scholarships to nonchurch members if there are no member applicants. The court will reform the trust if it finds that the testator had a general charitable intent to provide scholarships to Harvard University, and not an intent limited to the specified purposes. [Wesley United Methodist Church v. Harvard College, 316 N.E.2d 620 (Mass. 1974)]

4. **Spendthrift Trusts:** [§828]   A spendthrift trust is one in which the settlor imposes a valid **restraint on alienation**, providing that the beneficiary **cannot transfer** his interest **voluntarily** and that his **creditors cannot reach it** for the satisfaction of their claims. Despite the general invalidity of restraints on alienation (*see supra*, §396), the validity of spendthrift restrictions on **equitable** interests has been recognized in most American states. [Broadway National Bank v. Adams, 133 Mass. 170 (1882)]

   a. **Example:** S transfers a fund in trust to pay the income to A for life, remainder to B. The trust instrument provides: "Each beneficiary, A and B, is hereby forbidden to alienate his interest, nor shall the interest of any beneficiary be subject to claims of his creditors." A cannot transfer his life estate, and his creditors cannot reach it. B cannot transfer his remainder, and his creditors cannot reach it.

   b. **Rationale:** The legal title to the trust assets is in the trustee, and the specific trust assets are alienable by the trustee. The trustee can change investments if desirable. Therefore, the trust assets are not made inalienable by a restraint on the equitable interests. All the restraint on the equitable life estate does is to make the stream of income inalienable. The policy issue is then: Is it wise public policy to permit trust beneficiaries to enjoy a stream of income unreachable by creditors? Views on that matter have been sharply divided.

   c. **Exceptions:** [§829]   In some states, a beneficiary's former **wife and children** have been given the right to reach the beneficiary's interest for support. If this exception is applicable, the wife and children of A in the above example can have a court direct the trustee to pay the income of the trust to them to satisfy their support obligations. [Shelley v. Shelley, 354 P.2d 282 (Or. 1960)]

   d. **Discretionary trusts:** [§830]   If the spendthrift trust is not recognized, the settlor can give the beneficiaries some protection from their creditors by creating a **discretionary trust**. In a discretionary trust, the trustee has the discretion to withhold payment of income. The beneficiary has **no right** to the income and cannot legally force the trustee to give it to him. Thus, there is **no interest** for the creditors of the beneficiary to reach. The trustee can refuse to pay creditors just as she can refuse to pay the beneficiary.

5. **Defeating Spouse's Elective Share:** [§831]   In almost all common law property states, the surviving spouse is given a forced share (usually one-third or one-half) in the decedent's property owned at death (*see supra*, §781). Suppose that a husband wishes to defeat his wife's elective forced share, and during life he transfers all his property into a trust with income payable to him, remainder to others, with the **right to revoke** the trust at any time. After the husband's death, can the wife reach the trust assets to satisfy her elective forced share? If not, she may be left penniless. The states have divided into five groups.

   a. **Valid transfer test:** [§832]   The first group of states holds that if property has been validly transferred in trust during life, the surviving spouse cannot reach it. [Kerwin v. Donaghy, 59 N.E.2d 299 Mass. (1945)—*overruled prospectively by* Sullivan v. Burkin, 460 N.E.2d 572 (Mass. 1984)]

   b. **Intent test:** [§833]   The second group of states holds that if an inter vivos transfer is made with the **intent** to deprive the other spouse of her elective share, the property transferred is subject to the surviving spouse's elective share. Motive or intent is the controlling issue.

   c. **Fraud test:** [§834]   The third group of states holds that any transfer in **fraud** of the marital rights of the surviving spouse is subject to the surviving spouse's elective share. The fraud test weighs a wide variety of factors. *But note:* The intent and fraud tests have been rejected in most jurisdictions because they cast doubt on the validity of all transfers made by a married person outside of the regular course of business.

   d. **Illusory transfer test:** [§835]   A fourth group of states applies the illusory transfer test. A transfer over which the transferor retains substantial control is deemed illusory and subject to the surviving spouse's elective share. The key is the **amount of control** of rights retained. [Newman v. Dore, 275 N.Y. 371 (1937)—now abrogated by N.Y. Est. Powers & Trusts Law §5-1.1 (1981) (specifying types of inter vivos transfers reachable by surviving spouse)]

   (1) **Example:** H is married to W and owns $500,000 worth of stocks and bonds, and little else. H transfers all his stocks and bonds to X as trustee to pay the income to H for his life, and on H's death, to convey the trust property to A. H retains the power to revoke the trust. On H's death, W is entitled under state law to one-half of all property owned by H. The revocable trust is treated as illusory, and therefore owned by H. W can require the trustee to give her $250,000 in trust property.

   e. **Statutes:** [§836]   A fifth group of states has statutes on the subject. These statutes usually give the surviving spouse the right to reach any inter vivos transfer over which the deceased spouse retained a power of revocation or power of appointment. [N.Y. Est. Powers & Trusts Law §5-1.1 (1981)]

B. CONDOMINIUMS

1. **Introduction:** [§837]   The condominium form of ownership—which has been widely used in other parts of the world—was virtually unknown in this country until the early 1960s. Since that time, it has captured the popular imagination and is increasing rapidly in use. In this country, condominium ownership has taken the form of individual ownership of individual units organized with common areas, and mutual rights and obligations in the common areas. Statutes have been enacted in all states authorizing condominiums. The early statutes were called "Horizontal Property Acts" because the usual condominium involves the division of air space into horizontal layers, with separate fees simple in each layer piled one on top of another. The Uniform Condominium Act was approved in 1977 and has been adopted in many states, replacing the earlier acts. All condominium developments must conform to the state statute. A condominium usually consists of apartments, but it can consist of commercial units, separate houses, or town houses.

2. **Essential Features:** [§838]   Each condominium development consists of individual units, common areas, and perhaps "limited common areas."

    a. **Unit ownership:** [§839]   Each individual unit (apartment, office, store) is owned separately in **fee simple**. The boundaries of a unit are sometimes defined as the interior surfaces of the perimeter walls, floors, and ceilings. In interpreting deeds and plans, the physical boundaries of the unit as they actually exist control over any contradictory metes and bounds description or plans used prior to construction. The unit may include a space restricted to use by the unit owner, even if the space is not within the boundaries of the individual unit, *e.g.*, a parking space, storage room, balcony, or patio. [Uniform Condominium Act §2-102]

        (1) **Leasehold:** [§840]   Although the usual condominium unit is owned in fee simple, a unit can be held in any possessory estate, including a life estate and leasehold. Thus the unit owners may have ninety-nine-year leases, at the end of which title reverts to the original landowner.

    b. **Common areas:** [§841]   The entire condominium except the individual units is called common area. This includes walls, staircases, elevators, etc. The common area is owned by all owners of the units as **tenants in common**.

        (1) **No right to partition:** [§842]   Unlike the ordinary tenant in common, the condominium tenant has **no** right to partition the common areas so long as the structure remains intact.

        (2) **Easement for entrance and support:** [§843]   A nonexclusive easement for entrance and exit and for support, through the common areas, is appurtenant to each unit.

c. **"Limited common areas":** [§844] "Limited common areas" refers to common areas and facilities created so as to be available for the use of more than one but less than all unit owners. For example, a stairway or elevator giving access only to a certain apartment is a limited common area. Limited common areas are maintained by the management at the expense of all unit owners.

d. **Financing:** [§845] Each unit owner may finance the purchase of her unit independently of all other owners in the project. The unit owner gives the mortgage lender, who finances the purchase, a *separate mortgage* on her unit, for which she alone is responsible. The failure of one unit owner to make payments permits the mortgagee to foreclose on that unit. The other unit owners are not affected. Thus, so far as the mortgage is concerned, there is no financial interdependency with other owners. But there may be financial interdependency by virtue of monthly charges to keep up the common areas.

3. **Creation of a Condominium**

a. **Declaration of condominium or master deed:** [§846] A condominium is ordinarily created by a declaration or master deed stating that the owner is creating a condominium to be governed by the provisions of the state condominium act. Most states require that the declaration be recorded in the county recorder's office. The declaration may contain many details of the organization of the condominium—or alternatively, these may be set forth in separate bylaws signed by each unit owner at the time of purchase of the individual unit. The declaration and bylaws attempt to solve in advance problems that may arise from condominium ownership. Among the matters dealt with are the following:

(1) **Membership association:** [§847] All owners of units are members of the unincorporated condominium association. An elected board of directors runs the association. Until all the units are sold, the developer may keep control of the association and management. [Barclay v. DeVeau, 429 N.E.2d 323 (Mass. 1981)]

(2) **Management:** [§848] The board can manage the condominium or, more commonly, a professional manager is employed. One of the recurring problems with both condominiums and cooperatives arises where the manager has a long-term contract and a majority of the unit owners become dissatisfied with the management. Ordinarily, long-term management contracts cannot be abrogated without a vote of two-thirds or more of the unit owners. [Point East Management Corp. v. Point East One Condominium Corp., 282 So. 2d 628 (Fla. 1973)]

(3) **Owner's fraction:** [§849] Each owner's fractional share of the whole project is set forth. This usually fixes permanently the unit owner's proportionate interest in the common areas, including his share of the common expense and his interest in the whole project upon its destruction. Since each unit is taxed separately, the assessor may value the project as a whole and then use this fraction to compute the property tax on a unit.

b. **Promulgation of rules:** [§850] The membership association is empowered to make rules to govern the operation and use of the common areas and the conduct of unit owners within their units to prevent unreasonable interference with the use of other units by their owners. These rules may appear as bylaws of the condominium (and amendable by a two-thirds vote) or as rules of the association (amendable by a majority vote). The bylaws may even be amended to regulate use *within* a unit. [Breeve v. Plaza Tower Association, 310 N.W.2d 730 (N.D. 1981)]

(1) **Types of rules:** [§851] Promulgated rules of conduct have led to the most conflict among condominium owners, but they have been upheld by courts if reasonable. The rules may relate to use by children, keeping pets, use of alcohol, playing the piano or stereo, permissible plants for landscaping, or any other matter deemed in the interest of the unit owners. [Hidden Harbour Estates, Inc. v. Basso, 393 So. 2d 637 (Fla. 1981)]

c. **Deed to individual unit:** [§852] Each purchaser of an individual unit is given a deed, transferring title to him. The deed is a deed of real property and must comply with local recording statutes applicable to deeds. (*See* Recording Acts, *infra*, §§1984 *et seq.*)

4. **Administration of Common Areas**

a. **Expenses of maintenance:** [§853] The statute or condominium declaration should—and ordinarily does—provide that unit owners are liable for their shares of common expenses. Otherwise, the common law rule that a co-tenant cannot recover from another co-tenant except for necessary repairs applies (*supra*, §743). The provisions for financial contributions are covenants, and to be enforceable against subsequent purchasers must comply with the requirements for covenants to run with the land in law or equity (*infra*, §§1431 *et seq.*).

(1) **Enforcing payment:** [§854] Most declarations and some statutes provide for the imposition of a lien to enforce collection of assessments for common expenses. This lien may be foreclosed by the management in the same manner as a mortgage on real property.

b. **Improvements and renovation:** [§855] Inasmuch as it is unclear at common law whether, and to what extent, a majority of co-owners can authorize the cost of improvements to the building or common areas to be assessed against all, this should be, and ordinarily is, covered in the declaration or bylaws.

c. **Tort liability:** [§856] Individual unit owners are, of course, subject to tort liability for injuries occurring inside their respective units. In addition, all of the unit owners are jointly liable for injuries occurring in the common areas—which they own as tenants in common. The owners' association may also be liable for such injuries (on the ground that it has assumed management and control of the common areas), but this has no effect on the owners' personal liability. As a practical matter, each purchaser of a condominium unit will have to make sure the owners' association maintains adequate liability insurance to cover his personal liability for such injuries. Tortious conduct for which owners are liable includes failure to maintain common areas such as halls, elevators, and boilers; failure to supervise pools or playgrounds where children congregate; violation of housing codes. [Dutcher v. Owens, 647 S.W.2d 948 (Tex. 1983)—unit owners' liability for torts in common area limited to pro rata share of ownership]

(1) **Compare—cooperatives:** [§857]   The rule in cooperatives is just the opposite. The cooperative association owns the entire building, and, therefore, the injured party sues the cooperative *corporation* for injuries in common areas. The owner-tenant's liability is, in effect, *limited* to the value of his stock in the corporation. In a condominium, on the other hand, the association does not own the building, and thus all individual unit owners are subject to liability for injuries in the common areas.

5. **Restrictions on Transfer:** [§858]   Restrictions are often imposed on the transfer of a condominium unit. The restriction usually prohibits the transfer of the condominium unit without the consent of the association. These restrictions run into the following problems.

a. **Restraint upon alienation:** [§859]   In a condominium, the unit owner owns a fee simple. As previously discussed (*supra*, §§401 *et seq.*), direct restraints on transferring a fee simple have usually been held void, and the question arises whether a restraint on a condominium unit will be governed by the same rule as is usually applied to a fee simple. The courts appear to be developing a rule that the restraint is valid if reasonable.

(1) **What is reasonable:** [§860]   To date, there are not many cases defining what is reasonable. A restraint forbidding the sale to persons with small children has been upheld as reasonable. On the other hand, the cases are split over whether forbidding sale of a unit to several unrelated persons for use on a time-sharing basis is reasonable. [Seagate Condominium Association v. Duffy, 330 So. 2d 484 (Fla. 1976)—restriction reasonable; Laguna Royale Owners Association v. Darger, 119 Cal. App. 3d 670 (1981)—restriction unreasonable]

(2) **Administrative regulations:** [§861]   Where condominiums are subject to state regulation, the state regulatory agency may determine what is a reasonable restriction upon transfer. For example, California regulations provide that the Real Estate Commission will approve only "uniform and objective standards and qualifications for the sale or lease." If the unit owner cannot find a purchaser who meets such standards, he can be required to give the association an option to purchase which must be exercised within fifteen days. [Cal. Admin. Code tit. 10, ch. 6, art. 12, §2792.10] Identical regulations apply to cooperatives.

b. **Illegal racial discrimination:** [§862]   The Fair Housing Act [42 U.S.C. §3604 (*infra*, §962)] prohibits discrimination in sale or rental of housing on grounds of race, color, religion, sex, or national origin. The Civil Rights Act of 1866 [42 U.S.C.

§1982] bars all racial discrimination in the sale or rental of property. If it can be shown that the condominium association is using restrictions on transfer with the intent of discriminating illegally, the association can be enjoined from doing so, and may be liable for damages. [Robinson v. 12 Lofts Realty, Inc., 610 F.2d 1032 (2d Cir. 1979)]

   c. **Unconstitutional state action:** [§863] If the association refuses to approve a transfer for reasons that interfere with constitutional rights (particularly the right to marry and procreate and the right to freedom of association), it can be argued that it is unconstitutional state action for a court to enforce the restriction. The question, not yet authoritatively answered, is whether the principle of *Shelley v. Kraemer, supra,* §444, applies to judicial enforcement of nonracial covenants interfering with some constitutional right. (*See supra*, §444.) If judicial enforcement is ultimately held to be state action, the second question is whether the infringed constitutional right is subject to reasonable restriction in the public welfare.

6. **Conversion to Condominiums:** [§864] In order to maintain the stock of rental housing, many cities have enacted ordinances prohibiting or regulating the conversion of rental apartments to condominiums. Sometimes these ordinances have prohibited the eviction of any tenant who chooses not to buy. These ordinances have usually been upheld as a valid exercise of the police power. [Grace v. Town of Brookline, 399 N.E.2d 1038 (Mass. 1979); Flynn v. City of Cambridge, 418 N.E.2d 335 (Mass. 1981)]

C. COOPERATIVES

1. **Introduction:** [§865] A cooperative apartment house usually takes the following form: A corporation holds legal title to an apartment building. Shares of stock are sold to the persons who will occupy the apartments; the amount of stock required to live in the building depends upon the value of the apartment (size, location, etc.). In addition to owning stock in the corporation, the occupants receive leases from the corporation. The leases may be for long terms (ninety-nine years) or for short, renewable terms. Thus, the residents in a cooperative are ***both tenants*** (under their leases with the cooperative corporation) ***and owners*** of the cooperative corporation (by virtue of stock interests).

2. **Basic Characteristics:** [§866] The tenant-shareholders elect a board of directors which operates the building. Rent may be increased or decreased by the board of directors, depending on the operational costs.

   a. **Liability for mortgage payments:** [§867] The entire project (land and buildings) is normally subject to a blanket mortgage. This mortgage has priority over the occupancy leases, which means that, in event of foreclosure, the lender (mortgagee) will wipe out each tenant's interest. This is true even where the mortgage was executed after the lease. Each lease will be found to contain a provision "subordinating" the tenant's interest to the blanket mortgage. Although an individual tenant in the cooperative is not personally liable on the blanket mortgage, the risk of foreclosure of the blanket mortgage means that each tenant is in effect obligated to come up with any deficiency if other tenants fail to pay the rent. Because of the financial interdependency of the tenants, there is substantial risk to cooperative members if there are many rent defaults.

(1) **Capital improvements:** [§868] The board of directors can raise money to finance capital improvements simply by increasing the mortgage on the cooperative property. (This may be an advantage of the cooperative over the condominium.)

b. **Liability for taxes, maintenance, and repairs:** [§869] Repairs within each apartment are the responsibility of each tenant (lease normally so provides). Taxes and repairs to the building exterior and common areas are normally the responsibility of the cooperative corporation. If the rent payments are insufficient, the corporation raises the rent accordingly so that each tenant ends up paying his proportionate share.

3. **Restrictions on Transfer:** [§870] Normally both the lease and stock interest of each tenant are subject to restrictions on transfer. The purpose of these restrictions is to assure the remaining tenants that the new tenant will be compatible and financially responsible. Problems that arise are similar to those discussed in connection with condominiums (*supra*, §858). There may be more justification for a restraint in a cooperative than in a condominium, however, because the cooperative members are in a joint financial venture whereas the condominium owners are not. The cooperative has more need to be assured of the financial responsibility of the purchaser.

a. **Restraint upon alienation:** [§871] Older cases took a rather conceptual approach to whether a restriction on transfer was an unlawful restraint on alienation. They reasoned that inasmuch as a restraint on a *leasehold* is valid, as is a restraint on sale of stock, a restraint on sale of a cooperative apartment is valid. [Penthouse Properties, Inc. v. 1158 Fifth Ave., Inc., *supra*, §405] Furthermore, the cooperative corporation can arbitrarily withhold its consent to transfer. [Weisner v. 791 Park Ave. Corp., *supra*, §405]

(1) **Modern trend:** [§872] A few cases apply a reasonableness test to restrictions on transfer of a cooperative apartment. The restriction must be reasonably tailored to the purposes of assuring financial responsibility and social compatibility. The application of the restriction to particular buyers is reviewable by a court. [Mowatt v. 1540 Lake Shore Drive, 385 F.2d 135 (7th Cir. 1967)]

b. **Preemptive option:** [§873] Rather than retaining the right to veto the transfer, the cooperative corporation may retain the *right of first refusal* (a preemptive option) if any member wishes to sell his stock and lease. Preemptive options restrain alienation, and to be valid must be *reasonable* in purpose *and* in duration. Again, courts have been very liberal in upholding preemptive options in cooperative ventures. [Gale v. York Center Community Cooperative, *supra*, §406] Preemptive options in cooperatives and condominiums have been held not subject to the Rule Against Perpetuities.

    c. **Racial discrimination and unconstitutional action:** [§874] The discussion in connection with condominiums of restrictions interfering with statutory and constitutional rights (*supra*, §§862-863) is equally applicable to cooperatives.

4. **Termination of Lease:** [§875] The corporation may terminate the lease if the tenant fails to pay his assessed share of common expenses or violates rules of conduct established by the corporation. [Green v. Greenbelt Homes, Inc., 194 A.2d 273 (Md. 1963)]

    a. **Limitation:** [§876] The rules of conduct promulgated by the board of directors are unenforceable if they are arbitrary or unreasonable. [Justice Court Mutual Housing Cooperative v. Sandow, 50 Misc. 2d 541 (N.Y. 1966)—regulation prohibiting the playing of musical instruments after 8 p.m. and by any one person more than an hour and one half per day held unreasonable and unenforceable; hence termination of lease of pianist not allowed]

5. **Advantages Over Ordinary Leases:** [§877] The advantages of a cooperative over a landlord-tenant relationship include:

    a. **Tenant control:** [§878] The tenants, owning the corporation, control the building. They can set their own standards of maintenance and rules of conduct.

    b. **Capital gains:** [§879] If the value of the land and building rises, the capital gain goes to the owner-tenants in the form of rise in value of stock. When the owner-tenant sells his stock and moves out, he realizes this gain. Of course, he has the risk of loss as well, if the value of the apartment house goes down.

    c. **Income taxes:** [§880] Property taxes and mortgage interest assessed against the unit owners are ***deductible*** on income tax returns. In ordinary leases, these costs of operation are paid by the landlord and covered by the tenant's rent (which is not deductible by residential tenants).

VIII. LANDLORD AND TENANT

chapter approach

This chapter covers the major topics on landlord-tenant law. Of all the various areas of property, landlord-tenant law has undergone the most change during the last twenty years. On the whole, it has been revised to give tenants more rights and landlords less. Revisions have not been accepted in all states however nor, where accepted, have they had uniform content. These recent changes are discussed in this chapter.

As another general comment to this area of law, remember that landlord-tenant law is a blend of property law and contract law. Thus, even though a lease is a contract, it is also a transfer of a property interest; hence, depending upon the particular facts, sometimes property law will prevail over contract law, and at other times, the opposite will be true.

More specific considerations for study are:

1. **Types of Tenancies:** Be sure you can identify the four types of tenancies:

   —*Tenancy for years* (fixed period with beginning and ending dates; may be less than a year);
   —*Periodic tenancy* (period to period—*e.g.*, month to month—until notice of termination given);
   —*Tenancy at will* (no stated duration, continues until landlord or tenant desires an end); and
   —*Hold-over tenancy* or *tenancy at sufferance* (tenant remains after the end of his tenancy).

2. **Landlord's Duties:** The landlord has a duty:

   —*to deliver possession* at the beginning of the lease;
   —*not to interfere with the tenant's quiet enjoyment* (watch for issues of actual or constructive eviction); and
   —*to provide habitable premises* (at common law, the landlord generally had no duty, but courts today often find a duty imposed by an express warranty, implied covenant, or a statutory duty).

   A landlord is generally not liable for torts unless the tort is related to a concealed dangerous condition, common areas, public use, or if the landlord has a statutory or contractual duty to repair.

3. **Tenant's Duties:** The tenant *must pay rent*! Also, tenant has a duty:

   —*to repair in order to maintain* the premises and not to commit waste;
   —*not to disturb other tenants*; and
   —*not to use the property for illegal purposes*.

   Remember that these duties may be *independent* of duties of the landlord. Thus, the tenant will still have a duty to pay rent even though the landlord may have breached one of the landlord's duties.

4. **Landlord's Remedies:** The landlord may use the common law right of distress (abolished or statutorily altered in many states), statutory liens, security deposits, or rent acceleration clauses. Of course, the landlord's most common remedy is *eviction*.

5. **Assignment and Sublease:** Be sure you determine from the facts of your question whether there has been an *assignment* (a transfer of the entire interest under the lease) or a *sublease* (transferor retains an interest in the leasehold). Check to see whether the lease allows such a transaction. And also determine who is liable for rent and other obligations.

6. **Other Topics:** Recall that the landlord's right to select tenants may be limited by legislation (*e.g.*, Fair Housing Act, state laws, etc.); and for questions involving public housing, keep in mind that there are requirements for eligibility, notice and hearing, and site selection.

Finally, note that landlord-tenant questions on your property exam will involve issues touching on at least some of the above topics. Other topics may be reserved for other courses (*e.g.*, "real estate"). Obviously, which topics you'll see on your exam will depend on your professor.

A. INTRODUCTION

1. **Background:** [§881] Landlord-tenant law developed during feudal agrarian times to regulate the relationship between a landlord and his tenant farmer, an able-bodied man. The land itself was the important thing. Any buildings thereon were crude and could be fixed by the tenant. Because the law developed for the agricultural tenant, it imposed very few duties on the landlord. At early common law, the only duty the landlord had was not to evict the tenant so long as the rent was paid. In the second half of the twentieth century, this law has seemed in various respects unsatisfactory for the urban dweller, and it is now in the process of modernization and adaptation to the needs of the urban tenant.

    a. **Chattel real:** [§882] Although there is some dispute, the tenancy for years probably arose as a moneylender's device to avoid the church's strict prohibition against collecting interest on a loan. O, a landowner in need of money, would borrow a sum from a moneylender and in return transfer to the moneylender a portion of O's land for a period of time. The rents and profits from the land took the place of interest on the loan. Because of its beginning as a moneylender's device, a leasehold—like a mortgage today—was categorized as personal, not real, property. It was called a "chattel real." This peculiar categorization still lingers, and wherever it is necessary to classify a property interest as realty or personalty, a leasehold—a "chattel real"—is classified as personalty. For example, a statute of intestate succession might provide that decedent's children inherit real property subject to the widow's dower, whereas decedent's widow and children inherit personal property equally. Any leasehold owned by the decedent is personal property, and under such a statute goes to the widow and children equally.

    b. **Tenant does not have seisin:** [§883] A leasehold estate is not a freehold, and the tenant does not have seisin but only possession. In this way leaseholds differ from the freehold estates (fee simple, fee tail, life estate). The difference was historically important but matters very little today.

2. **Property Law and Contract Law Both Applicable:** [§884]   Landlord-tenant law is a blend of property law and contract law. This results from a lease being both a *conveyance of an estate in land* and a *contract containing promises* between landlord and tenant. Originally the lessee's rights were purely contractual, but from the sixteenth century onward the courts treated the lease as creating a possessory interest in land. For 400 years, property theory has dominated landlord-tenant law, but in the last twenty years, contract theory has been in the ascendant. It is important to see the difference between these two ways of analyzing the landlord-tenant relationship.

a. **Lease is a conveyance of leasehold estate:** [§885]   Landlord-tenant law traditionally rests upon a conception that the lease is a conveyance of property and that the tenant has purchased a leasehold estate in land. The parties to the conveyance can agree that the purchase price (known as rent) is payable at the beginning of the term, at the end, or in equal installments over the period. The tenant is entitled to possession of his estate, which he has the duty of maintaining. If a building on the land burns down, the tenant must continue to pay rent for the leasehold. The landlord has only the right to reenter and repossess the land upon breach of a covenant by the tenant (usually the covenant to pay rent). To put it in a nutshell, the traditional property rule is that the tenant has bought an estate in land and assumes the risks of caring for the estate.

(1) **Property rules apply:** [§886]   In some contexts a court will apply the property rule, in others the contracts rule. For example, a lease or conveyance of an estate in land must be *delivered* (handed over) to be effective (property rule), whereas a contract only has to be *executed* (signed). If the landlord signs the lease but does not deliver it, does the property rule or the contract rule apply? It has been held that the property rule applies; delivery of the lease is required to make it effective. [219 Broadway Corp. v. Alexander's, Inc., 46 N.Y.2d 506 (1979)]

b. **Lease is a contract:** [§887]   A lease is a contract containing promises (usually called covenants) of the parties. Most modern leases contain numerous covenants—promises to pay rent, taxes, or insurance, to repair, or to use the property for certain purposes. The lease is a document governing the relationship of landlord and tenant over the term of the lease. What happens when one party does not perform his promise? Can the other party withhold performance? Under contract law, covenants are deemed to be *mutually dependent*. If L does not do what he promises to do, T can refuse to do what he promises to do. The performance of one party's promise is dependent upon the performance of the other party's promises.

(1) **Independent covenant rule in leases:** [§888]   Promises in leases were, until the last twenty years, assumed to be *independent* of the other party's performance. The conception of a lease as creating a property interest was preferred to the conception of a lease as creating promises. For example, suppose that L rents T a house for four years; L promises in the lease to paint the house, and T prom-

ises to pay rent. After T moves in, L fails to paint the house. T is stuck for the rent. The performance of his promise to pay rent is not dependent upon the performance of L's promise to paint. The fundamental—and controlling—idea is that T purchased a four-year term in the land, and T must pay the agreed consideration for the specific thing for which he bargained. L's promise to paint is viewed as merely an incidental promise, enforceable in a lawsuit by T against L for damages. The disadvantage of the independent covenant rule is that T cannot break the lease upon L's failure to perform, but has to sue for damages. However, modern law is coming more and more to apply contract law where a landlord breaches a covenant.

c. **Property rights may be dependent upon taking possession:** [§889]   It is sometimes said that the tenant has only contract rights prior to taking possession, that his property rights begin when he takes possession. Or, to use an old-fashioned phrase, until the tenant enters he has only an *interesse termini*, a right to enter. There is not much merit in this contention because a tenant out of possession but entitled to possession may recover possession from the lessor or a third party in an action in ejectment, which is of course a possessory action and not an action in contract. Nonetheless, where a tenant breaks the lease before entering possession, courts have sometimes invoked the interesse termini idea to support a holding that the landlord can only pursue a contract remedy for damages and not hold the tenant for rent.

(1) **Example:** L and T execute a lease entitling T to occupy L's building for five years. The lease is to commence three months later after L renovates the building. Two months after executing the lease, T notifies L that T is breaking the lease. Under property law, T is liable for the rent payable for the five-year term T has bought, and L has no duty to mitigate damages by re-letting. Under contract law, L must relet to another tenant if he is able to do so, and mitigate damages. Because the contract rule lessens damages and saves costs, it is preferable to the property rule. A court not wishing to overrule the property rule can apply the contract rule, saying that T has no property interest until T moves in, and therefore the contract rule applies. [Arthur Treacher's Fish & Chips of Fairfax v. Chillum Terrace Limited Partnership, 327 A.2d 282 (Md. 1974)]

3. **Lease Distinguished From Other Relationships:** [§890]   To have a landlord-tenant relationship, the landlord must transfer to the tenant the *right to possession* of the premises. Apart from freehold estates, a leasehold is the only other interest that gives the holder the right to possession. Other interests, such as an easement, license, or profit, entitle the holder to *use* another's land, but do not give possession.

a. **Transfer of possession is the key:** [§891]   An instrument creating a landlord-tenant relationship contemplates that the lessee will control the leased property and exclude others from it. It is the right to possession that distinguishes the lessee's interest from an easement, license, or profit. Possession is, of course, a word of many meanings, and often refers both to facts and to the legal conclusion that a party should be protected by calling him a possessor. Whether a particular transaction results in a transfer of possession, and is a lease, depends primarily upon the intention of the parties. What the parties call the transaction is important, but **not conclusive**. Other guides to intention are:

(1) **Uses permitted:** [§892]   Since possession of a space implies that the space can be used for a wide variety of uses, the more the use of the space is limited, the more likely it is that a lease has **not** been created.

(2) **Defined area:** [§893]   Since possession implies possession of a defined area and not a right to wander at large, the more specific the description of boundaries, the more likely it is that a lease has been created.

(3) **Rent reserved:** [§894]   A lease usually calls for periodic payment of rent, whereas an easement is usually purchased with a lump sum payment. The reservation of a periodic rent indicates a lease.

(4) **Duration:** [§895]   A lease is usually limited in time, whereas an easement is not. A grant of a property right for a specific duration, not unlimited in time, indicates a lease.

b.   **Oil and gas lease:** [§896]   A landowner ordinarily transfers oil and gas rights to a well operator by an instrument denominated a "lease." A typical instrument conveys "the right to drill for oil and gas for five years and so long thereafter as oil or gas is produced." This "lease" does not create a landlord-tenant relationship between landowner and operator. Jurisdictions split over the nature of the lessee's interest. Some states hold that an oil and gas lease is a conveyance of a **fee simple determinable** in the minerals in place (determinable upon cessation of oil and gas exploration or production). Other states hold the lessee has a **profit a prendre** (the right to take away something that is affixed to or part of the land). Landlord-tenant law, developed in the contexts of farm leases, commercial leases, and residential leases, is inappropriate for regulation of the rights of the landowner and oil operator. A special body of law has developed for oil and gas interests.

c.   **Billboard lease:** [§897]   An instrument giving the lessee the right to erect signs or billboards, though denominated a "lease," does not ordinarily create a landlord-tenant relationship. It is usually deemed to give the sign company an **easement** to come on the land and erect and maintain a sign. Easement law is more appropriate to the context than landlord-tenant law. [Baseball Publishing Co. v. Bruton, 18 N.E.2d 362 (Mass. 1938)]

d.   **Lodging agreements:** [§898]   Agreements to furnish lodging may differ in a great many respects, particularly the following: the length of time of occupancy, the control exercised by the occupant, and the nature and extent of services furnished by the owner of the property. The test in each case is to determine whether the control of the occupant over the premises is so great as to make her a tenant or is so small as to make her a licensee. Whether the parties intend the consequences of a landlord-tenant relationship is an important factor in this determination. [Cook v. University Plaza, 427 N.E.2d 405 (Ill. 1981)]

(1) **Hotel guest:** [§899]   A guest in a hotel room is usually treated as a *licensee*. The brief duration of her stay, the large control usually retained by the hotel, and the services furnished indicate that the hotel did not intend to give the transient guest exclusive possession of the room. Nor does the hotel or the guest contemplate that the guest will have the remedy of ejecting the prior occupant who does not vacate.

(2) **Apartment hotel:** [§900]   Renting of a unit in an apartment hotel at a weekly or monthly rental, particularly where the renter supplies furniture for the rooms, may create a *landlord-tenant* relationship, even though maid service is furnished.

(3) **Rooming house:** [§901]   A lodger in a rooming house is usually treated as a *licensee*, not as a tenant. Courts emphasize that where the owner retains keys and furnishes maid service, he has retained general control, and thus the lodger is not a tenant. However, if the rented room is unfurnished or if maid service is not provided, a lease is probably created.

e. **Legal differences between leases and licenses and easements:** [§902]   The legal consequences of characterizing an instrument as creating a lease rather than a license or easement are chiefly: (i) a lease can be oral, but an easement is subject to the Statute of Frauds and requires a written instrument; and (ii) of these relationships, *only a tenant has a possessory interest in land* and can bring a possessory action such as ejectment, trespass, or nuisance. A holder of an easement or license must bring a different kind of lawsuit for interference with his rights.

B. TYPES OF TENANCIES AND THEIR CREATION

1. **Tenancy for Years**

a. **Definition:** [§903]   A tenancy for years is an estate that lasts for some *fixed period of time* or for a period of time computable by a formula which results in fixing *calendar dates* for beginning and ending, once the term is created or becomes possessory. The period may be a certain number of days, weeks, months, or years, but regardless of the period, the tenancy is called a tenancy for years or a term of years. Examples of terms of years: "Ten years from the date of this lease," "one year from next Christmas," "from the date of this lease until next Christmas." In all these examples, the beginning and ending calendar dates can be fixed.

(1) **Tenancy of no fixed period terminable upon some event:** [§904]   Although the definition of a tenancy for years requires that a calendar date be fixed or computable for its ending, in a few cases where the lease is terminable upon some event but of no fixed period, courts have held that a tenancy for years has been created. The primary example of this is where O leases to A "for the duration of the war." This type of lease does not fit easily within any of the permissible categories, but the tenancy for years is the closest approximation of the parties' intention. Why? Because a tenancy for years cannot be terminated unilaterally by either party prior to the event fixing termination, it gives the parties the

benefit of their bargain. (A periodic tenancy or a tenancy at will can be terminated prior to the event.) But there are some cases which hew strictly to the requirement that a term of years have a calendar date fixed for ending, and deem a lease terminable upon some event to create a periodic tenancy or a tenancy at will or, if the event is in the control of the tenant, a life estate determinable.

(2) **Term of years determinable:** [§905]   A term of years (and a periodic tenancy as well) may be made terminable upon some event or subject to condition subsequent, in the same manner as a freehold may be made terminable upon an event. Thus if L rents to T for ten years "so long as used for a sawmill," a ten-year term of years determinable is created.

(3) **Day of beginning and ending:** [§906]   Unless the parties specify otherwise, a lease begins on the earliest moment of the beginning day and ends immediately before midnight on the date set for termination. Thus a lease of one year "from July 1 next" is usually held to begin at 12:01 a.m. on July 1 and end at midnight the next June 30.

b. **Maximum permitted term:** [§907]   Unless there is a statute to the contrary, a term of years can be created for as long a period as desired (even for 1,000 years). Some jurisdictions by statute restrict the number of years for which a leasehold estate may be created.

c. **Termination of tenancy for years:** [§908]   Since the parties know precisely when a term of years will end, a term of years expires at the end of the stated period ***without either party giving notice***. This is the chief difference between a term of years and a periodic tenancy, which requires notice for termination.

2. **Periodic Tenancy**

a. **Definition:** [§909]   A periodic tenancy is a tenancy for a period of some fixed duration which continues for succeeding periods until either the landlord or tenant ***gives notice*** of termination. *Examples:* "To T from month to month," or "to T from year to year." If notice of termination is not given, the tenancy is automatically extended for another period. In this way the periodic tenancy differs from a term of years, which automatically ends on the day set.

(1) **Extensions are part of same tenancy:** [§910]   Although the tenancy carries over from one period to the next, it is basically the same tenancy and not a new tenancy each term. Consequently, all the conditions and terms of the tenancy are carried over and are applicable in each subsequent period, unless there are express provisions to the contrary.

b. **Creation of periodic tenancies:** [§911]   A tenancy from period to period may be created by agreement of the parties or by operation of law.

(1) **Creation by express agreement of the parties:** [§912] The landlord and the tenant may expressly create an estate that is to extend from period to period. For example, "L to T for one year, and at the end of such term, the lease shall continue in effect from month to month, unless one of said parties shall end this lease by notice in writing delivered at least one month prior to the end of the term in which such notice is given." At the outset, T has an estate for one year (a term of years), which at the expiration of the first year becomes an estate from period to period (month to month), which will continue as such until the requisite notice is given.

(2) **Creation by agreement only as to rent period:** [§913] More frequently, a tenancy from period to period arises by implication where land is leased with no set date for termination, but provision is made for payment of rent monthly, quarterly, annually, etc. The tenant has a periodic tenancy measured by the rental periods. Thus, if T rents an apartment beginning June 1 and pays monthly rent, T is a tenant from month to month.

   (a) **Annual rent payable monthly:** [§914] Where the lease provides for an *annual* rent *payable monthly* (*e.g.*, "$6,000 per annum, payable $500 on the first day of every month commencing January 1"), is the estate from year to year or month to month? At common law (and in most jurisdictions today), if an annual rent is specified, the estate is from year to year, even though the rent is required to be paid in monthly installments. It is said that the monthly payments are merely for the convenience of the parties. This view is sometimes applied only to leases of *agricultural land*, and not to leases of dwellings, on the theory that farm land is almost always rented on a yearly basis.

      1) **Minority view:** [§915] A contrary view holds that the payment of rent on a monthly basis presumptively makes the tenancy one from month to month—even where it is a one-twelfth installment of a specified yearly rent. But this view, where followed, is usually applied only to leases of *dwellings*, and not to leases of agricultural land.

      2) **Why it matters:** [§916] If the lease is from year to year, six months' notice is required for termination. If T holds over for any period of time after expiration of the year, L can hold T for another year's rent. If the tenancy is month to month, either L or T can terminate the tenancy upon a month's notice (below).

(3) **Creation by operation of law:** [§917] A tenancy from period to period may arise in certain cases even in complete absence of any agreement of the parties.

   (a) **Where tenant holds over after expiration of the term:** [§918] Where T holds over after the end of the term, L may elect to consent to T's staying over and hold her liable for further rent as a periodic tenant for an additional term. (*See infra*, §948.)

(b) **Where tenant takes possession under an invalid lease:** [§919]   If L leases Blackacre to T for ten years at $500 per month, but for some reason the lease is unenforceable or void—*e.g.*, due to lack of formalities required by the Statute of Frauds—but T nevertheless goes into possession under the invalid lease, what result? The mere entry into possession by T creates a *tenancy at will*. The *payment of rent* periodically, however, converts the tenancy at will into a tenancy from *period to period* arising by operation of law.

c. **Requirement of notice of termination:** [§920]   Probably the most distinctive feature of a periodic tenancy is that it continues *until proper notice* of termination is given. Except where required by statute or the lease, the notice can be either oral or written. The main problems are how much notice is required and at what time it must be given.

(1) **Common law rules**

(a) **How much notice need be given:** [§921]   To terminate an estate from period to period, notice must be *equal to the length of the period* itself (*e.g.*, month, week, etc.) with the *exception* that if the tenancy is from year to year, only *six months'* notice is required. By agreement, however, the parties to a periodic tenancy may shorten the amount of notice required, or eliminate the requirement of notice altogether.

(b) **Notice must specify last day of period:** [§922]   The notice must fix *the last day of period* as the date for termination and not some intervening date. Thus, in the case of a month-to-month tenancy commencing on the first day of each month, if notice is given on January 20, terminating the tenancy on February 20, the notice is insufficient to terminate on February 20. (Under the majority rule (below), the notice will not terminate the lease on the last day of February either, because it does not specify that date.)

(c) **When notice must be given:** [§923]   The notice must be given so that the tenant or landlord will receive the required amount of notice prior to the expiration of the current term. For example, in a year-to-year tenancy, commencing on January 1, the notice must be given sometime prior to July 1 in order to terminate the estate on the following December 31. If the notice is given on July 2, the year-to-year tenancy will not end on December 31 next. A majority of courts go even further and hold that an ineffective notice does not terminate the periodic tenancy at the end of the following period. Thus a notice given July 2, 1980, terminating the tenancy December 31, 1980, has no effect at all. It does not terminate the lease on the earliest date a termination is possible, December 31, 1981, because it does not specify that day. The tenant is stuck with the rent until proper notice is given. [Arbenz v. Exley, Watkins & Co., 50 S.E. 813 (W. Va. 1905)]

1) **Restatement position:** [§924]   The Restatement (Second) of Property declines to follow the majority rule and provides that "if the date stat-

ed in the notice for termination is not the end of a period or is too short a time before the end of a period, the notice will be effective to terminate the lease at the earliest possible date after the date stated." This rule seems more likely to carry out the terminating party's intention than the majority rule adverted to above. [Rest. 2d §1.5, comment f (1977)]

(2) **Statutory modifications:** [§925] Statutes in many states reduce the six months' notice required to terminate a tenancy from year to year to one month's notice. It is thought that six months' notice is unreasonably long. Statutes in a few states go further and provide that a month-to-month tenancy can be terminated on any day, and not only on the last day of the period, provided one month's notice before the day specified is given. [*See* Cal. Civ. Code §1946] This is a debatable change, since a landlord or a tenant may find it hard to rent an apartment in the middle of a month.

3. Tenancy at Will

a. **Definition:** [§926] A tenancy at will is a tenancy of no stated duration which endures only so long as *both* landlord and tenant desire. Either can terminate it at any time. Consequently, its potential duration is not very great. A tenancy at will can arise expressly or, more often, by operation of law when the intended tenancy fails for some reason.

(1) **Tenant's possessory rights:** [§927] A tenant at will is not merely a licensee; she has an estate in land. The tenant has *possession*. She can maintain an action of trespass against third persons who intrude upon the premises, or even against the landlord himself if the latter enters without having first terminated the tenancy.

(2) **Tenancy terminable by only one party:** [§928] A leasehold that is terminable at the will of *only one* of the parties is not a tenancy at will. By definition, a tenancy at will must be terminable by the landlord or by the tenant and not by one of them alone. The first step in determining what estate is created if only one party can terminate the tenancy is to ascertain whether the power to terminate is affixed to a term of years or periodic tenancy or not.

(a) **Lease for certain duration terminable by one party:** [§929] If a provision for termination by one party is grafted onto a term of years or a periodic tenancy, the lease creates a determinable tenancy, not a tenancy at will.

1) **Example:** L leases a house "to T for one year, with a proviso that L can terminate at any time." This creates a determinable term of years, terminable at the will of L.

2) **Example:** L leases land "to T from year to year for use as storage space. T has the right to terminate the lease at any time." L can termi-

nate the lease only in accordance with the law respecting periodic tenancies. T can terminate at any time.

(b) **Lease for no certain duration:** [§930] If a leasehold has no certain duration (*i.e.,*, is not an estate for years or a periodic tenancy by its terms), but is terminable at will by one party, the courts are split:

1) **Tenancy at will:** [§931] Some courts imply a power of termination in the other party, since there is no certain duration. Thus, a tenancy at will is created.

    a) **Example—termination by landlord only:** L leases land to T "for and during the pleasure of the landlord." This creates a tenancy at will, and L or T can terminate at any time.

    b) **Example—termination by tenant only:** L leases land to T "for as many years as T desires" at a yearly rent of $300. This creates a tenancy at will, and L also can terminate at any time. [Foley v. Gamester, 170 N.E. 799 (Mass. 1930)]

2) **Determinable life estate:** [§932] Other courts hold that if the agreement does not create a term of years or periodic tenancy, but the tenancy is to continue so long as the tenant wills, the tenant has a life estate determinable.

    a) **Example:** L leases land to T "so long as T should wish." This creates a life estate in T, determinable on his death or prior relinquishment of possession. [Thompson v. Baxter, 119 N.W. 797 (Minn. 1909)]

b. **Termination:** [§933] An estate at will may be terminated either by acts of the parties or by operation of law.

(1) **Termination by acts of the parties:** [§934] If either the landlord or the tenant manifests an intention that the estate come to an end, this terminates a tenancy at will. The usual manifestation by the landlord is a notice to quit; the usual manifestation by the tenant is abandoning the premises or giving notice.

(a) **Notice not required at common law:** [§935] At common law, neither landlord nor tenant had to give any notice for a period of time as a prerequisite to terminating a tenancy at will. The tenancy at will terminated on the day notice of termination was received by the other party.

(b) **Statutes require notice:** [§936] However, most states today have statutes that require some sort of notice to terminate a tenancy at will. Usually thirty days' notice is required, but often this requirement is imposed on the landlord and not the tenant. [*See, e.g.,* N.Y. Real Prop. Law §228]

(2) **Termination by operation of law:** [§937]   A tenancy at will can also terminate by operation of law, regardless of the intention of the parties. *Sale of the property* (conveyance of the reversion) by the landlord, or attempted assignment by the tenant, terminates a tenancy at will. Similarly *death* of either landlord or tenant terminates the tenancy. Statutory provisions for *notice*, however, are usually held still applicable, so that in effect the tenancy will not terminate until the statutory notice period has expired.

4. **Statute of Frauds:** [§938]   A term of years, periodic tenancy, or tenancy at will may be created by an express provision in a written lease. But where there is no written instrument, problems arise concerning the application of the Statute of Frauds and the type of tenancy that can be created by an oral agreement.

   a. **Short-term lease exception:** [§939]   The English Statute of Frauds (1677) provided that all leases must be in writing *except a lease for three years or less*. This is known as the "short-term lease exception," and was put in the statute to permit oral leases of short duration which are not uncommon. Most American states by statute have reduced the short-term lease exception to one year. An oral lease for more than one year (or whatever period measures the short-term lease exception) creates a tenancy at will only.

      (1) **No short-term lease exception:** [§940]   In a few states, the Statute of Frauds does not contain any exception for short-term leases. An oral lease of any duration (say, for two months) creates only a tenancy at will. However, each of these states requires a thirty-day notice to evict a tenant at will. Hence, as a practical matter, an oral lease creates a tenancy for at least a thirty-day period.

   b. **Oral lease to commence in the future:** [§941]   Suppose on July 15 a landlord orally leases to a tenant "for one year commencing next January 1." Is this lease valid? Under the lease provision of the Statute of Frauds referred to above, it is valid because it is for only one year. But the English Statute of Frauds had a section on contracts in addition to a section on leases. The section dealing with contracts required all agreements not to be performed within one year *from the making of the contract* to be in writing. As discussed above, a lease is a contract, and this contracts section could apply to leases. Under this section, the above lease would be void because it cannot be entirely performed within one year from July 15. The majority of courts hold that the contracts section of the Statute of Frauds is not applicable to leases because leases are expressly dealt with in the section on leases. Thus an oral lease to commence in the future is valid if the term does not exceed one year. The Restatement adopts this view. [Rest. 2d §2.1, comment f]

   c. **Option to renew oral lease:** [§942]   Where there is an oral lease that is renewable at the option of the lessee, the lease is usually treated as extending to the end of the option period. Thus, if the oral lease is for a one-year term, with an option to renew for another year, the lease is treated as a two-year lease and is void if the short-term exception in the Statute of Frauds is one year.

(1) **Minority view:** [§943]   A minority holds that the original period and the option period are separable, and only the option which extends the duration beyond the short-term exception is void. This minority view is adopted by the Restatement. [Rest. 2d §2.1, comment c]

d. **Entry and paying rent under an invalid lease:** [§944]   Although an oral lease not complying with the Statute of Frauds is void, entry by a tenant under an oral lease creates a *tenancy at will*. As soon as the tenant pays rent, *a periodic tenancy* is created. However, there is some difference of opinion as to what is the period of the periodic tenancy.

(1) **Year-to-year tenancy:** [§945]   The majority view is that a year-to-year tenancy is created, regardless of how the rent is calculated in the void lease and of how rent is paid. *Rationale*: Since the invalid lease was necessarily for a term exceeding one year, a year-to-year tenancy comes closest to approximating the parties' intention. (*But note*: The notice requirements for terminating a year-to-year tenancy might surprise the parties who think the (invalid) term will end automatically without notice.)

(2) **How rent is calculated:** [§946]   Another approach is to determine the length of the period by how the rent is calculated in the invalid lease. If the rent is calculated on an annual basis, even though payable monthly, a year-to-year periodic tenancy will be created.

(a) **Example:** T enters under a written ten-year lease, not signed by L or T, and therefore invalid. The lease is to end January 31, 1948. T makes rent payments specified in the lease, which are calculated on an annual basis, even though payable monthly. T is a year-to-year tenant, and at common law six months' notice is required to terminate the tenancy. (*Note*: No notice would have been required to terminate the ten-year term, but notice is required to terminate the periodic tenancy. Hence if L notifies T in November, 1947, to vacate on January 31, 1948, when the ten-year period expires, L has not given sufficient notice to terminate the periodic tenancy, and T is entitled to stay until January 31, 1949.) [Darling Shops Delaware Corp. v. Baltimore Center Corp., 60 A.2d 669 (Md. 1948)]

(3) **How rent is paid:** [§947]   A third approach is to determine the length of the period by the way the rent is actually paid, regardless of how it is calculated in the lease. The Restatement provides an unusual variation on this method. It provides that the initial period is determined by the interval between rent payments, but then goes on to provide that after a month of rent payments the tenancy becomes month-to-month, after a quarter of rent payments the tenancy becomes quarter-to-quarter, and after a year of rent payments the tenancy becomes year-to-year. Thus the tenancy period gradually increases, up to a year. [Rest. 2d §2.3, comment d]

5. **Hold-Over Tenant:** [§948]   When a tenant rightfully in possession wrongfully remains in possession (holds over) after termination of the tenancy, she is called a *tenant at*

sufferance. The tenant at sufferance is not really a tenant at all since she is not holding with the permission of the landlord. On the other hand, she is not a trespasser either, since her original possession was not wrongful. She is in a peculiar situation, called a tenancy at sufferance which lasts only until the landlord **evicts** the tenant **or elects to hold the tenant to another term**. The prior tenancy of the holdover tenant may be a tenancy for years, a periodic tenancy, or even a tenancy at will. Thus if T has a one-year lease expiring October 1, and T stays on until October 2, L can elect to hold T to another term. Or if T is a periodic tenant, and L serves T with notice to quit and T does not leave when required, L can hold T to another period. Even if T is a tenant at will, and holds over after notice to quit, T is a tenant at sufferance. In this last case, L cannot elect to hold T to another term or period because there is none, but L may be able to use self-help in evicting T or claim double rent under some statute applicable to hold-over tenants. [Donnelly Advertising Co. v. Flaccomio, 140 A.2d 165 (Md. 1958); Margosian v. Markarian, 192 N.E. 612 (Mass. 1934)]

a. **Rationale:** The hold-over doctrine, permitting the landlord to hold the hold-over tenant to another term, is justified as a deterrent to holding over, which is thought not to be in the best interest of tenants as a class who should be able to move in promptly upon expiration of an old tenancy. However, the hold-over doctrine has been criticized as imposing a penalty disproportionate to fault.

b. **Excuses:** [§949] The common law admitted no excuses for holding over. The tenant holding over was liable for another term regardless of extenuating circumstances.

    (1) **Example:** T's one-year lease expires October 1. T begins moving on September 26, but is taken sick. T's clerks continue moving, but do not finish until October 11. In the meantime, T dies on October 6. L elects to hold T's estate to another term of a year. T's illness is no excuse, and T's estate is liable for another year's rent. [Mason v. Wierengo's Estate, 71 N.W. 489 (Mich. 1897)]

    (2) **Modern law:** [§950] Most modern cases give a tenant relief where the tenant does not intend to hold over but is forced to do so by circumstances beyond her control. The relief is that the landlord cannot elect to hold the tenant to another term if the tenant vacates as soon as possible in light of the circumstances. This view, which relieves the tenant only when moving is a near-impossibility and beyond the tenant's control, is endorsed by the Restatement. [Rest. 2d §14.4, comment i] At least one court has gone further and has relieved the hold-over tenant even without extenuating circumstances where a dilatory tenant held over for a few hours, on the ground that the damage to the landlord was de minimis. [Commonwealth Building Corp. v. Hirschfield, 30 N.E.2d 790 (Ill. 1940)] The difficulty with this last view, of course, is where to draw the line in deciding what is de minimis. If the landlord has no new tenant in prospect, is he damaged much if the old tenant holds over fifteen days or thirty? If this last view is accepted, why not push it to its logical end and give the landlord only actual damages suffered from the hold-over plus reasonable rental value for the period held over? The calculation of actual damages might be

inefficient. An arbitrary penalty might be cheaper to administer. (*Compare* the penalty imposed by URLTA, *infra*, §955—three months rent or actual damages.)

c. **Length of new term:** [§951]   In most jurisdictions, holding over gives rise (at the landlord's election) to a periodic tenancy; in the rest, it results in a term of years. As to the basis for the length of the period or term, some courts hold it is the way *rent is reserved* in the original lease, and other courts hold it is the **length of the original term** or period—but the maximum length in each case is limited to one year. According to the Restatement, holding over results in a periodic tenancy measured by the way rent is computed, up to a maximum period of one year. [Rest. 2d §14.4, comment f]

(1) **Example:** L leases to T for five years, ending on November 4, 1984, reserving a yearly rent of $7,000. T holds over, surrendering possession on November 27, 1984, after the lease has expired. Under any of the above views, L is entitled to elect to hold T over as tenant for another year. (If T does not abandon the property but stays on and L accepts rent, T is a periodic tenant from year to year. A periodic tenancy with periods determined by how the rent is calculated in the lease usually results.) [Fetting Manufacturing Jewelry Co. v. Waltz, 152 A. 434 (Md. 1930); *but see*, Crechale & Polles, Inc. v. Smith, 295 So. 2d 275 (Miss. 1974)]

d. **Provisions of new term:** [§952]   Except with respect to length, the new tenancy is governed by the provisions in the old lease, including provisions for payment of rent and any covenants made by the parties.

(1) **Demand for higher rent:** [§953]   If the landlord notifies the tenant that she must pay a higher rent if she holds over, the hold-over tenant may be liable for the higher rent unless she notifies the landlord that she refuses to pay. Silence by the tenant is usually deemed implied consent. But there are cases holding that silence of the tenant cannot be construed as consent. [Maguire v. Haddad, 91 N.E.2d 769 (Mass. 1950)]

e. **Self-help in recovering possession:** [§954]   At early common law, a landlord could use self-help to evict a tenant. But expeditious summary proceedings for eviction (forcible entry and detainer) are now available to a landlord, and in most states a landlord cannot use self-help but must resort to judicial process for eviction. Nonetheless, a majority of courts, while forbidding self-help against a tenant not holding over, still permit a landlord to use self-help to evict a tenant holding over, provided the landlord uses no more force than is reasonably necessary to dispossess the tenant. [Gower v. Waters, 132 A. 550 (Me. 1926)] The Restatement leaves this matter up to local law, suggesting in the comment that self-help is unnecessary. The policy issue is, in terms of landlord's remedies: Why should self-help be allowed against a hold-over tenant but not against a tenant who does not pay rent? [Rest. 2d §14.2]

f. **Statutory modifications of landlord's remedies:** [§955] Statutory modifications of the landlord's remedies against the hold-over tenant are not uncommon. These modifications usually weaken the landlord's remedies in the belief that the penalties are disproportionate to the act. Uniform Residential Landlord & Tenant Act ("URLTA") section 4.301(c), adopted in about a dozen states, provides:

> If the tenant remains in possession without the landlord's consent after expiration of the term of rental agreement or its termination, the landlord may bring an action for possession and if the tenant's hold-over is willful and not in good faith the landlord may also recover an amount not more than [three] months periodic rent or [threefold] the actual damages sustained by him, whichever is greater, and reasonable attorney's fees. If the landlord consents to the tenant's continued occupancy [the tenancy is week to week in case of a roomer who pays weekly rent, and in all other cases month to month].

(1) **Holding over willfully:** [§956] URLTA section 4.301(c) only penalizes a tenant who willfully holds over. Some statutes imposing a double rent on a hold-over tenant are not expressly limited to willful hold-overs, but courts have construed these penalty statutes strictly and declined to apply them unless the hold-over is willful. [Jones v. Taylor, 123 S.W. 326 (Ky. 1909)] *See also supra*, §950, discussing the refusal of courts to apply the common law doctrine where the hold-over is excusable. The majority of courts believe an excusable holdover should not be penalized by statute or judicial doctrine, but willful holdovers should be.

C. SELECTION OF TENANTS

1. **Introduction:** [§957] Historically, a seller or a landlord was free to sell or rent to whomever he pleased. But federal and state statutes now prohibit discrimination in the sale or rental of property on various grounds—usually race, color, religion, or national origin. These statutes differ in many details, as outlined below. These statutes ordinarily apply to both *sale and rental* of property. Since it is convenient to treat them in one place in this Summary, they are treated here in connection with landlords and tenants because leasing is discussed first in this Summary, before sale.

2. **Civil Rights Act of 1866:** [§958] The 1866 Civil Rights Act, enacted by Congress after the Civil War, provides: "All citizens of the United States shall have the same right, in every State and Territory, as is enjoyed by white citizens thereof to inherit, purchase, lease, sell, hold, and convey real and personal property." [42 U.S.C. §1982] Although this act was long thought to bar only racial discrimination by states, the Supreme Court in *Jones v. Mayer*, 392 U.S. 409 (1968), held that the Act barred "all racial discrimination, private as well as public, in the sale or rental of property."

a. **Bars racial discrimination only:** [§959] The Act bars racial discrimination only. It does not bar discrimination against persons because of their religion or national origin. A person refused a lease because he is a Buddhist or of Italian origin cannot sue under the Civil Rights Act of 1866. (But he could sue under the Fair Housing Act, below.)

b. **Applies to all property transfers:** [§960] The Act applies to sale or rental of all property, not just to housing. Thus if a landlord refuses to rent a commercial building to a prospective tenant because he is black, the prospective tenant can sue under the Civil Rights Act of 1866. (But he could not sue under the Fair Housing Act, below, which deals only with housing.)

c. **Remedies:** [§961] Although the Civil Rights Act of 1866 was couched in declaratory terms and did not provide any explicit method of enforcement, courts have fashioned effective remedies. The remedies for a person discriminated against under this Act are an injunction against the landlord or seller, or damages.

(1) **Example:** Little Hunting Park, a membership corporation, operates a park and playground. Membership is open to all white residents of Fairfax County. A person owning a membership share is entitled to assign the share to his tenant when he rents his home. O, a member, leases his house to A, a black person. The board of Little Hunting Park refuses to approve the assignment to A because A is black. This is a violation of the Civil Rights Act of 1866 [42 U.S.C. §1982] because part of the monthly rental is for assignment of the membership share, and hence the board's action is an interference with A's right to lease houses in Fairfax County on the same terms as a white person. A is entitled to an injunction requiring the board to approve the assignment. Because O advocated A's cause, Little Hunting Park expelled O. O is entitled to damages from Little Hunting Park, because no one can be punished for trying to vindicate the rights of blacks under the Civil Rights Act of 1866. A white person may be the only effective adversary of unlawful discrimination of this sort. [Sullivan v. Little Hunting Park, 396 U.S. 229 (1969)]

3. **Fair Housing Act of 1968:** [§962] In 1968, Congress enacted the Fair Housing Act as part of a larger Civil Rights Act of that year. The Fair Housing Act makes it unlawful to refuse to sell or rent a *dwelling* to any person because of race, color, religion, or national origin. In 1974, the Act was amended to prohibit discrimination on the basis of sex. [42 U.S.C. §3604]

a. **Additional prohibitions:** [§963] In addition to prohibiting renting or selling, the Act prohibits *advertising* that indicates any discriminatory preference [42 U.S.C. §3604(c)], block busting by real estate agents [42 U.S.C. §3604(e)], discrimination by mortgage lenders in financing the purchase of a dwelling [42 U.S.C. §3605], and discrimination in furnishing brokerage services [42 U.S.C. §3606].

b. **Exemptions:** [§964] The Fair Housing Act provides that certain specified persons are exempt from the Act. The purpose of these exemptions is to protect some types of close personal relationships from what is thought to be an invasion of privacy.

(1) **Single-family dwelling:** [§965]   A person leasing or selling a dwelling he owns is exempt if he: (i) does not own more than three such dwellings, (ii) does not use a broker, and (iii) does not advertise in a manner which indicates his intent to discriminate. [42 U.S.C. §3603(b) (1)]

(2) **Small owner-occupied multiple unit:** [§966]   A person is exempt if she is offering to lease a room or an apartment in her building of four units or less, one unit of which she occupies, and she does not advertise in a discriminatory manner. This is known as the "Mrs. Murphy exception," an allusion to "Mrs. Murphy's boarding house." [42 U.S.C. §3603(b)(2)]

  (a) **Exemption under section 1982:** [§967]   The Civil Rights Act of 1866 [now 42 U.S.C. §1982] does not have any exemptions for a single-family dwelling or for "Mrs. Murphy." Section 1982 applies to sales or rentals by an owner of a single-family dwelling or by Mrs. Murphy. A person denied admittance to Mrs. Murphy's apartments must sue under section 1982 rather than the Fair Housing Act of 1968.

  (b) **Example:** O inserts an advertisement in a newspaper offering to rent a room in her house to a white person. O is in violation of the Fair Housing Act prohibition against discriminatory advertising. If O does not advertise, she is not in violation of the Fair Housing Act if she refuses to rent to blacks. However, if O refuses to rent to blacks, O is in violation of the Civil Rights Act of 1866 [42 U.S.C. §1982], which contains no exemption for owner-occupied dwellings.

(3) **Private clubs:** [§968]   The Fair Housing Act exempts private clubs, not open to the public, which own lodgings as an incident to their main activities and wish to restrict them to their members or members' guests. [42 U.S.C. §3607] Section 1982 contains no exemption for a private club. To date, the courts have avoided the issue of whether section 1982 applies to a private club by deciding that the organization sued is not a "private club." [Tillman v. Wheaton-Haven Recreation Association, 410 U.S. 431 (1973)—a swimming pool with membership open to white persons who own homes within three-quarters of a mile of the pool was not a private club; hence was covered by §1982 providing that blacks have the same rights as a white person who buys property]

(4) **Religious organizations:** [§969]   The Fair Housing Act also exempts religious organizations which own dwellings for members' use and not for commercial purposes, provided the organization does not exclude members because of race, color, or national origin. [42 U.S.C. §3607]

c. **Enforcement:** [§970] The Fair Housing Act provides several remedies for enforcement.

  (1) **Litigation by aggrieved party:** [§971]   An aggrieved person may sue the seller or landlord in federal court, without regard to the usual jurisdictional requirements as to diversity of citizenship and dollar amount in controversy, and with

the right to a court-appointed attorney if he cannot afford one. The court may give the plaintiff an injunction or actual damages plus no more than $1,000 in punitive damages. [42 U.S.C. §3612]

(2) **Administrative action by HUD:** [§972]   An aggrieved person may bring a complaint to the Department of Housing and Urban Development ("HUD") which may investigate and attempt to use conciliatory and persuasive methods on the seller or landlord. If there is no successful resolution of the complaint, the Department may, subject to certain limitations, bring a civil action against the seller or landlord. [42 U.S.C. §3610]

(3) **Litigation by Attorney General:** [§973]   The U.S. Attorney General may initiate suits if he or she feels issues of great public importance are involved. [42 U.S.C. §3613]

4.   Proving Discrimination

a.   **Prima facie case—discriminatory effect:** [§974]   Suppose that a landlord adopts a practice for screening tenants that has a racially discriminatory effect; it screens out proportionately more blacks than it does whites. In order to make out a prima facie case of discrimination, must a plaintiff show that the landlord acted with racially discriminatory motivation, or is it enough to show that the landlord's practices have a discriminatory effect? Proof of discriminatory impact is sufficient to make out a prima facie case that the Fair Housing Act or section 1982 is violated. Proof of discriminatory intent is not necessary. If an individual claims he is the victim of a discriminatory denial of housing, he can establish a prima facie case by proving that he is black (or is within some other class protected against discrimination); that he applied for and is qualified to rent or purchase the housing; that he was rejected; and that the housing opportunity remained available to white persons. [Robinson v. 12 Lofts Realty, Inc., *supra*, §862]

b.   **Shift of burden of proof:** [§975]   Once the plaintiff establishes a prima facie case of discrimination, the burden shifts to the defendant to come forward with evidence to show that his actions were not motivated by considerations of race. Defendant must come forward to testify under cross-examination. To rebut plaintiff's prima facie case, the defendant must convince the court or jury of the sincerity of the defendant's stated reasons and negative any discriminatory intent that can be inferred from the *sequence of events*. If race is even one of several motivating factors, the statute is violated. Thus if defendant's evidence shows that plaintiff was rejected because she was a lawyer and a troublemaker, the rejection is legal, but if, in addition, there was also a racial motivation, the rejection is illegal. On the other hand, if after a full trial of the case, the court fails to find racial motivation, the statute is not violated.

c.   **Exploitation liability:** [§976]   Traditional types of discrimination are not the only types covered by the statutes. Section 1982 also covers exploitation of blacks in housing prices. The Supreme Court in *Jones v. Mayer*, 392 U.S. 409 (1968), said that section 1982 was meant "to assure that a dollar in the hands of a Negro will purchase the same thing as a dollar in the hands of a white man." Hence it has been held that section 1982 is violated where, as a result of racial residential segregation, one housing market exists for white buyers and another one for blacks, and sellers take advantage of this situation by demanding from blacks prices in excess of those paid by whites for comparable housing. [Clark v. Universal Builders, Inc., 501 F.2d 324 (7th Cir. 1974)] To illustrate, suppose that because of racial discrimination, blacks in Chicago find it difficult to buy houses except on Chicago's south side, where they must pay $10,000 more for a new house than a comparable house would cost on Chicago's white north side. This makes out a prima facie case that builder-sellers of housing on the south side are violating section 1982.

5. **State Statutes:** [§977]   A number of states have statutes prohibiting discrimination in selling or renting because of race, color, religion, or national origin. These statutes were passed before the Federal Fair Housing Act of 1968 and differ in details respecting enforcement procedures and exemptions. Often, to enforce such state laws, an aggrieved party must complain to a state administrative agency which may be empowered to issue orders or to bring an enforcement action in the state court. In addition, some states have statutes prohibiting discrimination in the sale or rental of property on grounds of sex or marital status, tenant's having children, physical handicap, or tenant's age. [Marina Point, Ltd. v. Wolfson, 30 Cal. 3d 721 (1982)—interpreting statute to require landlords to rent to families with children; O'Connor v. Village Green Owners Association, 33 Cal. 3d 790 (1983)—applying statute to condominiums]

   a. **Eviction for sharing apartment:** [§978]   Even if a state prohibits discrimination in renting because of marital status, as New York does, a landlord can evict a tenant who violates a provision in her lease that the apartment will be occupied only by the tenant and her immediate family. If the tenant moves a lover in, or another person who is neither kindred nor spouse, the landlord can eject the tenant. The eviction is not because of marital status but because of violation of restrictions on occupancy. [Hudson View Properties v. Weiss, 56 N.Y.2d 733 (1983)]

D. LANDLORD'S DUTY TO DELIVER POSSESSION

1. **Legal Right to Possession:** [§979]   The landlord has the duty of transferring to the tenant at the beginning of the tenancy the *legal right* to possession. The landlord warrants that she has the legal right to possession and is transferring this to the tenant. If another person has *paramount title* and is legally entitled to possession, the landlord is in default.

   a. **Paramount title:** [§980]   "Paramount title" refers to any title or interest in the leased land, held by a third party at the time the lease is made, which is paramount to the interest of the landlord. *Examples:* Before leasing, L gives M a mortgage on the property, which M records; M has paramount title. Or L has given a prior recorded lease to another tenant. Or L does not own the property at all.

   b. **Tenant's remedies prior to entry:** [§981]   If on the commencement of the term, a paramount title exists which could prevent the tenant from enjoying the use contemplated by the parties, and which the tenant is **unaware** of when he signs the lease, the tenant **prior to entry** may **terminate the lease**. The tenant does not have to begin his tenure if after signing the lease he discovers a possibility that he will be evicted by a paramount claimant. If he **knows of the paramount title at the time he signs the lease**, he is presumed to **waive** the possibility of eviction by the paramount claimant. In other words, L must make full disclosure of the risks to T before the lease is signed.

c. **After the tenant enters into possession:** [§982]   After entry by the tenant, the mere existence of a paramount title does not breach the landlord's duties. The tenant has **no remedy** unless he is actually evicted by paramount title. Once T takes actual possession, he is assumed to have accepted the landlord's title as adequate for his use of the property. The traditional way of putting this is to say that, after entry by the tenant, the landlord's covenant of quiet enjoyment is not breached by the mere existence of a paramount claim. Actual interference by the claimant with the tenant's enjoyment is necessary to breach the covenant.

2. **Actual Possession**

a. **"English rule"** (majority view): [§983]   In most jurisdictions, the landlord **has** the duty to deliver **actual** possession, as well as the **right** to possession, at the beginning of the term. If the previous tenant has not moved out when the new tenant's lease begins, and the landlord does not remove the person within a reasonable period of time, the landlord is in default. This is known as the "English rule," and is adopted by the Restatement. [Rest. 2d §6.2; Dieffenbach v. McIntyre, 254 P.2d 346 (Okla. 1953); Adrian v. Rabinowitz, 186 A. 29 (N.J. 1936)]

(1) **Rationale:** This carries out the intention of the parties since the tenant bargains for **use** of property, not a lawsuit against the prior tenant. Furthermore, the landlord is more likely to know if the previous tenant will move out and is in a better position to pressure him to do so. Finally, the landlord is usually much more familiar with eviction procedures than the tenant, and can evict the hold-over tenant at less cost. The last two reasons suggest it is more efficient to put the duty on the landlord than on the tenant.

(2) **Tenant's remedies:** [§984]   For the landlord's failure to provide actual possession, the tenant has several remedies. The tenant can terminate the lease and recover damages sustained by having to obtain quarters elsewhere. Or the tenant can affirm the lease, refuse to pay rent for the portion of the term during which he was kept out of possession, and recover damages. Damages include costs of renting other premises in excess of the rent specified in the lease, costs of ousting the hold-over tenant, and loss of anticipated business profits proven to a reasonable degree of certainty which the landlord could have foreseen. [Rest. 2d §10.2; *but see* Adrian v. Rabinowitz, *supra*—lost profits of a newly established business were too speculative for recovery but, in the alternative, if recoverable, they had not been proven]

(3) **Part possession:** [§985]   If the hold-over tenant is only in possession of part of the premises, and the new tenant takes possession of the other part, the new tenant is entitled to an appropriate abatement in rent and damages.

   (a) **Contrast—subsequent eviction:** [§986]   If the landlord once puts the tenant into possession of the entire premises, and the landlord *thereafter evicts* the tenant from any part thereof, the tenant's rent obligation is *wholly abated* (*see* discussion of partial eviction, *infra*, §995). But for failing to put the tenant into possession of some portion of the premises at the beginning of the tenancy, there is no such whole abatement. The latter default is not seen as deserving such a drastic penalty.

(4) **Waiver in lease:** [§987]   Some standard form leases contain a provision that the tenant waives the landlord's duty to transfer actual possession. URLTA sections 1.403 and 2.103 provide that the tenant's right to actual possession at the beginning of the term cannot be waived. A few cases hold that waiver is *unconscionable* and unenforceable in ∩ long complex form lease, printed in small type, prepared by the landlord.

b. **"American rule" (minority view):** [§988]   In some jurisdictions, the landlord has no duty to deliver actual possession at the commencement of the term, and hence is not in default under the lease when the previous tenant continues wrongfully to occupy the premises. This is known as the "American rule"—although it is actually a *minority* view. [Hannan v. Dusch, 153 S.E. 824 (Va. 1930)]

(1) **Rationale:** Several reasons are advanced for the American rule. First, the lease conveys a leasehold to the tenant. It is up to the tenant to take possession of his property if he wants it. Second, the tenant has the right to evict the hold-over by summary proceedings and needs no additional remedy against the landlord. Third, the landlord should not be held liable for the tortious act of the hold-over. Fourth, since the landlord is not required to evict a trespasser after the tenant takes possession, she should not be required to evict a trespasser before the tenant takes possession. These reasons are either technical or question-begging and do not address the fundamental issues of fairness and efficiency.

(2) **Remedies against the hold-over tenant:** [§989]   Since the incoming tenant cannot sue the landlord when actual possession is not available, what remedies has the incoming tenant against the tenant holding over? The incoming tenant generally has the same rights against the hold-over as a landlord would have. He can sue to evict him, and recover damages. Or the incoming tenant can treat the hold-over tenant as tenant for another term, with rent payable to the incoming tenant (*supra*, §§948 *et seq.*). Since the purpose of the hold-over doctrine and penalty is to give the person with the right to possession more clout to recover possession, it should extend to the incoming tenant with the right to possession. [United Merchants' Realty & Improvement Co. v. Roth, 193 N.Y. 570 (1908)]

(a) **Landlord's remedies:** [§990]   Since the incoming tenant may oust the tenant holding over, and the landlord has no duty to do so, may the landlord oust the hold-over tenant? The logical answer under the American rule is that the landlord cannot sue because she has no right to possession and no duty to put the incoming tenant in possession. (The English rule gives the landlord the right to sue the hold-over in order to perform the duty of putting the incoming tenant in possession.) But logic would lead to an unfair result if the incoming tenant, deprived of possession, simply walked away and defaulted. Should the landlord have rights only against the defaulting new tenant, who might be hard to serve or judgment-proof? No, the landlord should be able to oust the hold-over tenant as an alternative to pursuing a legal remedy against the incoming tenant. [Eells v. Morse, 208 N.Y. 103 (1913)]

E. LANDLORD'S DUTY NOT TO INTERFERE WITH TENANT'S QUIET ENJOYMENT

1. **Covenant of Quiet Enjoyment:** [§991]   A tenant has a right of quiet enjoyment of the premises, without interference by the landlord. This right arises from the landlord's *covenant of quiet enjoyment*, which may be expressly provided in the lease. If not expressly provided, such a covenant is *always implied* in every lease.

   a. **Dependent covenant:** [§992]   As noted *supra* (§888), covenants in leases were, at common law, independent. But there was this exception: The tenant's covenant to pay rent was always dependent upon the landlord's performance of his covenant of quiet enjoyment. If the landlord breached this covenant, by evicting the tenant, the tenant's obligation to pay rent ceased.

   b. **Breach:** [§993]   The covenant of quiet enjoyment can be breached by either actual or constructive eviction.

2. **Actual Eviction:** [§994]   If a tenant is physically evicted from the *entire* leased premises—either by the landlord or by someone with paramount title—the tenant's rental obligation ceases. Having been deprived of possession of the entire premises, the tenant may treat the lease as terminated, and his liability for further rent under the lease as discharged.

   a. **Partial eviction by landlord:** [§995]   If the tenant is evicted from *any portion of* the leased premises by the landlord, his rent obligation *abates entirely* until possession thereof is restored to him. The tenant may stay in possession and refuse to pay rent. [Smith v. McEnany, 48 N.E. 781 (Mass. 1897)]

      (1) **Example:** L leases T a farm of forty acres. Subsequently L takes possession of an unused barn on the forty acres and stores corn in it. T may stay in possession and refuse to pay any rent until L gives up the barn.

      (2) **Rationale:** It is said that the obligation to pay rent rests upon tenant's possession of the entire leasehold, and that the landlord cannot apportion his own

wrong. But this is merely to state a conclusion. The result—and perhaps the reason—is to impose a penalty on the landlord who interferes with the tenant's use of any part of the premises. This rule may be an efficient way to protect a tenant. Other remedies available to the tenant may be costly or unsatisfactory. If the law gives the tenant damages, this requires a lawsuit. If the law gives the tenant the right to terminate the lease and leave, the tenant may not be able to find other equivalent quarters.

(3) **Restatement view:** [§996]   The Restatement rejects the rule of complete rent abatement for partial actual eviction on the grounds that this is unjust to the landlord. It adopts a rule of *partial rent abatement* and in addition gives the tenant the other usual remedies of termination or damages for breach of the covenant. [Rest. 2d §6.1]

b.   **Partial eviction by paramount title:** [§997]   Where the tenant is evicted from a part of the premises by a third party with paramount title, which interferes with the tenant's use contemplated by the parties, the tenant may terminate the lease, recover damages, or receive a *proportionate rent abatement*. If the tenant continues in possession, he remains liable for the reasonable rental value of the portion he possesses. [Rest. 2d §4.3]

(1) **Example:** L leases a lot and building to T, including an easement to cross an adjacent lot to reach a side entrance. In good faith, L assumes this easement exists, but after the lease is executed, litigation establishes that there is no such easement. The owner of the adjacent lot then prevents T from crossing it. This is an eviction by paramount title. T may stay on the premises and receive an abatement of the rent by the amount by which the agreed rent of the property exceeds its reasonable rental value without the easement.

(2) **Compare—partial eviction by landlord:** [§998]   If the landlord partially evicts the tenant, the tenant may stay in possession and pay no rent (*supra*, §995). But if a third party partially evicts the tenant, the tenant does not have the option of staying in possession and paying no rent. The reason for this distinction is this: Under the recording acts, a third party may have a paramount claim in the leased land only if the tenant has actual or constructive notice of the claim. If the tenant has notice, the tenant takes the leasehold with the knowledge that he may be ousted by a third party. It is unfair to penalize the landlord for a third party exercising paramount rights of which the tenant is aware, or, as in the example above, which the landlord does not believe to exist.

3.   **Constructive Eviction:** [§999]   Where, through the fault of the landlord, there occurs a substantial interference with the tenant's use and enjoyment of the leased premises, so that the tenant can no longer enjoy the premises as the parties contemplated, the tenant may terminate the lease, vacate the premises, and be excused from further rent liability. This is known as the doctrine of constructive eviction.

a.   **Dependent promises doctrine expanded:** [§1000]   The doctrine of constructive eviction applies where the tenant is left in possession but his use and enjoyment is disturbed. Using this doctrine, the courts expanded the application of the contract doctrine of dependent promises from cases of actual eviction to situations where the landlord prevented the tenant from getting the enjoyment bagained for. The doctrine serves to make the tenant's obligation to pay rent dependent upon the landlord's performance of his covenant of quiet enjoyment. It gives the tenant the remedy of termination of the tenancy. Without that remedy, the tenant could only sue for damages—a costly and inefficient remedy in many situations.

b. **Actual eviction distinguished:** [§1001]   Actual eviction requires physical expulsion or exclusion from *possession*. If the landlord changes the locks or bars entry, the eviction is actual. If the landlord interferes with *enjoyment*, but does not bar entry, the eviction is constructive.

   (1) **Example:** T, a lawyer, rents office space in a glass-enclosed, air-conditioned building. The windows are sealed. L promises comfortable use of the premises for twenty-four hours a day. L turns off the air-conditioning at 6 p.m. T wants to work late, but finds the office too hot and stuffy to work in after 6 p.m. T refuses to pay rent on the ground that this is an actual, partial eviction which results in the abatement of all rent (*supra*, §995). However, L's actions constitute a constructive, not an actual, eviction. Since this is not an actual partial eviction, T cannot stay in the office and not pay rent. T may claim constructive eviction, which releases the tenant from rent obligation, but to do so, T must abandon the premises. [Barash v. Pennsylvania Terminal Real Estate Corp., 26 N.Y.2d 77 (1970)]

   (2) **Partial constructive eviction:** [§1002]   Whether there can be a partial constructive eviction, with the tenant relieved of the obligation to pay rent, has not been considered in many cases. Suppose, for example, that T rents an apartment with a terrace. Because of L's misconduct, the terrace becomes unusable. Can T claim partial constructive eviction and—as in partial actual eviction—stop paying all rent while remaining in the rest of the apartment? It has been held that T can stop paying all rent and remain in the apartment. [East Haven Associates v. Gurian, 313 N.Y.S.2d 927 (1970)] It seems probable—with the development of the implied warranty of habitability (*see infra*, §1025)—that a doctrine of partial constructive eviction will be rejected by the courts in the future.

c. **Elements of constructive eviction**

   (1) **Substantial interference:** [§1003]   To have a constructive eviction, the tenant's use and enjoyment (as distinguished from possession) must be *substantially interfered with*. "Substantial interference" is measured objectively; it is what a reasonable person would regard as fundamentally incompatible with the use and enjoyment for which the parties bargained. Courts usually take into consideration the *purposes* for which the premises were leased, the *forseeability* of this type of interference, the *potential duration* of the interference, the *nature and degree of harm caused*, and the availability of *means to abate* the interference. Courts can and do differ over what is substantial interference.

[Reste Realty Corp. v. Cooper, 251 A.2d 268 (N.J. 1969)—water flooding basement office substantial interference; Jacobs v. Morand, 59 Misc. 200 (1908)—bedbugs, cockroaches, and ants not substantial interference and must be abated by the tenant]

(a) **Disclosure prior to lease:** [§1004]   If the landlord knows of defects in the premises (such as a leaky roof or the existence of cockroaches), he may be under a duty to disclose these to the tenant. Under tort law, the landlord is under a duty to disclose concealed dangers (*infra*, §1022). It is arguable that the landlord should be under a similar duty for contract purposes, even in the absence of physical injury. This argument usually states that it is fraudulent for the landlord not to tell the tenant of concealed and known substantial defects. [Leech v. Husbands, 152 A. 729 (Del. 1930)]

(b) **Tenant's knowledge:** [§1005]   If the tenant knows of the interference prior to taking possession, and subsequently takes possession, the tenant has *waived* the interference.

(c) **Notice to landlord:** [§1006]   Prior to claiming constructive eviction, the tenant must give notice to the landlord of the objectionable conduct and the landlord must fail to remedy the situation within a reasonable time.

(2) **Tenant must vacate premises:** [§1007]   A tenant cannot claim a constructive eviction unless and until he vacates the premises. He *cannot remain in possession* and refuse to pay rent or receive damages under this doctrine. If the tenant stays on, there is no eviction and the rent obligation continues. The tenant must determine at his peril that the circumstances amount to a constructive eviction, and must vacate the premises within a reasonable time, possibly at some expense, subject to the risk that the court will find no constructive eviction. [Thompson v. Shoemaker, 173 S.E.2d 627 (N.C. 1970)]

(a) **Declaratory judgment:** [§1008]   A tenant may be able to stay in possession and bring an equitable action for a declaratory judgment that the landlord's actions constitute a constructive eviction. Such declaratory relief permits the tenant to know, before vacating the premises, whether he is justified in vacating or not. [Charles E. Burt, Inc. v. Seven Grand Corp., 163 N.E.2d 4 (Mass. 1959)]

(b) **Damages after vacation:** [§1009]   If the tenant vacates the premises upon constructive eviction, this action terminates the lease. The tenant has no further rent liability. However, the tenant can recover from the landlord for damages suffered because of constructive eviction, including the difference between rent paid and reasonable rent value, expenses in obtaining substitute premises, loss of profits caused by landlord's actions, etc.

(c) **Vacation within reasonable time:** [§1010]   To claim constructive eviction, the tenant must vacate within a *reasonable time* after the landlord's acts justify vacating the premises. If the tenant does not abandon within a reasonable time, he has waived the landlord's breach of covenant. What constitutes a reasonable time depends upon the circumstances of the case.

(d) **Restatement view:** [§1011] The Restatement rejects the requirement that the tenant must abandon the property before claiming constructive eviction. The Restatement gives the tenant the right: (i) to terminate, or (ii) to stay on and receive damages or a rent abatement or employ certain self-help remedies. *Rationale:* The tenant should receive what he bargained for. If the tenant's only remedy is to vacate, the doctrine of constructive eviction has limited usefulness in giving the tenant what he bargained for, particularly the poor tenant who lacks the funds to find decent housing elsewhere. [Rest. 2d §6.1]

(3) **Fault of landlord:** [§1012] The interference with tenant's quiet enjoyment must result from some act or failure to act by the landlord. Generally, a tenant cannot claim a constructive eviction growing out of the wrongful acts of a third party (*e.g.*, another tenant) unless that party's acts were induced by, or committed with the express or implied consent of, the landlord.

(a) **Acts of landlord:** [§1013] Any act of the landlord—such as playing a stereo very loudly at 2 a.m.—which substantially interferes with T's use and enjoyment is sufficient for constructive eviction. The most significant modern cases concerning acts of the landlord involve *failure of the landlord* to furnish heat or services or to repair in violation of an express or implied covenant to do so. Where the tenant claims constructive eviction for the landlord's nonfeasance (failure to act), it is necessary that the landlord have some legal duty to act, the breach of which deprives the tenant of use and enjoyment, and thus breaches the covenant of quiet enjoyment.

1) **Example:** L leases a commercial building to T. The use of the basement is necessary for the conduct of T's business, which L knows. After every rainstorm the basement floor is covered by two inches of water. Finally, one rainstorm brings five inches of water. T moves out within a week. Even in the absence of an express covenant to keep the basement waterproof, most courts will imply such a duty as necessary to the tenant's enjoyment of the premises which the parties contemplated. T has been constructively evicted. [Reste Realty Corp. v. Cooper, *supra*, §1003—*overruling* Stewart v. Childs Co., 92 A. 392 (N.J. 1914)—agreement to pay rent and agreement to waterproof cellar were independent covenants]

(b) **Acts of other tenants:** [§1014] Whether the acts of other tenants will suffice for constructive eviction depends on whether the landlord can control the behavior of other tenants and can be regarded as at fault in not controlling it. As a general rule, the landlord is *not responsible* for one tenant causing annoyance to another tenant, even though the annoying conduct would be constructive eviction if done by the landlord himself, and even though the landlord can legally control the other tenant's conduct. [Stewart v. Lawson, 165 N.W. 716 (Mich. 1917)—neighboring tenants using foul and offensive language not constructive eviction; *but see* Bruckner v. Helfaer, 222 N.W. 790 (Wis. 1929)—loud music and foul language of neighbors held constructive eviction]

1) **Exceptions:** [§1015]   There are two recognized exceptions to the general rule. First, the landlord has a duty not to permit a **nuisance** on the premises. Hence, if the landlord rents to prostitutes, whose conduct is lewd or immoral, the landlord is in breach of his duty, and the conduct of others is attributable to him. [Dyett v. Pendleton, 8 Cow. 727 (N.Y. 1826); Milheim v. Baxter, 103 P. 376 (Colo. 1909)] Second, the landlord has a duty to control **common areas** under his control. If the objectionable conduct takes place in common areas, the conduct is attributable to the landlord. [Phyfe v. Dale, 72 Misc. 383 (1911)]

2) **Modern trend:** [§1016]   A modern trend appears to be developing that holds the landlord responsible for other tenants' acts if the landlord has the legal ability to correct the conditions and fails to do so. The reason is that the landlord is in a better position to stop the objectionable conduct than is the tenant. [Colonial Court Apartments v. Kern, 163 N.W.2d 770 (Minn. 1968); Rest. 2d §6.1, comment d]

a) **Example:** L leases an apartment to T, and also rents a cocktail lounge next door to X. The lease to X provides that L can terminate the lease if the noise disturbs the neighboring tenants. T complains to L of the loud noise of X. L does nothing. Since L can control the noise of X by terminating the lease, the noise is a constructive eviction. [Blackett v. Olanoff, 358 N.E.2d 817 (Mass. 1977)]

d. **Covenant not to compete:** [§1017]   A covenant by the landlord that he will not compete with or rent to a competitor of the tenant is usually deemed to be so important to the tenant's enjoyment of the property that breach of the covenant by the landlord is treated as a constructive eviction. [University Club v. Deakin, 106 N.E. 790 (Ill. 1914)]

(1) **Example:** L leases a store to T for four years. T is in the furniture business, and the lease provides that L will not rent space in the building for another furniture business. Three years after the lease begins, T becomes ill, retires from business, ceases to pay rent, but does not surrender the premises. Because of T's default in rent payments, L can elect to terminate lease, but does not do so. On April 2, L rents adjoining space to a competitor in the furniture business commencing May 1. On April 21, T gives notice to L that T is terminating the lease on May 1. T is entitled to terminate the lease because payment of rent is dependent upon L's performance of the noncompetition promise. T is not liable for rent after May 1. Constructive eviction is a defense even though T is in

default in the payment of rent at the time L's breach occurs. [Kulawitz v. Pacific Woodenware & Paper Co., 25 Cal. 2d 664 (1945)]

(2) **Dependent covenant analysis:** [§1018]   The extension of the constructive eviction doctrine to breach of noncompetition covenants means in effect that the payment of rent depends upon the performance of the noncompetition covenant. But why should a noncompetition covenant be singled out for such treatment? A noncompetition covenant is, after all, not favored by the law because it protects a monopoly. And why should commercial tenants be given rights denied to residential tenants? It has been suggested that the noncompetition cases rest upon a principle that all promises of the landlord which are *a significant inducement to the making of a lease* are dependent. It has been then argued that this principle logically extends to all types of promises, and not just to noncompetition promises. The Restatement adopts this view, and provides that all *significant promises, express and implied*, are dependent. Breach by the landlord relieves the tenant of performance. [Rest.2d §7.1] If this view is adopted by courts, then contract law will finally triumph over property law in the area of landlord and tenant. [*See* Teodori v. Werner, 415 A.2d 31 (Pa. 1980)—adopting Restatement view]

F. LANDLORD'S DUTY TO PROVIDE HABITABLE PREMISES

1. Landlord's Duty at the Inception of the Lease

a. **Common law:** [§1019]   Under the common law, there is no implied covenant by the landlord that the premises are in tenantable condition or are fit for the purposes intended. The rule is *caveat lessee*. Before he purchases his estate in land, the tenant is able to inspect the premises and thus protect himself. Unless the landlord gives an express warranty, the landlord has no duty to the tenant with respect to the condition of the premises. The tenant takes them "as is." [Franklin v. Brown, 118 N.Y. 110 (1889); Anderson Drive-In Theatre, Inc. v. Kirkpatrick, 110 N.E.2d 506 (Ind. 1953)]

(1) **Exceptions:** [§1020]   Three exceptions to the rule of caveat lessee are recognized.

(a) **Furnished house for short term:** [§1021]   Where there is a *short-term* lease of a *furnished house* (such as a summer cottage), a covenant is implied that the premises are tenantable. *Rationale:* The tenant in such a situation has no time to inspect or put the premises in tenantable condition. [Ingalls v. Hobbs, 31 N.E. 286 (Mass. 1892)] If the courts had wished to do so, they could easily have expanded this exception to cover unfurnished dwellings for immediate occupancy (the usual urban apartment or house) because the tenant has inadequate time to inspect and repair before signing the lease. Indeed, the reasoning underlying *Ingalls* might even have applied to a commercial lease for immediate occupancy. But the courts refused to so extend *Ingalls*. [Gade v. National Creamery Co., 87 N.E.2d 180 (Mass. 1949)]

(b) **Hidden (latent) defects:** [§1022] When defects or dangerous conditions are *known* to the landlord and *not easily discoverable* by an ordinary inspection, the landlord has a duty to disclose the defects. *Rationale:* The tenant cannot discover the defects in an ordinary inspection, and nondisclosure borders on fraud. (If the landlord fraudulently represents the condition of the premises, he is liable to the tenant.)

(c) **Building under construction:** [§1023] When a building is being constructed for a particular use, and the lease is executed *before the building is finished*, a covenant is implied that the building will be fit for the purposes intended. *Rationale:* The tenant has no opportunity to inspect the premises when the lease is executed.

(2) **Independent covenants rule:** [§1024] Even if there is an express warranty of suitability or habitability, or if the tenant comes within one of the exceptions, the tenant must overcome the independent covenants rule if the tenant wants to terminate the lease or be excused from rent. Under the independent covenants rule, the tenant is not excused from performance by the landlord's breach, and the tenant's remedy is to sue the landlord for damages. This remedy is time-consuming and the legal expenses may be costly. If the tenant desires to terminate the lease, he must—under the common law—prove constructive eviction, discussed above, and move out. Thus, if the roof leaks in a summer cottage, the tenant can (i) sue for damages, or (ii) move out if he proves a constructive eviction by a substantial interference with his use and enjoyment.

b. **Implied covenant of habitability:** [§1025] In recent years, a growing number of courts have held that there is an implied covenant of initial habitability and fitness in leases of urban dwellings, including apartments. They have further held that the dependent covenant doctrine applies, and that a tenant is relieved of his obligations when the landlord breaches the implied covenant of habitability. [Pines v. Perssion, 111 N.W.2d 409 (Wis. 1961); Lemle v. Breeden, 462 P.2d 470 (Hawaii 1971)] (Compare this implied covenant of habitability at the *inception* of the lease with a *continuing* covenant of habitability discussed *infra*, §1044. In most respects they are the same, but in some they differ.)

(1) **Restatement view:** [§1026] The Restatement implies a covenant of *suitability* "if the parties contemplate that the leased property will be used for residential purposes" which is breached if "the leased property, without fault of the tenant, is *not suitable for residential* use." The Restatement goes on to provide that after entry the landlord has a reasonable period of time to remedy the situation after being requested to do so by the tenant. [Rest. 2d §§5.1, 5.3]

(2) **Rationale:** [§1027] The implied covenant of habitability has been justified on several grounds. (i) A modern urban residential tenant does not have time to inspect the premises and put them in tenantable condition. (ii) The landlord knows more about the defects and is in a better position to remedy them. (iii) Housing codes, imposing duties on the landlord, have not been effectively enforced. More effective housing code enforcement will result from giving ten-

ants the right to sue when premises are untenantable. Constructive eviction, requiring vacation of the dwelling, is not a viable remedy in times of housing shortage. (iv) Because of the housing shortage, tenants have much less bargaining power than landlords. (v) Uniform Commercial Code sections 2-314 and 2-315 imply a warranty of fitness for the purpose intended in a sale by a merchant or where the buyer relies on the seller's skill. By analogy, similar warranties should be applied to the sale of a leasehold. (Analogy to the U.C.C. supports implying a warranty at the inception of the lease, but does not support implying a *continuing duty* on the landlord to maintain the premises.)

   (a) **Criticism:** The implied warranty of habitability has been criticized on economic grounds. It is claimed that placing this duty on the landlord will lead to increased rents to cover the upgraded housing, or to abandonment by the landlord, or to less investment in new housing. The end result of imposing obligations on the landlord, it is argued, is that the poor will lose more housing facilities. [27 Stan. L. Rev. 879] But this claim has been much disputed. Some argue that if imposing a duty on the landlord reduces the stock of low-income housing, perhaps this will result in the government's providing more housing for low-income persons. Under this view, the implied warranty of habitability is a strategic political move to put pressure on Congress to subsidize more low-income housing.

   (b) **Commercial leases:** [§1028]   The few cases on whether a covenant of initial suitability should be implied in commercial leases as well as in urban dwellings are split. Some of the reasons given above for the implied warranty in residential leases are equally applicable to commercial leases. Restatement (Second) of Property section 5.1 takes no position on this issue, but the Reporter's Note to section 5.1, item 2, says, "The Reporter is of the opinion that the rule of this section should be extended to nonresidential property. The small commercial tenant particularly needs its protection."

(3) **Scope of warranty:** [§1029]   The scope of the initial warranty of habitability has not received as much attention as has the scope of the continuing duty of habitability (*infra*, §1048). The cases have applied one of two standards.

   (a) **Latent defects only:** [§1030]   Some courts have held that the landlord is responsible for latent defects only. In one of the early cases implying the covenant, it was said: "[I]t is a covenant that at the inception of the lease, there are no *latent* defects in facilities vital to the use of the premises for residential purposes because of faulty original construction or deterioration from age or normal use." [Marini v. Ireland, 265 A.2d 526 (N.J. 1970)] This statement, limiting the warranty to latent defects, does not extend the warranty far beyond the second exception to the common law rule (*supra*, §1022). The statement has been repeated by several courts, but it does not seem to mean much in view of the imposition by these same courts of a continuing duty on the landlord to maintain the premises in tenantable condition, remedying patent defects as well as latent ones. If the landlord does not have to remedy patent defects initially, he has to remedy them thereafter. The latent-patent distinction might be important on the issue of waiver, however. If the defect is patent and seen by the tenant, the landlord may claim that the tenant waived it when he discovered it before signing the lease. (On waiver of the implied warranty, *see infra*, §1033.)

(b) **Housing code:** [§1031]   Some courts hold that the local housing code sets the standard of the landlord's duty. A substantial violation of the housing code is a violation of the implied covenant of habitability. The Restatement provides that leased property "is unsuitable for residential purposes if it would be unsafe or unhealthy for the tenant to enter on the leased property and use it as a residence." [Rest. 2d §5.1, comment e] It goes on to say that a "significant violation" of the housing code "which has a substantial impact upon safety or health" is conclusive that the premises are untenantable, but that other modes of proving untenantability are acceptable.

(4) **Remedies for breach:** [§1032]   The remedies for breach of a covenant of habitability include the usual contract remedies of damages, restitution, and rescission. In addition they may include using the rent for repair and rent withholding. The remedies are the same for the initial covenant of habitability as are provided for the continuing covenant of habitability and are discussed below in connection with the continuing covenant. The basic choice of the tenant in most cases is to move out and recover any prepaid rent *or* to stay in possession and recover damages (rent reduction). (How damages are calculated is discussed *infra*, §1054.)

(a) **Example:** T leases a house from L. T moves in and finds that the house is filled with rats, the roof leaks, and the toilet does not work. T can rescind the lease, move out, and sue for her rent deposit; *or* she can stay in possession and sue for damages; or, in some states, she can use a reasonable amount of the rent money to remedy the defects.

(5) **Waiver by tenant:** [§1033]   Suppose that a tenant is willing to take the premises "as is." May the tenant waive the implied warranty of habitability? The tenant can waive minor defects, but it may be against public policy to permit the tenant to waive defects that make the premises unsafe or unsanitary. Since one of the reasons for implying a covenant of habitability is to encourage enforcement of the housing code by tenants, tenants may not be able to waive code requirements. The cases so far decided do not permit waiver of a substantial breach. [Javins v. First National Realty Corp., 428 F.2d 1071 (D.C. Cir. 1970); Green v. Superior Court, 10 Cal. 3d 616 (1974)]

(a) **Restatement view:** [§1034]   The Restatement (Second) has two basic rules with respect to waiver. First, section 5.3, comment c provides that "the tenant as matter of law is unable to waive any remedies available to him at the time of entry, if at the time of entry it ***would be unsafe or un-***

healthy to use the leased property in the manner contemplated by the parties." Second, section 5.6 goes on to provide that any agreement modifying the landlord's duties is unenforceable if "***unconscionable*** or significantly ***against public policy***." In sum, in two situations the Restatement forbids waiver: (i) when the defect renders the premises unsafe or unhealthy; and (ii) when waiver is unconscionable or against public policy.

1) **Implied waiver:** [§1035]   If the defective condition does not make the premises unsafe or unhealthy, and waiver is not unconscionable nor against public policy, the defect can be waived. If the defect is ***patent*** and the tenant recognizes that the property is suitable for the contemplated use, the tenant impliedly waives the defect upon entry.

   a) **Example:** T leases a house in the country which has a roof badly in need of repair. When inspecting the house, T sees cracks and water stains in the ceiling and evidence of water having stood on the floor. T leases and enters. Upon the first rain T finds lots of leaks in the ceiling. T should have known from his inspection that the house was unsuitable for residential use. However, though unsuitable, the house is not unsafe or unsanitary with a leaky roof, and T has waived the breach by entry.

(b) **Analogy to contract law:** [§1036]   The duties imposed on the landlord under the implied warranty of habitability go beyond the bounds of ordinary contract law. Contract law permits the sale of property "as is." In refusing to permit tenants to waive the landlord's duty, courts are trying to put pressure on landlords to rehabilitate dwellings. The moving force is not contract law, but to find a way to upgrade the housing stock.

c. **Statutory duties:** [§1037]   In many states, statutes have been enacted which impose upon the landlord an affirmative duty to put residential premises in a tenantable condition prior to leasing them. [*See, e.g.*, Uniform Residential Landlord & Tenant Act §2.104, discussed *infra*, §1070, which specifically lists what defects will render leased premises untenantable] In a jurisdiction with such a statute, a tenant may be able to sue on the statute or on the judicially created implied warranty of habitability. [Foisy v. Wyman, 515 P.2d 160 (Wash. 1973)]

d. **Illegal lease:** [§1038]   A lease of premises which the ***landlord knows*** are in substantial violation of the municipal housing code is an illegal agreement ***if the code prohibits rental*** of premises in violation of the code. If the lease is an illegal agreement, the landlord cannot enforce any covenant to pay rent. [Brown v. Southall Realty Co., 237 A.2d 834 (D.C. 1968)]

(1) **Limitations on illegal lease defense:** [§1039]   A tenant cannot defend against an action for rent on the ground that the lease is illegal unless the violations exist at the time the lease is executed. The illegal lease defense also may not be available where the housing code does not prohibit rental of premises in violation of the code. The court may find in that case that the municipal legislature

intends to rely on administrative enforcement and does not intend to render void any contracts made in violation of the ordinance. [Posnanski v. Hood, 174 N.W.2d 528 (Wis. 1970)]

(2) **Tenant must pay reasonable rental value:** [§1040]   A tenant who enters under an illegal lease does not have to pay rent, but he does have to pay the reasonable rental value of the premises as they exist. [King v. Moorehead, 495 S.W.2d 65 (Mo. 1973)] As a practical matter, however, this gives the tenant an advantage. The landlord renting a particularly squalid apartment may find it difficult to prove that the premises have any reasonable rental value.

2. Landlord's Duty to Repair After Entry by Tenant

a. **Common law:** [§1041]   At common law, the landlord has no duty to maintain and repair the premises. At early common law, when the rule was formulated, most leases were agricultural leases, and the tenants were able-bodied men who could, and were expected to, make repairs on simple farm dwellings. The essential thing the tenant bargained for was possession of the land; the buildings were incidental.

(1) **Landlord's covenant to repair:** [§1042]   The parties can by agreement put the duty to repair on the landlord. But even where there is such an agreement, the landlord's covenant to repair is deemed *independent* of the tenant's covenant to pay rent. Hence, if the landlord fails to repair, this breach does *not excuse* the tenant from rent payments. The tenant's only remedy is to sue the landlord for damages or specific performance.

(a) **Duty to pay rent continues:** [§1043]   Even though the landlord is clearly in breach of the lease by failing to maintain the premises in proper repair, the tenant has to continue paying the rent in full. If he fails to do so, the landlord may either sue the tenant for the rent or institute summary proceedings to evict the tenant ("unlawful detainer," *infra,* §1207)—and the tenant may not defend on the basis that the landlord is in breach of the lease. Again, the duty to pay rent and the duty to repair are deemed *independent*.

b. **Implied covenant of habitability:** [§1044]   A large majority of courts have, since the 1960s, implied on the part of the landlord a *continuing* covenant of habitability in leases of urban dwellings. They have also held that the dependent-covenant doctrine of contract law applies, and thus a violation of the covenant by the landlord is a defense to an action by the landlord for payment of rent. For the landlord to sue on the tenant's covenant, he must have performed his own. The continuing covenant of habitability is similar to the covenant implied at the inception of the lease, which most states now imply. Thus under modern law in most states, a landlord has a duty of delivering habitable premises and of maintaining them in habitable shape. [Javins v. First National Realty Corp., *supra,* §1033; Green v. Superior Court, *supra,* §1033]

(1) **Restatement position:** [§1045]   The Restatement provides for an implied covenant of ***suitability*** continuing for the duration of the lease. If, without fault of the tenant, the premises become unsuitable for the use contemplated by the parties because of the landlord's conduct or failure to fulfill an obligation to repair or because of a sudden non-human-made force ("act of God"), the covenant is breached unless the landlord corrects the situation within a reasonable time after being requested by the tenant to do so. [Rest. 2d §5.4]

(2) **Rationale:** [§1046]   Almost all the reasons given for implying a covenant of habitability at the inception of the lease (*supra*, §1027) support the imposition of a continuing duty of maintenance upon the landlord. In addition, the tenant bargains for, and expects to get, continuing services, including maintenance, from the landlord.

    (a) **Commercial leases:** [§1047]   Covenants of habitability have in a few cases been implied in commercial leases when it appears that the commercial tenant has bargained for continuing maintenance by the landlord. This will more likely be the case where the landlord rents an office in a building than where the landlord rents the entire building. *Note:* Section 5.4 of the Restatement, implying a covenant of ***continuing*** suitability, is not expressly limited to residential use and therefore may apply to commercial use. Section 5.1, implying an ***initial*** covenant of suitability, is expressly limited to residential use.

(3) **Scope of warranty:** [§1048]   Courts differ on what standards are used to measure the landlord's duty. Generally they fall into one of two groups.

    (a) **Housing code:** [§1049]   Some courts hold that the standards are those of the housing code. If there is a substantial violation of the housing code, the landlord's warranty is breached. Minor violations not affecting habitability do not constitute a breach. [Javins v. First National Realty Corp., *supra*, §1044] The Restatement imposes on the landlord the obligation "to keep the leased property in a condition that meets the requirements of governing health, safety, and housing codes." [Rest. 2d §5.5]

    (b) **Fit for human habitation:** [§1050]   Some courts require that the premises be "fit for human habitation" or use similar language in respect to the standard. A violation of the housing code is compelling evidence of breach, but not conclusive. The standard as applied may be higher or lower than the housing code requirements. In these jurisdictions, continued loud noise could be a breach of warranty even though it is not a violation of the housing code. [Boston Housing Authority v. Hemingway, 293 N.E.2d 831 (Mass. 1973)]

    (c) **Notice to landlord:** [§1051]   If the landlord is unaware of the condition, must the tenant give the landlord notice of the condition and a reasonable time to repair? Several courts, assuming that the implied warranty incorporates a ***fault standard***, have stated that the landlord has a reasonable time to repair after notice is given. The Restatement agrees that the landlord is not in breach until a reasonable time has passed after the tenant has given the landlord notice. [Rest. 2d §§5.1, comment d, 5.4, comment g] But some cases hold that the landlord's duty is breached when the defect is discovered, not when the landlord fails to repair after being given notice. [Berman & Sons, Inc. v. Jefferson, 396 N.E.2d 981 (Mass. 1979)]

1) **Example:** On March 1, T moves into an apartment under a one-year lease. On October 8, the underground heating pipes break and T is without heat for two weeks. T withholds $35 from her November rent, as rent abatement (damages) for the failure to furnish heat. L brings eviction proceedings for failure to pay all the rent. T defends that she is entitled to a rent abatement and owes no more rent than she has paid. If fault is incorporated into the standard of L's duty, L does have a reasonable time to fix the heating pipes, and if two weeks is a reasonable time, L is not in breach of his duty. If fault is not part of the standard, L is in breach on October 8 and T is entitled to a rent abatement for the two weeks without heat. The latter theory, applied in *Berman & Sons, supra*, imposes strict liability (liability without fault) on the landlord.

(4) **Remedies for breach:** [§1052] The tenant's covenant to pay rent is dependent upon the landlord's performance of her duties under the implied warranty of habitability. Upon breach by the landlord, the tenant has the following remedies:

(a) **Terminate lease:** [§1053] The tenant may terminate the lease, vacate the premises, and recover damages. Damages may include relocation costs and the fair market value of the lease (the difference between the agreed rent and the fair market rent).

1) **Example:** L leases an apartment to T for two years at a rental of $300 per month. After six months, L breaches the warranty by failing to furnish heat. T terminates the lease. The reasonable rental value of the apartment is now $350 a month. T can recover $900 from L. This figure represents $50 a month for eighteen months, which is the advantage of the lease T is losing by terminating.

(b) **Continue lease and recover damages:** [§1054] The tenant may continue the lease and recover damages. Damages ordinarily will be a rent reduction. While there is general agreement on the foregoing, there is considerable disagreement regarding how damages are calculated. This is probably the most difficult technical problem to solve in the implied warranty area. The choice among the methods of calculating damages may ultimately be determined by which is the most effective in forcing rehabilitation of dwellings while being not unconscionably unfair to the landlord. The following are the most common methods of ascertaining damages. [1 A.L.R.4th 1182 (1980)]

1) **Pay-for-premises-as-is rule:** [§1055] One method of measuring damages has the purpose of making the tenant pay only for the value of what he is receiving (the premises as is). Damages are measured by the difference between the agreed rent and the fair market rental value of the premises *as they are* during occupancy by the tenant in the unsafe or unsanitary condition. [King v. Moorehead, *supra*, §1040] This method results in no damages if the agreed rental is the fair market rental for the premises as is, and thus it does not serve to goad landlords into rehabilitation.

   a) **Example:** T rents a slum apartment for $100 a month, which is the fair market rent for the apartment as is. If up to code, the apartment would rent for $200 a month. T should pay only for what he is receiving, which is worth $100 a month. Therefore T can claim no damages.

   b) **Compare—contract damages:** [§1056] This measure of damages is used in cases involving breach of warranty of personal property: If A sells a car to B, and warrants that the car will go 150 m.p.h., and the car will go only 90 m.p.h., B can rescind or receive the difference between the agreed price and a car that can go only 90 m.p.h. But A is not liable for the difference between the agreed price and what a car going 150 m.p.h. would cost (which is more or less the second method of measuring damages, below). A court adopting one of the following methods of measuring damages, which depart from the usual measure of contract damages, is consciously attempting to find a method that will pressure the landlord to fix up the property. Therefore, the goal of awarding damages may not be so much to give the particular tenant relief from an excessive price charged as to rehabilitate the housing stock.

2) **Loss-of-bargain rule:** [§1057] A second method is to attempt to give the tenant what he bargained for. This is achieved by measuring damages by the difference between the fair market rental value of the premises *if they had been as warranted* and the fair market value of the premises *as is*. The difference between the two multiplied by the months of untenantable occupancy is the figure for the tenant's damages. [Freedman v. Seidler, 194 A.2d 778 (Md. 1963); Teodori v. Werner, *supra*, §1018] (Observe that the agreed rent may be neither the market rent as warranted nor as is. At the inception of the lease, the agreed rent is probably the market rent for the property with patent defects but not with latent defects. As time goes on, with inflation, no rent increase, and deterioration, the agreed rent will bear less relationship to the market rent.)

   a) **Example:** T rents an apartment at $100 a month. The condition of the apartment deteriorates over several years. T sues for damages. The court finds the market rental for the apartment as warranted is $160 a month, and the market rental for the apartment as is is $80 a month. Therefore rent is abated to $20 a month. If the difference between the rental value as warranted and the rental value as is exceeds $100 a month, T can live in the apartment rent free! (Theoretically if damages are $110 a month, L should pay T $10 to live in the apartment, but probably no court would give damages in excess of the agreed rent.)

3) **Percentage diminution rule:** [§1058]   The third method assumes that the agreed rent is the proper figure for the premises **as impliedly warranted**. The agreed rent is then reduced by a percentage of use lost by the tenant in consequence of the landlord's breach. The percentage of use lost is determined—perhaps roughly or approximately—by a judge. [Cazares v. Ortiz, 109 Cal. App. 3d 23 (1980)] This method relies on the judge to do rough justice. Proponents of this method regard the first method of determining damages as unfair to tenants and the second as unfair to landlords. They are willing to accept the judge's discretion as the best among a choice of imperfect solutions.

    a) **Example:** T rents an apartment for $100 a month. The hot water and heat intermittently fail. A court finds that this results in a 33-1/3 percent reduction in habitability. Tenant's damages are $33.33 a month.

4) **Restatement method:** [§1059]   The Restatement method is a variation of the percentage diminution rule above. The Restatement attempts to give the tenant the benefit of his bargain in the same proportion as it was orginally made by the parties. Restatement (Second) of Property section 11.1 provides that the tenant's rent is abated to the amount of that proportion of the rent which the fair rental value as is bears to the fair rental value as warranted. This method has the same flaw as the first two in that it requires the establishment of fair rental value as is, which may not be feasible. In addition, it calls for expert testimony to determine two fair rental values, and hence is more costly to administer than the preceding proportional reduction method.

    a) **Example:** T rents an apartment for $100 a month. T is bargaining for the value of the apartment as warranted. After several years, the apartment becomes untenantable. The fair rental value of the apartment as warranted is now $160 a month, and the fair rental value as is is $80 a month. Since T is only getting fifty percent of his bargain (*i.e.*, the apartment as warranted would rent for twice as much as the apartment as is), T is entitled to a fifty percent abatement in rent. T's abatement is $50 a month.

5) **Damages for discomfort and annoyance:** [§1060]   This measure of damages is essentially a tort approach, and would give damages for

mental distress unaccompanied by physical injury. This measure of damages bears no relation to the value of the leased premises as is or as warranted, and has been avoided by the courts.

(c) **Continue lease and use rent to repair:** [§1061]   In some jurisdictions, if the landlord fails to repair after notice, the tenant may use a reasonable amount of rent to repair the defective conditions. [Marini v. Ireland, *supra*, §1030] This remedy is also provided for in the Restatement if the tenant first gives notice to the landlord and makes only reasonable expenditures. [Rest. 2d §11.2] This remedy will likely be more useful to a tenant holding a term of years than a month-to-month tenant. In a month-to-month tenancy, one month's rent may not cover the cost of repairs and if the tenant expends advance rent (assuming he has it), he may be evicted on thirty-day notice (provided eviction is not retaliatory) and lose the benefits of his expenditures. Then too, the tenant is subject to second-guessing by a court as to what expenditure is reasonable. A statutory repair and deduct remedy may be more specific than the judicial remedy of "reasonableness" and therefore be more useful to tenants. For example, California Civil Code section 1942 permits the tenant to use up to one month's rent for repairs (remedy available no more than twice in a year period).

(d) **Continue lease and withhold rent:** [§1062]   Section 11.3 of the Restatement provides that the tenant may, after notice to the landlord, place his rent in escrow until the default is eliminated. Apparently no case has specifically granted this as a judicial remedy, but a few have indicated that a total breach of warranty by the landlord may relieve the tenant of the responsibility for the rent. [Javins v. First National Realty Corp., *supra*, §1049] It seems likely that, with Restatement approval, this remedy will develop.

   1) **Compare—retaliatory eviction:** [§1063]   If the tenant claims the lease is illegal because of violations of the housing code, reports the violations to the authorities, and withholds rent, the landlord cannot evict the tenant if his motive is to retaliate for reporting housing code violations. (*See infra*, §1078.) However, even though the tenant can withhold rent and stay on the premises until the retaliatory motive disappears, the tenant is liable for the reasonable rental value of the premises as is.

(e) **Defense to landlord's rent action:** [§1064]   Set forth above are affirmative actions that a tenant may take upon the landlord's breach of the implied covenant of habitability. The tenant may also defend, in an action by the landlord for rent, that the agreed rent is not due because of the landlord's breach. This defense rests upon the dependent-covenants rule—that the duty to pay rent is dependent upon the landlord's performance.

   1) **Distinguish—non-rent action:** [§1065]   If the landlord brings an eviction action that is not based on failure to pay rent, but is based on her

right to possession at the expiration of the tenancy, the landlord's breach is not a defense. In a month-to-month tenancy, for example, the landlord can terminate it at any time for any reason upon thirty-day notice to quit. Breach of implied warranty is not a defense to a possessory action based on a notice to quit. Since the landlord is not suing for a breach of covenant by the tenant, which is dependent upon the landlord's performance, the landlord's breach is irrelevant. The only defense to an action to evict because the tenancy has terminated is that the landlord is retaliating against the tenant's acts. (*See infra*, §1078.)

(5) **Waiver by tenant:** [§1066]   According to the cases so far decided, a waiver of the landlord's obligations under the implied covenant of habitability is not permitted. The primary purpose of implying the obligation is to give tenants power to enforce the housing code, and it would be against public policy to permit tenants to waive that power (*see supra*, §1033).

(a) **URLTA view:** [§1067]   Uniform Residential Landlord & Tenant Act section 2.104(d) provides that the lease can shift the duty of repair to the tenant if (i) the agreement is not for the purpose of evading the obligations of the landlord and is set forth in a ***separate writing*** and supported by ***adequate consideration***, and (ii) the work is not necessary to cure noncompliance with the housing code. Hence, the parties can agree separately in consideration of a reduced rent that the tenant shall maintain the premises, provided the agreement does not shift to the tenant the burden of complying with the housing code. The tenant can be given the duty of painting and minor repairs, but not the duty of curing housing code violations.

(b) **Restatement view:** [§1068]   The Restatement provides that the parties may agree to decrease the landlord's obligations unless the agreement is "***unconscionable*** or significantly ***against public policy***." [Rest. 2d §5.6] An agreement is unconscionable when it would shock the conscience if enforced. This—as well as "against public policy"—is a vague and imprecise phrase, but the Restatement spells out seven factors to weigh in determining unconscionability or public policy. These include the extent to which the waiver interferes with the enforcement of the housing code; the type of property leased; whether the waiver serves a reasonable business purpose and is a result of conscious negotiations; whether the waiver is part of a boiler plate lease document (an adhesion contract); whether the waiver imposes unreasonable burdens on a tenant who is poor and has unequal bargaining power; and whether the parties were represented by counsel.

c. **Statutory duties of landlord:** [§1069]   Many states have enacted legislation imposing a duty on the landlord to maintain residential premises in habitable condition. The statutes usually spell out the standard of habitability, whether the duty can be waived, and the tenant's remedy for breach. In addition to the remedies mentioned above, developed by the courts, statutes often give the tenant additional remedies going beyond what the courts have so far approved.

(1) **URLTA:** [§1070]   The Uniform Residential Landlord & Tenant Act, enacted or copied in more than a dozen states, is a comprehensive residential landlord-tenant code that imposes duties on the landlord equivalent to those imposed by the judicially implied covenant of habitability. Section 2.104 of the Act imposes on the landlord the duty of keeping the premises "in a fit and habitable condition." No distinction is made between latent and patent defects. If the landlord violates his statutory duties, the tenant may send written notice to the landlord telling him to fix the problems or consider the lease terminated. If the landlord refuses, the tenant may, after written notice, sue for damages, sue for an injunction, or take advantage of the following self-help remedies. [URLTA §4.101]

   (a) **Repair and deduct:** [§1071]   If the defect can be cured by application of one-half the periodic rent, the tenant may correct the condition at the landlord's expense. [URLTA §4.103]

   (b) **Essential services:** [§1072]   If the landlord fails to supply heat, water, hot water, or other essential service, the tenant may procure the service and deduct the cost from the rent. In addition, the tenant may find substitute housing while the service fails and be excused from paying rent while the service failure continues. [URLTA §4.104]

(2) **New York statutes:** [§1073]   New York statutes enacted to deal with substandard housing provide the following remedies:

   (a) **Abatement of rent after six months' violation:** [§1074]   New York Multiple Dwelling Law section 302-a provides that if a serious housing code violation is not cured within six months after official notice by the building inspector, no rent shall be recovered if the tenant pays the rent due into court. None of the rent accruing after the end of the six-month period goes to the landlord, even if she ultimately corrects the violation. She forfeits the rent as a penalty. This remedy depends upon the enforcement agency issuing a citation. Tenants cannot proceed without this.

      1) **Welfare tenants:** [§1075]   New York's Spiegel Law [N.Y. Soc. Serv. Law §143b] provides that the public welfare department may withhold rent payments to landlords of substandard buildings. If the conditions are corrected, the department may pay the landlord the rent withheld. The law further provides that a welfare recipient cannot be evicted from a building with serious building code violations anywhere in the building.

   (b) **Rent withholding:** [§1076]   New York Real Property Actions and Proceedings Law section 755 provides for a stay of an action for nonpayment of rent or to evict a tenant for nonpayment when the premises have housing code violations serious enough to amount to a constructive eviction, provided the tenant deposits with the clerk of the court all rent due when the stay is issued. In other words, if there is a constructive eviction, the tenant does not have to move out, but may pay rent into court. The court then may release the rent to pay for repairs. If the code violations are cured, the deposited rent is paid to the landlord. There is no machinery for getting repairs made. All depends upon an individual tenant's initiative to repair her apartment. And rent is not suspended as under Multiple Dwelling Law section 302-a. Section 755, however, served as the basis for rent strikes in the 1960s.

(c) **Receivership:** [§1077]   New York Real Property Actions and Proceedings Law, article 7A, section 770, was enacted to cure the defects in sections 302-a and 755, above. It provides that upon application of one-third of the tenants of a building in dangerous condition, the court may order all rents from all tenants in the building paid to an administrator appointed by the court. The administrator is a rent receiver and uses the deposited rents to remedy the conditions found to exist in the building.

d. **Retaliatory eviction:** [§1078]   If a tenant reports the landlord for violation of the housing code, the landlord may try to evict the tenant or may refuse to renew the lease at the end of the leasehold term. For example, in a month-to-month tenancy, the landlord may try to evict the tenant after a thirty-day notice. Some recent cases hold that a landlord, acting under retaliatory motivation, cannot evict a tenant. Retaliatory action is a defense against eviction, even in summary eviction proceedings. [Edwards v. Habib, 397 F.2d 687 (D.C. Cir. 1968)] This defense is also adopted by the Restatement. [Rest. 2d §§14.8, 14.9]

(1) **Interference with statutory right:** [§1079]   Most of the retaliatory eviction cases involve a tenant complaining about violation of a *housing code*. In granting the tenant a defense against retaliatory eviction, the courts have emphasized that the retaliatory action frustrates the legislative policy underlying the housing codes. Enforcement of the codes depends in part upon tenants reporting violations. If landlords could inhibit enforcement by evicting tenants who report violations, the effectiveness of the housing codes—and the legislative intent—would be frustrated. The basic rationale underlying the doctrine of retaliatory eviction is that it is essential to the effectiveness of the housing codes. [Dickhut v. Norton, 173 N.W.2d 297 (Wis. 1970)]

(a) **Statute other than housing code:** [§1080]   If the landlord sues to evict the tenant in retaliation for filing suit under some statute other than the housing code, the retaliatory eviction defense may be allowed. If a statutory right unrelated to housing depends for its effectiveness upon private initiative of tenants, and would be rendered ineffective by allowing retaliatory eviction, the landlord may not evict in retaliation. [S.P. Growers Association v. Rodriquez, 17 Cal. 3d 719 (1976)—farmer-landlord cannot evict farm tenants in retaliation for their assertion of federal rights given to migrant farm workers]

(2) **Interference with judicially created right:** [§1081]   Cases to date have mostly involved retaliation by the landlord for reporting statutory violations or for involvement in a tenants' union. But it seems likely that courts will extend the retaliatory eviction defense to cases where the tenant complains to the landlord of violations of the implied warranty of habitability. URLTA section 5.101 extends the retaliatory eviction defense to complaints to the landlord of a violation of the landlord's obligations.

(3) **Interference with constitutional right:** [§1082]   It has been argued that retaliatory eviction would abridge the tenant's constitutional right of free speech or, if the tenant participates in a tenants' union or tenants' strike, right of free assembly. The courts have generally avoided ruling on the constitutional issue because of the difficulty of finding the requisite "state action." To hold retaliatory eviction interferes with constitutional rights, the courts must find that there is "state action" depriving the tenant of constitutional rights. (*See* the discussion of "state action" and *Shelley v. Kraemer, supra,* §444.) In *Edwards v. Habib* (*supra*, §1078), the court suggested (without holding) that the application by the judiciary of the state's common law constitutes "state action."

   (a) **Public housing:** [§1083]   If the tenants in a public housing project organize a tenants' union or report housing code violations, it would be state action for the public housing authority to evict the tenants exercising their constitutional rights. Similarly, it has been held that if the housing project is part of an urban renewal project and financed with public assistance, even though privately owned, the landlord's actions are state action. [McQueen v. Druker, 438 F.2d 781 (1st Cir. 1971)]

(4) **Proof of motive:** [§1084]   Whether a landlord's primary motivation is retaliation is a question of fact. The burden of proving a retaliatory motive is on the tenant. If the tenant can show that the landlord's action was discriminatory against the defendant tenant and followed the tenant's reporting of violations at the first opportunity, the burden shifts to the landlord to prove his primary motivation is not retaliatory. The Restatement provides that each case turns on its own facts. [Rest. 2d §14.8, comment f]

   (a) **Statutes:** [§1085]   Statutes sometimes provide presumptions to govern the question of retaliatory motives. Section 5.101 of the URLTA, for example, creates a presumption that action against a tenant within one year of the tenant's complaint to an official agency or to the landlord, or of the tenant's participation in a tenants' union, is retaliatory.

   (b) **Retaliation by rent increase:** [§1086]   The retaliatory eviction defense can be used in a suit where the landlord is not retaliating directly but retaliating indirectly. For example, if T reports housing code violations, and then L increases T's rent and moves to evict T for nonpayment of the increased rent, T can plead retaliatory eviction if T can show that the rent increase is retaliatory. [Schweiger v. Superior Court, 3 Cal. 3d 507 (1970)]

(5) **Tenant in default:** [§1087]   A tenant in default in payment of rent cannot assert a retaliatory eviction defense. However, a tenant is *not in default* if the tenant is acting legally in withholding rent. The tenant is acting legally if under a statutory right she is using the rent money to make repairs or is withholding rent. If the lease is illegal, because renting the premises is in violation of the housing code, the tenant is not in default if she refuses to pay rent.

(6) **When landlord can evict:** [§1088]   The landlord cannot evict if he has a retaliatory motive. When a court holds that the landlord's primary motivation is not retaliatory, he may evict. In the meantime, the tenant can remain in possession and withhold or abate rent. The tenant may have to pay the landlord the reasonable rental value of the premises as is, which the landlord must sue for. A suit for rental value is not a summary proceeding and may take years.

(a) **Example:** T refuses to pay rent because L is unwilling to make repairs on a dwelling which contains numerous housing code violations. L sues to evict T for nonpayment of rent. T defends that the lease is invalid under *Brown v. Southall Realty* (*supra*, §1038), and T does not owe any rent. T wins. Thereafter L serves T with a thirty-day notice to quit and subsequently sues T in unlawful detainer. T defends that the eviction is in retaliation for assertion of a *Southall Realty* defense. L alleges he is unwilling to make repairs and intends to take the dwelling off the market. *Held:* The retaliatory eviction defense is available to T. If L is removing the unit from the market for retaliatory motives, he cannot evict T, as that would inhibit private enforcement of the housing codes. L can evict T only if he makes the necessary repairs or takes housing off the market for *sound business reasons*. [Robinson v. Diamond Housing Corp., 463 F.2d 853 (D.C. Cir. 1972)]

(b) **Landlord stops utilities:** [§1089]   If the landlord cannot evict the tenant, can the landlord stop paying the utility bills? Statutes in a number of states prohibit the landlord from attempting to evict a tenant by refusing to pay for utilities. The landlord must evict the tenant by using the judicial process. Self-help measures are forbidden (*see infra*, §1222). These statutes sometimes impose severe penalties on a landlord who tries to evict a tenant by cutting off utilities. If the landlord abandons the building and is beyond the effective power of the court, it has been held that the city has the duty to provide utilities on a temporary and emergency basis until the tenants can be relocated. [Masszonia v. Washington, 321 F. Supp. 965 (D.D.C. 1971)]

(7) **Commercial tenants:** [§1090]   The case law has largely involved protecting residential tenants from retaliatory eviction. Does a commercial tenant have a retaliatory eviction defense? The Restatement takes no position on whether or not the retaliatory eviction defense should be extended to commercial tenants. [Rest. 2d §14.8] Most cases raising the issue have held against the commercial tenant, but in *Windward Partners v. Sarah Delos Santos*, 577 P.2d 326 (Hawaii 1978), the court held that commercial tenants were protected against re-

taliatory eviction where the landlord was evicting because tenants opposed a zoning change. The court thought that the effectiveness of land-use statutes calling for public notice and meeting to discuss changes would be frustrated by retaliatory eviction.

(8) **State statutes:** [§1091]   In many states, statutes prohibit retaliatory acts. The statutes vary, particularly on presumptions of retaliatory motive and the kinds of tenant acts protected against retaliatory eviction. Some of these statutes extend the retaliatory eviction defense to commercial tenancies. [*See* Rest. 2d §14.8, Statutory Note]

G. LANDLORD'S TORT LIABILITY

1. **Introduction:** [§1092]   The ordinary scope of duty in negligence cases is this: Where a person can foresee that if he does not use ordinary care and skill in a situation he will cause danger of injury to another person, a duty arises to use ordinary care and skill to avoid such danger. Negligence involves recognizing danger of injury and doing nothing about it. At common law, with a few recognized exceptions, the landlord had no duty to make the premises safe, because the law regarded the lease as equivalent to the sale of a term. The buyer (tenant) took the premises as is. *Caveat lessee* was the rule. After the tenant took possession, the tenant was responsible for tort injuries. The landlord had no right to possession; indeed, he could not even enter without the permission of the tenant. Hence the landlord had no responsibility for persons injured on the land as a result of conditions developing after the tenant took possession.

   a. **Contract and tort liability compared:** [§1093]   The preceding section of this chapter discussed the landlord's duty to provide the habitable premises, which the common law denied for more or less the same reasons it denied a duty of the landlord to act so as to protect others from injury. Modern courts have largely rejected the old reasoning and have implied a warranty of habitability. Oddly enough, however when it comes to tort liability, to liability for personal injury, the old conceptions still are adhered to. Even the Restatement (Second) of Property, which implies a nonwaivable covenant of habitability giving the tenant new rights to pressure landlords to rehabilitate dwellings, restates the old law on tort liability. The question now arises whether it is sound to continue to allow the landlord to escape liability for personal injury when the landlord is liable in damages for not maintaining the dwelling. There is this important difference in the two duties. A judgment for damages for breach of the duty of habitability cannot exceed the agreed rent. A judgment for personal injury can be as large as the injury suffered, perhaps thousands of dollars. Extending the landlord's tort liability would theoretically subject the landlord to the possibility of large costs, which he would pass along to the tenants in the form of higher rents. But this may be more theoretical than real, because landlords can and do insure against personal injury. The cost passed on to the tenant may be only the cost of the insurance premium. An impecunious tenant may not take out insurance, and if society wants personal injury insured against, the only practical solution may be to impose the burden on the landlord who may pass it on to the tenant. Thus, at bottom, the issue seems to be: Who should pay the cost of an accident? The party injured or the tenant class by way of an insurance premium built into the rent? Much of the old law was laid down without spreading of the risk through insurance in mind.

2. **Dangerous Condition Existing at Time of Lease:** [§1094]   As stated above, the common law general rule is *caveat lessee*—"let the lessee beware." The tenant is buying a term and takes it in the condition it is in. Therefore, the landlord is not liable for injuries to the tenant due to a dangerous condition of the premises. Nor is the landlord liable to the tenant's guests, since the tenant has assumed the risk of warning guests (*see infra*, §1096). (Tenant's "guests" include members of the tenant's family, invitees, licensees, and others lawfully on the premises.) There are several important exceptions to the general rule, narrowing its strict application. Dissatisfied with the general rule, courts have sometimes exercised considerable ingenuity in fitting facts into one of the following recognized exceptions.

   a. **Concealed dangerous condition (latent defect):** [§1095]   If the landlord knows of a dangerous condition, and also has reason to believe that the tenant will not discover this condition and realize the risk, the landlord has a duty to disclose the dangerous condition. If the landlord does not disclose, she is liable for injuries caused thereby to the tenant or the tenant's guests. Hence, if the tenant could not reasonably discover a latent defect known to the landlord, the landlord is liable for injuries resulting therefrom. *Rationale:* It is said that it is either negligent or fraudulent to fail to give a warning of a hidden danger, but this exception also has an economic basis. If the landlord discloses the defect to the tenant, the tenant can minimize the risk by remedying the defect or avoiding it. Both on grounds of fairness and efficiency, the tenant should not be held to assume the risk unless he can reasonably discover the defect upon inspection. [Johnson v. O'Brien, 105 N.W.2d 244 (Minn. 1960)]

     (1) **Example:** L owns two apartments, numbered 1 and 2, which are joined by a connecting door. L papers over the door, and it cannot be discovered from an inspection of apartment 1. T leases apartment 1 and L does not tell T of the door. Subsequently a person enters apartment 1 through the papered-over door, beats up T, and carries off T's stereo set. L is liable both for T's personal injuries and loss of property. [McIntyre, Ltd v. Chandler Holding Corp., 172 Misc. 917 (1939)]

     (2) **No liability after disclosure to tenant:** [§1096]   If the tenant is made aware of the defect and accepts the premises "as is," the tenant assumes the risk. Moreover, after disclosure to the tenant, the landlord is not liable to *guests* of the tenant. The tenant has not only assumed the risk for himself; he has assumed the duty to warn others. *Rationale:* It is said that the landlord cannot stand guard and warn visitors for the tenant is in possession. It is also said that the tenant's failure to remedy the defect is a superseding cause of the ultimate injury. [Rest. 2d of Torts §356] But these are not very satisfactory reasons. Nonliability to the tenant's guests is not consistent with negligence law generally which does not exonerate a negligent person simply because the dangerous condition she creates is no longer under her control.

(3) **Defect discovered after tenant enters:** [§1097]   If, after the tenant takes possession, the landlord learns of a latent dangerous defect which existed prior to the tenant's entry, the landlord has the duty of disclosing the existence of the condition to the tenant. The tenant then can minimize the risk.

(4) **Landlord did not know but should have known:** [§1098]   An old debate in torts law concerns whether a landlord should be liable only if she *actually knew* of a defect, or if she should be liable also if she possessed information which, as a reasonable person, *should have led her to discover the defect*. Proving actual knowledge is often quite difficult, and if this is the test, landlords may escape liability because of failure of proof. Proving that the landlord ought to have discovered the defect is easier but may be thought to be an unfair imposition of liability. Almost all courts now hold that the landlord is liable even if she does not have actual knowledge of the defect, if she should, as a reasonable person, have discovered the defect. [Johnson v. O'Brien, *supra*, §1095] Whatever position a court takes on the "knew or should have known" issue governs all instances of landlord's tort liability, and not just concealed defects.

b. **Public use:** [§1099]   Where the lease contemplates that the premises will be used as a place of public admission (store, restaurant, theatre, etc.), the landlord is liable for injury to members of the public *if* the landlord (i) knows or should know of the dangerous condition, (ii) has reason to expect that the tenant will probably not correct the condition before admitting the public, and (iii) fails to exercise reasonable care to remedy the condition. The reason for imposing liability on the landlord is that it will facilitate commerce and keep costs of doing business low if the public can go about its business in reasonably safe premises. Hence the landlord may not permit the land to be used in a manner which involves a *public, rather than a private*, danger. [Rest. 2d §17.2]

(1) **What is public use:** [§1100]   A few courts have limited the public use exception to situations where the lease contemplates use by a large number of persons at one time (*e.g.*, a store or lecture hall). But the majority do not so limit it and impose liability on the landlord when only two or three members of the public will be on the premises at only one time (*e.g.*, a doctor's office). It is the *nature of the use*, and the *expectations* of the public, and not the number of admissions, that creates the landlord's duty. Also, a few courts have defined public use to cover only situations where the public pays admission. The "paid admission" test is thought to be a cheap and easy way to determine what is a "public use," and hence to fix the limits of the exception. But this distinction has no relation to the public expectations underlying the exception, and the majority of courts reject it and hold the landlord liable whether admission is paid or not. It is possible that the public use exception will be widened by courts to include defects in almost all commercial buildings existing at the time of the lease.

(2) **Liability limited to persons entering for public purposes:** [§1101]   Since the landlord's liability is based upon her knowledge that the tenant plans to use the

premises for purposes involving entry by the public, before the defective condition is corrected, the landlord's liability extends only to persons who enter the premises for the purposes for which the public is invited.

(a) **Example:** T leases a lecture hall from L for a free public lecture. L knows that one of the steps at the entrance is defective and dangerous, and L points this out to T (thereby complying with L's duty under the first exception), and advises T to repair it. T replies that he does not think the step is dangerous and sees no need to repair it. A, coming to a lecture, slips on the step and is injured. L is liable to A. B, coming to paint the lecture hall when no lecture is being held, slips on the step and is injured. L is not liable to B.

(3) **Defect must exist at beginning of lease:** [§1102]   If the defect does not exist at the beginning of the lease, but arises after the tenant takes possession, the landlord has no liability under the public use exception.

(4) **Tenant's promise to repair:** [§1103]   If the tenant promises to repair the defect, the landlord may remain liable if she has reason to expect that the tenant will admit the public before repairing. The landlord's duty is not relieved unless she has no reason to expect that the public might be admitted to unsafe premises.

3. **Defects Arising After Tenant Takes Possession:** [§1104]   The general rule is that the landlord has no liability for personal injury from dangerous conditions that arise after the tenant takes possession. The duty of care to keep the premises safe rests upon the person in possession, the tenant.

  a. **Example:** L leases a house to T situated on a hill above the street. The house has a depressed passageway along the side, giving access to the rear of the house. The passageway is protected from the sloping bank of the hill by a retaining wall. At the time of the lease the retaining wall is in a safe condition. Subsequently a crack appears in the retaining wall, and two years later the wall falls on a young nephew of the tenant, injuring him. L is not under a statutory duty to repair. L has no liability for the injury. [Bowles v. Mahoney, 202 F.2d 320 (D.C. Cir. 1952)]

  b. **Repairs undertaken:** [§1105]   If the landlord voluntarily undertakes to make repairs, although not legally obligated to do so, she owes a duty to exercise reasonable care in the undertaking. If she makes repairs in a negligent manner, the landlord is liable to those who do not know of her negligence and are injured by her careless or unskillful workmanship. Some jurisdictions limit the landlord's liability to repairs that make conditions more dangerous or give them a deceptive appearance of safety. But the preferable view is that the landlord is liable if the repairs are ineffective. A showing of increased danger or deceptive appearance is not required. In any case, the very fact that repairs have been made usually gives rise to a deceptive appearance of safety. [Jordan v. Savage, 232 N.E.2d 580 (Ill. 1967)]

    (1) **Knowledge of tenant:** [§1106]   The landlord is not liable when she undertakes repairs if the tenant knows or should know that the repairs have been negli-

gently made. Liability is imposed under this exception to the general rule because of the *reliance of the tenant* on the landlord's acts, and where there is no reliance there is no liability. Oddly enough, knowledge by the tenant of the landlord's negligence also bars a suit by the tenant's guest, even though the guest relies on the deceptive appearance of safety. In such a case, the landlord can assume that the tenant will warn his guests.

(a) **Example:** In October, T leases a house from L. The roof leaks, and in repairing the roof, L removes the gutter. L knows that without a gutter rain will drain onto the front porch steps and freeze, resulting in icy steps. L intends to reinstall the gutter. T complains about the absence of the gutter. In January, before L reinstalls the gutter, rain falls and freezes, and a guest of T slips on the icy steps and is injured. L is not liable because T had knowledge of the danger and should have warned his guest. [Borders v. Roseberry, 532 P.2d 1366 (Kan. 1975)]

4. **Common Areas Controlled by Landlord:** [§1107] If the landlord leases part of the property and retains control of common areas (such as halls, walks, elevators, etc.), the landlord is liable for physical injury if the landlord could have reasonably discovered the condition and made it safe. This *duty of reasonable care* over common areas is the same as any owner-occupier has toward guests. [Crowell v. McCaffrey, 386 N.E.2d 1256 (Mass. 1979)]

a. **Example:** T slips and falls on the icy sidewalk leading to L's apartment house. L is liable if L knew or should have known of the ice and did not take reasonable steps to remedy it (by putting sand on it or otherwise).

b. **Criminal intrusion:** [§1108] If the landlord can reasonably foresee the risk of criminals coming into the building by way of common areas under the control of the landlord, the landlord may be liable for physical harm caused by criminal intrusion if necessary precautions are not made. Several cases hold the landlord liable if the premises are residential, but there are cases contra. It has also been held that the landlord is liable for criminal intrusion into the common area of commercial buildings, but there are cases to the contrary on this issue too. [Samson v. Saginaw Professional Building Inc., 224 N.W.2d 843 (Mich. 1975)—landlord liable for assault in commercial building lobby by mental patient receiving treatment in office there]

(1) **Example:** T is assaulted in the lobby of her apartment house, which is located in an area where such assaults are common, increasing, and foreseeable. L has no doorman on duty nor an adequate security system. Recent cases hold L is liable to T. The liability may be based on the landlord's control of common areas. Or, if the landlord has reduced security, the liability may be based on an implied contractual duty not to reduce security (tenant's expectations). [Kline v. 1500 Massachusetts Avenue Apartment Corp., 439 F.2d 477 (D.C. Cir. 1970)]

5. **Landlord Contracts to Repair:** [§1109]   If the landlord expressly promises to repair and maintain the premises, the older cases hold this promise does not carry with it tort liability. The injured tenant can sue only in contract, and damages may be limited to the cost of the repair or to the agreed rent. The reason is that the parties did not contemplate tort liability (which can be large) but only contractual liability. Carrying the contract analysis one step further, older cases also hold that guests of the tenant, who are not a party to the contract, cannot sue because of lack of privity of contract. (Even if the contract is construed to be a third party beneficiary contract, the tenant's guests may still be limited to contract damages and cannot recover damages for personal injuries.)

   a. **Modern law:** [§1110]   Although the old law is still followed in some jurisdictions, a majority of states now finds the landlord who contracts to repair liable in tort to the tenant and to his guests. By holding the landlord liable in tort to the tenant's guests, the privity of contract issue is circumvented. *Rationale:* Because of the landlord's promise, the tenant will rely on it and forego efforts to remedy the condition. Hence the tenant will not minimize the risk. Society wants the risk minimized. [Faber v. Creswick, 156 A.2d 252 (N.J. 1949); Rest. 2d §17.5]

6. **Landlord Under Legal Duty to Repair:** [§1111]   The landlord may have a statutory duty to repair the premises, or the jurisdiction may imply a covenant of habitability. This will probably be the case in most jurisdictions with respect to residential leaseholds. What effect does the legal duty to repair have upon the landlord's tort liability?

   a. **Statutory duty to repair:** [§1112]   If the landlord has a statutory duty to repair (such as imposed by a housing code), the landlord may be liable to the tenant and the tenant's guests who are injured as a result of the failure to repair. The jurisdictions divide into two groups.

      (1) **Negligence per se:** [§1113]   Some cases (and the Restatement) hold that the statute provides a legislative standard of conduct legally expected of the landlord, and violation of the statute constitutes negligence per se. [Rest. 2d §17.6] The court must instruct the jury that the standard of conduct is fixed by the legislature, and the jury's only function is to determine whether the landlord had a valid excuse. If the landlord has used reasonable care in complying with the statute, she is not liable. [Crowell v. McCaffrey, *supra,* §1107]

      (2) **Evidence of negligence:** [§1114]   Most courts hold that violation of the housing code is not negligence per se but is **evidence of negligence**, which the jury may or may not find conclusive. This permits the jury more leeway in setting the standard of care owed. A minor violation of the code known to the landlord might not be negligent. [Whetzel v. Jess Fisher Management Co., 282 F.2d 943 (D.C. Cir. 1960)]

         (a) **Assumption of the risk:** [§1115]   It is not a defense to breach of a statutory duty that the tenant assumed the risk. If it were, the responsibilities imposed on landlords by the legislature could be nullified. [Kanelos v. Kettler, 406 F.2d 951 (D.C. Cir. 1968)]

b. **Implied covenant of habitability:** [§1116]   Not many cases have considered whether the landlord should have tort liability for failing to comply with the implied covenant of habitability. But those that have have held the landlord is liable for negligence if personal injury results from a breach of the implied warranty. They have refused to impose a standard of strict liability, preferring the standard of reasonable care. The mere fact that the implied warranty is breached is not sufficient to bring on liability. The plaintiff must show that the landlord knew or should have known of the violation, and failed to correct the situation within a reasonable time. The courts may well split, however, over whether a violation of the implied warranty is negligence per se (as many courts hold a violation of a housing code is) or merely evidence of negligence (*see supra,* §1114). In either case, it appears likely that more and more courts will hold the landlord liable in tort if she fails to meet her implied warranty of habitability. It would be disturbing if the tenant who falls through a hole in the floor could withhold rent but not collect for personal injury. Such a result would not further either the purpose of rehabilitation or the tort objectives of minimizing the risk and distributing the loss. [Trentacost v. Brussel, 412 A.2d 436 (N.J. 1980); Rest. 2d §17.6—negligence per se]

7. **Modern Trend—Reasonable Care:** [§1117]   A few recent cases have thrown over the general rule and its elaborate exceptions. They have held that "landlords as other persons must *exercise reasonable care not to subject others to an unreasonable risk of harm.* A landlord must act as a reasonable person under all of the circumstances including the likelihood of injury to others, the probable seriousness of such injuries, and the burden of reducing or avoiding the risk. The questions of control, hidden defects, and common or public use, which formerly had to be established as a prerequisite to even considering the negligence of a landlord, will now be relevant only inasmuch as they bear on the basic tort issues such as foreseeability and unreasonableness of the particular risk of harm." [Sargent v. Ross, 308 A.2d 538 (N.H. 1973)] Under this reasonable care standard, a landlord is not liable in negligence unless she knows or reasonably should know of the defect and has a reasonable opportunity to repair it. In view of the imposition of the implied covenant of habitability, the reasonable care standard will likely be adopted by more and more courts in the future.

a. **Example:** T rents from L an apartment with a balcony. The balcony has a faulty railing, which the landlord knows about and warns T about. Several months later, T invites a young woman to a dinner party in his apartment. She steps out on the balcony, leans against the railing, which gives way, and she falls to the ground and is injured. L is liable to the young woman. [Young v. Garwacki, 402 N.E.2d 1045 (Mass. 1980)]

8. **Exculpatory Clauses:** [§1118]   An "exculpatory clause" is a lease provision that purports to exonerate the landlord from some or all responsibility and liability. The exculpatory clause may purport to relieve the landlord from all liability for personal injury resulting from the landlord's negligence. Courts are split on the validity of such provisions.

a. **Traditional view:** [§1119]   The traditional view is that an exculpatory clause relieving the landlord of liability for personal injury is **valid** because of freedom of contract. Thus, by inserting an exculpatory clause in the lease, the landlord can be effectively insulated from any liability to repair or maintain the premises. *Rationale:* Public policy is not offended by the parties bargaining to limit their rights and duties regarding each other at the time they enter into the leasehold. The tenant may contract to assume the risk for himself and his guests. [O'Callaghan v. Waller & Beckwith Realty Co., 155 N.E.2d 545 (Ill. 1959); *reaffirmed in* Sweney Gasoline & Oil Co. v. Toledo, Peoria & Western Railroad, 247 N.E.2d 603 (Ill. 1969); Ill. Rev. Stat. ch. 80, §91—reverses cases and provides exculpatory clauses relieving landlord of liability for personal injury unenforceable]

b. **Modern trend:** [§1120] Because of the disparity of bargaining power between landlord and tenant in modern times with a housing shortage, and where the tenant has no practical choice but to accept the lease as offered, several modern courts have held exculpatory clauses in residential leases are against public policy and void. The courts have objected to the fact that relieving the landlord of liability subjects others to an unreasonable risk of harm. The courts have thus held that the parties cannot relieve the landlord of tort liability by contract provisions in residential leases. [McCutcheon v. United Homes Corp., 486 P.2d 1093 (Wash. 1971)]

c. **Restatement position:** [§1121] The Restatement provides that an exculpatory clause is not effective to shift to the tenant the landord's duty owed to the *public,* where the premises are to be opened to the public (*see* exception discussed *supra,* §1099). The public has the right to expect that premises open to the public are reasonably safe. [Rest. 2d §17.2, comment j] Similarly, the Restatement provides that exculpatory clauses cannot relieve the landord of liability to *third parties,* who are not parties to the contract. On the other hand, the Restatement takes an equivocal position as to the validity of an exculpatory clause when the tenant is injured. It provides that such a clause "may" be valid to exonerate the landlord where the *tenant* is injured, unless "found to be ineffective as contrary to the policy of the law." [Rest. 2d §17.3, comment j]

d. **Statutes:** [§1122] Statutes in many states provide that exculpatory clauses relieving the landlord from liability in tort are void. Often these statutes apply to residential leases only, but some apply to all leases. [*See* Rest. 2d §17.3, Statutory Note—listing statutes in California, Illinois, Massachusetts, New York, and Ohio, among other states] URLTA section 1.403 provides that no residential rental agreement may relieve the landlord of tort liability.

H. TENANT'S DUTIES

1. **Duty to Pay Rent:** [§1123] The tenant has a duty to pay any rent reserved in the lease. Traditionally, the duty to pay rent is an independent obligation, not dependent upon the landlord's performance of her obligations. Thus if the landlord fails to repair, rent is still payable. In many jurisdictions the duty to pay rent is now dependent upon performance of the landlord's obligations if the premises are residential. If the landlord does not perform, the tenant can terminate the lease and move out, withhold rent, or receive a rent abatement (*see supra,* §§1052 *et seq.*).

a. **Implied agreement:** [§1124] If rent is not reserved, the tenant has a duty to pay the *reasonable rental value* of the use of the property (quantum meruit). [Gunn v. Scovil, 4 Day 228 (Conn. 1810)] The reasonable rental value is not rent, however, and the landlord's remedies upon default are not the same as her remedies upon default of rent. (*See infra,* §§1179 *et seq.*)

b. **Illegal agreement:** [§1125] If the rental agreement is illegal because the housing code forbids renting property in substandard condition, the tenant has no duty to pay rent. [Brown v. Southall Realty Co., *supra,* §1038] But the tenant must pay the reasonable rental value of the premises.

c. **Rent passes with reversion:** [§1126] The right to rent is attached to the landlord's reversion. If the landlord sells the property to another, the transferee is entitled to future rents. However, the right to rent is not inseparable from the reversion. The landlord can expressly reserve the right to rent when she transfers the reversion, or she can assign the rents without assigning the reversion.

d. **Nonapportionment of rent:** [§1127] In the absence of an agreement to the contrary, rent falls due only on the last day of the lease term. Rent does not accrue from day to day, but accrues and falls due simultaneously at the end of the term.

   (1) **Example:** On April 1, L leases Blackacre to T, with rent of $200 payable monthly. On June 18, L dies, and the will devises L's reversion in Blackacre to A, and leaves the residue of the estate to B. A, owner of the reversion on June 30, is entitled to the entire $200 due on June 30.

   (2) **Minority rule:** [§1128] In a very few states, courts have held that rent accrues from day to day and is apportioned. The Restatement adopts the minority rule. [Rest. 2d §12.1, comment e]

   (3) **Statutes:** [§1129] In many states, statutes have been enacted providing for apportionment of rent where the lease is terminated between lease days. [*See* Rest. 2d §12.1, Statutory Note, item 2]

e. **Rent control:** [§1130] Many cities have enacted rent control ordinances. The two big questions concerning these ordinances are: Is the ordinance constitutional in general? If it is, is the rent limitation constitutional as applied to a particular landlord?

   (1) **Constitutionality**

      (a) **Emergency test:** [§1131] Before rent control became popular (during and after World War II), the U.S. Supreme Court held that rent control is justifiable only under emergency conditions. Under this test, the Court is not bound by a legislative declaration that an emergency exists, but may review and reject the factual assertion. [Block v. Hirsh, 256 U.S. 135 (1921)]

(b) **Reasonableness test:** [§1132]   In several recent cases, the requirement of an emergency has been abandoned, and rent control has been held to be constitutional if (i) it bears a rational relation to a legitimate public purpose (the ordinary test for exercise of the police power), and (ii) the *landlord is given a just and reasonable return* on his investment. If the rent control law does not provide for procedural mechanisms that will give the landlord a fair return under changing economic conditions, it is confiscatory. An analogy is made to regulation of public utility rates. [Birkenfeld v. City of Berkeley, 17 Cal. 3d 129 (1976); *and see* Orange County Taxpayers Council, Inc. v. City of Orange, 416 A.2d 353 (N.J. 1980)—upholding ordinance that prohibited increases in rent unless dwelling is in substantial compliance with housing code]

(2) **Determination of fair return:** [§1133]   Problems arise in determining what is the landlord's investment upon which a fair return must be allowed. The investment might be either sunk capital or market value of the property. The former would result in different rents for similar apartments in different buildings, depending on what the landlord paid for the building. The latter might defeat the purpose of rent control by tying rents to the free operation of the housing market, deemed unfair to tenants. Other suggested methods of valuing the landlord's investment include depreciated replacement cost and capitalized income, but they too present problems.

2. Duty to Repair

a. **Common law duty:** [§1134]   In the absence of a duty on the part of the landlord to repair (imposed by statute, implied covenant of habitability, or express covenant), the tenant has a duty to make ordinary repairs to keep the property in the same condition as at the commencement of the term, ordinary wear and tear excepted. The tenant does not have to make substantial repairs, but he must protect the premises from damage, usually by the elements. He must treat the premises in such a way that no substantial injury is done to them during his tenancy. Sometimes the tenant's duty to repair is referred to as "liability for permissive waste." [Suydam v. Jackson, 54 N.Y. 450 (1873)]

(1) **Death and decomposition of tenant:** [§1135]   It has been argued that the tenant's estate is liable for damages if the tenant dies and his body decomposes in the apartment before it is discovered. The argument rests on the common law duty to redeliver the premises in the same general condition as they were at the time of letting. This argument has been rejected on the ground that the damages occurred as a result of unavoidable circumstances over which the tenant had no control. [Kennedy v. Kidd, 557 P.2d 467 (Okla. 1976)]

(2) **Tort liability:** [§1136]   To the extent that the tenant has a duty of repair, the tenant is liable to persons injured as a result of his failure to repair. [King v. Cooney-Eckstein Co., 63 So. 659 (Fla. 1913)]

b. **Duty not to commit affirmative waste:** [§1137]   Like a life tenant, a lessee is liable for waste. There are two kinds of waste: involuntary or permissive waste (waste from negligent *failure* to make normal repairs), and voluntary waste (*affirmative* acts which either substantially *damage* the premises or substantially *change* them). Permissive waste has been discussed *supra,* §1134. It results from the tenant's failure to use due care.

(1) **Damage to the premises:** [§1138]   If the tenant substantially damages the premises by an affirmative act, the tenant is liable to the landlord. The damage must be substantial, with effects extending well beyond the tenant's term. Attaching a wooden closet to a wall or putting a decorative frame around a window is not waste. Nor, it has been held, is it waste for the tenant to remove a defective ceiling and replace it with sheetrock (even it the sheetrock is insufficiently thick to satisfy the fire code). [Rumiche Corp. v. Eisenreich, 40 N.Y.2d 174 (1976)]

(2) **Improvement of premises:** [§1139]   If the structure is changed so as to *improve* its value, the act is known as *ameliorating waste*. Under the older rule, the tenant was liable for ameliorating waste, but in modern times a long-term tenant may be given the right to change the structure if the economic value is not diminished. For example, the replacement of old built-in cabinets with new ones is not waste. [Sigsbee Holding Corp. v. Canavan, 39 Misc. 2d 465 (1963); *cf.* Melms v. Pabst Brewing Co., *supra* §389]

(3) **Restatement position:** [§1140]   The Restatement provides that the tenant "is entitled to make changes in the physical condition of the leased property which are reasonably necessary in order for the tenant to use the leased property in a manner that is reasonable under all the circumstances." [Rest. 2d §12.2] Although older courts tended to be more technical, the Restatement position—if not now representative of the majority of modern courts—clearly states the strong modern trend.

c. **Covenant by tenant to repair:** [§1141]   The tenant may expressly covenant to repair and maintain the premises, and his covenant is enforceable (unless the lease is unconscionable). [Patton v. United States, 139 F. Supp. 279 (W.D. Pa. 1955)] If the tenant covenants without exception, the tenant is liable for repairs, whatever the cause. If the damage is by a third party or act of God, the tenant is liable. [Polack v. Pioche, 35 Cal. 416 (1868)]

(1) **Destruction of the premises:** [§1142]   If the tenant generally covenants to repair, making no exceptions, the tenant must rebuild the building if it burns down. [Chambers v. North River Line, 102 S.E. 198 (N.C. 1920)] Statutes in many states have changed this harsh rule. (*See infra*, §1165.)

(a) **Covenant by landlord:** [§1143]   If the landlord covenants to repair, he must rebuild the building if it is destroyed by fire. Thus, under modern law, a tenant who covenants to repair does not have to rebuild (statutes now so provide), but a landlord who covenants to repair has a duty to rebuild.

(b) **Insurance:** [§1144]   If the tenant insures the building against fire, and the building burns down, the majority of cases hold that the tenant is entitled to the entire insurance proceeds. That is so even though the leasehold interest is worth less than the insurance proceeds, and it is so whether or not the tenant has a duty to rebuild. The theory is that the tenant is insuring his interest, and the landlord can also insure his if he so desires. [Miller v. Gold Beach Packing Co., 282 P. 764 (Or. 1929)]

(2) **Repair to comply with building code:** [§1145]   If, after the tenant takes possession, repairs are required by a building code or other government regulation, the tenant who covenants to repair does not have to make *substantial* repairs. "Substantial" is a conclusory term reflecting the court's determination, after weighing all the factors, that the parties to the lease did not expect the lessee to assume this risk, despite the use of unqualified language. For example, in a long term commercial lease, repairs to an elevator would not be deemed substantial [Gaddis v. Consolidated Freightways, 398 P.2d 749 (Or. 1965)], but major structural repairs required to meet the building code would be [Scott v. Prazma, 555 P.2d 571 (Wyo. 1976)].

3. **Duty Not to Disturb Other Tenants:** [§1146]   Absent a covenant in a lease, there is no common law duty of a tenant not to make noise or otherwise disturb other tenants. The only duty of the tenant in this respect is not to commit a nuisance. All possessors of land have a duty not to commit a nuisance (*see infra*, §§1533 *et seq.*). It is common, however, for residential apartment leases to provide a covenant by the tenant that he will not substantially interfere with the enjoyment by other tenants of their apartments. Breach of such a covenant permits the landlord to evict the tenant. Covenants of this type tend to be judicially construed by a rule of reason. The amount of noise and disturbances permitted depends upon the particular context. Even if the covenant does not have a rule of reason written in it, but is a covenant to make "no noise or disturbance," a court will likely interpret it to mean "no unreasonable noise or disturbance." This construction in effect makes the court and not the landlord the arbiter of the defendant's conduct. [Louisiana Leasing Co. v. Sokolow, 48 Misc. 2d 1014 (1966)]

4. **Duty Not to Use for Illegal Purposes:** [§1147]   The tenant has a duty not to use the premises for an illegal purpose. But the landlord's remedies depend upon the landlord's complicity in the illegal use. Illegal uses most often litigated involve gambling or prostitution, or selling liquor, narcotics, or pornography. Sometimes they involve a use prohibited by a zoning ordinance.

a. **Landlord intends illegal use:** [§1148]   If the landlord and the tenant both intend that the property be used for an illegal purpose, the majority rule is that the lease is not enforceable by either of them. Both parties are tainted by participating in the illegal leasing. The landlord cannot recover rent from the tenant because the agreement cannot be enforced. [Brown v. Southall Realty Co., *supra*, §1125] The landlord can recover possession from the tenant, who has no valid lease (unless the landlord is retaliating unlawfully against the tenant, *see supra*, §1078). The Restatement follows the majority rule. [Rest. 2d §9.1]

(1) **Minority view:** [§1149]   Some courts do not think the majority rule discourages a tenant from entering into a lease for illegal use, since the tenant can get out of the lease at any time. These courts hold that the landlord may enforce the lease if he merely knows of the intended illegal use and does not thereafter participate in the illegal conduct. If the landlord participates in the illegal conduct, the lease is unenforceable. Because "participation" may be defined broadly, the landlord has an incentive to put a stop to the illegal conduct on the premises and hold the tenant to the lease.

   (a) **Example:** L leases a building to T with knowledge that T intends to conduct a gambling operation on the premises. L does not participate in any way in the operation. Under the majority rule, neither L nor T can enforce the lease. Under the minority view, L can enforce the lease against T (even if T's gambling business is shut down by the authorities).

   (b) **Further variation:** [§1150]   A few courts go further than the minority in permitting the landlord to enforce a lease. They hold that the landlord can enforce the lease unless (i) he actively participates in the illegal conduct, and (ii) the illegal conduct is particularly heinous or objectionable. Thus, in the above example, if gambling is not viewed as heinous, the landlord can participate in the gambling activity and still enforce the lease.

   (c) **Policy issue:** [§1151]   The policy question is: Which will most discourage leasing for illegal uses—stripping the landlord of his bargain, thus discouraging the landlord (majority view), or permitting the landlord to hold the tenant to his bargain, thus discouraging the tenant who is stuck with the rent if the illegal use is stopped by the landlord or the authorities? The minority courts assume the latter, but cannot stomach the landlord enforcing the lease if he participates in the illegal activity. Thus they stop short of the logical end of their assumption. It may also be said in favor of the majority rule that the law should not lend its support and authority to a transgressor.

b. **Landlord not a party to illegality:** [§1152]   If the tenant uses the leased property for an illegal purpose, not intended by the landlord, and the landlord is not a party to the illegal use, the common law rule is that the landlord cannot terminate the lease. The landlord can only sue for damages or sue for an injunction to stop the illegal activity. The lease is viewed as creating a term in the tenant, which is not an illegal bargain since the landlord did not intend an illegal use. Once created, the term cannot be forfeited except as provided in the lease. [Morris v. Austraw, 152 S.E.2d 155 (N.C. 1967)]

   (1) **Compare with foregoing rule:** [§1153]   This view may be logically consistent with the majority view above, but it leads to an odd result. If the tenant informs the landlord of the illegal use intended, making the landlord something of a co-conspirator, the lease is unenforceable. The landlord can evict the tenant and the tenant can abandon. If the tenant does not inform the landlord of the illegal

use intended, the landlord cannot evict the tenant when the illegal use takes place nor can the tenant abandon. Thus an innocent landlord is stuck with a tenant who performs illegal acts but a transgressing landlord is not.

(2) **Restatement position:** [§1154]   The Restatement takes the position that the landlord may terminate the lease if he acts while the illegal use is continuing or within a reasonable time after it is stopped by public authorities. [Rest. 2d §12.5] The termination remedy is justified on grounds of public policy and as a part of the dependent obligations doctrine adopted elsewhere in the Restatement.

(3) **Misrepresentation:** [§1155]   If the intended use is illegal, or perhaps not illegal but merely objectionable, the landlord may rescind the lease if the tenant has misrepresented the intended use. Thus if the tenant says during rental negotiations that he is going to sell gifts and novelties, and after moving in sells pornographic materials, L can rescind on the ground of misrepresentation. [Stroup v. Conant, 520 P.2d 337 (Or. 1974)]

5. **Acts of Third Party Relieving Tenant of Duty:** [§1156]   The tenant may be relieved of his duty to pay rent by acts of a third party which make it impossible or difficult to continue the lease. One must start from the proposition, however, that the tenant has purchased a term and assumed the risk. This was the old law. [Paradine v. Jane, 82 Eng. Rep. 897 (1647)—holding tenant assumed risk of war] Modern doctrines have carved exceptions in that proposition, but it still has considerable vitality.

a. **Use becomes illegal:** [§1157]   Where a use of property becomes illegal after the lease is made, a court may—in some circumstances—hold that the tenant may terminate the lease and stop paying further rent.

(1) **Where restricted to one use:** [§1158]   Where the parties intend that the premises be used for one particular use only, which becomes illegal, the tenant is excused from further liability for the rent. In effect the courts imply a condition that the lease is made on an implied condition that the one use intended remain legal. It is considered oppressive and unfair to hold the tenant when he can make no use of the property. [Walker v. Southern Trucking Corp., 219 So. 2d 379 (Ala. 1969); Rest. 2d §9.2]

(2) **Where several uses permitted:** [§1159]   Where the parties intend that the premises be used for one use, but the tenant is free to make other uses, and the intended use becomes illegal, the tenant cannot terminate the lease. It is not considered oppressive to hold the tenant when he can make other uses of the property than those intended. In this situation, the tenant takes the risk that the use will become illegal. The Restatement generally adopts this position, but adds that a tenant may terminate "if it would be unreasonable to place on the tenant the burdens of the lease after converting to the other use." [Rest. 2d §9.2(2)]

(3) **Permit required for use:** [§1160]   When the lease restricts the tenant to one particular use which is legal only if a permit or zoning variance is obtained from a governmental agency, the tenant cannot terminate the lease if the permit is not granted. The tenant assumes the risk of obtaining the permit. [Warshawsky v. American Automotive Products Co., 138 N.E.2d 816 (Ill. 1956)]

(a) **Minority views:** [§1161]   A minority of jurisdictions put the risk on the landlord and excuse the tenant from liability for rent if the permit is not granted. They reason that the burden on the tenant is too oppressive because he cannot make any further use of the land. The Restatement excuses the tenant if he makes a good-faith effort to obtain the permit. [Rest. 2d §9.2, comment a]

b. **Frustration of purpose:** [§1162]   The tenant may terminate the lease in case of extreme hardship if the purpose of the lease is frustrated. The most frequent form of frustration is governmental action that makes the intended use of premises extremely difficult. This doctrine originated as part of contract law and has been applied to *commercial* leases.

(1) **Requirements:** [§1163]   Courts have been more hesitant to relieve tenants of their bargains than promisors generally. They have imposed strict requirements on the frustration doctrine. For the tenant to be relieved of liability: (i) the use that has been frustrated must have been *contemplated by both* landlord and tenant as the use for which the premises were let; (ii) the frustration must be *total or near total*, imposing extreme hardship on the tenant; and (iii) the frustrating event must *not have been foreseen or foreseeable* by the parties. If it was foreseeable, the risk is ordinarily placed on the tenant.

(a) **Example:** In August 1941, L leases a building to T for the sole purpose of selling new cars. The lease is for five years. In January 1942, after the outbreak of war, the federal government restricts the sale of new cars to persons with preferential priorities, and orders Detroit to cut back on car production. L offers to waive the restriction on use, says he will accept an assignee if T can find one, and offers to reduce the rent if T cannot operate profitably. T refuses to stay on. On March 15, 1942, T vacates the premises, claiming frustration of purpose. The frustration doctrine does not apply to T, and T continues to be liable for rent. Why? First, the frustration has not been total, and the hardship is not extreme. Some new car sales are still possible. T has merely lost part of his expected profits. Second, the risk was reasonably foreseeable because in June 1940, Congress authorized the President to mobilize the automobile industry for national defense. The public anticipated that production would soon be restricted. T assumed the risk unless T can show the circumstances were wholly outside the contemplation of the parties. [Lloyd v. Murphy, 25 Cal. 2d 48 (1944)]

(2) **Impossibility of performance:** [§1164]   The frustration doctrine is similar to, but not identical with, the contract doctrine of impossibility of performance.

Both require the showing of extreme hardship. In the case of impossibility, performance must be literally impossible or extremely difficult or illegal. In the case of frustration, the *purposes* are frustrated, while performance is still possible. The doctrines are related, sometimes confused, and not always separable.

c. **Destruction of the premises:** [§1165]   At common law, destruction of the building on the leased property did not terminate the lease or relieve the tenant of his obligation to pay rent. *Rationale:* The leasehold (estate in land) survived the destruction, and the land was the important part of the bargain. The common law rule is unsuited to most urban leases where the lease is primarily of the building, not the land. Statutes in a large majority of states have been enacted providing that, if the lease does not provide to the contrary, the tenant may terminate the lease and cease paying rent if the premises are destroyed by fire, the elements, or any cause other than the tenant's own negligence. [*See* Rest. 2d §3.103, Statutory Note, item 2; URLTA §4.106]

(1) **Restatement position:** [§1166]   The Restatement provides that the tenant may terminate the lease if a change in condition "caused suddenly by a non-manmade force makes the leased property unsuitable for the use contemplated by the parties." [Rest. 2d §5.4] The reason is that a lease today is primarily a bargain for a building and not for land. The Restatement position shifts the risk of fire from the tenant to the landlord. It has been adopted by at least one state. [Albert M. Greenfield & Co., Inc. v. Kolea, 380 A.2d 758 (Pa. 1976)]

d. **Eminent domain**

(1) **Effect on continuation of lease**

(a) **Entire taking:** [§1167]   A permanent taking of all the leased property by condemnation proceedings *extinguishes* the leasehold. The leasehold is deemed merged into the reversion which is taken by the government. [3 A.L.R.2d 286 (1949)] (The lessee is entitled to compensation for the taking of the leasehold; *see* below.)

(b) **Temporary taking:** [§1168]   If the government takes the property for a limited period of time shorter than the duration of the lease (*e.g.*, to store munitions during an emergency), the lease is *not terminated*. The tenant's duty to pay rent continues unabated. The tenant is entitled to recover from the government the value of the occupancy taken. [Leonard v. Autocar Sales & Service Co., 64 N.E.2d 477 (Ill. 1964)]

(c) **Partial taking:** [§1169]   Where the government takes less than all the property, the lease continues in effect. The rent is *not abated* proportionately because of the partial taking. The tenant must continue to pay full rent to the landlord (but the tenant is entitled to recover compensation from the government). [Elliott v. Joseph, 351 S.W.2d 879 (Tex. 1961)]

1) **Criticism:** This rule is unfair to the landlord. It deprives the landlord of his security (the property) and substitutes only the tenant's unsecured obligation to pay rent. Where a tenant is evicted from part of the leased premises by the holder of paramount title, there is an apportionment of rent. The net effect of partial condemnation is no different; therefore, it would seem that rent should be apportioned on condemnation as well, but the majority rule is to the contrary. The Restatement provides that upon a partial taking, if the lease is not terminated, the rent is abated. [Rest. 2d §8.1(2)]

(2) **Condemnation award—rights of parties:** [§1170]   In most states, upon condemnation a lump-sum award is given for the entire fee simple. This award must be divided between the landlord and tenant, both of whom own interests in the property. Of this sum, the tenant is entitled to the fair market value of the unexpired term of the leasehold, minus the rent he would have paid under the lease. The landlord receives what is left. Hence, the tenant receives a share of the award only if his lease was for less than the fair rental value of the property for the balance of the term. [Great Atlantic & Pacific Tea Co. v. State, 22 N.Y.2d 75 (1968)]

(a) **Example:** T has a ten-year lease on property for $1,000 a year. After three years, the property is condemned by the government, and the condemnation award for the value of an unencumbered fee simple is $10,000. The property could lease for $1,200 a year now. T is entitled to the sum of $200 multiplied by seven years, or $1,400, discounted to its present value.

(b) **Proportional division:** [§1171]   Where the sum of the value of the leasehold and the reversion, appraised separately, exceeds the condemnation award, the method described above is unfair to the landlord, who receives less than the value of his reversion. In such a case, the court may order the condemnation award apportioned between landlord and tenant so that each suffers a deficiency proportionately. [Kentucky Department of Highways v. Sherrod, 367 S.W.2d 844 (Ky. 1963)] The Restatement provides for a proportional division of a lump-sum award. [Rest. 2d §8.2]

(c) **Other damages:** [§1172]   In addition to the value of the leasehold, the tenant may be entitled to *severance damages* to the part not taken or *relocation costs.* He is also entitled to compensation for fixtures that he is entitled to remove at the end of the term. [*In re* Allen Street & First Ave., 256 N.Y. 236 (1931)]

6. **Rights and Duties Relating to Fixtures:** [§1173]   When the tenant attaches a chattel to the premises, he may want to remove it upon termination of the lease. The common law made it difficult to do so. Two rules were applied: (i) fixtures belong to the landlord; and (ii) attached chattels that are not fixtures are forfeited to the landlord if they are not removed before the end of the lease.

a. **Fixtures belong to landlord:** [§1174] The common law rule is that fixtures cannot be removed from the premises by the tenant. Fixtures become part of the realty and therefore the property of the landlord. Thus the key question arises: What is a fixture?

(1) **Fixture defined:** [§1175] The word "fixture" has proven very difficult to define. The English view is that a chattel that has been **permanently attached** to land is a fixture. Thus the focus is on what is "permanent" and what is "attached." American courts have generally rejected the English view as unworkable and have held that whether a chattel is a fixture depends upon the intention of the tenant. The intention is determined by objective criteria, such as the nature of the article, the manner in which it is attached, and the amount of damage that would be caused by its removal. [Sigrol Realty Corp. v. Valcich, 12 App. Div. 2d 430 (1961)]

(2) **Exception—trade fixtures:** [§1176] An exception to the rule is recognized to allow a tenant to remove trade fixtures—*i.e.,* those installed for the purpose of carrying on a trade or business.

(a) **Rationale:** This encourages economic investment for trade. The tenant is liable to the landlord, however, for material damages caused by removing trade fixtures. [Cameron v. Oakland County Gas & Oil Co., 269 N.W. 277 (Mich. 1936); Handler v. Horns, 65 A.2d 523 (N.J. 1949)] To encourage investment, "trade fixture" has been broadly defined (*e.g.,* "trade fixtures" has been held to include improvements of property for agricultural purposes as well as for commercial trading or manufacturing purposes [Old Line Life Insurance Co. v. Hawn, 275 N.W. 542 (Wis. 1937)]).

(3) **Modern trend:** [§1177] The modern trend is to be very liberal in permitting the tenant to remove any chattel he installs on the leased premises, whether or not used in trade or business, so long as substantial damage is not caused. The Restatement provides that the tenant may remove his annexations "if the leased property can be and is restored to its former condition after the removal." [Rest. 2d §12.2(4)] The annexations may involve a considerable investment by the tenant, and there is no reason to require a gift of this investment to the landlord.

b. **Removal before end of term or forfeit:** [§1178] If the annexations do not belong to the landlord (*i.e.,* they are **not "fixtures"**), the tenant **must remove them before the end of his term** or they become the property of the landlord. The rule has been criticized on the ground that since the tenant does not lose title to his unattached chattels remaining behind, he should not lose title to attached chattels he is entitled to remove. On the other hand, if the tenant can foresee the need for removal, the landlord will be inconvenienced if the tenant does not remove his annexations before the end of the lease.

I. LANDLORD'S REMEDIES

1. **Means of Assuring Performance:** [§1179] The landlord has a number of means to assure performance of the tenant's duties. The principal concern of the landlord, of course, is the continuing payment of rent. The means available to the landlord to secure the rent may be provided by common law rule, by statute, or by a clause in the lease.

   a. **Distress (seizure of tenant's chattels)**

      (1) **Common law:** [§1180] At common law, if a tenant were in arrears in rent, the landlord could, without notice to the tenant, enter upon the premises and seize whatever chattels he could find and hold them as security until the rent was paid. This was known as the right of distress or the right of distraint. Because of the possibilities of injustice, some states have abolished the common law right of distress and have substituted no similar statutory right. [*See* Rest. 2d §12.1., Statutory Note, item 5c]

      (2) **Statutory distress:** [§1181] Statutes in many states have abolished the common law right of distress and have substituted therefor a statutory right similar to distress. These statutes usually eliminate the self-help feature or require peaceable entry. [*See* Rest. 2d §12.1, Statutory Note, item 5a]

         (a) **Constitutionality:** [§1182] The Constitution provides that no state shall deprive any person of his property without due process of law. Statutory or common law creditor remedies may be action by the state (*see* discussion of "state action" *supra*, §444). If so, these remedies must provide the debtor with due process. Principally, due process means the debtor must have prior notice and a judicial hearing before property is taken. In the early 1970s, statutes providing a remedy of distress were held to be state action and unconstitutional because the tenant has ***no prior notice and hearing*** by a public official before the property is taken. [Hall v. Garson, 468 F.2d 845 (5th Cir. 1972)] But the issues are not settled. First, it is not clear what kind of hearing due process requires. [*See* Mitchell v. W.T. Grant Co., 416 U.S. 600 (1974)—upholding statute providing for sequestration of the debtor's goods after an ex parte hearing.] Second, common law distress involves seizure by the landlord, not the sheriff or other public official. Seizure by the landlord acting alone may not be state action.

      (3) **Distress provided in lease:** [§1183] Standard form leases sometimes provide for distress even though it is not permitted by statute. The idea is to turn distress into a ***contract right***, bargained for by the parties. However, since this contract provision waives the constitutional right to notice and hearing before property is seized, the provision is not enforceable against the tenant, even though she has signed the lease, unless it is shown that the tenant knowingly and understandingly waived her rights. [Sellers v. Contino, 327 F. Supp. 230 (E.D. Pa. 1971)]

   b. **Statutory liens:** [§1184] Many states have statutes that create liens of one sort or another on the personal property of the tenant located on the rented premises. [*See*

Rest. 2d §12.1, Statutory Note, item 5] Some states create a general landlord's lien on all the tenant's personal property, which gives the landlord priority over other creditors; but no right to possession is conferred, and the landlord must institute judicial proceedings to foreclose his lien if the rent is in arrears. [Jordan v. Talbot, 55 Cal. 2d 597 (1961)]

c. **Security deposits:** [§1185]   Lease provisions commonly require the tenant to make a security deposit at the time the lease is executed to assure the tenant's performance. The landlord promises to return this money to the tenant at the end of the term if the tenant has not breached any covenant.

(1) **Landlord is debtor:** [§1186]   A security deposit creates a debtor-creditor relationship: The landlord owes the money to the tenant at the end of the lease. But the tenant, as a general creditor, has no priority over other creditors of the landlord. Statutes have been enacted in some states giving the tenant priority over any creditor with respect to the amount of the security deposit. Often the statutes state that the money is held by the landlord in trust or in escrow. [Mallory Associates, Inc. v. Barving Realty Co., 300 N.Y. 297 (1949); Mich. Stat. Ann. §26.1138(5)]

(2) **Upon termination of lease:** [§1187]   On the termination of the lease, the landlord must return to the tenant the amount of the security deposit that exceeds the landlord's actual damages (*e.g.,* cost of repossession and any unpaid rent). The tenant is due an accounting of the sum.

(a) **Interest:** [§1188]   Statutes in some states require the landlord to pay the tenant interest on the sum held as a security deposit. [*See, e.g.,* N.Y. Gen. Oblig. Law §§7-103, 7-105] But there is no general common law rule that the landlord must pay interest.

(b) **Liquidated damages:** [§1189]   The lease may provide that the landlord may keep the sum deposited as liquidated damages. Such a provision is a penalty, however, and is enforceable *only* if actual damages are not readily ascertainable and the deposit is reasonably related to the probable damages.

(c) **Penalty for not accounting:** [§1190]   Statutes in some states penalize landlords for failing to give tenants an itemized list of deductions from the security deposit. For example, the URLTA provides that the tenant may recover the sum due her together with damages in an amount equal to twice the amount wrongfully withheld, plus reasonable attorney's fees. [URLTA §2.101] These statutes sometimes apply to "prepaid rent" as well as to security deposits, if the purpose of the prepaid rent is to secure the tenant's performance.

(3) **Compare—"bonus":** [§1191]   If a payment is made to the lessor as a bonus for executing the lease, with no provision for any rebate to the tenant at the end of the lease, the landlord may retain the entire sum. The tenant has no right to the return of any portion thereof.

(4) **Compare—"prepaid rent":** [§1192]   If the rent is prepaid for some future period (*e.g.,* prepayment of $500 for the last month's rent), the prepaid rent may be retained by the landlord if the tenant terminates the lease prematurely. *Rationale:* The parties may make the rent payable at any time, and under the rule of nonapportionment of rent (*supra,* §1127), the advance payment belongs to the landlord upon premature termination by the tenant. Because forfeiting prepaid rent looks like a penalty, courts may construe agreements, when possible, as security deposits (requiring repayment to the tenant) rather than prepaid rent.

d. **Rent acceleration clause:** [§1193]   A standard lease usually contains a clause providing that the rent for the balance of the term shall become payable in full upon the tenant's default in payment of rent or some other obligation. This is known as a rent acceleration clause. Most courts uphold a rent acceleration clause. [Fifty States Management Corp. v. Pioneer Auto Parts, Inc., 46 N.Y.2d 573 (1979)] *Rationale:* Since the parties may contract for payment in advance of rent for the entire term, they have the right to contract that the entire rent shall become payable upon the happening of a contingency. The Restatement adopts this position. [Rest. 2d §12.1, comment k]

(1) **Minority view:** [§1194]   A minority of states hold that a rent acceleration clause is unenforceable, because it is an agreement for liquidated damages or a penalty. It is a penalty because its enforcement has the effect of increasing the total amount of rent payable under the lease: $100 payable in one year is not of equal value to $100 payable now because of the interest that can be earned during the year. By not discounting the rent for the remaining term that is accelerated, the clause—particularly in a long term lease—may impose a substantial penalty on the tenant. [Ricker v. Rombaugh, 120 Cal. App. 2d 912 (1953)]

(2) **Landlord cannot terminate lease and accelerate rent:** [§1195]   If a landlord elects to accelerate rent, the landlord cannot terminate the lease and demand possession also. Nor can he retake possession upon abandonment by the tenant and accelerate the rent. The landlord must choose to treat the tenant as a purchaser of the term for which he is demanding payment now by accelerating the rent, or choose to terminate the lease, thereby cancelling his claim for future rent. To allow the landlord to demand rent and at the same time take possession (equivalent in value to rent) would allow double recovery and be unconscionable.

(a) **Example:** L leases a store to T for five years at $1,000 a year with a rent acceleration clause. After two years, T defaults. L can elect to terminate the lease or to hold T to the lease and accelerate the rent (with $3,000 being due on T's default). If L collects $3,000 from T and thereafter relets the store for T's benefit (*see infra,* §1232), L must account to T for the rent received from the new tenant.

e. **Waiver of service and confession of judgment:** [§1196]   Standard form leases often provide that, upon default in rent, the tenant waives the right of service of process and authorizes anyone to confess judgment on her behalf. If this clause is effective, the landlord can get a judgment against the tenant for the total rent due for the remainder of the lease plus the costs and attorney's fees for the action *without the tenant receiving notice*. In most states, confession of judgment clauses are invalid. [*See, e.g.,* URLTA §1.403; Cal. Civ. Code §1953 (a)]

2. **Eviction of Tenant:** [§1197]   The landlord may wish to (i) evict the tenant *during the term of the lease* for nonpayment of rent or for other cause or (ii) evict the tenant who holds over *after the term expires*. The landlord's remedies may differ according to whether he is evicting during the term of the lease or after the lease expires. His remedies are usually more limited in the former case than in the latter.

a. **Termination for breach of covenant:** [§1198]   At old common law, the landlord had no power to terminate a lease if the tenant did not pay rent. The landlord's remedy was to sue for the rent due. [Brown's Administrators v. Bragg, 22 Ind. 122 (1864)] Statutes in most states now give the landlord power to terminate a lease for nonpayment of rent when due. As for other covenants such as a covenant to repair, the independent covenants rule still applies, and the breach of a covenant by the tenant does not give the landlord power to terminate the lease and evict the tenant.

(1) **Restatement position:** [§1199]   The Restatement adopts the dependent covenants doctrine and provides that the landlord may terminate the lease if the promise was "a significant inducement to the making of the lease." [Rest. 2d §13.1]

(2) **Lease provisions:** [§1200]   In view of the independent covenants rule, almost all leases contain express provisions authorizing the landlord to terminate the lease upon breach of *any* covenant by the tenant. The covenant might relate to payment of rent, repair, keeping dogs, making noise—whatever the tenant promises to do or not do. These provisions for termination are known as "forfeiture clauses." Forfeiture clauses are ordinarily construed as creating in the landlord an optional right of entry for breach of condition.

(a) **Notice of default and time to cure:** [§1201]   Where nonpayment of rent is the basis of forfeiture, the landlord must notify the tenant of default and demand rent, and then give the tenant a reasonable time to pay. If the tenant does not pay within a reasonable time, the landlord then can notify the tenant that he has elected to terminate the lease. "Equity abhors a forfeiture," and requires the landlord, *before exercising his right of entry*, to alert the tenant to the consequences of her failure to pay. If the dependent covenants doctrine applies to other covenants (*e.g.*, a covenant to repair), it is likely that the courts will similarly require the landlord to request the tenant to perform and give her a reasonable time to do so before declaring a forfeiture. Restatement (Second) of Property §13.1, comments h and k, so provide.

(b) **Phrased as determinable limitation:** [§1202] A forfeiture provision may be phrased as a determinable limitation, for example: "In the event of breach by the tenant, the landlord may terminate the lease by giving the tenant five days' written notice, and the term of this lease shall then expire upon the date mentioned in the notice." Under a determinable limitation, no exercise of a right of entry by the landlord is necessary to terminate the lease. It terminates ***automatically***, and the right to possession is in the landlord. (*Compare* "fee simple determinable," *supra,* §318.)

   1) **Note:** There may be advantages to the landlord in phrasing forfeiture as a limitation rather than a condition. First, at old common law, a landlord exercising a right of entry for breach could only use the ejectment remedy. This was cumbersome and time consuming (*see infra,* §1206). In order to permit the landlord to resort to summary proceedings (*infra,* §1207), where the only issue is who has the right to possession, the forfeiture clause had to be phrased so as to end the lease automatically, with the right to possession returning automatically to the landlord. Today, statutes in some states do away with this distinction; summary proceedings are available in either case. [Remedco Corp. v. Bryn Mawr Corp., 45 Misc. 2d 586 (1965)]

   2) **And note:** The limitation phrasing may avoid a requirement that the tenant be given an opportunity to cure default. The summary proceedings law in some states provides that where termination is ***for failure to pay rent***, the tenant has a grace period in which to pay after a judgment is issued and before the eviction order is issued, but where summary proceedings are against a hold-over tenant, no grace period is provided. In order to avoid the grace period, a landlord may claim that under a limitation clause, the lease terminates upon nonpayment of rent and the nonpaying tenant is a hold-over tenant. This claim is not likely to succeed however. The court will probably either construe the special limitation to be a condition subsequent, find a general intention in the lease to give the tenant an opportunity to cure, or find denial of an opportunity to cure to be against public policy. [Jamaica Builders Supply Corp. v. Buttelman, 25 Misc. 2d 326 (1960)]

(3) **Waiver:** [§1203] The landlord may expressly or impliedly waive his right to terminate upon breach. The landlord's acceptance of rent from the tenant ***with knowledge*** of the breach is generally held to constitute such a waiver.

(a) **Example:** T assigns the lease to X in breach of a covenant against assignment. Thereafter L accepts rent from X. L has waived the breach.

(b) **Reliance on practice of waiver:** [§1204] The landlord can waive the right to prompt payment by accepting delayed payment of rent. If he does this several times, then he must warn the tenant that he will insist on prompt payment in the future before he can terminate the lease because of delayed payment.

b.   **Eviction through judicial process:** [§1205]   If the landlord is entitled to evict the tenant for breach of a covenant or for holding over at the end of a lease, the landlord may resort to the following judicial remedies.

   (1)   **Suit in ejectment:** [§1206]   The landlord may bring an action in ejectment to recover possession of the premises. However, such an action does not take precedence over other civil litigation and may not come to trial for some time. As a result, a suit in ejectment is rarely brought by a landlord.

   (2)   **Summary proceedings:** [§1207]   Every state has a summary proceeding whereby the landlord can recover possession quickly and at low cost. Often this proceeding is called an action for "forcible entry and detainer" or "unlawful detainer." It is called forcible entry because the tenant is viewed as having tortiously, or wrongfully, acquired possession by holding over. [*See* Rest. 2d §14.1, Statutory Note]

      (a)   **Notice to quit:** [§1208]   Statutes usually require that before bringing a summary action, the landlord must give the tenant notice to quit, but the required notice may be very short (*e.g.*, three days) because it is assumed that the tenant knows that she is holding over unlawfully. If the landlord is terminating the lease under a forfeiture clause because of nonpayment of rent, the landlord usually must give the tenant notice that rent must be paid or the lease will be terminated after three days.

      (b)   **Issues that can be raised:** [§1209]   Because the proceeding is summary, the issues that can be raised are very limited. The landlord must prove that the lease has terminated, or that he has lawfully exercised his right to forfeit for nonpayment of rent. It is sometimes said that the sole issue is whether the landlord or the tenant has the right to possession. [People *ex rel.* Tuttle v. Walton, 2 Thompson & Cook 533 (N.Y. 1874)]

         1)   **Defenses:** [§1210]   The tenant can assert only those defenses which, if proven, would either preserve her possession as a tenant or preclude the landlord from recovering possession. The tenant cannot defend on the ground that the landlord had no title or that the lease was fraudulent, because, even if successful, the tenant would not be entitled to remain in possession. The landlord, as prior possessor, would have the superior right to possession. The tenant *can* defend on the ground that a landlord-tenant relationship does not exist because the lease is illegal, and therefore no rent is due, or that the landlord refused to accept a timely payment of rent.

         2)   **Modern trend:** [§1211]   In recent cases, where the landlord has been in breach of a statutory duty to repair or an implied covenant of habitability, courts have permitted the tenant to defend on the ground that no rent is due. The theory is that the duty to pay rent is dependent upon the performance of the landlord's duty to maintain the property

in habitable condition. [Jack Spring, Inc. v. Little, 280 N.E.2d 208 (Ill. 1972)] *Rationale:* Refusing summary eviction where the landlord is in breach of a duty of maintenance will give slum tenants a better bargaining position to enforce the landlord's repair obligations.

3) **Constitutionality:** [§1212]   If state law denies the tenant the right to defend on the ground that the landlord has breached his duty to repair, the statute is constitutional. Housing is not a fundamental right, and therefore no compelling state interest need be shown to justify the statute. [Lindsey v. Normet, 405 U.S. 56 (1972)]

(c) **Jury trial:** [§1213]   Many jurisdictions provide for jury trials of any fact issue in eviction proceedings. [Pernell v. Southall Realty, 416 U.S. 363 (1974)]

(d) **Appeal:** [§1214]   The tenant can get a stay of execution and appeal an adverse decision. The tenant may be required to post an appeal bond as security, but any bond-posting requirements must apply equally to an appeal by the landlord. Otherwise, the tenant is denied equal protection of the laws. [Lindsey v. Normet, *supra*]

(e) **Limitations on summary proceedings**

1) **Not allowed for purpose of retaliation:** [§1215]   Eviction for the purpose of retaliating against the tenant's assertion of her rights regarding maintenance of the premises may be forbidden. (*See supra,* §§1078 *et seq.*)

2) **Allowed only with showing of good cause in public housing:** [§1216] In public housing projects, tenants cannot be evicted unless the management shows good cause. In addition, notice and hearing may be required. (*See infra,* §1300.)

c. **Self-help:** [§1217]   The states take various positions on whether self-help by the landlord is permissible. If it is not, the landlord is liable for damages to the tenant and her chattels if he resorts to self-help.

(1) **Common law:** [§1218]   If the tenant had no right to continue in possession, the old common law permitted the use of such force as was necessary to expel the tenant. Because of too many breaches of the peace, the statute of 5 Richard II, ch. 8 (1381) made forcible entry by the landlord a crime. However, the courts did not change the rule in civil suits that the landlord was not liable for damages. Hence the landlord was liable only for a criminal offense. The criminal statute of Richard II has been accepted or reenacted in almost all American states.

(2) **Reasonable force permitted:** [§1219]   In this country, the majority rule apparently is still that the landlord may use ***reasonable force*** to expel the tenant, without court process of any kind. [Gower v. Waters, 132 A. 550 (Me. 1926)]

(3) **Peaceable entry permitted:** [§1220]   Some jurisdictions hold that the landlord can enter only by *peaceable* means. But what is peaceable? Definitions vary considerably. Changing the locks and locking out the tenant has been held forcible, not peaceable. This effectively guts the self-help rule as it is difficult to imagine circumstances which might be found peaceable if changing the locks is forcible.

   (a) **Constitutionality questionable:** [§1221]   The constitutionality of a self-help remedy, depriving the tenant of the leasehold without notice and judicial hearing, is not clear. Distress statutes, allowing self-help seizure of the tenant's chattels, have been held to deprive the tenant of due process (*see supra*, §1182). But the constitutionality of self-help repossession has not been decided.

(4) **Self-help not permitted:** [§1222]   A growing number of states prohibits self-help in recovering possession and requires the landlord to resort to a statutory remedy. If he does not, he is liable in damages. [Berg v. Wiley, 264 N.W.2d 145 (Minn. 1978)]

(5) **Lease provision authorizing self-help:** [§1223]   A lease may provide that the landlord is authorized to use self-help in retaking possession on the tenant's default. Most courts hold such a provision valid. A minority holds the provision void, as violating public policy against self-help. [Jordan v. Talbot, *supra*, §1184]

3. **Abandonment by Tenant:** [§1224]   If the tenant has no right to vacate the property but abandons it, the landlord may have several options: (i) terminate the lease; (ii) let the premises lie idle and sue the tenant for rent as it comes due; or (iii) retake possession and attempt to relet the premises. There is a great deal of conflict in the cases regarding the remedies available to the landlord.

   a. **Landlord terminates lease:** [§1225]   The landlord may terminate the lease upon the tenant's abandonment; this effects a *surrender*. The tenant is liable only for rent accrued and for damages caused by the abandonment. The landlord's remedy of distress and the landlord's lien (*supra*, §§1180-1184) cease upon termination of the lease. If the landlord keeps the lease alive under other options (below), these remedies do not cease.

   (1) **Common law rule—damages for anticipatory repudiation:** [§1226]   The common law rule, applicable to leases but not to other contracts, is that the landlord cannot terminate the lease (rescind) and receive damages for anticipatory breach of contract. The theory is that a covenant to pay rent does not create an enforceable obligation until the rent is due. If the landlord terminates the lease prior to the due date, he is not entitled to the rent. Hence, if the landlord wants damages, the landlord must keep the lease alive, wait until rent is due, and then sue. This rule is still followed in many states. [General Development Corp. v. Wilbur-Rogers Atlanta Corp., 273 N.E.2d 908 (Ohio 1971)]

(2) **Anticipatory repudiation allowed:** [§1227]   In some states, anticipatory repudiation of the contract by the landlord is allowed when the tenant makes it clear she will pay no further rent. If allowed, the landlord's damages are determined by the difference between the rent agreed upon in the lease and the fair rental value over the balance of the term. [Hawkinson v. Johnston, 122 F.2d 724 (8th Cir. 1941); Sagamore Corp. v. Willcutt, 180 A. 464 (Conn. 1935)]

(3) **Example:** T leases a building from L for five years at $1,000 a year. After two years, T abandons the building. L accepts the surrender and relets to another for $800 a year. Under the majority rule, T is not liable for the difference of $200 a year for three years or $600, which is L's damage. Under the minority rule, L can recover $600 from T, discounted to its present value.

b.   **Landlord stands by and does nothing:** [§1228]   Under this option, the landlord may leave the premises vacant and sue the tenant for rent as it comes due under the lease.

(1) **No duty to mitigate damages:** [§1229]   Most courts hold that the landlord does ***not*** have any duty to mitigate damages by finding another tenant. *Rationale:* The tenant has bought a term in the landlord's land. If the tenant chooses not to use it, it is not the landlord's fault. The tenant still owes the rent as it comes due. [Gruman v. Investors Diversified Services, Inc., 78 N.W.2d 377 (Minn. 1956); Whitehorn v. Dickerson, 419 S.W.2d 713 (Mo. 1967)] This rule is adopted by the Restatement, which offers in justification: "Abandonment of property is an invitation to vandalism, and the law should not encourage such conduct by putting a duty of mitigation of damages on the landlord." [Rest. 2d §12.1(3), comment i] This is silly because if the landlords had a duty to mitigate, they would have incentives to fill up abandoned properties so there would not be vandalism.

(a) **Example:** T leases a building from L for five years at $1,000 a year. After two years, T abandons the building. L does not reenter. L can sue T for the annual rent as it comes due.

(b) **Criticism:** This rule views the lease as a conveyance of property, and is inconsistent with modern cases which more and more view the lease as a contract. Moreover, it is wasteful of resources to permit the landlord to do nothing. Modern contract law imposes on promisees a duty to mitigate damages, reducing costs.

(2) **Minority view:** [§1230]   In a minority of states, the landlord has a duty to mitigate damages. A lease is treated as any other kind of contract and is not viewed, on this issue, through property glasses. If the landlord must mitigate damages, then this second option is not available to the landlord. [Sommer v. Kridel, 378 A.2d 767 (N.J. 1977); Lefrak v. Lambert, 89 Misc. 2d 197 (1976); United States National Bank of Oregon v. Homeland, Inc., 631 P.2d 761 (Or. 1981); Wright v. Baumann, 378 P.2d 119 (Or. 1965); *and see* URLTA §4.203—landlord must mitigate damages]

(3) **Rent acceleration clause:** [§1231] To avoid the rule that the landlord must wait to sue for rent as it falls due, a rent acceleration clause is often inserted in the lease. It provides that the rent for the balance of the term shall become payable in full upon the tenant's default of payment of rent or some other obligation. Most courts hold these clauses valid. (*See supra*, §1193.)

c. **Landlord repossesses and relets:** [§1232] Instead of standing by, the landlord may enter and repossess the property for the purpose of renting it out to another tenant. Courts are divided, however, on whether repossession by the landlord, which deprives the tenant of the right to possession, effects a surrender and thus terminates the lease. If it does, the tenant is excused from further rent liability. Courts can be divided into three categories.

(1) **Reletting effects surrender:** [§1233] One view is that repossession and reletting effects a surrender unless the tenant expressly or impliedly consents to the reletting. This view, coupled with the rule that damages for anticipatory breach are not allowed on surrender, strongly discourages reletting. [Gray v. Kaufman Dairy & Ice Cream Co., 162 N.Y. 388 (1900)]

(2) **Reletting without notice effects surrender:** [§1234] Another view is that *if the landlord gives the tenant notice* of the reletting and notice that he intends to hold the tenant for any loss in rental, the landlord may relet for the tenant's benefit. [Liberty Plan Co. v. Adwan, 370 P.2d 928 (Okla. 1962)]

(a) **Rationale:** The courts seem to be divided between two theories here. Some courts say that the repossession gives rise to a surrender but that the tenant's contract liability is not extinguished. The measure of damages is the difference between the rent reserved in the lease and the rent upon reletting. Other courts say that abandonment gives the landlord a power to relet on behalf of the tenant. This difference becomes important when the landlord relets at a higher rental.

(b) **Relets at a higher rental:** [§1235] Suppose L leases to T at $200 a month. T abandons, and L relets to A for $300 a month. If the theory is that T remains liable for contractual damages, L has not been damaged by the abandonment and L should be entitled to the $300 new rent. If the theory is that L has a power to rent on T's behalf, L should be entitled to only $200 of the new rental and T should be entitled to $100. [Eidelman v. Walker & Dunlop, Inc., 290 A.2d 780 (Md. 1972)]

(3) **Intent of landlord is test:** [§1236] A third view is that it is a question of fact in each case whether the landlord, by reletting, has intended to accept a surrender of the lease. Notice to the tenant is evidence of his intent not to effect a surrender, but failure to give notice is not conclusive of a contrary intent. The question is whether L intended to take possession for his own use or in his own interest. [Coffin v. Fowler, 483 P.2d 683 (Alaska 1971); First Wisconsin Trust Co. v. L. Wiemann Co., 286 N.W.2d 360 (Wis. 1980)]

(a) **Duty to mitigate damages:** [§1237] If the landlord is under a duty to mitigate damages (minority view), then the jurisdiction must necessarily follow the second or third view above.

(4) **Example:** The following example will illustrate the three views. L leases to T for five years at $1,000 a year. After two years, T abandons. L relets for $800 a year. Under the first view, L has accepted a surrender, and T is no longer liable for rent (and probably not for damages either). Under the second view, notice is controlling. If L gives T notice prior to reletting, T is liable for the difference of $200 a year. Under the third view, L's intent is controlling. Notice is evidence of intent, but if L gives T no notice the facts may show L still intends to hold T.

J. ASSIGNMENT AND SUBLETTING

1. **Assignment:** [§1238]   In the absence of a prohibition in a lease, a tenant or landlord may freely transfer his or her interest in the premises. If the tenant assigns her leasehold, the assignee comes into *privity of estate* with the landlord, which means that the landlord and the assignee are liable to each other on the covenants in the original lease which run with the land. Similarly, if the landlord assigns the reversion, the assignee and the tenant are in privity of estate.

   a. **Example:** L leases to T. T promises to pay $200 a month rent. T assigns the leasehold to T2. L can sue T2 on the promise to pay $200 a month rent. They are in privity of estate with each other.

   b. **Privity of estate:** [§1239]   Privity of estate is an ancient concept developed to give the landlord the right to sue the assignee of the tenant on the covenants in the lease, and to give the assignee the right to sue the landlord on the latter's covenants. In the example above, T promises to pay $200 a month rent. After assignment, L cannot sue T2 on a theory of privity of contract because T2 did not make the promise. To circumvent the lack of privity of contract, the courts invented the concept of *privity of estate.* Any assignee of the tenant is said to be in privity of estate and is liable on the covenants in the lease. Similarly, the landlord is liable to the assignee on the landlord's covenants (*e.g.,* the covenant to repair). If in the above example, L assigns his reversion to L2, L2 is in privity of estate with T2, and each is liable to the other on the covenants in the lease. Hence, parties who are in privity of estate have a landlord and tenant relationship.

   (1) **Privity of contract:** [§1240]   If there is privity of contract (*i.e.,* the plaintiff and defendant have agreed with each other to do or not do certain things), their obligations bind them regardless of whether or not they are in privity of estate. Thus, in the above example, after the assignment, L can sue T on her promise to pay rent, because T made the promise to L. L and T are in privity of contract. [Samuels v. Ottinger, 169 Cal. 209 (1915)] L can also sue T2 on the promise because L and T2 are in privity of estate. Being able to sue two persons is of course an advantage to L, because one of them, T or T2, might be judgment proof or difficult to get into court.

2. **Sublease Distinguished From Assignment:** [§1241]   If a tenant sublets the premises, and does not assign them, the tenant becomes the landlord of the sublessee. The sublessee is *not in privity of estate* with the landlord and cannot sue or be sued by him. Since the sublessee has made no contract with the landlord, he cannot sue or be sued on a contract either. The crucial question, then, is: When is a transfer an assignment and when is it a sublease?

   a. **Reversion retained:** [§1242]   At common law, a transfer by a tenant is a sublease if the tenant *retains a reversion* in the property after the transfer. If the tenant does not retain a reversion, the transfer is an assignment. A reversion is a period of time within the duration of the leasehold when the tenant will again be entitled to possession. The common law position is still adhered to in many states. [Amco Trust, Inc. v. Naylor, 317 S.W.2d 47 (Tex. 1958)]

      (1) **Example:** L leases to T for ten years. One month later T transfers a nine-year term to T2. This is a sublease, because T retains a reversion. T is T2's landlord. L is not in privity of estate with T2. L cannot sue T2 on covenants in the original lease, and T2 cannot sue L.

   b. **Right of entry retained:** [§1243]   Suppose that the tenant transfers the leasehold to another tenant and does not retain a reversion, but retains a *right of entry* for condition broken. The typical case is where the tenant transfers the entire remainder of the term to another, at a higher rent than she is paying, with a right to reenter if the rent is not paid.

      (1) **Example:** L leases to T for ten years with rent of $200 a month. Five years later, T transfers the remainder of the term to T2 for a rent of $250 a month. T retains the right to reenter and retake possession if T2 does not pay the rent promised. (This right is reserved in a forfeiture clause, discussed *supra,* §1200.) Is the transfer to T2 an assignment or a sublease?

         (a) **Common law view:** [§1244]   The common law view is that such a transfer is an assignment, not a sublease, because T retained no reversion. The right of entry reserved by T is viewed as merely a means of enforcing T2's contractual obligations. Since it is an assignment, there is privity of estate between L and T2, so that L can hold T2 personally liable for the rent reserved in the L to T lease ($200 per month).

         (b) **Right of entry makes it a sublease:** [§1245]   A substantial number of modern cases hold that such a transfer is a sublease, and not an assignment. The reservation of the right to enter for nonpayment of rent is deemed a "contingent reversionary interest," so that the transfer is a sublease even though no actual reversion is retained by T. Since it is a sublease, there is no privity of estate between L and T2. Thus, if T2 above fails to pay the rent, L cannot sue him directly. [Davis v. Vidal, 151 S.W. 290 (Tex. 1912)] This is the position of the Restatement. [Rest. 2d §15.1., comment i]

1) **Landlord's remedies:** [§1246]   This does not mean that L is without a remedy. L can sue T for rent based on privity of contract. L can evict T2 for breach of the promise to pay rent made in the L to T lease as readily as he could evict T. The distinction is that since this is only a sublease, there is no privity of estate, and hence L cannot hold T2 *personally* liable for rent.

2) **Criticism:** [§1247]   Some are critical of this view because a right of entry was merely a chose in action at common law, and even today, when it is treated as a property interest, it is not a "reversionary interest" (*see supra,* §440).

c. **Intention controls:** [§1248]   A few recent cases have rejected both the common law rule that retention of a reversion is necessary for a sublease and the rule that retention of a right of entry is sufficient to create a sublease. These cases hold that the *intent* of the parties determines whether a transfer is an assignment or a sublease, and that reservation of an additional rent by itself is an indication that the parties intended a sublease. On the other hand, the transfer of the lease for a lump sum, even if payment is to be made in deferred installments, indicates an assignment. [Jaber v. Miller, 239 S.W.2d 760 (Ark. 1951); Ernst v. Conditt, 390 S.W.2d 703 (Tenn. 1964)]

3. **Duty to Pay Rent:** [§1249]   A promise to pay rent is a covenant running with the land, which means the promisee can sue any person on the covenant with whom he is in privity of estate. Covenants running with the land are discussed more fully below, but the promise to pay rent is such an important covenant that it is singled out here for special attention. The general rule is that a landlord can sue for rent any person who is either in *privity of contract* with the landlord as to the rent obligation, *or* who has come into *privity of estate* with the landlord so as to be bound by the rental covenants in the lease.

a. **Assignment:** [§1250]   As already indicated, an assignment establishes privity of estate between the landlord and the assignee, so that the assignee is personally liable for the rent even though no mention is made of it in the assignment.

(1) **Liability of original tenant:** [§1251]   Although the assignee is liable for the rent, the *original tenant also remains liable* for the rent, in the event the assignee fails to pay, because the original tenant *contracted* with the landlord. The assignment terminates her interest in the leasehold, but does not affect her contractual liability to the landlord. [Samuels v. Ottinger, *supra,* §1240]

(a) **Example:** L leases to T. T promises to pay rent. T assigns her leasehold to T2. T2 is liable for the rent provided in the L to T lease. L can also sue T for rent because T remains liable on her promise to pay rent.

(b) **T is surety:** [§1252]   When the transferee, T2, becomes liable for the rent, T2 is *primarily* liable because he has the benefit of possession. T's liability, based on privity of contract, is **secondary**. This means that, although L can sue either T or T2, as between T and T2, the latter is responsible. T is said to be a surety. According to the rules of suretyship, if T2 and L materially change the terms of the lease, so as to prejudice T, T is released as a surety. [Gerber v. Pecht, 104 A.2d 41 (N.J. 1954)]

(c) **Release by landlord:** [§1253]   The only way T can escape from her duty to pay rent is by an express or implied **release** from her promise to L. The mere fact that L consents to the assignment and accepts rent from T2 is not an implied release of T. These acts give L additional rights against T2; from them, one **cannot** infer an intent to give up his rights against T.

(d) **Novation:** [§1254]   If L assents to the assignment to T2 and releases T, and in exchange for the release, T2 undertakes the promises in the lease, there is a **novation**. T is now out of the picture, and there is now privity of contract and privity of estate between L and T2.

(2) **Liability of assignee:** [§1255]   T2 is liable only for the rent accruing during the time he holds the leasehold. He is not liable for rent accruing prior to the assignment, nor for rent accruing after he reassigns—because the effect of any reassignment is to terminate the privity of estate with L. [A.D. Juilliard & Co. v. American Woolen Co., 32 A.2d 800 (R.I. 1943)]

(a) **Example:** L leases land to T for $200 a month. T becomes one month in arrears. T then assigns the leasehold to T2, who becomes four months in arrears. T2 assigns to T3, reserving a rent of $250 a month.

   1) **L recovers from T3:** [§1256]   L can recover $200 a month from T3 for the time T3 is assignee. During this time, L and T3 are in privity of estate. (L cannot recover the extra $50 reserved in the assignment to T3.)

   2) **L recovers from T2:** [§1257]   L can recover $800 from T2 because during the four months of default L and T2 were in privity of estate. One case, *Reid v. Wiessner Brewing Co.*, 40 A. 877 (Md. 1898), held that L could not sue T2 for rent **after** T2 assigned, even though the rent in arrears accrued while T2 was in privity of estate. However, this case is not in accord with decisions in other jurisdictions.

   3) **L recovers from T:** [§1258]   L can recover $1,000 (five months rent in default) from T because the parties are in privity of contract. In turn, T is **subrogated** to L's claim against T2 for the rental in arrears during the time that T2 held the leasehold, so that T could recover $800 from T2 if T pays L the rent due for these four months.

b. **Sublease:** [§1259]   If the tenant subleases, the sublessee is **not** personally liable to the landlord for rent.

(1) **Rationale:** There is neither privity of contract nor privity of estate between the landlord and the sublessee. The tenant-sublessor, of course, remains obligated to pay rent. If she does not pay, the landlord can terminate the lease and oust the sublessee. To prevent such ouster and forfeiture of the master lease, the sublessee may pay the landlord the rent due him from the tenant-sublessor (and offset this against any rental provided in the sublease).

(2) **Lien on rental:** [§1260]   Although the landlord cannot sue the sublessee for rent, he may have equitable remedies that protect him if he does not want to terminate the master lease. The landlord can assert an equitable lien on rent due under the sublease, so he has priority over the tenant-sublessor's creditors. In many states, the landlord can assert a statutory lien against the sublessee.

c.   **Third party beneficiary suits:** [§1261]   If an assignee or sublessee expressly assumes the covenants of the master lease, the assignee or sublessee is directly liable to the landlord as a third party beneficiary of the contract between the tenant and his assignee or sublessee. The liability of the assignee or sublessee for performance of his promise continues notwithstanding a further assignment. [Goldberg v. L.H. Realty Co., 86 So. 2d 326 (Miss. 1956)]

(1) **Example:** L leases to T. T sublets to T2, who promises to perform all obligations of T under the lease from L. T2 later assigns his interest to T3, who fails to pay the rent. L can sue T2 for the rent owed by T3. Having expressly assumed the lease obligations, T2 is bound to perform his contract notwithstanding the assignment of his entire interest to another. [Packard-Bamberger & Co. v. Maloof, 199 A.2d 400 (N.J. 1961)]

(2) **Landlord's agreements:** [§1262]   If a landlord expressly agrees to a sublease, the sublessee is a third party beneficiary to the covenant of quiet enjoyment in the master lease and has the right to go directly against the landlord for its breach. [Marchese v. Standard Realty & Development Co., 74 Cal. App. 3d 142 (1977)]

(a) **Example:** L leases to T. T sublets to T2, and L expressly agrees to the sublease. Subsequently, L cuts off the water supply to the property. T2 can sue L for breach of the covenant of quiet enjoyment.

4.   **Covenants Running to Assignees**

a.   **Introduction:** [§1263]   For the landlord to be able to enforce a covenant in the lease against the tenant's assignee, or for the tenant to be able to enforce a covenant in the lease against the landlord's assignee, the following requirements must be met. [*See* Rest. 2d §§16.1, 16.2]

(1) **Intention:** [§1264]   The parties to the lease must intend that the covenant run to assigns.

(2) **Privity of estate:** [§1265] The assignee must be in either privity of estate or privity of contract with the person who is suing or being sued. Privity of estate means, generally speaking, that the person succeeded to the estate of a party to the contract. (*See* discussion above.) If the assignee has **promised** to perform the covenant, the assignee's liability rests on privity of contract as well as on privity of estate.

(3) **Touch and concern:** [§1266] The covenant must touch and concern the interest that is assigned, be it the leasehold or the reversion. "Touch and concern" is an ambiguous expression that means, basically, that the covenant directly affects the party *in the use or enjoyment of the property*. "Touch and concern" is often conclusory, in the sense that the court determines that the covenant ought to run because of the parties' expectations, public policy, or some other factor. It is easier to see how it has been used than to define it.

   (a) **Two ends to covenant—burden and benefit:** [§1267] There are two "ends" to a covenant, the burden end and the benefit end. Whoever makes the promise has the burden end. Whoever has the benefit of the promise has the benefit end. For the burden or benefit end to run to assignees, the promise must touch and concern the interest of the assignee.

   1) **Example:** L leases to T. T promises to repair. T assigns her leasehold to T2. If L sues T2 on the covenant to repair, L must show that the **burden** touches and concerns the leasehold. If L assigned the reversion to L2, who sued T2, L2 would have to show also that the **benefit** touched and concerned the reversion.

   (b) **Generally both burden and benefit touch and concern leased land:** [§1268] In the great majority of covenants in leases, if either end touches and concerns, the other will also, because the covenant will have some direct relationship to the use or enjoyment of the leased property in which both parties have an interest. The covenant to pay rent, for example, touches and concerns the leasehold because it is the price paid for possession. It touches and concerns the reversion because it directly affects the value of (enjoyment of) the reversion.

   1) **Benefit or burden runs to other land:** [§1269] Occasionally, however, one end of the covenant may touch and concern the leased land, while the other end touches and concerns other land. The usual example of this is where the tenant does not want competition in a shopping center, and the landlord will promise that he will not permit a competing business on nearby property he owns. The benefit of the promise touches the leased land, because it affects its enjoyment, but the burden does not touch and concern the leased land because the promise relates to the use of *other* property. Similarly, if the lessee promises that he will not compete with the landlord's business next door, the burden is on the leased land but the benefit is with the business next door. [Thruston v. Minke, 32 Md. 487 (1870)] (On noncompetition covenants, *see supra*, §1017.)

a) **Example:** L owns two stores, store A and store B, located side by side. L runs a shoe store in store B. L rents store A to T, and T covenants that she will not sell shoes in store A. (This covenant relating to a physical act on the leased premises touches and concerns the leasehold and runs with the leasehold.) L sells the reversion in store A to L2. L2 cannot enforce the covenant against T because it does not benefit the reversion but rather store B. L, owner of store B, can enforce the covenant against T and her assigns.

(c) **Personal covenant:** [§1270]   If a covenant does not touch and concern the promisor's interest, it is personal to the promisor. The promisor continues to be liable on the personal promise after assignment if the parties so intend.

(4) **Notice:** [§1271]   To be liable, the assignee must have notice of the promise sued upon. Notice may be implied under circumstances where the assignee should have made reasonable inquiry and, if he had, would have discovered the promise.

b. **Covenant to do or not to do a physical act on the leased premises:** [§1272]   Covenants to do or not to do a physical act include covenants to repair, to conduct business in a certain manner, not to remove fixtures, to furnish heat and to deliver up premises in good condition.

(1) **Runs with leasehold:** [§1273]   A covenant by the *tenant* or by the *landlord* to do or refrain from doing a physical act *on the leased premises* touches and concerns the *leasehold* and runs with it.

(a) **Example:** L leases property to T for one year. T covenants to repair. T assigns to T2. L can enforce the covenant to repair against T2. If L rather than T had covenanted to repair, T2 could have enforced the covenant against L. The covenant runs with the leasehold.

(2) **Runs with reversion:** [§1274]   If L or T makes a covenant to do or not do a physical act *on the leased land*, such as to furnish heat or to repair, the covenant runs to assigns of the reversion.

c. **Covenant to pay money:** [§1275]   A covenant to pay money touches and concerns if it is paid for an improvement on the property or to protect the property to make it more valuable. Similarly, a covenant to pay taxes, which protects both landlord and tenant, runs both with the leasehold and reversion.

d. **Tenant's covenant to insure for benefit of landlord**

(1) **Insurance proceeds used for rebuilding:** [§1276]   A covenant by the tenant to insure the property touches and concerns *if* the lease requires the landlord to

use the insurance proceeds for rebuilding. In that case, the insurance proceeds are substituted for the building leased. ˑ

(2) **Insurance proceeds not used for rebuilding:** [§1277]   If the insurance proceeds can be pocketed by the landlord, who does not have to rebuild, the covenant is personal and does not touch and concern. [Masury v. Southworth, 9 Ohio St. 340 (1858); Burton v. Chesapeake Box & Lumber Corp., 57 S.E.2d 904 (Va. 1950)]

(a) **Restatement position:** [§1278]   The Restatement takes the position that a promise to insure touches and concerns even though the landlord does not have to use the proceeds to rebuild. The Restatement says the promise touches and concerns the tenant's leasehold because it affects her use and enjoyment (it is affected by the disaster insured against). It touches and concerns the landlord's reversionary interest because it enhances its value. [Rest. 2d §16.1, illustration 8]

e. **Landlord's covenant to return a security deposit:** [§1279]   A covenant by the landlord to repay a security deposit at the end of the lease has been held by some courts to be a personal promise which does not run. Hence, if L transfers the reversion to L2, L2 is not liable to T for the security deposit upon the expiration of the lease. [Federated Mortgage Investors v. American Savings & Loan Association, 47 Cal. App. 3d 917 (1975)] Other courts hold a promise to repay the security deposit does run with the reversion, and L2 must repay the amount to the tenant. If L2 is liable, she should, of course, request L to transfer the security deposits to her at the time L transfers the reversion to L2. The Restatement adopts this latter position. [Rest. 2d §16.1, comment c, illustration 13]

f. **Promise to arbitrate disputes:** [§1280]   A promise to arbitrate disputes arising under a lease touches and concerns the land. [Abbott v. Bob's U-Drive, 352 P.2d 598 (Or. 1960)]

g. **Implied covenants:** [§1281]   An implied covenant, such as the covenant of quiet enjoyment or an implied warranty of habitability can be enforced against whomever is the landlord at the time the covenant is breached. If L transfers the reversion to L2, L is not liable for a breach of the covenant occurring after the transfer.

5. **Covenants Against Assignment or Sublease:** [§1282]   Absent any covenant to the contrary, a leasehold is ***freely transferable*** by the tenant. It may be assigned or sublet without the landlord's consent.

a. **Express covenants:** [§1283]   Many landlords insist that the lease contain a covenant against transfers by the tenant. Such a covenant is valid, but, being a restraint on the transfer of land, it is strictly construed. Thus, a covenant "not to assign" does not prevent the tenant from subleasing, and a covenant "not to sublease" does not prevent an assignment. A transfer by will or by operation of law without a will is not a breach of the covenant; nor is an involuntary transfer (*e.g.,* by execution or bankruptcy).

b. **Implied covenants:** [§1284] A covenant against transfer may be implied where the landlord enters into the lease in reliance upon some special skill or ability of the lessee which will have a material effect upon the fulfillment of the landlord's reasonable contractual expectations. Thus if the owner of a fine hotel leases a hotel "to be operated in a first-class manner," and reserves as rent a percentage of the gross receipts, thus depending upon the ability of the tenant, the court may imply a covenant not to transfer without the landlord's consent. But courts are reluctant to imply covenants because they are restraints on alienation. [Rowe v. Great Atlantic & Pacific Tea Co., 46 N.Y.2d 62 (1978)]

c. **Arbitrary denial of consent:** [§1285] If there is a covenant against transfer, unless it provides that the landlord's consent to transfer cannot be unreasonably withheld, the majority view is that the landlord *may arbitrarily refuse to accept* a new tenant. He has no duty to mitigate damages, as he does under ordinary contract principles. The property conception of a lease as a conveyance of a term prevails. [Jacobs v. Klawans, 169 A.2d 677 (Md. 1961); Gruman v. Investors Diversified Services, 78 N.W.2d 377 (Minn. 1956); Dress Shirt Sales Inc. v. Hotel Martinique Associates, 12 N.Y.2d 339 (1963)]

(1) **Example:** L leases a building to T for $2,000 a month for ten years. T cannot make a profit in her business after two years. T produces X, a highly satisfactory and suitable person, and proposes that L agree that T can sublet to X for $1,750 a month. (This will cut T's losses to $250 a month.) L can refuse to accept X for any reason except an illegal reason such as violation of the civil rights laws.

(2) **Minority view:** [§1286] In a minority of jurisdictions, the landlord's denial of consent must be reasonable. [Homa-Goff Interiors v. Cowden, 350 So. 2d 1035 (Ala. 1977); Funk v. Funk, 633 P.2d 586 (Idaho 1981)] This is the position taken by the Restatement. [Rest. 2d §15.2]

(3) **Lease provisions:** [§1287] A lease may provide that the landlord may not unreasonably withhold his consent to a proposed transfer. Interpreting such provisions, courts have applied an objective test to determine whether the landlord is acting as a reasonably prudent person in withholding consent. The landlord may look at factors such as the financial responsibility of the proposed new tenant and his suitability for the building, but the landlord cannot consider his general economic advantage (*i.e.,* he cannot refuse consent as a stratagem to get T to terminate the lease). [Ringwood Associates, Ltd. v. Jack's of Route 23, Inc., 379 A.2d 508 (N.J. 1977)]

d. **Waiver of covenant:** [§1288] The landlord may expressly or, by his acts, impliedly waive the covenant against assignment of sublease. Implied waiver usually occurs when the landlord accepts rent from the assignees with the knowledge of the assignment.

(1) **Rule in Dumpor's Case:** [§1289] Where the landlord expressly consents to one assignment, the Rule in Dumpor's Case [76 Eng. Rep. 1110 (1603)] states

that the covenant thereafter becomes unenforceable. The rationale is that the covenant is single, and *once waived, the covenant is destroyed.*

(a) **Criticism:** The Rule makes no sense, as the obvious purpose of such a covenant is to assure the landlord that a responsible tenant is in possession throughout the term of the lease. Nonetheless, the Rule has been retained by a majority of courts in this country, though it is now abolished by statute in England. The Restatement rejects the Rule. [Rest. 2d §16.1, comment g]

(b) **Exceptions:** [§1290]   There are numerous exceptions to the Rule in Dumpor's Case, developed in attempts to avoid a questionable rule, of which the following are the most prominent:

   1) **Covenant binding lessee and assigns:** [§1291]   If the covenant not to assign without the landlord's consent is expressed as binding on the lessee *and her assigns*, an assignment by the lessee with consent of the landlord does not free the assignee from the binding force of the covenant. [Childs v. Warner Bros. Theatres, Inc., 156 S.E. 923 (N.C. 1931)]

   2) **Landlord's limited consent:** [§1292]   If the landlord, when consenting, expressly states that his consent is to this assignment only and not to future assignments as well, the Rule in Dumpor's Case does not apply.

K. PUBLIC HOUSING

1. **Public Housing Legislation:** [§1293]   The U.S. Housing Act of 1937 [42 U.S.C. §§1401-30] was the first important legislation authorizing government-owned housing in this country. The Act provides for public housing, financed by the federal government, but owned and operated by a local housing authority ("LHA"). To finance construction, the LHA sells tax-exempt bonds, which are paid off by the federal government. The government also subsidizes some part of each LHA's operating expenses. This Act established public housing, and the federal housing programs have since been expanded in many directions. A principal innovation was a program to provide financial assistance for privately owned housing for low and moderate income families.

2. **Site Selection**

   a. **Racial segregation:** [§1294]   Site selection decisions can perpetuate racial segregation in public housing and in the residential patterns of cities. Site selection of public housing must be approved by the local government, and the pattern in the past has been to approve public housing only in areas of racial concentration, though this may have violated Title 6 of the Civil Rights Act of 1964 [42 U.S.C. §2000d]. To remedy past illegal site selections, it has been held that a federal court can order governmental agencies to develop new public housing projects on a metropolitan-wide basis—*i.e.*, in the white suburbs as well as inside the city limits. [Hills v. Gautreaux, 425 U.S. 284 (1976)]

b. **Community approval:** [§1295]   A state constitutional requirement that a low-rent housing project can be developed only with the approval of a majority of the voters within the city has been upheld. *Rationale:* The referendum law is "neutral on its face" (*i.e.*, does not appear to be discriminatory) and is not in fact aimed at a racial minority. *Economic* classifications in housing are permissible, but *racial* classifications are suspect. [James v. Valtierra, 402 U.S. 137 (1971)]

3.   **Eligibility for Admission**

a.   **Federal requirements:** [§1296]   Federal statutes and regulations provide that low-rent housing shall be available to families of low income. Apart from preferences required to be given to veterans and persons displaced by urban renewal, the development of admission criteria was, until recently, left to each LHA. In 1982 the Department of Housing and Urban Development ("HUD") set forth broad "desirability criteria" to guide LHAs.

b.   **Local requirements:** [§1297]   Each LHA usually adopts "desirability standards" to determine eligibility. However, courts have held that a standard cannot exclude applicants as a class but can only be weighed in the individual's case. For example, persons with criminal records cannot be excluded as a class, but the particular record can be taken into account in weighing desirability. [Manigo v. New York City Housing Authority, 51 Misc. 2d 829 (1966)] Courts have also required LHAs to institute "objective scoring systems" to establish preferences. Chronological waiting lists have also been required.

4.   **Increase in Rent:** [§1298]   The tenant's interest in a public housing unit is a property interest within the protection of the fourteenth amendment. Thus, it has been held that tenants are entitled to certain due process rights before rents are raised. These include notice of proposed rent increase, opportunity to file written objections, and a statement of reasons by the LHA for its ultimate decision. [Burr v. New Rochelle Municipal Housing Authority, 479 F.2d 1165 (2d Cir. 1973)] On the other hand, if HUD approves a rent increase, the tenants do not have to be given notice and a hearing. Congress can diminish tenants' rights in public housing by leaving their protection to HUD.

5.   **Eviction**

a.   **Substantive grounds:** [§1299]   Tenants can be evicted for destroying the property, boisterous and disturbing conduct, and undesirable behavior imperiling the health, safety, or morals of the neighbors. Tenants can also be evicted for concealing ineligibility for continued residence. But a tenant cannot be evicted for exercising his constitutional rights, such as participating in a tenants' organization. [Thorpe v. Housing Authority, 386 U.S. 670 (1967)]

b. **Procedural rights**

(1) **Public housing—administrative hearing required:** [§1300]   A tenant cannot be evicted from *public housing* without *good cause*. Notice and hearing are required. The hearing must include the right to cross-examine witnesses and to have counsel. This requirement has been based on the theory that the tenants have a property interest and the government, as landlord, is still acting as the government and must provide persons with constitutional due process. [Swann v. Gastonia Housing Authority, 675 F.2d 1342 (4th Cir. 1982); Escalera v. New York City Housing Authority, 425 F.2d 853 (2d Cir. 1970); Geneva Towers Tenants Organization v. Federated Mortgage Investors, 504 F.2d 483 (9th Cir. 1974)]

(2) **Publicly assisted housing:** [§1301]   In publicly assisted housing, a hearing is required if the federal benefits to the project are such that the project's action is "state action" subject to the Due Process Clause of the fourteenth amendment. (On "state action," *see supra*, §444.) Recent cases hold that government financial assistance and state approval of the housing programs, together with the use of state eviction procedure, is sufficient "state action" to apply the fourteenth amendment. The landlord is treated as if he were a public landlord—*i.e.*, good cause to evict, notice and hearing must be given to the tenant. [Joy v. Daniels, 479 F.2d 1236 (4th Cir. 1973)]

6. **Implied Warranty:** [§1302]   Does a public housing project have the duty of complying with an implied warranty of habitability imposed on private landlords? It is one thing for a court to declare a duty and another to compel its performance by public housing officials, who may not have the funds to comply. Cases on this issue are few. Some hold that the public housing authority has *no* duty of habitability. [Alexander v. United States, 555 F.2d 166 (7th Cir. 1977)] Others recognize an implied warranty, and extend to public housing tenants the full range of remedies. [Boston Housing Authority v. Hemingway, 293 N.E.2d 831 (Mass. 1973)]

IX. EASEMENTS AND COVENANTS

chapter approach

Landowners often want to make agreements with their neighbors respecting the use of one or both of the parcels of land. These agreements can be divided into two broad categories: (i) rights arising from a *grant* of a right by one landowner to another (known as *easements* or *profits*), and (ii) rights arising from a *promise* respecting the use of land by one landowner to another (known as a *real covenant* or an *equitable servitude*). These rights are frequently found in subdivision developments and in condominiums, as well as between neighboring landowners.

1. As for *easements*, the most important questions relate to their *creation* and *termination*. An easement can be created by an express agreement, by estoppel, by implication from an existing use when land is divided, by necessity when land is divided, and by prescription. Pay particular attention to the requirements that must be met in order to have an easement of the designated type.

2. As for *real covenants*, the most important issue is whether they will *run to assignees*. Privity of estate is required for the covenant to run. Privity is a difficult concept. Concentrate on it and get it straight. Remember also that the remedy for breach of a real covenant is *damages.*

3. As for *equitable servitudes*, the most important issues relate to creation, enforcement by assignees or third parties, and termination. Note that unlike real covenants, equitable servitudes can be *implied* by a *scheme.* The rules for the running of equitable servitudes to assignees are technical and you should master them. Privity of estate is *not* required, but the covenant must touch and concern and, generally, the benefit must be to neighboring land. Also, look carefully at whether the assignee has notice of the covenant when she buys, for if she does not, she is not bound by the covenant. The remedy for breach of an equitable servitude is an *injunction* or enforcement of a *lien.*

The law in this chapter is technical, but if you concentrate on how these servitudes may be created, when they bind assignees, and when they may be terminated, you will be well prepared for any such question on your exam.

A. EASEMENTS

1. Introduction

    a. **Definition:** [§1303]   An easement is a grant of an interest in land which entitles a person to use land possessed by another.

    b. **Types of easements:** [§1304]   Easements are either affirmative or negative.

        (1) **Affirmative easement:** [§1305]   The owner of an affirmative easement has the right to *go onto* the land of another (the "servient land") and do some act on

the land. Most easements are affirmative. *Example:* O, owner of Blackacre, grants to A a right of way across Blackacre.

(2) **Negative easement:** [§1306]   The owner of a negative easement can ***prevent*** the owner of the servient land from doing some act on the servient land. Negative easements are rare and are generally not permitted unless one of four types recognized by early English law: easements for ***light***, for ***air***, for ***subjacent or lateral support***, or for the ***flow of an artificial stream***. These four negative easements permit two neighbors to agree that neighbor A will not block neighbor B's windows, will not dig so as to undermine B's house, or will not interfere with an aqueduct bringing water to B's farm. However, the list of negative easements is not necessarily closed, and new decisions may expand the list. Scenic easements and solar easements are two new types of negative easements recognized in recent years.

(a) **Example:** Blackacre, a hillside lot, has a view over Whiteacre to the sea. O, owner of Whiteacre, grants to A, owner of Blackacre, an easement of view beginning twenty feet above the ground level of Whiteacre. This will enable A to see the sea and prevent B from building above twenty feet and blocking the view. At common law this would not have been permitted as a negative easement, since it is not one of the four permitted types. However, in this country in modern times an easement of view or scenic easement has been permitted as a negative easement. Although the easement is not for light and air, it resembles the same. [Petersen v. Friedman, 162 Cal. App. 2d 245 (1958)]

(b) **Why types are limited:** [§1307]   Almost all types of purported negative easements can be treated as a ***promise*** by the servient owner not to use his land in a certain way. In the above example, O could have ***promised*** A not to build any structure over twenty feet high, in which case A would not have an easement but a covenant. (*Remember:* An easement is a ***grant*** of an interest in land; a covenant is a ***promise*** respecting use of land.) Courts have not found it necessary to expand the categories of permissible negative easements because they can classify the right to prevent a neighbor from doing something on his land as an equitable servitude (a "promise"). For example, if O grants A the right not to have commercial uses on adjacent Whiteacre, the court will likely classify this right as a restrictive covenant. Enforcement of this right as an equitable servitude works as well as enforcing it as a negative easement.

(c) **Compare—affirmative act on servient land:** [§1308]   If the owner of the servient land agrees to perform an affirmative act on the servient land (such as maintaining a flagpole), this is a covenant, not an easement. An easement involves either the right of A to go on O's servient land (an affirmative easement), or the right of A to prohibit O's use of his land in a way resembling one of the four traditional types of negative easements.

c. **Easements appurtenant or in gross:** [§1309] All easements are either appurtenant to other land or in gross.

(1) **Easement appurtenant:** [§1310] If an easement *benefits* its owner *in the use of another tract of land*, it is appurtenant to that land. The land benefited is called the *dominant tenement*; the land burdened is the *servient tenement*. The servient tenement usually is, but does not have to be, adjacent to the dominant tenement. [Kemery v. Mylroie, 506 P.2d 319 (Wash. 1973)]

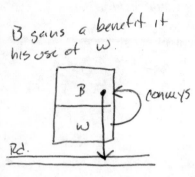

B gains a benefit it his use of W.

(a) **Example:** Whiteacre is located between Blackacre and a public road. O, owner of Whiteacre, conveys to A, owner of Blackacre, a right to cross Whiteacre to reach the public road. The easement over Whiteacre is appurtenant to Blackacre (the dominant tenement).

(b) **Passes with dominant tenement:** [§1311] An easement appurtenant is attached to the dominant tenement and passes with the tenement to any subsequent owner of the tenement. It cannot be separated from the dominant tenement and turned into an easement in gross, unless the owners of the dominant and servient tenements make a new agreement permitting that. In the above example, the benefit of the easement across Whiteacre will pass to any subsequent owner of Blackacre.

(c) **Negative easement:** [§1312] A negative easement is always appurtenant to land. It protects the owner of the easement in his enjoyment of his land. It cannot be in gross. (Recall what types of negative easements are permitted, and the reason for this statement will become clear.)

(2) **Easement in gross:** [§1313] If an easement does not benefit its owner in the use and enjoyment of his land, but merely *gives him the right to use the servient land*, the easement is in gross. "In gross" is the term used to signify that the benefit of the easement is not appurtenant to other land. (*Note well:* The term "in gross" means only that the easement is not appurtenant. It does not mean that the easement is personal to the holder and cannot be assigned. An easement in gross usually can be assigned if the parties so intend.) [Standard Oil Co. v. Buchi, 66 A. 427 (N.J. 1907)]

(a) **Example:** O, owner of Greenacre, grants to Heylook Billboard Co. the right to erect a sign on Greenacre. Heylook owns no land. The easement is in gross and can be assigned by Heylook if the parties so intend. If O sells Greenacre to A, the burden of the easement passes with the ownership to A. [Baseball Publishing Co. v. Bruton, *supra*, §897]

(b) **Not permitted in England:** [§1314] In England, an easement in gross is not permitted. An easement must have a dominant tenement. In the above example, an English Heylook Billboard Co. would merely have contract rights and a license to go on the land. But an easement in gross can be created in any American jurisdiction.

(3) **Easement appurtenant favored:** [§1315]   If an instrument creating an easement is ambiguous, courts generally construe it as creating an easement appurtenant rather than in gross. [Dunn Bros., Inc. v. Lesnewsky, 321 A.2d 453 (Conn. 1973); Martin v. Music, 254 S.W.2d 701 (Ky. 1953); Siferd v. Stambor, 214 N.E.2d 106 (Ohio 1966); Mitchell v. Castellaw, 246 S.W.2d 163 (Tex. 1952)]

  (a) **Rationale:** There are several reasons why courts prefer easements appurtenant. (i) *Intention*: In the usual factual situation, the parties have a dominant tenement in mind. If the easement serves to benefit its possessor in the use of a tract of land or enhance the value of a neighboring tract of land, the easement is considered to have been intended to be appurtenant. (ii) *History*: Although easements in gross are permitted in the United States, the English courts' refusal to recognize them influenced our courts to construe against them. (iii) *Elimination of obsolete easements*: It is thought to be easier to eliminate an obsolete easement appurtenant because the benefited party, who can release it, will be more easily ascertainable than the owners of an easement in gross (*see infra*, §1398). (iv) *Land value increased*: An easement appurtenant increases the value of the dominant land, presumably by more than it decreases the value of the servient land. To purchase an easement, the buyer will have to pay something more than the damage to the servient tenement in order to strike a bargain with the seller. Thus, an easement appurtenant increases the total value of land. An easement in gross does not increase the value of any land, and it in fact decreases the total value of land by the amount of damage to the servient tenement.

    1) **Example:** A, owner of Blackacre, wants to purchase an easement of way across Whiteacre, owned by O. Such an easement will increase the value of Blackacre by $100; it will damage Whiteacre by $60. At a price somewhere between $60 and $100, O and A will strike a bargain, which will make them both better off. If O sells the easement for $75, the total value of land has increased by $40. O has made a gain of $15 (the amount O receives in excess of his damage) and A has made a gain of $25 (the amount the easement is worth to A less what A pays). If A owns no land, so that the easement is in gross, the total value of land would be decreased by the amount of damage to Whiteacre ($60).

d. **Interest in land:** [§1316]   An easement is an interest in land. This means, among other things, that the burden passes to subsequent owners of the servient land. The owner of an easement does not have merely contract rights against the original grantor of the easement, but also has rights against all successors to the grantor.

e. **Profit compared:** [§1317]   A profit (or profit à prendre) is the right to *take something off* another person's land that is part of the land or a product of the land.

Profits include crops, timber, minerals, wild game, and fish. When a profit is grant-ed, an easement to go on the land and remove the subject matter is implied. The rules applicable to easements apply to profits with the following exceptions:

(1) **In gross preferred:** [§1318] Although a profit can be appurtenant to other land, the usual profit is in gross. Unlike most easements, profits have exchange value on the open market (*e.g.*, uncut timber can be bought and sold). A profit is usually not intended to benefit the owner of it in the use of adjacent land but rather intended to give the owner an economically valuable item. [Evans v. Holloway Sand & Gravel, Inc., 308 N.W.2d 440 (Mich. 1981)]

(2) **Assignment:** [§1319] Different rules may apply to assignment of profits in gross than apply to easements in gross. (*See infra*, §§1399 *et seq.*)

f. **License compared:** [§1320] A license is *permission* to go upon land belonging to the licensor. Licenses are very common: The plumber repairing a stopped-up drain, UPS delivering packages, guests at a party all have licenses. A license can be oral or in writing. A license is *revocable* at the will of the licensor.

(1) **Example:** O tells A that A can park on O's land. O's oral license gives A per-mission to park. O can revoke the license at any time.

(2) **Construction:** [§1321] Cases sometimes arise where the issue is whether a person has a license or an easement in gross. For example, an apartment house owner may give A the sole and exclusive right to install and maintain laundry machines in the owner's apartment house. If this is a license, it is not binding on a new owner of the apartment house; but if it is an easement, it is binding on a new owner who has notice of it. Reflecting a hostility to easements in gross, which clog title, courts usually construe agreements such as these, which do not give A exclusive possession of any definite space, as licenses. [Todd v. Krolick, 96 App. Div. 2d 695 (1983); Reliable Washer Service v. Delmar Associates, 49 Misc. 2d 348 (1966)]

(3) **Irrevocable licenses:** [§1322] A license may become irrevocable in certain limited situations.

(a) **License coupled with an interest:** [§1323] A license coupled with an inter-est cannot be revoked. A license coupled with an interest is one that gives the licensee the right to remove a chattel of the licensee, which is on the licensor's land. *Example:* O sells A an automobile located on O's land. A has an irrevocable license to enter and remove the car. [Bomberger v. McKelvey, 35 Cal. 2d 607 (1950)]

(b) **Estoppel:** [§1324] A license may become irrevocable under the rules of estoppel. If the licensee has constructed substantial improvements on ei-ther the licensor's land or the licensee's land, relying on the license, in many states the licensor is estopped from revoking the license. The theory is that it would be unfair to the licensee to permit revocation after he spends money in reliance. [Stoner v. Zucker, 148 Cal. 516 (1906); Holbrook v. Taylor, 532 S.W.2d 763 (Ky. 1976)]

1) **Example:** O gives an adjoining property owner, A, oral permission to go on O's land and erect a tile drain thereon to protect A's property from natural water drainage. A does so at substantial expense and with O's knowledge. O is estopped now to revoke permission. [Ricenbaw v. Kraus, 61 N.W.2d 350 (Neb. 1953)]

2) **Criticism:** When a court estops O in the preceding example, it is giving the entitlement to A at no cost, and permitting A to damage O to the extent of O's actual loss in value. O, being a good neighbor and casually saying yes, may not have realized the amount of damage he would suffer. Perhaps a fairer remedy would be to permit A to continue the license upon payment of damages to O. This remedy would mean that the good neighbor who gave permisson not anticipating any great harm by the license would not suffer any actual loss.

3) **How long irrevocable:** [§1325] The Restatement of Property says that irrevocability exists only for whatever time is required to enable the licensee to reap the fruits of his expenditures. [Rest. 2d §519] Some courts have held that irrevocability is limited to the life of the pertinent structure or improvement. A few courts hold that an irrevocable license is like an easement and is capable of lasting forever. [Cooke v. Ramponi, 38 Cal. 2d 282 (1952)]

4) **Minority view—estoppel rejected:** [§1326] Some courts hold that the licensor will not be estopped to revoke the license. *Rationale:* An oral irrevocable license, like an oral easement, falls within the Statute of Frauds. Refusing to enforce the oral agreement induces the parties to reduce their agreement to writing, avoiding lawsuits over oral statements and ambiguous expectations. Moreover, in fairness, a writing should be required so that the good neighbor who gives casual permission, without thinking of the permanent damage to his land, will not be bound. [Crosdale v. Lanigan, 129 N.Y. 604 (1892)]

(4) **Theatre tickets:** [§1327] A theatre ticket is something of an anomaly. A theatre ticket is a contract between the theatre owner and the buyer entitling the buyer to see a performance in a designated seat. The ticket, which is a memorandum that might satisfy the Statute of Frauds, could be held to create an easement, but this would give the ticket holder the right to use self-help to enter and to eject someone sitting in her seat. Courts have held that a ticket creates a revocable license, but this is not an interest in land so as to permit self-help. The ticket holder can be denied admission or ejected by the theatre owner. Her remedy is to sue the theatre owner for breach of contract. *Ratio-*

nale: The theatre owner does not want to incur ill-will, is likely to be fair in settling disputes between patrons, and is the most efficient "order keeper" in the situation. [Marrone v. Washington Jockey Club, 227 U.S. 633 (1913)]

(5) **Assignability:** [§1328]   A license is usually presumed to be personal and non-assignable, but if the parties so intend, it can be made transferable. A theatre ticket, for instance, is assignable. [McCastle v. Scanlon, 59 N.W.2d 114 (Mich. 1953)]

2. **Creation of Easements:** [§1329]   Easements may be created by *express grant or reservation*, by *implication*, or by *prescription*.

a. **Creation by express grant:** [§1330]   An easement over the grantor's land may be granted to another. This is known as an easement created by grant.

(1) **Statute of Frauds:** [§1331]   An easement, being an interest in land, must satisfy the Statute of Frauds. Unless one of the exceptions to the Statute applies, creation of an easement requires a *written instrument signed by the grantor*. If the grantor does not sign a written instrument but orally gives the grantee permission to enter land, the grantee has a *license* to use the land (*see supra*, §1320). The exceptions to the Statute of Frauds include the usual ones of fraud, part performance, and estoppel, as well as easements by implication and prescription.

(2) **Duration of easement:** [§1332]   An easement can be created to endure for a person's life, for a period of years, or forever. If it endures forever, it is called an easement in fee simple.

(3) **Construction of ambiguous instrument:** [§1333]   In some deeds it is difficult to tell whether the grantor intended to grant an easement or to grant a fee simple. Generally, a grant of a *limited use*, or for a *limited purpose*, or of an identified space *without clearly marked boundaries* creates an easement. Similarly a sale for less than the fair market value of a fee simple indicates an easement. If the owner of the servient land pays taxes, and the used space is not separately assessed, this also indicates an easement. [Northwest Realty Co. v. Jacobs, 273 N.W.2d 41 (S.D. 1978)]

(a) **Example:** O grants A a forty-foot strip "for a road." The limited purpose indicates that an easement is created. [Coon v. Sonoma Magnesite Co., 182 Cal. 597 (1920); Minneapolis Athletic Club v. Cohler, 177 N.W.2d 786 (Minn. 1970)]

(b) **Presumption of a fee simple:** [§1334]   Courts sometimes presume that the grantor conveys the largest interest he can convey, unless expressly limited. This presumption favors a fee simple construction. [Midland Valley Railroad v. Arrow Industrial Manufacturing Co., 297 P.2d 410 (Okla. 1956)—conveyance of "a strip of land for a right of way" conveys a fee simple because of presumption of fee simple]

b. **Creation by reservation:** [§1335] An easement may be reserved by the grantor over the land granted. If the grantor conveys land, reserving an easement, the land conveyed is the servient tenement.

(1) **Reservation in favor of grantor:** [§1336] An easement could not be reserved at early common law because only rights "issuing out of the land" (such as rents or feudal services) could be reserved. English courts eventually found a way around this restriction by inventing the *regrant theory*. Under the regrant theory, a deed from O to A purporting to reserve an easement in O was treated as conveying a fee simple absolute to A, who by the same instrument *regranted an easement* to O. Hence, A was treated as the grantor of a reserved easement. The fact that A, the grantee, had not signed the deed regranting an easement to O was initially bothersome, but courts ultimately held that the grantee had, by accepting the deed, bound himself to it. Although the conditions that gave rise to the regrant theory no longer exist, the regrant theory still plagues us.

(a) **Exception of an easement:** [§1337] At common law, a reservation differed from an exception. A reservation is the regrant of a *new easement*, not previously existing. An exception is a provision in a deed which excludes from the grant some *preexisting right*. *Example:* O, owner of Blackacre, conveys an easement over Blackacre to A. Subsequently O conveys Blackacre to B "except for an easement previously granted A." The *preexisting* easement in A is excepted. It could not be reserved because it has previously been granted to A. The distinction between an exception and a reservation has all but disappeared in American law, when a new easement has been retained, and the words exception and reservation are often treated as synonymous. Thus, today, if O "excepts" an easement in himself, it will be treated as a reservation.

(2) **Reservation in favor of a third party**

(a) **Common law:** [§1338] At common law, an easement could not be reserved in favor of a third party. The reasons for this prohibition lay in feudal notions of conveyancing and in the theory that the grantee *regranted to the grantor* the easement. This common law prohibition is still followed in a majority of states. [Vogeler v. Alwyn Improvement Corp., 247 N.Y. 131 (1928); Leidig v. Hoopes, 288 P.2d 402 (Okla. 1955); Pitman v. Sweeney, 661 P.2d 153 (Wash. 1983)]

1) **Solution—draft around:** [§1339] This rule serves only as a malpractice trap and ought to be eliminated. It can easily be circumvented by putting the third party in the position of the grantor. This can be done by using two pieces of paper. Suppose that O wants to convey Blackacre to A and reserve an easement for parking in favor of her church across the street. First, O conveys Blackacre to the church. Second, the church conveys Blackacre to A reserving an easement in itself. It is likely that a lawyer will be liable for malpractice if she does not use two pieces of paper and accomplish her client's wishes.

2) **Compare—covenants:** [§1340]   A covenant, unlike an easement, can be created to benefit a third party. (*See infra*, §§1418 *et seq.*)

(b) **Minority view:** [§1341]   Some modern cases hold that an easement may be reserved in favor of a third person. There is no reason to prohibit this in modern law. Moreover, if the easement is invalidated, the grantee is unjustly enriched by getting more than she bargained for (*i.e.*, she pays the value of land with an easement and gets land without an easement). [Willard v. First Church of Christ, Scientist, 7 Cal. 3d 743 (1972)]

c. **Creation by implication:** [§1342]   An easement by implication is created by *operation of law*, not by a written instrument. It is an exception to the Statute of Frauds. However, an easement can be implied only in very narrowly defined circumstances indicating that the parties intended an easement or that an easement is a necessity. Implied easements thus are limited to two kinds: (i) an intended easement based on an *apparent use existing* at the time the servient tenement is separated from the dominant tenement, and (ii) an easement by *necessity*.

(1) **Easement implied from existing use:** [§1343]   If, prior to the time a tract of land is divided into two lots, a use exists on the "servient part" that is reasonably necessary for the enjoyment of the "dominant part" and which the court finds the parties intended to continue after the tract is divided, an easement may be implied. The requirements for implication are discussed below.

(a) **Implied only over land granted or reserved when tract divided:** [§1344]   An easement can be implied only over land granted or reserved when a tract is divided into two or more parcels. If an easement is implied in favor of the *grantee*, the easement is created by *implied grant* to the grantee. If an easement is implied in favor of the *grantor*, the easement is created by *implied reservation* to the grantor.

1) **Example:** O owns Blackacre, a large tract of land. A house is built on the back of the tract, serviced by a driveway leading to the street. O divides Blackacre into two lots, and sells the back lot with the house on it (lot 1) to A. O retains the front lot with the driveway on it (lot 2). Provided the other requirements of implied easements are met, a court will imply a *grant* to A of an easement of way over lot 2. If O had retained lot 1, and sold lot 2 to A, a court would imply a *reservation* of an easement over lot 2.

2) **Implied only in favor of dominant tenement:** [§1345]   An easement in gross will not be implied. An easement by implication must benefit a dominant tenement created by dividing a tract into two or more lots.

(b) **Existing use at time of tract division:** [§1346]   At the time a tract is divided into two or more lots, a use of one part of the tract must exist from which it can be inferred that an easement permitting its continuation was intended. This existing use is often called a *quasi-easement*. It is not a legal easement, because O cannot have an easement in O's own land. It can arise as an easement only when O divides the land into two lots. However, a quasi-easement is a use of the land which would resemble an easement if the tract were divided into two lots. In the example above, the driveway on Blackacre, before division by O, is a quasi-easement. [Cheney v. Mueller, 485 P.2d 1218 (Or. 1971)]

1) **Apparent:** [§1347]   In order to have a quasi-easement, the previous use must be *apparent*. It is apparent if a grantee could, by a reasonable inspection of the premises, discover the existence of the use (*e.g.*, a "beaten path"). "Apparent" does not mean the same thing as "visible"; a nonvisible use may be apparent. Thus, for example, underground drains may be apparent even though not visible, if the surface connections would put a reasonable person on notice of their presence. [Romanchuk v. Plotkin, 9 N.W.2d 421 (Minn. 1943)]

   a) **Example:** O builds two houses on his property Blackacre. O installs a sewer line to service these houses; the sewer line runs from the street to house 1 and then to house 2. O sells house 1 to A. Although the sewer running under house 1 is not visible, A could discover that it serviced house 2 as well as house 1 by calling a plumber in for an inspection. It has been held that an implied sewer easement has been reserved to house 2 because the sewer is apparent. [Van Sandt v. Royster, 83 P.2d 698 (Kan. 1938); Westbrook v. Wright, 477 S.W.2d 663 (Tex. 1972)]

2) **Continuous:** [§1348]   The previous use must be *continuous*, not sporadic. The requirement of continuity is based upon the idea that the activities should be such that there is a great probability that the use was known to the parties at the time of the grant, from which an intent can be inferred that the parties wanted the use to continue. Thus, courts interpret "continuous" to include a permanent physical change in the land for a particular use. *Example:* The improvement of a roadway by paving is a permanent change of the land, and hence a continuous use, although the roadway is not used every day.

3) **Conveyance by paper plat:** [§1349]   If, before building a street, a subdivider conveys a lot by reference to an undedicated street or a paper plat, the requirement of a quasi-easement is *waived*. The purchaser receives an easement by implication at least in such streets as abut the purchaser's lot, and perhaps in all of the streets delineated on the plat, even though not yet in existence. *Rationale:* The purchaser buys in reliance upon the street being opened, and pays a price commensurate with a lot with easements. [Krzewinski v. Eaton Homes, Inc., 161 N.E.2d 88 (Ohio 1958); Putnam v. Dickinson, 142 N.W.2d 111 (N.D. 1966)]

(c) **Reasonable necessity:** [§1350]   The easement must be necessary for the enjoyment of the claimed dominant tenement. Necessity is an important circumstance in implying an easement on the basis of an existing use, because it probably affects the intention of the parties as to whether the existing use is to continue. In most jurisdictions *reasonable necessity*, and not strict necessity, is required. This is a flexible requirement. Relevant factors in determining reasonable necessity include cost and difficulty of establishing a new road or other alternate use, and whether the price paid reflects the expected continued use of the servient portion of the original tract. [Rose v. Denn, 212 P.2d 1077 (Or. 1949)]

1) **Necessity where easement reserved:** [§1351]   In older cases, courts were reluctant to imply an easement reserved by the grantor. An implied reservation was thought to be in derogation of the deed of the fee simple, and gave the grantee less than the deed called for. An implied grant of an easement, on the other hand, was not in derogation of the deed but gave the grantee some additional rights. In modern times, a few courts still refuse to imply an easement by reservation except in cases of strict necessity. [Mitchell v. Castellaw, *supra*, §1315] In many states, a stronger showing of necessity is required for an implied reservation than for an implied grant. [Adams v. Cullen, 268 P.2d 451 (Wash. 1954)] In perhaps the majority of states, the amount of necessity required is the same for both an implied reservation and an implied grant of an easement.

(2) **Easement by necessity:** [§1352]   An easement by necessity is implied if the owner of a tract of land divides the tract into two lots and by this division deprives one lot of access to a public road. An easement of way over the lot with access to the public road is implied. Usually an implied easement of way by necessity must be strictly necessary and not just a more convenient access. [Ward v. Slavecek, 466 S.W.2d 91 (Tex. 1971)] The doctrine of easements by necessity rests either on the ground that *public policy* requires a way of access to each separate parcel of land or on the ground that, since access is essential to use, the parties *intended* to create an easement but overlooked putting it in the deed.

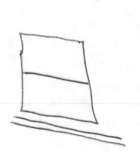

(a) **Example:** O owns Blackacre, the southern border of which fronts on a public road. O conveys the northern half of Blackacre to A. By this division, the northern half of Blackacre is deprived of access to a public road. An easement by necessity is implied over the southern half of Blackacre in favor of the northern half of Blackacre. [Berkeley Development Co. v. Hutzler, 229 S.E.2d 732 (W. Va. 1976); Finn v. Williams, 33 N.E.2d 226 (Ill. 1941)]

(b) **Implied only over landlocking parcel:** [§1353]   An easement by necessity is implied only when land is divided. The necessity must exist when the tract is severed. The easement is implied only over that portion of the divided tract that blocks access to a public road from the landlocked parcel. An easement by necessity cannot be implied over land that was never owned by the common grantor of the dominant and servient tenements. [Othen v. Rosier, 226 S.W.2d 622 (Tex. 1950)]

1) **Note:** In a few states, statutes give a landlocked landowner a right to force a way out over neighboring land, without proving the existence of an easement by necessity, but with payment of compensation to the neighbor. The Constitution provides that the power of eminent domain can be used only to take property for a public use. In Texas a statute giving a landlocked owner power to force a road out through a neighbor's land was held unconstitutional as permitting a taking of property for *private* use. [Estate of Waggoner v. Gleghorn, 378 S.W.2d 47 (Tex. 1964)]

(c) **No existing use required:** [§1354]   An easement by necessity, unlike an easement implied on the basis of existing use, does not require an existing use at the time a tract is divided into two lots. Even if the land is virgin timber land, and there are no roads on it, an easement by necessity is implied when it is divided so as to landlock a part.

(d) **Location of easement:** [§1355]   The owner of the servient parcel has the right to locate the easement by necessity, provided the location is reasonably convenient. The servient owner is best capable of locating the easement so as to do least damage to the servient land, thereby reducing costs. [Palmer v. Palmer, 150 N.Y. 139 (1896)]

(e) **Easements other than ways:** [§1356]   An easement by necessity might be implied in situations where an easement for something other than road access is claimed. For example, an easement for a sewer or for light and air might be implied when the severed parcel is deprived of access to a sewer or light and air. However, to date, courts have refused to imply such easements on the ground that sewage can be removed by truck and buildings can be equipped with artificial light and air. Moreover, it is far less likely that the parties intended, but forgot, to create an easement for sewage or light and air than that they intended to provide access to a landlocked lot, which is essential to its use. Inasmuch as the parties probably did not think sewage or light and air access was part of their bargain, the parties are left where they are. Thus, easements by necessity have so far been limited to easements of way. [Maiorello v. Arlotta, 73 A.2d 374 (Pa. 1950)]

(f) **Termination of necessity:** [§1357]   An easement by necessity lasts only so long as it is necessary. It terminates when the necessity ceases. [Palmer v. Palmer, *supra*]

1) **Compare:** An easement implied on the basis of a *quasi-easement* may continue forever, even after any element of necessity disappears.

d. **Creation by prescription**

   (1) **Historical development:** [§1358]   Statutes of limitations applicable to actions to recover possession of land did not apply to easements since an easement is a nonpossessory interest. Yet the same policies that underlie the law of adverse possession apply to long use of an easement. Thus the courts developed the doctrine that an easement could be acquired by prescription, *i.e.*, by an ***adverse user*** for a requisite period.

      (a) **English law:** [§1359]   Searching for a way to establish the doctrine of prescription, the English courts developed the ***fiction of the lost grant***. If a person had been using another's land for the requisite period, the court presumed that he was doing so under a grant from some former owner, which grant was now lost. The presumption of grant was conclusive, once the requisite period had passed, and was applied even though it was later admitted that no grant had ever been made.

      (b) **American law:** [§1360]   The fiction of the lost grant has been rejected in most American jurisdictions. In this country, the doctrine of prescription has been developed as a matter of public policy by analogy to the law of ***adverse possession***. If the statute of limitations for adverse possession is twenty years, the prescriptive period for acquiring an easement is likewise twenty years. Generally the same requirements for adverse possession are applied to an easement by prescription. Hence, the same period and same issues are generally involved in acquiring an easement by prescription as are involved in acquiring a fee simple by adverse possession.

   (2) **Elements of prescription:** [§1361]   For prescription, the usual elements required for adverse possession must be shown: ***open and notorious use; adverse and under a claim of right; continuous and uninterrupted*** throughout the requisite period. [Hunt Land Holding Co. v. Schramm, 121 So. 2d 697 (Fla. 1960)]

      (a) **Open and notorious use:** [§1362]   The use must be made without any attempt at concealment. This requirement is most often litigated in cases involving underground sewers and drains. If the sewer could be reasonably discovered upon inspection (*e.g.*, surface connections are visible), this requirement is satisfied.

      (b) **Under a claim of right:** [§1363]   A claim of a prescriptive easement must be under a claim of right, and not with permission of the owner of the land. But, as with adverse possession, a court may apply an objective or a subjective test to a "claim of right." Under the objective test, it is sufficient that the acts of the user appear to the community to be under a claim of right (*see supra*, §118). Under the subjective test, the user must in good faith believe that he has a right to use the servient land (*see supra*, §120).

         1) **Example:** A and B own adjoining lots. Pursuant to an oral agreement, A and B construct a cement driveway half on A's lot and half on B's

lot; each pays half the cost. Some twenty-five years later, A conveys her lot to C and B conveys his lot to D. C and D squabble, and D forbids C to use the driveway. C claims a prescriptive easement. Under the objective test, C and D have reciprocal prescriptive easements over the other's lot. If A and B believed they had a right to use the driveway because each contributed to construction, even under the subjective test C and D can have prescriptive easements. [Shanks v. Floom, 124 N.E.2d 416 (Ohio 1955)—prescriptive easement due to expense of constructing driveway (similar to estoppel to revoke license)] The courts are split in these common driveway situations, however; much depends upon the particular facts as to whether the user thought she had a right to use the common driveway or was using it permissively.

a) **Note—exclusivity not required:** [§1364] Adverse possession requires exclusive possession by the possessor, but prescription does *not* require exclusive use. The user can acquire a prescriptive easement even though using the land with the owner (*e.g.*, a common driveway).

2) **Permissive use changes to adverse:** [§1365] Prescriptive rights cannot be acquired where the use is permissive. However, if a person uses land of another with permission and subsequently begins to do acts which reasonably should put the owner on notice that the user is *claiming a right* to use the land, the use becomes adverse. For example, if O gives A permission to use a driveway, and A subsequently tears down a gate across the driveway or widens and paves the driveway, these subsequent acts begin adverse use. [Hester v. Sawyers, 71 P.2d 646 (N.M. 1937)] But if A merely repairs the driveway, this is insufficient to put O on notice that A is claiming use as of right. [Lunt v. Kitchens, 260 P.2d 535 (Utah 1953)]

3) **Color of title:** [§1366] In some states, statutes require color of title and payment of taxes for adverse possession. Neither is required for a prescriptive easement. These particular statutory requirements for adverse possession have been ignored by the courts in developing the analogous law of prescription.

(c) **Continuous use:** [§1367] The adverse use must be continuous, but this does not mean constant. Indeed, the use of an easement ordinarily involves only periodic use. Continuity requires a continuous claim of right and periodic acts which, given the nature of the type of easement claimed, give notice to the owner that an easement is being claimed. Thus driving or walking across another's land, whenever headed in that direction, is sufficient to establish a prescriptive easement, even though this is not done every day.

1) **Seasonal use:** [§1368] Grazing cattle on another's land during the grazing season every year establishes sufficient continuity, even

though the season is only a few months long. Similarly, hunting or fishing rights can be acquired by prescription although there are long intervals between use. The difficult thing in hunting and grazing cases is to distinguish between seasonal use with a claim of right to continue it season after season and, on the other hand, sporadic or occasional trespasses. The latter do not give rise to a prescriptive easement.

a) **Easement in gross:** [§1369]   It is possible to acquire a prescriptive easement in gross. For example, if a hunting club hunts on land of another every hunting season, the club members may acquire a prescriptive easement.

2) **Occasional trespasses:** [§1370]   Sporadic and occasional trespasses are not enough to establish a continuous use. For example, if A's house is located close to O's property line, and A walks on O's property occasionally to paint A's house or to put up and remove storm windows, these are occasional trespasses insufficient to establish continuity. They do not give notice to O that A is claiming a right to do these things. [Romans v. Nadler, 14 N.W.2d 482 (Minn. 1944)]

3) **Tacking:** [§1371]   Tacking is allowed in prescription, just as it is allowed in adverse possession. One prescriptive user can tack on to his period of use the prescriptive use of a predecessor in interest. Transfer of the dominant tenement establishes the necessary privity if the grantor intends to transfer with it the use-which-is-ripening-into-an-easement.

(d) **Uninterrupted use:** [§1372]   If the adverse use is interrupted by the owner of the land being used, the prescriptive period ends. If the adverse use begins again after interruption, a new prescriptive period begins. The central question is: What constitutes an interruption? In adverse possession the owner can interrupt the adverse possession only by entry upon the land or by bringing a lawsuit. But in prescription, there is some authority in jurisdictions following the fiction of the lost grant (*see supra*, §1359) that the owner can interrupt adverse use by merely protesting the use (*e.g.*, mailing a letter to the user). This authority assumes that the fiction of the lost grant is rebutted when the owner says, "I do not grant you an easement; stop using my property." [Dartnell v. Bidwell, 98 A. 743 (Me. 1916)] In jurisdictions rejecting the fiction of the lost grant, the owner must effectively interrupt the adverse use. A sign or oral protest will not suffice.

(3) **When prescriptive rights cannot be acquired**

(a) **Negative easements:** [§1373]   In the United States, negative easements (for light and air, support, drainage) *cannot* arise by prescription. The reason is that prescription bars a *cause of action*, and where the owner has no cause of action, prescription does not apply.

1) **Example:** In 1960, A builds a house four inches from her property line adjoining B's land. A's windows overlook B's land. In 1984, B proposes to erect a building on B's side of the property line, six inches away from A's windows. Although B's building will block A's light and air, A does not have a prescriptive negative easement for light and air over B's land and cannot stop B from building. *Rationale:* Since between 1960 and 1984 B did not have a cause of action against A (to force A to close up her windows), B had no cause of action on which the statute of limitations has run. It would be unfair to give A a prescriptive right that B could not prevent from arising. [Parker & Edgarton v. Foote, 19 Wend. 309 (N.Y. 1838)]

(b) **Easement by necessity:** [§1374]   The use of an easement by necessity *cannot* give rise to a prescriptive easement. This is because the use of an easement by necessity is by right and not wrongful. However, when the necessity ends, the easement by necessity also ends. At the time the necessity ends further use of the easement becomes adverse and can give rise to a prescriptive right if continued thereafter for the prescriptive period.

(c) **Public lands:** [§1375]   Generally prescriptive rights, like adverse possession, *cannot* be obtained in public lands.

(4) **Public easements:** [§1376]   In most jurisdictions, the public at large can acquire a public easement in private land by prescription if members of the public use the private land in a manner meeting the requirements for prescription. If the public uses land for a roadway, the presumption is that the use is adverse (under a claim of right), just as it is for an individual claim of easement. [Svoboda v. Johnson, 281 N.W.2d 892 (Neb. 1979)] On the other hand, if the public uses vacant, undeveloped land, the presumption is that the use is permissive. It is deemed not to give notice to the owner of a claim of right. Therefore, except for a public road, it is difficult to acquire a public easement by prescription. [*But see* Gion v. City of Santa Cruz, 2 Cal. 3d 29 (1970)—no presumption of permissive use of unimproved land]

(a) **Minority view:** [§1377]   In some states, the general public *cannot* acquire prescriptive rights in private property. *Rationale:* The owner's cause of action runs against the specific trespassing individuals and not against the public at large. Therefore the statute of limitations only bars the owner from suing the individuals who trespassed. [Haman v. Fox, 594 P.2d 1093 (Idaho 1979)]

(b) **Customary rights:** [§1378]   In Florida, Hawaii, and Oregon, courts have revived the medieval doctrine of customary rights in beaches. If the public has used the beach (the dry sand area in private ownership) for so long that "the memory of many runneth not to the contrary," the public has a customary right to use the beaches. [State *ex rel.* Thornton v. Hay, 462 P.2d 671 (Or. 1969)]

3. **Scope of Easements:** [§1379]   After an easement is created, questions may arise about what use the easement owner can make of the easement or about what interference by the servient owner is permissible. These questions are treated as questions of the scope of the easement.

   a. **General rule:** [§1380]   The scope of an easement depends upon the intention of the parties. In ascertaining this intent, a court may examine whether the easement was created expressly or by prescription, what changes in use might reasonably be foreseeable by the parties, and what changes in use are required to achieve the purpose of the easement under modern conditions and preserve the usefulness of the easement to the dominant tenement. The court will also look at whether the increase in the burden is unreasonable. [Farnes v. Lane, 161 N.W.2d 297 (Minn. 1968)]

   b. **How easement was created**

      (1) **Express easement:** [§1381]   If the easement was *expressly* created, the court will look at the language of the instrument, together with the surrounding circumstances, in order to determine the parties' intent.

         (a) **Easement of way:** [§1382]   An easement of way is a favorite of the law because surface access is essential to the use and productivity of land. An easement of way is given a scope that permits it to meet the needs of the dominant tenement as it normally develops. It may be used in ways reasonably foreseeable by the parties or, if not foreseeable, by ordinary means of transportation as those means normally evolve. There is a strong public policy that land have access necessary to make it useful under contemporary conditions.

            1) **Example:** In 1876, O grants A a right of way over Blackacre to reach Whiteacre, which is used for a slaughterhouse. Animals are brought in by cart, slaughtered, and animal products removed by cart. After thirty-five years, the slaughterhouse burns, and Whiteacre is used for farming. Farm machinery is moved in and out over the easement. Whiteacre is then sold for commercial use. Modern vehicles can use the easement to reach Whiteacre. The easement is not limited to the modes of transportation (horse and cart) in use in 1876. Nor is the easement limited to vehicles reaching land used only for a slaughterhouse or for a farm. If the use of the dominant tenement changes to commercial use, trucks may use the easement. The purpose of the easement is to gain access to the dominant tenement, however it is used. [Cameron v. Barton, 272 S.W.2d 40 (Ky. 1954)]

            2) **Adding utilities:** [§1383]   The owner of an easement of way may desire to install electric poles and wires on the easement, so as to bring electricity to the dominant tenement. The courts are split on whether installation of electric poles and wires comes within the purpose of the

easement. [Kelly v. Schmelz, 439 S.W.2d 211 (Mo. 1969)—permitting installation of poles; Ward v. McGlory, 265 N.E.2d 78 (Mass. 1970)—denying right to install poles]

(b) **Other easements:** [§1384]   The scope of easements that are not easements of way may be more strictly limited by the courts to the use in existence at the time the easement was created. For example, suppose that O grants A an easement for a ditch to convey water to A's land. At the time of the grant the ditch is open and earthen. Several years later, A wants to concrete the ditch to reduce loss of water through seepage. A cannot do this because this change would damage O's land by reducing the water seeping through the soil and nourishing O's trees on the ditch bank. [Krieger v. Pacific Gas & Electric Co., 119 Cal. App. 3d 137 (1981); *but compare* Big Cottonwood Tanner Ditch Co. v. Moyle, 174 P.2d 148 (Utah 1946)—state policy of water conservation justified concreting]

(2) Implied easements

(a) **Existing use:** [§1385]   If an easement is implied on the basis of a use existing at the time of severance of a tract into two parcels, which the parties intended to continue, the scope is generally the same as an express easement. Changes that reasonably might have been expected or that are necessary to preserve the utility of the easement are permitted.

(b) **Easement by necessity:** [§1386]   In case of an easement by necessity, the extent of necessity determines the scope. Since an easement by necessity is imposed as a matter of public policy, courts are reluctant to expand the scope beyond what is strictly necessary.

(3) **Easements by prescription:** [§1387]   It is more difficult to increase the burden of an easement by prescription than any other kind of easement. The uses that give rise to the easement can continue, but there is no basis for assuming the parties intended the easement to accommodate future needs. After all, the owner of the servient land (O) might not have objected to A crossing O's land to pick apples on A's land which use gave rise to the prescriptive easement, but the owner would have objected to a whole stream of traffic generated by a subdivision on A's land. Thus if a prescriptive easement is acquired by use to reach a house, and the use of the dominant tenement is changed from residential to commercial, the added burden of traffic probably will not be permitted on the prescriptive easement. [S.S. Kresge Co. v. Winkelman Realty Co., 50 N.W.2d 920 (Wis. 1952); Cushman v. Davis, 80 Cal. App. 3d 731 (1978); *but compare* Glenn v. Poole, 423 N.E.2d 1030 (Mass. 1981)—prescriptive easement acquired to haul wood and gravel and to reach land for truck storage could continue to be used when dominant land was used for garage and repair shop and increase in burden was moderate]

c. **Subdivision of dominant tenement:** [§1388]   As a general rule, if the dominant estate is subdivided, each subdivided lot has a right to use easements appurtenant to the dominant estate. An easement is appurtenant to every part of the dominant tenement. However, there is an important limitation on use of an easement by sub-divided lots: The servient estate is not to be burdened to a greater extent than was contemplated at the time the easement was created. Obviously it is a question of judgment, weighing all the circumstances, as to when the increase in burden be-comes unreasonable. Use by four subdivided lots may be permitted but use by forty lots may be viewed as excessive. [Bang v. Forman, 222 N.W. 96 (1928)—subdivid-ing three lots into twenty-six lots creates unreasonable burden; Cushman Virginia Corp. v. Barnes, 129 S.E.2d 633 (Va. 1963)—subdividing 126-acre tract not un-reasonable burden; Cox v. Glenbrook Co., 371 P.2d 647 (Nev. 1962)—subdividing into forty to sixty lots may constitute unreasonable burden, but court refuses to declare in advance]

d. **Use for benefit of nondominant land:** [§1389]   An easement granted for the bene-fit of lot 1 cannot be used for the benefit of lot 2, even though the same person owns lots 1 and 2. The dominant owner cannot increase the scope of the easement by using it to benefit a nondominant tenement. [S.S. Kresge Co. v. Winkelman Realty Co., *supra*; Kanefsky v. Dratch Construction Co., 101 A.2d 923 (Pa. 1954)]

(1) **Example:** O, owner of Whiteacre, grants to A an easement of way over Whi-teacre for the benefit of Blackacre, which A owns. Subsequently A buys Greenacre, adjacent to Blackacre, and erects a building on Greenacre and Blackacre. Access to this building is across the easement on Whiteacre. O can enjoin A, preventing the use of the easement to provide access to the portion of the building on Greenacre. [Penn Bowling Recreation Center, Inc. v. Hot Shoppes, Inc., 179 F.2d 64 (D.C. Cir. 1949)] If it is impossible for an injunc-tion to be effective in preventing the use of the easement for access to Green-acre, the easement will be extinguished entirely. A will pay the penalty of for-feiture if A extends the easement to other land in such a way that use for the dominant tenement only cannot be effectively policed. [Crimmins v. Gould, 149 Cal. App. 2d 383 (1957)]

e. **Change in location of easement:** [§1390]   If an easement has been granted in a specific location, or has been located by mutual agreement of the parties, the loca-tion cannot thereafter be changed by one party acting unilaterally. The location can be changed only by mutual consent.

(1) **Example:** O, owner of Whiteacre, grants A an easement of way in a specific location on Whiteacre. Subsequently O wants to erect a building in this loca-tion and move the easement to another location on Whiteacre, which would be just as convenient to A. O cannot move the location of the easement without A's consent. [Sakansky v. Wein, 169 A.1 (N.H. 1933)]

(2) **Widening of easement:** [§1391]   If the width of an easement is specified in the grant, or if it existed at the time of the grant so that it can be inferred that the parties intended it to remain the same width, the easement cannot be widened without the consent of the servient owner.

f. **Use by servient owner:** [§1392] The servient owner has the right to use the servient land in ways that do not unreasonably interfere with the easement. The servient owner may erect a structure over an easement of way, provided enough headroom is provided for the passage of vehicles below. Similarly, the owner of the servient land may use the easement itself, provided it is not an exclusive easement and the use does not unreasonably interfere with the rights of the owner of the easement. [Alban v. R.K. Co., 239 N.E.2d 22 (Ohio 1968)]

  (1) **Example:** O grants to a water company an easement to lay water pipes across O's land. O can grant similar rights to others for the same purpose, provided these subsequent rights do not interfere with the rights of the water company. [City of Pasadena v. California-Michigan Land & Water Co., 17 Cal. 2d 576 (1941)]

g. **Easements in gross:** [§1393] Easements in gross present special problems about excessive use, since the use is not limited by the needs of a dominant tenement.

  (1) **Nonexclusive use:** [§1394] If an easement in gross is nonexclusive (*i.e.*, it is enjoyed both by the beneficiary and the servient owner), it cannot be "apportioned." Absent authority in the grant, the owner of the easement cannot convey to others the right to share in its use, for that would constitute competition with the servient owner for the sale of easement rights, not contemplated by the grant.

  (2) **Exclusive use:** [§1395] If the easement in gross is exclusive, *i.e.*, the beneficiary has the exclusive right to enjoy the easement, the easement can be apportioned or divided by its owner. The owner of the easement can grant the right to others to share the easement, if the original grant does not provide to the contrary. [Jolliff v. Hardin Cable Television Co., 269 N.E.2d 588 (Ohio 1971)] However, if the easement in gross is assigned to two or more persons, who can use the easement independently of each other, the resulting use may greatly burden the servient land. To prevent this, courts have applied to easements in gross the "one stock" rule, originally invented to prevent the over-use of profits in gross (below). The one stock rule is: When two or more persons own an easement in gross, they must use the easement as one stock. Neither can operate independently of the other. One owner can veto use by the other because consent of all is required.

    (a) **Example:** O grants A and his heirs the exclusive right to boat and bathe in O's lake. A assigns the right to B and C. B and C must use the easement as "one stock," both agreeing on the amount of use. [Miller v. Lutheran Conference & Camp Association, 200 A. 646 (Pa. 1938)]

h. **Profits in gross—the "one stock" rule:** [§1396] Almost all profits are held in gross; they are not appurtenant to land. A usual profit is the right to take timber, minerals, or sand on O's land. Suppose that A has the right to take sand from Blackacre. If A desires, A can extract all the sand now, but A will not do so because what A extracts and sells today A cannot extract and sell tomorrow. If A were to sell the sand today, A would bear the loss if prices rose tomorrow. A will set an optimum rate of extraction based upon the present price of sand relative to its expected future price. If A assigns the right to dig sand to B and C, B and C must act as "one stock" in extracting sand and not as independent owners. B and C both must agree on the rate of extraction. Why? Without this rule, B and C would have an economic incentive to take as much sand as fast as possible, before the other took it. If B took all the sand today, the cost of having no sand tomorrow would be borne by B and C and not by B alone. If B and C must act as a single owner, agreeing on the rate of extraction, they will set a rate of extraction that takes into consideration future demand and prices. The "one stock" rule thus inhibits consuming natural resources without regard to future needs.

4. Transfer of Easements

a. **Easement appurtenant:** [§1397]   When the dominant tenement is transferred, any easements appurtenant are transferred with it. Similarly, the burden of an easement appurtenant passes with the servient land when transferred. An easement appurtenant is thought of as "attached" to the dominant land, and it benefits the possessor of that land, including an adverse possessor. Of course, the owners of the servient and dominant tenements may make a contrary agreement if they wish. By mutual consent, they can "detach" the easement and either "attach" it to other dominant land or convert it into an easement in gross, but neither party acting alone can do this.

b. **Easements in gross:** [§1398]   Easements in gross may present special problems regarding transferability. If the benefit of an easement in gross is inherited by or assigned to a large number of persons, it may be difficult to locate these persons (or their heirs upon their deaths), making it difficult to secure a release of the easement or to clear up title. (Compare an easement appurtenant, where the dominant owner is always known and available to bargain with.) With this danger in mind, courts have sometimes restricted the transfer of the benefit of an easement in gross.

(1) **Easement not assignable:** [§1399]   In some old cases, courts held that the benefit of easements in gross was neither assignable nor inheritable. [Stockdale v. Yerden, 190 N.W. 225 (Mich. 1922)—right to pass over lands of another not assignable] It is probable that in most jurisdictions this rule is no longer followed, at least with respect to commercial easements and maybe with respect to all easements in gross. [Johnston v. Michigan Consolidated Gas Co., 60 N.W.2d 464 (Mich. 1953)—easement to install pipelines assignable]

(2) **Commercial easements in gross assignable:** [§1400]   Sections 489 through 492 of the Restatement of Property (1944) say that the benefit of a commercial easement in gross is assignable, and a noncommercial easement in gross is assignable if the parties so intend. Commercial easements in gross are those that have primarily *economic benefit* rather than personal satisfaction. The large majority of easements in gross are of this kind: railroad rights-of-way, gas pipe lines, utility easements. *Rationale:* It would be unacceptable public

policy for a transportation or utility company to lose its easements when it merged with another company. Moreover, the problem of locating multiple unknown owners does not arise with most commercial easements in gross, which are held by utility companies or railroads. Finally, if commercial easements in gross are not assignable, utility companies will buy a fee simple for their lines, rather than easement; this is undesirable because a fee simple, unlike an easement, cannot be terminated by abandonment or by acts of the owner. [Geffine v. Thompson, 62 N.E.2d 590 (Ohio 1945)]

(3) **All easements assignable:** [§1401]   In some jurisdictions, all easements in gross may be assignable, but very little litigation on the question of assignability of noncommercial easements in gross has arisen.

c.   **Profits in gross:** [§1402]   Profits in gross (*e.g.*, the right to take timber or minerals) have always been assignable. Inasmuch as profits in gross could give rise to the same problem of multiple and unknown owners, it is odd that courts put more restrictive rules on easements. Perhaps the fact that assignability of profits has resulted in no serious problems is an argument for holding all easements in gross assignable.

5.   **Termination of Easements:** [§1403]   An easement may be terminated in any of the ways provided below.

a.   **By unity of title:** [§1404]   An easement is a right in the land of **another**. If the title to the easement and title to the servient tenement come into the hands of one person, the easement is extinguished. This usually happens when one person buys the dominant tenement and the servient tenement. Once the easement is extinguished, it is **not revived** by subsequent separation of the tenements into two ownerships. [Witt v. Reavis, 587 P.2d 1005 (Or. 1978)]

(1) **Example:** O, owner of Blackacre, conveys an easement over Blackacre to A, owner of Whiteacre. Subsequently B buys both Blackacre and Whiteacre. The easement is extinguished. If B then sells Blackacre to C, the easement is not revived. A new easement may, however, be created expressly or by implication.

b.   **By act of dominant owner**

(1) **Written release:** [§1405]   The owner of an easement may release the easement to the servient owner by a written instrument.

(2) **Oral release:** [§1406]   An easement is an interest in land, and because of the Statute of Frauds, it cannot be conveyed by merely an oral release from the dominant owner to the servient owner. However, if the oral agreement is accompanied by an **act** showing intent to abandon, the easement may be extinguished by abandonment (*see infra*, §1410).

(a) **Estoppel:** [§1407]   If the owner of an easement orally releases it to the servient owner, and the servient owner **expends money in reliance** on the oral release (such as erecting a building on the easement), the easement owner is estopped to plead the Statute of Frauds. The easement is extinguished by the oral release and action in reliance.

(3) **Nonuse:** [§1408]   Mere nonuse of an easement, like nonuse of a fee simple, does **not** extinguish the easement. A power company, for example, which has an easement for electric lines across Blackacre, does not lose the easement merely because the lines are not built. The easement is not extinguished no matter how long the nonuse continues. [Lindsey v. Clark, 69 S.E.2d 342 (Va. 1952)]

   (a) **Clog on title:** [§1409]   An old, unused easement may be a clog on transferring title to the servient estate. It is not discoverable by inspecting the land, and may be discoverable only by searching the land records back many, many years.

(4) **Abandonment:** [§1410]   Although neither oral release nor nonuse alone is sufficient to terminate an easement, if the owner of an easement **acts** in such a way as to indicate a **clear intent** to abandon the easement, the easement is abandoned. Such acts can include an oral release or nonuse coupled with failure to maintain the easement or permitting the easement to be blocked by others or establishing a substitute easement elsewhere. [Flanagan v. San Marcos Silk Co., 106 Cal. App. 2d 458 (1951); Hatcher v. Chesner, 221 A.2d 305 (Pa. 1966)]

   (a) **Example:** A, owner of Blackacre, has an easement to use a common driveway located half on adjacent Whiteacre. A builds a barn on the part of the driveway located on Blackacre, which makes further use of the driveway impossible. The easement is abandoned. [Carr v. Bartell, 9 N.W.2d 556 (Mich. 1943)]

   (b) **Rationale:** A fee simple cannot be abandoned. Why can an easement be abandoned? The abandonment of an easement removes an encumbrance on title and makes land more marketable. The doctrine of abandonment to some extent compromises the Statute of Frauds, but it furthers marketability.

(5) **Alteration of dominant tenement:** [§1411]   If an easement is granted for a particular purpose, and an alteration of the dominant tenement makes it impossible to achieve the purpose any longer, the easement is extinguished.

   (a) **Example:** O, owner of Blackacre, grants to A, owner of the adjacent lot, an easement of view from the windows of A's present house across Blackacre to Main Street (on the other side of Blackacre). A subsequently moves her house to the rear of her lot, where it has no view of Main Street from any of its windows. The easement is extinguished. [Hopkins the Florist, Inc. v. Fleming, 26 A.2d 96 (Vt. 1942)]

(b) **Particular purpose:** [§1412] Whether an easement is limited to a particular purpose may, in any individual case, be debatable. However, courts are reluctant to construe an easement to be limited for a particular purpose when this is not clearly and unequivocally stated. An easement for light and air "for the windows of A's dwelling," for example, is usually construed to be for the benefit of A's ***building***. "Dwelling" describes A's present use, but does not limit the purpose of the easement, and the easement is not extinguished if A uses the building for something other than a dwelling. [First National Trust & Savings Bank v. Raphael, 113 S.E.2d 683 (Va. 1960)]

(6) **Easement by necessity:** [§1413] An easement by necessity terminates when the necessity ends. Since an easement of surface access by necessity is imposed on the servient estate as a matter of public policy (in order to make land usable), it is deemed fair to extinguish the easement when the dominant owner acquires another way out of the landlocked lot. If the dominant owner acquires other access by conveyance or prescription, the easement by necessity is extingished. (*See supra*, §1357.)

(7) **Excessive use:** [§1414] As a general rule, excessive use or misuse of an easement does ***not*** extinguish an easement. The remedy against excessive use is an injunction forbidding improper use. [Wetmore v. Ladies of Loretto, 220 N.E.2d 491 (Ill. 1966)] However, when it becomes impossible or impractical to police the excessive use, the easement may be extinguished by a court. (*See supra*, §1389.)

c. **By act of servient owner**

(1) **Destruction of servient tenement:** [§1415] An easement in a structure (*e.g.*, a right to use a stairway) is terminated if the building is destroyed without fault of the owner of the servient estate (*e.g.*, by fire or act of God). If the building is destroyed by the ***intentional*** act of the servient owner, the easement is not extinguished. The servient owner is liable in damages to the owner of the easement, and a court may require the servient owner to create in any new building a stairway for the use of the dominant owner. [Rothschild v. Wolf, 20 Cal. 2d 17 (1942)] One state holds an easement can be destroyed by the intentional destruction of the building by the servient owner. [Union National Bank of Lowell v. Nesmith, 130 N.E. 251 (Mass. 1921)]

(2) **Prescription:** [§1416] If the servient owner interferes with an easement in an adverse manner (*e.g.*, by erecting a fence across a roadway), the servient owner can extinguish the easement by prescription. The requisite elements of adversity are the same as for the creation of an easement by prescription.

d. **By change of conditions:** [§1417] The doctrine of change of conditions in the neighborhood, which may prevent the enforcement of a real covenant or equitable servitude (*see infra*, §1529) is ***not*** applicable to easements. [Waldrop v. Town of Brevard, 62 S.E.2d 512 (N.C. 1950)]

B. REAL COVENANTS

1. Introduction

a. **What covenants are about:** [§1418]   A covenant is a *promise* to do or not to do a certain thing. The covenants considered in this chapter are promises relating to the *use* of land. Typically they are promises to do something on land (*e.g.*, a promise to maintain a fence) or a promise not to do something on land (*e.g.*, a promise not to erect a commercial building). The promise to do something is an *affirmative promise*. The promise not to do something is a *negative promise*. If the promisee sues the promisor for breach, the law of contracts is applicable. If, however, a person who buys *the promisee's land* is suing or a person who buys *the promissor's land* is being sued, then the law of property, as set forth in the rest of this chapter, is applicable. These property rules determine when a successor owner can sue or be sued on an agreement to which he was not a party.

b. **Remedies for breach:** [§1419]   If the promise is breached, the promisee or his successor may want one of two things: (i) money damages, or (ii) an injunction or decree requiring specific performance of the promise. If the promisee wants money damages, he must sue *in law*. If the promisee wants an injunction or specific performance, he must sue *in equity*. In England (and still in a few states in this country), law and equity are separate courts. In most American jurisdictions, law and equity have been merged into one court. Nonetheless, even with one court, the plaintiff must ask for legal relief (money damages) or equitable relief (injunction or specific performance). If the plaintiff asks for money damages, the rules developed by the old law courts are applicable. If the plaintiff asks for equitable relief, the rules developed by the equity courts are applicable.

c. **Real covenant defined:** [§1420]   A real covenant is a covenant that runs with the land *at law*, so that, generally speaking, each person who owns the land subsequently is entitled to enforce or is burdened by the covenant. A real covenant is one that is enforceable at law by a successor owner of the promisee's land and, concomitantly, is enforceable against a successor to the promisor's land. If the plaintiff wants money damages, the plaintiff must show that the covenant qualifies as a real covenant. The plaintiff must satisfy the requirements for the covenant to run at law.

(1) **Personal liability only:** [§1421]   A real covenant gives rise to personal liability only. It is enforceable only by an award of money damages, which is collectible out of the general assets of the defendant.

(a) **Example:** O conveys Blackacre to A, and A promises for herself, her heirs and assigns not to erect a slaughterhouse on Blackacre. The covenant is for the benefit of adjacent Whiteacre, owned by O. The deed is recorded, giving notice to subsequent purchasers. A sells Blackacre to B. B erects a slaughterhouse. O decides to enforce the promise as a real covenant. O is entitled to money damages from B in the amount that Whiteacre is devalued by having a slaughterhouse next door. (This promise can also be enforced as an equitable servitude in equity. Equity will enjoin B, prohibiting erection of the slaughterhouse, if O sues for an injunction before the slaughterhouse is erected.)

d. **Historical background:** [§1422]   At early English law, the only person who could sue to enforce a promise was the promisee, and the only person who was liable on the promise was the promisor. English judges found these restrictions unsatisfactory as applied to landlords and tenants. Suppose that L leased land to T, and that L promised to repair the premises and that T promised to pay rent. Subsequently L transferred his interest to L1. Under the old rule L1 was not obligated to repair. Similarly, if T transferred his leasehold to T1, T1 was not obligated to pay rent. To remedy this situation, the law courts invented the "real covenant." They said the promise to pay rent attached itself to T's leasehold (the realty, hence real covenant), and ran with the leasehold to T1. T1 was thus liable for rent. Similarly, L's promise to repair attached itself to L's reversion and ran with the reversion to L1. The new landlord was thus liable on the promise to repair. The English courts never extended the concept of the real covenant outside of the landlord-tenant context. American courts, however, extended it to promises between fee simple owners or neighbors. The real covenant considered in this chapter is a promise made by a fee simple owner. (For covenants running in leases, *see supra*, §§991 *et seq.*)

(1) **Runs with estate in land:** [§1423]   From the above historical development, it should be clear that the real covenant is conceptualized as being attached to the *estate* in land (originally the tenant's leasehold). The burden passes to anyone who takes that estate. Although a covenant is said to "run with the land," in fact the covenant runs with an estate in land. This distinction becomes important where the exact estate is not conveyed to the new possessor. For example, suppose that O, owning a fee simple, promises A that O will erect a wall on O's land. Subsequently O dies before erecting the wall. O devises her land to B for life, remainder to C. B is not liable at law on the promise because B has not succeeded to the estate (fee simple) owned by O. (*See infra*, §1453.)

e. **Distinguished from other interests**

(1) **Equitable servitude:** [§1424]   An equitable servitude is a covenant enforceable *in equity* by or against successors to the land of the original parties to the contract. Hence, if the plaintiff wants equitable relief (injunction or specific performance), the plaintiff must show that the covenant qualifies as an equitable servitude. Different rules may be applicable to the enforcement of covenants in equity than are applicable in law. (Equitable servitudes are discussed *infra*, §§1461 *et seq.*)

(2) **Easement:** [§1425]   A covenant is a *promise* respecting the use of land; an easement is a *grant* of an interest in land. An affirmative easement gives someone the right to go on another's land, which a covenant never does. On the other hand, a negative easement (*e.g.*, right to light and air) resembles a promise not to do something (*e.g.*, a promise not to block light and air). Inasmuch as English courts limited negative easements to four types existing at early law (*see*

supra, §1306), negative promises that are not one of the four permitted types of negative easements are given effect as real covenants or equitable servitudes. (In England, which does not recognize real covenants between fee owners, negative promises are enforceable only as equitable servitudes.)

(3) **Condition:** [§1426]   Land use may be controlled by a condition as well as by a covenant. A condition provides for *forfeiture* upon breach of the condition, whereas a covenant is enforceable only by an award of money damages (real covenant) or an injunction (equitable servitude). A condition is imposed when the grantor conveys a *fee simple determinable* or a *fee simple subject to condition subsequent* (*see supra*, §§318, 326).

(a) **Ambiguous language:** [§1427]   A deed may be ambiguous, with some language pointing to a covenant and other language suggesting that a condition is imposed. If the deed is ambiguous, courts ordinarily construe against a forfeiture and hence in favor of a covenant. [W.F. White Land Co. v. Christenson, 14 S.W.2d 369 (Tex. 1928)]

f.   **Benefit and burden explained:** [§1428]   In the law of easements, one parcel is the servient or burdened tenement, another parcel the dominant or benefited tenement. If the easement does not benefit land, the benefit is said to be in gross. Similar distinctions are made in the law of covenants, but we do not talk of servient and dominant tenements. We talk of burden and benefit. One tract is burdened for the benefit of another tract. If the benefit does not touch and concern land, the benefit is in gross. However, unlike an easement, which cannot impose a burden in gross (a servient tenement is always required), the burden of a covenant can be in gross.

(1) **Example:** Cable TV Co. has the benefit of an easement in gross across Blackacre. Cable promises the owner of Blackacre to maintain and repair the cable lines. Blackacre has the benefit of a covenant; the burden of Cable to perform the promise is in gross.

2.   **Creation**

a.   **Writing required:** [§1429]   At common law a real covenant had to be in writing and under seal. The requirement of a seal has been abrogated, but a writing is still required. Note that a real covenant will not be implied, nor can it arise by prescription.

b.   **Grantee bound without signing:** [§1430]   Most deeds are signed only by the grantor. Such a deed is known as a deed poll. By accepting a deed poll, the grantee is bound by any covenants in the deed to be performed by the grantee.

3.   **Enforcement By or Against Assignees:** [§1431]   The major issue involving real covenants is whether the covenant can be enforced by a successor to the promisee or against a successor to the promisor. This issue is often framed in terms of whether the benefit or the burden will run to assignees. There are two ends of every covenant: the

burden end and the benefit end. The requirements for the burden to run to assignees are more exacting than for the benefit to run. For reasons to be mentioned later, the law deems it more objectionable for burdens to run than for benefits to do so.

a. **Requirements for burden to run at law:** [§1432]   The requirements for the burden to run are:

(1) **Intent:** [§1433]   The contracting parties must intend that successors to the promisor be bound by the covenant. This is usually indicated by language binding the promisor's "heirs and assigns." (*See infra*, §§1442-1443.)

(2) **Privity of estate:** [§1434]   A majority of courts are said to require privity of estate (meaning a grantor-grantee relationship) between the original promisor and promisee, as well as privity of estate (meaning succession to the *estate* of the promisor) between the promisor and his assignee. (*See infra*, §§1444 *et seq.*)

(3) **Touch and concern:** [§1435]   The covenant must touch and concern the burdened land. In a majority of states, the covenant must touch and concern the benefited land as well; the burden will not run if the benefit is in gross. (*See infra*, §1456.)

(4) **Notice:** [§1436]   A subsequent purchaser of the promisor's land is not bound by the burden unless he has notice of the covenant before buying. (*See infra*, §1457.)

(5) **Example:** O, owner of Blackacre and Whiteacre, sells Whiteacre to A. In the deed A promises for herself, her heirs and assigns to use Whiteacre only for residential purposes. Blackacre is benefited thereby, and Whiteacre burdened. The deed is recorded, giving constructive notice to all subsequent purchasers of Whiteacre. A sells Whiteacre to B, who erects an auto service station on the parcel. B is liable for damages to O because: (i) the parties intended to bind assigns, (ii) O and A were in a grantor-grantee relationship, and A assigned his estate to B, (iii) the covenant relates to the use of Whiteacre and benefits Blackacre, thereby touching and concerning both parcels, and (iv) B had notice from the recorded deed from O to A.

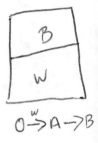

b. **Requirements for benefit to run at law:** [§1437]   The requirements for the benefit to run are:

(1) **Intent:** [§1438]   The contracting parties must intend that the benefit run to successors of the promisee. (*See infra*, §1442.)

(2) **Privity of estate:** [§1439]   Restatement of Property section 548, in accordance with most authority, states that horizontal privity of estate between the contracting parties is not required for the benefit to run. However, vertical privity (meaning being a successor in interest of the promisee) is required. (*See infra*, §§1444 *et seq.*)

(3) **Touch and concern:** [§1440]   The benefit must touch and concern land owned by the promisee. (*See infra*, §1456.)

(4) **Compare—burden:** [§1441]   There are three principal differences in the requirements for the running of the burden and the benefit: (i) the benefit will run without horizontal privity of estate, required for the burden to run; (ii) the meaning of vertical privity may differ depending upon whether the burden or benefit is alleged to run; and (iii) the benefit will run if the burden is in gross, whereas in most states the burden will not run if the benefit is in gross (*see infra*, §1497).

c. **Intention of the parties:** [§1442]   The intention of the parties that the burden and benefit run is usually found in the language of a deed or contract. The instrument may read "these covenants shall run with the land," or "the grantee promises for herself, her heirs and assigns." If the instrument is unclear, the court will look at the purpose of the covenant and all the circumstances to ascertain the parties' probable intent.

(1) **Necessity of word "assigns":** [§1443]   In *Spencer's Case*, 77 Eng. Rep. 72 (1583), the court laid down three requirements for the burden of a covenant to run at law. The first pertained to the intention to bind assigns: If the covenant concerns a *thing that is not in being* at the time the covenant is made but is to be built or created thereafter, the burden of the covenant will not bind assigns unless they are *expressly mentioned*. For example, if A promises B that A will build a wall, A's assignee is not bound unless A promises on behalf of herself *and her assigns*. This technical rule has been abolished in the large majority of states, which hold that intention is to be gathered from the whole instrument and not from the presence or absence of the word "assigns."

d. **Privity of estate:** [§1444]   In the analysis of privity of estate, it is necessary to keep separate two kinds of privity of estate: horizontal privity and vertical privity. *Horizontal privity of estate* refers to the relationship that exists between the original promisor and promisee. Early judges thought that for a covenant to run to successors, the original parties must be in a special relationship—though exactly what the relationship had to be was in dispute. *Vertical privity of estate* refers to succession by an assignee to the estate held by, or an interest created by, one of the original parties to the promise. Thus, if A, the owner of Blackacre, promises B, the owner of Whiteacre, that no commercial building will be erected on Blackacre, and A thereafter transfers an interest in Blackacre to C, the burden of the covenant will run to C if A and B are in *horizontal privity* and A and C are in *vertical privity*.

(1) **Horizontal privity—running of the burden:** [§1445]   For the *burden* of a covenant to run to assignees, the majority rule is that the original parties to the covenant must be in privity of estate. This requirement was laid down in *Spencer's Case, supra*. Privity of estate was not defined in that case, and later courts had to decided what the phrase meant. In *Spencer's Case*, the original parties were landlord and tenant, the covenant by the tenant to build a wall was in the lease, and the landlord was trying to enforce the covenant against the assignee

tenant. The court found on these facts that there was privity of estate. But which was the important fact that put the parties in privity of estate? It could be (i) that they were landlord and tenant, (ii) that they both had interests in the land, or (iii) that the promise was in a conveyance of a term of years.

(a) **English view:** [§1446]   In England it was ultimately decided that the parties to a promise are in privity of estate only if they are in a landlord and tenant relationship. [Keppell v. Bailey, 39 Eng. Rep. 1042 (1834)] The judges wanted to curtail restrictions on a fee simple, largely because England at the time had no recording system and covenants could not be discovered by a prospective purchaser from an inspection of the land. Hence, in England, the burden of a covenant runs at law only if it is contained in a lease; the burden of a covenant given by a fee owner does not run at law to assignees. A covenant by a fee owner is enforceable against assignees only in equity as an equitable servitude.

(b) **Mutual interest:** [§1447]   Massachusetts and a few other states took the position that what put the parties in privity of estate in *Spencer's Case* was the fact that the landlord and the tenant both have an interest in the property. Hence, applying this view of privity to a covenant by a fee owner, the burden will run if one party has an interest (apart from the covenant) in the land of the other. For example, if O divides Blackacre into two lots, and sells one lot to A, reserving an easement for the benefit of the other lot, a promise by A to maintain a fence along the lot line will be enforceable against A's successors. O and A both have interests in A's land: A owns the fee simple and O owns an easement. If O had not reserved the easement, the promise would not be enforceable against A's successors. In effect, then, for the burden of a covenant to run at law in Massachusetts, the covenant must be coupled with an easement. [Morse v. Aldrich, 36 Mass. 449 (1837)]

(c) **Successive relationship:** [§1448]   A third view of privity—perhaps the majority—is that the important fact in *Spencer's Case* was that the covenant was contained in a ***conveyance*** of an interest in land. Applying this view to a covenant by a fee owner, privity of estate is present where the promise is contained in a conveyance of the fee simple, that is, where one of the original parties to the promise succeeds to an estate previously owned by the other party. [Wheeler v. Shad, 7 Nev. 204 (1871)]

1) **Example:** O, a developer, conveys lot 1 to A. A promises not to use lot 1 for commercial purposes. A sells lot 1 to B. The burden of the covenant runs to B because the promise was in the deed from O to A. If A had made the promise to O in a separate instrument a week after the conveyance from O to A, the burden of the covenant would not run to B because O and A were not in privity of estate (a grantor-grantee relationship) when the promise was made.

2) **Malpractice trap:** Inasmuch as the large majority of covenants by fee owners are contained in deeds, this view of privity of estate greatly diminishes the importance of the privity requirement. Nonetheless, the privity requirement remains a malpractice trap for lawyers drafting covenants between neighbors. In the example immediately above, where A makes the promise a week after the conveyance, the lawyer should have O and A convey their lots to a straw person, who conveys A's lot back to A by a deed containing a promise to the grantor (the straw person), her heirs and assigns, for the benefit of the lot or lots formerly owned by O. Then the straw person conveys O's lot or lots back to O. In other words, put the parties in a grantor-grantee relationship, using a straw person, when the promise is made.

(d) **Restatement view:** [§1449] Restatement of Property section 534 says privity of estate is satisfied by either a mutual relationship or a successive relationship. In some cases both relationships will be present. If, for example, O conveys an easement over Blackacre to A, and in the conveyance A promises to fence the easement, there is privity in two senses: O and A are in a grantor-grantee relationship, and O and A both have interests in Blackacre. [Carlson v. Libby, 77 A.2d 332 (Conn. 1950)]

1) **Restatement policy:** The Restatement of Property sections dealing with covenants were very controversial. The Restatement objected to the **burden** of covenants running **at law**, and put as many technical roadblocks in the way as arguably could be supported by the cases. The Restatement had no policy objection to the benefit running at law or to burden and benefit running in equity. Why? The Restatement theory was that a judgment for damages—which could result in unlimited personal liability—was much more objectionable than an injunction or foreclosing a lien—which limited the defendant's liability to the value of the land. This theory is, of course, of very dubious soundness since in most cases a judgment for damages will result in a smaller loss to the defendant than would an injunction (*see infra*, §1470). Because an injunction is usually worth more to the plaintiff, it is the remedy usually sought.

2) **Criticism:** The outstanding authority on covenants, Judge Charles E. Clark, was highly critical of the Restatement. Clark thought that technical roadblocks to running, which applied to good and bad covenants alike, should be removed, and that the Restatement should focus on how to remove socially undesirable covenants. Clark wanted to shift the emphasis from technicalities to public policy. Clark argued that requiring horizontal privity was historically dubious, prevented many socially desirable covenants from running, and had been repudiated by many cases. He thought only vertical privity should be required. [Clark, Covenants and Interests Running with the Land 116-137 (1947)] A recent New York case agrees with Judge Clark and

says that the only privity of estate required for running of the burden is vertical privity. [Orange & Rockland Utilities, Inc. v. Philwold Estates, 52 N.Y.2d 253 (1981)]

(e) **Caveat:** [§1450]   It is not easy to say to what extent horizontal privity of estate is required in the various states. The cases are few, and the reasoning of the cases is often obscure. In a few states, the horizontal privity requirement has been abolished by statute. The horizontal privity requirement is rarely litigated today for two reasons: (i) covenants are usually contained in deeds, satisfying any alleged privity requirement; and (ii) plaintiffs almost always go into equity and seek an injunction rather than damages (for reasons given *infra* at §1470), and horizontal privity is not required in equity (*see infra*, §1472). Hence, although we operate on the assumption that horizontal privity is required at law, it is a very shaky assumption.

(2) **Horizontal privity—running of the benefit:** [§1451]   At common law, the *benefit* of a covenant could run without the covenanting parties being in privity of estate. [Pakenham's Case, Y.B. Hil. 42 Edw. 3, pl. 14 (1368)] What primarily motivated the courts was the desire to keep land free of burdens undiscoverable by a purchaser upon inspection of the land. A benefit did not adversely affect marketability. Restatement section 548 restates the common law view that horizontal privity is not required for running of the benefit, and this is the position taken by most modern cases. [165 Broadway Building, Inc. v. City Investing Co., 120 F.2d 813 (2d Cir. 1941); *but compare* Albright v. Fish, 394 A.2d 1117 (Vt. 1978)—privity necessary for running of benefit, but court found both horizontal and vertical privity existing on the facts]

(3) **Vertical privity—privity between a covenanting party and an assignee:** [§1452] For an assignee to sue on a covenant at law, the assignee must be in privity of estate with the original promisee. Likewise, for an assignee to be sued on a covenant, the assignee must be in privity of estate with the original promisor. Privity here means succession to the estate of one of the original parties. The covenant attaches to the estate and runs with that estate. Strictly speaking, it does not run with land but with an estate in land.

(a) **Running of the burden:** [§1453]   When the assignment of the burden is in issue, the Restatement maintains its hostility to burdens running at law. Section 535 draws support from a few old cases and states that privity of estate requires that the assignee succeed to the ***identical estate*** owned by the promisor: If the promisor had a fee simple, the covenant runs only to a person who succeeds to that fee simple. Hence, if A, the original promisor and owner of Blackacre in fee simple, devises Blackacre to B for life, remainder to C, the burden does not run to B at law. This definition of privity of estate is similar to the idea in landlord-tenant law that the landlord is in privity of estate only with assignees of the tenant who succeed to the whole term (*see supra*, §1239). Judge Clark was sharply critical of this Restatement position; he pointed out that an easement would not disappear if the servient land were transferred to B for life, and a covenant was analogous to an easement. "[T]he rule should be broad and untechnical. Wherever there is an assignment whereby the assignee *for any length of time*, no matter how limited, assumes in large measure legal relations with respect to the land which are similar to those which his grantor had, the necessary privity should be held to be supplied." [Clark, *supra*, p. 135] It is debatable whether modern courts would follow the Restatement or Judge Clark.

(b) **Running of the benefit:** [§1454] When the running of the benefit is in issue, Restatement section 542 says the benefit will run to assigns of the original estate or of a lesser estate, such as a life estate. The owner of the succeeding possessory estate can enforce the benefit at law. This is the meaning Judge Clark would assign to privity of estate when the running of the burden is at issue as well as when running of the benefit is at issue.

1) **Homeowner's association:** [§1455] A homeowner's association may sue to enforce the benefit of a covenant even though the homeowner's association succeeds to no land owned by the promisee. The homeowner's association is regarded as the agent of the real parties in interest who own the land. [Neponsit Property Owners Association v. Emigrant Industrial Savings Bank, 278 N.Y. 248 (1938)]

e. **Touch and concern:** [§1456] For the burden to run with the burdened land, the covenant must touch and concern the burdened land. Likewise, for the benefit to run with the benefited land, the covenant must touch and concern the benefited land. Inasmuch as this is a requirement in equity as well as in law, and as most of the cases involve equitable servitudes, this requirement is discussed in connection with equitable servitudes, *infra*, §§1461 *et seq.*

f. **Notice:** [§1457] A bona fide purchaser of the burdened land is not bound at law if he has no notice of the covenant. The same notice requirement is applicable to equitable servitudes, discussed *infra*, §§1461 *et seq.*

g. **Liability of original promisor after assignment:** [§1458] After the promisor assigns the land, does the promisor remain personally liable on the contract? The answer depends upon the type of promise made.

(1) **Promise to perform act:** [§1459] If the covenant is a promise to do or not to do some act on the burdened land, the covenantor has *no liability* after assignment. The covenantor has no control over the land after assignment, so it would be unfair to hold him liable for performance of the covenant by the assignee or subsequent assignees. With this type of covenant, the courts imply that the parties intended that the covenantor's liability cease with assignment.

(2) **Promise to pay money:** [§1460] If the covenant is a promise to pay money, the covenantor *may* be liable after assignment on the theory that his personal credit may have been important to the deal, or that his lack of control over the land does not prevent performance. However, it is doubtful that the parties

intend that covenantors in a subdivision or condominium intend to remain liable on a promise to pay for maintenance of common spaces after they have transferred the land, and it is probable that courts will not find them liable.

C. EQUITABLE SERVITUDES

1. Introduction

a. **Definition:** [§1461]   An equitable servitude is a covenant, whether running with the land at law or not, that **equity** will enforce against **assignees** of the burdened land who have **notice** of the covenant. The usual equitable remedy granted is an **injunction** against violation of the covenant.

b. **Historical development:** [§1462]   As noted above (*supra*, §1446), the law courts in England refused to permit a covenant by a fee simple owner to run with the land to an assignee. The main reason for this was that England had no recording system that would permit subsequent purchasers to discover what covenants were applicable to the land. It was deemed unfair to subject purchasers to such risks. On the other hand, the industrial revolution had demonstrated the need for enforceable running covenants. One tract of land might need to have power supplied by the owner of a neighboring tract and his successors. The owner of one tract might want to prevent economic loss by a factory or incompatible use locating next door. As urban land use intensified, it was seen that benefits could be gained from running covenants. In the middle of the nineteenth century, equity stepped in to resolve these conflicting considerations by holding that a covenant would be enforced in equity against a subsequent purchaser **with notice** of the covenant (thus obviating the main objection of the law courts).

(1) **Tulk v. Moxhay:** [§1463]   The famous case of *Tulk v. Moxhay*, 41 Eng. Rep. 1143 (1848), originated equitable servitudes. In this case, Tulk sold Leicester Square in London to Elms, who promised for himself, his heirs and assigns not to build on the Square. Elms conveyed the Square to Moxhay, who had notice of the covenant. Moxhay proposed to build on the Square, and Tulk sued for an injunction. The chancellor granted the injunction. The chancellor deemed it inequitable that a covenant should be unenforceable against a subsequent purchaser where the purchaser acquired the land with knowledge of the restriction. The purchaser, Moxhay, probably supposed himself bound by the covenant and probably paid less for the land than he would have had to pay for unburdened land. To hold the covenant unenforceable would give Moxhay an advantage he did not bargain for and would unjustly enrich him. From this acorn developed a new servitude known as an equitable servitude.

(2) **Theory of enforcement:** [§1464]   The theory underlying an equitable servitude was at one time disputed. Some early courts and scholars said that equity was merely granting specific performance of a contract against an assignee with notice. Ultimately, however, most courts shifted away from this theory. The right to specific enforcement of the contract (like equitable conversion,

infra, §1811) was deemed to give the promisee an interest in the land. When the promise was negative (not to do something), the right was thought of as an "equitable interest analogous to a negative easement." [Trustees of Columbia College v. Lynch, 70 N.Y. 440 (1877)] The Restatement and practically all the recent cases now take the view that an equitable servitude is an interest in land. As a consequence, the owner of the servitude—like the owner of an easement—is entitled to an injunction without being required to prove that damage to him will result from breach of the agreement.

c. **Equitable servitude compared with real covenant:** [§1465] The principle differences between an equitable servitude (enforceable in equity) and a real covenant (enforceable in law) are as follows:

(1) **Remedy:** [§1466] Different remedies are available for breach of an equitable servitude than are available for breach of a real covenant. If a promisee seeks *damages* or a *money judgment* from an assignee, the promisee must go into law and attempt to enforce the promise as a real covenant. If the promisee seeks an *injunction*, the promisee must go into equity and ask for enforcement of an equitable servitude.

(a) **Enforcing a lien:** [§1467] If a promisee seeks to enforce a lien against the burdened land, it is necessary to distinguish between *judicial liens* and *consensual liens* in order to determine whether the promisee must go into law or into equity.

1) **Judicial liens:** [§1468] A judicial lien is an equitable remedy available to a person who first has secured a money judgment at law and is trying to satisfy the judgment by selling the defendant's land. Once the judgment is secured, equity puts a lien on the defendant's property. If the judgment is not paid, the plaintiff can sell the defendant's land to pay the judgment. If the plaintiff is attempting to enforce a judicial lien, the covenant must run at law (giving the plaintiff a judgment) before equitable relief to satisfy the judgment can be granted.

2) **Consensual liens:** [§1469] A consensual lien is one that arises from an agreement by the parties. A person who gives a mortgage on her house, for example, gives the lender a consensual lien on the house to secure the debt. If the house is subsequently sold, the buyer may not assume (be liable for) the mortgage debt, but if the debt is not paid, the lender can foreclose the lien by selling the land. Similarly, a person who promises to pay money for the upkeep of common spaces in a condominium may, in the purchase agreement, give the promisee a lien to secure performance of the promise. If the promisee does not pay, the lien is foreclosed in equity, the burdened land is sold, and the proceeds are applied to payment of the sum due. Under the theory of consensual liens, the land can be reached by equitable process without first obtaining a personal judgment in law against the assignee. Hence, where the burden of the covenant does not run with the land, because

of lack of privity of estate or failure to touch and concern or otherwise, so that the assignee is not personally liable in contract, the land may be liable for foreclosure of the consensual lien. [Restatement of Property §540; *cf.* Neponsit Property Owners Association v. Emigrant Industrial Savings Bank, *supra*, §1455—finds covenant satisfies requirements for running but does not make clear whether it is enforcing a judicial lien or a consensual lien]

(b) **Remedies compared:** [§1470]   In the usual case, the plaintiff wants an injunction, not damages. An injunction is worth more to the plaintiff than damages. For example, assume a subdivision is restricted to residential use. A wants to put a commercial building on her lot. If A's lot is available for commercial use, the value of A's lot will increase from $25 to $100. A will make a gain of $75. On the other hand, commercial use of A's lot will damage B's house next door, causing a $30 loss in value. If B sues for and is awarded damages, B gets $30. If B sues for and gets an injunction, B has a right which B can sell to A for more than $30. Since A will make a gain of $75 if she can build commercially, and B will be damaged only $30 by A's commercial building, B should "sell his injunction" to A for a price somewhere between $30 and $75 and A and B are both better off. The difference between the damage to B and the value to A ($45) is an economic gain available to the parties by trading. If A buys B off for $55, B has a profit of $25 and A has a profit of $20. As a general rule, then, an injunction permits B to reap some of the gain from trading with A, whereas a judgment for damages gives all the gains from trade ($45) to A. A naturally would prefer to have a judgment for damages, rather than an injunction, awarded to B.

(2) **Creation:** [§1471]   A real covenant must be in writing. In many states an equitable servitude will be *implied* (*see infra*, §1474).

(3) **Privity of estate:** [§1472]   Neither horizontal nor vertical privity of estate is required in equity. The court, in enforcing an equitable servitude, is enforcing an interest in land analogous to an easement against any person who interferes with it (*see infra*, §1484).

(4) **Identical requirements:** [§1473]   Both real covenants and equitable servitudes require that the covenant touch and concern land. Neither is enforceable against a bona fide purchaser without notice thereof.

2. **Creation:** [§1474]   Inasmuch as an equitable servitude is an interest in land, most courts hold that the Statute of Frauds requires a writing signed by the promisor. As with real covenants, acceptance of a deed signed only by the grantor binds the grantee as promisor (*see supra*, §1430). However, there is one important exception to the requirement of a writing: Negative equitable servitudes may be implied from a common scheme for development of a residential subdivision. This exception, followed in a majority of states, is discussed below.

a. **Negative servitude implied from a scheme:** [§1475]   In the case of a restricted residential subdivision, many courts will imply a negative servitude on a lot even though there is no writing creating the servitude on that lot. This is usually done on the theory of equitable estoppel: Where a purchaser, buying a lot restricted to residential use, relies upon the promise of the subdivider to restrict the other lots and makes a substantial investment, the subdivider and any assignee of the other lots are estopped to plead the Statute of Frauds.

(1) **The circumstances:** [§1476]   Suppose that a developer is marketing a tract of fifty lots. The developer sells off thirty lots by deeds containing covenants by the respective grantees that each will use his lot for residential purposes only. The developer orally assures all thirty grantees that this will be an exclusively residential development and that similar restrictions will be inserted in subsequent deeds. Then the developer sells off two corner lots to gasoline companies by deeds containing no covenants. The gasoline companies want to erect service stations. If (i) the developer had a *scheme* of an exclusively residential subdivison, *and* (ii) the gasoline companies had *notice* of the covenants in the thirty prior deeds, the court will imply a covenant in the deeds to the gasoline companies restricting their lots to residential purposes only. [Sanborn v. McLean, 206 N.W. 496 (Mich. 1925); Buffalo Academy of the Sacred Heart v. Boehm Bros., Inc., 267 N.Y. 242 (1935)]

(a) **Scheme required:** [§1477]   A court will imply a reciprocal negative servitude only if the evidence shows that the developer had a reasonably uniform scheme for development of all lots of the same character. On the basis of this scheme, it is inferred that the purchasers bought in reliance on the scheme and in the expectation of being able to enforce subsequently-created equitable servitudes similar or identical to the restrictions imposed on their lots. Almost always the alleged scheme is for an exclusively residential subdivision, into which some subsequent buyer wants to intrude with a commercial use.

(b) **Evidence of scheme:** [§1478]   The scheme must exist at the time the developer sells the first burdened lot within the scheme. If the scheme arises later, it cannot impose burdens on lots previously sold without the burdens. [Arthur v. Lake Tansi Village, Inc., 590 S.W.2d 923 (Tenn. 1979)] Evidence of a scheme includes a recorded plat with restrictions, the developer exhibiting to buyers a map or plat of the entire tract on which restrictions appear, oral representations of the developer with respect to restrictions to be imposed on the remaining land, and statements made in sales brochures or advertising. Or, a scheme can be shown by the fact that the developer inserted similar covenants in a substantial number of the deeds in the subdivison *prior* to the deed to defendant. Restrictions inserted in other deeds *after* the deed to defendant do not show a scheme at the necessary time.

1) **Example:** Subdivider CG (common grantor) sells off lot 1 to A. No restrictions appear on any plat or map. Subsequently, CG sells off the remaining lots in the subdivision, restricting them to residential use.

Lot 1 is not bound by the restrictions. If a number of lots in the subdivision are sold off before the scheme arises, the court may find "no scheme" because of the apparent inequity of enforcing burdens against only some, and not all, owners in the subdivision. [Petersen v. Beekmere, Inc., 283 A.2d 911 (N.J. 1971)]

(2) **Kind of servitude implied:** [§1479]   A servitude similar to a ***reciprocal negative easement*** is implied. This label is quite descriptive. The servitude must be ***reciprocal***; *i.e.*, a similar covenant must bind other lots in the subdivision. It must be a ***negative*** or ***restrictive*** covenant, forbidding some use of land; the court will not imply affirmative covenants, requiring the purchasers to do something. And the servitude is in the nature of an ***easement***; *i.e.*, it is an interest in land.

(3) **Covenants not implied:** [§1480]   Some courts refuse to imply reciprocal negative servitudes in a residential subdivision. California holds that the deed constitutes the final understanding of the parties and cannot be varied by oral or written agreements not incorporated therein. [Werner v. Graham, 181 Cal. 174 (1919)] Under this principle, servitudes cannot be established by a recorded declaration of restrictions not referred to in the deed. [Riley v. Bear Creek Planning Commission, 17 Cal. 3d 500 (1976)] Massachusetts holds that estoppel does not apply because there is no misrepresentation of an existing fact, only a broken promise, and thus will not imply negative servitudes. [Sprague v. Kimball, 100 N.E. 622 (Mass. 1913)]

b. **Real covenants:** [§1481]   Real covenants, unlike equitable servitudes, will not be implied in any state. The reason is that the courts deem it unfair to impose unlimited personal liability upon a person without an express agreement. An implied servitude, enforceable only by injunction or lien, limits liability to the value of the land.

3. **Enforcement By or Against Assignees:** [§1482]   For an equitable servitude to be enforced by a successor to the promisee or against a successor to the promisor, certain requirements must be met.

a. **Intent:** [§1483]   The contracting parties must intend that the servitude be enforceable by and against assignees. No technical words such as "assigns" (possibly required for a covenant to run at law) are required. (*See supra*, §1443.) The court ascertains intent from the purpose of the covenant and the surrounding circumstances. [Sun Oil Co. v. Trent Auto Wash, Inc., 150 N.W.2d 818 (Mich. 1967)]

b. **Privity of estate**

(1) **Between covenantor and covenantee:** [§1484]   Privity of estate between the covenantor and the covenantee (horizontal privity, *see supra*, §§1444 *et seq.*) is not required for the burden of a covenant to run to assigns in equity. Equity is enforcing a property interest analogous to an easement, and no special relationship between the parties who created the property interest is necessary. [Fitzstephens v. Watson, 344 P.2d 221 (Or. 1959)]

(2) **Between covenanting party and assignee:** [§1485]   Equity does not require vertical privity of estate between a covenanting party and an assignee. In law, the court views the covenant as attaching to and running with an estate in land. Equity, on the other hand, is enforcing a servitude in the nature of an easement in the servient land. Anyone who takes a property interest in the *burdened* land is obliged to comply with the servitude. The *benefit* of a servitude is, like an easement, appurtenant to the benefited land and enforceable by any successor possessor of that land.

(a) **Adverse possession:** [§1486]   An adverse possessor of the *burdened land* takes subject to the servitude, just as he takes subject to an easement. The statute of limitations begins to run against the servitude owner when the adverse possessor violates the servitude. Thus, if a person acquires title by adverse possession to a house with residential restrictions on it, the servitude remains on the land until the adverse possessor violates the servitude and the statute of limitations runs on the violation. [*In re* Nisbett & Potts' Contract, [1960] 1 Ch. 386] The adverse possessor of the *benefited land* might take the benefit of the servitude (as he takes the benefit of an affirmative easement), but there are practically no cases on the point.

c.   **Touch and concern requirement**

(1) **General rule:** [§1487]   For the burden to run with the burdened land in equity as well as in law, the covenant must touch and concern the burdened land. And likewise, for the benefit to run with the benefited land, the covenant must touch and concern the benefited land. Equity generally applies the same touch and concern test as is applied at law. It is difficult to give any but the most generalized statement of the meaning of "touch and concern." Early cases asked whether the covenant burdens or benefits a party in the *physical use or enjoyment* of particular land, but this proved too narrow a test. Some covenants, particularly negative covenants, merely *enhance the value* of the benefited land, but they have been held to touch and concern the benefited land as well as the burdened land. Perhaps Judge Clark put it best: "Where the parties, as laymen and not as lawyers, would naturally regard the covenant as intimately bound up with the land, aiding the promisee as landowner or hampering the promisor in similar capacity, the requirement should be fulfilled." [Clark, *supra*, p. 99; *but see* Restatement §537—burden will not run at law unless benefit is to promisee in physical use or enjoyment of land (a position lacking much case support)]

(a) **Function of requirement:** [§1488]   The function of the touch and concern requirement is to permit courts to stop covenants from running when the social utility of the covenant is outweighed by the fettering of the burdened property. A market economist would say that if there are no harmful third party effects, the court, in deciding whether a covenant touches and concerns, should try to approximate the decision the present landowners would reach in a negotiation free of transaction costs. If the value of the benefit exceeds the burden, the present landowners would reimpose the covenant because it would be to the advantage of both. Since the benefited party values the right more, the benefited party would pay the burdened party for the right. Under this theory, the relative values of the benefit and burden are very important in deciding whether a covenant touches and concerns. The Restatement appears to have some such theory in mind when it states, "the burden will not run if the burden imposed is obviously greater than the benefit given. There must be such a relation between benefit and burden that the performance of the promise has, in the particular case, some reasonable prospect of promoting land utilization as a whole." [Restatement §537, comment h]

(2) Specific applications

(a) **Negative covenants:** [§1489]   Covenants not to do a physical act (*e.g.*, not to erect commercial buildings) touch and concern. These covenants affect the burdened owner in the physical use of his land. Restrictive covenants also **enhance the value** of the benefited land, even though it is hard to say they affect the benefited owner in the physical use of his land. Covenants containing building restrictions, enhancing the value of the benefited land, have always been held to touch and concern.

1)   Covenants not to compete

a)   **Burden side:** [§1490]   A covenant not to compete restricts the promisor in the **physical use** he may make of his land. Hence, it touches and concerns the **burdened** land as much as a covenant restricting the property to residential use. Most courts have so held, provided the covenant is reasonable in its duration and in the area it encompasses. [Dick v. Sears, Roebuck & Co., 160 A. 432 (Conn. 1932); Hall v. American Oil Co., 504 S.W.2d 313 (Mo. 1973); Oliver v. Hewitt, 60 S.E.2d 1 (Va. 1950)]

b)   **Benefit side:** [§1491]   The benefit of a covenant not to compete clearly enhances the value of the covenantee's land, but it is debatable whether it affects him in the physical use of his land. Nevertheless, a majority of courts hold that **enhancement of commercial value** is enough to satisfy the requirement of touch and concern. Massachusetts formerly held that the benefit of a covenant not to compete does not touch and concern land. This holding, coupled with the rule that the burden will not run if the benefit is in gross (*see infra*, §1497), meant that the burden of a covenant not to compete would not run. However, the old Massachusetts cases have now been overruled; reasonable covenants not to compete now run in Massachusetts when they facilitate orderly and harmonious commercial development. [Whitinsville Plaza Inc. v. Kotseas, 390 N.E.2d 243 (Mass. 1979)]

c) **Restatement:** [§1492] The Restatement of Property took the view that the *burden* of a covenant not to compete does not touch and concern in *law* [Restatement §537, comment f], but does in *equity* [Restatement §539, comment k]. It says the *benefit* touches and concerns *both* in law and equity. The Restatement's view has practically no case support, but is simply the logical extension of its basic position to put roadblocks to the running of the burden at law, but not elsewhere.

d) **Example:** O has a furniture store on Blackacre. O sells Whiteacre, located across the street, to A. In the deed, A promises for himself, his heirs and assigns not to conduct a furniture business on Whiteacre. Most courts would hold that O can enforce the covenant against A's successors. Under the Restatement position, A's successors can be enjoined by O, but they are not liable for damages.

(b) **Affirmative covenants:** [§1493] In England, only negative covenants are enforceable as equitable servitudes. This refusal rests either upon the idea that an equitable servitude is in substance a negative easement or upon the perceived difficulty of supervising performance by a mandatory injunction. In some early cases in this country, particularly in New York and New Jersey, this English restriction on equitable servitudes was influential. Today, however, this position has been largely abandoned. Most courts permit affirmative covenants to run both in law and equity; they usually are held to touch and concern the land. [Petersen v. Beekmere, Inc., *supra*, §1478; Nicholson v. 300 Broadway Realty Corp., 7 N.Y.2d 240 (1959)] Nonetheless, if an affirmative covenant (like a negative covenant) is of limited social utility and constitutes an undesirable fettering of land, a court may find it does not touch and concern. [Eagle Enterprises, Inc. v. Gross, 39 N.Y.2d 505 (1976)]

1) **Performance off land:** [§1494] If the act is to be performed off the burdened land, without benefiting the burdened land, the covenant does not touch and concern the burdened land. *Example:* O conveys Blackacre to A, who promises to keep a house on Whiteacre in repair. The benefit touches and concerns Whiteacre, but the burden does not touch and concern Blackacre. On the other hand, if the act to be performed off the burdened land benefits the burdened land, the covenant does touch and concern. A typical covenant of the latter type is a promise to perform (or not perform) an act regarding maintenance of common areas in a condominium.

(c) **Covenants to pay money:** [§1495] Covenants to pay money for some improvement that benefits the promisor by enhancing the value of his property touch and concern even though the improvements are on other land. Typically these covenants provide that the landowner or condominium owner will pay a certain sum each year to maintain common spaces. If the formula for calculating the sum is reasonably clear, a covenant to pay an annual fee is enforceable against assigns. [Kell v. Bella Vista Village Property Owners Association, 528 S.W.2d 651 (Ark. 1975); Neponsit Property Owners Association v. Emigrant Independent Savings Bank, *supra*, §1469]

1) **Lien:** [§1496]   A covenant to pay money is normally enforced by an action at law for breach of contract. To give the promisee an additional remedy, a deed often will retain a lien on the land to enforce the promise. If the burden of the covenant does not run, the ***land*** can be reached by equitable process to satisfy the consensual lien, although no personal judgment can be obtained against the assignee of the promisor. (*See supra*, §1469.)

(3) **Covenant with benefit in gross:** [§1497]   When the benefit of a covenant does not touch and concern land (*i.e.*, is in gross), the majority rule is that the burden will not run. In other words, the burden will not run unless it is tied to land. What is the reason for this rule? A brief historical explanation will show its origin and its misapplication in the United States.

(a) **English rule:** [§1498]   English courts refused to recognize an easement in gross (*see supra*, §1314), which is the equivalent of saying that the burden of an easement in gross will not run to assigns of the burdened land. When the equitable servitude developed, they viewed it as an "interest analogous to a negative easement." Therefore, quite logically, the English courts held that the burden of an equitable servitude (analogous to a legal easement) will not run if the benefit is in gross. For a servitude to run, there must be both a servient and a dominant tenement. [London County Council v. Allen, [1914] 3 K.B. 642]

1) **Example:** The Urban Housing Commission sells land to A, extracting a promise from A that A will use the land only for residential purposes. A sells the land to B. If the Urban Housing Commission owns no land benefited by the promise, the covenant is not enforceable against B.

(b) **American law—equitable servitudes:** [§1499]   In this country, easements in gross are recognized, and the burden of the easement runs with the land. Therefore, if an equitable servitude is an "interest analogous to an [American] easement," the burden should run even if the benefit is in gross. Most courts, however, followed the English view, paying no mind to its basic assumption that equitable servitudes were analogous to easements. [Snow v. Van Dam, 197 N.E. 224 (Mass. 1935); Neponsit Property Owners Association v. Emigrant Industrial Savings Bank, *supra*, §1469]

1) **Rationale:** The rule possibly can be justified on the following grounds: (i) Where a burden devalues land, public policy requires an accompanying benefit to other land, resulting in a net increase in land value. (ii) Public policy disfavors covenants that do not have the purpose of

dealing with externalities affecting other land. (iii) Where the benefit is in gross, finding the owner or owners to buy them out is more difficult than when the benefit is in the owner of neighboring land.

2) **Minority view:** [§1500]   Some courts hold that the burden of a covenant will run even though the benefit is in gross. They see no reason to distinguish between covenants and easements. [Merrionette Manor Homes Association v. Heda, 136 N.E.2d 556 (Ill. 1956); Pratte v. Balatsos, 113 A.2d 492 (N.H. 1955)] Section 539 of the Restatement of Property takes the view that in equity the burden will run even though the benefit is in gross.

(c) **American law—real covenants:** [§1501]   Although the analogy to legal easements is not made with respect to real covenants, it has been held that the policies underlying the rule in equity (*see supra*, §1499) are applicable to covenants at law. Thus if a covenant will not run in equity because the benefit is in gross, neither will a covenant run at law. [*In re* Turners Crossroad Development Co., 277 N.W.2d 364 (Minn. 1979); Caullett v. Stanley Stilwell & Sons, Inc., 170 A.2d 52 (N.J. 1961)] Consistent with its general position (*see supra*, §1449), Restatement section 537 takes the view that if the benefit is in gross, the burden will not run in law but will run in equity.

(d) **Developer sells out:** [§1502]   Suppose that the developer of a subdivision imposes restrictive covenants on the lots in the subdivision. The covenants are for the benefit of the other lots in the subdivision. When the developer sells all the lots, can the developer enforce the burden of the covenants against assignees? If the benefit of the covenants runs with the land, the usual answer is no. The developer has assigned the benefit. But it has been held that where the developer owns nearby land that could be adversely affected, even though it is not the benefited land, the developer retains the right to enforce the restriction in equity. [Christiansen v. Casey, 613 S.W.2d 906 (Mo. 1981)]

d. **Notice:** [§1503]   If the assignee is a subsequent purchaser for valuable consideration without notice of the servitude, he does not take subject to it. If the assignee has notice, he is bound if the servitude is otherwise enforceable. Notice can be actual, record, or inquiry.

(1) **Actual notice:** [§1504]   If the assignee has actual knowledge of the covenant in a prior deed, he clearly has notice.

(2) **Record notice:** [§1505]   If the covenant is in a deed to the assignee's lot, he has record notice. If the covenant is in a deed or deeds to other lots in a subdivision conveyed by the developer to prior grantees, the assignee has record notice if the deeds to neighboring lots are in the assignee's **chain of title** (*i.e.*, he must read them because by operation of law he has notice of their contents). However, there is a split of authority as to whether covenants contained in prior deeds out to other grantees in the same tract from a common grantor, and purporting

to restrict use of all lots in the tract, are in a subsequent grantee's chain of title (*infra*, §1509). Some courts hold that prior deeds out from a common grantor to other purchasers in a subdivision are in the chain of title of a subsequent purchaser from the developer. [Guillette v. Daly Dry Wall, Inc., 325 N.E.2d 572 (Mass. 1975)] Other courts hold they are not in the chain of title, and the subsequent grantee does not have record notice of their contents. [Buffalo Academy of the Sacred Heart v. Boehm Bros., Inc., *supra*, §1476]

(a) **Example:** Developer CG sells off forty lots by deeds containing identical residential restrictions. CG sells off lot 41 to A without restrictions. A has no actual notice of the contents of prior deeds. If the prior deeds are in A's chain of title, A may be subject to an implied restriction if there is a scheme, or A will be subject to an express restriction if the prior deeds expressly bind the common grantor's retained land. If the prior deeds are not in A's chain of title, A is not subject to an implied covenant nor to an express covenant contained in those deeds.

(3) **Inquiry notice:** [§1506]   At least one court has held that a purchaser buying into a built-up residential area where the houses appear to have been built in accordance with a plan should look at the other deeds out from the developer to see if any basis for an implied covenant exists. Regardless of whether such prior deeds are in the purchaser's chain of title, the lay of the land puts him on inquiry notice to look at the deeds of the neighboring lots from the developer. [Sanborn v. McLean, *supra*, §1476]

4. **Enforcement by a Third Party or Prior Purchaser:** [§1507]   In the above material, the discussion involved the question of whether *assignees* of one of the original parties to the covenant could sue or be sued. Now we turn to another question: Can a covenant be enforced by a *third party or by a prior purchaser* in a subdivision? Distinguish carefully between suits by *assignees* of the original promisee, who have a right to sue by virtue of stepping into the shoes of the promisee, and suits by *third party beneficiaries*. It is these latter suits that now concern us.

    a. **Contract law:** [§1508]   The issue of whether third party beneficiaries can enforce a covenant in law or in equity is best analyzed by first looking at contract law. Historically, contract law resisted the enforcement of contracts by third parties; the law required that the consideration for the promise must move to the promisor from the person who had the right to enforce the promise. Beginning with *Lawrence v. Fox*, 20 N.Y. 268 (1859), the American courts began to permit some third party beneficiaries to enforce contracts. Gradually, over a hundred years, the courts broadened the types of contracts so enforceable until today, in almost all jurisdictions, a third party beneficiary may enforce a contract if the parties so intend. [Restatement (Second) of Contracts §302; Farnsworth, Contracts §§10.2-10.3 (1982)] Although contract law has now moved to a position of clarity and rationality, its reluctance to enforce third party beneficiary contracts affected the development of property law, and certain restrictive notions still survive.

b. **Third-party must be grantee of party imposing covenant:** [§1509] The restrictive rule followed in many states is that the person seeking to enforce the promise must be a grantee of the person who imposed the covenant, either directly or through mesne conveyances. The enforcer thus must trace title to the party imposing the covenant. Sometimes, in explaining this, it is said that the enforcer must be in "privity of estate" with the party imposing the covenant, meaning the two must have been at one time in a grantor-grantee relationship. Under this restriction, *prior purchasers in a subdivision* may be given the right to enforce restrictions imposed by the developer on lots later sold, but a person who owns the lot next door cannot enforce a covenant unless he bought the lot from the person imposing the covenant.

(1) **Example:** Developer, owner of fifty lots in Greenacres Subdivision, conveys lot 1 to A. Lot 1 is restricted to residential use, but the remaining lots are not so restricted. Subsequently Developer conveys lot 2 to B, restricting lot 2 to residential use. If Developer intends to give the right to enforce the restriction on lot 2 to the owner of lot 1, the owner of lot 1 can enforce the restriction. The owner of lot 1 acquired title from Developer, who imposed the covenant. If, on the other hand, Developer intends to give the right to enforce the restriction to the Sierra Club, which owns no land acquired from Developer, or to owners of a neighboring subdivision developed by another subdivider, the Sierra Club or the owners of the neighboring subdivision cannot enforce the restriction.

(a) **Malpractice trap:** The rule that a third party beneficiary cannot enforce a covenant unless he succeeded to land once owned by the party imposing the covenant is a malpractice trap. The lawyer with a client (O) who wants to convey Blackacre to A and impose a covenant for the benefit of neighbor B (who owns land never owned by the client) should go this safe route: (i) Have B convey his land to O; (ii) then O conveys this land back to B; then (iii) O conveys Blackacre to A, imposing a covenant for the benefit of B's land. Since B received title from O, B can enforce the covenant.

(2) **Showing intent:** [§1510] If the deed is silent as to who can enforce a covenant, prior purchasers in a subdivision can enforce the covenant if they can show that the developer had a *scheme* of substantial uniformity in land use *at the time the prior purchasers bought*, which the prior purchasers relied upon in buying in the subdivision. From the uniform scheme it is inferred that the developer intended to confer a benefit upon the other purchasers in the subdivision. [Snow v. Van Dam, *supra,* §1499]

(3) **Compare—scheme to imply burden:** [§1511] Previously, we discussed the use of a scheme to imply a burden on land where the covenant was *not in writing* (*see supra*, §1475). The problem there was the Statute of Frauds. Here we consider the use of a scheme to imply who has the benefit of a covenant *that is in writing*. Even though a jurisdiction will not imply a burden from a scheme, it may imply who has the benefit of written covenants. Massachusetts is such a jurisdiction. In the preceding example, if Developer had a scheme at the time he sold lot 1, but he did not restrict his remaining lots when he sold lot 1,

Massachusetts will not imply a restriction on lots 2 through 50. If Developer does not subsequently restrict lot 2, the owner of lot 1 cannot sue the owner of lot 2. On the other hand, if Developer subsequently restricts lot 2, the owner of lot 1 can sue the owner of lot 2 because of the scheme.

(a) **In states where burden implied:** [§1512]   In states that imply a burden on all lots in a subdivision where there is a scheme, the benefit is for all owners in the subdivision. If, in the preceding example, Developer had had a scheme from the beginning, and had restricted lots 1 through 15, but thereafter sold off lots 16 through 50 without restrictions, restrictions would be implied on lots 16 through 50 as soon as lot 1 is sold. The owner of lot 1 would then be enforcing an *implied* restriction on lot 16, not a written restriction.

(4) **Developer's right to modify:** [§1513]   If the developer retains the right to modify the restrictions imposed on lots to be sold in the future, some cases have held that this is evidence of intent to benefit the developer personally and not the neighbors in the subdivision. The retention of this right may negate the idea of development according to a scheme. [Suttle v. Bailey, 361 P.2d 325 (N.M. 1961)] However, there are cases holding that the reservation by the developer of a right to modify must be exercised in good faith, and the reservation of this right does *not* show an intent not to give enforcement power to the other subdivision owners. [Berger v. Van Sweringen Co., 216 N.E.2d 54 (Ohio 1966)]

(5) **Where no subdivision:** [§1514]   If there is no subdivision, but the person attempting to enforce the restriction previously bought his lot from the person imposing the restriction, it may be more difficult to show that the latter intended to benefit the former. Courts favor restrictions in subdivisions, where benefits flow to many persons and preserve the character of the neighborhood, but the ancient hostility to covenants surfaces when only two lots are involved and development is impeded. [Rodgers v. Reimann, 361 P.2d 101 (Or. 1961)]

(6) **No benefit implied:** [§1515]   California will not imply who has the benefit of a covenant, by a scheme or otherwise. The deed constitutes the final understanding of the parties. Only the grantor can enforce the restrictions unless the neighbors are expressly given the right to enforce. [Werner v. Graham, *supra*, §1480]

c. **No restrictions on third party beneficiaries:** [§1516]   Restatement of Property section 541 states that any third party beneficiary can enforce a covenant in law or in equity if the contracting parties so intend. This reflects the view of modern contract law, embodied in the Restatement of Contracts. A few jurisdictions (notably New York) follow this theory. [Zamiarski v. Kozial, 18 App. Div. 2d 297 (1963)]

d. **Compare—easements:** [§1517]   At common law, an easement cannot be reserved in favor of a third party (*see supra*, §1338). This remains the majority view, even in

New York, which freely permits third parties to enforce real covenants and equitable servitudes. [Vogeler v. Alwyn Improvement Corp., *supra*, §1338]

5. **Construction of Covenants:** [§1518]   A covenant will be construed so as to carry out the intention of the parties in light of the purpose of the covenant. Some of the more frequently recurring construction problems involve the following matters.

   a. **Single-family dwelling:** [§1519]   Covenants in residential subdivisions usually prohibit construction or maintenance of other than one single-family dwelling on each lot. There has been much litigation over what is a single-family dwelling. An apartment house or condominium is not; a detached single-family house is. There is a divergence of judicial opinion over what types of "group homes" constitute a single-family dwelling. The most recent cases involving "group homes" hinge on whether the group mirrors the stability and structure of the traditional family. If the group has two parents supervising dependent children who are relatively permanent residents, very likely the group will be classified as a single family. [Saunders v. Clark County Zoning Department, 421 N.E.2d 152 (Ohio 1981)] But if the children are transients, staying only a few months, or if a large part of the supervision is performed by outsiders who come and go, the group will probably not be classified as a single family. If the group is composed exclusively of adults who are severely retarded (and thus may be as dependent as children), the cases are split. [*See* Crane Neck Association v. New York City/Long Island County Services Group, 61 N.Y.2d 154 (1984)—home for eight severely retarded adults not a single-family use; *but see* Crowley v. Knapp, 288 N.W.2d 815 (Wis. 1980)—home for eight developmentally retarded adults is a single-family use]

   b. **Whether residential use only implied:** [§1520]   A covenant may *not specifically* limit use of land to residential, but it may do so inferentially by providing, "no dwelling house shall be built closer than twenty feet from the street or costing less than $25,000," or something similar. Some older courts, hostile to covenants, construed them literally and refused to imply a general prohibition against nonresidential use from specific restrictions on dwelling size, cost, or location. [Holliday v. Sphar, 89 S.W.2d 327 (Ky. 1935)] But more modern cases construe the restrictions in a manner to achieve their purpose of protecting the character of the neighborhood. These cases imply a general restriction for residential use from specific restrictions on dwellings. [Joslin v. Pine River Development Corp., 367 A.2d 599 (N.H. 1976)]

   c. **Architectural controls:** [§1521]   Many modern subdivisions contain covenants that every building to be erected shall be approved by an architectural control committee. The standards governing approval may be very general or vague. Courts have held that specific standards are not necessary, but the architectural control committee must act reasonably and in good faith. [Rhue v. Cheyenne Homes, Inc., 449 P.2d 361 (Colo. 1969); Jones v. Northwest Real Estate Co., 131 A. 446 (Md. 1925)] This good faith rule has been criticized for failing to protect against arbitrary action in fact, because the burden of establishing bad faith is too costly for most landowners to undertake.

d. **Exclusion of churches:** [§1522]   Churches and religious schools can be excluded from residential areas by restrictive covenants. The majority of courts hold that it is not state action for a court to enjoin religious use of residentially restricted land. [Ginsberg v. Yeshiva of Far Rockaway, 45 App. Div. 2d 334, *aff'd* 36 N.Y.2d 706 (1976); *but see* West Hill Baptist Church v. Abbate, 261 N.E.2d 196 (Ohio 1969)—contra]

e. **Restraint on sale:** [§1523]   A covenant restraining sale of a house or a condominium unit must pass scrutiny as a restraint on alienation (*see supra,* §§396 *et seq.*). If the covenant gives a group a veto power on sale, the covenant is void as an unreasonable restraint on alienation. [Kenney v. Morgan, 325 A.2d 419 (Md. 1974); Tuckerton Beach Club v. Bender, *supra,* §404]

6. **Termination of Covenants and Servitudes**

a. **Merger:** [§1524]   If the title to the land benefited and the title to the land burdened come into the hands of one person, real covenants and equitable servitudes, like easements, merge into the fee simple and cease to exist. *Rationale:* The owner of the benefited land cannot sue himself for damages or an injunction; therefore, there is no enforceable covenant. If one parcel is subsequently sold, new covenants will have to be imposed if the owner wants a covenant.

b. **Equitable defenses to enforcement:** [§1525]   Any of the following may be asserted as defenses to enforcement where an equitable servitude is claimed.

   (1) **Acquiescence:** [§1526]   If a benefited party acquiesces in a breach of the servitude by one burdened party, he may be deemed to have abandoned the servitude as to others similarly burdened. An equitable servitude, like an easement, can be abandoned. [Morris v. Nease, 238 S.E.2d 844 (W.Va. 1977)]

   (2) **Estoppel:** [§1527]   If a benefited party acts in such a way as to lead a reasonable person to believe that the covenant was abandoned, and the burdened party acts in reliance thereon, the benefited party may be estopped to enforce the covenant.

   (3) **Relative hardship:** [§1528]   As a general rule of equity, a court of equity may deny an injunction when the hardship to the defendant is great and the benefit to the plaintiff small. But where the right to the benefit of a servitude is clear, the defense of disproportionate harm and benefit is usually not persuasive to a court in covenant cases. [Loeb v. Watkins, 240 A.2d 513 (Pa. 1968)]

   (4) **Change of conditions in neighborhood:** [§1529]   The most frequently asserted defense to equitable enforcement of a servitude is that the character of the neighborhood has so changed that it is impossible any longer to secure in substantial degree the benefits of the restrictive covenants. If this is shown, equity will refuse to enforce the covenant. [Trustees of Columbia College v. Thacher, 87 N.Y. 311 (1882)] However, for the defense of change of conditions to succeed, most courts require either that (i) the change *outside* the subdivision

must be so pervasive as to make **all lots** in the subdivision unsuitable for the permitted uses, or (ii) substantial change must have occurred **within the subdivision** itself. Change outside the subdivision that affects only the border lots in a subdivision is not sufficient to prevent enforcement of the covenant against the border lots. [Osborne v. Hewitt, 335 S.W.2d 922 (Ky. 1960); Western Land Co. v. Truskolaski, 495 P.2d 624 (Nev. 1972); Cilberti v. Angiletta, 61 Misc. 2d 13 (1969); Albino v. Pacific First Federal Savings & Loan Association, 479 P.2d 760 (Or. 1971); Cowling v. Colligan, 312 S.W.2d 943 (Tex. 1958)]

(a) **Example:** Developer restricts a subdivision to residential use. Subsequently, commercial development and traffic increase on the borders of the subdivision. The owner of a border lot within the restricted tract wants to develop commercially. The courts refuse to permit the border lot owner to develop commercially unless the purposes of the restrictions can no longer be achieved for any owner because of changed conditions. *Rationale:* If the purchaser of a border lot has paid a lower price because it is a buffer lot, to permit the border owner to develop would give him a benefit he did not bargain for and deprive the owners of inner lots of a benefit paid for. But in reply it can be said there is no evidence in the cases that, as a general rule, purchasers of border lots paid less for their lots. The change in surrounding uses is usually unexpected.

(5) **Effect on right to damages:** [§1530] Theoretically, the above defenses are equitable defenses, and if successful the plaintiff still may have a right to damages. But in fact the damage remedy is rarely used. The all-or-nothing approach of the doctrine of changed conditions (injunction granted or denied) has been criticized as unfair or inefficient. It has been suggested that efficiency and fairness would be better served by giving the owners of interior lots damages rather than an injunction in the usual case of changed conditions. It is asserted that, in many cases of change in the neighborhood, society would maximize its wealth if it compensated the inner lot owners and permitted development to proceed on the border. It is also argued that this would be fairer than putting the entire loss from changed conditions upon the border owners, as is done by granting an injunction. [Comment, 31 UCLA L. Rev. 226 (1983); *and see* Mass. Gen. Laws ch. 184, §30—denying injunctive relief and giving damage remedy only if any of several enumerated conditions are found to exist; held constitutional in Blakeley v. Gorin, 313 N.E.2d 903 (Mass. 1974)]

c. **Eminent domain:** [§1531] When the government by eminent domain takes title to the burdened land and condemns the covenant as well, the majority rule is that the government must pay damages to the owner of the benefited land. The measure of damages usually is the difference in value of the benefited lot with and without the benefit of the covenant. The underlying theory is that a real covenant or equitable servitude is a property interest analogous to an easement, and it must be paid for when removed by the government. [Southern California Edison Co. v. Bourgerie, 9 Cal. 3d 169 (1973)]

(1) **Minority view:** [§1532] A few older cases have taken the view that a real covenant or equitable servitude is only a contract enforced by the courts (*see supra*, §1464). Under this view, not being a property interest, the benefit of a covenant is not compensable under eminent domain. This view makes it cheaper for the government to condemn land in a restricted subdivision.

X. RIGHTS IN THE LAND OF ANOTHER ARISING BY OPERATION OF LAW

chapter approach

The law has long given the possessor of land various rights against neighbors. These rights include the right to be free of a *nuisance* nearby, the right to *support* so that the land does not fall in, rights in streams and in surface and underground *water*, and rights in *air space*.

For questions concerning these rights, consider the following:

1. For *nuisance*, be sure to distinguish between a nuisance (interference with the use and enjoyment of land) and a trespass (invasion of the possessor's interest in exclusive possession). Also consider the *remedies* available (injunction and damages) and whether one is more appropriate than another in a particular case.

2. Regarding the *right to support*, remember that the right extends to both lateral support (support from adjacent land) and subjacent support (support from ground below).

3. *Water rights* may vary depending on the type of water—*i.e.*, whether it is a stream or lake, percolating ground water, or surface water.

4. *Air space* issues may arise in questions about navigable airspace and flight paths (remember that the government sets the standards), or those about solar enjoyment (where the type of use—solar power source vs. garden requirements—may determine whether the right will be enforced).

In all of these areas, *economic analysis* theories may well influence the courts' decisions, and thus should probably be considered in your answer.

A. NUISANCE

1. **In General:** [§1533]   A "nuisance" is an unprivileged interference with a person's use and enjoyment of his land. Relief from nuisance was awarded at common law under the basic maxim that *one must use his property so as not to injure that of another*. A nuisance is termed a "*private nuisance*" when it involves interference with the private use and enjoyment of one or a number of nearby properties. It is a "*public nuisance*" when the interference is with a right which is common to the general public.

2. **Private Nuisance**

   a. **Definition:** [§1534]   A private nuisance is conduct that causes a *substantial* interference with the private use of land and is either (i) *intentional and unreasonable*, or (ii) *unintentional but negligent*, reckless, or resulting from an abnormally dangerous activity (for which there is strict liability). [Restatement (Second) of Torts

§822] A person cannot sue claiming a private nuisance unless he has a **property interest** that is affected or alleges bodily harm as the result of the activities complained of.

(1) **Intentional nuisance:** [§1535]   The usual type of nuisance is an intentional and unreasonable act that continues over time and is known to interfere with another's enjoyment of land. The primary factor in determining an intentional nuisance is the **unreasonableness of the interference** with the neighbor's use and enjoyment. Restatement (Second) of Torts section 826 lays down a utilitarian test of reasonableness: Any intentional invasion of an interest in the private use and enjoyment of land is unreasonable "if (a) the **gravity of the harm outweighs the utility of the actor's conduct,** or (b) the harm caused by the conduct is serious and the financial burden of compensating for this and similar harm to others would not make the continuation of the conduct not feasible." Balancing the gravity of the harm against the utility of the conduct requires an examination of particular factors in each case. [McCarty v. Natural Carbonic Gas Co., 189 N.Y. 40 (1907)]

    (a) **Gravity of harm:** [§1536]   The Restatement lists the following factors to be considered in determining **the gravity of the harm**: (i) the **extent** of the harm; (ii) the **character** of the harm; (iii) the **social value** of the use or enjoyment invaded; (iv) the **suitability** of the use invaded to the locality; and (v) the **burden** on the person harmed of avoiding the harm. [Rest. 2d, Torts §827]

    (b) **Utility of conduct:** [§1537]   The Restatement lists the following factors to be considered in determining the **utility of the conduct of the invader**: (i) the **social value** of the primary purpose of the conduct; (ii) the **suitability** of the conduct to the character of the locality; and (iii) the **impracticability** of preventing or avoiding the invasion. [Rest. 2d, Torts §828]

    (c) **Fault:** [§1538]   The fault of the defendant is not controlling, but the failure of defendant to use due care in avoiding the harm may be a ground for imposing liability. In some cases, courts have imposed liability upon the defendant even though he has taken all reasonable precautions and is in no way at fault. They have concluded that the gravity of the harm outweighed the utility of the conduct. [Pendoley v. Ferreira, 187 N.E.2d 142 (Mass. 1963)—existing well-operated piggery enjoined as nuisance when new homes built in area]

        1) **Comment:** There may be an **economic** justification for this result in that total value to society will be increased by the cessation of the defendant's activity, but the question of whether it is **fair** to put the cost of abating the conflict on the defendant is another matter.

    (d) **"Nuisance per se" vs. "nuisance in fact":** [§1539]   Courts sometimes distinguish between a "nuisance per se" (an activity that is a nuisance no matter how reasonable the defendant's conduct) and a "nuisance in fact" (an activity that is unreasonable under the particular facts). However, the distinction is of dubious value, because it conflicts with the basic concept that a nuisance is determined by whether the activity causes an **unreasonable interference** with the use of another's land—not whether the activity is unreasonable regardless of the use of the other land. The tendency of courts that have found nuisances per se is to limit them to unduly hazardous activities (*e.g.*, storage of explosives), unlawful activities, or highly objectionable uses in the particular district.

(2) **Unintentional act:** [§1540]   An unintentional act may give rise to a nuisance when the risk of harm makes the conduct unreasonable. When the act is unintentional, "unreasonableness" does not involve weighing the utility of the conduct against the harm caused, but refers to the **actor's conduct** (whether negligent or reckless) as well as the gravity of the harm. The utility of the conduct is seldom a defense. Nuisances of this type are uncommon, but an example is the storage of dangerous explosives.

b.   **Types of unreasonable interference:** [§1541]   The practical meaning of the term "nuisance" can best be grasped by looking at the particulars of various cases in which the interference has been held to be a nuisance.

(1) **Character of the harm**

(a) **Depreciation of property value:** [§1542]   Use of property in a manner that depreciates the value of surrounding property is **not** enough **by itself** to constitute a nuisance. Even so, it is an important factor in proving that there is substantial injury to the plaintiff. In the case of "psychological" nuisances (cemeteries, funeral homes, etc.), depreciation of neighboring property values may be the underlying or controlling factor.

(b) **Discomfort:** [§1543]   Serious discomfort and inconvenience in the use of land is another important factor in determining a nuisance. Objectionable noise, odors, or smoke are frequently the interference complained of. The standard of unreasonable interference is measured by the sensibilities of the average person. [Rose v. Chaikin, 453 A.2d 1378 (N.J. 1982); Morgan v. High Penn Oil Co., 77 S.E.2d 682 (N.C. 1953)]

1)   **Sunlight:** [§1544]   Older cases held that cutting off a neighbor's sunlight by building next to the property line was not a nuisance. [Fontainebleau Hotel Corp. v. Forty-Five Twenty-Five, Inc., 114 So.2d 357 (Fla. 1959)] But this view may change as a result of the development of solar collectors, which provide cheap energy. It has been held that blocking a neighbor's roof solar collector can be enjoined as a nuisance. [Prah v. Maretti, 321 N.W.2d 182 (Wis. 1982)]

2)   **Spite fences:** [§1545]   A spite fence, erected solely to harm the neighbor and of no economic benefit to the erecting party, can be enjoined as a nuisance. Such conduct has no social utility.

(c) **Fear of harm:** [§1546] If the use is a dangerous one which puts the adjoining neighbor in fear of harm, this is a significant factor in declaring a nuisance (*e.g.*, storage of high explosives, mental hospital, leprosarium). The reasonableness of the fear is tested by general community beliefs and extrinsic evidence based upon experience. And, of course, even though people fear a use, it may be permitted to exist because it has high social value.

1) **Example:** The owner of Blackacre wants to put a "half-way house" on Blackacre to provide temporary residence for selected parolees from state prison. It has been held that a half-way house, which has a high social value, is not a nuisance in a residential area because the fear of bringing criminal activity to the neighborhood is speculative. Until established and tried, the half-way house is an "unknown quantity." [Nicholson v. Connecticut Half-Way House, 218 A.2d 383 (Conn. 1966)]

(2) **Character of the neighborhood:** [§1547] The character of the neighborhood is of great importance in determining a nuisance. Residential areas are often given a preferred status and are protected against incompatible uses.

(a) **Use authorized by zoning ordinance:** [§1548] A zoning ordinance is admissible in court to show community policy with respect to desirable land use within a neighborhood. However, the fact that the defendant's use of her land is consistent with local zoning is *not controlling* in an action for private nuisance. Even though the ordinance may permit the use generally, the specific activity may be carried out in such a manner as to constitute an unreasonable interference with the particular adjoining properties. [Boomer v. Atlantic Cement Co., 26 N.Y.2d 219 (1970)—cement plant located in industrial district declared a nuisance]

(3) **Social value of the conflicting uses:** [§1549] One of the primary objects of nuisance law is to avoid the more serious harm. Society does not want to resolve conflicts in such a way as to make it poorer. If one party's conduct has great social value (*e.g.*, a factory employing many people), a court will be reluctant to enjoin it as a nuisance. On the other hand, if the harm is serious and the payment of damages will not shut down the plant, the court may order the payment of damages for nuisance and refuse to enjoin the activity. This possibility is referred to in section 826(b) of the Restatement (Second) of Torts, *supra*, §1535.

(a) **Example:** Atlantic Cement Co. has invested $45 million in its plant, which employs 300 people. Dirt and smoke emanating from the plant cause $185,000 in permanent damage to A's property. It has been held that A cannot enjoin Atlantic for this nuisance, but can collect $185,000 damages. [Boomer v. Atlantic Cement Co., *supra*]

(4) **Priority in time:** [§1550]   Another important factor is which of the conflicting uses was first located in the vicinity. If the defendant's use was first, the plaintiff has "*come to the nuisance*" and has a less appealing case because he could have avoided the harm. [Bove v. Donner-Hanna Coke Corp., 236 App. Div. 37 (1932)] Economic analysis supports the "coming to the nuisance" defense in many cases (*see infra*, §1565).

c.   **Nuisance compared to trespass:** [§1551]   A *physical invasion* of another's land can be either a trespass or a nuisance. A trespass is an actionable invasion of a possessor's interest in exclusive *possession* of land. A nuisance is an actionable invasion of a possessor's interest in the *use and enjoyment* of land. In trespass, the plaintiff is entitled to relief upon showing an *intentional*, unprivileged physical intrusion. No showing of substantial injury is required; a court does not balance the equities in trespass. In a *nuisance* action, plaintiff must show (i) unreasonable conduct; (ii) substantial injury; and (iii) in most jurisdictions, that the equities balance in plaintiff's favor. In terms of remedies, in trespass the plaintiff is entitled, usually as a matter of right, to damages for past conduct and an injunction against future trespass. In nuisance, the court may, in its discretion, give damages for past conduct or *permanent damages for future conduct* or an injunction. The remedies for nuisance are more flexible than for trespass.

(1) **Air pollution:** [§1552]   Air pollution can be classified as a trespass on the theory that unseen but measurable particles are entering on the plaintiff's land. Or it can be classified as a nuisance, an interference with plaintiff's enjoyment of clean air. Restatement (Second) of Torts section 826(b) (*supra*, §1535) permits a court to treat air pollution as a nuisance—even if the utility of the conduct outweighs the gravity of the harm—if the harm is serious and the defendant can afford to pay those damaged. One of the purposes of section 826(b) is to give courts, in cases where they would be very reluctant to close down a plant having great utility to the public, the option of treating a suit for air pollution as a suit in nuisance, and giving permanent damages.

d.   **Economic analysis:** [§1553]   Economic analysis is increasingly used by modern courts in solving problems of nuisance, including what remedy to give. Indeed, the law of nuisance is hardly ever taught any more without an economic analysis; therefore, a brief exposition is appropriate. Suppose that landowner A has a factory on her land belching smoke into the air, which flows across to landowner B, who has an amusement park on his land. The smoke interferes with the patrons' enjoyment of the park. This simple hypothetical case is useful to focus the economic issues. [*See* Rabin, 63 Va. L. Rev. 1299 (1977)]

(1) **Who is at fault?** [§1554]   Neither A nor B is solely the cause of the harm. Both are responsible, because of the conflicting uses A and B make of their respective parcels. If B's land were most valuable when devoted to some use where smoke is unobjectionable, there would be no conflict and no harm. Now, given B's use as an amusement park, should the court allow B to harm A (by enjoining A's smoke emission as a nuisance) or allow A to harm B (by refusing

to enjoin A)? The economic problem is to avoid the more serious harm, though other factors, particularly fairness, may be important in a judicial determination of the appropriate solution.

(a) **Neither party alone causes conflict:** [§1555]   Under economic theory, the party emitting the smoke is no more the cause of the conflict than the party sensitive to the smoke. The conflict requires the presence of both parties. Courts have sometimes talked about "higher uses," usually in protecting a residential area from noise or smoke or such, giving the "higher use" an advantage, but this does not make economic sense. If the factory has a greater market value than the homes, then society values the factory higher; it is worth more to society.

(b) **Externalities:** [§1556]   An externality is a cost (or benefit) of any given action that is not taken into consideration by the actor in determining the level of that activity that is optimal from the actor's point of view. Economic theory suggests that resources will generally be allocated more efficiently if the costs (and benefits) of different actions are "internalized," *i.e.*, taken into account by economic actors in determining the optimal level of their activities. It is economically inefficient for a business to impose a cost of doing business upon others and not internalize it. In the above example, an external cost of the factory, which A imposed on B, is that B's land is made unsuitable for uses sensitive to smoke. An external cost of B's use of land as an amusement park is that A's land is made unsuitable for activities that conflict with an amusement park.

(2) **The Coase theorem:** [§1557]   The economic problem in all cases of harmful effects is how to maximize the social value of production by putting land to its most valuable use while internalizing costs. Suppose the cost to A of installing smoke abatement equipment is $100, and the damage to B's land is $50. If the right to belch smoke is given A, A will continue to do so because B will give A only $50 to stop, and it is worth $100 to A to continue. If the right to stop the smoke is given B, B will sell the right to smoke to A at somewhere between $50 and $100, because the right is worth only $50 to B and is worth $100 to A. A sale will make them both better off. Thus, regardless of whether A or B is given the right, it will end up in A's hands by operation of the market, at least in most cases where costs of conducting transactions are low. If the figures are reversed, so that installing smoke abatement equipment would cost A $50 and the smoke damage to B's land is $100, A would install the smoke equipment no matter where the right is initially assigned. If assigned to A, B will pay A something between $50 and $100 to install the equipment. If assigned to B, A would install the equipment for $50 rather than buy out B's right for $100. Thus the *market* determines whether the activity (smoke emission) will continue, not the initial allocation of rights by the courts. The initial allocation only makes one party richer and will not stop pollution. This argument was first made by Professor Ronald Coase and is known as the Coase theorem. [3 J. Law & Econ. 1 (1960)]

(3) **Transaction costs:** [§1558] The Coase theorem, which provides that the market will move the right to the highest valued use, depends upon the assumption that transaction costs are zero or low. It assumes that A and B can easily transfer rights to each other at little or no cost. This may be an unrealistic assumption. Transaction costs include costs of obtaining ***information*** about persons with whom one must deal, conducting ***negotiations***, ***coming to terms*** with the other party or parties, and ***enforcing*** any bargains made. The more parties involved, the higher the transaction costs.

(a) **The holdout problem:** [§1559] Suppose that A's factory belches smoke over a large residential area so that fifty neighbors (and not just B) suffer damage. Assume the total damage to the neighbors is $50 ($1 each) and the cost of smoke abatement equipment is $100. If each neighbor is given the right to enjoin A, A has to buy all the neighbors out. It would be to the economic benefit of everyone if this occurred, but A is not likely to be able to buy ***all*** fifty neighbors out at a price under $100. Each neighbor would have an incentive to ***hold out*** for an exorbitant price, more than the $1.99 A would be willing to pay each neighbor. If A were to buy up the right from forty-nine neighbors for $97.51, it would be worthless unless A were to also buy out the final neighbor. Knowing that A will lose $97.51 if he (the final neighbor) will not sell, the last neighbor holding out will price his right higher than $1.99, which means the total cost to A would exceed $100. Therefore, A will not buy out the neighbors and the right to enjoin A will stay with the neighbors, where it was initially allocated. The market does not work to modify the initial allocation.

1) **Caveat:** A can avoid the holdout if she does not make a firm commitment to buy any rights until she is sure that all sellers will agree to sell at a total price of less than $100. But negotiating with fifty neighbors is time-consuming and costly. The deal may not be made because the information cost of finding out at what price each of the fifty neighbors will sell and A will buy exceeds the possible gain of $50 from the trade.

(b) **The free rider problem:** [§1560] Suppose that in the above example the damage to the fifty neighbors was $100 and the cost of smoke abatement equipment was $50. Suppose also that A's activity was not deemed a nuisance by the court, thus allocating the right to A. To achieve the least economic harm, the fifty neighbors should get together, pay A something between $50 and $100, and get A's agreement to install smoke abatement equipment. A and the fifty neighbors will all be better off if this is done. However, there is a tendency for each neighbor to desire a ***free ride*** and not to cough up his or her share: "Let the others do it." Thus, it is difficult to bring about the transfer, transaction costs are too high, and the right stays where allocated. A continues to belch smoke.

(c) **The strategic behavior problem:** [§1561] If A or B behaves in a "strategic" way in an effort to get as much of the gains from trade as possible, bargaining may be difficult to achieve. Suppose that A's smoke damages B's land in the amount of $50, that the cost to A of installing smoke abatement equipment is $100, and that B is entitled to an injunction. Both A and B are better off if a trade takes place with A paying B a sum more than $50 and less than $100. The difference between the value of the right to B and the value to A is called "gains from trade." The question is who will get how much of the gains from trade by bargaining. If B holds out for $90, and A offers "a top" of $80, no trade will take place, and haggling can go on and on—with transactions costs mounting. Parties may behave in a strategic way, particularly where they can only trade with each other (*i.e.*, A is the only person who will pay B more than $50, and B is the only person who can prevent the $100 loss to A; this situation is called a bilateral monopoly).

(d) **Query—are transaction costs ever low?** [§1562]   The holdout and free rider problems mean that when there are many parties, the costs of transacting are high. When there are few parties, transaction costs may be made high by strategic behavior.

(4) **Initial allocation:** [§1563]   The initial allocation of the right is called the "entitlement." How should the initial allocation of the right be made? Should A be given the entitlement? Or should B be given the entitlement? Below are some suggested solutions. Economic arguments are given in (a) and (b), moral arguments in (c) and (d).

(a) **Give to highest valued user:** [§1564]   If the market says that the right is going to end up with the party who most values it, allocate it there initially and avoid transaction costs. By eliminating transaction costs, the ***total wealth*** of society is increased. Economic analysis favors reduction of costs. Another way of phrasing this argument is to say: Allocate the liability (not the right) to the cheapest cost avoider, the person who can eliminate the conflict at the least monetary cost. This will reduce ***total costs to society***.

(b) **First in time prevails:** [§1565]   If one of the conflicting uses is established before the other, the first user may have an irretrievable or "sunk" cost of investment, which the second user may not now have. The first user should prevail at least to the extent that the second user should be forced to buy out the first user. This will require the second user to internalize the cost imposed on the first user and to choose among competing location sites, knowing it must bear this cost. [Spur Industries, Inc. v. Del E. Webb Development Co., 494 P.2d 700 (Ariz. 1972)] Thus, the second user chooses a location on the basis of the cheapest cost, which is to society's benefit. Also, by permitting established uses to continue unharmed, the court avoids "demoralization costs," which might arise if a court enjoins a long-established use because of incompatibility with some use newly arrived on the scene. [*See* Wittman, 9 J. Legal Stud. 557 (1980)]

1) **Criticism:** Awarding the entitlement to the first in time might be efficient and fair where (i) the defendant established his use at a time when he could not reasonably foresee the conflict, and (ii) the activity was not a nuisance at the time it was established. But if there were external costs at the time the activity was begun, it seems both inefficient and unfair not to require the defendant to take these into account by giving damages to the damaged parties.

(c) **Wealth redistribution:** [§1566]   Assume the cost to A of installing smoke abatement equipment is $100, and the smoke damage to B is $50. If the right is given to A to continue to belch smoke, A is $100 richer and B is $50 poorer. The market will not reallocate the right. If the right is given to B to enjoin A, B is richer by $50, or, if the market subsequently reallocates the right, by some amount between $50 and $100 (whatever price A and B come to for transferring that right) and A is poorer by the same amount. Thus the initial allocation affects the wealth position of A and B. A court might decide to allocate the right to A if B is very rich and A poor, or to allocate the right to B if the situation were reversed. The theory would be that society prefers to equalize wealth. This is not an economic argument but a public policy argument based upon *fairness*.

1) **Fairness in other contexts:** [§1567]   Fairness may also be argued in other contexts. If A can pass the cost of abating the harm on to the consumers, so that the cost is spread, this may be deemed fair. If B bought the land at a market price for smoky land and did not pay the price for unsmoky land, it may be deemed unfair to give the right to stop the smoke to B on the ground that B will reap a benefit B did not bargain for. (The economic loser is the person who initially suffered the decrease in land value because of A's smoke, though of course in determining net loss, it is necessary to determine if the "harmed" land rose in value because A's use as a factory brought more people into the area and increased the value of land.)

(d) **Healthy environment:** [§1568]   Another noneconomic argument for allocation of the property right (or entitlement) is that it is morally right for society to guarantee a minimally healthy environment. A person should not be subject to certain health risks, no matter how economically inefficient such a policy might be. Thus, if A's smoke is deemed "unhealthy," allocate the entitlement to B. This argument usually has a strong appeal when phrased in words such as "healthy environment," "air quality," and the like, but the costs of achieving these goals cannot be disregarded. A variation on this argument is to set up an order of preferred activities, as is done in cumulative zoning which prefers housing over commercial uses. This, in effect, makes the allocation in accordance with how "harm" is intuitively perceived by the court or legislature.

e. **Remedies**

(1) **Judicial remedies:** [§1569] In determining what remedy to give in cases of land use conflict, a court has the four choices below. The basic choice of remedy is between injunctive and damage relief. When an injunction is granted, the plaintiff receives the entitlement or property right; the plaintiff can refuse to sell this right if the defendant does not offer enough. When damages are given, the invader is in effect given power to destroy the entitlement of plaintiff upon payment of its value, objectively determined by a jury. Thus the remedy has an important impact on the wealth position of the parties (if not on whether the activity will cease). To illustrate, assume A is a factory owner and B is the owner of an amusement park.

(a) **Enjoin A:** [§1570] The court may grant B an injunction forbidding A to emit smoke. B then has the right. A and B can then bargain, and, according to the Coase theorem, transfer the right to A. B is made richer by the entitlement and is also in a strong position to get most of the gains from trade. [Estancias Dallas Corp. v. Schultz, 500 S.W.2d 217 (Tex. 1973)]

1) **High transaction costs:** [§1571] If transaction costs are very high (if, *e.g.*, the plaintiffs were fifty neighbors), the right as initially allocated would probably not be transferred, even though it would be to society's economic advantage (*see supra*, §1559). For this reason, some have suggested that the second or third remedy, which leaves the right with the highest valued use while giving damages to the other party, is appropriate in such a situation.

(b) **Give B damages:** [§1572] The court may refuse an injunction but grant B damages. This has the effect of giving the right to B, but forcing a sale of it to A (damages). Since the forced sale is at the price of B's damage, B gets his damages but A gets all the possible gains from trade. [Boomer v. Atlantic Cement Co., *supra*, §1548]

1) **Taking for private use:** [§1573] It is arguable that this remedy results in A "taking" B's property. Since the Constitution prohibits taking of private property for private use, this remedy is arguably unconstitutional. However, if it is assumed that neither party alone is at fault in conflicting land use (*see supra*, §§1554-1555), this argument begs the question of whose property is being taken. A might claim that an injunction against her would be the taking of her property. In recent cases, this argument has been rejected on the ground that the question is what *remedy* a court of equity should fashion, not whether A is taking B's property.

(c) **Enjoin A and give A damages:** [§1574] The court may grant B an injunction against A *and* require B to pay A damages. This has the effect of giving the right to B, but forcing B to pay A for it. This solution tends to bring about efficient resource allocation because B, who claims the right is worth more to B than to A but is unwilling to or cannot bargain with A for transfer of the right, is forced to back up his claim for a judicially enforced transfer with cash. However, this solution may not be feasible when there are many potential Bs, and high transaction costs. [Spur Industries, Inc. v. Del E. Webb Development Co., *supra*, §1565]

(d) **Refuse B any remedy:** [§1575]   The court may refuse to grant B any remedy—either an injunction or damages.

3.   Public Nuisance

a.   **Definition:** [§1576]   A public nuisance affects the ***general public***, whereas a private nuisance affects only particular individuals. "A public nuisance is a nuisance which is so widespread in its range or so indiscriminate in its effects that it would not be reasonable to expect one person to take proceedings on his own responsibility to put a stop to it, but that it should be taken on the responsibility of the community at large." [Attorney-General v. P.Y.A. Quarries, Ltd., [1957] 2 Q.B. 169 (per Denning, L.J.)] Uses classified as public nuisances include gambling, prostitution, nude sunbathing, air pollution, and rock festivals. [Town of Preble v. Song Mountain, Inc., 62 Misc. 2d 353 (1970)] The underlying test of a public nuisance is the same as for private nuisance: ***substantial*** harm caused by ***intentional and unreasonable*** conduct or by conduct that is ***negligent or abnormally dangerous***. Unreasonableness turns primarily on the gravity of the harm balanced against the utility of the activity.

b.   **Enforcement by private persons:** [§1577]   A private individual may act against a public nuisance ***only*** if he can show that the nuisance is ***specially injurious*** to him. The person does not have to own any affected land (as in private nuisance), but he must show that the damage to him is of a ***different kind*** than damage to the public at large. It is not enough to show that he suffers the same kind of harm as the general public but to a greater extent.

(1) **Example:** A pollutes a navigable stream so that it is no longer fit for drinking and swimming. This is a public nuisance. A fish hatchery downstream whose business is ruined thereby is entitled to bring suit.

(2) **Standing to sue:** [§1578]   The reason for the requirement of "special injury" is to avoid an excessive number of lawsuits seeking to enforce public rights. The suit should be brought by a public official. However, in recent years, under pressure from environmentalists, standing to sue for public nuisance has been liberalized by statutes and decisions. In some states, a private person can sue as ***representative*** of the general public or in a class action.

c.   **Use authorized by statute:** [§1579]   If a use is authorized by statute or ordinance, it is not a public nuisance and cannot be enjoined. Even so, what would be a public nuisance (in the absence of a statute authorizing it) may be treated as a private nuisance if special injury is shown. Zoning ordinances are not defenses to a private nuisance suit (*see supra*, §1548).

B. RIGHT TO SUPPORT

1. **In General:** [§1580] The right to support of one's land from the lands adjoining is one of the incidents of ownership. It is sometimes called a "natural right." There are two kinds of support involved. "Lateral support" is support that land receives from the adjacent land. "Subjacent support" is support that land receives from underlying strata.

2. **Right to Lateral Support**

   a. **Right to support of land:** [§1581] A landowner is ***strictly liable*** if he changes his land use so as to withdraw lateral support from his neighbor and cause his neighbor's land to slip or fall in. It is no defense that the excavator acted with the utmost care and not negligently. The absolute right to support of land is based on the idea that fairness requires that adjacent landowners not disturb the natural conditions so as to deprive the other's land of lateral support.

      (1) **Retaining walls:** [§1582] If an excavator builds a retaining wall to support the adjoining parcel, he and his successors in interest have the duty thereafter to maintain the wall. Although a landowner is not liable for failure of support because of an act of God (erosion, storm, flood, etc.), decay or deterioration of a retaining wall is not an act of God so as to relieve the excavator from liability. Once a landowner changes the natural conditions and erects an artificial support, he and all subsequent owners of the changed property have a duty to maintain such support. [Gorton v. Schofield, 41 N.E.2d 12 (Mass. 1942); Noone v. Price, 298 S.E.2d 218 (W. Va. 1982)]

   b. **Right to support of buildings on land**

      (1) **Majority view:** [§1583] Strict liability for withdrawal of lateral support to a neighbor's property does not extend to buildings on the neighbor's land. There is no obligation to support the added weight of buildings that the land cannot naturally support. Where an adjacent landowner excavates and provides sufficient support to sustain the weight of the neighboring land in its natural state, ***but the neighboring land slips because of the weight of the buildings on it,*** the excavator is not liable in the absence of negligence. On the other hand, if land in its natural state can support the weight of a building, the neighbor who withdraws support to the land, resulting in damage to the building, is ***strictly liable*** for damage to the land and the building. The crucial fact is whether the weight of the building placed so much pressure on the land that the building caused the subsidence when the neighbor withdrew support. If it did, the neighbor is liable only for negligence. [Noone v. Price, *supra*]

         (a) **Improvement on burdened land:** [§1584] In jurisdictions imposing liability only for negligence, the developer may wish to shore up an adjacent building to protect himself from a possible claim of negligence. The developer must pay the cost; the owner of a building is not obliged to shore up his own building and may let it collapse if he wishes. [Warfel v. Vondersmith, 101 A.2d 736 (Pa. 1954)]

(2) **Minority view:** [§1585]   In England and by case law in a minority of states, an adjacent landowner has the same strict liability for failing to support neighboring buildings as he has with respect to land. Statutes and city ordinances adopt this position in many states. It is likely that this view is the law in all the large cities in this country.

(a) **Policy issues:** Strict liability, protecting the person who builds first, encourages development. In protecting the first developer, strict liability for lateral support of buildings is efficient because it imposes the costs on the second developer, who more easily can avoid them (*see supra,* §1565). It may appear unfair, however, because it allows the first developer to increase the support burdens on neighbors and perhaps devalue their land. The same conflict in policy appears in nuisance law over whether priority in time controls what is a nuisance (*see supra,* §1565).

c. **Subsidence from withdrawal of water:** [§1586]   As discussed *infra* (§1607), a landowner usually has absolute ownership of all the percolating ground water under the land. He can sink wells, drying up neighboring wells, with impunity. If the landowner sinks wells and causes subsidence of neighboring land, is he liable? Some courts have applied the absolute-ownership-of-percolating-water rule, and have held that the landowner is not liable unless he carries off some soil in the process or reduces the lateral support of the land. This seems unfair and inefficient because it does not require the owner of the well to take adequate precautions. More modern cases hold that an owner of a well is liable for negligence if he causes adjacent land to subside. [Finley v. Teeter Stone, Inc., 248 A.2d 106 (Md. 1968); Friendswood Development Co. v. Smith-Southwest Industries, Inc., 576 S.W.2d 21 (Tex. 1978)—applying new rule prospectively]

3. **Right to Subjacent Support:** [§1587]   Whenever mineral estates are severed from the surface, the surface occupant has a right of subjacent support against the mineral owner. This right differs from the right to lateral support in two respects: (i) the mineral owner must support the land with the buildings existing on it when the mineral estate is severed (*i.e.,* the mineral owner is strictly liable for subsidence of the land and any existing buildings); and (ii) the mineral owner is liable for negligently damaging springs and wells, but under the usual rule that an adjacent owner has absolute ownership of the percolating water under his land (*see infra,* §1607), the adjacent owner is not liable for interfering with percolating ground water of his neighbors.

C. RIGHTS IN WATER

1. **Streams and Lakes:** [§1588]   Rights in streams and lakes adjoining land are different from rights in percolating ground water under the owner's land and surface water on the land. In most jurisdictions, adjacent landowners have *riparian rights* in streams or lakes, but in some states adjacent landowners have only *prior appropriation rights.* In some states, these two distinctly different approaches to allocating water rights are both used.

a. **Riparian rights—in general:** [§1589]   In the large majority of states, land adjacent to streams or lakes has riparian rights. A stream is a *flowing* body of water contained *within a definite course*. The stream can be above ground or underground. Riparian rights include rights in the *quantity*, *quality*, and *velocity* of the water. Riparian owners have swimming, boating, and fishing privileges as well as the right to use or take the water onto riparian land. The extent of riparian rights depends upon whether the jurisdiction follows the natural flow theory or reasonable use theory (discussed below).

(1) **Riparian land:** [§1590]   Riparian land is all land under a unit title contiguous to a body of water—provided it is within the watershed of the body of water. The reason for this proviso is that water used in the watershed will return to the body of water and be available for the other riparian owners. [Stratton v. Mt. Hermon Boy's School, 103 N.E. 87 (Mass. 1913)] In a few jurisdictions, the unit of title is the smallest tract of land that has always been contiguous to the water, but in most states, a riparian owner can buy contiguous land within the watershed and extend riparian rights to it.

   (a) **Use on nonriparian land:** [§1591]   A riparian right is "attached" to the riparian land and can never be transferred to a nonriparian owner. The right runs with the land, so to speak. This is not to say, however, that water can never be used on nonriparian land by the riparian owner. Under the reasonable use theory, use of water by a riparian owner for nonriparian purposes (*e.g.*, selling it to the public as drinking water) or to irrigate nonriparian land may be permitted. (*See infra,* §1597.)

(2) **Pollution:** [§1592]   There is no riparian right to pollute waters, but most pollution problems have been handled as questions of nuisance. Downstream riparian owners usually sue an upstream polluter alleging a nuisance. Hence this discussion deals largely with *diminishing the quantity* of water, although riparian doctrine traditionally speaks of quality and quantity.

(3) **Public rights:** [§1593]   A riparian owner may not exercise her rights so as to infringe on public rights in public waters. Public waters include navigable waters of all kinds and great lakes and streams. Public rights include boating, swimming, and fishing. Such public rights may be exercised by any person *with legal access to the water.* In most jurisdictions, the state can regulate the public rights under the police power and can permit a riparian owner to impair public rights. In some states, however, the state holds public waters *in trust* for the public and cannot permit uses that violate public rights. [National Audubon Society v. Superior Court, 33 Cal. 3d 419 (1983)]

b. **Natural flow:** [§1594]   In determining the extent of riparian rights, the English courts developed the natural flow theory, which was well suited to an agrarian society and the early days of the Industrial Revolution when many mills were powered by water. Under this theory, one riparian owner can use the water but must return it to the stream in its natural condition. Each riparian owner is entitled to the *natural flow of water, without material diminution in quantity or quality.* In determining what is "natural," courts have held that each riparian owner has the privilege of using water for domestic needs. In addition, each riparian owner can use water for "artificial" or commercial needs, provided such uses do not materially affect the quantity or quality of the water.

(1) **Limitations:** [§1595] A riparian owner is not permitted to use water on nonriparian land. Also, a riparian owner, limited to uses that do not interfere with natural flow, cannot deplete the quantity of water *even though no one is harmed.* Water storage is not permissible.

(2) **Criticism:** [§1596] The natural flow theory severely limits the use of water for irrigation and commercial use. It inhibits the full utilization of water since, even though no one is harmed and the water would otherwise be wasted, a riparian owner cannot deplete the natural quantity of water. Because it is not utilitarian, the large majority of states reject the natural flow theory as it is applied to streams and follow the reasonable use theory. A few states still (theoretically) follow the natural flow theory, but the language of reasonableness has crept into the court opinions in recent years.

c. **Reasonable use:** [§1597] Most American courts follow a reasonable use theory. The riparian owner is entitled to a reasonable use of the water, and downstream owners cannot enjoin the owner or recover damages unless they are not receiving enough water for their needs or the upstream owner is substantially interfering with their needs. If the downstream owner is not harmed, he cannot enjoin the upstream owner's use. [Dumont v. Kellogg, 29 Mich. 420 (1874)]

(1) **Domestic use preferred:** [§1598] Although in theory no one factor is controlling in determining reasonableness, in most states domestic uses are preferred over others. The upstream owner can take whatever water is necessary for domestic purposes—without regard for its effect on the natural flow or level of the water or the needs of lower riparians. For domestic use, the upstream owner has a preferred status. "Domestic use" includes water for drinking and bathing, for farm animals on a small farm, and for irrigation of a garden to supply produce to the riparian owner.

(a) **Rationale:** "Domestic uses" are necessary to maintain life. They usually involve taking only small quantities of water. A preferred domestic use can be established at any time, interfering with existing nondomestic uses. In times of drought, nondomestic users must cut their use of water to accommodate domestic users.

(2) **Commercial use:** [§1599] The upstream owner cannot take water for commercial purposes unless there is enough water for the domestic wants of all. To the extent that water is in excess of everyone's domestic needs, it can be used for commercial purposes. Irrigation of a large farm is deemed a commercial riparian use, not a domestic use. In some reasonable use jurisdictions, especially in the arid West, irrigation is favored over all other commercial uses and may even impair rights of lower owners for water power use.

(3) **Use for nonriparian land:** [§1600]   Some, but not all, courts adhering to the reasonable use theory have permitted a riparian owner to use water on nonriparian land if this does not cause harm to a reasonable use of another riparian owner. Courts that permit this are usually in states where irrigation of land is important. [Smith v. Stanolind Oil & Gas Co., 172 P.2d 1002 (Okla. 1946)]

(4) **Economic justification:** [§1601]   Although the reasonable use theory favors development and use of water, any theory of reasonable use—with the resulting uncertainty—has costs that a fixed definition of rights does not. Ad hoc balancing of the interests has high judicial costs and costs of legal advice and litigation. On the other hand, it is economically better if a right passes to the user who values it most (*see* Coase theorem, *supra*, §1557). A fixed definition of riparian rights, as under the natural flow theory, will not result in the right passing to the highest valued user because of high transaction costs. Usually there are many persons along a stream with riparian rights who would be necessary parties to a bargain. Hence, the economic justification for the reasonable use doctrine is that the court should intervene to achieve efficiency because of the high transaction costs that will prevent a bargain.

d. **Prior appropriation doctrine:** [§1602]   In the eight most arid western states (Arizona, Colorado, Idaho, Montana, Nevada, New Mexico, Utah, and Wyoming), common law riparian rights have been rejected as unsuitable because they hinder investment in irrigation and other water uses. Riparian rights have been replaced by the "prior appropriation" doctrine. Under this doctrine, water rights are determined by priority of beneficial use. The water can be used on land far away from the water ("nonriparian"). The prior appropriation doctrine grew out of the custom of miners in diverting water for their needs, sometimes miles away from the source. Once a right to water is established, it is an interest independent of the land and ***can be severed*** from the land and sold to another for use on other land. [Coffin v. Left Hand Ditch Co., 6 Colo. 443 (1882); Baker v. Ore-Ida Foods, Inc., 513 P.2d 627 (Idaho 1973)]

(1) **Economic justification:** [§1603]   The prior appropriation doctrine is a rule of capture and has the advantages of such a rule (*see supra,* §6): It encourages development of water uses and is predictable; it is efficient in that it permits the transfer of a prior appropriation right to a user who puts a higher value on it; and transaction costs are low.

(2) **Supplemental to reasonable use theory:** [§1604]   For many years, in nine western states including California and Texas the prior appropriation doctrine has existed along with the reasonable use theory. In these states, water law is quite complex because the prior appropriation doctrine is fundamentally inconsistent with the reasonable use doctrine. State administrative boards have been established in these states to resolve conflicts between the two principles so as to conserve (not waste) water. [People v. Shirokow, 26 Cal. 3d 301 (1980)] Since the 1960s, a limited application of the prior appropriation doctrine has

been adopted by legislation in several southeastern and midwestern states. This legislation has usually established a state water resources board to regulate water uses in the public interest.

e. **Taking by government:** [§1605]   If the government takes riparian rights by eminent domain, it must pay the owner for them. However, the federal government has the power under the Constitution to regulate all navigation in navigable waters. Under this power, it can build dams across rivers, interfering with the natural flow of the river. A riparian owner has no right to maintenance of a river at any given level below high-water mark, as against improvements of navigation. The government may raise the level of the river to high-water mark or lower it. Lands above the high-water mark are fast lands, and to flood them requires compensation. [United States v. Willow River Power Co., 324 U.S. 499 (1945)]

2. **Percolating Ground Water:** [§1606]   Recognized *underground streams* are subject to the same riparian rights as surface watercourses (discussed above). *Ground water* (*i.e.,* water moving through the ground diffusely, rather than in a channel) is subject to different rules, which usually give the owner of the soil more rights than a riparian owner would have.

a. **Absolute ownership:** [§1607]   The oldest rule is the English, which deems ground water, like minerals, to be part of the soil. Accordingly, the surface owner has the right to pump water either for her own use or for commercial use. Unless done with malicious intent, an owner can with impunity sink a well and cause a neighbor's well to go dry. In a sense, this is a rule of "capture"; the captured water can be sold to another. [Acton v. Blundell, 12 Mees. & W. 324 (1843)]

(1) **Applied in eastern states:** [§1608]   The rule is still followed in many of the eastern states, where underground water is plentiful. (Compare this rule granting absolute ownership of percolating water with the natural flow theory, still applied in some eastern states, which gives the owner very limited rights in a flowing stream.) In the arid west, which has a strong public policy against wasting water, the rule has usually been rejected.

b. **Reasonable use doctrine:** [§1609]   In most western states and some eastern ones, the surface owner is limited to the reasonable use of percolating ground water. The test of reasonable use is similar to the reasonable use doctrine applied to streams. An overlying owner can pump water for use on her own land for reasonable uses in unlimited quantities—even if it causes a neighboring landowner harm. [Bristor v. Cheatham, 255 P.2d 173 (Ariz. 1953)] An overlying owner cannot divert water from her well to noncontiguous land if another owner within the water basin would be harmed. [Farmers Investment Co. v. Bettwy, 558 P.2d 14 (Ariz. 1976); Higday v. Nickolaus, 469 S.W.2d 859 (Mo. 1971)] In an arid climate, this limitation poses a serious obstacle for cities attempting to supplement their water supplies by purchasing land and sinking wells.

(1) **Example:** A, a dairy farmer, has a well on her property which provides water for her cattle. On one side of A's farm, B, an adjoining owner, sinks a powerful

well that provides water to B's pulp mill, which is discharged back into the source basin. City Water Co. sinks pumps on the other side of A's land for a city water supply. A's well dries up. City Water Co. is liable to A, but B is not.

c. **Correlative rights doctrine:** [§1610]   In California, the surface owners over a common aquifer (underground water basin) own the water jointly, and each is allowed a proportionate *quantity* of water. Surplus water not needed on the basin lands can be used on other land. Any use that lowers the water table is prohibited.

d. **Prior appropriation doctrine:** [§1611]   In some arid western states, the prior appropriation doctrine (*see supra,* §1602) applies to ground waters as well as to streams.

3. **Surface Water:** [§1612]   Diffused surface water refers to water that has no channel but passes across the surface of land. The source may be rainfall, melting snow, or seepage. The rights of the land owner depend upon whether the water is beneficial and wanted, or not wanted. In the first case, the owner wants to capture the water; in the second, she wants to expel it.

a. **Capture:** [§1613]   If a person wants to, she may capture surface water. Once captured, by a dam or in barrels, it can be diverted by the owner to any use she sees fit, on or off the land. The only limitation is that the capturing owner not unnecessarily harm owners below her.

(1) **Example:** O builds an earthen dam on her farm to catch water seeping across her land for her livestock. Subsequently, a farm owner on higher ground builds a dam and creates a pool. This lowers the level of O's water. O has no right to the continued flow of the surface water, and the other farmer is within his rights in capturing the water.

b. **Expelling:** [§1614]   More often the landowner will try to get rid of surface waters by changing the natural drainage. Liability to the landowner's neighbors depends on whether the state follows the "common enemy" doctrine or the "natural servitude" doctrine.

(1) **Common enemy doctrine:** [§1615]   Under the common enemy view, surface water is a common enemy, and any owner theoretically has an unqualified right to fend off surface waters by changing the drainage or building a dam. The common enemy doctrine is rarely applied in its extreme form any more. Almost all modern decisions applying the doctrine modify it by requiring that the interference with the neighbors be *reasonable* or at least not negligent. The landowner must avoid unnecessary or disproportionate harm to the neighbors. [Tucker v. Badoian, 384 N.E.2d 1195 (Mass. 1978); Armstrong v. Francis Corp., 120 A.2d 4 (N.J. 1956); Pendergast v. Aiken, 236 S.E.2d 787 (N.C. 1977)]

(2) **Natural servitude doctrine:** [§1616]   The natural servitude doctrine, sometimes known as the "civil law doctrine," is followed in about half the states. It

provides that lower lands are servient to the natural flow of surface waters. The owner cannot obstruct or change the flow so as to injure others either above (by building a dam and backing up water on the upper owner) or below (by digging a channel so as to hasten the flow of water).

(a) **Criticism:** Although having the advantage of predictability, this doctrine limits development or improvement of land. In most states, it is being changed to permit reasonable changes in the flow from the servient land (such as channeling drainage), particularly in urban areas. Under the natural servitude doctrine, as well as under the common enemy doctrine, courts are gradually introducing a reasonableness test, and it is likely that ultimately both of these doctrines will disappear and be replaced by a reasonableness test. The same trend is taking place in riparian rights, where the reasonable use test is replacing the natural flow doctrine.

D. RIGHTS IN AIRSPACE

1. **Navigable Airspace:** [§1617]   The surface owner may be protected against intrusions in the overlying airspace that impair his present or potential use of the surface. He may be able to recover in trespass or, where there are repeated intrusions, in nuisance.

   a. **Navigational servitude:** [§1618]   An ancient maxim says that the surface owner has a right to exclusive possession to the heavens. However, the modern world pays little heed to this maxim. Aircraft have a navigational servitude (right to cross airspace) above the surface land. The distance above surface land at which the servitude begins may be set by proper government authority. The real test of a surface owner's rights is whether use of airspace *harms the surface owner.* If it does not harm the surface owner, intrusions in airspace by aircraft are not actionable.

   b. **Noisy flights as inverse condemnation:** [§1619]   If the noise of airplanes flying over land constitutes a direct and continuing interference with the enjoyment and use of the surface, a governmental body may have taken property for which compensation must be paid under the Constitution.

   (1) **Example:** Low-flying military aircraft from a nearby field fly directly over a chicken farm and frighten the chickens, causing production to fall off. The chicken farm is forced to go out of business. The federal government has taken, by inverse condemnation, an easement for noisy flights over the farmer's land and must pay damages. [United States v. Causby, 328 U.S. 256 (1946)]

   (2) **Inverse condemnation:** [§1620]   Inverse condemnation is an action brought by an owner against a governmental body having the power of eminent domain. The purpose of the action is to recover the value of property that in effect has been taken by the government, although no formal exercise of the power of eminent domain has occurred. (*See infra,* §1717.)

   (a) **Public body must be sued:** [§1621]   This theory can be applied only to governmental units with the power of eminent domain. The *government* or *airport commission* must be sued—*not* the airlines.

(3) **Rights of neighboring landowners:** [§1622] A landowner whose land is near, but not directly under, the flight path may suffer nearly as much noise and air pollution as those owners directly under the flight path. However, since an aircraft has not entered the landowner's airspace, it may be difficult for the landowner to claim a taking of an easement for noisy flight. A federal court has not permitted the neighboring landowners to recover damages, reasoning that there must be a trespass by the airplane before there can be a taking of property. [Batten v. United States, 306 F.2d 580 (10th Cir. 1962)] On the other hand, a few state courts **have permitted** a recovery on the theory that the **noise** constitutes a physical invasion interfering with the neighboring owner's enjoyment of the surface. [Thornburg v. Port of Portland, 376 P.2d 100 (Or. 1962); Martin v. Port of Seattle, 391 P.2d 540 (Wash. 1964); *but see* Ferguson v. City of Keene, 238 A.2d 1 (N.H. 1968)—cause of action in nuisance, but not inverse condemnation, would lie]

c. **Noisy flights as a nuisance:** [§1623] If noise pollution from airplanes is classified as a nuisance, the landowner can collect damages. [Ferguson v. City of Keene, *supra*]

(1) **Injunction not available:** [§1624] Note however that a court cannot issue an injunction, as this would interfere with the regulation of air traffic by the appropriate governmental agencies. In addition, an injunction would be an economically inefficient way to allocate airspace, because it would require the airline to buy out the landowners, each of whom might hold out for an unreasonable price. The award of damages means that the landowners are forced to sell a navigational servitude for noisy flights at a price set by a jury.

(2) **Neighboring landowners may recover:** [§1625] Since a nuisance does not necessarily involve a physical invasion of the landowner's space, this theory permits recovery of damages by landowners whose airspace is not entered by the airplanes, but whose enjoyment and use is substantially harmed.

(3) **Nongovernmental defendant:** [§1626] Under this theory, a nongovernmental defendant (such as an airline) can be sued by the landowner. Because of governmental immunity from tort in some states, this theory might not be available against a governmental defendant (which would have to be sued under the inverse condemnation theory).

2. **Solar Enjoyment:** [§1627] Whether a landowner has a cause of action in nuisance for his neighbor's blocking of sunlight is a question on which there is, to date, a split of judicial opinion. It has been held that such a cause of action does not lie. [Fontainebleau Hotel Corp. v. Forty-Five Twenty-Five, Inc., *supra,* §1544—neighboring hotel blocking sun on swimming pool] It has also been held that a cause of action in nuisance does lie for blocking sunlight. [Prah v. Maretti *supra,* §1544—blocking neighbor's solar collector] If such a cause of action does lie, it is probable that the court, in balancing the utility of the conduct against the harm, will give more protection to solar collectors than to sunlight for gardens or swimming pools.

a. **Economic issue:** [§1628]   The economic issue, discussed earlier in other contexts is whether it is more efficient to have a fixed definition of solar rights, which can be easily transferred to the higher valued use if there are low transaction costs, or a reasonableness test. If only two neighbors are involved, under the Coase theorem (*supra,* §1557), the right will end up with the party who values it more regardless of whether the court says solar blockage is or is not a nuisance. If so, judicial costs can be saved by having a fixed rule. However, when many parties are affected, the reasonableness test of nuisance, which lets the court determine who has the right, has greater economic justification because of the high transaction costs involved (*see supra,* §1558).

3. **Weather Modification:** [§1629]   In recent years, weather modification has sometimes been undertaken. Forms of such modification include cloud seeding and hail suppression. If a private person not acting in a governmental capacity flies over land he does not own in an attempt to modify the weather, the landowner is entitled to an injunction against weather modification. An entry for this purpose, unlike air travel generally, is *not* privileged. It interferes with the plaintiff's right to the natural clouds and natural rainfall over the plaintiff's land, which aircraft generally do not disturb. [Southwest Weather Research, Inc. v. Rounsaville, 320 S.W.2d 211 (Tex. 1959)] Whether a landowner can prevent weather modification attempts by persons who do not enter his airspace, but fly over neighboring lands, is more doubtful. At the very least, the plaintiff must prove harm—by analogy to a nuisance being committed on neighboring property. To date, injunctions have been denied on the ground that the harm has been too speculative. [Pennsylvania Natural Weather Association v. Blue Ridge Weather Modification Association, 44 Pa. D. & C.2d 749 (1968)]

XI. PUBLIC LAND USE CONTROLS

chapter approach

The use of land is often controlled by local governments. The primary tool used by government is the *zoning* ordinance. But governments may also use *subdivision regulation* and *eminent domain*.

For purposes of study:

1. Remember that the authority for zoning comes from the state, and so a zoning ordinance must conform to the state's enabling act or it is *ultra vires* (void because it is beyond the authority of the local body).

2. Also consider the constitutional limitations on these land use controls:

    — Zoning power may be limited by procedural or substantive due process, equal protection considerations, or the Taking Clause of the fifth amendment. Current "hot" topics, raising difficult and unsettled constitutional issues, include regulatory takings and aesthetic regulations. Be sure to look for constitutional problems when you see *exclusionary zoning*—zoning that excludes a particular group.

    — Although the power of eminent domain is usually upheld, recall that when the government takes land it must be for a *public use* (defined broadly by the Supreme Court) and there must be *just compensation* paid (generally fair market value).

A. ZONING

1. **Theory of Zoning:** [§1630]   By dividing up a city into use zones from which harmful uses are excluded, zoning purports to prevent one landowner from harming his neighbor by bringing in an incompatible use. In a sense, zoning is nuisance law made predictable by declaring in advance what uses are harmful and prohibited in the various zones. Indeed, this is the theory used in the classic case upholding zoning from constitutional attack, *Village of Euclid v. Ambler Realty Co.,* 272 U.S. 365 (1926). But zoning has purposes beyond preventing harm. Modern zoning often regulates uses to achieve public benefits or to maximize property values (the tax base) in the city. Zoning also has a darker side: It has been used to exclude low income groups who cannot afford the housing permitted in the city.

    a. **Separation of uses:** [§1631]   The most fundamental means by which zoning accomplishes its purposes is the separation of conflicting uses, which are classified on a scale from "highest" use to "lowest" use. The highest use is deemed the least harmful to others, the lowest the most harmful. Separation of uses into different districts is sometimes called "Euclidean zoning," after the *Euclid* case holding it valid.

        (1) **Highest use—housing:** [§1632]   Zoning laws embody the assumption that wholesome housing (the central objective) must be protected from harmful

neighbors. Thus commerce and industry are excluded from residential zones because they are deemed harmful to housing. Even within residential zones there is a hierarchy of desirable uses. A single-family house, the "highest" use, is protected by being in an exclusive single-family house zone from the harmful effects of less desirable housing being nearby. Excluded are two-family houses and apartments. Similarly, in a two-family house district, lower residential uses such as apartments are excluded.

(a) **Classifying uses:** [§1633]   Sometimes it is difficult to determine whether a use is more properly permitted in a residential district or in a commercial district. The question is one of compatibility of appearance, purpose, noise, and traffic. Any classification *reasonably related* to the legitimate purpose of segregating residential and commercial uses will be upheld. Thus, boarding houses and rooming houses are usually permitted in a residential district, but hotels and motels are not. The latter are thought to have commercial appearances, to be more public in character, and to generate more noise and traffic. [Pierro v. Baxendale, 118 A.2d 401 (N.J. 1955)]

(2) **Commercial and industrial districts:** [§1634]   Commercial use is "lower" than residential. Zoning codes typically divide commercial districts into several different kinds. C-1, for example, might provide for convenience shopping (grocery, drugstore, etc.), C-2 for a regional shopping center, and C-3 for a downtown commercial district. Industrial uses, which are "lower" than commercial, are similarly divided. The purpose of such divisions is to separate light from heavy industry and commerce.

(3) **Principle of cumulative uses:** [§1635]   The principle of cumulative uses underlies zoning law. It states that *higher* but not lower uses are permitted in any district. Accordingly, in an apartment district, single-family and two-family houses can be erected, but no commercial or industrial uses are permitted. In certain situations, however, the ordinance may not be cumulative and may exclude higher uses. For example, it is rather common today for a zoning ordinance to forbid residential or commercial use in an industrial park district. The purposes of such noncumulative ordinances are to prevent discord between houses and industry and to keep land available for industry in the industrial park.

b. **Density controls:** [§1636]   Density controls are rules that indirectly control the number of people using an area of land. They may include height limitations, setback requirements, and minimum lot and house sizes.

2. **Source of Zoning Power:** [§1637]   Zoning ordinances are usually enacted by a city or a county to apply to land within its local jurisdiction. But under our governmental scheme, the state legislature is the sovereign power, and a city or county has no power to zone unless given such power by the state legislature. The act giving power to zone is called the *enabling act*. All zoning ordinances must be authorized by and must conform to the state's enabling act. Any zoning ordinance that does not conform to the enabling act is *ultra vires* (*i.e.*, beyond the authority of the local body) and is therefore void.

a. **Delegation of power:** [§1638]   Under our constitutional theory, a legislature cannot delegate discretionary power to an administrative body unless it lays down standards to govern the exercise of the power. A delegation without standards is improper. At the heart of the delegation of powers doctrine is the desire of courts to restrict discretionary administrative powers so far as may be practical in view of the job to be done. Courts fear discretionary power because of the potential for abuse. Thus in zoning cases, where the standard to be applied is vague, the delegation of authority can be attacked (sometimes successfully) as an improper delegation of power.

(1) **Note—argument not in vogue:** The delegation of powers without standards argument was more successful formerly than it is today. With the increasing complexity of society came increased bureaucratic decision-making. Since World War II we have grown accustomed to the exercise of broad powers by administrators. The delegation of powers argument is not as appealing to judges as it formerly was.

3. **Constitutional Limitations:** [§1639]   When a state enacts an enabling act, it does so under the authority of its "police power," the legislative power a state has to regulate human affairs so as to effect the purposes of government. The power of states to authorize regulation of property use by zoning laws and the power of local governments to enact such laws have been specifically upheld as valid use of the police power. [Village of Euclid v. Amber Realty Co., *supra*, §1630] Although zoning laws enjoy a presumption of validity, like any other legislation, zoning laws must not violate the Constitution. The constitutional requirements must be met with respect to *each individual lot*. Thus an ordinance might be valid in general, but be *invalid as applied* to a particular lot. [Nectow v. City of Cambridge, 227 U.S. 183 (1928)] Any argument that a zoning ordinance is unconstitutional must usually be based on one of the following clauses.

a. **Due Process Clause:** [§1640]   The Due Process Clause of the fourteenth amendment provides: "No State shall . . . deprive any person of life, liberty, or property, without due process of law. . . ." A rough conceptualization of the effect of this clause divides it into *procedural* and *substantive* due process. Zoning actions may violate either form of due process.

(1) **Procedural due process:** [§1641]   A landowner may argue that a zoning action has deprived him of procedural due process if it has been enacted without notice to him and without his having had an opportunity to be heard. However, courts have drawn a distinction between *legislative* actions (such as enacting a zoning ordinance for the entire city) and *administrative* actions. For legislative actions, notice does not have to be given to each landowner affected, whereas for administrative actions, it does have to be given. Administrative actions include variances and special exceptions, which are granted by the zoning board of adjustment (*infra*, §1698). In some states, zoning ordinance amendments by the city council affecting a few lots are treated as administrative decisions, on the theory that it is fair and reasonable to require notice to affected parties (including neighbors) where the action affects only a few. [Fasano v. Board of County Commissioners, 507 P.2d 23 (Or. 1973)]

(2) **Substantive due process:** [§1642]   Substantive due process must be defined with separate reference to the Federal Constitution and state constitutions. Prior to the mid-1930s, the United States Supreme Court struck down legislation deemed unwise on the ground that it violated (substantive) due process of law. The court was severely criticized for requiring legislatures to conform with its notions of proper public policy, which it read into the Due Process Clause. In the 1930s, the court beat a retreat, and with rare exceptions since then has not struck down economic and social legislation on grounds of violation of due process. The current test for whether federal substantive due process has been violated is: Does the ordinance bear a **rational relationship to a permissible state objective**? If so, the ordinance is valid under the Due Process Clause. The ordinance must be *a* rational way of achieving the objective, not necessarily the best way. [Village of Belle Terre v. Boraas, 416 U.S. 1 (1974)] Legitimate state objectives have been held to include public health, safety, and general welfare. Inasmuch as almost all zoning ordinances involve a means of achieving these objectives that is not wholly irrational, few zoning ordinances are struck down under the rational relationship test.

    (a) **Strict scrutiny standard:** [§1643]   If the zoning ordinance infringes upon a **fundamental right** (*e.g.*, the right to vote, the right to free speech, the right to interstate travel, etc.), the burden is on the state to justify the legislation by showing it has a **compelling state interest** in the legislation's objective. This standard is called strict scrutiny, because it requires that a statute be examined very closely. However, strict scrutiny is rarely applied under the Due Process Clause to zoning ordinances, because housing has been held *not* to be a "fundamental" right. [Lindsey v. Normet, *supra*, §1214; *but see* Moore v. City of East Cleveland, 431 U.S. 494 (1977)—constitutional protection given to the right of traditional family to live together (*see infra*, §1674)] Even though exclusionary zoning ordinances may infringe upon the right to travel and settle in the community, it is difficult to raise that issue in federal courts (*see infra*, §1682).

(3) **State due process requirements:** [§1644]   Like the Federal Constitution, state constitutions also require that legislation not deprive a person of due process of law. As to a state constitution, the state supreme court is the final arbiter of its meaning. Although the United States Supreme Court has interpreted the Due Process Clause in the Federal Constitution in such a way as to limit severely its application to laws regulating the use of property, state supreme courts have continued to recognize that the **state** due process clause has **considerable substantive** as well as procedural content. Under this clause, state courts strike down legislation they deem "arbitrary" or "unreasonable," even though it may be *a* rational way of achieving the objective. State courts, interpreting state constitutions, give a broader reach to the state due process clause than does the U.S. Supreme Court interpreting the Federal Constitution.

    (a) **Adequate return on investment required:** [§1645]   State courts require that the ordinance not deprive the landowner of a reasonable return from his investment. If the possibility of any adequate return from the land is denied by the ordinance, the regulation is unreasonable and therefore a violation of due process. [Arverne Bay Construction Co. v. Thatcher, 287 N.Y. 222 (1938)] Note that a state court may characterize an extreme reduction in value either as a "taking" or as in violation of substantive due process. [Fred F. French Investing Co. v. City of New York, 39 N.Y.2d 587 (1976)—great destruction of economic value is a deprivation of due process]

b. **Equal Protection Clause:** [§1646]   The Equal Protection Clause of the fourteenth amendment provides: "No State shall . . . deny to any person within its jurisdiction the equal protection of the laws." As applied to zoning, this clause requires that landowners who are similarly situated be similarly treated, except where treating them differently can be justified. The difference between the Due Process Clause and the Equal Protection Clause is generally this: Under the Due Process Clause the question is whether the government can take away the right. Under the Equal Protection Clause, the question is whether the government can take away the right from these persons and not from others. In order to establish a violation of the Equal Protection Clause, the plaintiff must prove a *discriminatory purpose or intent*. Discriminatory effect is not enough. [Village of Arlington Heights v. Metropolitan Housing Development Corp., 429 U.S. 252 (1977)]

(1) **Rational relationship standard:** [§1647]   The validity of most zoning regulations under the Equal Protection Clause is measured by the rational relationship test that is also applicable under the Due Process Clause. The legislation only has to bear a *rational relation* to a *permissible state objective*. [Village of Belle Terre v. Boraas, *supra*, §1642]

(2) **Strict scrutiny standard:** [§1648]   If the zoning ordinance operates by reference to a *suspect classification* (*i.e.*, race, national origin, religion, and possibly age and sex), the burden is on the state to justify the legislation by showing it has a *compelling state interest* in the legislation's objective. The ordinance is strictly scrutinized. Thus, a zoning ordinance that restricts blacks to one district and whites to another would violate the Equal Protection Clause. However, strict scrutiny is rarely applied under the Equal Protection Clause to zoning ordinances because they rarely operate by reference to a suspect classification.

c. **Taking Clause:** [§1649]   The fifth amendment to the Constitution provides: ". . . nor shall private property be taken for public use without just compensation." Although this amendment is expressly applicable only to the federal government, it has also been held applicable to the states under the fourteenth amendment, which requires the states to provide citizens with due process of law. Because of this, courts sometimes do not clearly indicate whether they regard the issue as one of taking or as one of due process. They mix the two. But this is confusing because due process is basically a question of rational relationship between means and ends (or substantive due process) whereas taking involves rather different matters, such as whether the ordinance prevents harm or secures a benefit (discussed *infra*, §§1727 *et seq.*). So, too, the remedy for a violation of due process and the remedy for a taking may be different. If an ordinance violates due process, it is void and the landowner may have a cause of action in damages under the Civil Rights Act of 1871 (*infra*, §1726). If an ordinance is a taking, the landowner's only remedy may be a declaration that the ordinance is void. (*See* the discussion of remedies under regulatory takings, *infra*, §1722.) For clarity, it is wise to keep the due process issue and the taking issue separate.

    d. **Summary:** [§1650]   To sum up, the arguments made against zoning actions are principally these:

        (1) **Ultra vires:** [§1651]   The action is not authorized by, or violates an express provision of, the enabling act.

        (2) **Improper delegation:** [§1652]   The action is unconstitutional because the delegation of discretionary authority to the local decision-maker is without any governing standards.

        (3) **Procedural due process:** [§1653]   The action—an administrative decision—was taken without notice and hearing to the affected parties.

        (4) **Substantive due process:** [§1654]   The action deprives persons of due process of law because (i) it lacks a rational relationship to a permissible state objective, or (ii) it infringes upon a fundamental right and cannot be justified by a compelling state interest. Or, under a state due process clause, the action is arbitrary or unreasonable.

        (5) **Equal protection:** [§1655]   The action deprives persons of equal protection of the laws because (i) it has no rational relationship to a permissible state objective or (ii) it operates by reference to a suspect classification and cannot be justified by a compelling state interest.

        (6) **Taking:** [§1656]   The action takes the plaintiff's property without compensation.

        (7) **New arguments:** [§1657]   New arguments against zoning actions have appeared in the last decade. They are (i) that a zoning action depriving a landowner of property rights gives the landowner the right to sue under the Civil Rights Act of 1871 [42 U.S.C. §1983]; and (ii) that zoning actions restricting competition are in violation of the federal antitrust laws. These arguments have had some limited success and have stirred up considerable comment in the law reviews, but it is too early to tell how successful these arguments will turn out to be. [*See infra*, §1726—on 42 U.S.C. §1983; *and see* Mason City Center Associates v. City of Mason City, 671 F.2d 1146 (8th Cir. 1982)—on antitrust laws and zoning]

   4. **Purposes of Zoning:** [§1658]   Although zoning legislation with the purpose of protecting the public health or safety is clearly within the police power, three other purposes have been much litigated in recent years: zoning for aesthetic objectives; zoning against adult bookstores and cinemas; and zoning for preservation of historic buildings and open space.

a. **Zoning for aesthetic objectives**

(1) **Old doctrine:** [§1659]   In the late nineteenth century, the courts laid down the rule that the police power cannot be used to accomplish objectives that are primarily aesthetic. There is no statutory or constitutional basis for this doctrine; it is simply a restriction that the courts, cognizant of the subjectivity of what is beautiful, imposed on the legislatures, usually municipal legislatures. The doctrine may owe something to the fact that zoning was originally conceived as a scheme to deal with nuisance. Older nuisance cases drew a distinction between offenses to the sight, which are not actionable because they are considered to be neither substantial nor tangible, and offenses to the other senses, which are actionable. [United States v. County Board, 487 F. Supp. 137 (E.D. Va. 1979)]

  (a) **Avoidance of old doctrine:** [§1660]   In some cases, courts avoid the old doctrine by finding that the challenged zoning ordinance is not in fact motivated primarily by aesthetic objectives but rather by considerations of health and safety (*e.g.*, a city's ban on billboards within specified areas of the city may be upheld on the ground that the ban promotes highway safety by preventing motorists from being distracted).

(2) **New doctrine:** [§1661]   In recent years, many state courts, discarding the old doctrine, have held that cities may enact regulations primarily for aesthetic objectives. Some of these courts, attempting to put some limitation on what can be legislated in the name of beauty and to read some standard into the delegation of power, have said that the standard to be applied to aesthetic ordinances is whether the prohibited use offends the sensibilities of the *average person* and tends to *depress property values*. Inasmuch as the sensibilities of the average person will be reflected in property values, this standard boils down to whether the prohibited uses deemed ugly will lessen property values. This tends, it is alleged, to make aesthetic judgments more objective. [People v. Stover, 12 N.Y.2d 462 (1962)—ban on clotheslines in residential front yards upheld] Recently, the U.S. Supreme Court declared it "well settled that the state may legitimately exercise its police powers to advance esthetic values." Thus, there is nothing in the Federal Constitution that stands in the way unless the regulation impinges upon some other constitutional right. [Members of City Council of Los Angeles v. Taxpayers for Vincent, 104 S. Ct. 2118 (1984)] This declaration by the highest court is bound to be very influential in state courts.

  (a) **Architectural review boards:** [§1662]   Most courts now uphold the power of city architectural review boards to deny building permits for proposed buildings that the board disapproves. Because the standards these boards apply are often vague and difficult to apply, they raise problems of improper delegation of power and equal protection of the laws. A favorite standard is that the building must "conform to the existing character of the neighborhood and not cause a substantial depreciation in neighboring property values." Such a standard has been upheld, even when the "existing character" of the neighborhood is not entirely uniform. [State *ex rel.* Stoyanoff v. Berkeley, 458 S.W.2d 305 (Mo. 1970); Reid v. Architectural Board of Review, 192 N.E.2d 74 (Ohio 1963)]

(b) **Advertising signs:** [§1663]   It has long been held that commercial advertisements may be prohibited in residential areas, on the theory that they are harmful to the quiet and tranquility sought in residential areas. If the commercial use itself can be excluded, the advertisement of it can also be excluded. But problems arise when ***political*** advertisements are banned or when ***commercial billboards*** are banned from ***commercial areas***. Here the zoning ordinance may conflict with the first amendment right of freedom of speech.

1) **Political advertisements:** [§1664]   Political speech occupies a preferred position and is given greater protection than most other kinds of speech. Political speech includes comment on any matter of public interest. Political speech can be regulated only if the regulation (i) can be justified without reference to the content of the speech (*e.g.,* all signs, regardless of content, are banned), (ii) is narrowly tailored to serve a significant governmental interest, and (iii) leaves open ample alternative channels of communication. Recently, the U.S. Supreme Court upheld the prohibition of ***all*** private signs—including political signs—on public property. The Court held that there was no hint of bias against political speech in the ordinance, that it curtailed no more speech than necessary to accomplish its "weighty, essentially esthetic" purpose, and that there were ample alternative modes of communication in the city, such as the right to distribute literature on public property. [Members of the City Council of Los Angeles v. Taxpayers for Vincent, *supra,* §1661] On the other hand, ordinances prohibiting political signs entirely in front yards of residential areas have usually been held void, because adequate alternative means of communication are not available to the owners. [State v. Miller, 416 A.2d 821 (N.J. 1980)]

2) **Commercial advertisements:** [§1665]   First amendment protection of commercial speech is an emerging area of the law. Although not protected at all until 1975, in that year, the U.S. Supreme Court held that commercial speech enjoys a substantial amount of first amendment protection, but the Court has yet to carve out exactly what that amount is. The most recent pronouncement on the regulation of billboards from the Supreme Court is *Metromedia, Inc. v. City of San Diego,* 453 U.S. 490 (1981), and that case settled little. San Diego had enacted an ordinance banning outdoor advertising signs throughout the city, with a few exceptions. Signs advertising goods sold on the premises ("on-site" advertising) were allowed, as were signs falling into twelve specific categories (one of which was "temporary political campaign signs"). Seven justices explicitly concluded that the city's interest in avoiding visual clutter was sufficient to justify a prohibition

of billboards, but a majority of justices voted to invalidate the specific ordinance as in violation of the first amendment. The reasoning of the justices differed considerably. Four justices in a plurality opinion concluded that the ordinance was void because it was not content-neutral. The ordinance contained an exception for on-site commercial advertising but lacked a similar exception for noncommercial messages. There were four other separate opinions expressing different views.

b. **Zoning against adult entertainment:** [§1666]   Cities have adopted various measures to deal with adult bookstores, cinemas, and other places of entertainment. Some cities have prohibited live entertainment, including nude dancing, throughout the city, but entertainment (including plays, films, and nude dancing) is within the protection of the first amendment. A total ban on live entertainment is overbroad and has been held to run afoul of the first amendment. [Schad v. Borough of Mount Ephraim, 452 U.S. 61 (1981)] However, a zoning ordinance that permits adult entertainments, but disperses or limits them to certain zones, is constitutional. The chief constitutional difficulty with such ordinances is not lack of due process, because regulation of location is a rational way of dealing with their harmful effects. The chief problem is equal protection because adult theatres are discriminated against whereas other theatres are not. That appears to be discrimination on the basis of content of speech (impermissible), but nonetheless such classification has been held constitutional. [Young v. American Mini Theatres, Inc., 427 U.S. 50 (1976)]

c. **Zoning for preservation:** [§1667]   In recent years, there has been increasing public demand to preserve open spaces, wildlife areas, and historic structures. In cases challenging legislation threatening these areas and structures, plaintiffs used to argue that the legislation violated due process. Now, however, there is a trend toward analyzing these problems in terms of whether a "taking" of property has occurred. Whether property is "taken" depends upon an analysis of the economic loss to the landowner weighed against the reasonable need for the legislation to accomplish a substantial public purpose. (*See infra,* §1727.)

(1) **Historic preservation**

(a) **Historic districts:** [§1668]   Ordinances directed toward preservation of historic districts are generally valid. The standard usually applied in judging a new building's conformity with the "character of the district" is much clearer in a historic district than in the ordinary city residential district because the existing architecture is normally of a uniform character (*e.g.,* Georgian or French Quarter, etc.). This standard minimizes the likelihood that an architectural board will violate equal protection in its decisions. Furthermore, control of historic preservation districts is not a taking of property. The preservation of a historic district often results in *gain*, not loss, to the landowners, so there is a reciprocity of benefit from the regulation. (*See infra,* §1738.)

(b) **Individual landmarks:** [§1669]   Preservation of individual buildings that are deemed historically important but are not in a historic district raises serious equal protection and "taking" problems not raised by general district-wide regulations. Since there is no historic district with many owners affected, the designation of a single historic building can impose a large cost on one individual who reaps no reciprocity of benefit. In state courts, these landmark ordinances have had a mixed reception. [State *ex rel.* Powderly v. Erickson, 285 N.W.2d 84 (Minn. 1979)—sustaining ordinance; Lutheran Church in America v. City of New York, 35 N.Y.2d 121 (1974)—invalidating ordinance as applied to building that had become unusable by church for its purposes] The landmark case is now *Penn Central Transportation Co. v. City of New York,* 438 U.S. 104 (1978). The Supreme Court, sustaining New York City's landmark law, which prohibited building an office tower above Grand Central Terminal, held that the owners could not establish a "taking" merely by showing that they had been denied the right to exploit the air space, a valuable property interest. The court held the taking issue in this context must be resolved by focusing on the uses *permitted*, not on the uses prohibited (*i.e.,* on what has been left the owner, not on what the owner has lost). The uses permitted included *continuing use* as a terminal containing office space, which the Court regarded as Penn Central's *primary expectation concerning use.* In addition, subject to certain limitations, Penn Central could sell its development rights in its air space to other developers in the neighborhood. Altogether, the income from the terminal and the possible sale of development rights provided Penn Central with a *reasonable return* on its investment. This case is bound to have wide repercussions on similar problems facing state courts. Some of the more restrictive state court decisions may be rendered obsolete.

(2) **Preservation of open space**

(a) **Urban zoning:** [§1670]   An ordinance that prohibits the development of a tract of land is unconstitutional if the owner has no adequate return from his investment. Thus, an ordinance that restricts the use of a tract to parks open to the public is void. [Fred F. French Investing Co. v. City of New York, *supra,* §1645—such an ordinance violates due process (rather than being a taking)]

(b) **Wetlands zoning:** [§1671]   Ordinances have been enacted regulating and sometimes prohibiting fill of wetlands, usually defined as swamp, marsh, beach, or land subject to tidal action or storm flooding. The public purpose is preservation of ecological systems and the natural environment, and the aesthetic enjoyment. Some state courts struck down such legislation as a "taking" of property without compensation or as unreasonable (*i.e.,* a denial of substantive due process). [State v. Johnson, 265 A.2d 711 (Me. 1970); *but see In re* Spring Valley Development, 300 A.2d 736 (Me. 1973)—upholding new wetlands site location law] However, more courts now appear to uphold wetlands preservation legislation. The theory used to

sustain wetlands preservation legislation is that it is not a "taking" to prohibit future activities that would be **harmful** to the public. It does not matter that the existing uses of wetlands—wildlife observation, hunting,
haying, shellfish harvesting, and aesthetic enjoyment—may be of little
economic value, if the purpose of the ordinance is to prevent public harm.
[Just v. Marinette County, 201 N.W.2d 761 (Wis. 1972)] (*See* discussion
of harm theory of taking, *infra,* §1728.)

5. **Exclusionary Zoning:** [§1672]   Zoning can be used to purposefully exclude various
groups from the community or from certain districts. Excluded persons may be unmarried or unrelated persons who live together as a family, low-income persons, or racial
minorities. Even where there is no intention to exclude these persons, the zoning ordinance may in fact result in exclusion. Bear in mind the difference between intentional
and de facto exclusion, which may be an important distinction in some cases.

a. **Nontraditional families:** [§1673]   At the heart of the zoning system is the protection of the single-family home. But what is a "single family"? How is it defined?
Legislatures have defined it in various ways, usually in terms of persons being related by blood or marriage. If the definition of single family bears a rational relationship to the objective of preserving "family values" and "the blessings of quiet
seclusion and clean air" in a single-family residential area, the definition is constitutional. Thus, the **rational relationship** test is used to determine whether the definition of family is constitutional. [Village of Belle Terre v. Boraas, *supra,* §1647—
upholding ordinance excluding a household of more than two unrelated persons;
but see City of Santa Barbara v. Adamson, 27 Cal. 3d 123 (1980)—holding limitation of household to five unrelated individuals violates right of privacy guaranteed
by California Constitution]

(1) **Excluding traditional family:** [§1674]   If the definition of family excludes the
traditional family, including the extended family, the ordinance requires a
higher standard of justification than rational relationship (but less than strict
scrutiny). The Supreme Court has struck down, as violating substantive due
process, an ordinance defining a family so that a grandmother could not live
with her son and her two grandchildren where the grandchildren were not both
children of the son. The court held the ordinance intruded into the traditional
family and had only a marginal relationship to the permissible zoning objectives of preventing overcrowding and congestion. The Court thus has given
constitutional protection to the tradition of uncles, aunts, cousins and grandparents sharing a household—a protection it has not extended to students or
unmarried persons living together. [Moore v. City of East Cleveland, *supra,*
§1643]

b. **Low income persons:** [§1675]   Various types of land use controls may be enacted
which have the purpose or effect of limiting housing to the affluent in a particular
district, or excluding low income persons entirely from the community. Ordinances
may stipulate a minimum house size, minimum lot size, or minimum front foot-
age—all of which may have the effect of limiting development to more expensive
homes and excluding cheaper types of housing from the community. Excessive sub-

division requirements for off-site and on-site improvements can also drive up the cost of housing. Zoning ordinances may prohibit entirely certain cheaper types of housing units—usually apartments and mobile homes. A conflict thus arises between preserving the character of the community and making housing available to all persons.

(1) Validity of density controls

(a) **Rational relationship test:** [§1676]   The older cases tended to uphold density controls under the rational relationship test. Inasmuch as such controls tended to prevent overcrowding and bore a rational relationship to density, they were valid, even though they operated to exclude low income groups from entry into the community or portions thereof. [Bilbar Construction Co. v. Board of Adjustment, 141 A.2d 851 (Pa. 1958)—upholding one-acre requirement] Since the 1960s, particularly in New Jersey, New York, and Pennsylvania, courts have begun to scrutinize the rationality of density controls more carefully when they have an exclusionary effect. It has been held that a four-acre minimum lot requirement imposed by a township in a growth area to prevent newcomers from coming in and burdening public services bears no rational relationship to public health, safety, or welfare. The community cannot irrationally prevent growth. [National Land & Investment Co. v. Kohn (Easttown Board), 215 A.2d 597 (Pa. 1965); *but see infra,* §1679] Similarly, it has been held a violation of substantive due process to exclude all apartments from a developing city. [Appeal of Girsh, 263 A.2d 395 (Pa. 1970)] So too a minimum house size requirement has been struck down as not rationally related to preventing overcrowding because occupancy of the house is not limited. [Home Builders League of South Jersey, Inc. v. Township of Berlin, 405 A.2d 381 (N.J. 1979)]

(b) **Enabling act violation:** [§1677]   Another theory for invalidating some exclusionary devices is that the enabling act, authorizing the division of the city into zoning districts, requires the city to provide space somewhere for each type of housing. Thus, it is argued that under the enabling act a newly developing city must provide for all types of housing within its borders. This argument has not been as successful as arguments on constitutional grounds.

(c) **Fair share test:** [§1678]   The *Mount Laurel* decision of the New Jersey Supreme Court has become famous for laying down a requirement that each community must provide its fair share of housing needs in the region. *Mount Laurel I* [Southern Burlington County NAACP v. Township of Mount Laurel, 336 A.2d 713 (N.J. 1975)] held that a city's zoning regulations, which did not provide opportunity for a fair share of the region's need for low- and moderate-income housing, were in violation of the *state* constitutional requirements of *substantive due process* and *equal protection* because the regulations were not concerned with the general welfare of all persons. The intent of the town legislature is not controlling; the effect of excluding low-income persons is. Eight years later, after the township did very little to comply with the constitutional mandate of providing housing opportunities for low-income persons, the court in *Mount Laurel II* [Southern Burlington County NAACP v. Township of Mount Laurel, 456 A.2d 390 (N.J. 1983)] reaffirmed the requirement of opportunities for constructing a fair share of low-income housing. In a long and detailed opinion, the court dealt with how this requirement would be implemented. The obligation is imposed on any area designated as a growth area in the State Development Guide Plan, and all litigation over fair share is to be channeled to a small group of judges, who will administer a broad group of remedies, including ordering a revision of the zoning ordinance and using incentives and bonuses for builders of low-income housing. Although a court cannot build housing, it can remove any legal impediments to low-cost housing.

(2) **Timing of development:** [§1679] Ordinances with the purpose of slowing growth of housing, so that construction of necessary public facilities such as schools and sewers can keep pace, have an obvious exclusionary impact on out-siders trying to settle in the city. These ordinances have been attacked primar-ily (i) as being in violation of due process because lacking a rational relation to the public welfare, and (ii) as being a taking of property inasmuch as some landowners may not be able to develop for ten or more years. However, growth control ordinances have been *upheld* if the purpose is not exclusionary, and the ordinance is a rational method of timing development according to a compre-hensive plan. The purpose is not exclusionary if not aimed at excluding low-income housing and if growth is not permanently halted but is put on a time-table. And as for rationality, the courts find it rational to time development of housing so that it does not outrun the building of schools, sewers, and other public facilities. [Golden v. Planning Board of Ramapo, 30 N.Y.2d 359 (1972); Construction Industry Association v. City of Petaluma, 522 F.2d 897 (9th Cir. 1975)] Slow-growth ordinances, if reasonable from a regional per-spective, have also been held not to unlawfully interfere with the constitutional right to travel and settle. [Associated Home Builders v. City of Livermore, 18 Cal. 3d 582 (1976)] At the heart of these cases is a conflict between protecting the natural environment and opening suburbia to low-income housing. Clearly, judges are of different views as how best to draw the balance, but so far (except in New Jersey and to a lesser extent in New York and Pennsylvania) courts have usually deferred to the judgment of the legislative branch.

c. **Racial exclusion:** [§1680] A zoning ordinance that has an exclusionary effect is not ***unconstitutional*** solely because it has a racially disproportionate impact. A ra-cially discriminatory ***intent or purpose*** must be shown—as evidenced by such fac-tors as disproportionate impact; a clear pattern of discrimination, unexplainable on grounds other than race; the historical background of the challenged ordinance; departures from normal procedures; and the statements of the local legislators. If such intent is shown, the ordinance violates the Equal Protection Clause. [Village of Arlington Heights v. Metropolitan Housing Development Corp., *supra,* §1646]

(1) **Fair Housing Act:** [§1681] Even though a discriminatory intent is required to bring an action under the Equal Protection Clause, under the Fair Housing Act [42 U.S.C. §§3601-3619] plaintiffs need only show that there is a discriminatory **effect** in the municipality's refusal to rezone to allow low income housing. A discriminatory effect makes a prima facie case of statutory, but not constitutional, violation. Thus, it may be easier to prove a statutory violation than a constitutional violation. [Metropolitan Housing Development Corp. v. Village of Arlington Heights, 558 F.2d 1283 (7th Cir. 1977)] What the courts are trying to do is to encourage litigants to litigate **statutory** (defined) rights rather than litigating **constitutional** rights, which are harder for the courts to handle.

d. **Federal courts:** [§1682] It is difficult to litigate exclusionary ordinances in federal courts. To have **standing** to litigate a municipal ordinance in federal court, a plaintiff must show a "**case or controversy**" between himself and the defendant. The controversy cannot be hypothetical. To challenge a zoning ordinance as exclusionary, the plaintiff must allege "specific, concrete facts demonstrating that the challenged practices harm **him**," *i.e.,* that he suffers some injury in fact. Harms that are suffered by others or by the public at large, or that are speculative, are not sufficient. Thus **nonresidents** of a city, housing developers, and nonprofit groups interested in promoting low-income housing cannot sue the city in federal court, alleging that exclusionary zoning denies them the opportunity of finding housing in the city, unless they can show a substantial probability that the injury complained of would be redressed if the zoning were struck down. For standing, a plaintiff must (i) have a current involvement, contractual or otherwise, with a **specific housing proposal on a specific lot**, which is prevented by the ordinance, and (ii) be within the **zone of interest** protected by the particular constitutional provision involved. The constitutional right to travel or migrate, for example, **cannot** be asserted by a **builder's association** or by **residents within the city** because their right to travel is not being interfered with. Thus, they cannot challenge the exclusionary zoning in federal court on that ground. Only a resident outside the city who wants to move into the city and has contracted to buy (or has bought) a specific lot in the city can raise the right to travel issue. [Construction Industry Association v. City of Petaluma, *supra,* §1679—building association could attack ordinance on due process grounds, not on right to travel grounds]

(1) **Fair Housing Act:** [§1683] Standing to litigate a **federal** statute, such as the Fair Housing Act, is governed by a different rule than the rule on standing to litigate state legislation in federal courts. Standing requirements are much more liberal. Courts have permitted third parties to sue to vindicate rights of minorities under the Fair Housing Act, on the theory that Congress intended to define standing broadly. [United States v. City of Parma, 661 F.2d 562 (6th Cir. 1981)] It seems clear that the federal courts, by maintaining tight standing requirements, are trying to channel exclusionary zoning litigation into the state courts.

6. **Nonconforming Uses:** [§1684] A nonconforming use is a **use in existence when the zoning ordinance is passed** which is not permitted in the zone in which the property is

located. Nonconforming uses are permitted to remain; requiring immediate termination would be either a violation of substantive due process or an unconstitutional taking of property rights. (*See infra,* §1727.) However, nonconforming uses may be limited or terminated under certain conditions (below).

a. **Limits on expansion and rebuilding:** [§1685]   A zoning ordinance may limit the expansion of a nonconforming use. It may stipulate that the use cannot be extended beyond the precise space the use took at the time the ordinance was passed. Or it may stipulate that a nonconforming building, if destroyed by fire, cannot be rebuilt without compliance with the ordinance. Or it may prohibit changing one type of commercial use to another type of commercial use. [Belleville v. Parrillo's Inc., 416 A.2d 388 (N.J. 1980)—restaurant cannot be changed to discotheque]

b. **Amortization:** [§1686]   A zoning ordinance may provide that the nonconforming use must terminate after a specified period of time. The ordinance may provide for different amortization periods, depending upon the amount of investment in the use and building. These ordinances have been challenged as being unconstitutional, sometimes successfully.

   (1) **Majority view—amortization valid:** [§1687]   The majority of courts has held such ordinances constitutional as a reasonable exercise of the police power, not in violation of due process nor a taking. Nonetheless, the ordinance must be reasonable *as applied* to each nonconforming use terminated. If not reasonable as applied to each particular landowner, it is unconstitutional as to that landowner. [City of Los Angeles v. Gage, 127 Cal. App. 2d 538 (1954)—five years for removal of plumbing business reasonable; Board of Supervisors of Cerro Gordo County v. Miller, 170 N.W.2d 358 (Iowa 1969)—five years for removal of auto wrecking business reasonable; Harbison v. City of Buffalo, 4 N.Y.2d 553 (1958)—upholding amortization generally; Town of Hempstead v. Romano, 33 Misc. 2d 315 (1963)—three-year amortization period for junkyard in residential district unreasonable]

   (2) **Minority view—amortization unconstitutional:** [§1688]   A minority of courts has held amortization ordinances unconstitutional as a taking of property without compensation. [Mayor & Council of New Castle v. Rollins Outdoor Advertising, Inc., 459 A.2d 541 (Del. 1983); Hoffman v. Kinealy, 389 S.W.2d 745 (Mo. 1965)]

7. **Administration of Zoning Ordinance**

a. **Comprehensive plan:** [§1689]   Section 3 of the Standard Zoning Enabling Act requires that local zoning ordinances "be made in accordance with a comprehensive plan." To prepare the plan, the enabling act requires that a planning commission composed of citizens be appointed by the mayor or other executive officer. The commission employs a staff of expert professional planners to prepare plans and give it advice. The commission also recommends to the local legislative body a zoning ordinance to implement the comprehensive plan.

(1) **Legal effect of plan:** [§1690]   A master or comprehensive plan is a guide for development within the city; it states policies and guiding principles. Its adoption by the commission or by the local legislative body does not have the legal consequence of restricting the use of property. To restrict the use of property, the plan must be implemented by the local legislature enacting a zoning ordinance or subdivision regulations, which have legal effect. A comprehensive plan places an important constraint on exercise of discretionary powers. Because of abuses in zoning, courts are emphasizing more and more the importance of a comprehensive plan in reviewing discretionary zoning techniques. [Cochrane v. Planning Board, 210 A.2d 99 (N.J. 1965); Udell v. Haas, 21 N.Y.2d 463 (1968)]

(2) **Conflict between plan and prior ordinance:** [§1691]   Once a city adopts a comprehensive plan, the city has a duty to conform any preexisting zoning ordinance to the plan. At least one court has held that the plan is controlling if the city does not act and the ordinance violates the plan. [Baker v. City of Milwaukie, 533 P.2d 772 (Or. 1975)]

   (a) **Example:** In 1978, the city adopts a zoning ordinance permitting thirty-nine units per acre on lot A. In 1985, the city adopts a new comprehensive plan which allows only seventeen units per acre in the zone applicable to lot A. Even though the ordinance is not amended, the plan is controlling and no more than seventeen units per acre are permitted on lot A.

(3) **Existence of comprehensive plan:** [§1692]   Many cities have not prepared written comprehensive plans, but have enacted zoning ordinances. The requirement in the enabling act that zoning be in accordance with a comprehensive plan was, until recently, construed narrowly by courts. Zoning ordinances not based on plans were generally held valid on the theory that a separate, comprehensive plan is not required; the zoning ordinance itself is the plan. Indeed, even if a separate plan is required, it has been held that the plan can consist of policies of the planning commission, as evidenced by documents or testimony of the commission members. It does not necessarily have to consist of a formal document. Under this interpretation, a comprehensive plan means comprehensive *planning.* [Bartram v. Zoning Commission, 68 A.2d 308 (Conn. 1949)]

b. **Amendment of zoning ordinance:** [§1693]   The enabling act provides that the zoning ordinance can be amended by the local legislative body rezoning a particular parcel of land. The local legislative body is advised by the planning commission on amendments, but it does not have to follow the commission's advice.

(1) **Spot zoning:** [§1694]   An amendment not in accordance with the comprehensive plan is "spot zoning." Spot zoning is unlawful. Although spot zoning usually involves rezoning one lot in violation of the plan, the zoning of one lot differently from its neighbors could, in a particular context, be in accordance with a comprehensive plan. In determining what is spot zoning, size or number of lots rezoned—while important—is not controlling; deviation from the plan

is controlling. [Kuehne v. City of East Hartford, 72 A.2d 474 (Conn. 1950); Langer v. Planning & Zoning Commission, 313 A.2d 44 (Conn. 1972); Schubach v. Silver, 336 A.2d 328 (Pa. 1975); City of Pharr v. Tippett, 616 S.W.2d 173 (Tex. 1981)]

(2) **Amendments generally presumed valid:** [§1695]   The traditional view is that zoning amendments, like zoning ordinances, are presumptively valid, and the burden is on persons objecting to the amendment to prove it is not in accordance with a comprehensive plan. However, abuses in the zoning amendment process have caused some courts in recent years to tighten up the standards applicable to zoning amendments. These standards are generally designed to make it harder for a proponent to procure a zoning amendment. They are not yet widely followed.

(a) **"Change or mistake rule":** [§1696]   One way to tighten up on amendments is to shift the burden of proof. Accordingly, it has been held that there is no presumption of validity of piecemeal amendments. The original zoning is presumptively valid and **correct.** To sustain a piecemeal change therein, the proponent must show strong evidence of **mistake** in the original ordinance or of a **substantial change in conditions.** [MacDonald v. Board of County Commissioners, 210 A.2d 325 (Md. 1965)]

(b) **Must show public need:** [§1697]   Another way of tightening up is to narrow the applicable standards for amendments. Accordingly, it has been held that in proving that the proposed amendment is in accordance with the comprehensive plan, the proponent must show that there is a **public need** for a change of the kind proposed, and that such need will be best served by changing the zoning of proponent's parcel **as compared with other available parcels.** [Fasano v. Board of County Commissioners, *supra*, §1641; Green v. Hayward, 552 P.2d 815 (Or. 1976)]

c. **Variances:** [§1698]   Because of the difficulty in drawing a general zoning ordinance that takes into account all the various existing shapes, sizes, topographical features, and peculiar conditions of every lot in the city, zoning enabling acts provide for a **board of adjustment** (sometimes called the board of zoning appeals) to grant relief by way of variance where the restrictions contained in the ordinance cause the owner "**practical difficulty**" or "**unnecessary hardship.**" The board of adjustment is composed of citizens appointed by the mayor or other chief executive and is a body different from the planning commission.

(1) **Standards for variances:** [§1699]   The standards for a variance are **practical difficulty** or **unnecessary hardship,** for which the evidence should be strong since the variance is a departure from the uniform plan. The hardship must be due to unique circumstances, *i.e.,* peculiar to the particular lot. If the hardship conditions generally exist in the neighborhood, an amendment to the zoning ordinance, not a variance, is proper. The owner must not be able to get a reasonable return on the land if it is used in compliance with the zoning ordinance. The hardship must **not** be **self-created.** The variance must not result in substan-

tial detriment to the public health, safety, or welfare, and it must not be a substantial departure from the comprehensive plan. [Puritan-Greenfield Improvement Association v. Leo, 153 N.W.2d 162 (Mich. 1967); Application of Devereux Foundation, Inc., 41 A.2d 744 (Pa. 1945); Clark v. Board of Zoning Appeals, 301 N.Y. 86 (1950)]

(a) **Example:** The zoning ordinance requires a twenty-foot building setback from the street. Because of the shallowness of the lot, which was created before the zoning ordinance was enacted, it is not practicable to set back a new building twenty feet. This is a proper case for a variance. If the shallow lot were created *after* the enactment of the zoning ordinance, the difficulty would be self-created, and a variance would be improper. [Commons v. Westwood Zoning Board of Adjustment, 410 A.2d 1138 (N.J. 1980)]

1) **Compare—use vs. bulk variance:** [§1700] In the above example, a *bulk* variance is illustrated. A *use* variance, permitting a use prohibited in the district, is much more destructive of the master plan and in effect is an amendment. In some states, use variances cannot be granted by the board of adjustment.

(2) **Are standards followed?** [§1701] The variance process provides a means for introducing flexibility into zoning procedures that have proven too rigid, but it also opens the door to favoritism, venality, and unequal protection of the laws. Considerable evidence has accumulated that boards of adjustment do not adhere closely to the legal standards for granting variances, probably because the pressure for flexibility in a fairly rigid system is too great for boards to resist. The variance is the easiest mechanism to provide that flexibility. Because of the abuses in granting variances, some courts have attempted to require more formalities by the board of adjustment, which ordinarily does not write an opinion or give written reasons. Courts have required that the board *render findings* to support its ruling. And it has been held that a court will scrutinize the granting of a variance to see if the legal standards are followed. [Broadway, Laguna, Vallego Association v. Board of Permit Appeals, 66 Cal. 2d 767 (1967)] In the vast majority of cases, however, the granting of a variance is never appealed by the neighbors, and the decision of the board is final.

d. **Special exception:** [§1702] A special exception to a zoning ordinance is one allowable where certain conditions specified in the ordinance are met. It has frequently been confused with a variance, but a theory other than individual hardship underlies the special exception. The theory is that certain uses can peacefully coexist with their neighbors when specified conditions occur. The board of adjustment is empowered to determine whether the conditions specified in the ordinance are met. Sometimes the special exception is called a "special use" or "conditional use." [Kotrich v. County of DuPage, 166 N.E.2d 601 (Ill. 1960); North Shore Steak House, Inc. v. Board of Appeals of Thomaston, 30 N.Y.2d 238 (1972)]

(1) **Example:** A zoning ordinance specifies that a nursery school is permitted in a residential district if adequate off-street parking is provided, if no more than thirty students are enrolled, and if play space is fenced and screened by a hedge. This is a special exception.

(2) **Standards for special exception:** [§1703] Legislative power cannot be delegated to an administrative agency unless the standards are sufficiently clear to prevent gross arbitrariness. Delegation of power without standards is improper. Sometimes the standards set forth in the ordinance for granting a special exception are especially vague. For example, a nursery school might be permitted in a residential district "when compatible with the neighborhood" or "with permission of the board of adjustment." Despite the lack of procedural safeguards and standards, the majority of courts have usually upheld provisions for special exceptions without clear standards. They have held that the general purposes in view ("health, safety, and general welfare of the community") are a sufficient safeguard to control the board's discretion. [Value Oil Co. v. Town of Irvington, 377 A.2d 1225 (N.J. 1977)]

e. **Discretionary or non-Euclidean zoning:** [§1704] Under the zoning ordinance upheld in the *Euclid* case, the only means of flexibility provided were variances and special exceptions. These proved to be insufficient. More flexibility was required than the early planners thought. As a result, cities have experimented with various types of non-Euclidean or discretionary zoning, which have generally been upheld after some initial judicial objection. The gist of the judicial objection is that these techniques give planners great discretion, and open the door to favoritism, unfairness, and unpredictability. However, the trend is to uphold these discretionary devices as necessary to effective public land planning.

(1) **Contract zoning:** [§1705] Where a city agrees to zone or rezone a particular tract of land upon condition that the owner execute a contract or covenant restricting the use of the tract in specified ways, this is called "contract zoning" or "conditional zoning." It is a method whereby, upon application by the owner, the city can tailor planning considerations to the particular tract, permitting the owner to develop the land in ways that do not harm the neighborhood. Planners consider it useful in bringing flexibility to zoning. [Sylvania Electric Products, Inc. v. City of Newton, 183 N.E.2d 118 (Mass. 1962); Collard v. Incorporated Village of Flower Hill, 52 N.Y.2d 594 (1981); State *ex rel.* Zupancic v. Shimenz, 174 N.W.2d 533 (Wis. 1970)]

(a) **Example:** A landowner wishes to put a light manufacturing plant on a lot zoned residential. If the owner will agree by covenant to provide a buffer strip park to protect nearby houses, the city will agree to rezone the land for light industrial use. The owner executes the covenant in favor of the city; the city rezones the land.

(b) **Criticism:** It has been argued that contract zoning is illegal because the city is not authorized to bargain with individual landowners. This procedure lacks standards to govern administrative discretion and fails to give interested parties notice. It is also claimed that this is in essence spot zoning, because it is not in accordance with a uniform comprehensive plan. Some courts have agreed and have struck down contract zoning. [Baylis v. City of Baltimore, 148 A.2d 429 (Md. 1959)]

(2) **Density zoning:** [§1706]   After World War II, developers often desired to develop large tracts of land and use their spaces in a way different from that permitted by the zoning ordinance. Typically, the developer wanted to build houses on smaller lots (clustering them) and use the space saved for some recreational use for the homeowners—a park, riding trails, tennis courts. The overall density would remain the same, as under traditional development, but the homeowners would have some common amenity that made the subdivision more desirable. To permit this, cluster zoning or density zoning laws were enacted. Thus, density zoning provides developers with an option to use spaces in various ways, provided a specified overall density of population is maintained. [Chrinko v. South Brunswick Township Planning Board, 187 A.2d 221 (N.J. 1963)]

(3) **Floating zones:** [§1707]   Another method of introducing flexibility is the floating zone. A floating zone is a zone provided in the ordinance to which no land is assigned on the zoning map until a landowner makes such a request and is granted that zoning classification. Such reclassification is made by amendment to the zoning map. Such a zone is said to "float" over the city; no one knows where it will land. The planners argue that this allows them to postpone making a specific site selection until a specific proposal is made; it prevents over-zoning for uses before they are needed. And it offers the extra dollars that might come from giving the floating zone to the first landowners to come up with an acceptable proposal.

(a) **Example:** The city council decides it needs a limited industrial district somewhere in the city. The zoning ordinance is amended to create a limited industrial district (F-1), which sets forth the requirements (twenty-five acres minimum), conditions (sufficient off-street screened parking; 200-foot setback from street, with grassy front lawn) and uses permitted (non-noisy light industry). No land in the city is placed in an F-1 district. The zone "floats" over the city. Subsequently landowner A, whose tract is in a residential district, applies for rezoning to F-1. A's tract meets the criteria set forth in the ordinance. The city council rezones the tract F-1.

(b) **Criticism:** It has been asserted that floating zones are in violation of the requirement of a comprehensive plan, which gives predictability as to future use. Thus, it is argued, floating zones are not permitted by the enabling act. It is also claimed that floating zones deny equal protection of the laws, because when and where the zone will "come to rest" lies in the arbitrary discretion of the planning commission. Some courts agreed in the early days of floating zones and struck them down. But now courts uphold floating zones by analogizing them to the variance and special exception procedures, where a comparable amount of discretion is permitted. [Rodgers v. Village of Tarrytown, 302 N.Y. 115 (1951)]

(4) **Planned unit development:** [§1708] In a planned unit development (PUD) district, the developer with a large tract of land can mix uses—*e.g.,* some single-family houses, some apartments, some neighborhood shopping, even an unobjectionable industry. The developer can ignore specific lot and density requirements if the overall density of the development does not exceed that of standard lot-by-lot development. The requirements for a PUD classification may be set forth in the ordinance, and ordinarily require a large amount of land. The test, as with an amendment, is whether the rezoning is in accordance with a comprehensive plan. [Cheney v. Village 2 at New Hope, Inc., 241 A.2d 81 (Pa. 1968)]

(a) **Criticism:** It has been argued that the PUD district violates the enabling act on the theory that by mixing uses and ignoring lot lines it violates the essence of zoning, which is lot by lot development. And, like the floating zone, it does not give predictability to what is permitted in the neighborhood (a virtue of Euclidean zoning). It is unlikely that such arguments would succeed today where the market demand for planned unit developments, thought to represent advanced ideas for flexible planning, is strong. Planned unit development, however, gives largely discretionary powers to the planning authorities, which is to some extent the antithesis of the zoning upheld in the *Euclid* case (*see supra,* §1630).

f. **Zoning by referendum:** [§1709] Because of public hostility to certain types of uses, mainly certain types of multiple dwellings, zoning ordinances in some cities in recent years have been amended to provide that a zone change *amendment* can be made only by a public referendum. Although the requirement of a referendum may have the effect of excluding low-income housing and may have a disproportionate effect on one race, mandatory referendums have been upheld as constitutional. It has been held that a referendum is a legislative act that cannot, by itself, violate the Due Process Clause. To violate that clause the *result* of the referendum must not be a rational method of achieving a permissible public objective. Nor is a referendum an unconstitutional delegation of legislative power to a limited group uncontrolled by any standard; it is direct legislation by the voters. [City of Eastlake v. Forest City Enterprises, Inc., 426 U.S. 668 (1976)] The reasoning of the Supreme Court in *Eastlake* is not necessarily applicable to *administrative* decisions (such as variances and special exceptions). A referendum for administrative decisions may be an improper delegation of power without standards.

B. SUBDIVISION CONTROL AND MAPS

1. **Subdivision Regulations:** [§1710] Pursuant to an enabling act, cities may enact subdivision regulations to govern the development of new tracts of land. Subdivision regulations apply when land is to be divided for development. Subdivision regulations differ

from zoning ordinances: Zoning ordinances regulate land *use*, while subdivision regulations lay down **conditions for approval of a subdivision plan**. Ordinances usually provide that a building permit will not be granted unless there is compliance with subdivision regulations. Subdivision regulations may lawfully give the planning authority considerable discretion in determining whether the layout of a proposed subdivision satisfies the needs of public health and safety. [Durant v. Town of Dunbarton, 430 A.2d 140 (N.H. 1981)] Inasmuch as subdivision layout approval is and always has been so largely discretionary, the arguments against non-Euclidean zoning (*supra*, §§1630 *et seq.*) as giving too much discretion lose a lot of their force.

a. **On-site beneficial improvements:** [§1711] Subdivision regulations generally require the subdivider to put in paved streets with curbs and gutters in an approved layout, and to install street lights, water mains, and sewers. If these requirements, which benefit the subdivision buyers in the physical use of their homes, are reasonable, they are valid. [Blevens v. City of Manchester, 170 A.2d 121 (N.H. 1961)]

b. **Parks and school sites:** [§1712] If authorized by the enabling act, subdivision regulations may require the developer to dedicate a certain amount of land for a public park or school site, or, in lieu thereof, to contribute a sum to a public fund to purchase land for such purposes. Such regulations have met with a mixed judicial reception.

   (1) **"Specifically and uniquely attributable" test:** [§1713] Some courts hold that school and park dedication requirements are proper only if the need for such facilities is "specifically and uniquely attributable" to the developer's activity. Under this test, dedication for school and park sites has been held improper, since the need for more schools and parks is not specifically and uniquely attributable to the developer's activity. (It is also attributable to activity of other developers in the area and to procreation by the new residents.) [Board of Education v. Surety Developers, Inc., 347 N.E.2d 149 (Ill. 1976)]

   (2) **Elimination of open space theory:** [§1714] Dedication for a park is valid on the ground that a city can require dedication for park or open space needs commensurate with the increased need for such facilities created by the subdivision. Since the subdivision decreases open space, using up raw land, the city can require reasonable exactions for the purpose of acquiring open land elsewhere. The regulation is viewed as similar to density regulations (*see supra*, §1676) designed to preserve open spaces (setback requirements, height limitations, and such), and the fact that the open spaces may incidentally benefit persons other than the subdivision residents does not matter. This theory, while useful in sustaining park dedication requirements, seems inapplicable to school site dedication requirements. [Associated Home Builders v. City of Walnut Creek, 4 Cal. 3d 633 (1971); Jenad, Inc. v. Village of Scarsdale, 18 N.Y.2d 78 (1966)]

2. **Official Maps**

a. **Street maps:** [§1715] The enabling act may provide that if a city adopts a street plan, locating future streets on maps, no one will be permitted to build in the location of a mapped street. The purpose of an official map locating unbuilt streets is to save costs in the future, when the city exercises eminent domain and condemns the land. (If the land is not built upon, the city will not have to pay for improvements.) The question arises whether mapping future streets is a "taking" of the private property that is mapped for future use as a street. It has been held that the mere mapping of future streets is not a "taking" because it does not divest the owner of title and does not interfere with any present use of the property. However, **when the owner applies for and is denied a building permit** in the mapped street, denial is a "taking" unless there is a special hardship procedure in the act whereby an owner is permitted to build in a mapped street if the owner is substantially damaged by denial of a permit to build. Thus, most map acts require the municipality to allow the owner, upon application, to build something that will give a reasonable return. [State *ex rel.* Miller v. Manders, 86 N.W.2d 469 (Wis. 1957)]

b. **Park maps:** [§1716]   The enabling act may provide that a city can map land to be acquired in the future for a public park or playground, which mapping freezes development of the land for a set period, usually one year. This gives the city a right to prevent development for one year of lands it wants to acquire for a park. If the city elects to map land for acquisition in this way, it may have to pay the landowner the price of an "option" to purchase land for one year, for this is what, in effect, the city has taken from the landowner. [Lomarch Corp. v. Mayor & Common Council of Englewood, 237 A.2d 108 (N.J. 1968)—requiring compensation for the "option" taken] But most courts have upheld these "freeze ordinances" without payment of compensation if reasonably limited in time. [Rancho La Costa v. County of San Diego, 111 Cal. App. 3d 54 (1980)]

C. EMINENT DOMAIN

1. **In General:** [§1717]   The federal, state, and local governments have the power of eminent domain, *i.e.*, the power to take title to property against the owner's will. The fifth amendment to the Constitution provides ". . . nor shall private property be taken for public use, without just compensation." Although the fifth amendment is expressly applicable only to the federal government, it has been held applicable to the states as well under the Due Process Clause of the fourteenth amendment. Under the Taking Clause there are three major questions: (1) What is a "taking"? (ii) What is "public use"? (iii) What is "just compensation"?

2. **What Is a "Taking"?**

   a. **Taking title:** [§1718]   If the government formally exercises the power of eminent domain to take title to the land, the government has taken property and must pay for it.

   b. **Physical invasion:** [§1719]   If the government physically invades property, without taking title, it has taken property and must pay for it. Sometimes this is called "**de facto**" taking or inverse condemnation (*see infra*, §1724).

      (1) **What constitutes invasion?** [§1720]   Physical invasion includes moving soil, water, or physical bodies onto plaintiff's property. It includes opening private

property to the public. [Kaiser-Aetna v. United States, 444 U.S. 164 (1979)] It has been held that a statute authorizing private cable TV companies to install cables in apartment buildings, over the landlord's objections, is a physical invasion and a taking. [Loretto v. Teleprompter Manhattan CATV Corp., 458 U.S. 419 (1982); *but see* Pruneyard Shopping Center v. Robins, *supra*, §185—state court decision that persons may exercise free speech rights in large private shopping center not a taking; the physical invasion did not "unreasonably impair the value or use of their property as a shopping center," indicating invasion for free speech may not be a taking when other types of invasions may be]

(2) **Example:** United States military airplanes fly over A's chicken ranch, causing so much noise that A's chickens quit laying and A is forced out of business. This would be a nuisance if committed by a private person, but an action in nuisance does not lie against the government unless sovereign immunity in tort has been waived. Here, however, the government has taken a navigational servitude by inverse condemnation. [United States v. Causby, *supra*, §1619] (On noisy overflights, *see supra*, §1623.)

(a) **Compare—negative restriction:** [§1721]   In the *Causby* case, the government in effect took an affirmative easement (*see supra*, §1305) over A's land. Suppose that the government forbids any structure over thirty feet high in a zone around an airport. This restriction is very similar to a negative easement (*see supra*, §1306). Has there been a taking of a negative easement by regulation? If the government has not taken all value out of the land, the answer is no. The owner is prohibited from exploiting the airspace, but the government cannot exploit it and the courts treat these two cases differently. Thus, one could say that the government must pay if it takes an affirmative easement permitting the government to use the land, but does not necessarily have to pay if it takes a negative easement by regulation.

c. **Regulatory takings**

(1) **Causes of action available to landowner:** [§1722]   The landowner may have a legal remedy or an equitable one.

(a) **Suit for injunction:** [§1723]   A landowner may sue, asking a court to *invalidate* regulatory legislation on the ground that it "takes" the property without compensation and hence is an invalid exercise of the police power under the Due Process Clause. If a court declares that the land use regulation is a "taking," this is a metaphor meaning that the regulation is beyond the scope of the police power and is *void*. Enforcement of the ordinance is enjoined. If the regulation is deemed not a "taking," it is within the scope of the police power and is valid. Thus, in a suit for an injunction (usually called an action for mandamus or declaratory relief), finding that a regulation is a "taking" is synonymous with enjoining its enforcement. (This was the conventional interpretation of the meaning of "taking" until the Brennan dissent, *infra*, §1725.)

(b) **Suit for damages:** [§1724]   A landowner may sue, asking a court to award *damages* because the government regulatory activity has taken the property. The landowner is asking, in effect, that the government be required to pay for an interest in the property similar to a negative easement. The landowner's action is called a suit in *inverse condemnation*. Why "inverse condemnation"? Because the landowner is suing for compensation instead of the government instituting formal condemnation proceedings. Inverse condemnation has rarely been allowed in state courts where zoning or land use regulation goes so far as to be a taking. It has been thought that awarding money damages would have a chilling effect on land-use planning, because planners would have to be extremely cautious in drawing regulations. [Agins v. City of Tiburon, 24 Cal. 3d 266 (1979)—landowner's only remedy is a suit for invalidation of the regulation, *aff'd*, 447 U.S. 225 (1980)—no taking because owner was not deprived of substantially all reasonable use and therefore the court did not reach question whether a damages remedy was available] However, two new developments indicate that damages may be allowed in the future.

1) **Brennan dissent—damages for a taking:** [§1725]   In *San Diego Gas & Electric Co. v. City of San Diego*, 450 U.S. 621 (1981), the issue of permitting a remedy of damages for invalid land use regulation was again before the Court. Five justices thought the Court lacked jurisdiction in the case because the judgment below was not final. They did not reach the issue of the availability of a damages remedy. Justice Brennan, writing for four dissenting justices, indicated that if a taking is found, the effect is not merely that the ordinance is void. Instead, the government must pay *interim damages* for the "period commencing on the date the regulation first effected the 'taking' and ending on the date the government entity chooses to rescind or otherwise amend the regulation." If—after the ordinance is declared a taking—the government decides to keep the regulation in force, it then must pay *permanent damages*. Justice Rehnquist, who concurred with the majority decision to dismiss the case, noted that if the court had jurisdiction, "I would have little difficulty in agreeing with much of what is said in the dissenting opinion." Hence, at least four of the current justices now take the view that an action in inverse condemnation can be brought for *damages* for a regulatory "taking." The Brennan dissent is now being followed in some courts. [Burrows v. City of Keene, 432 A.2d 15 (N.H. 1981); Martino v. Santa Clara Valley Water District, 703 F.2d 1141 (9th Cir. 1983); Hamilton Beach v. Williamson County Regional Planning Commission, 729 F.2d 402 (6th Cir.), *cert. granted*, 53 U.S.L.W. 3202 (Oct. 2, 1984)] Because certiorari has been granted in the *Hamilton Beach* case, the Court will probably rule on this issue in 1985.

2) **Damages under Civil Rights Act of 1871:** [§1726]   Even if a landowner has no cause of action in inverse condemnation under the fifth and fourteenth amendments for damages for an unconstitutional zoning

action, the landowner may have a cause of action for damages under the Civil Rights Act of 1871 [42 U.S.C. §1983] where the landowner is ***deprived of substantive due process*** or ***equal protection***. Section 1983 of this Act provides that a person may sue in law or equity any person who, acting under color of any statute or ordinance, deprives the plaintiff of a right, privilege, or immunity secured by the Constitution or federal law. Deprivation of due process is included within section 1983. In 1979, the U.S. Supreme Court held that a cause of action for damages under section 1983 can be based on overregulation of land depriving the landowner of substantive due process. [Lake Country Estates, Inc. v. Tahoe Regional Planning Agency, 440 U.S. 391 (1979)] (Carefully distinguish between an action in inverse condemnation for damages for an unconstitutional taking and an action under section 1983 for damages for deprivation of due process.) An action under section 1983 can be brought in state or federal court. A city or other local governmental unit, which is deemed a "person" under section 1983, can be sued for damages. [Wheeler v. City of Pleasant Grove, 664 F.2d 99 (5th Cir. 1981), *cert. denied*, 456 U.S. 973 (1983)] A municipality is not immune from liability merely because its officials acted in good faith. [Owen v. City of Independence, 445 U.S. 622 (1980)] But the city may be immune from liability when the city officials act in a legislative (rather than an administrative) capacity. The extent of the liability of the city and its officials for damages under section 1983 and how this liability relates to an action for damages for a taking is in an evolving and uncertain state. Until these uncertainties are resolved, a landowner seeking damages should sue both in inverse condemnation and under section 1983.

(2) **Tests of a taking:** [§1727] Whether government regulatory activity should be considered a "taking" is a most difficult question. There is no set formula, but there are several tests and analyses that are fruitful in dealing with the problem. The Supreme Court has, at one time or another, applied each of the tests set forth below in an attempt to determine when, based on the particular facts, justice and fairness require that economic injuries caused by public action be compensated by the government.

(a) **Harm test:** [§1728] Courts have sometimes said that the difference between the police power and eminent domain is this: When the regulation has the purpose or effect of protecting the public from ***harm*** (or prohibiting a ***nuisance***), it is an exercise of the police power and noncompensable; when the regulation has the purpose of extracting a ***public benefit***, it is an exercise of eminent domain, and the owner must be compensated. The public cannot extract a public good without paying for it, but it can prohibit an owner from making a nuisance of himself. This theory was the basis for the decision in *Hadachek v. Sebastian*, 239 U.S. 394 (1915), which upheld a zoning ordinance prohibiting the continuation of a brickyard in a residential area. The brickyard was looked upon as a "harmful" or "noxious" use, which, like a nuisance, could be abated.

1) **Distinction may be illusory:** [§1729] The distinction between preventing harm and acquiring a benefit may be illusory. All restrictions preventing A from harming B confer a benefit on B. If a brickyard is prohibited from continuing operation, a benefit is conferred upon the neighbors. Also, as in nuisance situations (*see supra*, §§1533 *et seq.*), when two landowners have incompatible uses, it is not proper to say only one is inflicting harm upon the other. Each harms the other in the sense that each interferes with the other's use of his land. If the brickyard were in the midst of a heavy industrial district, it would not be harming its neighbors. Harm arises only when the neighbors want to make an incompatible use. To decide that one of two competing land uses is "noxious" is merely a conclusion reflecting a judgment about which of two incompatible property uses ought to be preferred. However, the harm or noxious use test can be made to work if there is a rule of neutral conduct or legislated preferences to determine what is harmful.

2) **Neutral benchmark:** [§1730] The harm theory can be made to work if there is a neutral rule about who is harming whom. Such a rule might be that the second use in time, which is incompatible with an established use, harms the first use (*see* discussion *supra*, §1550). Or a neutral rule might be that natural, undeveloped land is the benchmark, and any change from the natural state that is harmful can be prohibited. [Just v. Marinette County, *supra*, §1671] Such a rule may be reasonably applied to wetlands (*supra*, §1671), but if applied to all land, it would mean that all new development can be regulated out, leaving the landowner with only existing use value. This, indeed, is the position taken in England—that all development can be forbidden by the state, but taking an existing use requires compensation.

3) **Cases sometimes do not apply distinction:** [§1731] Cases have sometimes permitted a public benefit to be acquired by the police power, even though the prohibited use is not more harmful than the permitted use. The state may properly make a choice between preserving one class of property vs. another. [Miller v. Schoene, 276 U.S. 272 (1928)—Virginia statute ordered landowners to cut down ornamental cedar trees (without compensation) because they produced cedar rust fatal to apple trees cultivated nearby]

(b) **Test of severe economic loss:** [§1732] The most famous case setting forth the difference between an invalid taking and a valid exercise of the police power is *Pennsylvania Coal Co. v. Mahon*, 260 U.S. 393 (1922). In that case, the Supreme Court struck down a Pennsylvania statute forbidding coal mining that caused the subsidence of any house. Before the statute was enacted, the coal company had sold the surface right to land it owned to Mahon, reserving the right to remove the coal thereunder. Because the statute made it commercially impracticable to mine the coal, and thus had nearly the same effect as the complete destruction of the mineral rights, the Court held the statute invalid as a taking without compensation. Said Justice Holmes: "The general rule at least is, that while property may be regulated to a certain extent, if regulation goes too far it will be recognized as a taking. . . . this is a question of degree—and therefore cannot be disposed of by general propositions." Holmes had in mind that if *diminution in economic value goes too far* it will be a "taking." Thus, large damage to the owner is compensable, but small damage is not.

1) **Nuisance—test does not apply:** [§1733]   If the use is held to be a nuisance, and enjoinable as such, large noncompensable losses can be suffered. Thus, the economic diminution test in *Mahon* may *not* apply to nuisances.

2) **Severity of loss:** [§1734]   Notwithstanding the *Mahon* test, severe losses resulting from government regulation have been held *noncompensable*. [Village of Euclid v. Ambler Realty Co., *supra*, §1639—prohibition of industrial use reduced value of land by 75 percent]

3) **Landowner must be left with reasonable return:** [§1735]   In *Mahon*, the regulation deprived the coal company of *all* value of its property (mineral rights). Hence, it is sometimes said that the *Mahon* test requires that the landowner have some *reasonable economic value left* in the property. [*Cf.* Fred F. French Investing Co. v. City of New York, *supra*, §1670—deprivation of reasonable use was not a taking but a violation of due process] This interpretation is supported by the most recent Supreme Court case, *Penn Central Transportation Co. v. City of New York, supra*, §1669, which said the test was not what the owner had lost, but what the owner had left. The Court, holding that the owner was entitled to a reasonable return on its investment, viewed as particularly important "the extent to which the regulation has interfered with distinct investment-backed expectations."

a) **Calculation of reasonable return:** [§1736]   When courts say that property must be left a reasonable return, it is often unclear what property base is to be used in calculating reasonable return. Is it reasonable return on original cost, or on present economic value, or on present economic value less the amount of value attributable to community activities and not to activity of the landowner? In *Penn Central, supra*, the Court held that the plaintiff had a reasonable return on its "investment," probably referring to sunk investment or cost.

4) **What "property" is focused upon:** [§1737]   When one asks what proportion of "the property" is destroyed, it is necessary to define "property" in order to say what "property" one is looking at. In *Mahon*, the Court looked only at the coal rights, which had been severed from the surface. The value of the coal had been almost completely destroyed by the statute. The Court did not look at the fee simple in the surface

and the coal together. If it had, it would see there were many valuable uses left to which the surface could be put. Perhaps the reason the Court looked only at the coal rights is that these rights had been separated from the surface rights and were in different ownerships. In *Penn Central*, the Court focused on the surface rights and the air rights together (which were in common ownership) and held that even though the air rights were devalued, valuable surface rights remained.

(c) **Reciprocity test:** [§1738]   Another test stemming from Holmes' opinion in *Mahon* is that regulations that involve reciprocal advantages are **not** a taking. If the regulated owners obtain some advantage, though it be less than the advantage obtained by others, the regulation is within the police power. An example is zoning. Although a landowner with a residentially-zoned lot loses the economic value of commercial uses, he is protected from possible economic loss by commercial loss next door. There is "an average reciprocity of advantage," to use Holmes' phrase. If the landowner obtains **no** advantage from the regulation, the regulation is more likely to be held a taking.

(d) **Balancing test:** [§1739]   In applying the *Mahon* test, courts often say that in testing the validity of the police power action they must balance private loss against public gain. If the gain outweighs the loss, the landowner is not compensated. Courts often do not give specific content to the balancing test. If the test means that when the totality of society's welfare gains is greater than the individual's loss no compensation is due, the test can be used only rarely to strike down legislation because the legislature is better equipped than courts to determine economic efficiency, *i.e.*, that aggregate social values will be increased by the legislative action. However, as applied, the test indicates the court is not balancing exclusively economic gains and losses, but is adding to the scales its notions of fairness. The more doubtful the efficiency of the legislation, and the more unfair it seems, the more compelling must be its justification.

1) **Michelman's utility and fairness tests:** [§1740]   In a very influential article, Professor Michelman has proposed two tests grounded respectively in utility and fairness for determining when compensation should be offered. These are balancing tests, but stated with much greater specificity than is found in judicial opinions. Although not yet in general use by courts, these tests have been influential in refocusing the questions. [80 Harv. L. Rev. 1165 (1967)]

a) **Utility test:** [§1741]   Compensation should be made when it is a **means** of maximizing overall social utility, which is measured in terms of economic value. There are three items to be considered:

(i) "Net efficiency gains" (the excess of economic benefits over losses resulting from regulation);

(ii) "Demoralization costs" (the present capitalized value of lost future production caused by the demoralization of persons who think they might be subject to similar treatment someday); and

(iii) "Settlement costs" (the costs of paying off persons damaged in an amount sufficient to avoid demoralization costs).

When the net *efficiency gains are less than the sum* of demoralization costs and efficiency costs, the regulation is inefficient and should not be pursued. When the net efficiency gains *are greater than such sum* and the *demoralization costs exceed settlement costs*, compensation should be required. When settlement costs exceed demoralization costs, no compensation should be required. [80 Harv. L. Rev. at 1208-1215 (1967)]

b) **Fairness test:** [§1742]   The second test of Michelman is concerned with fairness: A denial of compensation "is not unfair so long as the disappointed claimant ought to be able to appreciate how such decisions might fit into a consistent practice which holds forth a lesser long-run risk to people like him than would any consistent practice which is naturally suggested by the opposite decision." Thus, if a person can reasonably see that denial of compensation will place him in a worse position over the long run than he would be in under alternative land use practices, compensation must be paid. [80 Harv. L. Rev. at 1223 (1967)]

3. **What Is Public Use?**

a. **Constitutional requirements:** [§1743]   The fifth amendment to the U.S. Constitution provides: ". . . nor shall private property be taken for public use, without just compensation." The Supreme Court has read this provision to mean that a taking must be for a *public purpose*. If not, it is beyond the power of eminent domain and is void.

(1) **Public use or purpose?** [§1744]   The fifth amendment speaks of public use, and some courts, construing similar provisions in state constitutions, have held that to exercise eminent domain, the public must have the *right to use* the condemned property. This might be called the "narrow reading" of the public use requirement. Other courts including the U.S. Supreme Court have held that the term "public use" means the condemnation must *benefit the public*. Under the broader construction, most condemnations are permissible.

(a) **Example:** The state enacts a law permitting a private person to erect a dam on a stream, which will collect water and flood riparian upstream land. The dam builder must compensate the upstream owners. In effect, the lower riparian is given a right to flood an upper riparian for the purpose of erecting a dam to provide power. Under the narrow construction—the right to use by the public—the law is void. Under the public purpose construction, the law is valid: The public purpose is the generation of hydroelectric power.

(2) **Urban renewal:** [§1745] The problem of whether exercise of the power of eminent domain is for a public purpose was much litigated in the context of urban renewal. Basically, urban renewal involves the government exercising eminent domain, condemning title to a tract of land, and transferring the title to a private redeveloper to develop in accordance with an urban renewal plan. The fundamental issue was whether the power of eminent domain can be used to take property away from one private owner and transfer it to another private owner.

   (a) **Validity of urban renewal:** [§1746] Condemnation for urban renewal has been upheld as for a public purpose. It is not necessary that urban renewal be limited to the removal of dilapidated slum dwellings (a public purpose). It may extend to the removal of sound buildings that are in a substandard neighborhood that is to be cleared. In a very influential opinion, the U.S. Supreme Court held: "Appellants argue that this makes the project a taking from one businessman for the benefit of another businessman. . . . The public end may be as well or better served through an agency of private enterprise than through a department of government—or so the Congress might conclude. We cannot say that public ownership is the sole method of promoting the public purposes of community redevelopment projects." [Berman v. Parker, 348 U.S. 26 (1954); *and see* Miller v. City of Tacoma, 378 P.2d 464 (Wash. 1963)]

   (b) **Economic justification:** [§1747] The use of eminent domain in acquiring land for urban renewal has been justified on the ground of the holdout problem. Because of the holdout (*see supra*, §1559), it is alleged that the private market cannot acquire title to all the various parcels in a slum clearance project at a cost of fair market value. It is then argued that the failure of the private market to clear the slum and make the most efficient use of land justifies the government "lending" its power to private redevelopers. But it must be kept in mind that the use of eminent domain to transfer title from one private person to another forces a sale at a jury-determined price; it deprives the landowner of possible gains from trading with the buyer. Eminent domain might be limited to cases where it may be warranted on economic grounds—where there is a holdout problem—but it has not been.

(3) **Revitalizing economy:** [§1748] Eminent domain can be used to condemn private land for use in a scheme to revitalize the economy and promote commerce. It is sufficient if the purpose of eminent domain is the well-being of the city and has a significant economic advantage for the city. [Courtesy Sandwich Shop, Inc. v. Port of New York Authority, 12 N.Y.2d 379 (1963)] It has even been held that the land, after condemnation, can be resold to a private corporation to build an industrial plant. [Poletown Neighborhood Council v. City of Detroit, 304 N.W.2d 455 (Mich. 1981)]

(4) **Reducing concentration of ownership:** [§1749]   In Hawaii, as a legacy of its feudal land tenure system, almost half of its land is owned by a tiny group of private landowners. Almost all homes are on rented land. To break up this concentration of land ownership which prevented people from buying homes, the Hawaii legislature enacted a statute providing for the condemnation of private lands and transferring ownership of the condemned fees simple to existing lessees. This act has been held to be for a public purpose and upheld by the U.S. Supreme Court. The Court stated that the Court's role in reviewing a legislature's judgment of what constitutes a public use is "an extremely narrow" one. "Where the exercise of the eminent domain power is rationally related to a *conceivable public purpose*, the Court has never held a compensated taking to be proscribed by the Public Use Clause." Judicial review is limited to cases where the legislative declaration of public purpose is "palpably without reasonable foundation." [Hawaii Housing Authority v. Midkiff, 104 S. Ct. 2321 (1984)]

4.   What Is Just Compensation?

a.   **Market value:** [§1750]   Generally speaking, the requirement of just compensation means that the owner must be paid fair market value for the property taken. Fair market value is the price in cash for which the property would change hands in a transaction between a willing buyer and a willing seller (*i.e.*, neither acting under any compulsion to buy or to sell). Fair market value does not mean the value to the owner, who might place a higher value on the property than other persons do. Property may have subjective value to the owner that is not compensated in the market. Thus the owner whose property is condemned may be penalized.

(1) **Justification for market value test:** [§1751]   The market value test is justified on efficiency grounds. It is the easiest, least costly test to apply. If just compensation required that the owner be given the value the owner placed on the property, it would be difficult to ascertain the value and there would be potential for fraud.

(a) **Criticism:** The fair market value test does not award objectively verifiable costs to the owner (*e.g.*, moving expenses). It also imposes on the owner who does not agree with the government's offer the cost of hiring a lawyer to fight out fair market value in court. Apart from depriving the owner of the unique value the property has for the owner, the fair market value test leaves the owner at a substantial disadvantage. This has been called, however, "part of the burden of common citizenship." [United States v. 564.54 Acres of Land, 441 U.S. 506 (1979)]

(b) **Exceptions—special purpose property:** [§1752]   Where there is no relevant market for the property, *any just and equitable method* of valuation may be employed. A special purpose property (school, church, park) for which no realistic market exists may be valued by replacement cost, depreciated original cost, capitalization of income, or some other just and equitable method.

(2) **Expectations about possible future uses:** [§1753]   The market value test takes into account the possibility of future uses as well as existing uses. A buyer, believing there is some possibility of different and more valuable use in the future, is willing to pay something extra for this speculation. In ***instructing the jury***, the judge must tell the jury to consider any evidence that a willing buyer would have considered the possibility of rezoning and would have paid more based on the possibility of future use. The jury must determine for itself whether it thinks the zoning change is reasonably probable. If not reasonably probable, that element of value should be disregarded. [H. & R. Corp. v. District of Columbia, 351 F.2d 740 (D.C. Cir. 1965)]

(a) **Expectations about leasehold renewal:** [§1754]   When the government condemns a leasehold interest with improvements, it must pay the lessee the value of the leasehold with improvements. The expected useful life of the improvements and expectations that the landlord will renew the lease must be considered as part of market value. [Almoto Farmers Elevator & Warehouse Co. v. United States, 409 U.S. 470 (1973)]

(b) **Expectations about rights revocable by government:** [§1755]   Some Supreme Court cases seem to establish that the government does not have to pay the owner for a value the government has created, or that the government can take away by regulation. [United States v. Fuller, 409 U.S. 488 (1973)—government condemned land adjacent to federal land on which condemnee possessed revocable government grazing permits; government did not have to pay for element of value based on use of condemnee's lands in combination with federal permit lands] The theory excluding this element of value (because the government could destroy it) could logically be applied to condemnation of property subject to zoning regulations. If that were done, whatever value that could be removed by regulation would not be compensable upon a taking by eminent domain.

1) **Example:** O owns farmland zoned for residential purposes (and for those purposes worth $100 an acre). The state could lawfully rezone O's land to agricultural purposes (and for those purposes worth $40 an acre). The state condemns O's land. Under present law, the state must pay O $100 an acre. Under the above theory, the state would pay O $40 an acre, assuming any regulation more restrictive than an agriculture-only zone would be going too far.

b. **Effect of condemnation action on values**

(1) **Condemnation blight:** [§1756]   The government may announce its intention to take property in a certain area for some government purpose, perhaps urban renewal. Until it files a suit or an appropriation map, or does some other act asserting dominion over the property, ***title*** to the property has not been taken. Nonetheless, the ***value*** of the property may decline because of the threat of condemnation. Prospective buyers may shy away because of the threat of condemnation. This is called "condemnation blight." When the government actu-

ally condemns the property, it must pay the market value of the property at the time of the taking, as if the value-depressing acts of the government had never taken place. [City of Buffalo v. J.W. Clement Co., 28 N.Y.2d 241 (1971)]

(2) **Increase in value from project:** [§1757]   The government's announcement of a project may increase the value of the land in the area, because of population increase or other factors. The owner is not entitled to the increase in market value that comes from government action preparatory to filing a condemnation suit.

c.   **Loss of business:** [§1758]   When there is a business on the condemned land, the business itself is not condemned and thus it must move. It may be, for various reasons, that the business cannot be moved successfully to another location. The owner is *not* entitled to be paid for the taking of the business, which, if destroyed, is merely an unintended incident of the taking of land.

d.   **Loss of goodwill:** [§1759]   The federal rule (which is followed in most states) is that compensation for loss of business goodwill is not allowed to the owner of a business conducted on the property taken unless provided for by statute. Goodwill includes the benefits that accrue to a business as a result of its *location* and as a result of the *proprietor's skill or business acumen*. [Community Redevelopment Agency v. Abrams, 15 Cal. 3d 813 (1975)]

e.   **Partial taking:** [§1760]   If only part of the property is taken, the owner is entitled to recover for resulting damages to the part not taken. These are called "severance damages." There are two basic methods (with variations thereof in the several states) of determining the owner's compensation where there is a partial taking.

(1) **Before and after rule:** [§1761]   The owner is entitled to the difference between the value of the *entire tract* before taking and the value of the *remainder* left in him after taking. This rule is the easiest to apply and is more consistent with realistic market appraisal techniques.

(a) **Example:** O owns a tract of land in the country, on which his house is situated. The tract is worth $400,000. The state takes a portion of the tract for an expressway, which will depreciate the value of the house because of the noise from the expressway. The value of the land taken is $75,000. The remainder, after taking, is worth $150,000. Thus there is consequential damage (damage resulting from the state's use of the portion taken as a freeway) of $175,000. Under the before and after taking rule, O is entitled to $250,000—*i.e.*, $400,000 (original value) less $150,000 (value of remainder). [Dennison v. State, 22 N.Y.2d 409 (1968)]

(2) **Value plus damage rule:** [§1762]   The second method of determining what the owner gets on partial taking is to give him the sum of the value of the part taken and any net damages to the remainder after offsetting benefits. Unlike the before and after rule, this method evaluates separately the value of the tract taken and the damages to the remainder. [Merrill Trust Co. v. State, 417

A.2d 435 (Mo. 1980)] The two methods reach the same result in the preceding example—*i.e.*, $175,000 (consequential damage) plus $75,000 (value of land taken) equals $250,000. They lead to different results where net special benefits are realized by the remainder. Under the value plus damage method, any special benefits to the remainder are set off against the remainder only; under the before and after test, special benefits are set off against the value of the entire property.

(a) **Example:** O's land is worth $400,000. The state takes a portion of O's land in order to create a park. The land taken was worth $75,000. The remainder after the taking is worth $350,000, since proximity to the park has increased the value of the land. Therefore, under the value plus damage method, O is entitled to $75,000 (value of land taken). The special benefit of $25,000 to the remainder can be offset only against damage to the remainder, not against the value of the land taken.

XII. THE SALE OF LAND

___chapter approach___

The sale of land is ordinarily a two-step process: First, a **contract of sale** is signed by the buyer and seller. Then, after a couple of months or more, the **closing** takes place. At the closing, the seller **delivers a deed** to the buyer, and the buyer hands the seller a **check for the purchase price**. This two-step process is necessary because the buyer—after signing the contract but before paying the purchase price—needs time to check out the seller's title (discussed *infra*, §§1785 *et seq.*), to arrange financing, and to take steps to move onto the premises.

Problems regarding the sale of land (both on exams and in "real life") generally arise, if at all, during the period between the signing of the contract and the closing date. The buyer may learn of title defects or the premises may burn down. For these and other reasons, the buyer (or seller) may wish to rescind the contract while the other party wants to enforce it. Remember that **specific performance** (as well as **rescission** and **damages**) is a remedy for the breach of a land sale contract. Also keep in mind that the **doctrine of equitable conversion** may determine who bears the loss if the property has been destroyed.

At the closing, another party may be represented—the **mortgagee**. To pay for the property, the buyer may have secured a purchase money mortgage, or the seller may have previously mortgaged the property. In any case, remember that a mortgagee has a major interest in the land; any time a question mentions a mortgage, don't overlook this interest in your answer. Consider the **mortgagee's rights** upon sale or transfer of the property (*i.e.*, whether the transferee takes subject to the mortgage or assumes the mortgage, effect of a due-on-sale clause, etc.) and upon default by the mortgagor. Also consider the duties the mortgagee has regarding the **mortgagor's judicial or statutory rights of redemption**.

After closing, questions may arise as to the seller's liabilities if title proves defective or if the building proves defective. Review the **seller's warranties** (contained in the deed) at the end of this chapter.

Favorite topics for examination include risk of loss before closing, delivery of the deed, and seller's warranties after closing.

A. THE CONTRACT FOR SALE OF LAND

1. **Broker's Role:** [§1763]   Almost all houses and a large percentage of other real property are sold through a broker. The seller signs a contract with the broker, giving the broker the right to list and show the property to prospective buyers and, if the property sells, to collect a commission out of the purchase price. The broker's commission may run from five to eight percent of the selling price. Three major legal issues involving brokers are:

    a. **Authority to sell:** [§1764]   Most contracts with brokers give the broker "the exclusive right to sell the property at the price and upon the terms set forth in the contract *or at such other price or terms as the parties may agree upon*." This type of contract does not give the broker the power to bind the seller to a contract to convey, but only the power to find a buyer with whom the seller is to conduct the final negotiations. The emphasized words above, giving the broker the right to sell upon terms agreeable to the seller, are the basis of this construction. Only if the contract expressly gives the broker the power to sell on definite, fixed terms, leaving no discretion in the seller, will it be construed as giving the broker the authority to bind the seller. [Forbis v. Honeycutt, 273 S.E.2d 240 (N.C. 1981)]

b. **When commission earned:** [§1765]   The traditional rule is that the broker is entitled to a commission if she produces a customer ready, able, and willing to buy upon the terms and for the price set by the seller in the brokerage contract. Once the buyer is accepted by the seller, the seller owes the broker a commission. This means that if the seller enters into a contract with the buyer and the sale falls through because of the buyer's default, the broker gets a commission. This rule does not carry out the expectations of sellers, who ordinarily expect that the broker will take the commission out of the sale proceeds. Almost all courts that have considered the matter in recent years have discarded the traditional rule and have held that the broker earns a commission only when the buyer completes the transaction by paying the purchase price. If the sale falls through because of the buyer's fault, the seller is not liable to the broker. On the other hand, if the sale falls through because of the *seller's* fault, the seller is liable to the broker. [Tristam's Landing, Inc. v. Wait, 327 N.E.2d 727 (Mass. 1975)] If the contract is drafted by the broker and provides a different rule, such as giving the broker a commission even though the buyer defaults, a modern court may refuse to enforce it because it is unconscionable or against public policy.

c. **Practicing law:** [§1766]   Because brokers draft contracts of sale, which change the legal relationships of the parties, the broker's work borders on the practice of law. The courts have had some difficulty in drawing the line between practicing law and offering brokerage services. Courts say that brokers can prepare simple real estate contracts but must refrain from inserting provisions in a contract that require the exercise of legal expertise. (The legal effect of detailed financing provisions usually requires the advice of a lawyer.) A broker who practices law without a license may be liable in damages, enjoined, or penalized in some other way by the court. [Chicago Bar Association v. Quinlan & Tyson, Inc., 214 N.E.2d 771 (Ill. 1966); Duncan & Hill Realty, Inc. v. Department of State, 62 App. Div. 2d 690 (1978)]

2. **Statute of Frauds:** [§1767]   Once the buyer and seller have come to an agreement, the Statute of Frauds requires that the contract for the sale of land be in writing, signed *by the party to be charged thereby*. Otherwise, the contract is not enforceable. This means, in general, that both buyer *and* seller must sign the contract of sale.

a. **Kind of writing:** [§1768]   The necessary writing can be a formal contract, signed by the seller and buyer, or it can be an informal memorandum signed by them. It can even consist of several documents taken together to be a contract (*e.g.,* an agreement by the seller with a broker to sell for $30,000 if the broker produces a buyer, and a separate acceptance by the buyer to buy at $30,000, together may constitute a written contract). [Ward v. Mattuschek, 330 P.2d 971 (Mont. 1958)]

(1) **Negotiations:** [§1769]   If the parties are negotiating with an understanding that the terms of the contract are not fully agreed upon and a written formal agreement is contemplated, a binding contract does not come into existence until the formal contract is executed. Preliminary informal agreements do not constitute a binding contract if the parties do not intend to be bound until the formal contract is signed. [King v. Wenger, 549 P.2d 986 (Kan. 1976)]

b. **Essential terms:** [§1770]   The writing must contain all essential terms. "Essential terms" are identification of the *parties*, description of the *property*, and *terms* and *conditions* (such as price and manner of payment, if agreed upon). Parol evidence (*i.e.*, evidence other than the written document itself) is admissible to clear up ambiguities.

(1) **Price:** [§1771]   If the price has been agreed upon, it must be set forth. Failure to put it in the memorandum makes the contract unenforceable. However, if no price has been agreed upon, the court may imply an agreement to pay a reasonable price, where such an agreement is inferable from all the circumstances.

(2) **Conditions**

(a) **Financing:** [§1772]   Many contracts to purchase contain a clause providing that the offer to purchase is contingent upon the purchaser obtaining the necessary amount of financing. This "subject to financing" clause may be held void for vagueness unless the surrounding circumstances indicate what amount and terms the parties had in mind. [Gerruth Realty Co. v. Pire, 115 N.W.2d 557 (Wis. 1962)] If the clause is interpreted to mean that the loan must be in such amount and on such terms as the buyer considers necessary, the buyer must act in good faith and use reasonable diligence in procuring a loan. [Bushmiller v. Schiller, 368 A.2d 1044 (Md. 1977)]

(b) **Building permit:** [§1773]   A contract may be conditioned upon the buyer obtaining from the public authorities all the necessary permits for erecting a building or obtaining a zoning change. As with a condition about obtaining financing, the buyer must use reasonable efforts to obtain the permits or zone change. If the buyer does not submit any plans to the public authority or apply for a zone change, the buyer is in default. [Sechrest v. Safiol, 419 N.E.2d 1384 (1981)]

c. **Part performance:** [§1774]   Part performance is an equitable doctrine that allows a court of *equity*, under certain circumstances, to specifically enforce an *oral* contract for the sale of an interest in land. If a buyer or seller sues *at law* for damages, the doctrine of part performance is not applicable in most states; the doctrine is applicable only in a suit in equity for specific performance.

(1) **Acts of "unequivocal reference to a contract":** [§1775]   What acts constitute part performance, taking the contract out of the Statute of Frauds and making it enforceable, vary considerably from state to state. But most courts require acts of unequivocal reference to a contract, *i.e.*, acts done by the parties that make sense only as having been done pursuant to a contract. Thus, if the buyer (i) *pays* all or part of the purchase price, *and* (ii) enters into *possession, and* (iii) *makes improvements*, the contract is enforceable, because the court assumes the buyer would not do these acts without a contract. Such acts supply sufficient evidence of the contract. Inasmuch as the purpose of requiring acts of "unequivocal reference to a contract" is to give reliable evidence of the contract, the requirement is not insisted on if the seller admits to making the contract or the contract is clearly proved. [Shaughnessy v. Eidsmo, 23 N.W.2d 362 (Minn. 1946)]

    (a) **Variations on part performance:** [§1776]   In some states, the contract is enforceable if the buyer merely takes *possession* under circumstances referable to a contract. This is known as the English rule. Other states require that the buyer also *make payments or improvements*. Still other states require the buyer to go further and show, in addition to these acts of part performance, *irreparable injury if the contract is not enforced*. Usually this is shown by the buyer's making valuable improvements that cannot be compensated in money.

    (b) **Injurious reliance theory:** [§1777]   Another theory of part performance is that it is a theory to prevent injurious reliance on the oral contract. Restatement (Second) of Contracts section 129 adopts this theory. It provides that a contract may be specifically enforced if the party seeking enforcement proves the contract and, *in reasonable reliance on the contract*, "has so changed his position that injustice can be avoided only by specific enforcement." This position is in line with the modern trend to relax the Statute of Frauds. [Hickey v. Green, 442 N.E.2d 37 (Mass. 1982)] But the requirement of unequivocal acts probably survives in most states.

(2) **Suit by seller:** [§1778]   Most suits for specific performance alleging part performance are brought by the buyer against the seller. Suppose that the buyer performs some acts of part performance, enough to justify specific performance by the buyer, and then the buyer wants to back out of the deal. Can the seller sue the buyer for specific performance of an oral contract? Some older cases refused to grant the seller specific performance based on the buyer's acts that caused economic loss to the buyer. The seller, seeking to circumvent the Statute of Frauds, could not take advantage of the buyer's acts. However, most courts now hold that if the property has been changed by the buyer so as to lessen its value or to prevent the seller from being restored to his original position, specific performance will be granted. Other courts go further and hold the seller can sue under the principle of "mutuality" of remedies: If the buyer can sue for specific performance, the seller can also. [Pearson v. Gardner, 168 N.W. 485 (Mich. 1918)]

(3) **Contracts to devise:** [§1779]   The doctrine of part performance may be applied to oral contracts to devise land at death in exchange for services. However, courts are more reluctant to enforce oral contracts to devise than to enforce oral contracts to sell, because in the former case one party is dead and cannot testify. When oral contracts to devise are enforced, courts emphasize that the proof of the promise is clear and convincing, the promisee changed to a detrimental position in reliance on the promise, and failure to enforce would be unconscionable (*i.e.*, is grossly harsh or would work a fraud).

(a) **Example:** A alleges that T, an old man, promised to devise A his house if A moved in and looked after T for the rest of his life. A moved in and looked after T, who subsequently died, leaving a will devising the house to B. If a court finds that A's acts are not unequivocally referable to a contract (but that A acted merely in the expectation of reward), A is not entitled to enforce the alleged contract. If A is denied specific performance, A has an action in law for quantum meruit (the monetary value of services rendered). [Burns v. McCormick, 233 N.Y. 230 (1922)]

(b) **Uniform Probate Code:** [§1780]   In an effort to reduce litigation, Uniform Probate Code section 2-701, adopted in many states, takes a hard line against enforcing oral contracts to devise. The Code requires that the will must set forth the material provisions of the contract, the will must expressly refer to the contract and to extrinsic evidence proving its terms, or a separate writing signed by the decedent must evidence the contract.

d.   **Estoppel:** [§1781]   In a few states, part performance is not recognized. In these states, estoppel is the theory used to enforce an oral contract to sell land. Estoppel applies where unconscionable injury would result from denying specific performance after one party has been induced by the other seriously to change his position in reliance on the contract. [Baliles v. Cities Service Co., 578 S.W.2d 621 (Tenn. 1979)]

e.   **Revocation:** [§1782]   A written contract for the sale of land can be *revoked* by *oral* agreement of both parties in a majority of states. *Rationale:* The Statute of Frauds applies to the *making* of a contract, not to the *revocation* thereof. [Niernberg v. Feld, 283 P.2d 640 (Colo. 1955)] However, in some states, the revocation must be in writing; the theory is that the contract creates equitable title in the buyer (*see* "equitable conversion," *infra*, §1811), and revocation of the contract is in reality a *transfer* of this equitable title back to the seller.

3.   **Time of Performance:** [§1783]   Even though the contract sets a specific date for performance ("the closing date"), the contract is enforceable in equity *after* that date if performance is offered within a reasonable period thereafter. The time for performance is treated as a formal rather than an essential term of the contract. [Kasten Construction Co. v. Maple Ridge Construction Co., 226 A.2d 341 (Md. 1967)]

a.   **Effect of "time of essence" provision:** [§1784]   Because the rule in equity can leave the liabilities of the parties uncertain for a substantial period of time, well-drafted contracts always provide that *"**time is of the essence**."* If this clause is in the contract and one party does not tender performance by the specified date, the other party is thereby *excused* from performance.

(1) **Example:** In one case where payment was to be made before 2:30 p.m. on December 19, and time was stated to be of the essence, and the buyer produced the payment at 3 p.m. on December 19, it was held that the buyer could not enforce the contract. [Doctorman v. Schroder, 114 A. 810 (N.J. 1921)]

4. **Marketable Title**

a. **Implied in contract:** [§1785]   Unless there is a provision in the contract of sale to the contrary, it is implied that the seller must furnish the buyer with good and marketable title at closing. This implication will be made even though the contract calls for a conveyance by quitclaim deed (without any warranties of title). The reason is that the contract calls for a conveyance of land, and the seller cannot convey land unless he has title to it. [Wallach v. Riverside Bank, 206 N.Y. 434 (1912)]

(1) **Contract provisions:** [§1786]   If the contract requires the seller to provide the buyer with an *insurable* title, only a title insured by a title insurance company and not a marketable title is required. If the contract calls for a "good *record* title," the seller must offer a marketable title based upon recorded documents alone, not upon adverse possession. [Tri-State Hotel Co. v. Sphinx Investment Co., 510 P.2d 1223 (Kan. 1973)]

b. **Marketable title defined:** [§1787]   A marketable title is a title reasonably free from doubt, one which a prudent purchaser would accept. Although a perfect title is *not* required, the title must be such that there is no reasonable probability that the buyer will be subjected to a lawsuit. In cases where the seller asks for specific performance, the courts tend to be very exacting in looking at the seller's title.

(1) **Example:** Seller contracts to sell land to buyer. The record shows an ancient mortgage that has never been released on the record. This makes title unmarketable. Even though it is highly probable that the statute of limitations has run on the mortgage debt, it might not have. The running of the statute may have been tolled by an unrecorded agreement of the parties or by payments. [Douglass v. Ransom, 237 N.W. 260 (Wis. 1931)]

(2) **Good record title:** [§1788]   A seller can show marketable title by producing a good *record title* or, in many states, by showing title by *adverse possession*. Good record title means, generally speaking, that there was a conveyance (usually many years ago) by a sovereign state then holding ownership, and thereafter there are, on record, transfers of title from the original grantee to the seller. In addition, good record title means that there are no recorded encumbrances, such as mortgages and easements, on the property. A person who has a good record title has an unencumbered fee simple, provable from the public records.

(a) **Record search:** [§1789]   Because of the burden of searching title back to its original source, local practice may limit backward search to some definite period, such as sixty years. Title searchers assume that the statute of limitations will bar any earlier defect, though of course this is not necessarily the case. The risk of limiting search to a sixty-year period is deemed acceptable, in view of the high cost of further search back to the inception of private title. The risk may be covered by the seller's warranties of title (*see infra*, §§1935 *et seq.*) or by title insurance (*see infra*, §§2087 *et seq.*). In determining whether the seller has good record title, courts usually consider local practices regarding the period of record search.

(3) **Adverse possession:** [§1790]   Unless marketable title "of record" is called for, many states hold that marketable title can be based upon adverse possession. Adverse possession must be clearly proven. The seller must offer the buyer written evidence or other proof admissible in court which the buyer can use to defend any lawsuit challenging title. [Rehoboth Heights Development Co. v. Marshall, 137 A. 83 (Del. 1927); Conklin v. Davi, 388 A.2d 598 (N.J. 1978)] *But note:* About an equal number of states follow a contrary rule: Marketable title requires the seller to produce a good record title. [Simis v. McElroy, 160 N.Y. 156 (1899)]

c. **Defects in title**

(1) **Defects in record chain:** [§1791]   Title may be unmarketable because of a defect in some prior instrument constituting part of the chain of title. For example, a deed might not be acknowledged before a notary (required for recordation), or the land descriptions in the chain may not match, or an old mortgage is not discharged on the records.

(2) **Private encumbrances:** [§1792]   As a general rule, marketable title means an unencumbered fee simple. Mortgages, liens, covenants, and easements make title unmarketable unless the buyer waives them. However, a mortgage is not an encumbrance if the seller pays it off before closing.

(a) **Easements:** [§1793]   An easement that lessens the value of the property (such as an easement by a neighbor for a right of way) makes title unmarketable. An easement that benefits the property (*e.g.*, a utility easement to service the property) does not necessarily make title unmarketable. Although a ***majority holds that such easements are encumbrances***, a ***minority*** holds that an open and visible easement for the benefit of the property known to the buyer before he makes the contract is not an encumbrance. Under the minority view, much depends upon the expectations of the buyer, including what future use he plans to make of the property.

(b) **Covenants:** [§1794]   Restriction on the use of property, imposed by private covenant, makes title unmarketable. It is assumed that the buyer wants to use the property for any purpose permitted by zoning regulations, and not merely continue its present use. On the other hand, if the contract expressly states that the property has been purchased for a particular use, and such use is permitted by the private covenants, title may be held marketable.

(c) **Express waiver:** [§1795]   The contract of sale may enumerate the encumbrances and the buyer may waive them. Or the contract may provide that the seller shall furnish the buyer with a list of encumbrances prior to closing, and failure of buyer to disapprove within a few days after receipt will be deemed a waiver. However, a waiver of an encumbrance in the contract of sale is not a waiver of a *violation* of the encumbrance when the buyer does not know of the violation. Thus, if in the contract the buyer waives building restrictions, and it is then found that the building on the property violates the restrictions, the buyer can rescind. [Lohmeyer v. Bower, 227 P.2d 102 (Kan. 1951); Hebb v. Severson, 201 P.2d 156 (Wash. 1948)]

(3) **Zoning restrictions:** [§1796]   Zoning laws and subdivision restrictions generally do *not* make title unmarketable. They are not considered encumbrances. Even though zoning regulations do not generally affect marketability of title, if zoning restrictions are imposed *after* the buyer signed the contract, and these restrictions would materially interfere with or frustrate the buyer's contemplated use of the property, many courts will refuse to enforce the contract against the buyer. Some courts proceed on the theory of frustration of purpose. Others proceed on the ground that it would be unfair to grant specific performance in such event. [Clay v. Landreth, 45 S.E.2d 875 (Va. 1948)]

(a) **Violations of zoning regulations:** [§1797]   If the property is in violation of a zoning ordinance or subdivision law, and the correction of such violation can be demanded by the government, the title is usually held unmarketable. *Rationale:* To force the purchaser to take the property may force a lawsuit on the purchaser. The purchaser may be sued by the government to correct the violation.

1) **Example:** P contracts to buy land and a building thereon from V. The land is in a single-family residence zone. After the zoning ordinance was passed, V cut up the house into two apartments in violation of the ordinance. P can rescind on the ground that title is unmarketable. (If the land were in an apartment zone, the title would be marketable.)

5. **Remedies for Breach of Contract:** [§1798]   Unless a contrary intention is clearly manifested, payment of the purchase price and delivery of the deed are dependent promises. Neither party can place the other in default unless he himself *tenders his own performance* and *demands* that the other party perform. Thus, to place the seller in default, the buyer must, on closing day, tender payment and demand title from the seller. Unless the contract contains a "time is of the essence" provision, the seller has a reasonable period of time thereafter within which to tender performance. If one party breaches the contract, the remedies of the other party are *rescission, specific performance,* and *damages.*

a. **Remedies of the buyer**

(1) **Rescission:** [§1799] Upon breach by the seller, the buyer may rescind the contract and recover her down payment. However, if, as is customary, the seller has agreed only to furnish title at date of closing (law day), the buyer *cannot rescind prior to closing* on the ground that seller does not have title. The seller may be able to acquire title before closing and hence be able to perform. [Luette v. Bank of Italy National Trust & Savings Association, 42 F.2d 9 (9th Cir. 1930)] If before closing the buyer notifies the seller that title is defective and the buyer therefore rescinds the contract, the buyer—not the seller—is in breach. The seller is entitled to attempt to make his title good before closing. [Cohen v. Kranz, 12 N.Y.2d 242 (1963)]

(2) **Specific performance:** [§1800] Land is considered unique, making money damages for failure to convey land inadequate. Therefore, the buyer has a right to specific performance if the seller breaches the contract. Specific performance is an *equitable* remedy, however, and there are equitable defenses available to the defendant. If the defendant would suffer undue hardship, or if circumstances have so changed that specific performance would be inequitable, specific performance will be denied.

(a) **Abatement in price:** [§1801] Although the buyer is entitled to specific performance, a court will not ordinarily require the seller to cure a defect in title. Where there is a defect and the buyer wants the property, the buyer's only remedy is to ask for an abatement in price. If the seller cannot perform fully, *e.g.* because of an easement across the premises, or a deficiency in acreage contracted for, the buyer is entitled to specific performance, with abatement in the agreed price compensating for the deficiency. [Bartos v. Czerwinski, 34 N.W.2d 566 (Mich. 1948)]

(3) **Damages:** [§1802] If the buyer chooses, the buyer can sue the seller *at law* for money damages rather than for specific performance.

(a) **Benefit of bargain:** [§1803] In most states, the buyer seeking damages is entitled to the difference between the contract price and the market value of the land on the date performance is due. This is known as the "benefit of the bargain" rule, because it gives the buyer the benefit of the bargain.

1) **Example:** On July 1, V contracts to sell Blackacre to P for $20,000. Closing is to take place on October 1. Oil is discovered under the land in September. The land is worth $45,000 on October 1. V sells Blackacre to a bona fide purchaser (*i.e.,* one who pays value and takes without notice of any defect) on September 15 for $35,000. P is entitled to recover $25,000 as damages from V. [Smith v. Warr, 564 P.2d 771 (Utah 1977)]

(b) **Exception—good faith of seller:** [§1804] Note that in the preceding example, V is a "bad person" who intentionally breached the contract. But suppose that V does not act in bad faith. Suppose that the deal falls through because V's title is unmarketable. A deed in V's chain of title, unbeknownst to V, is a forgery. Is it fair to stick V for $25,000 damages? About half the states say no, and follow this exception to the general rule: If the seller acts in good faith, the buyer is limited to recovery of any money paid to the seller, plus interest and expenses in examining the title ("money out of pocket"). In other words, where the seller is not acting in bad faith, the buyer is entitled only to be restored to her original position (as in rescission). [Kramer v. Mobley, 216 S.W.2d 930 (Ky. 1949)]

b. Remedies of the seller

(1) **Rescission:** [§1805] Upon breach by the buyer, the seller can rescind the contract.

(2) **Specific performance:** [§1806] A seller, like a buyer, is entitled to demand specific performance upon the other party's breach of contract. If there is a defect in the seller's title that is insubstantial and not material, the seller can enforce the contract specifically with an abatement in the purchase price to compensate the buyer for the deficiency.

    (a) **Defenses:** [§1807] There may be a new trend to deny specific performance to the seller when damages at law are adequate. [Centex Homes Corp. v. Boag, 320 A.2d 194 (N.J. 1974)—denying specific performance to seller of condominium unit] Uniform Land Transactions Act section 2-506(b) gives the seller the right to specific performance only if the seller cannot resell the property at a reasonable price.

(3) **Damages:** [§1808] If the seller prefers to keep the land, the seller can do so and still sue the buyer for money damages—the difference between the contract price and the market price when performance is due. If, for example, the seller contracts to sell land for $20,000, and the market price is $15,000 on the date of closing, the seller is entitled to $5,000 damages if the buyer does not perform. (If the value has increased or stayed the same, the seller can recover only nominal damages—*e.g.,* one dollar—for the breach.)

    (a) **Liquidated damages:** [§1809] The contract may provide that the seller can keep the down payment. If the parties intended this provision to be an agreement for liquidated damages, it is enforceable if the amount stipulated does not greatly exceed the injury that will be suffered. Generally, if the amount of down payment bears some *reasonable relationship* to the *actual* damages the seller sustains as a result of the buyer's breach (*e.g.,* any decline in value; costs of reselling property, if any; loss of other prospects; loss of interest on expected purchase price, etc.), such a provision for liquidated damages will be upheld. On the other hand, if the parties did not intend the provision that the seller can keep the down payment to be in lieu of compensatory damages, nor did they intend to deprive the seller of other remedies, the seller may recover actual damages. [Frank v. Jansen, 226 N.W.2d 739 (Minn. 1975)]

(b) **Installment land contracts:** [§1810]   An installment land contract is one where the purchaser agrees to pay the purchase price over a period of time to the seller, and when all the payments are made, the seller will give the buyer a deed. Until all the payments are made, title remains in the seller. The installment land contract is a substitute for a sale to the buyer with the seller taking back a purchase money mortgage. If the parties had used a purchase money mortgage, the seller-mortgagee could only *foreclose* the mortgage in case of buyer default. Under foreclosure, the land is sold and from the proceeds the mortgagee gets the amount of the debt, and the mortgagor gets the rest. Foreclosure is expensive, time-consuming, and subject to extensions of time for payment granted by common law or statute. Thus, the installment land contract is used where the seller wants to avoid the foreclosure remedy if the buyer defaults, but such an arrangement is loaded in favor of the seller because the seller will claim, as liquidated damages, forfeiture of all payments made by the buyer upon breach. If the buyer has paid a substantial amount, this can be unjust. As a result, courts more and more are refusing to decree forfeiture when the buyer would suffer exorbitant monetary loss under an installment land contract and are requiring the seller to foreclose (thus treating the contract as an equitable mortgage). [Skendzel v. Marshall, 301 N.E.2d 641 (Ind. 1973)] Or the courts may relieve against forfeiture by restoring the buyer her rights under the contract or awarding the buyer restitution of payments made in excess of the seller's damage. [Union Bond & Trust Co. v. Blue Creek Redwood Co., 128 F. Supp. 709 (N.D. Cal. 1955)]

6. **Equitable Conversion:** [§1811]   The doctrine of equitable conversion may be invoked to solve problems resulting from the two-step method of conveyancing: First there is the contract of sale, and second, some weeks later, the closing. During this period, various problems may arise which depend upon who has "title" to the real property. The doctrine of equitable conversion was invented to treat the buyer as having title for certain purposes prior to the date set for closing.

a. **Statement of doctrine:** [§1812]   The doctrine of equitable conversion is based on the idea that equity *regards as done that which ought to be done* (since either party can demand specific performance of the land sale contract). Thus, the buyer is regarded in equity as the owner of the land; the seller has a security interest for payment of the purchase price, not unlike a mortgage. Sometimes it is added that the seller holds the legal title in trust for the buyer as security for the debt owed the seller. [Griggs Land Co. v. Smith, 89 P. 477 (Wash. 1907)]

(1) **Example:** On July 1, O contracts to sell Blackacre to A for $5,000, closing to take place on September 1. As of July 1, in equity A is regarded as the owner of Blackacre; O is regarded as having a debt of $5,000 owed her and a security interest in Blackacre to protect the debt.

(2) **Application:** The doctrine of equitable conversion was applied rather rigorously by the English courts to govern all relationships between buyer and seller during the period before closing. In this country, however, there is much diver-

gence of view about its application; many courts say they apply equitable conversion only to carry out the presumed intent of the parties and to do equity. Hence, they might apply it in one context and not in another.

b. **Devolution on death**

(1) **Early history:** [§1813] The doctrine of equitable conversion originated in cases having to do with devolution of interests upon death of one of the parties to a contract for sale of land. In England, real property descended to the primogenitary heir (eldest son); personal property was distributed to the next of kin (all the children equally). If the seller's interest were real property, it descended to the heir. The courts, however, held that the seller's interest was personal property, which descended to all the children equally. The doctrine of equitable conversion was the device invented to accomplish this result. Having invented the doctrine in this context, the English courts extended it logically to other contexts as well.

(2) **Modern law:** [§1814] Equitable conversion is widely applied in the United States to questions of both testate and intestate devolution, *i.e.*, to distribution of property both with and without a will. The seller's interest is treated as personal property secured by a lien; the buyer's interest is treated as real property.

(a) **Example:** O, owner of Blackacre, executes a will devising "real property" to A and "personal property" to B. Subsequently, O contracts to sell Blackacre to C for $5,000. Before closing, O dies. Applying the doctrine of equitable conversion, O's interest in Blackacre is treated as personal property, and hence B is entitled to the $5,000 when paid. [Shay v. Penrose, 185 N.E.2d 218 (Ill. 1962)] Likewise, if C defaults and cannot pay the $5,000 on closing, B is entitled to Blackacre. Equitable conversion took place the moment the contract was signed; hence, at O's death, his interest, which passed under his will, was personal property. [Clapp v. Tower, 93 N.W. 862 (N.D. 1903)]

c. **Right to possession:** [§1815] Although the buyer has *equitable* title, he does *not* have the right to *possession*, which follows *legal* title. The contract, especially an installment sale contract, may put the buyer into possession. If it does, the buyer may not commit waste that would impair the security of the seller. In questions of waste, the seller under an installment land contract is treated as having a security interest in the property, similar to a mortgage. [Moses Bros. v. Johnson, 7 So. 146 (Ala. 1890)]

d. **Risk of loss:** [§1816] Suppose that before the date set for closing, the property is destroyed or damaged by fire, flood, or other cause not the fault of either party. Who has the risk of loss? The parties may cover this matter in their contract, but if they do not the court will apply a rule.

(1) **Majority—buyer has risk of loss:** [§1817]   The majority of courts follows the old English rule enunciated in *Paine v. Meller*, 6 Ves. 349 (Ch. 1801), which applied equitable conversion and put the risk of loss on the buyer. By virtue of equitable conversion, the buyer owns the land, and the seller has only a security interest. If the buyer refuses to take the damaged property, the seller can sue for specific performance at the contract price or sue for damages. The amount of damage is the loss in value of the property due to the fire or other cause. [Bleckley v. Langston, 143 S.E.2d 671 (Ga. 1965)]

  (a) **Unmarketable title:** [§1818]   If the seller's title is unmarketable, and the seller cannot obtain specific performance, equitable conversion will not take place, and the risk of loss will not shift to the buyer. To shift the loss to the buyer, the seller must prove that he is entitled to specific performance. [Sanford v. Breidenbach, 173 N.E.2d 702 (Ohio 1960)]

  (b) **Contract terms:** [§1819]   The contract can, of course, put the risk of loss on the seller. If it does so, the buyer can get specific performance with an abatement in the purchase price in the amount of the damage suffered. [World Exhibit Corp. v. City Bank Farmers Trust Co., 270 App. Div. 654 (1946)]

  (c) **Insurance:** [§1820]   If the risk of loss is on the buyer, should the buyer be entitled, in the event of loss, to the proceeds of the seller's insurance policy? The English rule was that the insurance policy is a personal contract of indemnity, and hence the seller is entitled to the insurance proceeds and does not have to credit them against the purchase price. American courts have looked upon this rule with marked disfavor. Most reject it completely on the ground that it gives the seller a windfall: He pockets both the insurance proceeds and the purchase price through specific performance. These courts require the seller to credit the insurance proceeds against the purchase price in an action for specific performance. They usually say the seller holds the insurance proceeds in a constructive trust for the buyer. A few states follow the English rule, but have created two exceptions that cover most cases that arise: (i) if the seller is required by the contract *to keep the property insured* for the benefit of the buyer, or (ii) if the buyer is required by the contract *to pay the premiums* on the seller's policy, the insurance proceeds are credited against the purchase price. [Raplee v. Piper, 3 N.Y.2d 179 (1957)]

(2) **Minority—seller has risk of loss:** [§1821]   A minority of courts follows the so-called "Massachusetts rule," which puts the risk of loss on the seller. These courts reject equitable conversion in this context. They imply a *condition in the contract* that (i) *if the loss is substantial*, and (ii) *the terms of the agreement show that the building constituted an important part of the subject matter* of the contract, the contract is not binding. If the building is destroyed, the buyer can rescind and recover any earnest money. [Anderson v. Yaworski, 181 A. 205 (Conn. 1935)]

(a) **Specific performance with abatement:** [§1822] If the damage is **insubstantial**, the buyer can get specific performance with an abatement in the purchase price for the amount of damage. But where the damage is **substantial**, logical application of the Massachusetts theory will not permit specific performance with an abatement in the purchase price. Specific performance is inconsistent with the theory that the contract is not binding if damages are substantial. (Indeed, strict application of the Massachusetts theory would mean that the seller could refuse to convey where there is substantial damage even though the purchaser tendered the full purchase price.) Nonetheless, one court purporting to follow the Massachusetts rule has decreed specific performance to the buyer with abatement in the purchase price—not by the amount of actual damages, but by the amount of insurance received by the seller. [Skelly Oil Co. v. Ashmore, 365 S.W.2d 582 (Mo. 1963)] This does not make much theoretical sense, but it may be equitable to give the buyer an abatement and efficient to treat the insurance proceeds as equivalent to damages (thus avoiding proof problems). This result is hardly distinguishable from the majority view that the buyer has the risk of loss, but the seller holds any insurance proceeds as trustee for the buyer.

(b) **Buyer's insurance:** [§1823] Buyers sometimes take out insurance to protect themselves when they sign a contract to purchase real property. This is a common practice, particularly when commercial property is purchased. If the building is destroyed, the buyer is paid by the insurance company. A seller who has the risk of loss **cannot** reach the proceeds of the buyer's insurance. This accords with the common understanding of the parties that, although the continuation of the seller's insurance during the contract period may be for the protection of the buyer, the buyer's purchase of insurance is solely to protect the buyer. [Sanford v. Breidenbach, *supra*, §1818]

(3) **Party in possession has risk of loss:** [§1824] Some courts have held that the **party in possession** has the risk of loss. If the seller is still in possession, he bears the risk; if the buyer has gone into possession, she bears the risk. The Uniform Vendor and Purchaser Risk Act (adopted in California, Illinois, Michigan, New York and a few other states) adopts this position.

e. **Application to options:** [§1825] In the United States, equitable conversion does not apply to an option to purchase **until** the option is exercised. *Rationale:* An option is specifically enforceable only by the buyer (optionee) and not by the seller (optionor). Equitable conversion applies only where there is a mutually specifically enforceable contract.

(1) **Example:** O gives A a ninety-day option to buy Whiteacre for $30,000. Within the ninety-day period, O dies leaving a will executed two years previously which devises B a life estate in Whiteacre. At O's death, equitable conversion has not occurred. At her death, O has legal title to Whiteacre subject to an option, and B takes a life estate in Whiteacre subject to that option. If A exer-

cises the option, O's interest is converted into money, and at that time equitable conversion takes place and B takes a life estate in the $30,000. [Eddington v. Turner, 38 A.2d 738 (Del. 1944)]

7. **The Closing:** [§1826]   At the closing, a third party (either a lawyer or escrow agent) is usually in charge. A check for the purchase price is handed by the buyer to the party in charge; a deed executed by the seller is also handed over. Any mortgage given to the seller or to a third-party lender is executed by the buyer and handed to the party in charge. The party in charge makes various agreed-upon adjustments in the amount owed, such as proration of taxes, utility bills, and mortgage payments to the date of closing. The party in charge then records the deed and any mortgage. Finally, the party in charge hands a check to the seller. The deal is closed.

B. THE MORTGAGE

1. **Why a Mortgage Is Used:** [§1827]   Most people do not have cash available to pay for the real property they are purchasing. They must go to a lender and borrow money. The lender—usually a bank or savings and loan association—has money to lend at the market rate of interest. If the borrower is an acceptable credit risk (has a job, pays bills on time, etc.), the lender will lend money to the borrower, to be paid back with interest over time. To secure the debt owed the lender, the borrower will give the lender a mortgage on the property. If the debt is not paid, the lender will "foreclose the mortgage." Foreclosing the mortgage means that the property will be sold, and from the proceeds the lender will be paid the amount of the debt and anything left will be given to the borrower. Mortgages are extremely useful in real estate transactions because they enable persons without capital to borrow capital from others and acquire real property for themselves. *Caveat*: In a brief synopsis such as is set forth here, only the general outline of mortgage law can be given. Although the outline is accurate, a detailed treatment would include numerous qualifications. Mortgage law is complex, and there are many local variations. The purpose of this synopsis is to give you information sufficient for an understanding of the mortgage problems that arise in a first-year property course.

2. **Nature of the Mortgage Transaction:** [§1828]   The mortgage transaction consists of two documents: (i) the note and (ii) the mortgage. A note is a document that evidences the debt: "I, Borrower, promise to pay Lender $10,000 on June 1, 1990, with interest to be paid annually at ten percent per annum." The note is a personal obligation of the borrower, and the lender can sue the borrower on the note if the borrower does not pay. The note is sometimes called the debtor's *bond*. The second document is the *mortgage*. It is the agreement that the land will be sold if the debt is not paid, and the lender reimbursed from the proceeds of sale. The mortgage gives the lender *security*. In case of default on the note, the lender does not have recourse only against the general assets of the borrower—which may be few. The mortgage gives the lender recourse against the land. Thus, the lender's risk is limited; only if on foreclosure the land sells for less than the debt will the lender lose money. The mortgage ordinarily will be *recorded* in the county courthouse at the time it is given, which recordation will give the lender priority over subsequent purchasers of the land. Once the mortgage is recorded, any subsequent purchaser or creditor takes subject to the mortgage.

a. **Caveat:** Although we say two documents are involved in a mortgage transaction in order to emphasize the difference between the *note* and the *mortgage*, in many states, only one document is used. This one document contains *both* the note and the mortgage.

3. **Terminology:** [§1829] Before discussing the law of mortgages, it is useful to define some of the common terms used in mortgage law.

a. **Mortgagor:** [§1830] The borrower or debtor is the mortgagor. Where a person buys land and gives a mortgage on the land to a lender, the buyer is the mortgagor.

b. **Mortgagee:** [§1831] The lender is the mortgagee.

c. **Equity:** [§1832] The borrower's interest in the land is called the equity (short for equity of redemption). This word came into common usage historically because it referred to the interest of the debtor protected by equity courts (*see infra*, §1840).

d. **Deficiency judgment:** [§1833] If, on foreclosure sale, the land does not bring enough to pay the debt, the lender can sue the borrower on the note for the deficiency. A judgment for this deficiency, collectible out of the general assets of the borrower, is called a deficiency judgment.

e. **Purchase money mortgage:** [§1834] A mortgage given to secure the purchase price of land is called a purchase money mortgage. If the borrower already owns the land and gives a mortgage to secure a debt, this mortgage is not a purchase money mortgage. If the debt is incurred to finance improvement of a house, the mortgage will be a *home improvement* mortgage.

f. **Balloon payment mortgage:** [§1835] A balloon payment mortgage is one that calls for periodic interest payments until the due date of the debt, when the *whole principal sum* must be paid at once. *Example:* Bank lends A $10,000, due in five years, with interest at ten percent per year. At the end of each of the first four years, A must pay the bank $1,000 interest. At the end of the fifth year, A must pay the bank $1,000 plus $10,000 (the principal).

g. **Amortized payment mortgage:** [§1836] The typical home mortgage is not a balloon payment mortgage, but a mortgage for twenty-five or thirty years with even monthly payments over the period. The last monthly payment, in the same amount as the earlier ones, pays off the mortgage. There is no balloon payment at the end. The monthly payments are calculated so as to return principal as well as interest to the lender over the period of the mortgage. This type of mortgage, developed by the Federal Housing Authority in the 1930s, has made borrowing for home purchase easier—or, at least, seem easier. Home buyers think it is like paying rent, and since the mortgage interest is deductible on the federal income tax, buying a house may not be much more expensive than renting.

h. **Second mortgage:** [§1837] More than one mortgage can be given on a tract of land. A mortgage given second in time, with notice of the earlier mortgage, is called a second mortgage. The second mortgagee's rights are **subject to** the rights of the first mortgagee. If the first mortgagee forecloses a mortgage debt of $20,000, for example, and the land sells for $15,000, all the proceeds go to the first mortgagee. The second mortgagee has a right to the proceeds only after the first mortgagee is paid off. As a result, second mortgages are riskier than first mortgages and command a higher interest rate.

i. **Deed of trust:** [§1838]   In a large number of states, particularly in the South and West, the mortgage takes the form of a deed of trust. Instead of the borrower giving the lender a mortgage, the borrower gives the lender a deed of trust. By this arrangement the borrower transfers title to a third person **as trustee** for the lender to secure the debt. (The third person is often the nominee of the lender.) If the debt is not paid, the trustee sells the land under a power of sale in the trust deed, pays off the debt, and pays over anything left to the borrower. The essential difference between a mortgage and a deed of trust relates to the power to sell the land upon default. In some jurisdictions, the mortgagee must resort to **judicial foreclosure**, which is time-consuming and costly; a clause in the mortgage giving the mortgagee power to sell the land upon default, without going through judicial proceedings, is void. In other jurisdictions, if the mortgage gives the mortgagee a **power of sale**, the power of sale is valid. The mortgagee can foreclose by his own public sale after notice to all parties, avoiding judicial foreclosure, but—at least in earlier times— the mortgagee could not bid on the property at the sale (thought to be self-dealing). To avoid judicial foreclosure and the rule that a mortgagee could not bid at his own sale, the deed of trust was invented. Under the deed of trust, upon default by the buyer and request by the lender, the trustee can sell the land at a public sale out of court and the lender can bid at the trustee's sale.

(1) **Note:** Modern statutes now permit the mortgagee to bid at his own sale when he has a power of sale, and have largely eliminated the difference between a deed of trust and a mortgage with power of sale. In other respects, the rights of the borrower under a deed of trust are practically the same as under a mortgage.

j. **Installment land contract:** [§1839]   An installment land contract is an agreement by the buyer to buy land and to pay for it over a period of years—maybe twenty or thirty years. In the contract the seller agrees to deliver title at the end of the period. The buyer goes into possession, and the seller keeps title until the final payment. Keeping title is the seller's security. The installment land contract was once thought to have two particular advantages for a seller: (i) the seller can repossess upon default without going through judicial foreclosure; and (ii) the seller can keep all payments made under the contract as damages upon the buyer's default. However, the installment land contract functions as a mortgage, and courts more and more are extending the traditional rights of a mortgagor to the buyer under an installment land contract. The history of mortgage law is that equity stepped in to relieve borrowers from unconscionable contracts drafted by lenders and to give borrowers rights they could not contract away, and this history is now repeating itself with installment land contracts. [*See* Skendzel v. Marshall, *supra*, §1810; *and* Sebastian v. Floyd, 585 S.W.2d 381 (Ky. 1979)—both holding installment land contract should be treated like a mortgage and judicial foreclosure required; forfeiture of payments is limited to situations where equitable (*i.e.*, where roughly equal to fair rental value); *and see* Union Bond & Trust Co. v. Blue Creek Redwood Co., *supra*, §1810—buyer has right to make payments in default and continue contract, in effect giving buyer an equity of redemption]

4. **History of the Mortgage:** [§1840]   In order to better secure the debts owed, money lenders in England by the seventeenth century had invented the ancestor of the modern mortgage. The lender insisted that the borrower convey the land *in fee simple* to the lender, *subject to a condition subsequent*: If the loan was repaid on the agreed date, the lender would reconvey the fee simple to the borrower. This condition subsequent was called a "proviso for redemption." The agreement was strictly enforced by the law courts, and if the borrower could not pay (redeem the land) *on the agreed date*, the land could never be redeemed. Upon default, the mortgagee was the absolute owner. Equity, however, viewed that result as excessively harsh on the borrower, who might, for good reason, be unable to present himself at the lender's office with the money on the due day. Equity intervened to give borrowers a right to redeem *at any time*, even years after the agreed date. Equity took the position that the borrower should be treated as the owner in equity, and the mortgage should be deemed no more than a device to secure the debt. This right to redeem was called "the equity of redemption." Because the right to redeem without limitation of time made it very difficult for the lender to sell the land upon default, equity gave the lender the right to *foreclose the right of redemption*. (Note that today we speak of "foreclosing the mortgage," but technically we mean "foreclosing the equity of redemption.") Foreclosure is a judicial proceeding that orders the property sold at public sale, the equity of redemption barred, the debt paid, and any excess proceeds given to the mortgagor.

a. **Equitable mortgage:** [§1841]   Sometimes lenders try to avoid the protection equity has extended to borrowers by devious procedures. A lender, rather like the early English lenders, may insist on the borrower giving the lender a deed to the land in fee simple, with a lease back to the borrower with an option to repurchase. Or the lender may insist on a deed to the lender in fee simple absolute, and the lender promises to return the deed when the debt is paid. Courts have been astute to look through these forms to the *substance* of the transaction; when they find the parties intended the land to be security for a debt, they have declared the deed or other conveyance to be an *equitable mortgage*—that is, in equity, it will be *treated as a mortgage*. Extrinsic evidence is admissible to show the intent of the parties. [Mid-State Investment Corp. v. O'Steen, 133 So. 2d 455 (Fla. 1961); Koenig v. Van Reken, 279 N.W.2d 590 (Mich. 1979)]

b. **Statutory period of redemption:** [§1842]   In many states, by *statute* borrowers have a period of time *after judicial foreclosure* during which they can redeem from the purchaser at foreclosure sale. A two year period is typical. These statutes were enacted to protect debtors by giving them more time to come up with the money and save their property. Do not confuse the *statutory right to redeem* the property from the purchaser at the foreclosure sale with the *judicially created equity of redemption*, which is cut off at the foreclosure sale. Ironically, the post-foreclosure-sale redemption period chills the bidding at the foreclosure sale, because the purchaser does not get a clear title until the period expires. This harms the debtor by lessening the value of his equity. Because of this, the Federal Housing Authority has preempted local law with respect to FHA guaranteed mortgages; *i.e.*, the state redemption statutes do not apply to foreclosures by the FHA. [United States v. Stadium Apartments, Inc., 425 F.2d 358 (9th Cir. 1970)]

5. **Theory of the Mortgage:** [§1843]   Because the historical form of a mortgage purported to give title to the lender, with an equity of redemption in the borrower, the early American cases—from eastern states—treated legal title as being in the mortgagee. States adopting this theory are known as *title theory* states. Later cases—principally from the West—looked through form to substance and declared that legal title remained in the mortgagor and the mortgagee had merely a *lien* on the property to secure the debt. States adopting this theory are known as *lien theory* states. (Note that even in lien theory states, however, the mortgagor's interest is still known as "the equity.")

   a. **Difference in theories:** [§1844]   The basic distinction between these two theories is that under the title theory the mortgagee, having title, is *entitled to possession*, whereas a lienor is not. However, in almost all mortgages given in title theory states, the mortgagee agrees that the mortgagor shall have the right to possession, so the distinction makes little difference in practice. Other differences have all but disappeared. In title theory states, for almost all purposes, the courts have come to the same results as would be reached by treating the mortgage as a lien. Therefore, though they may say they are title theory states, they in fact treat the mortgage as in substance a lien.

6. **Transfer of the Mortgagor's Interest**

   a. **Sale subject to the mortgage:** [§1845]   The mortgagor can transfer his interest ("the equity") *subject to the mortgage*. If the sale is "subject to the mortgage," the new buyer takes the land subject to the lien upon it, but the new buyer is *not personally liable on the debt*. If the debt is not paid, the mortgagee can foreclose on the land, but the mortgagee cannot sue the new buyer on the debt. Thus, the mortgagee cannot get a deficiency judgment against the buyer who takes "subject to the mortgage." The original mortgagor remains liable on the debt, of course.

      (1) **Remedies of mortgagee:** [§1846]   If the debt is not paid, in most states the mortgagee has a choice: He can sue the mortgagor personally or proceed against the land by foreclosure and sale. If the mortgagee elects to sue the mortgagor personally, the mortgagor is *subrogated* to the mortgagee's rights and can obtain reimbursement by foreclosing on the land. In other words, when land is sold subject to the mortgage, the land is primarily liable for the debt, and the mortgagor is a surety for the debt.

   b. **Sale with assumption of the mortgage:** [§1847]   The mortgagor can transfer his interest to a new buyer who assumes the mortgage. If the new buyer "assumes the mortgage," she becomes personally liable on the debt. The mortgagee can sue either the new buyer or the original mortgagor on the debt (as between them, the new buyer is primarily liable). Both are subject to a deficiency judgment if, upon foreclosure sale, the land does not bring a sum sufficient to discharge the debt. If the mortgagee elects to sue the original mortgagor on the debt, the mortgagor in turn can sue the new buyer, who assumed the mortgage, for the debt or foreclose upon the land.

(1) **Assumption implied:** [§1848]   Assumption of the mortgage debt can be implied from the circumstances surrounding the sale to the new buyer. In the absence of an express contrary agreement, an assumption may be implied when the amount due under the trust obligation has been deducted from the purchase price. [Daugharthy v. Monritt Associates, 444 A.2d 1030 (Md. 1982)]

   (a) **Example:** A buys a building for $125,000 and gives B a mortgage for $75,000. Subsequently, A sells the building to C for $140,000 minus $75,000, or $65,000 (the value of A's equity). If the settlement statement shows the buyer elected to deduct the $75,000 from the purchase price, this may constitute an agreement to assume the mortgage. The buyer, C, should protect herself with an express provision that the sale is subject to the mortgage if that is what is intended.

c. **Due-on-sale clauses:** [§1849]   Lenders often insert due-on-sale clauses in their mortgages. A due-on-sale clause provides that, at the mortgagee's election, the *entire mortgage debt is due upon sale* of the mortgagor's interest. In other words, the mortgagee can accelerate the due date if the land is sold, requiring payment of the mortgage at that time. The purpose of this clause is two-fold: (i) by requiring the lender's consent to assign the mortgage, the lender is protected against assignment to an unsatisfactory credit risk; and (ii) when the market interest rate rises, the clause permits the mortgagee to force the new buyer to refinance at a prevailing higher rate of interest. With rapidly rising interest rates in the 1970s, some state courts intervened to give borrowers protection. They took the position that the due-on-sale clause was an unreasonable restraint on alienation because it hampered the mortgagor from transferring his equity (at the old lower rate of interest). They refused to enforce such a clause unless the lender could show that its risk would increase or its security would be impaired by the transfer. In other words, they limited the clause to its first purpose given above. [Wellenkamp v. Bank of America, 21 Cal. 3d 943 (1978); Malouff v. Midland Federal Savings & Loan Association, 509 P.2d 1240 (Colo. 1973)] Responding to the outcry of lenders that the due-on-sale clause was an important device in maintaining their portfolios at current interest rates, and making money available to new borrowers for housing, Congress in 1982 enacted a statute preempting state law prohibitions of due-on-sale clauses. This legislation generally provided that due-on-sale clauses are enforceable. An exception (a "window") was provided for existing mortgages made or assumed *after state action* had prohibited the enforcement of due-on-sale clauses but *before* the enactment of the federal act. [Garn-St. Germain Act of 1982, Pub. L. 97-320, 96 Stat. 1469]

d. **Prepayment penalty:** [§1850] Many mortgages provide a penalty if the mortgage debt is paid *before* the end of the mortgage term. The purpose of the penalty is to discourage refinancing when the market rate of interest falls below the rate of interest specified in the mortgage.

7. **Transfer by the Mortgagee:** [§1851] The mortgagee can transfer the note and the mortgage to another person. However, as the mortgage is only security for the debt, the mortgage cannot be transferred to one person and the note (debt) to another. Any transfer of the mortgage by itself is void. Any transfer of the note by itself also, by operation of law, transfers the mortgage to the assignee. This is summed up in this rule: *The mortgage follows the note*.

   a. **Secondary mortgage market:** [§1852] Mortgages are often assigned by the primary lender (the original mortgagee) to financial institutions operating the secondary mortgage market. These institutions include large banks, insurance companies, and the federal government operating through the Federal National Mortgage Association ("Fannie Mae") and the Federal Home Loan Bank. These large institutions attempt to make credit available in smaller localities for building. The government agencies stabilize the market and keep mortgage money available by buying mortgages from private lenders when credit is tight and selling them when private funds are flowing into the market. Thus, if A obtains a loan and gives a mortgage to her local Home Savings & Loan Association, Home may sell the mortgage on the secondary market to a lender in New York. The monthly payments continue to be made to Home, which remits them to the new owner of the mortgage in New York.

8. **Default by the Mortgagor:** [§1853] Upon default by the mortgagor, the mortgagee can sue on the debt or foreclose on the mortgage. In a minority of states, the mortgagee must foreclose the mortgage and exhaust the security before suing on the debt. After either a judicial foreclosure or a sale under a power of sale in the mortgage, the mortgagee can get a deficiency judgment against the mortgagor for the difference between the amount of the debt and the amount realized from the sale. The mortgagor has been given various remedies against price inadequacy on foreclosure sale. The inadequacy may result from depressed real estate prices or from the fact that few bidders were at the sale. At many sales, the mortgagee is the only bidder.

   a. **Legislation:** [§1854] To protect the mortgagor in default, legislatures in some states have enacted various kinds of legislation.

      (1) **Fair market value limitations:** [§1855] A statute may provide that the mortgagee can get a deficiency judgment only for the difference between the debt and the judicially determined fair market value of the property at foreclosure. This legislation is designed to protect the mortgagor from foreclosure sales in the time of depressed real estate prices.

      (2) **Anti-deficiency judgment:** [§1856] A few states have legislation prohibiting the mortgagor from getting a deficiency judgment on purchase money mortgages. This legislation was usually enacted in the Great Depression, after persons had bought real estate in the 1920s in various promotion schemes.

(3) **Statutory right of redemption:** [§1857] The statutory right of redemption after foreclosure has been discussed *supra* (§1842). Under this statutory right, the mortgagor can in some states stay in possession until the redemption period has expired.

b. **Judicial decisions:** [§1858] Courts have set aside foreclosure sales for inadequacy of price where the price is so low as to shock the conscience of the court. [Central Financial Services, Inc. v. Spears, 425 So. 2d 403 (Miss. 1983)] And they may scrutinize the sale to make certain that proper notice was given and other safeguards complied with.

C. THE DEED

1. Formalities

a. **Statute of Frauds:** [§1859] To transfer an interest in land, the Statute of Frauds requires a writing signed by the party to be bound. The writing is usually in the form of a deed, but it may be an informal instrument. A letter evidencing a present intent presently to vest title in the grantee is sufficient. [Metzger v. Miller, 291 F. 780 (N.D. Cal. 1923)—letters saying "house is now yours," coupled with grantee moving in, evidenced intent to pass title]

(1) **Signature of grantor only:** [§1860] The writing must be signed by the party to be bound—the *grantor*. It is neither necessary nor customary that the *grantee* sign the deed. A deed signed by the grantor only is called a "deed poll"; a deed signed by both grantor and grantee is called an "indenture." If a deed poll contains covenants by the grantee (*e.g.*, to use the property only for residential purposes), the grantee is bound by the covenants, even though he does not sign the deed, if the grantee *accepts* the deed.

(a) **Forged deed:** [§1861] No interest passes under a forged deed. Unless estoppel comes into play because of the purported grantor's acts, the deed is not legally effective at all.

(b) **Executed parol gift:** [§1862] A parol gift of land has sometimes been upheld in spite of the Statute of Frauds. To take a parol gift out of the Statute of Frauds, the grantee must take possession in reliance on the gift and *make valuable improvements* so that a substantial injustice would result from rigorously applying the Statute of Frauds. The doctrine of executed parol gift bears substantial similarity to the doctrine of part performance of a contract (*supra*, §1774). [Hayes v. Hayes, 148 N.W. 125 (Minn. 1914)]

(2) **Acknowledgment:** [§1863] Acknowledgment by the grantor in front of a notary public or attestation by witnesses is usually not necessary for an effective deed. However, acknowledgment or attestation is desirable for two reasons:

(a) **Recordation:** [§1864] Acknowledgment or witnessing is usually required for recordation of a deed. In most states, an unacknowledged deed cannot be recorded (*see infra*, §§1984 *et seq.*).

(b) **Authentication:** [§1865] In most states, an acknowledged or witnessed deed is self-authenticating, meaning that it can be admitted into evidence in any legal action even though no one can testify to its execution or delivery. An unacknowledged or unwitnessed deed may not be admitted into evidence without direct testimony regarding its execution. In addition, proof of delivery of the deed may be required, and this may be difficult if there were no witnesses.

(3) **Seal:** [§1866] At common law, a "deed" was defined as an instrument under seal. Today a seal is not required for a valid transfer, and unsealed instruments are commonly called deeds.

(4) **Signature of spouse:** [§1867] The spouse may have property rights accruing from marriage, such as dower, curtesy, homestead, or community property rights in the property. To release these, the spouse must join the deed.

b. **Words of grant:** [§1868] Any words indicating an intent to make a transfer will suffice. Words of grant include "I give, grant, bargain and sell, convey, quitclaim, assign." Only one word of grant is necessary, but deeds often contain many of the technical terms used at common law, which are no longer necessary for an effective deed.

(1) **Modern deeds:** [§1869] At common law there were numerous kinds of deeds, each adapted for a particular set of circumstances. Common law deeds included a "bargain and sale deed," a "covenant to stand seised," a "feoffment," and a "lease and release," among others. Today these deeds are no longer used. Modern deeds are of two types: (i) *warranty deeds*, by which the grantor warrants title, and (ii) *quitclaim deeds*, by which the grantor does not warrant title. (*See infra*, §§1936-1940.)

c. **Consideration:** [§1870] Consideration is *not* necessary to transfer land; a person can *give* land away. It is neither necessary nor customary to recite the true consideration, if any, in the deed. The purchaser usually wants to keep the purchase price secret. However, it is customary to recite that the deed is given "for one dollar and other good and valuable consideration." This rebuts any implication of a resulting use or trust in favor of the grantor and raises a presumption that the grantee is a purchaser, not a donee, and hence entitled to protection under the recording acts (*see infra*, §§1984 *et seq.*).

d. **Parts of the deed**

(1) **Granting clause:** [§1871] The initial clause in a deed, setting forth the parties, the consideration, words of grant, the description of the land and its appurtenances, is known as the granting clause.

(2) **Habendum clause:** [§1872] The habendum clause is usually introduced by the words "to have and to hold" ("habendum et tenendum" in Latin). This ordinarily follows the granting clause and in feudal times was very important because it contained the name of the person (lord) from whom the land was held, the services due, and the kind of estate held. After feudalism declined and trusts arose, any declaration of trust was inserted in the habendum clause (*e.g.*, "to have and to hold to the use of B for life, then to the use of B's children"). If no trust is intended, the habendum clause in a modern deed will say that the grantee holds for his own use, thus negating a trust.

(a) **Inconsistency:** [§1873] If the habendum is inconsistent with the granting clause, they will be reconciled, if possible. It was sometimes said, in older cases, that a granting clause will prevail over a habendum in case of conflict, on the theory that the grantor could not cut back on the interest earlier conveyed. But modern courts usually find a means of reconciling the conflict by looking "within the four corners of an instrument" (*i.e.*, looking at all the terms of the document itself) to ascertain intent. [Barrier v. Randolph, 133 S.E.2d 655 (N.C. 1963); First National Bank of Oregon v. Townsend, 555 P.2d 477 (Or. 1976)]

1) **Example:** An elderly couple executed a deed to their land. The granting clause said "to our son, George," the consideration being that "George is to take care of the grantors as long as they live." The habendum clause said "to have and to hold the land to George and his wife Mae and their heirs and assigns." Looking at all parts of the deed, the court inferred that the deed was made in consideration of both George and Mae looking after the old couple, since the wife would be performing the household duties. Thus the court held that the habendum clause controlled, and the conveyance was to George and Mae by the entirety, and not to George alone. [Grayson v. Holloway, 313 S.W.2d 555 (Tenn. 1958)]

(b) **Not used in statutory forms:** [§1874] The habendum clause is superfluous today and is omitted from all statutory forms of deeds.

(3) **Exceptions and reservations:** [§1875] A clause in the deed may except or reserve some rights in the *grantor*. An exception excludes from the grant some land or *existing interest*. For example, if O conveys to A "500 acres except the twenty-foot strip on the east side now used for a road," O retains the fee simple in the twenty-foot strip. A reservation, on the other hand, allows the entire property to pass to the grantee, with a fictional grant back from the grantee to the grantor of a *new interest*. Thus if O conveys to A "500 acres reserving twenty feet on the east side for a right of way," A takes a fee simple and grants back to O an easement over the twenty feet. (On the difference between exception and reservation, *supra*, §§1335-1337.)

(a) **Third party:** [§1876] At common law, there could be no reservation or exception in favor of a third party, only in favor of the grantor or the grantor's spouse, because it was necessary to use words of grant to convey an interest to a third party. Thus O could not say, in a deed granting land to A, "reserving a life estate in B." O had to say, "I **grant** to B for life, remainder to A." The rule is still followed in some states. Because the rule is easily avoided by using appropriate words of grant, it serves no public policy and is only a malpractice trap for lawyers.

(4) **Grantor's covenants:** [§1877]   A final paragraph of the deed may include covenants of warranty by the grantor. (*See infra,* §§1935 *et seq.*)

(5) **Signature and acknowledgment:** [§1878]   The grantor's signature and acknowledgment before a notary come at the end of the deed.

e. **Description of the grantee:** [§1879]   If the instrument names a grantee, the grantee must be described with sufficient particularity so that it can be determined who is to take the grant. If the named grantee is a nonexistent or unascertained person, the deed may be invalid either for uncertainty or for failure to make delivery.

(1) **Sufficient description required:** [§1880]   The grantee need not be actually named, as long as a sufficient description is given. A grant to the "wife" or "oldest living child" of a named person is valid.

(2) **Grantee's name left blank:** [§1881]   A grantee is an essential part of a deed. If the grantee's name is left blank in the deed, some older cases held that the deed is a legal nullity. Under this view, the intended grantee can only sue in equity for specific performance of the contract to sell.

(a) **Implied authority:** [§1882]   A majority of modern cases hold that if the grantee's name is blank, the intended grantee is the agent of the grantor with implied authority to fill in his own or another name. The deed is a nullity when executed, but when the name is filled in, the instrument becomes operative as a deed. [Board of Education v. Hughes, 136 N.W. 1095 (Minn. 1912)]

1) **Death of grantor:** [§1883]   Although the death of a principal usually terminates the power of the agent to act, if the grantor dies before the agent fills in the grantee's name, the agent can fill in the grantee's name after the grantor's death even in the case of a gratuitous transfer. Thus courts bend the rules to make a deed in blank effective—and why not when they hold a blank check valid? [Womack v. Stegner, 293 S.W.2d 124 (Tex. 1956)]

2. **Description of Land Conveyed**

a. **Admission of extrinsic evidence:** [§1884]   The property passing under a deed can be described by: metes and bounds (meaning "measurements and boundaries"); reference to a government survey, a recorded plat, or adjacent properties; a street and number system; or the name of the property. If the description in a deed furnishes any means of identification of the property involved, the description is sufficient. Extrinsic evidence is usually admissible to clear up any ambiguity. [Bybee v. Hageman, 66 Ill. 519 (1873); Hoban v. Cable, 60 N.W. 466 (Mich. 1894)]

(1) **Part of larger tract:** [§1885]   A conveyance of "one acre off the western end of my thirty-acre tract" (the thirty-acre tract being adequately described) would probably fail for uncertainty. "Off the western end" is too vague to tell **which** acre, and the admission of parol evidence to clear up the ambiguity here would probably be held to violate the Statute of Frauds. However, if there is an **underlying contract** for sale, written or oral, which specified the particular acre, the grantee may bring a suit in equity to change the deed to comply with the contract.

(2) **No ambiguity—extrinsic evidence not admissible:** [§1886]   If the description of a deed is not ambiguous—such as "the northeast quarter of the northeast quarter" or "the west fifty feet of lot 13"—extrinsic evidence, such as action of the parties in locating fences or oral agreements, is not admissible to contradict the deed. Such evidence is admissible only to show a mutual mistake in the description in a suit to reform the deed to carry out the parties' original intent. [Loverkamp v. Loverkamp, 45 N.E.2d 871 (Ill. 1943); Walters v. Tucker, 281 S.W.2d 843 (Mo. 1955)]

b. **Canons of construction:** [§1887]   Where there is a mistake or inconsistency in the description, as where the deed leaves in doubt the exact location of a boundary line or gives two different locations for the line, canons of construction are applied to ascertain the parties' intent. These canons are designed to give effect to what the parties most likely intended, but they yield to any clear manifestation of the parties' intent. The order is: **original survey monuments** prevail over **natural monuments,** which prevail over **artificial monuments,** which prevail over **maps,** which prevail over **courses,** which prevail over **distances,** which prevail over a **name,** which prevails over **quantity.** [Pritchard v. Rebori, 186 S.W. 121 (Tenn. 1916)]

(1) **Survey monuments:** [§1888]   A survey monument is a specially placed stake or some natural object used in marking the lines and corners of a survey. When land is conveyed by reference to a survey, the survey monuments prevail over a less certain description if the original survey monuments can be found. [Arnold v. Hanson, 91 Cal. App. 2d 15 (1949)—surveyor's stakes prevail over filed subdivision plat]

(2) **Natural and artificial monuments:** [§1889]   A description based on natural or artificial monuments prevails over a description based on maps, courses and distances, or quantity. Thus, a call from "Point X to the old oak tree" prevails over a call from "Point X north 150 feet." *Rationale*: Property is normally bought in reliance on what can be seen, not on paper calculations. Furthermore, people cannot measure distances very accurately with the naked eye.

(a) **Natural vs. artificial monuments:** [§1890] Natural monuments (*e.g.,* tree, river) are regarded as more reliable than artificial, easily moved monuments (*e.g.,* surveyor's stake, fence). Hence, natural monuments prevail over artificial monuments if they are of greater permanence.

(3) **Maps:** [§1891]   If a survey map has been made of the property, but the marks of the original survey have disappeared or were never made, the survey map describing courses and distances can be used to establish boundaries. A description based on a survey map prevails over a description by courses and distances or quantity.

(4) **Courses and distances:** [§1892]   A description by courses and distances gives a starting point and the direction and length of the lines to be run. Courses (*e.g.,* angles) prevail over distances. If the parcel will not close as described, but will close by following the courses and lengthening or shortening the distances, this will be done. It is assumed that an angle, which fixes the shape of the lot, is more obvious to the parties than length. [Hall v. Eaton, 29 N.E. 660 (Mass. 1885)]

(5) **Name or quantity:** [§1893]   All the foregoing prevail over descriptions by name (*e.g.,* "Walker's Island") or quantity (*e.g.,* "being 300 acres"). As between these two, description by name prevails over description by quantity. Quantity is regarded as the least reliable description.

c. **Streets and railways as boundaries:** [§1894]   If land is described as being bounded by a public or private right of way—or if the land conveyed is otherwise described but actually is bounded by such right of way—there is a rebuttable *presumption that the title of the grantee extends to the center of the right of way* (assuming the grantor owns to the center) or to the full width of it if the grantor owns the width of it and retains no land on the other side. [Smith v. Hadad, 314 N.E.2d 435 (Mass. 1974); Parr v. Worley, 599 P.2d 382 (N.M. 1979)]

(1) **Rationale:** This accords with (i) the presumed intention of the parties that the grantor not retain a narrow strip underlying the right of way; and (ii) the greater public convenience in having the land underlying the right of way owned by the abutters.

(2) **Presumption not applicable:** [§1895]   The general presumption that a deed conveys title to the center of an adjoining street or right of way owned by the grantor does ***not*** apply where the ***side*** of the street is described as one of the boundaries of the tract (*e.g.,* "running along the side of Main Street"). Nor does it apply where a city or other public body owning a street or highway conveys land referring to the street or highway as a boundary. It is assumed the public body intends that the street or highway should remain in public ownership.

d. **Water boundaries:** [§1896]   A description of a tract so framed as to have a water boundary carries title to the appurtenant land under water if owned by the grantor. A grantee of land abutting water normally expects access to the water; therefore, the deed is construed to give him the land under the water.

D. DELIVERY OF THE DEED

1. **In General:** [§1897]   A deed is not effective to transfer an interest in land until it has been delivered by the grantor. "Delivery" requires words or conduct of the grantor which show an *intent to make the deed operative* and to pass an *interest* immediately to the grantee. In other words, the conduct must show an intent to make the deed legally effective now. The usual method of delivery is handing over the deed from the grantor to the grantee, but handing over a deed without the concurrent intent is not an effective delivery. On the other hand, if the grantor intends to make delivery, manual transfer is not necessary. The crucial issue is intent—not what physically happens to the deed. Nonetheless, physical transfer of the deed is compelling evidence of intent.

   a. **Examples**

      (1) **No intent, but manual transfer:** [§1898]   O executes an instrument conveying Blackacre to A, and hands the instrument to A "for safekeeping." Even though it is handed to the named grantee, this is not a valid delivery. There is no evidence that O intended the instrument to have any present operative effect.

      (2) **Intent, but no transfer:** [§1899]   O executes an instrument conveying Whiteacre to B. O attempts to give the instrument to B personally, but is unable to find B. Nevertheless, O quits possession of Whiteacre, tells other people B owns the land, and thereafter treats B as the owner thereof. Most courts would hold that there has been a sufficient delivery. [McMahon v. Dorsey, 91 N.W.2d 893 (Mich. 1958)]

   b. **Presumptions:** [§1900]   Courts have laid down, and usually follow, presumptions with respect to whether delivery has occurred. Delivery is presumed: (i) if the deed is *handed* to the grantee, (ii) if the deed is *acknowledged* by the grantor before a notary, or (iii) if the deed is *recorded.* No delivery is presumed if the grantor retains possession of the deed. However, these are presumptions only, and can be rebutted by any type of extrinsic evidence—including the grantor's conduct or statements made after the alleged delivery.

      (1) **Deeds effective at death:** [§1901]   In a surprising number of cases, grantors—wishing to avoid probate and lawyers—execute a deed of land in favor of a beneficiary and put the deed away in a safe deposit box. The deed is intended as a substitute for a will. If the grantor intended the deed to be legally effective *before* death, it is a validly delivered deed (creating a springing executory interest or remainder in the grantee). On the other hand, if the grantor did not intend the deed to be effective *until* death, the deed is not delivered during life and is no good as a deed. If not executed with the formalities required of wills,

the document cannot be probated as a will either—and the grantee does not get the land. The cases involving this situation are hard to predict, but if it appears that the grantor never formed a definite crystallized intention to do a legally effective act and did not believe himself bound by the deed, there has been no delivery. [Shroyer v. Shroyer, 425 S.W.2d 214 (Mo. 1968); Erbach v. Brauer, 206 N.W. 62 (Wis. 1925)] On the other hand, if the grantor tells third persons "that he had deeded that land to Pat," and the evidence suggests that the grantor kept the deed merely for safekeeping, a delivery probably has been made. The grantee's case is helped if the deed is kept in the grantor's safe deposit box to which the **grantee** has access. [McMahon v. Dorsey, *supra*] In these cases, the courts are much affected by the equities of the case and often stretch to find a delivery when the grantee is deserving of the land. [Ferrell v. Stinson, 11 N.W.2d 701 (Iowa 1943)]

c. **Cancellation of delivery ineffective:** [§1902]   After there has been an effective delivery of a deed in fee simple, the title has passed to the grantee and a return of the deed to the grantor has no effect as a cancellation or reconveyance. The Statute of Frauds requires a **writing** to move title back to the grantor. *Example*: O hands deed to grantee A, intending to make delivery. O changes her mind, asks A for the deed back. A gives the deed back to O. A still owns the land.

2. **Conditional Delivery to Grantee**

a. **Written condition:** [§1903]   Where a deed contains a provision that it is to take effect only upon the happening of a condition precedent, it is possible to interpret it in one of two ways: (i) the provision may mean there is **no delivery** and the **deed is not effective at all until the condition happens;** or (ii) the provision may mean that grantor intends the deed **to be legally effective now, but passing only an interest that is subject to a condition precedent.** Under the first construction the deed is a nullity, because it has not been delivered. Under the second, the grantee receives a valid springing executory interest (compare a common law conveyance "to my daughter upon her marriage," which created a springing executory interest in the daughter, *supra,* §582). This is a very subtle distinction, which produces litigation. But most litigation involves deeds used as will substitutes.

(1) **Will substitutes:** [§1904]   A deed can be intended to operate as a substitute for a will. A will must be probated, with attendant costs of probate administration including lawyers' fees. A deed, *if effective,* avoids those costs. The will substitute cases usually involve one of three sets of facts: (i) where the deed is absolute on its face but the grantor retains possession of the deed, discussed *supra,* §1901; (ii) where a written condition in a deed handed to the grantee provides that the deed is not effective until the grantor's death or that the deed is revocable, (*see* below); or (iii) where the deed is handed to an escrow agent with oral instructions to deliver the deed to the grantee at the grantor's death (discussed *infra,* §1911).

(a) **Conditions relating to death of grantor:** [§1905]   Where the deed is handed to the grantee, and a written provision in the deed says the deed is on condition, the particular words of condition may be crucial in determining intent to deliver. If the deed says, "O conveys to A, reserving a life estate in O," there is no problem. The deed is delivered. If, however, the deed says, "this deed shall be effective only upon my death," the cases are split. Some hold that, although these words may be intended to be the equivalent of reserving a life estate, the word "effective" suggests the instrument is not to be effective at all until death. Under this reading, the instrument can be given effect only if executed as a will. [Butler v. Sherwood, 233 N.Y. 655 (1922)] Other cases hold the deed is validly delivered, creating a springing executory interest in the grantee. The word "effective" is construed to mean "effective to transfer possession"; it does not indicate an intent not to create a legal future interest. [Abbott v. Holway, *supra*, §582]

1) **Surviving grantor:** [§1906]   If the deed says, "O conveys to A if A survives O," this looks very much like a will, except a will can be revoked and this deed, if effective, cannot be. Most cases take the position that, inasmuch as the condition of survivorship is not within O's control, O intends to presently create a contingent executory interest (or contingent remainder) in A. The deed is thus held good. [Abbott v. Holway, *supra*; Thomas v. Williams, 117 N.W. 155 (Minn. 1908)]

(b) **Grantor retains power to revoke:** [§1907]   If the grantor retains the power to revoke the deed, the courts are split over whether the delivery is effective. Some courts hold the deed is void either on the theory that the grantor must surrender control in order to make an effective delivery or on the theory that the deed is a testamentary instrument and is void as a deed. Neither reason is persuasive (*see* below). Probably most modern courts will give effect to the deed as creating an interest in the grantee that can be revoked. [St. Louis County National Bank v. Fielder, 260 S.W.2d 483 (Mo. 1953)]

(c) **Criticism:** [§1908]   Much confusion results in the will substitute cases from the failure of courts to make a consistent policy analysis. The fact that the deed is a will substitute ought to be irrelevant. Many other will substitutes are legally permitted when a written instrument is signed by the grantor: life insurance, joint bank accounts, inter vivos revocable trusts, and designation of beneficiaries on government bonds, pension plans, and savings accounts. If these inter vivos instruments serving as will substitutes are permitted, there is no reason why a delivered deed should not be valid as a will substitute. The written provisions of a deed are as reliable as provisions of these other written instruments. The policies the courts should be concerned with are the two underlying the Statute of Frauds and the delivery requirement, applied to inter vivos transfers, which policies also underlie the Statute of Wills: (i) the law requires the transferor to do something (perform a *ritual*) that indicates the transferor intends to do a legally effective act, *i.e.*, intends to be bound (this is the *ritual policy*); and (ii) the law requires *evidence* of the transferor's intent that is reliable and free of room for fraudulent allegations after the grantor's death (this is the *evidentiary policy*). Where the grantor *signs* a deed *with written conditions*, and *hands it over* to the grantee, experience indicates that the grantor intends the deed to be legally effective (otherwise, why would he do this?). The signed written instrument is reliable evidence; dangerous parol evidence is not necessary to give it effect. Thus all deeds manually delivered with written conditions intended as will substitutes should be valid. Also, inasmuch as the death beneficiary named in other will substitutes can be revoked, there is no reason why a deed with the written power to revoke should be invalid. As with a life insurance beneficiary designation, the grantor intends to be bound unless he changes his mind and performs another ritual revoking the transfer. Nonetheless, so long as courts say the grantor must put the deed beyond his control for an effective delivery, no lawyer should use a deed as a will substitute. A revocable inter vivos trust, valid everywhere, is the preferred route, Thus, instead of executing a revocable deed in favor of A to be effective at O's death, O should execute a trust instrument providing, "O hereby declares he holds Blackacre in trust for O for life, and upon O's death, Blackacre is to go to A. O retains the right to revoke this trust at any time." This is a valid revocable trust. O can subsequently change his mind, revoke the trust, and get title to Blackacre back, if he desires.

b. **Oral condition:** [§1909] Although there is little reason in policy to refuse to give effect to written conditions in a deed, the policy of the Statute of Frauds is offended by oral conditions. Where the grantor hands over to the grantee a deed absolute on its face, with a contemporaneous oral understanding that the deed shall not take effect until some condition is performed, the general rule is that the delivery is valid, and the oral condition is void. Courts do not like oral conditions contradicting a written instrument because of the possibilities of fraud and fabrication of evidence and the resulting uncertainty of real estate titles. [State *ex rel.* Pai v. Thom, 563 P.2d 982 (Hawaii 1977); Takacs v. Takacs, 26 N.W.2d 712 (Mich. 1947)]

(1) **Example:** O delivers to A a deed absolute on its face. O and A have an oral understanding that the deed is to be effective only if A survives O. A now owns the land. The delivery is good; the oral condition is void. [Sweeney v. Sweeney, 11 A.2d 806 (Conn. 1940)]

(2) **Compare—escrows:** [§1910] A deed delivered to a third party (an escrow agent) upon an oral condition is valid (*infra*, §1911). In an exceptional case, where a great injustice would otherwise take place, a court might hold that delivery of the deed directly to the grantee on an oral condition makes the grantee an escrow agent. Under this theory, a fictional escrow is invented to give effect to the oral condition to prevent injustice. [Chillemi v. Chillemi, 78 A.2d 750 (Md. 1951)]

3. **Deed Given to Third Party Custodian (Escrow Agent):** [§1911] Although generally a deed delivered directly to a grantee cannot have oral conditions attached, a deed can be delivered in escrow with oral conditions attached. However, the rules regarding effective escrows may differ depending upon whether the escrow is *donative* or *commercial.*

a. **Donative escrow:** [§1912] A donative escrow is one where the grantor is giving the land to the grantee, but desires to postpone the grantee's right to possession until a later date, usually the grantor's death. Typically a donative escrow involves this situation: O executes a deed naming A as grantee; O hands the deed to X, a trusted friend, and says, "Deliver this deed to A at my death." When O hands the deed to X, O has made an effective delivery, X becomes the agent of O and A, and O cannot recall the deed. X must deliver the deed to A at O's death. [Stone v. Duvall, 77 Ill. 475 (1875); Smith v. Fay, 293 N.W. 497 (Iowa 1940)]

   (1) **Grantee's rights:** [§1913] At the time of the delivery in escrow, the grantee (A in above example) receives a future interest in the property—properly classified as a springing executory interest but sometimes classified as a remainder. (For more on the grantee's rights, *see* the discussion of the relation-back doctrine, *infra, §§1923 et seq.*)

   (2) **Writing not required:** [§1914] The instructions to the custodian X can be *oral* or *written.* The Statute of Frauds is to some extent violated by oral instructions, but courts have believed that the testimony of X, a disinterested party, is sufficiently reliable so as to justify not applying the Statute. Also, in donative transfers in escrow (unlike commercial escrows), the oral instructions are usually inferable from the deed, the surrounding circumstances, and experience—*i.e.,* the grantee ordinarily is a natural object of the grantor's bounty, the custodian a trusted friend, and experience indicates that the usual instruction is to deliver on the death of the grantor. Because of these considerations, the escrow agent's testimony is permitted to substitute for written instructions.

   (3) **Effect of grantor's reserving power to revoke:** [§1915] If, in the escrow instructions, the grantor retains the power to recall the deed, the escrow is invalid. No delivery occurs—regardless of whether the power of revocation is ever exercised. The courts reason that the grantor must give up control to have an effective delivery in escrow. If the grantor can recall the deed, the escrow agent is *solely the grantor's agent,* and no delivery takes place when the deed is put in escrow because it is not beyond the grantor's control. [Johnson v. Johnson, 54 A. 378 (R.I. 1903)]

      (a) **Compare—contingent right to recall:** [§1916] If the grantor retains a contingent right of recall ("return the deed to me if I survive the operation" or "or return the deed to me if the grantee predeceases me"), some cases, with unsound reasoning, hold the escrow fails because there was no intent presently to convey an unconditional interest. The reasoning is unsound inasmuch as the law permits contingent future interests to be created. [Atchison v. Atchison, 175 P.2d 309 (Okla. 1946)] Other cases, however, hold a conditional right of recall does not make the escrow invalid, because the condition is outside the control of the grantor.

      (b) **Criticism:** [§1917] A revocable escrow is invalid not for any reason of policy, but only because of unreasoning adherence to the ancient dogma that the grantor must surrender control to effect a delivery. The fact that a revocable donative escrow operates very much like a will is not objectionable in policy (*see supra,* §1908); if the ritual and evidentiary requirements of the Statute of Frauds and delivery are satisfied, the inter vivos transfer should not be called testamentary and subject to the Statute of Wills. Inasmuch as revocable trusts are permitted, there is no policy reason why revocable escrows should not be permitted. If the escrow custodian were called a "trustee," the revocable transfer would be permissible. The ban on revocable escrows discriminates against persons (usually poorer persons) who do not consult lawyers but try to arrange their affairs by themselves. Lawyers will advise a revocable trust.

b. **Commercial escrow:** [§1918] A commercial escrow is a common and useful arrangement in buying and selling land. Typically, the seller hands a deed naming the buyer as grantee to an escrow agent with instructions to hand the deed to the grantee when and if, before a fixed date, the grantee hands over a cashier's check for the purchase price. This arrangement protects both the buyer and the seller: Money and title change hands at the same time.

(1) **Fiduciary obligation:** [§1919] An escrow agent is a fiduciary and owes obligations to ***both*** the grantor and grantee. If the agent violates the instructions or acts without reasonable prudence, the agent is liable to the parties. The law holds fiduciaries to a high standard and interprets any clause relieving the fiduciary of liability very strictly against the fiduciary. [Miller v. Craig, 558 P.2d 984 (Ariz. 1976)]

(2) **Oral instructions:** [§1920] Where the escrow agent is given written instructions, the grantor is bound by the delivery to the agent. On the other hand, where the grantor deposits the deed in escrow under ***oral instructions,*** most courts hold that the grantor may countermand the instructions and recall the deed while still in the escrow agent's hands, ***unless there is a written contract of sale.*** [Campbell v. Thomas, 42 Wis. 437 (1877)]

(a) **Example:** O orally agrees to sell Blackacre to A. O executes a deed in A's favor and hands the deed to Bank with ***oral*** instructions to deliver the deed to A if A pays $10,000 within thirty days. Ten days later, O has a better offer for Blackacre from B. O tells Bank not to deliver the deed to A. A brings $10,000 to Bank one week later. A has no enforceable contract right (Statute of Frauds), and A is not entitled to the deed. O still owns Blackacre.

(b) **Rationale:** O can revoke because the oral escrow instructions violate the Statute of Frauds. The purchase price is an indispensable part of a contract of sale. From the mere deposit of a deed into escrow, one cannot infer what is the purchase price. Since there is no underlying written contract of sale on which to sue, A has no rights against O.

1) **Compare—donative escrows:** [§1921] In donative escrows, the oral instructions can reasonably be inferred from the facts (delivery upon

death is almost always the instruction), so relying on the escrow agent's testimony is not dangerous. In commercial escrows, the price cannot be inferred from experience, and it is dangerous to let it depend upon the agent's testimony.

(c) **Minority contra:** [§1922] A minority of courts considers an underlying written contract not necessary, and will enforce an oral commercial escrow without one. The textwriters also favor this minority view. *Rationale:* The deed is not a contract of sale but a conveyance; delivery is merely a question of grantor's intent, which can be proved by parol evidence.

c. **Relation-back doctrine:** [§1923] In escrow cases, courts often talk about the "first delivery" and the "second delivery." Suppose O executes a deed to A and puts it in escrow with X. The first delivery is when O hands the deed to X; the second delivery is when X hands the deed to A. When a valid delivery in escrow (either donative or commercial) has occurred, it is clear that neither the grantor nor the grantee has full title until the second delivery. Nonetheless, under some rules, legal rights depend upon who has "title." In order to do justice, courts have invented the relation-back doctrine: Although title does not pass to the grantee until the second delivery, upon that delivery title will "relate back" to the first delivery so that the law assumes that it *passed at the first delivery.* The relation-back doctrine is a fiction applied only "where equity and justice require."

(1) **Application:** [§1924] Assume a valid delivery by O to X of a deed to Blackacre, naming A as grantee, to deliver to A upon the occurrence of some condition. The relation-back doctrine applies in the following cases:

(a) **Death of grantor:** [§1925] Assume O dies after first delivery. Only a will can pass title at death. To avoid this rule, the relation-back doctrine says title passed during O's life at first delivery. O's heirs take subject to the grantee's rights. [First National Bank & Trust Co. v. Scott, 156 A. 836 (N.J. 1931)]

(b) **Incompetency of grantor:** [§1926] Assume O becomes incompetent after first delivery and cannot convey title. Under relation-back doctrine, title passed at first delivery, when O was competent.

(c) **Creditor of grantor attaches:** [§1927] Assume a creditor of O attaches Blackacre after first delivery. Relation-back doctrine says O did not own Blackacre at time of attachment, so A prevails over the creditor. *Rationale*: O's creditor should have no greater right than O with respect to the property.

(2) **Not applicable as against subsequent bona fide purchaser:** [§1928] The relation-back doctrine does *not* apply where the grantor subsequently executes and delivers a deed or mortgage to a bona fide purchaser or mortgagee. If the subsequent purchaser has no knowlege of the deed in escrow, the subsequent pur-

chaser prevails. The person who claims to be a subsequent bona fide purchaser has the burden of showing that he had no notice of the prior escrow and that he gave valuable consideration. [Hood v. Webster, 271 N.Y. 57 (1936)]

4. **Estoppel of Grantor:** [§1929]   Although delivery of a deed is required to make it effective, in some cases, the grantor may be estopped to deny delivery even though no delivery was intended. These cases involve the grantor's entrusting the deed to another and the other breaching the trust so that a bona fide purchaser—a person without notice of the fact of nondelivery—acquires the land.

    a. **Delivery to grantee:** [§1930]   When the grantor gives possession of a deed voluntarily to the grantee (*e.g.*, to examine it), and the grantee violates the grantor's confidence and conveys the land to a bona fide purchaser, the grantor may be estopped to deny delivery. The grantor may be deemed negligent in so entrusting the deed. A rule applied in many situations where there are two honest persons and one dishonest one is: As between two innocent persons (grantor and bona fide purchaser), the one who could have prevented the loss to the other should bear it. Since the grantor could have prevented the loss to the subsequent purchaser by not entrusting the grantee with a deed, the grantor must bear the loss.

    b. **Delivery in escrow:** [§1931]   Suppose that the grantor puts a deed into escrow and the grantee wrongfully obtains possession of the deed from the escrow agent. Then the grantee sells the land to a bona fide purchaser who has no knowledge of the fraud. Is the grantor estopped from proving no delivery? The cases are split.

        (1) **Grantor not estopped:** [§1932]   About half the cases hold that the grantor is not estopped, and hence the grantor prevails against the bona fide purchaser. *Rationale:* The grantor has acted reasonably in putting a deed into escrow, and the difficulties in resolving the true bona fides of the purchaser may be considerable. [Clevenger v. Moore, 259 P. 219 (Okla. 1927)]

            (a) **Grantor's knowledge:** [§1933]   Under this view, however, if the grantee wrongfully obtains possession of the deed and records it, **and the grantor has knowledge of these facts,** the grantor will be estopped against a bona fide purchaser unless the grantor acts to expunge the deed from record within a reasonable time.

                1) **Example:** O delivers a deed to X naming A as grantee. O instructs X to deliver the deed upon payment of $10,000. X delivers the deed to A without receiving the $10,000. A records. O is informed of these facts and does nothing. One year later, A conveys to B, a bona fide purchaser who has no notice of O's claim. O is estopped to prove nondelivery, and B prevails. [Mays v. Shields, 45 S.E. 68 (Ga. 1903)]

        (2) **Grantor is estopped:** [§1934]   About half the cases hold that the grantor is estopped against a bona fide purchaser. *Rationale:* Where the custodian is chosen by the grantor, he is the grantor's agent, and the grantor is bound by the

acts of his agent. Also, inasmuch as the grantor could have prevented the loss to the bona fide purchaser by selecting a more trustworthy agent, the grantor should suffer the loss. [Micklethwait v. Fulton, 196 N.E. 166 (Ohio 1935)]

E. SELLER'S WARRANTIES

1. **Covenants of Title:** [§1935]   Normally, the extent of the seller's liabilities for some defect in title is governed by the covenants of title contained in the deed. If the deed contains no covenants of title, the seller is not liable if title fails. No covenants of title are implied in the deed.

    a. **Types of deeds:** [§1936]   Various types of deeds are used in the several states to convey interests in property. Some warrant title, some do not. Although some jurisdictions have peculiar local terminology, under standard classification deeds can be divided into three types, depending upon the warranties included. These types are: general warranty deeds, special warranty deeds, and quitclaim deeds.

        (1) **General warranty deed:** [§1937]   A general warranty deed normally contains all six of the "usual" covenants (listed below). It warrants title against defects arising *before* as well as *during* the time the grantor had title.

        (2) **Special warranty deed:** [§1938]   A special warranty deed also normally contains all six of the usual covenants listed below; however, the warranties cover only defects arising *during the grantor's* tenure, and not defects arising prior to that time. Hence, the grantor guarantees only that *he* has done nothing to make title defective.

            (a) **Example:** O, owner of Blackacre, gives A a mortgage on Blackacre. O then forges a release of the mortgage, which is recorded. O then conveys to B by quitclaim deed. B then conveys to C by a special warranty deed. A still holds a valid mortgage on the property. B is not liable to C for the mortgage since B did nothing to make title defective. If B had given C a general warranty deed, B would be liable.

        (3) **Quitclaim deed:** [§1939]   A quitclaim deed warrants nothing. The grantor merely transfers whatever right, title, or interest he has, if any. A quitclaim deed is useful in clearing an apparent defect in title, where the grantor is not pursuing the claim.

        (4) **Statutory warranty deeds:** [§1940]   Statutes in a number of states provide for shortened forms of deeds, and in many cases, specific words of conveyance are deemed to include certain enumerated covenants. For example, the words "grant," "bargain," "convey," or "sell" often, by statute, presumptively connote general warranties of title.

    b. **Covenants for title in warranty deeds:** [§1941]   A warranty deed usually contains all six of the following covenants, but it may contain less than six.

(1) **Covenant of seisin:** [§1942]   The grantor covenants that he owns the estate or interest that he purports to convey.

(2) **Covenant of right to convey:** [§1943]   The grantor covenants that he has the power to make the conveyance. This covenant is satisfied if the grantor has title and is under no disability, or if he is acting as trustee or agent for the owner.

(3) **Covenant against encumbrances:** [§1944]   The grantor covenants that there are no easements, covenants, mortgages, liens, or other encumbrances on the property.

(4) **Covenant of quiet enjoyment:** [§1945]   The grantor covenants that the grantee will not be disturbed in possession or enjoyment of the property by a third party's lawful assertion of superior title.

(5) **Covenant of warranty:** [§1946]   The grantor covenants that he will defend on behalf of the grantee any lawful claims existing at the date of conveyance, and will compensate the grantee for any loss sustained by the assertion of superior title. For all practical purposes, this covenant and the covenant of quiet enjoyment amount to the same thing.

(6) **Covenant of further assurances:** [§1947]   The grantor covenants to perform whatever acts are reasonably necessary to perfect the purchaser's title, if it turns out to be imperfect. This covenant is not much used in the United States, and is often omitted from deeds. It is called a "usual covenant," but in fact it is rather unusual.

c. **Merger of contract into deed:** [§1948]   When the seller and buyer sign a contract for the sale of land, the contract may call for a marketable title or the seller may make various promises with respect to title (*see supra*, §1785). Once the buyer accepts the deed, the usual rule is that the buyer can sue only on the covenants in the deed. Acceptance of the deed discharges the seller from his obligations under the contract. The contract is said to "merge" into the deed. *Rationale*: When the buyer accepts the deed, it is assumed the buyer accepts the deed as containing terms of compliance with the sales contract. The buyer cannot thereafter sue on the contract (though the buyer can sue on an express collateral undertaking not contained in the contract, such as a promise by the seller that "I will have that door fixed"). The merger rule is designed to carry out the assumed intention of the parties. [Reed v. Hassell, 340 A.2d 157 (Del. 1975)]

d. **Breach of covenants**

(1) **Covenants of seisin, of right to convey, and against encumbrances:** [§1949] These covenants are called ***present covenants***. This means that they are breached ***when made***, if at all. At the time a covenant of seisin is made, for example, either the grantor has or does not have title. If he has title, the covenant is not, and can never be, breached. If he does not have title, the covenant

is breached when made. Similarly, at the time a covenant against encumbrances is made, either an encumbrance exists (in which case the convenant is broken), or it does not exist (in which case the covenant can never be broken).

(a) **What constitutes breach:** [§1950]   The covenant of seisin is breached if the grantor does not own the interest he purports to convey. The covenant against encumbrances is breached if there is an encumbrance on the property at the time the covenant is made. No eviction or disturbance of the grantee's possession is required to establish a breach.

   1) **Grantee's knowledge of defect:** [§1951]   The usual rule is that covenants of seisin and against encumbrances are breached even though the grantee knew of the defect in title or of the encumbrance. Knowledge of the defect may be the very reason for insisting on a covenant against it. If the grantor does not expressly exclude a defect from the covenants, the grantor is liable for the defect, whether it is known or unknown.

      a) **Minority views:** [§1952]   A minority of jurisdictions holds a covenant against encumbrances is not breached if the buyer had actual or constructive knowledge of an *open and visible* encumbrance, such as a railroad easement. The theory is that the parties must have contemplated the continued existence of the encumbrance when they struck their bargain. This theory is not applied to an "invisible" encumbrance such as a mortgage or lien, and it is sometimes limited to public highways and public utility easements. [Leach v. Gunnarson, 619 P.2d 263 (Or. 1980)]

(b) **When breach occurs:** [§1953]   If there is a breach it occurs *at the time of the conveyance.* The grantee has an immediate cause of action, and the statute of limitations begins to run immediately. *Note:* The statute of limitations (usually four to six years) begins to run when the present covenant is made. Thus, present covenants offer protection to the grantee only for a limited period of time and cannot be sued upon many years later.

(c) **Whether the covenant "runs":** [§1954]   If a covenant for title can be enforced against the covenantor by a transferee of the covenantee, it is said to "run with the land." The majority rule is that *present* covenants do *not* run with the land and *cannot* be enforced by remote grantees. At the time of breach, the covenant becomes a chose in action (*i.e.,* a personal right to sue for breach) in the grantee and ceases to be a covenant. Hence, there is no covenant to attach to and run with the land conveyed to the second grantee, and—most important—the *chose in action is not impliedly assigned.*

   1) **Example:** A purports to convey Blackacre to B by a deed containing a covenant of seisin. In fact, O owns Blackacre. Therefore, the covenant of seisin is breached, and B has a chose in action (a right to sue A). B

subsequently purports to convey Blackacre to C. The chose in action is not assigned to C, and C cannot sue A. *Criticism:* The rule developed at a time when choses in action were not assignable, a rule now repudiated. Today there is no reason why the chose in action should not be impliedly assigned from B to C. It is C, after all, who will be in possession when O shows up and who needs the protection of the warranty.

2) **Minority rule:** [§1955] In some states, the chose in action is impliedly assigned by the original grantee to a subsequent grantee; thus, in the preceding example, C could sue A. [Schofield v. Iowa Homestead Co., 32 Iowa 317 (1871); Rockafellor v. Gray, 191 N.W. 107 (Iowa 1922)]

(2) **Covenants of quiet enjoyment, warranty, and further assurances:** [§1956] These covenants are *future covenants.* This means the covenant is not breached until the grantee is actually or constructively *evicted* sometime in the future.

(a) **What constitutes breach:** [§1957] A covenant of quiet enjoyment or warranty is breached only when the covenantee is evicted or disturbed in possession. The mere existence of a superior title does not constitute a breach of the covenant, and the grantee has no cause of action if she is not disturbed in some way. [Brown v. Lober, 389 N.E.2d 1188 (Ill. 1979)]

1) **Constructive eviction:** [§1958] Actual eviction is not necessary for a breach of a future covenant. Constructive eviction will suffice. *Example:* The grantee is constructively evicted if she must buy the superior title to prevent eviction or is enjoined from using the property in violation of a restrictive covenant on the property. If the grantee's right to possession is interfered with by a paramount owner of some interest in the property, the grantee is constructively evicted.

2) **Grantee's knowledge of superior title:** [§1959] Knowledge by the grantee of a potentially superior title does not bar her claim for breach of covenant upon eviction. As with a covenant against encumbrances (*see supra,* §1951), the covenants of quiet enjoyment and warranty may have the very purpose of protecting the grantee from the potentially superior claim. [Foley v. Smith, 539 P.2d 874 (Wash. 1975)]

3) **Defending lawsuits:** [§1960] A covenantor has the duty of defending against *lawful* superior claims, but he has no duty to defend title against a wrongful claim by a third party. Refusal to defend against unlawful claims does not breach the covenant. The burden is thus put upon the grantee to defend all claims; she can recover against the covenantor only if she loses. If she wins, she may be out a large sum of money in legal fees, but she cannot recover these from the covenantor. If the grantee loses, she can recover from the covenantor damages plus legal fees. The covenantor is not bound by the result of the lawsuit, however, unless the covenantee gives the covenantor notice of a lawsuit brought by an adverse claimant and requests the covenantor to

defend it. Thus, in any litigation by a third party claiming paramount title, a covenantee should notify the covenantor and give him a chance to defend. If the covenantee does so, the covenantor will be bound by the result.

(b) **When breach occurs:** [§1961]   A future covenant is not breached, and the statute of limitations does not begin to run, until the covenantee is disturbed in possession. This may be many years after the covenant is made. After the statute of limitations has run on present covenants (which are breached, if at all, when made), the grantee of a general warranty deed is protected only by the future covenants. If the grantee then discovers some defect in title, the grantee must wait until eviction to sue. (In the meantime, the covenantor may die, and the covenantee may not be able to sue anyone upon later eviction.)

(c) **Whether covenant runs:** [§1962]   A future covenant runs with the land if there is *privity of estate* between the original grantor-covenantor and the remote grantee. In this context, "privity of estate" means that the covenantor conveyed either *title or possession* to his grantee, who conveyed it to the remote grantee. The covenant attaches to the fee simple estate or the possessory estate and runs with it to subsequent grantees.

   1) **No estate transferred:** [§1963]   If the grantor did not convey either title or possession, there is no "estate" (neither "fee simple estate" nor "possessory estate") to which the covenant can attach. In that case, in theory the covenant will not run. There must be an "estate" with which the covenant runs—or so goes the ancient metaphor.

      a) **Example:** Blackacre is unoccupied forest land owned by O. In 1980, A executes and delivers a deed of Blackacre to B with a covenant of warranty. In 1982, B quitclaims her interest in Blackacre to C. In 1985, C attempts to enter Blackacre but is prevented from doing so by O. C can recover from A only if there is privity of estate between them. However, since A had neither title nor possession, there is no privity and C cannot recover from A.

   2) **Criticism:** [§1964]   The requirement of having an "estate" for the covenant to run with is purely metaphorical and makes no sense. Inasmuch as C can sue A if Blackacre is a house occupied successively by B and C, no reason appears why C cannot sue A if Blackacre is unpossessed land. Endowed with great powers of imagination in finding an "estate," some modern courts have found that A does indeed transfer an "interest" to B. The interest may be B's right, under the doctrine of estoppel by deed (*see infra,* §1974), to receive any title to Blackacre that A might subsequently acquire. Or the "interest" transferred by A may be the "constructive possession" of the land which arises when the grantor has apparent record title. Thus does legal fiction come to the rescue of a metaphor taken too literally. [Solberg v. Robinson, 147 N.W. 87 (S.D. 1914)]

(3) **Damages for breach:** [§1965]   The basic remedy for breach of contract is an award of damages, and the basic principle used in ascertaining those damages is that the injured party should be put into as good a position as she would have been had the contract been performed. In other words, the injured party is entitled to the benefit of the bargain. This principle has never been applied consistently to damages for breach of covenants of title. Courts have developed different rules, largely because of the expectations of the parties, notions of fairness, and the perceived difficulty of establishing the market value of land.

(a) **Basic limitation:** [§1966]   Except in a few New England states, the grantee cannot recover more than the covenantor received as consideration. The amount received by the covenantor (in most cases the purchase price) sets the maximum liability of the covenantor. When land increases sharply in value, or the grantee improves it, the loss to the grantee upon eviction several years after purchase may be far greater than the amount of the purchase price. Under this maximum liability rule, the grantee is certainly not in as good a position as she would be if the covenant had not been breached. Nonetheless, courts, believing that it would be unfair or not in accordance with the covenantor's expectations, refuse to require the covenantor to reimburse the grantee for her improvements or capital appreciation lost. If the covenantor had to pay the value of the land at the time of recovery (giving the grantee the benefit of the bargain), the resulting liability might be huge and wipe out a covenantor who received a small amount for the land. [Davis v. Smith, 5 Ga. 274 (1848)]

1) **Gifts and exchanges:** [§1967]   If the land is a gift by the covenantor to the grantee, some courts allow no recovery for breach. Others allow the grantee to recover the market value of the land at the time the covenant is made. In case of exchange of land, the maximum liability is the market value of the land given up by the grantee. [Maxwell v. Redd, 496 P.2d 1320 (Kan. 1972)]

2) **Interest:** [§1968]   Interest on the purchase price may be awarded to the grantee, but there is a conflict as to whether interest should be given from the date the covenant is made or only from time of eviction. Where the grantee has been in possession, some courts deny interest on the theory that possession of the land is the equivalent of interest on the purchase price. It unjustly enriches the grantee to give her both possession and interest. Other courts give the grantee interest on the theory that the grantee in possession is liable to the paramount owner for the fair rental value of the land, and interest is an approximate compensation for that liability. Of course, the paramount owner may not sue within the period of the statute of limitations, and under this solution, the grantee may end up with interest and no liability to the paramount owner. [Hilliker v. Rueger, 228 N.Y. 11 (1920)] A third view, not apparently taken by any court, is to require the covenantor to pay interest into court, which will pay it to the grantee *if* the grantee is

called upon to pay fair rental value to the paramount owner within the period of limitations and, if not, will return the interest to the covenantor.

(b) **Present covenants**

1) **Covenant of seisin:** [§1969]   If title to the entire tract fails, the grantee is entitled to recover the full purchase price. If the grantee recovers, the grantee must reconvey her possessory interest to the covenantor. The grantee may decide not to sue on the covenant of seisin and to stay in possession until evicted, when she can sue on the covenant of general warranty. If the grantee stays in possession long enough, she may acquire title by adverse possession.

   a) **Partial breach:** [§1970]   If title to only part of the land fails, the grantee is entitled to recover as damages a proportionate part of the purchase price commensurate with the value of the land to which title fails. [Knudson v. Weeks, 394 F. Supp. 963 (D. Okla. 1975)] Or, if the portion to which the grantee received title is not a usable parcel of land, the grantee can rescind and recover the entire purchase price. The grantee must give up possession of the portion to which title failed in order to recover more than nominal damages. [*But see* Hilliker v. Rueger, *supra*—grantee can recover damages and remain in possession (which seems unfair to the covenantor, for possession is a valuable right that can ripen into title)]

2) **Covenant against encumbrances:** [§1971]   Where a covenant against encumbrances is breached by the existence of a restrictive covenant or easement or other encumbrance not removable by the grantee, damages are the difference in value, at the date of sale, of the land with the encumbrance and the value of the land without it (subject to the maximum liability stated above). If, however, the grantee has the right to remove the encumbrance for a specific amount, such as paying off a mortgage, the measure of damages is the amount spent to remove the encumbrance. If the grantee does not remove a removable encumbrance, the grantee is entitled only to nominal damages unless she can prove actual damage by selling the property for less than market value. This rule is designed to induce the grantee to pay off the mortgage and establish damages clearly, thus avoiding speculative damages. [McGuckin v. Milbank, 152 N.Y. 297 (1897)]

(b) **Future covenants:** [§1972]   For breach of a future covenant, which usually takes place some years after the covenant is made, the grantee is entitled to recover the consideration paid, or the amount spent in buying up a paramount claim, if reasonable. The grantee is not entitled to the value of the land at the time of eviction. Of course, the amount of the purchase price is the maximum liability of the covenantor.

1) **Suit by remote grantee:** [§1973] When a remote grantee sues the covenantor, the courts have split on the measure of damages. The question arises whether the remote grantee should recover the amount received by the covenantor or, if he pays less, the amount paid by the remote grantee. One view is to give the remote grantee his actual damages (what he paid), but not exceeding the amount received by the covenantor. [Taylor v. Wallace, 37 P. 963 (Colo. 1894)] Another view takes the position that, because the basic measure of damages deprives the remote grantee of the value of the land at the time of eviction, the remote grantee should recover the amount received by the covenantor even though the consideration paid by the remote grantee was less. The covenantor is stripped of his profit, which goes to compensate in a rough way the grantee, who is unfairly treated by the basic rule set forth *supra* at §1966.

a) **Example:** Blackacre is owned by O. A conveys Blackacre to B by general warranty deed for $10,000. Subsequently, B conveys Blackacre to C by general warranty deed for $5,000. O ousts C. C can sue B for $5,000, or C can sue A. Under the first view set forth above, C can recover only $5,000 from A. Under the second view, C can recover $10,000 from A.

e. **Estoppel by deed:** [§1974] Where a grantor purports to convey an estate in property that he does not then own, if the grantor subsequently acquires title, the title passes by operation of law to the grantee under the earlier deed. By executing a deed without title, the grantor is deemed impliedly to have covenanted that, when he obtains title, he will immediately convey it to the grantee. The doctrine of estoppel gives the grantee the thing bargained for, the land itself—and not merely damages.

(1) **Example:** A, having no title (or a defective title), purports to convey a good title to B. Subsequently, A receives a good title from O. Under the doctrine of estoppel by deed, A is estopped to assert that he had no title at the time of his deed to B and therefore B did not take any title. Rather, A's after-acquired title inures to the benefit of B, and B owns the property. [Robben v. Obering, 279 F.2d 381 (7th Cir. 1960); Aure v. Mackoff, 93 N.W.2d 807 (N.D. 1958)]

(2) **Application:** [§1975] Originally, the doctrine of estoppel developed as an outgrowth of the covenants for title in a warranty deed. If A executed a warranty deed without title, A would be liable to B on the covenants for warranty. But if A later obtained title, it would avoid unnecessary litigation, and give B what B bargained for, to hold that A's title inured to B, rather than to force B to sue A for specific performance. Although originally applied to warranty deeds only, the doctrine has been applied in modern cases to quitclaim deeds that expressly purport to convey a fee simple. It is a doctrine to carry out probable intent, and if the parties thought the grantor was conveying title, the doctrine will be applied to carry any after-acquired title to the grantee.

(3) **Subsequent purchasers from grantor:** [§1976]   Whether estoppel by deed applies, so that the grantee prevails over subsequent purchasers from the grantor, is discussed in connection with the recording system, *infra*, §§2048-2050.

2.   Liabilities for Defects in Houses

a.   **Builder's liability:** [§1977]   At common law, the builder of houses had no liability to the buyer, absent an express warranty. Caveat emptor was the rule. In the last thirty years, influenced by the development of implied warranties in sales of personal property and in leases, the law has changed. In almost all jurisdictions, courts now imply a warranty of habitability in the sale of new homes. The builder impliedly warrants that the building is free from defective materials and is constructed in a sound and workmanlike manner. *Rationale:* The builder's greater ability to prevent defects, the home buyer's reliance on the builder's skill, the unequal bargaining power of the parties, and the importance to society of soundly constructed housing justify imposing liability for defects upon the builder. [Wawak v. Stewart, 449 S.W.2d 922 (Ark. 1970); Petersen v. Hubschman Construction Co., 389 N.E.2d 1154 (Ill. 1979); McDonald v. Mianecki, 398 A.2d 1283 (N.J. 1978); Yepson v. Burgess, 525 P.2d 1019 (Or. 1974); Humber v. Morton, 426 S.W.2d 554 (Tex. 1968)] Important issues respecting the warranty remain to be worked out; the more important are mentioned below.

(1) **Tort or contract?** [§1978]   The implied warranty of habitability is a hybrid, resting on both tort and contract theory with confusing and inconsistent results. If tort theory is applied: the warranty is a duty imposed by public policy; it runs to all persons who buy the product; liability cannot be waived or disclaimed by a provision in the sales contract or conveyance; and the statute of limitations runs from the time of the discovery of the defect. On the other hand, if contract theory is applied: the implied warranty arises from the bargain; it runs only to those in privity of contract with the builder; it can be disclaimed by a provision in the conveyance; and the statute of limitations begins to run from the date of the conveyance. The courts have not consistently applied either theory; the implied warranty has developed more or less on an ad hoc basis.

(2) **Subsequent purchasers:** [§1979]   Subsequent purchasers of a house may have difficulty in recovering from the builder on a contract theory because of lack of privity of contract. On a tort theory, they may have difficulty recovering because both negligence liability and strict liability in tort are usually limited to physical injury and not mere economic loss. Nonetheless, because the builder is placing a defective house in the stream of commerce, and owes a duty of care to those who subsequently buy it, about half the courts that have considered the question have held that the builder has liability to subsequent purchasers regardless of any lack of privity. [Blagg v. Fred Hunt Co., 612 S.W.2d 321 (Ark. 1981); Gupta v. Ritter Homes, Inc., 646 S.W.2d 168 (Tex. 1983)]

(3) **Disclaimer:** [§1980]   In a few cases, courts have permitted the implied warranty of liability to be disclaimed or waived by the buyer. [G-W-L, Inc. v.

Robichaux, 643 S.W.2d 392 (Tex. 1982)] But it probably can be expected that courts will require a knowing disclaimer. The effect of the first buyer's disclaimer upon the rights of a subsequent purchaser who does not know of the disclaimer is not settled.

(4) **Commercial buildings:** [§1981]   The cases so far have implied a warranty of habitability *only* in the sale of housing, but in the future the warranty may be extended to sale of commercial buildings, just as the implied warranty has been extended from leases of rental housing to leases of commercial buildings.

b. **Lender's liability:** [§1982]   Buyers of defective housing have, in recent years, attempted to hold liable the mortgage lender who negligently supervised the construction of a house. If the lender exercises substantial control over the builder, and its activities become entangled with the builder's, the lender has been held liable. [Connor v. Great Western Savings & Loan Association, 69 Cal. 2d 850 (1968)] However, where the lender's activities do not exceed those necessary to protect its security, courts have not held the lender liable to the purchaser. If the lender reserves the right to approve plans and specifications and make periodic inspections of the construction, this is for the protection of the lender's security and creates no duty to subsequent purchasers.

c. **Seller's liability:** [§1983]   The seller of a used house who is not a builder has no liability based upon an implied warranty of habitability. Nonetheless, the seller is liable for misrepresentation and fraud. If the seller knowingly makes any false statement to the buyer as to some fact which materially affects the value of the premises to the buyer, and the buyer relies upon such statement in purchasing, the buyer is entitled to relief. Similarly, the seller is liable for defective conditions that the seller has concealed. The traditional view is that the seller is not liable for failure to disclose defective conditions, but this view is changing in many states. Modern cases hold the seller must disclose known defects that are not readily discoverable by the buyer, such as termites or roof leaks. A recent California case even holds that, if the seller of a house fails to tell a buyer that a murder occurred in the house ten years prior to sale, the buyer can rescind and recover damages. [Reed v. King, 145 Cal. App. 3d 261 (1983)] The law in this area is moving in the direction of requiring the seller to divulge all known information that has a significant and measurable impact on market value.

XIII. METHODS OF TITLE ASSURANCE

chapter approach

Four methods of title assurance are used in the United States:

1. _Grantor's express warranties of title contained in deed_—this is the oldest method, inherited from the English (and discussed _supra_, §§1935 _et seq._).

2. _System of recording land titles_—this involves an actual search of public records in the county recorder's office. Each state has some kind of recording system.

3. _Title registration_ (sometimes called _Torrens system_)—this is available in only a few states and registers title to land, rather than evidence of title (as with recording statutes).

4. _Title insurance_—this method is increasing in use and insures good title, _i.e._, insures the accuracy of the records by agreeing to defend the record title if litigated.

Title assurance questions often are found in fact situations where the landowner conveys the property to one person and later conveys it again to another. To determine the rights of the parties in this situation (or in any other title assurance question), consider:

1. The _language_ of the recording act (race, notice, race-notice) or registration statute.

2. Whether any party has BFP status (is a _purchaser or mortgagee_ who had _no_ actual, record, or inquiry _notice_ at the time he gave _consideration_).

3. The effect of any _unrecorded or unregistered_ instruments, any _errors_ in recording or registration, and who bears the _costs_ of those errors (grantor, grantee, title insurer).

A. RECORDING SYSTEM

1. **Common Law Rule—Prior in Time: [§1984]** All states today have recording acts providing for recordation of documents affecting land title. These acts are designed to protect bona fide purchasers of land from secret unrecorded claims. Prior to these acts, the common law rule gave legal effect to conveyances in accordance with the time of execution. Thus, a grantee who was _prior in time_ prevailed over one subsequent in time. For example, if O conveyed Blackacre to A, and later O conveyed Blackacre to B (who knew nothing of A's deed), A prevailed over B on the theory that O had conveyed title to A and had nothing left to convey to B. Under this rule, the purchase of land was risky, because B had no reliable way to assure that there was no prior deed. The recording acts now give B a way of discovering A's prior deed.

   a. **Exception in equity: [§1985]** Equity, noting that the legal rule tended to encourage fraud, developed one important exception to the "prior in time" rule. If the prior interest was *equitable*, and therefore within the jurisdiction of the equity court, equity would not enforce it against a subsequent purchaser of a *legal* interest who did not know of the prior equitable interest and paid valuable consideration. Thus, suppose that O contracts to sell Blackacre to A; under the doctrine of equitable conversion, the contract gives A equitable title (*see supra*, §1811). Later O conveys legal title to Blackacre to B, and B is a purchaser for value who has no notice of A's equitable interest. The subsequent conveyance to B cuts off the prior equity in A. This was called the equitable doctrine of bona fide purchaser.

2. **Recording Acts—In General:** [§1986]   In many cases, allowing the first grantee to prevail encouraged fraudulent acts by a grantor and imposed losses on innocent subsequent grantees. Consequently, as early as the Massachusetts Bay Colony in the seventeenth century, statutes were enacted in this country to require some sort of recordation to give "notice to the world" that title to property had been conveyed, and thus to put subsequent purchasers on guard. Such statutes are known as recording acts and are in effect in some form in every state. In general, such statutes set up a system that permits the recordation in each county of any deed (or other instrument affecting title) to property located in that county. Recordation is not essential to the validity of a deed, as between the grantor and the grantee. However, if a grantee does not record the instrument, he may lose out against other purchasers from his grantor.

3. **Mechanics of Recording:** [§1987]   The following is a brief description of how the recording system works. Although a deed is used as an illustration, other instruments affecting title to land, such as mortgages, can also be recorded.

   a. **Filing copy:** [§1988]   The grantee or grantee's agent presents the deed to the county recorder, who stamps the date and time of filing thereon and makes a copy (usually a photocopy or microfilm). The recorder files this copy in an official "deed book," which contains copies of prior recorded deeds. After the official copy is made, the original deed is returned to the grantee.

   b. **Indexing:** [§1989]   The recorder *indexes* the deed by entering a notation in the "index book" showing in which deed book the deed can be found reproduced in full. Just as the card or on-line catalog is the key to finding books in a library, the index is used to find the deed in subsequent title searches. The usual index system includes an index for grantors and an index for grantees; tract indexes exist in a few localities.

      (1) **Grantor and grantee indexes:** [§1990]   Separate index volumes are maintained for grantors and grantees, enabling a title searcher to locate an instrument by searching under either the grantor's name or the grantee's name. In the grantor index, entries are made chronologically, as instruments are filed, under the name of the grantors, listed alphabetically. The entry will include first the grantor's name, then the name of the grantee, then a description of the property and the type of instrument, and finally a reference to the volume and page of the deed books where the recorder's copy of the instrument can be found. The grantee index will contain the identical information, except that it will be entered alphabetically under the name of the grantee.

(2) **Tract index:** [§1991] In urban areas where land has been platted and broken down into blocks and lots, the recording office may keep a tract index. Entries are made under block and lot number. All instruments are indexed on a page that deals only with the lot to which the instruments relate. This greatly simplifies title search, for all the entries dealing with a specific parcel of land are kept together, rather than being found under the names of the many grantors and grantees who have previously owned the property.

c. **Title search:** [§1992] In order to understand the legal problems arising under the recording system, it is helpful to know how a title search is made. Suppose that O contracts to sell Blackacre to A. Prior to closing, a title search is made to assure A that O owns Blackacre and to determine if there are any encumbrances on O's title. How is this title search done?

(1) **Tract index search:** [§1993] If there is a tract index, the job is easy. The searcher looks at the page, indexed by block and lot, describing Blackacre, and at a glance can see prior recorded instruments conveying, mortgaging, or otherwise dealing with Blackacre.

(2) **Grantor-grantee index search:** [§1994] Where there are grantor and grantee indexes only, title search is much more complicated. The title searcher first uses the grantee index to discover from whom each previous owner took title. Then the title searcher uses the grantor index to ascertain what transfers each owner made during his tenure on the land.

(a) **Grantee index:** [§1995] The searcher, S, goes first to the grantee index, and looks under O's name—starting at the present date and going backward—to find out who was O's grantor. (O's grantor was N.) When S finds the deed from N to O indexed under O's name in the grantee index, S then does not look any further under O's name but instead looks backward under N's name in the grantee index until S finds the deed by which N acquired title, which names the grantor. S repeats this process until a "***chain of title***" of previous owners for a period of years acceptable in the jurisdiction (usually sixty years or some other time well in excess of the period of the statute of limitations) has been established.

(b) **Grantor index:** [§1996] Now, having discovered the previous owners of Blackacre, S turns to the grantor index to determine whether any of these previous owners conveyed any interest in Blackacre before conveying the fee simple to the next owner. In the grantor index, S looks under each of the owner's names from the day title came into the owner until the day of recordation of a deed from the owner. (In some jurisdictions, S will have to search a longer period of time under each owner; *see infra*, §§2043 *et seq.*)

(c) **Example:** K, owner of Blackacre, conveyed it to L in 1900. In 1930, L conveyed Blackacre to M. In 1955, M conveyed Blackacre to N. In 1975, N gave B Bank a mortgage on the property. In 1980, N conveyed Blackacre to O. O contracts to sell the land to A. Assume a title search back to

1900 is required. The title searcher, S, will look in the *grantee* index under O's name from the present back to 1980, when S finds the deed from N to O, then under N's name from 1980 to 1955, when S finds the deed from M to N, then under M's name from 1955 to 1930, then under L's name from 1930 backward. S will then look in the *grantor* index under L's name from 1900 to 1930, under M's name from 1930 to 1955, under N's name from 1955 to 1980, and under O's name from 1980 to the present. In this manner, S will pick up the mortgage to B Bank which is recorded in 1975 under N's name in the grantor index.

(d) **Death of owner:** [§1997]   In the preceding example, we have assumed deeds from one owner to the next. But title can pass also by will or intestacy. Assume that in 1930 L died, devising Blackacre to M, and that in 1955 M died, leaving N as her sole heir. L's will can be found in the recorder's office or in the office of the probate court clerk; it will be indexed in a testators' or decedents' index, to which S must turn if S cannot find M's grantor in the index to deeds. N, who took title from M by intestate succession, has no recordable document signed by M. To perfect title, M's heir, N, will file in the recorder's office an affidavit of heirship, prepared by N, which will state that N is the sole heir of M. However, if N is lying and there are in fact two heirs, this affidavit cannot adversely affect another heir who is not disclosed thereon. The burden is on the subsequent purchaser to make sure that he has a deed from *all* persons who are M's heirs. Any heir who does not sign the deed retains his or her interest.

(3) **Negligence in search:** [§1998]   A lawyer or abstractor who undertakes a title search owes a duty to the client to make a careful examination of the records. The title searcher is liable for negligence in this search. If the search is negligently made by an agent for the seller, who furnishes an abstract of title to the buyer, the buyer can sue the agent as a third party beneficiary of the contract between seller and searcher. The search is made for the benefit of the buyer, not the seller, and the searcher can foresee the reliance by the buyer. [Williams v. Polgar, 215 N.W.2d 149 (Mich. 1974); Slate v. Boone County Abstract Co., 432 S.W.2d 305 (Mo. 1968)]

4. **Types of Recording Acts:** [§1999]   There are three major types of recording acts: (i) "race," (ii) "notice," and (iii) "race-notice" statutes. (A fourth type, giving the purchaser a period of grace (such as ninety days) in which to record, was common in the last century but is largely outmoded today.)

a. **"Race" statutes:** [§2000]   The earliest statutes were race statutes. Under a race statute, as between successive grantees to the same land, priority is determined solely by *who records first*. Whoever wins the race to record prevails over a person who has not recorded or who subsequently records. Notice is irrelevant.

(1) **Example:** On January 1, O conveys Blackacre to A. A does not record. On February 1, O conveys Blackacre to B. B *knows* of the deed to A. B records. Then A records. B prevails over A because B recorded first. It is immaterial that B had actual notice of A's interest.

(2) **Rationale:** Determining who has actual notice depends upon extrinsic evidence, which may be unreliable. To bar use of such evidence, race statutes protect whoever wins the race to the recorder's office. Thus, the title searcher may rely upon the records to determine priorities. However, because it is deemed inequitable for a person with notice of a prior claim to prevail, very few states have race statutes today.

b. **"Notice" statutes:** [§2001]   Notice statutes developed from race statutes. American courts, applying the early race statutes, thought that it was fraudulent and unfair for a second purchaser with notice of a prior claim (B in the example above) to prevail over the prior claim. The courts construed the race statutes to apply only to a subsequent purchaser for a valuable consideration without notice. This judicial construction became codified in time, and thus developed modern notice and race-notice statutes. Under a notice statute, a subsequent bona fide purchaser prevails over a prior grantee who fails to record. The subsequent purchaser wins under a notice statute if he has *no actual or constructive notice* of a prior claim at the time of the conveyance. A typical notice statute provides: "A conveyance of an estate in land (other than a lease for less than one year) shall not be valid against any subsequent purchaser for value, without notice thereof, unless the conveyance is recorded." About half the states have notice statutes.

> (1) **Example:** On January 1, O conveys Blackacre to A. A does not record. On February 1, O conveys Blackacre to B, who gives valuable consideration and has no notice of the deed from O to A. B prevails over A. [Wilson v. Schneiter's Riverside Golf Course, 523 P.2d 1226 (Utah 1974)]

c. **"Race-notice" statutes:** [§2002]   Race-notice statutes, like notice statutes, protect only subsequent purchasers *without notice* of the prior claim. But they do not protect all such subsequent purchasers. They protect a subsequent bona fide purchaser *only if he records before the prior grantee*. Under a race-notice statute, in order for a subsequent purchaser to win, he must *both* be without notice *and* win the race to record. A typical race-notice statute provides: "A conveyance of an estate in land (other than a lease for less than one year) shall not be valid against any subsequent purchaser for value, without notice thereof, *whose conveyance is first recorded*." Race-notice statutes exist in about half the states.

> (1) **Example:** On January 1, O conveys Blackacre to A. A does not record. On February 1, O conveys Blackacre to B, a bona fide purchaser. On February 3, A records. On February 15, B records. A prevails over B because B's conveyance was not first recorded.

5. **Effect of Recordation**

a. **What recordation does:** [§2003]   Proper recordation gives the grantee the protection of the recording system. After recordation, all persons who deal with the land thereafter have constructive notice of the existence and contents of the recorded instrument, and no subsequent purchase without notice can arise. Also, in race-notice jurisdictions, because a grantee is not protected against prior unrecorded claims until he records, recordation protects the grantee from prior unrecorded claims as well as eliminates the possibility of a subsequent bona fide purchaser.

b. **What recordation does not do**

(1) **Validate invalid deed:** [§2004] Recordation is not necessary for a valid conveyance. A deed is valid between grantor and grantee if it is delivered. Recordation raises a rebuttable *presumption* that the instrument has been validly delivered and that it is authentic (*see supra*, §1900), but if forged or not delivered, recordation will not validate it. [Stone v. French, 14 P. 530 (Kan. 1887)]

(a) **Deed fraudulently procured:** [§2005] Where a deed has been procured by fraud, the deed is void or voidable between the grantor and grantee. If the grantee conveys to a bona fide purchaser, the bona fide purchaser prevails over the grantor if the grantor was sufficiently negligent to create an estoppel. [Hauck v. Crawford, 62 N.W.2d (S.D. 1953)]

(2) **Protect against interests arising by operation of law:** [§2006] Recordation does not protect a subsequent purchaser against prior interests that have arisen by *operation of law* (*e.g.*, dower rights, prescriptive and implied easements, title by adverse possession). Why not? The answer lies in a careful reading of the recording statute; it states that "a *conveyance* shall not be valid against a subsequent bona fide purchaser. . . . " Therefore, the statute applies only to *unrecorded conveyances*. Because interests arising by operation of law do not arise by conveyance, the recording acts do not apply, and subsequent purchasers take subject thereto. [State v. Meeker, 294 P.2d 603 (Wyo. 1956)]

(a) **Example:** A adversely possesses Blackacre for the period of the statute of limitations. O, the record owner, then conveys Blackacre to B, a bona fide purchaser. Even though A's interest has never been recorded and a look at the premises would reveal nothing of A's claim, A prevails against B. [Mugaas v. Smith, 206 P.2d 332 (Wash. 1949)]

c. **Effect of failure to record**

(1) **Prior-in-time rule:** [§2007] If a person does not record and thereby come within the protection of the recording act, the common law rule of "prior in time, prior in effect" is applicable.

(2) **Power to defeat left in grantor:** [§2008] If a person does not record, the person leaves in her grantor (and the grantor's heirs and devisees) the *power* to defeat the deed by executing a subsequent deed in favor of a bona fide purchaser. This is the logical and necessary consequence of the recording acts. This can be dramatically seen from the following illustration.

(a) **Example:** O, prior to death, executes a deed of Blackacre to A, who does not record. O dies, leaving H as O's heir. (H does not prevail over A because H has not given valuable consideration.) H conveys to B, a bona fide purchaser, who records. B prevails over A. [Earle v. Fiske, 103 Mass. 491 (1980)] Even though A had title at O's death, and therefore no title passed to H, the title *shown on the records* was in O at O's death. Relying upon the record, a bona fide purchaser can buy from O's heir and defeat A. Thus, though O had no title, the recording system gives O and O's heir the *power* to convey to a bona fide purchaser until A records her deed. Any other result would render the recording system useless because the records could not be relied upon.

(3) **Suit against double-dealing grantor:** [§2009]   If a person fails to record and loses title to a subsequent purchaser, the person may sue her grantor who conveyed twice, and recover under the theory of unjust enrichment the amount that the grantor received from the subsequent purchaser. The grantor, exercising the power left in him by the unrecorded deed, is selling the prior purchaser's property, and the grantor holds the proceeds as constructive trustee for the prior purchaser. (*See* Remedies Summary.) [Patterson v. Bryant, 55 S.E.2d 849 (N.C. 1939)]

6.   **Requirements for Recordation**

a.   **What can be recorded:** [§2010]   Practically every kind of deed, mortgage, contract to convey, or other instrument creating or affecting an interest in land can be recorded. A judgment or decree affecting title to property can also be recorded. And, even before judgment, where a pending lawsuit may affect title to property, any party to the action can record a lis pendens (notice of pending action) which will effectively put third parties on notice of all claims pending in the lawsuit.

b.   **Acknowledgments:** [§2011]   Most recording statutes provide that, in order to be recorded, a deed must be acknowledged by the grantor before a notary public. This requirement offers protection against forgery. In a few states, an instrument must be witnessed *as well as* acknowledged before a notary in order to be recorded. In a few states, an instrument must be witnessed *or* acknowledged.

c.   **What constitutes "recordation":** [§2012]   The fact that an instrument has been copied and entered in the recorder's office does not necessarily mean the instrument has been "recorded." The instrument must be entered in the recorder's books in a manner complying with the applicable statute or judicial decisions.

(1) **Failure to index:** [§2013]   Occasionally, a clerk in the recorder's office fails to index the instrument properly. Is the grantee of such an instrument protected against a subsequent bona fide purchaser? The cases are split: One view protects the grantee, on the theory that, by delivering the deed for recordation, the grantee has done all that she could reasonably be expected to do to give "notice to the world" of her interest. The other view protects the subsequent bona fide purchaser on the theory that only a properly indexed instrument imparts sufficient constructive notice to a subsequent purchaser. [Mortensen v. Lingo, 99 F.

Supp. 585 (D. Alaska 1951); Hanson v. Zoller, 187 N.W.2d 47 (N.D. 1971)—deed indexed in tract index but not in grantor-grantee index sufficient to impart notice] The latter is believed to be the better view, because as a practical matter until an instrument has been properly filed **and** indexed, there is no reasonable way to locate it. Further, the grantee of the prior instrument could have prevented the harm to the subsequent purchaser by seeing that the instrument was properly recorded. Accordingly, under the rule that as between two innocent persons, the one who could prevent the loss to another loses, the grantee, rather than the subsequent bona fide purchaser, should bear the loss.

(a) **Mother Hubbard clauses:** [§2014]   A Mother Hubbard clause is a provision in a deed that attempts to sweep within it other parcels not specifically described. *Example*: O gives a mortgage on Blackacre "and all other land I own in Henry County." O also owns Whiteacre in Henry County. In the grantor index, this mortgage will be noted as affecting Blackacre. Generally, Mother Hubbard clauses are not valid against subsequent purchasers of the undescribed land, and a bona fide purchaser of Whiteacre would not take subject to the mortgage. The reason is that since the mortgage will be indexed only as affecting Blackacre, it is an undue burden to require a title searcher to read all conveyances of other lots by an owner of the subject lot to see whether the conveyances affect the subject lot. [Luthi v. Evans, 576 P.2d 1064 (Kan. 1978)]

(2) **Recording unacknowledged instrument**

(a) **No acknowledgment:** [§2015]   As noted above, the recording acts generally require that in order to record any instrument it must first be acknowledged by the grantor before a notary. What happens if the recorder, by oversight, records a deed that has **not been acknowledged**? Since an unacknowledged deed does not qualify for recordation, it does **not** give constructive notice to subsequent purchasers. Unless the subsequent purchaser has actual or inquiry notice of the earlier deed, the subsequent purchaser prevails.

(b) **Defective acknowledgment:** [§2016]   Where the recorded instrument has been acknowledged but the acknowledgment is defective for some reason **not apparent on the face** of the instrument, the better view is that the recordation imparts constructive notice. [Mills v. Damson Oil Corp., 437 So. 2d 1005 (Miss. 1983)] However, there is contrary authority holding that if an instrument is defectively acknowledged, it is not entitled to be recorded and hence cannot impart constructive notice. It has even been held that under a race-notice statute, if an instrument in the chain of title bears a defective acknowledgment, **no later instrument** in the chain can be deemed properly recorded so as to defeat a prior unrecorded claim.

1) **Example (race-notice statute):** O conveys Blackacre to A, who does not record. O later conveys to B by a deed that appears to bear a valid acknowledgment, but which is in fact defective (because O did not

appear personally before the notary). B records this deed, and then sells to C, who records. Thereafter, A records his prior deed. *Held:* A prevails—because even though C recorded first, C's title is derivative of B's, and the defective acknowledgment in B's deed means that B's deed has never been "recorded." [Messersmith v. Smith, 60 N.W.2d 276 (N.D. 1953)]

2) **Criticism:** A hidden defect in an acknowledgment should not make the deed unreliable. For the recording system to work efficiently, purchasers must be able to rely on what *appears* to be a perfectly recorded document.

7. Who is Protected by Recording Acts

a. **In general:** [§2017]   Only a bona fide purchaser is entitled to protection under notice and race-notice statutes. To attain this status, a person must satisfy three requirements: (i) the person must be a *purchaser* (or mortgagee, or creditor if the statute so allows), (ii) who takes *without notice* (including actual, record, or inquiry notice) of the prior instrument, and (iii) gives a *valuable consideration*. If a person does not meet these requirements, he is not protected by the recording acts. The common law rule of first in time prevails. In a race jurisdiction, notice is irrelevant, but a race statute protects only subsequent purchasers for a valuable consideration who win the race to record.

b. **Purchasers**

(1) **Purchasers and mortgagees:** [§2018]   All recording acts protect purchasers of the fee simple or any other interest in the property. Some recording acts expressly apply to mortgagees as well as to purchasers. But even if the statute does not expressly apply to mortgagees, mortgagees are treated as purchasers under judicial decisions because mortgagees take a security interest in the property in exchange for value.

(a) **"Shelter rule":** [§2019]   A person who takes *from* a BFP will prevail over any interest over which the BFP would have prevailed. This is true even where such person had actual knowledge of the prior unrecorded interest.

1) **Example:** O conveys to A, who fails to record. O then conveys to B, a BFP, who records. B then conveys to C, who has *actual knowledge* of the O to A deed. Inasmuch as B prevails over A, B's assignee, C, prevails over A. This is true whether C is a donee or purchaser. C is "sheltered" by the BFP.

2) **Rationale:** If the rule were otherwise, a BFP would not receive the full protection of the recording statute. The statute has the purpose of giving a BFP the value of the bargain, which includes the right to enjoy, convey, or devise his interest. Accordingly, the transferee from a BFP

is not protected only if he is meritorious. The transferee is protected, whether meritorious or not, in order to give the BFP his expectations arising from his reliance on the records.

(2) **Donees:** [§2020]   Generally, donees do not come within the protection of the recording system because they do not give value. It is considered unfair to take property away from A and give it to B if B does not give consideration for the property. It has been held, however, that where the recording statute is broadly worded to include "any class of persons with any kind of rights," donees are entitled to the protection of the recording system. [Eastwood v. Shedd, 442 P.2d 423 (Colo. 1968)]

(3) **Creditors:** [§2021]   The recording acts vary considerably in the protection afforded creditors. Thus, the acts, as well as the judicial interpretations, must be examined carefully.

(a) **Creditors not protected:** [§2022]   Some acts do not mention creditors nor extend protection to "all persons," and under such acts, a creditor can claim protection, if at all, only when he *purchases* the debtor-owner's interest *at a judicial sale* following an action to enforce the debt.

(b) **Act extends to "creditors" or "all persons":** [§2023]   In some states, the recording act protects "all creditors" or "all persons" against an unrecorded instrument. However, because creditors do not ordinarily rely upon the record when extending credit, courts have held that, in spite of the statutory language, general creditors are *not* protected. Only *judgment or lien creditors* are protected. Bear in mind that the recording act protects judgment or lien creditors only against prior interests arising under instruments *capable of being recorded* (*see supra,* §2006). If the recording act is inapplicable in determining priorities, because the prior interest arises by operation of law, a court of equity may follow whatever rule of priority it deems equitable.

1) **Example:** Seller deeds land to Buyer, taking back a note for the purchase price. Buyer promises that he will execute and record a mortgage on the property to secure the note, but Buyer does not do so (thereby acting fraudulently). A constructive trust arises on the land in favor of Seller at the time of the fraud. Subsequently, creditors of Buyer obtain judgments which become liens on the property. The recording act provides that an unrecorded conveyance (or mortgage) shall not be valid against creditors, but the recording act is inapplicable because the constructive trust arose by operation of law. The court can do what it regards as fair. It has been held that a subsequent creditor will be protected against a defrauded seller if and only if the creditor shows he affirmatively relied upon the records at the time he extended credit. [Osin v. Johnson, 243 F.2d 653 (D.C. Cir. 1957)]

(c) **Purchaser at execution sale:** [§2024]   A purchaser at a creditor's execution sale who does not have notice of a prior unrecorded instrument takes free of any claim under such instrument. If a judgment creditor is protected under the recording act from time of judgment, and after judgment a prior unrecorded deed is recorded, the purchaser at the execution sale is protected because he is sheltered under the creditor.

c. **Without notice:** [§2025]   To be protected by a notice or race-notice statute, a subsequent purchaser must be without notice. "Without notice" means, in its most comprehensive sense, that the purchaser has no *actual, record,* or *inquiry* notice of the prior claim *at the time he paid consideration* and received his interest in the land.

(1) **Actual notice:** [§2026]   If a subsequent grantee actually knows of the prior instrument, he has actual notice and is not a BFP. Proof of actual notice depends upon extrinsic evidence.

(2) **Record notice:** [§2027]   If an instrument is properly recorded, any subsequent purchaser has record notice and is therefore not a BFP. Record notice is one form of "constructive notice," *i.e.,* notice that the law imputes to the purchaser whether he actually knows or not.

(3) **Inquiry notice:** [§2028]   Inquiry notice is another form of constructive notice. Under certain circumstances, a purchaser is required by law to make reasonable inquiries. He is charged with notice of whatever the inquiry would reveal, even though he made no inquiry. In a few states, such as Massachusetts, inquiry notice is irrelevant because the court has quite literally interpreted the recording act, which protects subsequent purchasers unless they have "actual notice" or record notice. [Toupin v. Peabody, 39 N.E. 280 (Mass. 1895)]

(a) **Inquiry from quitclaim deed:** [§2029]   Although some courts hold that a purchaser under a quitclaim deed must make inquiry concerning possible unrecorded prior conveyances because a quitclaim deed is a suspicious circumstance, in a majority of states, a grantee under a quitclaim deed is treated the same as a grantee under a warranty deed. No inference is made that a quitclaim deed is given because the grantor had some doubt about the validity of his title.

(b) **Inquiry from possession:** [§2030]   Suppose that O conveys Blackacre to A, who does not record but goes into possession of Blackacre. O then conveys Blackacre to B. To be a bona fide purchaser, must B inquire of the possessor (A) as to A's possible claim to Blackacre?

1) **Majority view:** [§2031]   B, the subsequent purchaser, is charged with knowledge of whatever an inspection of the property would have disclosed. Hence, B is on constructive notice of A's possession and what

would be uncovered by inquiring of A. [Wineberg v. Moore, 194 F. Supp. 12 (N.D. Cal. 1961); Galley v. Ward, 60 N.H. 331 (1880); Miller v. Green, 58 N.W.2d 704 (Wis. 1953)]

2) **Minority views:** [§2032]   There are a number of minority views imposing a lesser inquiry burden on B. These views usually rest on language in the applicable recording act, especially language saying an unrecorded deed is void against persons having "actual notice." Some courts hold that B must make inquiry of A only if B *actually knows* A is in possession. [Brinkman v. Jones, 44 Wis. 498 (1878)—construing unusual statute applying to mortgages only, which provides unrecorded mortgage is invalid against person with actual notice] Another view is that if A's possession is *consistent* with record title, B does not have to make inquiry. Thus, suppose that T devises Blackacre to A for life, remainder to B. B then conveys her remainder to A, which conveyance is not recorded. B subsequently conveys her remainder to C. A's possession (as a life tenant) is consistent with A's record title of a life estate. Hence, C does not have to inquire of A to determine if he claims more than a life estate. [*But see* Toland v. Corey, 24 P. 190 (Utah 1890)—rejecting this view]

(c) **Inquiry from neighborhood:** [§2033]   Deeds out from a common grantor (subdivider) to buyers of other lots in a residential subdivision may contain express written restrictions on land retained by the common grantor and later sold to a subsequent purchaser without any restrictions. Or, under the doctrine of implied reciprocal negative easements (*see supra,* §1479), a negative restriction on use may be imposed *by implication* on a lot in a subdivision, where there is a uniform scheme for development of the subdivision, even though the deed to that lot may contain no restrictions. If the restriction is not contained in a deed in the direct chain of title of the subject lot, the only way a purchaser can find such a restriction is to read all the deeds to other lots from the common grantor. Must a purchaser do this? Some courts have held that the purchaser has constructive notice of the contents of these other deeds out (discussed *infra,* §2054). At least one court has held that if, from the looks of the neighborhood, a purchaser should reasonably conclude that a restriction on use of the subject lot might exist, the purchaser is put on inquiry notice of the contents of other deeds out from the common grantor. These deeds may show a scheme from which a restriction will be implied on the purchaser's lot. [Sanborn v. McLean, 206 N.W. 496 (Mich. 1925)]

1) **Example:** CG, owner of a subdivision of twenty lots, conveys lots 1 through 19 to various purchasers. Each deed restricts the lot to residential use only. Single family houses are built on these lots. Under the doctrine of implied reciprocal negative easements, there is a scheme whereby lot 20 is impliedly restricted to residential use. CG conveys lot 20 to A. If A is a purchaser without notice, A will not take subject

to the restriction. However, if the looks of the neighborhood should reasonably put A on inquiry, A must read the deeds from CG of lots 1 through 19 and, finding a scheme of residential development, take the risk that a court will imply a restriction on lot 20.

(d) **Inquiry into unrecorded instruments:** [§2034]   If a recorded instrument refers *expressly* to an unrecorded instrument, in most states, the purchaser has an obligation to make inquiry into the contents of the instrument. The purchaser has constructive notice of its contents. [Harper v. Paradise, 210 S.E.2d 710 (Ga. 1974); Gagner v. Kittery Water District, 385 A.2d 206 (Me. 1978); Baker v. Mather, 25 Mich. 51 (1872); *but see* Tramontozzi v. D'Amicis, 183 N.E.2d 295 (Mass. 1962)—no inquiry required in Massachusetts because recording act requires *actual* notice]

1) **Statutory changes:** [§2035]   In an attempt to limit inquiries off the record, statutes have been enacted in some states providing that no burden of inquiry is placed upon a purchaser by an "indefinite reference." An indefinite reference generally is a reference to interests not created by a properly recorded instrument. [Stroh & Sons, Inc. v. Batavia Homes & Development Corp., 17 App. Div. 2d 385 (1962)]

2) **Notice of lease:** [§2036]   Statutes in some states permit the recordation of a "notice of lease," without reproducing on the public records the entire lease (which might be very long). If a notice of lease is recorded, a subsequent purchaser has the duty of examining the original lease. [Mister Donut of America, Inc. v. Kemp, 330 N.E.2d 810 (Mass. 1975); *but see* Howard D. Johnson Co. v. Parkside Development Corp., 348 N.E.2d 656 (Ind. 1976)—no duty to inquire into contents of commercial lease on neighboring land within shopping center of which purchaser had actual knowledge]

d. **Valuable consideration:** [§2037]   To be protected under the recording acts, a purchaser must give valuable consideration. A person qualifies as a purchaser only when consideration is given, and is protected against unrecorded prior conveyances only from that time. If the deed is delivered and some time later the purchaser gives consideration, the purchaser does not prevail over deeds recorded before consideration is given. [Lown v. Nichols Plumbing & Heating, Inc., 634 P.2d 554 (Alaska 1981)]

(1) **What is valuable consideration:** [§2038]   A valuable consideration must be more than merely nominal, but it does not have to equal the market value of the property. It must be sufficient for a court to deem it equitable to deprive the prior purchaser of the land. "Love and affection" is *not* a valuable consideration. [Kindred v. Crosby, 100 N.W.2d 20 (Iowa 1959)] But an agreement to work and support a person in old age, if performed, is a valuable consideration. [Larkins v. Howard, 39 So. 2d 224 (Ala. 1949)]

(a) **Compare—contract law:** [§2039]   The test of valuable consideration is different from that of contract law, where any consideration—even a peppercorn—suffices to make a contract enforceable. Here the law is trying to differentiate between a donee (not protected) and a purchaser (protected), and thus the consideration must be of substantial monetary value so that it is equitable to deprive another person of the land. [Allaben v. Shelbourne, 212 S.W.2d 719 (Mo. 1948)—one dollar is not a valuable consideration; this case casts doubt on Strong v. Whybark, 102 S.W. 968 (Mo. 1907)—where five dollars was a valuable consideration]

(2) **Antecedent debts:** [§2040]   A person who receives a deed or mortgage as *security* for a preexisting debt has not given a valuable consideration at the time the deed or mortgage is executed. The person is not at that time a bona fide purchaser for value. [McDonald & Co. v. Johns, 114 P. 175 (Wash. 1911); Gabel v. Drewrys, Ltd., 68 So. 2d 372 (Fla. 1953)]

(a) **Example:** O becomes indebted to A. O conveys Blackacre to B, who does not record. O then gives A a mortgage on Blackacre to secure the indebtedness, and A records. B prevails over A.

(b) **Creditor gives new consideration:** [§2041]   If the creditor gives new valuable consideration, usually in the form of worsening his legal position, this will be sufficient consideration. Thus, in the preceding example, if A extends the time of payment of the debt when he takes the mortgage, he gives valuable consideration. Or if a debtor conveys the property to the creditor in *satisfaction* of the debt, so that a suit cannot thereafter be brought on the debt, the creditor has given valuable consideration.

(3) **Partial payment:** [§2042]   Where the purchaser has paid only part of the purchase price and has given a note to the grantor for the balance, most courts protect the purchaser only to the extent of payment made. Depending upon the equities, the court will either give the subsequent purchaser a lien on the land for the amount paid *or* give the prior grantee a lien to the extent of the balance still owed the grantor by the subsequent purchaser. Under the first alternative, the subsequent purchaser loses the land, but he receives his money back. [Durst v. Daugherty, 17 S.W. 388 (Tex. 1891)]

8. **Chain of Title Problems:** [§2043]   Even though an instrument has actually been recorded and indexed in the recording office, the instrument might not be recorded in such a way as to give notice to subsequent purchasers. The deed may not be in the "chain of title." To give notice to subsequent purchasers, a deed must be in the "chain of title," as that term is defined in the jurisdiction. (*Note:* The problems that are discussed below do not arise if the jurisdiction has a tract index. They arise only where grantor and grantee indexes are used.)

a. **Chain of title defined:** [§2044]   The "chain of title" includes, and is co-extensive with, those documents of which the purchaser has constructive notice. In all jurisdictions using a grantor-grantee index system, a purchaser is charged with notice of those conveyances of the property by her grantor *recorded after the grantor acquired the property from his predecessor in title and recorded before a deed is recorded conveying title from that grantor to another.* Likewise, the purchaser is charged with notice of conveyances made by the various predecessors in title during similar periods of ownership. This is the standard title search, and all documents found in a standard title search are in the chain of title.

(1) **Extended chain:** [§2045]   As noted below, in some jurisdictions "chain of title" is defined to include, in addition to the above conveyances, other conveyances that can be picked up by a more extensive record search.

(2) **"Wild deeds":** [§2046]   A "wild deed" is a recorded deed to the property which is not recorded within the chain of title. Sometimes the term "wild deed" is used in a narrower sense, meaning a recorded deed from a grantor who is not connected to the chain of title.

b.   **Grantor not connected to chain of title:** [§2047]   If a deed entered on the records has a grantor unconnected to the chain of title, such a deed is not recorded within the chain and does not give constructive notice.

(1) **Example:** O conveys to A, who does not record. A conveys to B, who promptly records his deed from A. O conveys to C, a BFP, who records. *Result:* C prevails over B. The A to B deed is not connected to the chain of title; the O to A link is missing. There is no feasible way for C to discover the A to B deed; therefore, C prevails. [Board of Education v. Hughes, 136 N.W. 1095 (Minn. 1912); Losey v. Simpson, 11 N.J. Eq. 146 (1856)]

c.   **Deeds recorded before grantor obtained title—estoppel by deed:** [§2048]   Must a purchaser search the index under the name of a grantor prior to the date title came into the grantor to see if the grantor gave an earlier deed to the property to which the doctrine of estoppel by deed (*supra,* §1974) applies? Or to put the question another way, does a recorded deed from a grantor who has no title, but who afterwards otbains title, give constructive notice to a subsequent purchaser from the same grantor? Suppose that on June 1, O owns Blackacre, but on that day, A conveys Blackacre by warranty deed to B who promptly records. On July 2, O conveys Blackacre to A, and this deed is also promptly recorded. Under the doctrine of estoppel by deed, title moves from O to A to B on July 2. No problems will arise if A does not convey the land to a subsequent purchaser. But, suppose that on August 3, A conveys Blackacre to C, a bona fide purchaser who has no actual notice of the prior A to B deed. Will estoppel by deed apply against a subsequent bona fide purchaser? Now who prevails?

(1) **Majority—limited search required:** [§2049]   Most courts hold that C prevails over B on the theory that a deed from A to B, recorded prior to the time title came to A, is not in the chain of title. *Rationale:* It would put an excessive burden on the title searcher to require a search of the index under each grantor's name ***prior*** to the date the grantor acquired title. [Sabo v. Horvath, 559 P.2d 1038 (Alaska 1976); Ryczkowski v. Chelsea Title & Guaranty Co., 449 P.2d 261 (Nev. 1969)]

(2) **Minority—extended search required:** [§2050] A minority of courts protect B over C. *Rationale:* Under the doctrine of estoppel by deed, if a grantor who does not have title later acquires it, it passes by operation of law immediately to the grantee. When A acquires title from O, title is transferred automatically to B by virtue of the estoppel arising from A's earlier deed to B. Therefore, A had nothing left to transfer to C. [Ayer v. Philadelphia & Boston Face Brick Co., 34 N.E. 177 (Mass. 1893)] Under this theory, C must search title prior to the time each grantor acquired title to ascertain whether an estoppel applies against the grantor.

d. **Deeds recorded late:** [§2051] Must a purchaser search the index under the name of a grantor **after** the recordation of a deed by that grantor transferring title? Or to put the question another way, does a deed recorded after the grantor is shown by the record to have parted with title give constructive notice? Suppose that on January 1, O conveys to A, who does not then record. On February 2, O conveys to B, a donee, who records. B, being a donee, does not prevail over A. On March 3, A records. On April 4, B conveys to C, who has no actual notice of A's deed. C records. Who prevails?

(1) **Limited search required:** [§2052] In most states, C prevails over A. *Rationale:* If A prevails, the title searcher would have to look in the indexes under the name of each grantor in the chain of title to the present date (not just to the date of the first recorded deed from each grantor) to see if there was a deed executed before the first recorded deed but recorded later. This puts an excessive burden on the title searcher. [Morse v. Curtis, 2 N.E. 929 (Mass 1885)] In jurisdictions following this rule, the title searcher looks under O's name in the grantor index only to February 2. The searcher looks under B's name after that date and does not find the O to A deed, recorded on March 3, and does not take subject to it.

(2) **Extended search required:** [§2053] In a minority of states (including California and New York), A's deed gives notice to subsequent purchasers, although recorded after B's deed. [Woods v. Garnett, 16 So. 390 (Miss. 1894)] In these states, the title searcher must search **to the present date** under the name of **each person who ever owned** the property in order to pick up deeds recorded late. As this extended search would greatly increase the cost of conveyancing, title searchers in practice often ignore the law and take the risk.

e. **Deeds from common grantor of adjacent lots:** [§2054] Must a purchaser look at deeds to other lots from a grantor who owned the subject lot? Or to put the question another way, and narrow it somewhat, does a deed by a subdivider to another lot in a subdivision give constructive notice of any covenants or easements reserved over the neighboring lots? Suppose that subdivider O is developing a residential subdivision. O sells lot 1 to A and the deed provides that lot 1 is restricted to residential use. The deed also provides that "O on behalf of himself, his heirs and assigns, promises to use his remaining lots (2, 3, etc.) for residential purposes only." Then O sells lot 2 to B. The deed to B contains no restrictions. B wishes to erect a gasoline station. Is B bound by the restrictions in the O to A deed, of which he had no actual notice? The courts are split: Some hold that because the burden of title search would be excessive, deeds out to other lots from the common grantor are ***not*** in B's chain of title, and B is not bound by them. [Glorieux v. Lighthipe, 96 A. 94 (N.J. 1915); Buffalo Academy of the Sacred Heart v. Boehm Bros., Inc., 267 N.Y. 242 (1935)] Others charge B with reading all deeds out from a common grantor, not just the deeds to his particular tract. Under this view, B has constructive notice and is bound by the restriction. [Guillette v. Daly Dry Wall, Inc., 325 N.E.2d 572 (Mass. 1975)]

9. **Defects in the Recording System:** [§2055] The recording system has numerous defects and has been much criticized.

   a. **Criticisms:** [§2056] The recording system has been primarily criticized for the following reasons:

      (1) **Public records contain incomplete information:** [§2057] Even with good record title, a person can be defeated as a result of a defect of fact or law not ascertainable from the recorded documents. Among such defects are: forged deed; deed with faulty acknowledgment by the notary public; deed by grantor who is described as single but who is in fact married and whose spouse has dower or community property rights; claims of heirs who have been omitted from affidavit of heirship and whose claims are not barred; will produced for probate after conveyance by heirs at law; claimants of title who supposedly have been barred by tax sale, foreclosure, or execution sale but who have not been barred because of lack of jurisdiction of court; statutory liens and implied easements and servitudes not required to be of record; notice imputed from possession but not discovered by the purchaser yet considered notice by the courts; and claims arising from adverse possession.

      (2) **Public records are inefficiently organized:** [§2058] Grantor-grantee indexes are antiquated, inefficient, and can be searched only with great difficulty and expense. A tract index is needed.

      (3) **Expense:** [§2059] Every time a piece of property is sold, a record search back to the inception of title is required. This record search by a different title searcher each time a new sale or mortgage occurs is wasteful and costly.

   b. **Remedies:** [§2060] The following remedies have been proposed to cure the defects in the recording system:

      (1) **Title standards:** [§2061] Title standards deal with the very exacting examiner. They are adopted by the local or state bar association and provide, in effect, that specified kinds of defects should not be challenged. They determine risks that are reasonable to take, but title standards are merely a form of "gentlemen's agreement," not binding upon the courts nor upon lawyers. Title standards have been promulgated by bar associations in half the states.

(2) **Curative acts:** [§2062]   A curative act is like a short statute of limitations, curing some ancient irregularity of record. For example, a curative act may provide that an unacknowledged deed that has been of record for ten years is deemed properly recorded. Curative acts have been enacted in many states, but they cure only specified defects and are of limited usefulness in clearing title.

(3) **Tract index:** [§2063]   A tract index solves most of the problems relating to whether an instrument is in the chain of title (*see supra,* §2043), but it does not solve problems of inquiry notice (*see supra,* §2028) or of whether an instrument has been effectively recorded and indexed (*see supra,* §2013). Tract indexes exist in very few states, and even then are usually limited to certain counties within the state.

(4) **Marketable title acts:** [§2064]   Marketable title acts, adopted in eighteen states, attempt to limit record search to a specified number of years—typically twenty, thirty, or forty years. (For explanation here, a thirty-year period will be assumed.) Under a thirty-year marketable title act, if a good record chain of title is found based on a "root of title" more than thirty years old, any claims arising prior to the root of title (with some exceptions) are nullified. If there were no exceptions, a title searcher in 1985 would have to search back only to a root of title more than thirty years old (*i.e.,* a deed executed before 1955). Hence, if A conveyed a fee simple to Blackacre to B in 1952, that deed would be the root of title. All interests created prior to 1952 by whatever manner—deed, inheritance, or adverse possession—are deemed void. If A's claim rested upon an earlier forged deed, say from F to A in 1948, that fact is irrelevant. [Marshall v. Hollywood, Inc., 236 So. 2d 114 (Fla. 1970), *cert. denied,* 400 U.S. 964]

   (a) **Root of title updated:** [§2065]   The root of title may change as the years go by. *Remember:* The root is a conveyance more than thirty years old at the date of search. If Blackacre is conveyed in 1990, and the records show a deed from B to C in 1958, that deed—and not the 1952 deed from A to B—is the root of title.

   (b) **Pre-root interests:** [§2066]   A pre-root interest is valid if it is referred to in the root of title or in a post-root instrument. Thus, in the 1985 search in the example above, if the 1952 deed from A to B said "subject to an easement in D created in 1920," D's easement would remain valid. On the other hand, if the search took place in 1990 and D's easement was not mentioned in the B to C deed (the new root of title), D's easement is extinguished.

      1) **Rerecording:** [§2067]   Pre-root interests can be preserved by being rerecorded within the thirty-year period. Thus, it is wise to rerecord all claims every thirty years.

      2) **Exceptions:** [§2068]   Marketable title acts usually contain a number of exceptions for pre-root interests. These may include public ease-

ments, observable easements, utility easements, restrictive covenants, and mineral interests. These exceptions impair the usefulness of the marketable title act, for the title searcher must go beyond the root of title to ascertain the existence of these interests.

(c) **Possession:** [§2069]   Under most of the marketable title acts, rights of a possessor are not barred. Thus, a purchaser should make a physical inspection of the land.

(d) **Two chains of title:** [§2070]   Under a marketable title act it is possible to have two chains of title existing simultaneously. Suppose that in the preceding example, F had forged a deed to Blackacre to A in 1948. The 1952 A to B deed serves as the root of title for this chain. Suppose also that O, the true owner, had conveyed Blackacre to M in 1954. The deed from O to M serves as the root of title for this chain. There is practically no authority on how to resolve problems involving two conflicting chains of title.

(e) **Constitutionality:** [§2071]   Marketable title acts have been held constitutional on the ground that the social usefulness outweighs the impairment of old private rights. They operate like a statute of limitations, barring enforcement of a right unless the right is rerecorded within the period of the search. [Presbytery of Southeast Iowa v. Harris, 226 N.W.2d 232 (Iowa 1975)]

B. TITLE REGISTRATION

1. **In General:** [§2072]   Title registration is a system of title assurance entirely separate from the recording system. It is sometimes known as the "Torrens system" (after Sir Richard Torrens, who invented it). The basic principle of title registration is to register *title* to land, instead of recording *evidence* of title (as under the recording system). Title registration is built around three ideas: (i) getting title adjudicated by a court, then keeping it up to date by (ii) installing a tract index, and (iii) making the public records conclusive. This system is available in Colorado, Georgia, Hawaii, Illinois, Massachusetts, Minnesota, New York, North Carolina, Ohio, Virginia, and Washington.

2. **How Title Registration Works**

a. **Initial registration:** [§2073]   First, a judicial proceeding in rem is started by the owner to clear away all past claims and adjudicate present title. A title searcher is appointed by the court to investigate the records and report to the court. Notice is given to all interested parties, after which the court approves the report of the situation of the title. The court issues a *certificate of title* binding, with few exceptions, upon all the world. The certificate is issued in duplicate; the official copy stays in the recorder's office. A duplicate copy is given to the owner. The certificate states who owns title and also lists as "memorials" all encumbrances (mortgages, covenants, easements, etc.) to which the title is subject. [State v. Johnson, 179 S.E.2d (N.C. 1971)]

b. **Tract index:** [§2074]   Once a certificate of title is issued, it is indexed in a tract index. Thereafter, anyone wishing to see the state of the title will look up the lot number in the tract index and see, on the face of the certificate of title, who has title and memorials of all encumbrances on the lot. The searcher can then go to the books containing the originals or copies of all documents listed as memorials and examine them. Title search is vastly simplified.

c. **Subsequent transfer:** [§2075]   Suppose that O has the title to Blackacre registered in her name. The certificate of title shows O as fee owner and also lists all mortgages, liens, easements, etc. Suppose that O wants to convey title to A. O delivers to A her duplicate certificate of title together with a deed to Blackacre. A submits the certificate to the recorder, who cancels O's certificate on the books, registers a new official certificate in favor of A, and delivers to A a new duplicate certificate. If A should later grant a mortgage to B, B would present her mortgage and A's duplicate certificate to the recorder, and the recorder would issue a new official certificate showing B's mortgage. Thus the certificate is kept up to date.

d. **Indemnity fund:** [§2076]   If any person's rights to the land are cut off without notice in the initial registration proceeding, she is paid from an indemnity fund established from title registration fees. If, subsequently, any person is harmed through the recorder's mistake (*e.g.,* omission of an encumbrance on a new certificate), she is likewise entitled to indemnification from the fund. [Hoffman v. Schroeder, 186 N.E.2d 381 (Ill. 1962)]

e. **Records conclusive:** [§2077]   With few exceptions, the title certificate is conclusive. The certificate of title *is* title. Exceptions may include tax and mechanic's liens and public easements, which do not have to be entered on the certificate. Federal tax liens are valid without being entered on the certificate. [United States v. Rasmuson, 253 F.2d 944 (8th Cir. 1958); *reversing* United States v. Ryan, 124 F. Supp. 1 (D. Minn. 1954)]

   (1) **Adverse possession:** [§2078]   Title to registered land ***cannot*** be claimed by adverse possession where the possession begins after the title is registered. The certificate of title is conclusive.

3. **Defects in Conclusiveness:** [§2079]   Although by making the certificate conclusive title registration in theory offers great protection to the buyer, in practice this protection is less conclusive than it appears. Motivated by a desire to do equity, courts have resisted the idea that the certificate is conclusive and have lessened its reliability. The following are the major attacks that can be made on the conclusiveness of the certificate.

a. **Defect in initial registration**

   (1) **No notice given:** [§2080]   The Constitution requires that a person be given notice and hearing before being deprived of property. Reasonable efforts must be made to give notice reasonably calculated to reach the owner. If notice is not given, the court lacks jurisdiction, and its decree can be attacked afterward. A person in possession of the land at the time of the initial registration is easily

located, and it has been held that he must be given personal notice of the registration proceedings. If not so notified, the possessor can set aside the decree in a suit against the original registrant. [Konantz v. Stein, 167 N.W.2d 1 (Minn. 1969)] Whether the unnotified possessor can set aside the decree against a bona fide purchaser from the original registrant has not been decided.

(2) **Fraud:** [§2081]   If the initial registration was procured by fraud or forgery, the decree can probably be set aside against the original registrant. If not, the person defrauded can have a constructive trust imposed upon the person who fraudulently registered the title, if he still owns it. [State Street Bank & Trust Co. v. Beale, 227 N.E.2d 924 (Mass. 1967)] Whether the initial registration can be set aside for fraud after the title has come into the hands of a bona fide purchaser has not been decided.

   (a) **Subsequent transfer:** [§2082]   If fraud is involved in a subsequent transfer of title (*e.g.,* the registered owner entrusts his duplicate certificate to a person who forges a deed and acquires a new official certificate), the new certificate is valid if relied on by a subsequent bona fide purchaser. The person who registers title, or buys registered title, voluntarily enters into the Torrens system and can lose title unwillingly because of the conclusiveness of the certificate. (This cannot be said of a person who loses title by fraud or forgery in the initial registration.) [Eliason v. Wilborn, 281 U.S. 457 (1930)]

b. **Bona fide purchasers:** [§2083]   Courts have introduced into the title registration system the idea that the title certificate protects only subsequent bona fide purchasers who rely on it. This, of course, is a basic principle of the recording system, but it is not part of the title registration statute. Applying this principle, courts have held that a person with *actual* notice of an unregistered interest (*e.g.,* a lease) does not prevail over it. [Killam v. March, 55 N.E.2d 945 (Mass. 1944); Butler v. Haley Greystone Corp., 198 N.E.2d 635 (Mass. 1964)] Similarly, a person who does not make adequate inquiry into the validity of a signature on a deed is not in good faith and is not protected by the issuance of a certificate. [Hoffman v. Schroeder, *supra,* §2076] These decisions are reminiscent of early courts that construed the race recording statutes (also designed to make the records conclusive) not to apply to a person with notice of a prior claim. The battle between an efficient title transfer system decreed by the legislature and judicial notions of fairness (the concept of bona fide purchaser) continues.

   (1) **Possession as constructive notice:** [§2084]   The majority holds that possession does not give constructive notice to a person who purchases relying on a title certificate.

      (a) **Example:** O registers title in his name. Then, O deeds the property to A, but does not give A the certificate of title. A takes possession and records her deed in the grantor-grantee index. Later, O deeds the property to B, a bona fide purchaser who does not know A is on the land. O gives B the certificate of title. B prevails over A. The earlier recording of A's deed is not constructive notice, where B has been given the certificate of title. [Abrahamson v. Sundman, 218 N.W. 246 (Minn. 1928)]

(2) **Judgment creditors:** [§2085]   It has been held that although bona fide purchases can rely upon the certificate, a judgment creditor cannot. If a judgment creditor attaches property registered in the name of the debtor, which the debtor has previously conveyed to another by an unregistered instrument, the judgment creditor loses because he did not rely on the registered state of title when extending credit. [Echols v. Olsen, 347 N.E.2d 720 (Ill. 1976)]

4. **Comment:** [§2086]   Even where available, title registration has proceeded very slowly on a voluntary basis. The main objection is the cost of the initial registration proceeding. As a result, three situations account for most registrations: (i) where the record title is defective; (ii) where the owner wants to prevent adverse possession of the land (*e.g.,* wild timberland); or (iii) where a subdivider registers title to a large tract before subdividing, passing the cost along to the buyers (which is cheaper than having each buyer pay the cost of an individual title search). (For a proposal to change the system so that title can be registered without an expensive judicial proceeding, *see* 29 UCLA L. Rev. 661 (1982).)

C. TITLE INSURANCE

1. **In General:** [§2087]   Title insurance is available in almost all states, but it is used more in some states than in others. There are two types of title insurance systems in general use.

    a. **Lawyer-title policies:** [§2088]   Suppose that A wants to buy Blackacre from O. A hires a lawyer to search the record. In addition to giving A an opinion as to the title, the lawyer furnishes an abstract of the record to a title insurance company. On the basis of this abstract, rather than its own independent investigation, the company insures title. This system keeps the lawyer in the picture as a title examiner.

    b. **Title-plant policies:** [§2089]   Some title insurance companies maintain duplicate records of all instruments in the county recording office. They have a separate title plant, with a tract index, and carry out their own independent title search. The lawyer does not search title for them. The employment of this kind of title insurance eliminates the lawyer from the title examination process.

2. **Who Is Insured:** [§2090]   Title insurance can be taken out either by the owner of the property or by the mortgage lender. The insurance protects only the ***person who owns the policy.*** The policy does not run with the land to subsequent purchasers.

3. **Extent of Coverage**

    a. **Record title insured:** [§2091]   The title insurance company or its agent ordinarily conducts a search of record title only and does not go outside the records nor inspect the premises. Accordingly, the standard policy insures only a **good record title** as of the policy's date. In essence, the policy insures only the accuracy of the records, and agrees to defend the record title if litigated.

(1) **What is record title:** [§2092] "Record title" is generally coextensive with instruments properly recorded within the insured's "chain of title" as defined in the particular jurisdiction (*see supra,* §2044). An instrument not in the insured's chain of title is not insured against. Thus, a deed to a neighboring lot from a common grantor which purports to affect the insured lot is not insured against if the deed is outside the chain of title.

(2) **Duty to disclose:** [§2093] Some courts have held that, where a title insurance company undertakes to conduct a search of title, the company has a **duty to disclose** to the purchaser specific impediments to title. Thus, the title insurance company's obligations go beyond that of an insurer, which has no duty to disclose the risks it is taking. For example, where the policy states that "rights of way for existing roads" are not insured, and the existing road is fifteen feet, but a lawsuit has been filed claiming a forty-foot right of way, which lawsuit is not brought to the purchaser's attention by the company, the company is liable. The purchaser's expectations include both **search and disclosure.** [Shotwell v. Transamerica Title Insurance Co., 558 P.2d 1359 (Wash. 1976)] But there are cases to the contrary, holding the insurance company has no duty to disclose defects it discovers. [*See* Horn v. Lawyers Title Insurance Co., 557 P.2d 206 (N.M. 1976)]

(3) **Giving legal advice:** [§2094] If the title insurance company goes beyond insuring the purchaser against loss, and advises the purchaser as to the legal marketability of title, the company is giving legal advice and assumes responsibility therefor. If the legal advice is wrong and the company is negligent in giving such advice, the company is liable in damages (not limited to the amount of insurance liability stated in the policy). [Glyn v. Title Guaranty & Trust Co., 132 App. Div. 859 (1909)]

b. **Exclusions:** [§2095] The standard title insurance policy does not insure against loss arising from the following defects, among others:

(1) **Liens imposed by law but not shown on the public records:** [§2096] This exception may include various statutory liens, such as a mechanic's or builder's lien. It also may include street assessments assessed to abutters, which by law become liens on the abutting property, without recordation.

(a) **Example:** On January 1, 1985, the city council authorizes improvements to Green Street, to be assessed against the abutters in 1985 and to become liens upon their property as of July 1, 1985. In March, 1985, the title insurance company issues a policy to A, who buys a lot abutting Green Street. Since the lien does not arise until after the policy is issued, the company has no liability on the policy. [Metropolitan Life Insurance Co. v. Union Trust Co., 283 N.Y. 33 (1940)] Nor does the company have a duty to disclose the assessment, which, although not yet a lien and not an encumbrance or defect, the purchaser would certainly like to know about. [Mayers v. Van Schaick, 268 N.Y. 320 (1935)]

(2) **Claims of parties in possession not shown on the public records:** [§2097] The insurance company does not physically inspect the property, and therefore does not insure against claims by adverse possession or possessory claims that could be found by inspection of the premises. [Bothin v. California Title Insurance Co., 153 Cal. 718 (1908)]

(3) **Boundary disputes:** [§2098] The insurance company does not survey the property, and therefore does not insure against encroachments and boundary disputes that would be disclosed by a correct survey or inspection of the premises. However, a correct survey is one that corresponds to the description in the deed, and if the description in the deed is wrong, the company is liable. In other words, the company insures the accuracy of the records. [Lawyers Title Insurance Corp. v. McKee, 354 S.W.2d 401 (Tex. 1962)]

(4) **Easements or servitudes not shown on the public records:** [§2099] Implied easements or covenants and easements by necessity or by prescription are not covered by the policy.

(5) **Zoning or building ordinances:** [§2100] The policy does not insure against any law or government regulation restricting the use of land. This includes building codes, zoning ordinances, and subdivision regulations.

4. **Amount of Liability**

a. **Maximum liability:** [§2101] The maximum liability of the company is the amount set in the policy. Ordinarily, this is the purchase price of the property. Unless there is an inflation clause in the policy, the policy does not insure the present value of the property where such value exceeds the amount set in the policy.

b. **General rule of liability:** [§2102] The company is liable for the difference in value of the property with and without the defect, up to the maximum set by the policy. Values at the date of issuance of the policy are usually held to control. [Southern Title Guaranty Co. v. Prendergast, 494 S.W.2d 154 (Tex. 1963)]

(1) **Example:** O sells Blackacre to A for $9,000. A takes out a title insurance policy for $7,000, which insures against any easements on Blackacre. Subsequently, A discovers that B has an easement over Blackacre. The true market value of Blackacre without the easement is $15,000 on the date of issuance of the policy (A bought at a great bargain). The value of Blackacre with the easement on the date of issuance of the policy is $5,000. A has been damaged $10,000, and can collect the maximum $7,000 under the policy. [Beaullieu v. Atlanta Title & Trust Co., 4 S.E.2d 78 (Ga. 1939)]

REVIEW QUESTIONS

1. Mable and Ichabod are both licensed to hunt on Olga's land. Mabel has a fox under pursuit.

    a. Ichabod overtakes Mable and shoots the fox first. Can Ichabod keep the fox?   _____

    b. Mable captures an ordinary red fox and pens it in her yard. The fox escapes. Eric, who does not know the fox has been captured by Mabel, captures the fox. Can Eric keep the fox?   _____

2. Ima Lukkin finds a ring owned by Opal Essent on property owned by Anna Mossity. Anna has never seen the ring before, but claims it as owner of the locus where the ring is found.

    a. If Ima finds the ring in Anna's private home while a guest there, is Ima entitled to the ring, as against Anna?   _____

    b. If Ima finds the ring on the wash basin in the women's room of Anna's store, is Ima entitled to the ring, as against Anna?   _____

    c. If Ima finds the ring in the ground while digging on Anna's farm, is Ima entitled to the ring, as against Anna?   _____

    d. Ima finds the ring on the floor of Anna's shop. She gives the ring to Anna to look at and Anna refuses to give it back. Is Ima entitled to the full value of the ring from Anna?   _____

    e. Suppose that Ima is adjudged to have better rights than Anna to the ring. Ima lends the ring to Natalie Attired. The ring is wrongfully taken from Natalie by Izzy Strong. Can Natalie recover the full value of the ring from Izzy?   _____

3. Jack hands his watch to the Ace Watch Repair Co. to repair, taking back a claim check. Jack puts the claim check in his law school locker, from which it is stolen by Paul. Paul presents the claim check to Ace and receives the watch. Is Ace liable to Jack?   _____

4. Professor Marcia Law says, "A person who by an innocent mistake takes a chattel belonging to another and improves it with her labor is entitled to ownership of the chattel, but she must compensate the previous owner for the value of the chattel before improvement." Is this correct?   _____

5. Alita occupies Greenacre in the belief that it is Brownacre, which she has purchased from Bly. The statute of limitations for ejectment is 10 years.

    a. Is Alita's possession hostile for purposes of adverse possession?   _____

    b. If Alita occupies Greenacre for 3 years then "sells" it to Charlie, who occupies it for 7 years, is the owner barred from ejecting Charlie?   _____

6. David plants a hedge on what he believes to be the true boundary between his property and that of his neighbor, Ellen. In fact the hedge is 20 feet inside Ellen's property. If David occupies the land inside the hedge for the requisite period of adverse possession, does he obtain title to the 20-foot strip?   _____

7. Without George's permission, Fanny occupies a lake cabin owned by George each summer for 21 years; the cabin is unoccupied during the remainder of the year. The statutory period for adverse possession is 20 years.

a. Does Fanny now have title to the cabin? _____

b. Would the result be the same if George occupied the cabin for 2 weeks each winter during this period? _____

8. Helen occupies Whiteacre openly, continuously, and hostilely to the true owner, Isaac, for 10 years. Thereafter she conveys the property to Jane, who occupies Whiteacre under the deed for 8 years. Jane leaves the property to move to Mexico, and Karl—learning of Jane's intentions from Jane's friend Lulu—moves in on the day of Jane's departure and continues in open, continuous, and hostile possession for 3 years.

a. If the statutory period for adverse possession is 20 years, does Karl have title to Whiteacre? _____

b. Would the result be different if Jane had told Karl of her departure and invited him to occupy Whiteacre? _____

9. Paul purports to convey a 40-acre tract of land, known in the community as "Birnham Woods," to Quincy. Paul does not own Birnham Woods. Birnham Woods is forest land, not occupied by anyone. Quincy occupies 15 of the 40 acres and continues in possession for the statutory period for adverse possession. Does Quincy have title to all the property described in the deed? _____

10. In each of the following cases is there a valid gift? Dolly, in bed ill and dying, is in a room with Bea and Sally.

a. Dolly says: "Sally, I want to give Bea my insurance policy in the bureau there, so please get it and give it to her." Sally, however, leaves the insurance policy where it is. Dolly dies. Does Bea own the policy? _____

b. Dolly says: "Bea, I want to give you my little jewelry box here on the table and the diamond ring and bracelet locked in it. Here is the key." Bea takes the key but the box stays where it is. Dolly dies. Does Bea own the diamond ring and bracelet? _____

c. Dolly says: "Sally, I want to give Bea my jewelry in this box when I die. Take the box and give it to Bea on my death, but if I change my mind, return the box to me." Sally takes the box and hides it in her house. Dolly dies without changing her mind. Does Bea own the jewelry in the box—

(1) if Sally is deemed to be Dolly's agent? _____

(2) if Sally is deemed to be a trustee? _____

d. Dolly says: "Bea, I want you to have the proceeds in my savings account; the passbook is in my safe deposit box." Dolly then gives Bea the key to the box. Is Bea entitled to the savings account on Dolly's death? _____

11. Are the following accurate statements of law?

a. The tenant of a freehold has seisin; the tenant of a nonfreehold estate does not hold seisin. _____

b. Words of purchase indicate that consideration has been paid for the property. _____

c. A future interest, unlike a present possessory interest, is not a presently existing interest. _____

12. Alice conveys Blackacre to Bob "so long as Blackacre is used for agricultural purposes."

   a. If Blackacre is used for industrial purposes, and the next day Bob conveys "to Carol and her heirs," does Alice have any rights against Carol? _____

   b. If the conveyance from Alice to Bob had concluded, "and if Blackacre is used for nonagricultural purposes, Alice has a right of entry," would Carol have a fee simple determinable? _____

13. In 1960, Kenneth conveys Blackacre to Liza "upon condition that Blackacre never be used for commercial purposes, and if it is so used, Kenneth has a right to reenter." Two years later, Matt, an adverse possessor, occupies the property and constructs a drive-in restaurant. The adverse possession period is 20 years.

   a. If Matt continues in possession until 1985, does he have good title against Kenneth? _____

   b. Would Matt have a good title against Kenneth if the conveyance had been "to Liza so long as Blackacre is not used for commercial purposes"? _____

14. Dot conveys Blackacre "to School Board so long as it uses the land for school purposes, then to Mercy Hospital."

   a. Does Mercy Hospital have a possibility of reverter? _____

   b. Suppose there were no gift over to Mercy Hospital. After the conveyance Dot conveys her interest in Blackacre to Errol. Does Errol have a possibility of reverter? _____

   c. Suppose the conveyance had been "to School Board, but if it ceases to use the land for school purposes, Dot has a right to reenter." Subsequent to the conveyance Dot conveys her right of entry to Errol. Does Errol have a right of entry? _____

15. Harry devises property "to my wife Ida so long as she does not marry, and if she does marry, to Jack." If Ida marries, will she lose the property? _____

16. Ned devises Brownacre "to Olivia and the heirs of her body."

   a. At common law, would this create a fee tail in Olivia, which Olivia could devise to her oldest child, cutting out her other children? _____

   b. Under modern law, can Olivia convey a fee simple absolute in Brownacre? _____

   c. If the devise had been "to Olivia and the heirs of her body, but if she dies without surviving issue to Penelope and her heirs," can Olivia convey a fee simple absolute today? _____

17. Indicate whether each of the following acts would probably constitute waste by a life tenant.

   a. Life tenant replaces outmoded pipes with the same type of tubing, even though improved pipes are available at the same cost. _____

   b. Life tenant plows under a vineyard and converts the property to industrial use, substantially increasing the value of the property. _____

18. Yogi devises his summer cabin "to Zeta, but if Zeta attempts to transfer the property without the consent of Rock, then to Susan." Zeta subsequently sells the cabin without Rock's consent.

    a.   Is Zeta's conveyance valid?

    b.   Would the result be the same if a condominium were involved, and the consent of the condominium board of directors were required?

19. Addie, owner of Blackacre, conveys Blackacre to Bill for life. Bill subsequently leases Blackacre to Casey for a 25-year term, which is greater than Bill's life expectancy.

    a.   Do Addie and Bill have reversions in Blackacre?

    b.   Will Casey's leasehold continue if Bill dies within the 25-year period?

20. Rhoda conveys Whiteacre "to Arnie for life, then to Bob and his heirs, but if Bob dies before Arnie, to Arnie's children who survive Arnie and their heirs." Arnie has a child, Carolyn. No other child is born to Arnie. Bob dies intestate. Carolyn dies intestate. Then Arnie dies. Does Rhoda own Whiteacre?

21. Grace conveys her house "to Henry for life, then to Irene, but if Irene predeceases Henry, then to Irene's children who survive Henry." Irene has one child, Jill, alive.

    a.   Does Irene have a contingent remainder?

    b.   Does Jill have a contingent remainder?

    c.   Suppose the conveyance were "to Henry for life, remainder to Irene's heirs." Irene is alive. Do Irene's heirs have a vested remainder?

22. Karen devises property "to Lloyd for life, then to Lloyd's children, and if Lloyd dies without children surviving him, to Marvin." At Karen's death, Lloyd has a son, Norman, alive.

    a.   Does Norman have a vested remainder?

    b.   Does Marvin have a contingent remainder?

    c.   Suppose Karen had devised the property "to Lloyd for life, then to Lloyd's children who survive Lloyd, and if Lloyd dies without children surviving him, to Marvin." Does Marvin have a contingent remainder?

    d.   Suppose that Marvin dies while Lloyd and Norman are alive. Is Marvin's interest destroyed?

23. Rose conveys Greenacre "to my husband Sam for life, remainder to my children and their heirs." At the time of the conveyance Rose has no children, and before any are born Rose transfers to Sam "all my right, title, and interest in Greenacre." The jurisdiction has not abolished destructibility of contingent remainders.

    a.   Do Rose's children have any interest in Greenacre?

    b.   Would the result be different if Rose had a child, Toby, when the conveyance was made?

    c.   If Rose had no child, would Rose's unborn children have any interest in the land if the jurisdiction has abolished destructibility of contingent remainders?

24. Ottilie conveys Whiteacre "to Xavier for the life of Portia in trust to pay the income to Portia, and upon Portia's death to convey the principal to Portia's heirs." The jurisdiction applies the Rule in Shelley's Case.

    a. Does the Rule in Shelley's Case apply? _____

    b. Would the result be different if the conveyance were "to Xavier in trust to pay the income to Portia, and upon her death to convey the principal to Portia's heirs"? _____

25. Quinn conveys property "to Xavier in trust for Quinn for life, then to the heirs of Quinn." Subsequently Quinn seeks to terminate the trust, alleging that he owns all the equitable interest in the trust, is also the settlor, and therefore can terminate the trust. Can Quinn terminate the trust? _____

26. Eunice conveys Whiteacre to Veronica and her heirs at such time as Veronica "becomes a lawyer." Veronica is aged 2.

    a. Prior to the Statute of Uses (1536), would Veronica have a legal interest in Whiteacre? _____

    b. Would the result be different after the Statute of Uses? _____

    c. Suppose the conveyance after the Statute of Uses had been "to Winston and his heirs, but at such time as Veronica becomes a lawyer, to Veronica and her heirs." Does Veronica have any interest in Whiteacre? _____

27. Do any of the following devises violate the Rule Against Perpetuities?

    a. T devises property "to the first child of A to become a lawyer." A's eldest child, B, is in law school. _____

    b. T devises property "to A for life, then to A's children who reach 25." A has no children living. _____

    c. T devises land "to Library Board, but when it ceases to use the land for a library to A and his heirs." _____

    d. T devises land "to Library Board so long as used for library purposes, then to A and his heirs." _____

    e. T devises property "to A for life, then to A's widow for life, then to A's issue." _____

    f. T devises property "to A for life, then to A's widow for life, then to A's children." _____

28. Ann conveys Blackacre "to Ann, Ben, and Celia as joint tenants."

    a. Would this create a joint tenancy between the three at common law? _____

    b. Would this create a joint tenancy between Ben and Celia at common law? _____

    c. If Ben died, would Ann and Celia hold equal shares as tenants in common? _____

    d. Would the conveyance create a joint tenancy under modern law if the conveyance were "to Ann, Ben, and Celia"? _____

29. Don conveys Blackacre to Estelle, Fred, and Grant as joint tenants.

    a. Thereafter Estelle dies, devising to Harvey "all my interest" in Blackacre. Does Harvey take Estelle's interest? _____

b. If thereafter Fred mortgages his interest in the property, then dies, does Grant hold Fred's share? _____

c. Suppose prior to his death, Fred's creditor sued him for breach of contract and obtained judgment against Fred. Before the creditor takes any other action, Fred dies. Is the creditor entitled to levy upon and sell Fred's interest? _____

30. Minna Skewel and Millie Grazie buy property together, taking title "as joint tenants with right of survivorship." Minna contributes two-thirds of the purchase price.

a. Has a joint tenancy been created? _____

b. If Minna brings an action in partition, is she entitled to two-thirds of the selling price? _____

31. Sally Forth devises lakefront property to her daughter Marian Haste and Marian's husband Art Fuldodger, as tenants by the entirety. Thereafter Art accumulates substantial debts. Can Art's creditors reach the lakefront property to satisfy the debts? _____

32. Nina and Orlando purchase several hundred acres of farmland as tenants in common. Nina remains in the city and conducts her law practice while Orlando moves onto the land, cultivates it, and produces a crop which he sells.

a. Is Nina entitled to a share in the sales proceeds? _____

b. Is Nina entitled to one-half the fair rental value of the farm? _____

c. Would your answer to b. be different if Orlando had rented the land to Peter, who farmed it and paid $100 rent to Orlando? _____

d. Suppose Orlando discovers a uranium deposit under the farm, whereupon he excavates the ore and sells it. Is he liable to Nina for a portion of the sales proceeds? _____

e. Can Orlando obtain a contribution from Nina for his costs in improving and enlarging various buildings upon the property? _____

33. Steven purchases Lazy Acres while married to Tricia. Subsequently Steven sells Lazy Acres to Uranus, a bona fide purchaser with no knowledge that Steven is married. Then Steven dies. The jurisdiction has common law dower.

a. Does Tricia have dower in Lazy Acres? _____

b. Suppose Steven had not sold Lazy Acres. Under a statutory elective share would Tricia's interest be greater than her dower interest? _____

34. Frances purchases stock in a cooperative apartment house and leases an apartment in the building. When she attempts to do calisthenics in the morning, the directors inform her that no prolonged jumping or running is permitted in the apartment.

a. If Frances continues her exercises, can her lease be terminated? _____

b. Suppose Frances decides to sell her stock and lease to Gary. The corporation rules provide that a tenant cannot assign her stock or lease without approval of the directors. If the directors refuse to consent to the assignment, with no evidence of illegal discrimination, can Frances obtain judicial review of their decision? _____

35. Bjorn leases space in a shopping center to Clark for 100 years.

a. At common law is this a valid lease? _____

b. Would the result be different if the lease to Clark were "until the war is over"? _____

c. Would the result be different if the lease were an oral lease for two years, and Clark occupied the space after paying one month's rent? _____

36. Delia rents an apartment to Eliza "at a rental of $250 per month payable on the 15th."

a. Does this create a month-to-month tenancy? _____

b. Suppose Delia decides to terminate Eliza's lease and on April 17th notifies Eliza to quit the premises on May 17th. Can Delia require Eliza to vacate the premises on May 17th? _____

37. L leases an office to T from year to year. At the end of the second year, T moves out without giving L any notice. Can L hold T for another year's rent? _____

38. L leases land to T "for as long as T may desire."

a. Does this create a tenancy at will? _____

b. Would the result be different if the lease were to T "for as long as L may desire"? _____

c. Can T assign the lease to A? _____

39. L leases his farm to T for 5 years. When the 5-year period expires, T remains on the farm.

a. Can L elect to treat T as a tenant for a further 5-year period? _____

b. Must L give T notice before evicting him from the farm? _____

40. L places a sign in the window of her home, advertising a basement apartment for rent. A, a black student, asks to rent the apartment but L refuses to do so because of A's color.

a. Can A obtain damages or injunctive relief against L? _____

b. Would the result be different if L refused to rent to A because A was a woman? _____

41. L leases a warehouse to T. Shortly after T moves in, L informs T that L plans to use a 10 square foot area in one corner of the building for his own storage and proceeds to close off this area.

a. Does T's obligation to pay rent thereby abate? _____

b. Would the result be different if the corner space were occupied by a third party, B, under a valid claim of title to the building? _____

42. L rents an apartment to T. When T occupies the apartment, T discovers that he is temporarily without hot water while the water heater is being repaired.

a. Can T move out and refuse to pay rent, on grounds of constructive eviction? _____

b. Assuming T claims constructive eviction, can T remain in the apartment and claim an offset against rent for the lack of hot water? _____

c. Would the result be different if the absence of hot water were a chronic problem and T claimed a breach by L of his duty to provide habitable quarters?

43. After occupying the apartment for several months, T discovers shorts in several electrical outlets. The lease does not expressly require L to make repairs on the apartment.

   a. Can T obtain an injunction requiring L to repair the faulty wiring?

   b. Can T elect either to make the repairs herself and deduct them from the rent, or to have the rent reduced to the fair market value of the premises "as is"?

   c. Would the result be the same in most courts if the lease contained an express waiver by T of any rights against L for failure to make repairs?

   d. Suppose T is a month-to-month tenant and reports the violation of the housing code to public authorities. L thereupon sues to evict T. Assuming L gave T the requisite notice to quit, does T have any defense to the action?

44. L rents an apartment to T. The first night on the premises, T steps out on the balcony, the balcony collapses, and T is injured.

   a. Is L liable to T in tort under common law rules?

   b. Would the result be different if it were T's girlfriend, A, who was injured?

   c. Is L liable to T in tort if there is an implied warranty of habitability?

45. L rents to T a warehouse for storage of high explosives.

   a. Shortly after the lease is signed, a substantial part of the warehouse is destroyed by a tornado. Will this terminate the lease?

   b. Would the lease be terminated if, sometime after signing, the area were rezoned so as to prohibit storage of high explosives?

   c. Suppose that the lease is terminated and T wants to remove special fireproof divider panels in the warehouse which T has installed. Can T remove them?

46. L rents her house on a month-to-month tenancy to T, who moves his furnishings and other belongings onto the premises. T pays his rent during the first three months, but fails to pay in the fourth month.

   a. Can L thereupon enter the house and seize T's belongings to hold until the rent is paid?

   b. If the rental agreement required T to pay two months' rent in advance as a security deposit, can L retain this amount when T fails to pay the fourth month's rent?

   c. Can L enter the house and forcibly eject T?

   d. Suppose L brings an unlawful detainer action against T. Can T defend on the ground that L has violated an implied covenant to repair, for which T has spent the rental owed?

47. L leases an office to T for 3 years, with rent payable on a monthly basis. The terms of the agreement provide that the breach of any covenant therein by T allows L to declare a forfeiture. T fails to pay rent during the term of the lease.

a. If L declares a forfeiture, is T liable for the remaining rent for the term (as well as arrearages)? _____

b. If T abandons the office after one year, can L leave the office vacant and sue T for rentals due? _____

48. L leases his summer cabin to T for 5 years. After one year T transfers her entire interest in the cabin to A, who pays no rent to L.

a. Can L sue either T or A for the rent due? _____

b. Would the result be different if T had transferred possession to A for 3 years? _____

c. Would L be able to sue A if T had transferred possession to A for 3 years and A assumed all the covenants in the L-T lease? _____

d. Is T's 3-year transfer to A invalid if the L-T lease contains a covenant not to assign? _____

49. Professor Claire Voyant tells her students that "affirmative easements are much more widely recognized than negative easements, which are usually limited to those recognized in early English law."

a. Is Professor Voyant correct? _____

b. Voyant also comments that "in doubtful cases, courts incline toward finding an easement to be in gross rather than appurtenant, because an easement in gross benefits the owner personally." Is this an accurate statement? _____

50. Arlene, owner of two adjoining lots, Lots 1 and 2, sells Lot 1 to Bill.

a. If the deed to Bill conveys "Lot 1, excepting the 15-foot strip thereof bordering Lot 2 to be used as an irrigation ditch by Arlene," would this probably be held to except a fee rather than an easement? _____

b. Would the result be different if the deed had reserved the 15-foot strip for an irrigation ditch to be used by Cary (another adjacent landowner)? _____

c. Suppose that Lot 2 is situated on higher ground than Lot 1. If the deed is silent on the subject, can Arlene claim drainage rights across Bill's property? _____

d. Prior to the sale of Lot 1, Arlene constructs an access road from Lot 2 to the public highway; part of the access road crosses a corner of Lot 1. If the deed to Bill makes no mention of the road, does Arlene continue to have an easement across Lot 1? _____

e. Would the results in c. or d. be different if Bill conveys Lot 1 to Dolly? _____

51. Earl purchases Greenacre from Felicia, who tells Earl that there is a path across adjoining property to a public park (which Felicia has been using for 15 years).

a. If Earl continues to use the path for an additional 5 years, and the period of limitations is 20 years, does he acquire an easement to reach the park? _____

b. Would the result be different if the owner of the adjacent property posts a "no trespassing" sign at the boundary of Greenacre? _____

c. Would the result be different if Greenacre were landlocked after being separated from the adjoining property, and the path gave it access to a public road? _____

52. In his deed to Blackacre, Garland is given an easement across the adjoining land of the grantor, Herman, "for right of way purposes." Garland proceeds to construct a factory on Blackacre and moves trucks in and out over Herman's land 24 hours a day.

    a.   Can Herman enjoin such travel over his property? _____

    b.   Suppose that Herman grants Garland the use of an existing road across his property as an express easement. Garland constructs buildings on Blackacre to make use of the road. Herman later decides to build on the existing right of way. Can he move the road elsewhere on the property? _____

    c.   If Garland sells Blackacre to Irene, does Irene have an easement across Herman's property? _____

    d.   If Herman gives Joe an easement to maintain a billboard on Herman's property, can Joe assign it? _____

53. Shirley Eugeste is granted the right to use an access road across Romana Clay's land to reach a public street. If Shirley fails to use the road for 20 years, is her easement extinguished? _____

54. Opal agrees with Peter that Opal will sell all timber cut on her land to Peter, although Peter is free to purchase from others as well. Is this a covenant in gross as to both Opal and Peter? _____

55. Professor Polly Onymous notes that "a primary difference between a real covenant and an equitable servitude is that the remedy for breach of a real covenant is damages and the remedy for breach of an equitable servitude is an injunction." Is this correct? _____

56. Quick covenants with his neighbor, Ralph, not to remove trees on the common boundary of their properties unless Ralph agrees thereto. Thereafter Quick sells the property to Tricia, who uproots the trees. Can Ralph sue Tricia for damages? _____

57. Uriah sells Blackacre to Victor, and Victor covenants not to use the property for commercial purposes of any kind. Victor later conveys a life estate in Blackacre to Wayne, who enters upon the property and commences a truck farm operation.

    a.   Can Uriah sue Wayne for damages? _____

    b.   If Wayne had occupied Blackacre as an adverse possessor, would Uriah be able to get damages from him? _____

58. Yetta grants Zelda an easement of way across Yetta's property in town and Zelda covenants to keep the right of way in good repair.

    a.   If Yetta never uses the road, can her assigns enforce the covenant against Zelda? _____

    b.   Would the result be the same if Zelda had covenanted instead to keep Yetta's mountain cabin in good repair? _____

59. Anthony, a restaurant owner, contracts with Bolla Co. to use only Bolla products on the premises. Anthony then sells the restaurant to Catherine, who knows of the contract.

    a.   In the majority of courts, can Bolla enjoin Catherine from using a competitor's products? _____

    b.   Assuming the burden of the covenant runs, can Anthony be held liable for Catherine's refusal to purchase Bolla products? _____

60. Delta Land Co. develops a tract of 300 lots, called Washington Park. In the first 280 deeds, the grantees all agree to use their lots for single-family dwellings only, and Delta's representatives assure each grantee that Washington Park will be developed only for residential single-family dwellings. Erin, who has notice of the prior deeds, offers to purchase the remaining 20 lots at a premium price to erect an apartment complex.

   a. If Delta conveys the lots to Erin with no covenants, can the neighbors prevent Erin from building the apartment houses?

   b. Suppose the earlier 280 deeds had also contained a promise by each grantee to plant trees on his lot, and Delta had conveyed the final 20 lots to Erin without a covenant. Can Erin be compelled to plant trees on her property?

   c. Suppose Erin's deed had contained an express covenant not to build multi-family housing, but Erin nevertheless files plans to construct an apartment house. Can the prior grantees enjoin the contruction in most courts?

   d. Would the result in a. and c. be different if Delta had reserved the right to modify restrictions as to each lot?

61. Sherry D. Cantor, a residential developer of a large parcel called Eden Acres, sells Lot 1 to Phyllis Teen. In the deed of Lot 1 Phyllis promises (i) that she will use the property for residential purposes only, (ii) that she will build a fence 6 feet in height along her side boundaries, and (iii) that she will pay the Eden Acres Property Owners Association $100 a year to maintain a swimming pool for use of all buyers into Eden Acres. These covenants are stated in the deed to be covenants running with land, binding upon assignees, and enforceable by other owners in Eden Acres and the Property Owners Association. Sherry sells Lot 2 to Maude Lynn, and the remaining lots to other purchasers. The deeds to all the other parcels contain covenants identical to those in Lot 1. Subsequently Phyllis sells Lot 1 to Coco Vann. Coco, who is in the chicken business, plans to build a chicken ranch on Lot 1, and she refuses to build the side fences and to pay the $100 a year assessment.

   a. If Coco builds the chicken ranch, can Maude recover damages from Coco?

   b. In most states is Maude entitled to an injunction compelling Coco to build the fences?

   c. If the deed to Lot 1 creates a lien against the lot to enforce the covenant to pay money, can the Property Owners Association enforce the lien against Coco in states that define privity of estate as a mutual relationship?

62. James, a developer, sells all 50 lots in a residential tract to grantees, each deed containing a covenant to use the property only for residential purposes. Houses are erected on most lots. Kerry, one of the grantees, now wants to construct a store on his lot.

   a. If property adjacent to Kerry's lot outside the subdivision is being used for commercial purposes, can a neighbor in the subdivision enjoin construction of the store?

   b. Would the result be the same if Kerry's lot were zoned for commercial use?

63. Maggie is a hog farmer. Nigel, a neighboring homeowner, objects to the odor and noise from the hogs.

   a. If keeping hogs is permitted under the local zoning ordinance, does Maggie have a defense to a nuisance action?

b.   If Maggie were raising hogs when Nigel first purchased his property, would Maggie have a defense? _____

c.   Could Ophelia seek relief from the nuisance if she were a relative house-sitting for Nigel? _____

64.   Bella Kose sues to enjoin Qua Corporation, a nearby industrial plant, from polluting the air with soot and noxious gas.

a.   Will the importance of Qua Corp. to the community be considered in a nuisance action? _____

b.   If Bella is denied an injunction, is it possible for her to obtain damages from Qua Corp.? _____

c.   If Bella is denied an injunction, but awarded damages, has she received a share of the "gains from trade"? _____

65.   Theo conveys one-half of Whiteacre to Underground Explorers, Inc., which proceeds to excavate a fish pond near the border of Theo's property.

a.   If the fish pond causes Theo's surface soil to subside, is Underground Explorers liable for damages? _____

b.   Would the result probably be different if Theo had a house bordering the fish pond, which collapsed when the pond was excavated? _____

c.   Suppose Theo grants Underground Explorers the right to remove minerals from Theo's portion of Whiteacre. Underground Explorers does so, and in the process negligently pollutes a well on the property. Is Underground Explorers liable to Theo? _____

66.   Victoria Farms owns a parcel of land adjacent to Running River. May Victoria Farms properly take river water to irrigate its farmland that is not adjacent to the river and does not adjoin the parcel on the river? _____

67.   Willie owns Greenacre, which is at a lower elevation than the surrounding property. In order to prevent flooding, Willie constructs a dike which diverts surface runoff onto the adjacent land. In a state following the common enemy doctrine, can the adjoining property owners recover from Willie for damage to their land? _____

68.   Axel is a homeowner in Main Street, U.S.A. The Main Street City Council passes a zoning ordinance permitting 3 types of "nonobjectionable" commercial use (a nursery school, a liquor store, and a bank) in a residential area where Axel's property is located.

a.   If Axel sues to challenge the validity of the ordinance must Axel bear the burden of proving it invalid? _____

b.   Can Axel successfully challenge the ordinance as an uncompensated "taking" of his property? _____

c.   Suppose that Barry, who operates a funeral parlor and would like to locate in a residential district, challenges the ordinance as a denial of equal protection. Must the city show that the ordinance promotes a compelling state interest? _____

69.   Scenic City has an ordinance requiring approval of all proposed construction by a board of architects, in order to insure that no ugly buildings are built. Dan's proposed building plan is rejected, and he challenges the ordinance as unconstitutional.

a. If the ordinance provides that the board may refuse a building permit to a building "not conforming to the character of the neighborhood," will Dan probably prevail? _____

b. Scenic City also has an ordinance providing that historic buildings cannot be torn down. Is this constitutional? _____

c. Emma, a real estate developer, plans to build a subdivision in the city. Can the city council require that Emma dedicate certain space for a public playground within the subdivision? _____

70. Snob Hills, a suburb next to Big City, has an ordinance that excludes apartments from the city and an ordinance that requires a minimum lot size of 5 acres in all residential areas. Lolly Gagging wants to erect apartments and erect single-family homes on one-half acre lots.

a. Is the exclusion of apartments constitutional? _____

b. Is the 5-acre requirement constitutional? _____

c. If Lolly is a developer who lives in Big City, who has no present plans to build in Snob Hills and owns no land there, but is looking to the future, can Lolly sue Snob Hills in federal court? _____

71. Crystal operates a meat market in Tiny Township. A zoning ordinance is passed which prevents any commercial use of property in the area where Crystal's market is located. The ordinance provides that any existing commerical use must be terminated within 30 days.

a. Must Crystal move within 30 days? _____

b. Can Crystal succeed in an action for inverse condemnation? _____

72. Big City amends its zoning map so as to reclassify Gentry's land, previously in a residential district, to a light industry zone.

a. Can Hattie, Gentry's neighbor, enjoin the amendment if it does not conform to Big City's master plan? _____

b. If Hattie brings suit, does Big City have the burden of proof? _____

73. Ike owns a lot in Star Pines; the zoning ordinance permits construction only upon the 50 percent of each parcel farthest from the street. Ike's lot has drainage problems making construction away from the street extremely expensive.

a. Is it possible for Ike to get a permit to build closer to the street? _____

b. Would the result be different if many lots in the area had the same problem? _____

c. If the city agreed to let Ike build closer to the street on condition that Ike dedicate 10 feet to the city for street widening, would this be constitutional? _____

74. Kelly owns Blackacre, a tract in the country.

a. If the government takes one foot of Blackacre, must it pay Kelly for damage to the remainder? _____

b. If the state prohibits the use of Blackacre for any use except as a public park, is the state liable in inverse condemnation? _____

c. Suppose Blackacre is wetlands, and the state prohibits development. Is the state liable in inverse condemnation? _____

75. Lyle owns Whiteacre, located in Greenville. The Greenville city council decides Greenville needs a McDonald's, and Whiteacre is just the place for it. The city brings an action to condemn Whiteacre for the purpose of reselling it to McDonald's, which plans to build a hamburger emporium on the land. Can Lyle enjoin the city's action? _____

76. Nina owns Greenacre, which is prime agricultural land at the edge of suburbia; it has great potential for development. For agricultural use only the land is worth $100 an acre; for subdivision use, $500 an acre. The land is presently zoned for agricultural use. The county condemns two acres of Greenacre for a fire station. It argues that it should pay Nina $200, and not $1,000, because the government could destroy the $800 difference by refusing to rezone Blackacre. Is this sound? _____

77. Louise executes a written contract to sell her apartment house to Martin, with title to pass upon closing in 60 days.

a. The contract calls for Martin to tender the purchase price on September 14. Martin submits the price on September 15. Can Martin enforce the contract? _____

b. If the contract makes no provision therefor, is there a warranty that Louise will convey marketable title to Martin? _____

c. Prior to closing Martin discovers that Nick is the record owner of the property but that Louise can prove title by adverse possession. Can Martin cancel the escrow? _____

d. Suppose Martin discovers that the apartment has been constructed with insufficient sewer outlets, in violation of local building codes, and that legal action has begun regarding this violation. Can Martin back out of the deal? _____

78. Orville contracts to sell Woodacre to Paula. On the date of closing, Paula tenders the purchase price but Orville refuses to convey the property and further discloses that the land is subject to an easement held by the Quashee Co., an adjoining landowner.

a. Can Paula obtain specific performance of the agreement? _____

b. If Orville tenders title to the property subject to the easement of Quashee Co., but Paula refuses to pay the purchase price, can Orville compel specific performance of the contract? _____

c. Suppose that by the date of closing the title to Woodacre is found to be held by Ross rather than Orville. Between the date of contract of sale and date of closing, the property has increased $50,000 in value. If Orville did not know that title was in Ross, is Paula entitled to $50,000 in damages? _____

79. Wendy contracts to sell her house to Yuri. Shortly before closing, the house is destroyed by flood.

a. Assuming Yuri has not yet occupied the house, can Wendy obtain specific performance of the contract? _____

b. If Wendy has insurance on the property, must she credit the proceeds against the purchase price if the buyer bears the risk of loss and Wendy obtains specific performance? _____

80. In return for $5,000 Felix gives Gary a 30-day option to purchase an office building which Felix owns. Felix dies 4 days later, leaving a will which devises all of his real property to Herbie and the remainder of his estate to Iris. If Gary decides to exercise the option, is Iris entitled to the purchase price?

81. Professor Vera Similitude states that acknowledgment or attestation of a deed is not required to make it effective, but should be done wherever possible. Is she correct? _____

82. Sarah Yayvo conveys Blackacre to "the heirs of my deceased friend, Ferdinand Hapsburg." Is this a valid deed? _____

83. Juan conveys to Geoffrey "that portion of Whiteacre bounded on the south by the fire road."

    a.   If Juan also owns the land over which the fire road runs, does Geoffrey have title to any portion of the road? _____

    b.   Would the result be different if the grantor were a municipality? _____

    c.   Would the result be different if Juan had conveyed "that portion of Whiteacre extending 500 yards south from the south edge of the fire road"? _____

84. Helen Highwater prepares a deed of her house to Moira Less and has the deed recorded. She does not hand over the deed to Moira.

    a.   Will this, without more, establish delivery of the deed to Moira? _____

    b.   Can Helen introduce evidence that, despite recording the deed, she had no intent to make a present transfer to Moira? _____

85. Norma executes a deed conveying Blackacre to Omar, "upon condition that title pass next January 10th."

    a.   If Norma hands the deed to Omar, has there been a valid delivery? _____

    b.   Would the result probably be the same if the condition were stated orally by Norma when she handed the deed to Omar? _____

86. Pierre executes a deed conveying Whiteacre to Quintin and hands the deed to Quintin's friend, Robin, with instructions to give the deed to Quintin. Can Pierre recall the deed before Robin gives it to Quintin? _____

87. On July 1, pursuant to an oral contract of sale, Scott hands Tamar a deed naming Unity as grantee of his ski cabin and orally instructs Tamar to give the deed to Unity "if Unity pays $5,000 before October 30."

    a.   On August 1, Scott seeks to recall the deed so that he can sell the cabin to Virginia. Can he do so? _____

    b.   Suppose that on July 10, Unity steals the deed from Tamar and sells the cabin to Walter, a bona fide purchaser. Does title pass to Walter? _____

88. Liza conveys her farm, Possum Acres, to Meta by a general warranty deed. Unknown to the parties, Liza's title to the property was defective at the time she acquired it.

    a.   Is Liza liable to Meta for the defect? _____

    b.   Would the result be different if the conveyance were by a special warranty or quitclaim deed? _____

c. If the soil on Possum Acres is no longer arable, is Liza liable to Meta under the warranty deed? _____

89. Ned purports to convey his house in fee simple to Olive, but Ned actually is a life tenant of the property. Olive occupies the house for 20 years until her death, devising the house to Phil.

   a. Can Phil sue Ned for breach of covenant? _____

   b. Would the result be different if Ned had a fee simple title to the house, but it was subject to a mortgage? _____

   c. In either case, would Ned be liable if Olive knew of the title defects and sued promptly? _____

   d. Suppose that Quinn brings a quiet title action against Phil, establishes paramount title to the house, and ejects Phil. Can Phil sue Ned for breach of covenant? _____

90. Mario sells Blackacre to Eduardo, giving him a general warranty deed. Eduardo is subsequently evicted by Alicia in a quiet title action.

   a. If Eduardo successfully sues Mario for a breach of a covenant of quiet enjoyment, can Eduardo recover the amount he paid for Blackacre? _____

   b. Assuming Eduardo made improvements to Blackacre, can Eduardo recover the fair market value of the property at the time of eviction if it exceeds the purchase price paid? _____

91. Fay conveys her truck farm to Gladys as a gift, but Gladys does not record the deed. Fay dies intestate, and her heirs sell the truck farm to Homer, a bona fide purchaser without notice of the gift to Gladys.

   a. If Homer records immediately, will he prevail over Gladys in a quiet title action? _____

   b. Would the result be different in a "notice" state, if Homer likewise had failed to record? _____

   c. Would the result be different if Fay's heirs conveyed the property to Homer as a gift? _____

   d. If Fay's heirs had decided instead to keep the farm, would they prevail over Gladys in a quiet title suit? _____

92. Isaiah conveys Blackacre to John on June 1, and John records on June 15. On June 10, Isaiah conveys Blackacre to Kathy, a bona fide purchaser without knowledge of the deed to John. Kathy records on June 18.

   a. Will John prevail over Kathy in a "notice" jurisdiction? _____

   b. Will John prevail over Kathy in a "race-notice" or "race" jurisdiction? _____

93. Lucy is the grantee of property under a deed from Manuel, who had previously conveyed the same land to Nellie.

   a. If Manuel tells Lucy that he previously conveyed to Nellie, but that Nellie's title is unenforceable because not recorded, does this prevent Lucy from being a subsequent BFP? _____

b.   Would the result be the same if Manuel had told Lucy nothing, but Nellie had moved onto the property?   _____

c.   Suppose Manuel had deeded the property to Lucy as security for a preexisting debt he owed Lucy. Would Lucy be a BFP?   _____

d.   Would Lucy be a BFP if Lucy had obtained the property for less than its market value?   _____

94.   Olivia conveys Whiteacre to Pedro, who immediately presents the deed to the recorder for filing. Unknown to Pedro, the deed is not indexed under Olivia's name in the recorder's office. Olivia subsequently sells Whiteacre to Quincy, a bona fide purchaser.

a.   Will Pedro prevail over Quincy?   _____

b.   If Pedro's deed is properly recorded but contains no acknowledgment, will Pedro prevail over Quincy?   _____

95.   Ramon conveys Blackacre to Sarah, who does not record. Sarah conveys Blackacre to Tim, who promptly records his deed from Sarah. Ramon then conveys to Ursula, a BFP, who records. Does Ursula prevail over Tim?   _____

96.   Vincent resides on Whiteacre, which is owned by his father, Wilbur. Vincent deeds Whiteacre to Yvonne on March 10, and Yvonne records immediately. On March 25, Wilbur dies, devising Whiteacre to Vincent. Vincent then sells Whiteacre to Zachary, a BFP who knew nothing of the Vincent-Yvonne conveyance.

a.   In most states does Yvonne prevail over Zachary?   _____

b.   Would Yvonne prevail against Vincent if Vincent had not sold the property to Zachary?   _____

97.   On January 1, Abe mortgages Greenacre to Bob, who does not then record. On February 1, Abe mortgages Greenacre to Carol, who knows of Bob's mortgage. Carol records. Bob, learning of Carol's mortgage, records his mortgage on February 8. On March 1, Carol assigns her mortgage to Diana, a BFP. Does Diana prevail over Bob in most states?   _____

98.   Evelyn, the owner of adjoining hillside parcels 1 and 2, conveys the upper parcel, number 1, to Felipe with a covenant by Evelyn that she, her heirs and assigns will not use parcel 2 to obstruct the view that parcel 1 commands over parcel 2. Evelyn later conveys parcel 2 to Gene, without mention of any restriction. Does Gene take parcel 2 subject to Felipe's rights?   _____

99.   Harry conveys Brownacre to Iva, who registers title under the Torrens system. Thereafter Jerry enters the property and remains in adverse possession throughout the requisite 20-year period. Has Jerry established title to Brownacre?   _____

100.   Title Insurance Company insures title to Kenny's house in the amount of $50,000. Subsequently Kenny finds that his title is defective; the property is now worth $75,000. Can Kenny recover $50,000?   _____

ANSWERS TO REVIEW QUESTIONS

1.a. **YES**   The person who takes prior possession of the fox wins. A person must capture a wild animal, or mortally wound it, to take possession. [§6]

b. **YES**   Although Mabel captured the fox, and thus took possession, she lost possession when the fox escaped. [§13]

2.a. **NO**   The prior possessor wins. As against a guest, Anna has prior constructive possession of all objects in her home, even though unaware of them. [§27]

b. **PROBABLY NOT**   The ring has probably been mislaid by the owner intentionally placing it there. She has left it in the custody (possession) of the owner of the shop. [§32]

c. **NO**   Unless classified as treasure trove, property found under the surface of the soil is in the prior possession of the owner of the locus, even though the owner is unaware of it. A ring is not treasure trove. [§25]

d. **YES**   Anna is not in prior possession. The ring has been lost, not mislaid. [§§30-32]

e. **YES**   Izzy cannot assert the defense of jus tertii (*i.e.*, cannot claim that Ima, not Natalie, owns the ring and has the cause of action). Izzy must pay Natalie full damages. Because Natalie is a voluntary bailee, a recovery by Natalie bars a suit by Ima against Izzy. [§§49-51, 74]

3. **YES**   A voluntary bailee has strict liability for delivering the goods to the wrong person. [§84]

4. **NO**   The innocent improver acquires title only if there is so great a disparity between the original and improved values of the chattel that it would be unfair to award it to the owner. If the owner gets the chattel, the innocent improver may be awarded the value of her labor where an injustice would otherwise result. [§90]

5.a. **YES**   Even though acting on a mistaken belief, Alita has a good faith belief the land is hers and she intends to claim the land as her own. If she stays in possession long enough, she wins under either the objective or subjective test of claim of title. [§§118, 120-121]

b. **YES**   Charlie can tack Alita's possession on to his own if he is in privity of estate with Alita. Even though Alita had no color of title to Greenacre, voluntary transfer of ***possession*** of Greenacre by Alita to Charlie puts Charlie in privity of estate with Alita. Thus together they have held adversely for 10 years. [§148]

6.a. **SPLIT OF AUTHORITY**   Some courts say David is not an adverse possessor if he would not have occupied the 20-foot strip if he had known it was not his. If he would not have occupied it had he known of the mistake, he does not have a hostile intent. Most courts reject this subjective view of hostile intent, and find that David acted hostilely when, believing the 20-foot strip was his, he performed objective acts claiming ownership. [§§128-130]

7.a. **YES**   Fanny has title by adverse possession if summer occupancy is the use an average owner would make of the property, which appears to be true in this case. [§145]

b. **NO**   George's use tends to show that an average owner would use the property in the winter time (as well as in the summer). It also interrupts possession by the adverse possessor. Either will defeat Fanny's attempt to gain title by adverse possession. [§145]

8.a.	**NO**	Privity of estate is present between Helen and Jane, but not between Jane and Karl. Hence, Karl's possession cannot be tacked onto Jane's, and a new 20-year period begins with Karl's possession. [§§148, 149]
b.	**YES**	An oral, voluntary transfer of possession is sufficient for privity of estate and tacking between successive adverse possessors. Hence, a total of 21 years in possession by Helen, Jane, and Karl gives Karl title to the property. [§149]
9.	**YES**	Where possession is under color of title, the adverse possessor is deemed to occupy all of the land described in the instrument, provided the land described is viewed in the community as one tract, possession is taken of a significant part, and no one is in possession of the part not actually occupied. [§§164-165]
10.a.	**NO**	The insurance policy has not been delivered, either actually, constructively, or symbolically. [§§193, 200-201]
b.	**NO**	Constructive delivery (by a key) is not allowed when the object is capable of manual delivery. Dolly could easily hand over the box. [§202]
c.(1)	**NO**	A revocable escrow is invalid, because the donor has not surrendered control of the object. [§208]
(2)	**YES**	A revocable trust is valid. [§210]
d.	**YES**	Constructive delivery is allowed where a person is dying and is physically unable to go to the bank. [§202]
11.a.	**YES**	A person is seised of land only if he has a freehold estate in possession. [§275]
b.	**NO**	Words of purchase state the name of the person or persons who are given an estate by grant or devise. For example, in a grant "to A and her heirs," the words "to A" are words of purchase, the words "and her heirs" are words of limitation. [§282]
c.	**NO**	A future interest is a presently existing interest, but the holder is not entitled presently to possession. It can be passed by will or intestacy, and usually can be seized by creditors. [§285]
12.a.	**YES**	The fee simple determinable has ended, and Alice, as owner, has the right to possession. [§§318-319]
b.	**NO**	The deed can be construed as creating either a determinable fee or a fee simple subject to a right of entry. If construed as the former, the fee simple terminated upon industrial use. If construed as the latter, Carol has a fee simple subject to Alice's right of entry, which is now exercisable. [§332]
13.a.	**SPLIT OF AUTHORITY**	Some courts hold that the statute of limitations does not begin to run on Kenneth until he exercises his right of entry. Other courts hold the statute runs from the time of breach of condition. Also, the equitable doctrine of laches may run against Kenneth if his failure to assert his right would cause damage to Matt. [§336]
b.	**YES**	When the fee simple determinable ends in 1962, title automatically reverts to Kenneth. Since 1962 Matt has been an adverse possessor. [§§103, 324, 434]
14.a.	**NO**	A possibility of reverter cannot be created in a transferee. It is an interest retained by the *grantor* if created by deed, or retained by *testator's heirs* if created by a will. Mercy Hospital has an executory interest, which is not subject to the Rule Against Perpetuities because all interests in Blackacre are given to charities. [§§399, 435]

b.	**SPLIT OF AUTHORITY**	In most jurisdictions a possibility of reverter is alienable, but in some it is not. In the latter, the conveyance to Errol is void. [§§436-438]
c.	**SPLIT OF AUTHORITY**	Jurisdictions go three ways. In some, the right of entry is alienable (thus Errol has it). In others, the right of entry cannot be alienated (thus Dot still has it). In still others, the mere attempt to alienate the right of entry destroys it (thus the School Board has a fee simple absolute). [§§441-442]
15.	**DEPENDS**	If the *intent* of Harry is to give Ida support only until she marries and becomes supported by her second husband, the condition restraining marriage is valid. If the intent of Harry is to penalize Ida for marrying, the restraint is void and Ida has a fee simple absolute. A fee simple determinable upon remarriage has often been held indicative of an intent to support, not to penalize, and thus the restraint is probably valid. [§§337-338]
16.a.	**NO**	This would create a fee tail in Olivia, but she could not devise it by will. It was inherited under primogeniture by her eldest son (not eldest child, who might be a daughter). [§340]
b.	**SPLIT OF AUTHORITY**	In some states the fee tail remains, and the fee tail tenant can convey a fee simple absolute by deed. In other states, the language in Ned's will would create a fee simple in Olivia. But in still other states, the language in Ned's devise would create a life estate in Olivia, remainder to her issue. In these states Olivia could not convey a fee simple. [§§363-367]
c.	**SPLIT OF AUTHORITY**	Where the fee tail remains, Olivia can bar the entail and remainder in Penelope by conveying a fee simple. Where fee tail is abolished, Olivia can convey a fee simple absolute only in those states which construe the language in Ned's will as giving Olivia a fee simple absolute. [§§363-367]
17.a.	**NO**	Life tenant's obligation is to maintain the property, not to make permanent improvements. [§384]
b.	**DEPENDS**	This is voluntary waste, but since it is *ameliorative*, the holder of the remainder may not have an action for damages if the property value is increased and the grantor had no intent to pass the vineyard itself to the remainderman. Depends on grantor's intent. [§§386, 388]
18.a.	**YES**	The purported restraint on alienation is void, and Zeta can freely transfer the cabin to whomever he pleases. [§398]
b.	**NO**	A restraint on the transfer of a condominium unit is valid, provided it is not used to violate the Civil Rights Laws (i.e., to discriminate because of race, religion, or ethnic origin). [§§405-407]
19.a.	**YES**	Addie has a reversion, which becomes possessory upon Bill's death. Bill has a reversion, which becomes possessory, if at all, upon the expiration of 25 years within Bill's lifetime. [§§418, 428]
b.	**NO**	Bill cannot convey a larger estate than he has. Therefore, the leasehold will expire at Bill's death or after 25 years, whichever happens first. [§428]
20.	**NO**	Rhoda does not have a reversion in Whiteacre because a vested remainder in fee simple was given Bob. Since Bob was never divested, Bob's heirs now own Whiteacre. [§456]
21.a.	**NO**	Irene's interest is a vested remainder subject to divestment (i.e., by Irene's failing to survive Henry). [§§467-468]

b.	**NO**	Jill has an executory interest, which can become possessory only by *divesting* Irene's vested remainder. [§§424, 468]
c.	**NO**	Irene's heirs cannot be ascertained until her death. Hence the remainder is contingent because the takers are unascertained. [§477]
22.a.	**YES**	Norman's remainder is vested subject to open up and let in other children, and also subject to complete divestment if Lloyd dies without children surviving him. [§462]
b.	**NO**	Marvin has an executory interest because his interest can vest only by divesting Norman's vested remainder. [§§424, 468-469]
c.	**YES**	Marvin has a contingent remainder because his interest *can* become possessory *without divesting* anyone. If Norman had a vested remainder, as in the principal hypothetical, Marvin could take possession only by divesting Norman, and thus would have an executory interest. [§§424, 473]
d.	**NO**	Marvin's interest in both the principal hypothetical and in c. is transmissible at his death to his heirs. It is not contingent upon surviving anyone. [§471]
23.a.	**NO**	The children have a contingent remainder, which is destroyed by merger of Sam's life estate into Rose's reversion. [§494]
b.	**YES**	Toby has a vested remainder in fee simple subject to open. Rose has no reversion. A vested remainder cannot be destroyed by merger. [§§494, 504-505]
c.	**YES**	If destructibility of contingent remainders is abolished, Sam has the life estate and reversion, subject to the indestructible interest in Rose's children. If Rose has a child, that child will take the property on Sam's death. [§§511-512]
24.a.	**NO**	Portia's life estate is equitable; the remainder in Portia's heirs is legal. Hence the Rule does not apply. [§§514, 536]
b.	**YES**	Portia has an equitable life estate. Her heirs have an equitable remainder, which by the Rule in Shelley's Case is given to Portia. These merge and Portia has the equitable fee simple. [§536]
25.	**DEPENDS**	Under the Doctrine of Worthier Title, the remainder in Quinn's heirs is void, and Quinn has a reversion. If the Doctrine applies, Quinn has all the equitable interests in the trust and can terminate the trust. There is a rebuttable presumption that the Doctrine applies, but it can be overcome by contrary evidence of intent. In some states the Doctrine has been abolished. In these states Quinn cannot terminate the trust. [§§548, 551, 554]
26.a.	**NO**	Because Eunice has not made present livery of seisin to Veronica, Veronica has no legal freehold interest. Before 1536, a freehold could not be created at law to spring out in the future. [§§568, 570]
b.	**YES**	If, in the hundred or so years after the Statute of Uses, Eunice had used a feoffment to uses, a bargain and sale deed, or a covenant to stand seised, Veronica would have a legal *springing* executory interest that may divest the *transferor* (Eunice). Under modern law a springing executory interest can be created by any kind of deed. [§§581-582, 604]
c.	**YES**	Veronica has a *shifting* executory interest that may divest a *transferee* (Winston). [§583]

27.a. **YES**   The devise is void. B might die tomorrow, and the first child of A to become a lawyer might be an afterborn child. The first child of A to become a lawyer might become a lawyer more than 21 years after A's death. [§§606, 608]

b. **YES**   The devise to A's children is void. All of A's children will not necessarily reach age 25 within 21 years after A's death. A might die leaving a child under the age of 4. [§§608, 611]

c. **YES**   The executory interest to A violates the Rule because it might become possessory centuries hence. It is struck out. The Library Board has a fee simple absolute. [§623]

d. **YES**   The executory interest to A violates the Rule and is struck out. The Library Board has a determinable fee, and O has a possibility of reverter. [§620]

e. **YES**   The unborn widow case. The remainder in A's issue may vest at the death of A's widow, a woman not necessarily now alive. [§628]

f. **NO**   The remainder in A's children will *vest in interest*, if at all, at A's death. No children can be born to A after that time. (In e., above, the remainder to A's *issue* cannot vest in interest until the widow dies because the class of *issue* will not close until then. Remember: "children" includes only one generation; "issue" includes all descendants.) [§607]

28.a. **NO**   Because Ann had an interest in Blackacre when the conveyance took place, there is no unity of time and title between Ann and her co-tenants. [§§655-657]

b. **YES**   The common law presumed a joint tenancy so Ben and Celia take their two-thirds share as joint tenants between themselves; they hold with Ann as tenants in common. [§664]

c. **NO**   Celia would have Ben's one-third share plus her own, giving her two-thirds. Ann now holds one-third interest with Celia as tenants in common. [§652]

d. **NO**   Under modern law, the presumption is that a tenancy in common is created unless a joint tenancy is expressly stated (or in some states, unless an express right of survivorship is stated). [§666]

29.a. **NO**   The attempted testamentary disposition is ineffective; the surviving joint tenants have the whole, relieved of Estelle's participation. [§652]

b. **SPLIT OF AUTHORITY**   In "title theory" states, Fred has transferred title to his interest to the mortgagee, thus severing the joint tenancy. In "lien theory" states, Fred has given the mortgagee only a lien on his interest, and the joint tenancy is not severed. Fred owns Blackacre. (The lien states divide over whether Fred owns Blackacre subject to the mortgage or not.) [§§682-684]

c. **NO**   The judgment creditor must sever the joint tenancy during Fred's life in order to reach Fred's interest. To sever, the creditor must levy execution. (In some states severance does not occur until the judicial sale or until the redemption period expires.) [§710]

30.a. **YES**   Joint tenants must have equal shares. This is presumed by taking title as joint tenants, regardless of who pays the consideration. [§661]

b. **MAYBE**   Partition is an equitable proceeding, and the presumption that joint tenants are entitled to equal shares on partition can be overcome by evidence that Minna did not intend a gift to Millie and that this was a business venture. [§661]

31.	**SPLIT OF AUTHORITY**	In most states, the creditors of the husband cannot reach the property because the husband cannot alienate his interest without his wife's consent. In a few states, the husband's creditors can reach the husband's interest; however, they cannot deprive the wife of her interest in the property, including the right of survivorship. [§§708-710]
32.a.	**NO**	Nina is not entitled to share in the proceeds, nor is she liable for any net loss from farming. [§735]
b.	**SPLIT OF AUTHORITY**	In a majority of states, Nina is not entitled to one-half the reasonable rental value unless Orlando has ousted her (refused to admit her in possession). In a minority of states, Orlando must pay Nina one-half the reasonable rental value. [§§722-729]
c.	**YES**	Orlando must pay Nina one-half of any rent he receives from third parties. [§730]
d.	**YES**	Orlando must pay one-half the net amount received to Nina. [§§733-734]
e.	**NO**	A co-tenant cannot require other co-tenants to contribute for improvements to property. However, upon partition Orlando will receive whatever increase in value of the property is attributable to his improvements. [§744]
33.a.	**YES**	The dower attached immediately upon Steven's purchase of the land, and cannot be defeated by a subsequent transfer by Steven to a BFP. [§767]
b.	**YES**	The statutory elective share gives the surviving spouse a fractional share (usually one-half or one-third) in fee simple of property owned by the decedent spouse at death. Dower is only a *life estate* in one-third of Lazy Acres. [§781]
34.a.	**DEPENDS**	The corporation can establish reasonable rules of conduct, and terminate leases upon violation. If alternative facilities (gym, etc.) are available, and Frances is clearly disturbing surrounding tenants, the restriction may be reasonable. [§§875-876]
b.	**SPLIT OF AUTHORITY**	Some courts refuse to review a refusal to consent provided it is not based on discriminatory grounds. Others will review the reasonableness of the refusal. [§§870-872]
35.a.	**YES**	A lease at common law can be for any number of years. In some states, however, a maximum period is set by statute. If a lease exceeds this period, it is either void entirely or void as to the years in excess of those permitted. [§907]
b.	**NO**	Most courts would consider this a tenancy for years, even though the termination date is indefinite. This classification comes closest to carrying out the parties' intention. [§904]
c.	**YES**	The lease would be unenforceable as a tenancy for years because of failure to comply with the Statute of Frauds. However, Clark's entry plus payment of rent would create a *periodic* tenancy (the period being the same period for which rent is calculated in the invalid lease). [§§939, 944]
36.a.	**YES**	The period is determined by the rental period in the agreement. [§913]
b.	**NO**	By common law, the lease has to be terminated at the end of a rental period. However, statutes may give landlord or tenant the right to terminate on any day with 30 days' notice. [§§920-925]
37.	**YES**	A periodic tenant must give notice to terminate the tenancy. A tenant for a term does not have to give notice. [§§908, 923]

38.a.	**SPLIT OF AUTHORITY**	Some courts hold T has a life estate determinable upon T's death. Others say T is a tenant at will. [§§931-932]
b.	**YES**	This would probably create a tenancy at will, terminable by either L or T at any time. [§931]
c.	**NO**	A tenancy at will is personal, and any attempted assignment by the tenant terminates the tenancy. [§937]
39.a.	**NO**	Where the term exceeds one year, the tenant can be held over to a new term up to a maximum of one year. [§951]
b.	**NO**	Assuming there is a tenancy at sufferance (*i.e.,* no implied consent by L to holdover for a period), L can evict T without prior notice. [§948]
40.a.	**YES**	The 1968 Fair Housing Act exempts L from its terms ("Mrs. Murphy" exception), but the 1866 Civil Rights Act gives A relief. [§§958-961, 964-967]
b.	**YES**	The 1866 Civil Rights Act has no application to sex discrimination. [§959]
41.a.	**YES**	Actual eviction by L from any portion of the premises causes T's rent obligation to abate entirely while L occupies the corner space. [§995]
b.	**YES**	Here T's rent would only abate proportionately to the space occupied by B. T would remain liable for rent on the remainder of the building. [§997]
42.a.	**NO**	Since the lack of hot water is only temporary, there is probably insufficient interference with T's use and enjoyment to establish constructive eviction. The result would be contra if the problem occurred repeatedly or the delays were extended. [§§999, 1003]
b.	**NO**	The general rule is that T must vacate the premises before he can claim constructive eviction. [§1007]
c.	**YES**	In this situation, the absence of hot water could result in constructive eviction or breach of an implied covenant of habitability. If a breach of a covenant of habitability is found, T could elect to stay in the apartment and abate the rent. [§§1025, 1032]
43.a.	**NO**	If there is no express covenant to repair, T cannot compel L to make repairs. [§1042]
b.	**PROBABLY YES**	Modern cases give T the right to have her rent abated when the implied covenant of habitablility is breached. In some states, T can use a reasonable portion of the rent money to make repairs. [§§1055, 1061]
c.	**SPLIT OF AUTHORITY**	Some courts uphold a waiver, unless unconscionable or against public policy. (Waiver of electrical defects, which make house dangerous for habitation, might be against public policy.) Other courts hold a waiver of the implied covenant of habitability in urban residential leases is void. [§§1033-1035, 1066]
d.	**YES**	Recent cases and statutes give T a defense of retaliatory eviction—which may permit T to remain in the apartment until L can show sound business reasons for the eviction. [§§1063, 1078-1091]
44.a.	**DEPENDS**	If L knew or should have known of the defective balcony, and did not warn T, L is liable in tort. Otherwise T is not liable. [§§1095, 1098]

b.	**NO**	The trend of modern law is to extend L's tort duty to T's visitors as well as to T. [§1095]
c.	**DEPENDS**	Answer same as under a. above. Strict liability in tort is not imposed for violation of implied warranty, only reasonable care. [§1116]
45.a.	**YES**	Statutes in almost all states would permit termination by T unless the lease required him to make substantial repairs. [§§1134, 1141, 1165-1166]
b.	**DEPENDS**	If T cannot make any other reasonable use of the warehouse, and if the zoning change was unforeseeable, the lease may be terminated because of frustration of purpose. However, upon the particular facts, T may have assumed the risk. [§§1162-1163]
c.	**YES**	Under the modern trend, T has the right to remove such fixtures (and this might also be true under the earlier rule respecting "trade fixtures"). However, removal must occur within a reasonable time (if not prior to T's termination of the lease), and T must pay for any damage to the warehouse caused by the removal. [§1177]
46.a.	**NO**	Even where L has a statutory lien on such property, L must first obtain a court order before seizing. Any seizure without a court order is unconstitutional. [§§1182-1184]
b.	**NO**	L can retain only the amount necessary to cover rental due, costs of eviction, etc. [§1187]
c.	**NO**	A few states still permit such self-help remedies, but the growing trend is strongly contra, even where the lease provides that L can use self-help. [§§1217-1223]
d.	**YES**	Up until recent years, this defense was not permitted in unlawful detainer actions, but the modern cases permit this defense. [§§1207-1212]
47.a.	**NO**	Since forfeiture terminates the lease, T is not liable for future rent unless some other valid lease provision binds him to pay notwithstanding termination of the lease. [§§1200-1204]
b.	**SPLIT OF AUTHORITY**	The old rule is that L can do nothing. However, the modern trend is to require L to mitigate damages by reletting. [§§1228-1230]
48.a.	**YES**	L can sue T on the contract. L can sue A, assignee, because there is privity of estate between L and A. [§§1238-1240]
b.	**YES**	This is a sublease, not an assignment, and L can sue T but not A for the rent. A sublessee is not in privity of estate with L. [§§1241-1242]
c.	**YES**	L is a third party beneficiary of A's promise to T. [§1261]
d.	**NO**	Such a transfer is a sublease, and the covenant, strictly construed, only prohibits assignment. [§§1282-1283]
49.a.	**YES**	Negative easements are generally limited to the four common law types: light, air, support, and stream flow. But equitable servitudes, analogous to negative easements, are very common. [§§1304-1308]
b.	**NO**	Courts favor easements appurtenant because they benefit land and increase its economic value, and the owner of an easement appurtenant is more easily located than is the owner of an easement in gross. [§§1310, 1313, 1315]

50.a.	**NO**	Although the description of the strip is quite definite, indicating a fee simple, the deed says "to be used," indicating an easement. [§1333]
b.	**YES**	Most courts would not permit reservation of an easement in favor of a third party. A few courts would permit such an easement by reservation. [§§1338-1341]
c.	**NO**	Arlene has reserved no rights. An easement will be implied only if there is a quasi-easement (existing visible use) the parties intended to continue. Drainage does not appear to qualify as a quasi-easement. [§§1346-1347]
d.	**DEPENDS**	If Lot 2 were landlocked, Arlene would have an implied easement by necessity. If the road is merely convenient access to the highway, there is a split of authority. Some courts would deny Arlene an implied easement by reservation, but the majority would give her an implied easement by reservation on the basis of a quasi-easement if a replacement road would be costly and the facts indicated the parties intended the use to continue. [§§1350, 1352-1353]
e.	**NO**	If an implied easement exists in either case, it is valid against a subsequent purchaser of the servient estate, even if she is without notice. An implied easement does not arise from a recordable document, and is not within the recording system. [§§1342-1347]
51.a.	**YES**	Assuming the use by Felicia and Earl was hostile, open, notorious, and continuous, a prescriptive easement can be acquired over the path. Tacking is permitted. [§§1361-1368, 1371]
b.	**SPLIT OF AUTHORITY**	Some courts, following the "lost grant" theory, hold that a sign indicates nonacquiescence, negating an implied lost grant. Others hold that the owner of the servient estate can break the running of a prescriptive easement only by erecting a permanent obstruction to bar further use of the path. [§§1359-1360, 1372]
c.	**YES**	If Greenacre was formerly a part of a parcel containing the adjoining property, and if when separated from it Greenacre was landlocked, Greenacre would have a way of necessity over the adjoining parcel. (If Greenacre was not landlocked by separation from the adjoining parcel, no way of necessity exists over it; if Greenacre did not have a way of necessity, Earl would have to rely upon prescription—or bargain his way out.) [§1374]
52.a.	**DEPENDS**	The amount of Garland's use of the easement depends upon the burden to Herman's property contemplated when Blackacre was sold and the reasonableness of any change in use of the property and easement. [§§1380, 1382]
b.	**NO**	If the easement was specifically described in the deed, Herman cannot move it elsewhere for his own convenience. [§1390]
c.	**YES**	The easement is appurtenant and hence is assignable. [§1397]
d.	**YES**	Although this is an easement in gross, it is of a commercial character and thus would be held assignable by most courts. [§§1398-1401]
53.	**NO**	Mere nonuse of an easement does not extinguish the easement regardless of how long the nonuse continues. [§1408]
54.	**NO**	Peter's end is in gross; Opal's end burdens land. [§§1402, 1418]
55.	**YES**	The remedy available is a primary difference. Another difference is that privity may be required for a covenant to run at law but not in equity. [§§1419-1420, 1423, 1466]

56.	**NO**	There must be privity of estate between Quick and Ralph in order for the burden of the covenant (on Quick's land) to run at law. There is no privity here, in any of the meanings of that term. [§1434]
57.a.	**SPLIT OF AUTHORITY**	Vertical privity of estate is necessary in order for Uriah to sue Wayne at law. In some states Wayne is not in vertical privity of estate unless he succeeds to Victor's entire estate. In others, Wayne may be considered as in privity of estate when he succeeds to a possessory estate. [§§1444, 1452]
b.	**NO**	No privity of estate between Victor and Wayne exists. [§1444]
58.a.	**YES**	Both the benefit and burden touch and concern the land, since good repair enhances the value of the property (whether or not Yetta makes use of same). [§§1432-1441, 1456]
b.	**NO**	Here the covenant calls for performance on Yetta's mountain cabin, and assigns of the land in town cannot enforce this covenant because it does not touch and concern the land in town. [§§1435, 1456]
59.a.	**NO**	The benefit is in gross; therefore, according to most courts, the burden will not run. [§§1428, 1435]
b.	**NO**	Anthony has no control over the restaurant following the sale, and a cessation of his liability will be implied. [§1459]
60.a.	**SPLIT OF AUTHORITY**	Most courts would hold that Delta's common scheme of single-family dwellings creates an implied reciprocal negative servitude on the remaining 20 lots, which Erin has notice of, and which the subdivision neighbors can enforce. But some courts (California and Massachusetts are examples) will not imply a restrictive covenant on Erin's lots. In these jurisdictions she can build the apartment houses. [§§1461, 1475-1478, 1480]
b.	**NO**	Only *negative* reciprocal servitudes will be implied; courts will not imply affirmative promises. [§1479]
c.	**YES**	The prior grantees can enforce the covenant either on the ground that an implied reciprocal servitude on the 20 lots arose when the subdivision was first developed or on third-party beneficiary rationale. (California would not permit prior grantees to enforce unless they were expressly granted that right.) [§§1507-1510, 1515]
d.	**YES**	This probably negates any "common scheme," so that a restriction will not be implied in a. It also may establish that the benefit of the covenant runs to Delta and not to the neighbors (so that Delta alone can enforce the covenant). [§1513]
61.a.	**SPLIT OF AUTHORITY**	If Sherry was in horizontal privity of estate with Phyllis, Maude can recover damages from Coco. Under the majority view, a grantor-grantee relationship provides privity, and Maude would win. Under the tenurial or mutual interest view, there is no privity. (Maude could get an injunction, because privity is not required in equity.) [§1509]
b.	**YES**	In most states, equity will enforce an express affirmative covenant against a subsequent purchaser. In a few, equity will enforce only a negative covenant against a subsequent purchaser. [§§1493-1494]
c.	**YES**	The Association can sue in equity to enforce the express lien, even though an action at law for damages will not lie. [§§1469, 1496]

62.a.	**YES**	An injunction will be granted if the benefits of the restriction can still be achieved for the other lots in the subdivision. An injunction will be denied only if the entire 50-lot tract is now unsuitable for residential purposes. [§1529]
b.	**YES**	A cumulative zoning ordinance is not in conflict with the private restriction because residences are permitted in commercial zones. (A zoning ordinance prohibiting residences in commercial zones might be held to override the private restriction, or it might be unenforceable as a taking of private property. Courts are split.) [§1635]
63.a.	**NO**	In most states, the fact that the use is authorized by zoning ordinances is no defense for a private nuisance. However, a few states make it a presumptive defense. [§1548]
b.	**DEPENDS**	Plaintiff's coming to the nuisance is one factor, but not the sole controlling factor, in determining whether relief for a nuisance will be granted. [§1550]
c.	**NO**	The complainant must have a property interest affected by the nuisance, unless she suffers bodily harm from the activity (which is unlikely here). [§§1534, 1542-1546]
64.a.	**YES**	The utility of the conduct is an important factor. The character of the neighborhood, the importance of Qua Corp. to the economy, the severity of the damage to Bella, and the available means of controlling pollutants are probably determinative. [§§1537, 1549]
b.	**YES**	If the pollution is found to be a nuisance but the activity is too important to be enjoined, a court may refuse an injunction and award damages to Bella. [§1552]
c.	**NO**	If damages are given Bella, all the gains from trade are given to Qua Corp. [§1572]
65.a.	**YES**	Underground Explorers has strict liability for damage to neighboring land by withdrawing lateral support. [§1581]
b.	**MAYBE**	Some courts extend the duty of absolute support of adjoining land to buildings thereon. However, the majority holds the excavator liable only for negligence in excavating the pond, where the building slips because of the weight of the building. The question then is whether Underground Explorers was negligent. [§1583]
c.	**YES**	Since Underground Explorers was negligent in removing minerals, it is liable for damaging the neighbor's well. [§1587]
66.	**DEPENDS**	In a natural flow jurisdiction, Victoria Farms can use water only on riparian land. In some reasonable use jurisdictions, Victoria Farms can use water on nonriparian lands if this does not harm other riparians. In prior appropriation jurisdictions, Victoria Farms can use the water on nonriparian land. [§§1594, 1597]
67.	**DEPENDS**	States following the common enemy doctrine allow diversion of surface waters onto adjacent land, but they require that Willie's diversion be reasonable, avoiding disproportionate damage to his neighbors. [§1615]
68.a.	**YES**	There is a presumption of validity that the ordinance is an exercise of the state's police power. [§1639]
b.	**NO**	Axel is not deprived of all reasonable use (he has residential and 3 commercial uses available). However, Axel might have an argument that the ordinance violates the enabling act or is a denial of substantive due process or equal protection. [§§1642, 1646]

c.	**NO**	Since this does not involve a suspect classification, the standard of review is whether the ordinance bears a rational relationship to a permissible state objective. [§§1647-1648]
69.a.	**NO**	The modern trend is to uphold such architectural review boards where the applicable standard is the "existing character of the neighborhood." [§1662]
b.	**YES**	If the existing use gives the owner a reasonable return on his investment, the ordinance will be upheld, according to most recent cases. [§§1668-1669]
c.	**SPLIT OF AUTHORITY**	Most courts uphold dedication requirements only where the need is specifically and uniquely attributable to the developer's activities, and frequently they limit the types of dedication to improvements that benefit the subdivision residents and not the public generally. A few courts would uphold such a requirement on the theory that the subdivider is using up open space and creates the need for playground. [§§1712-1713]
70.a.	**NO**	Recent cases hold that the complete exclusion of apartments from a suburban city is unconstitutional. [§1676]
b.	**DEPENDS**	Some courts uphold such requirements where the character of the area is being preserved. Other courts strike down large acreage requirements as unrelated to the proper objectives of zoning and as unreasonably interfering with housing development. [§1676]
c.	**NO**	Lolly has no standing in federal court because she has no personal stake in the matter and the injury is too speculative. [§1682]
71.a.	**NO**	Amortization ordinances have been upheld in most states if they are reasonable as applied. A 30-day period appears to be too short a time, even if Crystal's only investment is in the business. If she owns the nonconforming building, a 30-day period is clearly too short for amortization. [§§1686-1687]
b.	**MAYBE**	The old rule was that a suit in inverse condemnation is not permitted when the alleged taking results from governmental regulation, but some courts are now allowing such suits. [§§1724-1725]
72.a.	**YES**	Any amendments that do not comply with the master plan may be attacked as "spot zoning." [§1694]
b.	**SPLIT OF AUTHORITY**	The older cases held a zoning amendment is presumptively valid, but some new cases put the burden of proof on the city to justify a zoning amendment. [§§1695-1697]
73.a.	**YES**	Ike may obtain a variance allowing him to build closer to the street. [§§1698-1699]
b.	**YES**	The hardship required for a variance must be unique and not general to the area. The proper remedy is an amendment, not a variance. [§1699]
c.	**POSSIBLY**	If Ike's building helps to create the need for street widening, the city may require him to pick up some of the cost in this way. On the other hand, if dedication is not a general ordinance requirement for a variance, but is bargained for individually, it may violate the Equal Protection Clause or be struck down as contract zoning. [§1705]
74.a.	**YES**	This is known as severance damage. [§1760]

| b. | **YES** | The requirement that Kelly admit the public on his property, if he use it at all, is a taking. Kelly has no reasonable private use left in Blackacre. [§1734] |
| c. | **NO** | Recent cases uphold wetlands zoning on the theory that existing uses permitted are reasonable and development is harmful. [§§1671, 1730] |

75. **YES** The government has no authority (apart from a formal redevelopment scheme of an area) to condemn the property of one person solely to resell it to another. [§§1744-1745]

76. **NO** Even though the government can regulate out value by refusing to rezone, fairness requires that it pay the market value (including speculative value about the probabilities of rezoning) on the date of condemnation. [§§1750-1753]

77.a. **YES** Unless a "time is of the essence" clause is in the contract, this probably constitutes performance within a reasonable period. [§§1783-1784]

b. **YES** There is an implied warranty that the seller will furnish marketable title at the closing. [§1785]

c. **SPLIT OF AUTHORITY** Unless the contract specified marketable record title, some courts hold the seller can prove title by adverse possession. Others hold record title is required. [§§1787-1790]

d. **YES** Building code violations usually do not make title unmarketable, but a legal action commenced to enforce the building code does. [§1787]

78.a. **YES** If the value of Quashee's easement can be calculated (so that a proper abatement in the purchase price can be made), Paula is entitled to specific performance. [§1801]

b. **DEPENDS** If the easement is a substantial defect, specific performance is not available to the seller. If insubstantial, then the seller is entitled to specific performance with a reduction in purchase price for the easement. [§1806]

c. **SPLIT OF AUTHORITY** Where the seller's breach is unintentional (not known when the contract is signed), the courts are split. Many states would give the buyer $50,000, but others would give Paula only monies paid to Orville plus out of pocket costs (title search, etc.). *Compare:* If Orville knew all along that title was in Ross, Paula would get $50,000 in all states. [§§1802-1804]

79.a. **SPLIT OF AUTHORITY** In most states, Yuri is deemed to have title through equitable conversion and he bears the risk of loss. Hence Wendy can enforce the contract. Other states follow the Massachusetts rule and put the risk of loss on the seller, or have a statute putting risk of loss on the party in possession. In these states, Wendy cannot get specific performance. [§§1811-1812, 1816, 1821]

b. **YES** Most courts require the seller to credit the insurance proceeds against the purchase price if the buyer bears the risk of loss. [§1820]

80. **NO** Felix, at death, had title subject to an option, and this title passes to Herbie, not Iris. Since the option is not exercised until after Felix's death, equitable conversion does not take place. [§1825]

81. **YES** While not necessary for an effective deed, acknowledgment or attestation may be required for recordation and is always helpful in authenticating the deed. [§§1863-1865].

82.	**YES**	Since Ferdinand is dead his heirs can be determined, and delivery can be made. If Ferdinand were alive, the deed might be void for uncertainty or for want of delivery (since Ferdinand's heirs are not presently ascertainable). [§1879]
83.a.	**YES**	Geoffrey presumptively takes title to the northern half of the road. [§§1884, 1894]
b.	**YES**	Presumably the city intended to retain title to the road. [§1895]
c.	**YES**	Where the measurement is *from* the side of a road, the presumption is that the grant does not include the road. [§1895]
84.a.	**YES**	If Helen demonstrates an intent that the deed have present operative effect, handing over the deed is not required to make delivery. Recordation raises a presumption of delivery. [§§1897, 1900]
b.	**YES**	The presumption is rebuttable by evidence of the grantor's intent not to make delivery. [§1900]
85.a.	**YES**	Where the condition is stated in writing, there has been a valid delivery of a deed creating a future interest in the grantee. [§1903]
b.	**NO**	Most courts would not admit parol evidence of Norma's statement to show that delivery was subject to a condition. [§1909]
86.	**NO**	Unless Robin is acting *solely* as Pierre's agent (which does not appear to be the case here), there is a valid delivery to Robin for Quintin when Robin receives the deed, and it cannot be recalled. [§§1909-1913]
87.a.	**SPLIT OF AUTHORITY**	When the escrow instructions are oral, some courts allow Scott to recall the deed, unless there is an underlying *written* contract of sale. Other courts do not require a written contract and enforce the escrow if Scott had the requisite intent to transfer on July 1. [§§1920-1922]
b.	**SPLIT OF AUTHORITY**	If Scott had no knowledge of the theft and conveyance to Walter, some courts hold that no title passes to Unity until the conditions of escrow are met, and hence Walter loses. Other courts hold that a bona fide purchaser prevails because Scott made it possible to defraud a person by placing the deed in escrow; therefore, Scott is estopped to plead no delivery. [§§1929-1934]
88.a.	**YES**	A general warranty deed protects against defects arising before, as well as during, the grantor's tenure on the land. [§1937]
b.	**YES**	A special warranty deed warrants only against defects arising while the warrantor has title. A quitclaim deed warrants nothing. [§§1938-1939]
c.	**NO**	The usual covenants of title in a warranty deed do not include a covenant of fitness for intended use. For Liza to be liable, an express covenant of fitness would have to be included in the deed. [§§1935, 1941-1947]
89.a.	**NO**	Phil has not been evicted, and cannot sue on a future covenant. A covenant of seisin is breached when made; the cause of action on this covenant is barred by the statute of limitations. [§§1949, 1953]
b.	**NO**	A covenant against encumbrances is breached when made; the statute of limitations has run. [§1949]
c.	**YES**	If Olive files within the limitations period, she can hold Ned for damages even though she knew of the defects. [§§1951, 1959]

d.	**YES**	Phil can sue on the covenants of quiet enjoyment and general warranty, which are breached when Phil is evicted. These future covenants run with the land to Olive's successor, Phil. [§§1956-1957]
90.a.	**YES**	Since Eduardo is the covenantee, he is entitled to his purchase price. If Eduardo had been a remote grantee, there is a split of authority. Some courts would give the remote grantee the amount received by Mario, which might be more than the remote grantee paid; others would limit the remote grantee to his purchase price or the amount received by Mario, whichever is less. [§§1965-1966]
b.	**NO**	The maximum Eduardo can recover is the amount he paid Mario. [§1966]
91.a.	**YES**	By recording, Homer prevails under all types of recording acts. [§§1984-1986]
b.	**NO**	In a "notice" state, Homer still prevails since Gladys failed to record. In a "race-notice" or "race" state, however, Gladys would prevail. [§§1999-2002]
c.	**YES**	Recording acts protect only subsequent purchasers (not donees); therefore the common law rule of prior in time gives the land to the first grantee in time, Gladys. [§2006]
d.	**NO**	The heirs stand in Fay's shoes. Recordation is not required to establish the validity of a deed as between grantor and grantee. [§1986]
92.a.	**NO**	Kathy had no notice on June 10 (the time of conveyance) and thus prevails over John. [§2001]
b.	**YES**	John prevails in both, because he has recorded before Kathy. [§§2000, 2002]
93.a.	**YES**	Regardless of enforceability, the prior conveyance is known to Lucy. [§2025]
b.	**SPLIT OF AUTHORITY**	Most courts would charge Lucy with inquiry notice of the possessor's claim, and Nellie would prevail. A minority would not require Lucy to inspect the premises, and if she did not, she would prevail over Nellie. [§§2030-2032]
c.	**NO**	A conveyance as security for an antecedent debt of the grantor is not a conveyance for a valuable consideration. [§2040]
d.	**YES**	The consideration paid by the subsequent purchaser must be of substantial pecuniary value, but need not be the full market value of the property. [§2038]
94.a.	**SPLIT AUTHORITY**	The better view allows Quincy to prevail, on the ground that he lacked constructive notice. However, some courts protect Pedro on the theory that indexing is not part of recordation. [§2013]
b.	**NO**	If the deed was not acknowledged, it cannot be recorded and does not give notice to subsequent purchasers. Quincy prevails. [§2011]
95.	**YES**	Tim's recorded deed does not give constructive notice because its grantor was not connected to the chain of title. It is "wild." Ursula, who has no notice of it, prevails. [§2046]
96.a.	**NO**	Most courts protect the subsequent BFP, Zachary, on the theory that the Vincent-Yvonne conveyance is not in the chain of title because it was recorded prior to the date Vincent obtained title. A minority is contra, and applies the theory of estoppel by deed against the subsequent purchaser. [§§2048-2050]

b.	**YES**	As between Vincent and Yvonne, all courts protect Yvonne using the theory of estoppel by deed. [§2048]
97.	**YES**	Most courts protect Diana on the theory that Bob's deed, recorded after Carol's recordation, does not give notice to Carol's assignee. A minority protects Bob on the theory that his mortgage is recorded, and with extended search Diana can find it. [§§2051-2053]
98.	**SPLIT OF AUTHORITY**	Some courts hold that the deed to Felipe is not in the chain of title of parcel 2, and hence, Gene is a BFP who prevails. Other courts hold that Gene has constructive notice of the contents of deeds to other lots from a common grantor to other persons. Under this latter view, Felipe prevails. [§2054]
99.	**NO**	Title to registered land cannot be claimed by adverse possession where such possession begins after title is registered. [§2078]
100.	**YES**	Kenny can recover actual market loss up to the limit of the policy. [§§2101-2102]

SAMPLE EXAM QUESTION I

In 1970, Olivia, owner of Blackacre, an eighty-acre parcel, executed, delivered, and recorded a deed transferring two acres of Blackacre to Lincoln County. The relevant language of this deed stated:

> Olivia hereby grants two acres of Blackacre, located in the corner and adjacent to the road, to Lincoln County to be used as the site of a highway weighing station. This deed is on the condition that if said use does not commence within six months from this date, or, having commenced, ceases, the conveyance to be null and void.

In 1980, Olivia executed a deed to Blackacre and delivered it to Alan. This deed described Blackacre as it had been described in the deed by which Olivia had acquired Blackacre. It made no mention of the deed to Lincoln County. In 1981, Olivia died intestate survived by Bob, her sole heir.

The two-acre parcel conveyed to Lincoln County was improved as a highway weighing station site within sixty days from the date of the 1970 deed. It was continually used as such until 1984 when Lincoln County removed the weighing equipment and sold its interest in the land to Carol. Alan learned of the County's action before Carol took possession. Alan removed the fences which had separated the two-acre parcel from Alan's land and fenced the outside boundaries of Blackacre so as to include the two-acre parcel with his land.

In 1985, who is entitled to the two-acre parcel and why?

SAMPLE EXAM QUESTION II

Dan and Earl pooled their life savings and purchased Greenacre. The deed named the grantees as "Dan, Earl, Fanny, and George, as joint tenants and not as tenants in common."

Subsequently Dan died. The administrator of his estate brought an action against Earl, Fanny, and George for the purpose of determining the respective interests in the property, if any, of the estate and the three defendants. Harry intervened claiming an interest in the property.

At the trial, Harry established by competent evidence that Dan wanted to borrow $10,000 from Harry but had no security other than Dan's interest in Greenacre; that Dan would not grant a mortgage of Greenacre because he did not want George to know about the loan; that after considerable negotiation, Dan executed a deed purporting to grant all his interest in Greenacre to Harry; that Dan then handed the deed to a mutual friend with instructions to give it to Harry after Dan's death; and that Harry then loaned Dan the $10,000.

What are the respective interests of Earl, Fanny, George, and Harry in Greenacre? Discuss.

SAMPLE EXAM QUESTION III

In June 1982, Helga, who owned a neighborhood grocery store and a large apartment house, leased a fourth floor apartment to Ike for five years at a monthly rental of $150. The lease was on a standard printed form containing language requiring the landlord to maintain all common areas in a "safe and sanitary condition" and making all terms of the lease binding on the successors and assigns of both parties. The following two clauses were added in handwriting:

> 27. Landlord agrees to leave Tenant a pint of milk and a newspaper every morning except Sunday.

28. Landlord will repaint the kitchen and bathroom during the second year of the lease and replace the kitchen sink with a new one within the first six months of the lease.

When Ike and Helga signed the lease a doorman and a garage attendant were on duty twenty-four hours a day. All entrances not under their direct observation were kept securely locked and were checked periodically by a guard from dusk to dawn.

In June 1983, Helga sold and conveyed the apartment house to Jack. In August 1984, Jack sold and conveyed the apartment house to Karl. Ike has not received any milk or newspapers since the sale by Helga. The repainting has never been done, and the sink has not been replaced.

Since Karl became the owner, conditions have deteriorated. Karl discharged the garage attendant and there has been no doorman on duty except in the afternoon and early evening. The 100-watt light bulbs in the hallways have been replaced with twenty-five-watt bulbs. The locks on the doors from the fire escapes have fallen into disrepair. The responsibility for checking doors has been left to the local police, who are overburdened because of numerous thefts and violent crimes in the neighborhood. Recently Ike was robbed and severely beaten in the hall just outside his apartment.

At the time of their respective purchases of the apartment house, Jack and Karl were aware of the printed form lease which Helga used but they had no knowledge of the two clauses added to Ike's lease.

A.   What are Ike's rights against Jack? Discuss.

B.   What are Ike's rights against Karl? Discuss.

SAMPLE EXAM QUESTION IV

On June 1, 1983, in accordance with a written contract of sale, Leon deeded some land to City. On the land was a small open bandstand used for summer concerts. The deed contained this language: "To have and to hold so long as City uses the land for park purposes, and should City at any time stop using said land for park purposes, said land shall revert to the heirs of Leon."

The deed was placed in escrow with Local Loan on the oral understanding that the city would deposit the purchase price within sixty days after the date of the deed. Before the deposit was made, the bandstand was destroyed by a fire of unknown origin. The city deposited the purchase price in time, but contended that it was entitled to a deduction because of the fire loss. Leon disagreed but authorized delivery of the deed and consented not to withdraw the money until they could negotiate the matter.

The city took the deed and recorded it at once, but, because of the loss of the bandstand, began using the land for storage of City Street Department trucks. Leon immediately wrote to the city objecting to the use of the land and advising the city that he would instruct Local Loan to return the purchase price to the city if the city would immediately give up possession of the land and reconvey it to Leon. Three days later, before the city had taken any further action, Leon died.

The city then caused the execution and recordation of a deed of the land to Leon, removed all of the trucks from the land and requested Leon's executor to instruct Local Loan to release the escrowed funds to the city.

Leon's executor wants to know whether he should comply with the city's request and whether the city would have a valid claim to either the land or the funds if he did not. What should he be advised? Discuss.

SAMPLE EXAM QUESTION V

For many years prior to June 13, 1981, Moe operated a tavern on property owned by him at 13 Exeter Street, in the City of Columbus. On June 13, 1981, Moe broke his leg and closed the tavern but did not remove any of the merchandise or fixtures. He reopened the tavern on September 10, 1981.

Effective July 1, 1981, Columbus adopted a zoning ordinance restricting use of property on Exeter Street to single family dwellings but providing for continuation of any existing nonconforming uses by the owner or successors in title subject to the following provision:

> No nonconforming use, once abandoned, shall be reinstituted. For the purpose of this section "abandoned" is defined as cessation of the nonconforming use for six months or more.

On March 15, 1983, Moe executed and delivered a deed to 13 Exeter Street to Dr. Nell to pay a past due bill for medical services she had rendered to him. Dr. Nell allowed Moe to continue to operate the tavern and did not immediately record her deed.

On September 15, 1983, Moe, for valuable consideration, executed and delivered a conveyance of "all my right, title and interest" in 13 Exeter Street to Olga who had no knowledge of Dr. Nell's deed. Dr. Nell recorded her deed on October 1, 1983, and Olga recorded her deed two days later.

Olga operated the tavern continuously from September 15, 1983 to January 10, 1985, when she closed the tavern because her liquor license was then suspended for nine months by the state board of liquor control.

A.   Who should prevail in a quiet title action between Nell and Olga? Discuss.

B.   If Olga prevails, will she be legally entitled to reopen the premises as a tavern when the suspension of her liquor license terminates? Discuss.

SAMPLE EXAM QUESTION VI

Peter, owner of Blackacre, told his friend, Quincy, that he wanted to avoid probate and would like for his heirs to take Blackacre on his death without the expense and delay of probate. Quincy, who had been to law school, suggested that if Peter conveyed Blackacre to him, and he conveyed it back to Peter for life, remainder to Peter's heirs, Peter's heirs would take Blackacre at Peter's death without going through probate. Peter accepted the suggestion. He executed and delivered a deed "to Quincy and his heirs." Quincy then executed and delivered a deed "to Peter for life, and then to his heirs." Not certain that he had conveyed all his interest, Quincy then executed a third deed quitclaiming all his right, title, and interest to Peter. All three deeds were acknowledged and properly recorded.

A few months later Peter leased Blackacre, which was commercial rental property, to Rosie for ten years at a monthly rental of $500. The lease contained a covenant that the tenant would repair and maintain the premises. Rosie opened up a leather goods store on Blackacre.

After a year Rosie thoughtlessly threw a lighted cigarette in the waste basket, causing a fire which resulted in total destruction of the building on Blackacre. Peter was uninsured and when he saw the fire, he had a heart attack and died. Rosie abandoned the premises after the fire.

Peter left a will, devising all his property to Sue, who is not Peter's heir.

Sue wants to know what her rights are with respect to Blackacre. Discuss.

SAMPLE EXAM QUESTION VII

Easement

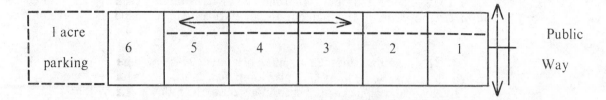

Terry owned the tract of land described above, consisting of lots 1-6. In 1968, he sold lots 1-5. The deeds to lots 1-5 imposed an easement over the northerly 15 feet of lots 1-5 for the use and benefit of lots 2-6. This easement provides the only access to lots 2-6. The deeds to lots 1-5 also contained the following restriction: "To preserve high quality, this lot is conveyed on condition it be used solely for residential purposes, and any other use may be enjoined and shall be cause for forfeiture." Residences were immediately built on lots 1-4. Lot 5 remained vacant. Terry sold lot 6 in 1969 without any use restrictions in the deed conveying it, and a residence was built on that lot.

In 1982, Ugo, a rock music promoter, purchased lot 6 and since then has operated a discotheque in the house on that lot. In 1977, Victor purchased lot 5 and built a family home, but experienced frequent noise disturbance from Ugo's club.

All of the deeds were recorded.

In 1983, a zoning ordinance was enacted and lots 1-6 were zoned "Single Family Residential."

Ugo's club prospered. In 1984, by quitclaim deed, Ugo acquired from Wayne, who owned sixty acres of rural land surrounding the tract on the north, west and south, a one-acre parcel adjoining lot 6 on the west for use as a parking lot. Ugo now plans to use a few rooms in the residence on lot 6 for a mortuary featuring rock funerals. In 1985, despite Victor's appearance and objections, the County Commissioners, stating that Wayne's adjacent land was a likely shopping center site, rezoned lot 6 and the parking lot to "Commercial." This would permit their use for mortuaries and discotheques. As Victor left the meeting, he told Ugo that he would use every means legally available to prevent or hinder Ugo's discotheque and mortuary operation on lot 6 and the parking lot.

Ugo consults you before investing any more money in lot 6 or paving the parking lot. He wants to know what legal actions Victor and the owners of lots 1-4 might reasonably be anticipated to take, what defenses he might reasonably assert, what his chances of success are, and whether there is any other legal proceeding he might take to obtain alternate access to the parking lot. Discuss.

NOTE: Each sample exam question is designed to be read and answered in fifty minutes. Thus the answers given here cannot and do not discuss all the issues in detail. They are not presented as perfect answers, or as answers that could be written if eight hours were allowed for each. The answers are merely illustrations of acceptable answers that can be organized and written in the time allotted.

ANSWER TO SAMPLE EXAM QUESTION I

Alan, Bob, and Carol each have plausible claims which will be explored separately.

1. **Alan's claim:** Olivia conveyed to Lincoln County either a fee simple determinable or a fee simple subject to a condition subsequent. The conveyance is ambiguous because it uses both the words "on the condition that" (normally creating a condition subsequent), and the words "the conveyance to be null and void" (indicating the automatic termination of the interest characteristic of a fee simple determinable). In cases of ambiguity, courts usually interpret the interest to be a fee simple subject to a condition subsequent, so as to require an affirmative action of forfeiture and also to permit more equitable defenses to be asserted.

The conditions in the conveyance were (a) that the site be used for a weighing station within six months of the conveyance (which was fulfilled) and (b) that the land continue to be so used (which was not fulfilled). The interest Olivia retained was not subject to the Rule Against Perpetuities (regardless of whether it was a right of entry or a possibility of reverter) because all interests retained by the grantor are deemed vested and hence exempt from the Rule.

When Olivia later conveyed Blackacre to Alan, describing it as including the two-acre parcel, she evidently intended to convey her reversionary interest in that parcel to Alan. In most states, both the possibility of reverter and the right of entry are transferable inter vivos, but in some states these interests are both inalienable, or the possibility of reverter is and the right of entry is not; in others, the mere attempt to convey a right of entry destroys it.

If the possibility of reverter and right of entry are alienable (or if only the possibility of reverter is alienable and the court so classifies Olivia's interest), Alan is in a very strong position. When Lincoln County violated the condition of continued use, the title either reverted directly to Alan or Alan had a right of entry which he exercised by removing the fences around the two-acre parcel.

2. **Bob's claim:** The analysis of Bob's claim is similar to that of Alan's except that he would argue that Alan's deed did not include Olivia's reversionary interest in the two-acre parcel and that it descended to Bob as sole heir of Olivia when Olivia died intestate. Bob would argue that Olivia did not show an intent to convey the reversionary interest merely by repeating the old description, and that Alan did not expect to receive an interest in view of the obvious presence of the weighing station at the time of the conveyance.

Alternatively, Bob could argue that the possibility of reverter or right of entry retained by Olivia could not be transferred inter vivos, and, hence, it resided in Olivia at Olivia's death, and was inherited by Bob.

3. **Carol's claim:** Carol's major argument would be that Olivia's conveyance presumptively created a fee simple subject to a condition subsequent (*see* paragraph (1) above) so that the reversionary interest retained by Olivia was a right of entry. Carol could then argue that such interest could not be conveyed, and Olivia's attempt to convey it to Alan (*see* analysis above) resulted in its *destruction.* The result would thus be that Lincoln County had its interest enlarged to a fee simple absolute because of the removal of the condition subsequent, and Carol is now the owner of such interest.

Conclusion: The answer depends, first, upon how the court classifies Olivia's retained interest (possibility of reverter or right of entry) and, after such classification, upon what rule is followed in the jurisdiction as to the alienability of such interest. Probably in a majority of states Alan would win, because this is a right of entry which can be alienated, but local law varies considerably on alienability, as stated above.

ANSWER TO SAMPLE EXAM QUESTION II

Interests created by deed: The first question is whether the deed from the owner of Greenacre created a joint tenancy or a tenancy in common in Dan, Earl, Fanny, and George. In almost all states, a joint tenancy can be created by appropriate language indicating an intent to create a joint tenancy; the language here is appropriate to create a joint tenancy. In a few states, it is necessary to state expressly that the tenants have the right of survivorship, which is not done here, and in these states, the parties would hold as tenants in common. In a very few states, the joint tenancy has been abolished, and the parties hold as tenants in common unless the deed is construed to give them life estates for their joint lives, remainder to survivor.

If a joint tenancy is created, Harry's fight is first with the surviving joint tenants (Earl, Fanny, and George) and, only if he wins this, will he fight Dan's administrator. If a tenancy in common is created, Earl, Fanny, and George have no rights in Dan's one-fourth share of Greenacre and Harry's rights depend upon how the escrow transaction is dealt with.

The escrow transaction: This is a very strange escrow transaction because the facts indicate a ***commercial negotiation*** took place between Dan and Harry, but the deed was put into escrow with oral instructions to deliver upon Dan's death, which are the common instructions in a ***donative escrow.*** A donative escrow is a substitute for a will. But rather clearly there was no donative intent here; a bargain of some kind was intended. What was it? Parol evidence is admissible to show the conditions of delivery where a deed is put into escrow. Harry's rights depend upon how this escrow transaction is characterized.

The escrow can be viewed as an arrangement to give Harry security for a loan; hence the deed in escrow was in essence a mortgage, executed in exchange for a loan. Courts can look through the form of a deed to substance and declare that the deed, though absolute on its face, is really intended to be a mortgage and will be so treated by the court. If this is done, then the mortgage (deed) is held by the escrow agent as security until Dan dies, and then is to be given to Harry. This seems the most likely intent of the parties.

If this is a mortgage, a serious Statute of Frauds problem arises. There is authority (but much criticized) that where there is a commercial escrow with oral instructions to the escrow agent, the escrow fails unless there is an underlying written contract. It is too dangerous to permit the escrow agent to fill in essential terms, such as price, by oral testimony. Here, however, extrinsic evidence that $10,000 was loaned (*e.g.,* by cancelled check) may be reliable; and part performance (handing over of the $10,000) may take the underlying agreement out of the Statute of Frauds. On the other hand, there is so much else about this escrow transaction that is questionable; the evidence of a donative escrow may not be reliable, and may be an attempt to characterize the escrow as noncommercial to get around this Statute of Frauds problem. A court may very well conclude that the escrow cannot be enforced because it violates the Statute of Frauds. (If this were a donative escrow, no written instructions or agreement would be necessary, and the escrow would be valid but there seems to be no donative intent here.)

There is also a question of delivery. If the grantor had an absolute right of recall, the escrow is void. This does not appear to be the case here. If the grantor had a conditional right of recall (upon repayment of the loan, for instance), some cases (again, much criticized) would hold that the grantor lacks the necessary intent to convey a present interest unconditionally when the deed is put into escrow. For delivery to occur, the deed must pass beyond control of the grantor. If the grantor can get the deed (mortgage) back upon payment of money, it is arguable that there is no delivery because of the grantor's control. But, if this is viewed as a mortgage, this is specious, since it is the nature of a mortgage that it is released upon payment of money.

The escrow transaction can also be viewed as the sale of an executory interest to Harry by Dan for $10,000 if the "loan testimony" is ignored and the escrow instruction is emphasized, or it could be viewed as a sale of an executory interest, to become possessory upon Dan's death if Dan had not repaid the $10,000. Under the first of these views, there is the same Statute of Frauds problem discussed above; under the second, there is, in addition, the delivery problem discussed above.

If the escrow transaction is void because of the Statute of Frauds or lack of delivery, Harry is a general creditor of Dan's estate, but has no interest in Greenacre.

Effect on joint tenancy: If the escrow transaction is void, Dan did not sever the joint tenancy during life and the three survivors now own Greenacre. If the escrow is valid, the rights of Earl, Fanny, and George depend upon whether the escrow severed the joint tenancy. If not severed during Dan's life, they now own the property free of the mortgage.

If the escrow was in reality a mortgage, and treated as such, the escrow severed the joint tenancy only if the *title theory* of mortgages is followed, *i.e.,* that the mortgagee takes title, thereby breaking the four unities. If the *lien theory* is followed, no severance occurred because the mortgage is only a lien upon Dan's title, which disappears at Dan's death (the four unities of time, title, interest, and possession are not destroyed during Dan's life). If the theory of *partial severance* is used, the surviving joint tenants take the whole subject to the mortgage.

If, on the other hand, the deed in escrow is viewed as a conveyance of an equitable executory interest to Harry, there is probably no severance. Legal title remains in Dan during the escrow, subject to Harry's equitable interest.

Conclusion: Though there are several other possible results, the court will probably hold a joint tenancy was created, the deed in escrow was in substance a mortgage, and that the mortgage did not effect a severance of the joint tenancy. If the court is in a "title theory" state, it may avoid that theory by holding the escrow fails for lack of delivery or violates the Statute of Frauds. Therefore, Earl, Fanny, and George own Greenacre free of the mortgage.

This result seems equitable and carries out the expectations of the joint tenants. Harry is little deserving of sympathy because he entered a secretive oral escrow transaction that disguises or confuses the truth. He could have easily protected himself in a mortgage transaction by having Dan convey his interest to a straw person (thus severing joint tenancy), who after mortgaging to Harry, conveyed equity back to Dan. Harry has caused the confusion, and brought the loss on himself. He is asking equitable relief, and is not totally blameless himself.

ANSWER TO SAMPLE EXAM QUESTION III

A. Ike vs. Jack

There are three claims that Ike may raise against Jack.

1. Failure to deliver milk and newspapers

Helga, a grocer, promised to deliver the milk and newspaper every morning. Does this burden run with the landlord's reversion, so that Helga's assignee, Jack, is liable for it? For a covenant to run with the land, the parties must *intend* that it run, they must be in *privity* of estate, the covenant must *touch and concern* the land, and the defendant must have *notice.* There is privity of estate because Jack succeeded to Helga's reversion by assignment, but there are problems with the other three requirements.

Intent: Although the lease expressly stated all terms of the lease were binding on assigns, it does not necessarily follow that the first of the two clauses added was intended to bind assignees. The printed statement might apply only to printed terms, and not to added clauses. The covenantor, Helga, was a grocer who could conveniently leave milk and newspapers for tenants, and because of this the parties might not have intended that this added covenant run to assignees. This argument is buttressed by the fact deliveries were not to occur on Sunday, if it can be shown that Helga's grocery was closed on Sunday.

Touch and concern: The promise is to do a physical act on the leased premises. Ordinarily this type of promise, such as a promise to repaint, repair, or furnish heat, touches and concerns because it is directly related to the enjoyment of the premises. Here, however, it is probable that the promise by Helga was intended to be a personal obligation of Helga, not touching and concerning the land.

Notice: Jack had no notice of the added clauses and therefore, as assignee, is not subject to them unless notice is *implied.* This five-year lease should have been recorded, but was not. The question does not state whether the copy in the landlord's office, as well as the copy given the tenant, contained the added clauses. The purchaser should make inquiry of the prior landlord, and be deemed to have constructive notice of the leases as they appear in the landlord's office. He may be required to make inquiry of tenants as well, since they are in possession, but the cases differ on whether a purchaser can be a BFP without inquiring of tenants. Here, the apartment house was "large," and inquiry might be an unreasonable burden.

Conclusion: Jack is not liable on the covenant to deliver milk and newspapers because it was a personal promise by Helga.

2. Failure to paint rooms

The kitchen and bathroom were to be painted during the second year of the lease, when Jack owned the building. Does the burden of the covenant run to Jack? The above analysis is applicable to the running of this covenant, except: There seems to be no argument that the parties intended this covenant to be a personal one which would overcome the express language in the lease; and, the covenant touches and concerns because it affects the use and enjoyment of the premises.

If the notice problem can be hurdled, Ike can sue Jack on the covenant to repaint. It was breached while Jack was the landlord. Ike can receive damages from Jack.

3. Failure to replace sink

This covenant was to be performed within the first six months, before Jack took title. This covenant was breached while Helga owned the building, and became a chose in action in Ike. There was no longer any covenant to run with the land. One cannot sue a successor upon an obligation which falls due and is breached during the tenure of a predecessor.

B. Ike vs. Karl

1. Failure to deliver milk and newspapers

Karl is not liable on this covenant for the same reasons Jack is not.

2. Failure to paint rooms and replace sink

Karl is not liable for failure to paint and replace the sink because these obligations fell due and were breached during the tenure of predecessors. Karl is not liable for Jack's failure to repaint during the second year nor for Helga's failure to replace the sink during the first six months.

3. Deterioration

The obligation of the landlord to maintain security was an express obligation in the lease; in addition, the landlord has a legal duty to maintain common areas in a safe condition.

Express obligation in lease: The express obligation in the lease to maintain common areas in safe and sanitary condition affects the use and enjoyment of the property, and touches and concerns. The lease provision binding successors and assigns clearly applies to printed covenants in the leases. Karl had notice of the form lease containing this provision. Therefore, it runs with the land and Karl can be sued on this covenant. If the present conditions are found not to be "safe and sanitary" (a jury question), Karl is liable for damages, and may be enjoined to perform an express covenant. If the covenants are deemed dependent, Ike can rescind the lease. Karl also is liable for personal injuries suffered by Ike if (a jury believes) they resulted from Karl's breach of covenant.

Duty with respect to common areas: Landlord has a duty to maintain common areas, and must take precautions against the foreseeable acts of third parties. This liability is based on tort, not on breach of contract. Whether Ike's personal injuries were foreseeable (numerous crimes and thefts in neighborhood) and whether Karl's precautions were reasonable are questions for the jury, but there is a good case against Karl here, and the modern trend is in Ike's favor.

Implied warranty: Many recent cases have implied a continuing warranty of habitability in urban residential leases. If this were done, Ike might be able to recover for breach if the apartment house violated the city housing code or fell below some other applicable standard of habitability. Using this theory, Ike could possibly have a statutory remedy of paying rent into escrow for repairs in addition to the remedies of damages and rescission. The modern trend again favors Ike.

Covenant of quiet enjoyment: The landlord covenants quiet enjoyment of the premises, which appears to be breached here by failure of the landlord to make the premises safe and by letting them deteriorate substantially below the level at the time of signing the lease. Breach of this covenant may constitute constructive eviction, which permits tenant to rescind lease and move out within a reasonable time.

Conclusion: Using one or more of the above theories, Ike can rescind the lease, recover damages (rent abatement) from Karl, recover damages for personal injuries from Karl, and possibly elect some other statutory remedy.

ANSWER TO SAMPLE EXAM QUESTION IV

What estates were created by deed: The deed executed by Leon granted the city a fee simple determinable, with a purported executory interest in the heirs of Leon. It is an executory interest because it is a future interest following a fee simple, and is created in transferees described as "heirs." The executory interest violates the Rule Against Perpetuities because it is possible for it to become possessory long after lives in being plus twenty-one years. The executory interest is therefore struck out. This does not increase the determinable fee in the city. Since Leon has not granted the entire fee simple, Leon has a possibility of reverter. Upon cessation of park use by the city, title automatically reverts to Leon.

Deed placed in escrow: The deed was placed in escrow with oral instructions to deliver upon deposit of the purchase price within sixty days. There was an underlying written contract of sale; therefore the Statute of Frauds is satisfied. The contract is specifically enforceable, and the escrow is valid. (If there were no underlying written contract, some cases hold that a deposit of a deed in commercial escrow on an oral condition is void—it violates the Statute of Frauds.)

Bandstand destroyed by fire: When the property is destroyed while the deed is in escrow, the majority of courts hold that the risk of loss is on the buyer. Since the contract is specifically enforceable, the doctrine of equitable conversion applies, and the buyer is treated as the owner of the property subject to the seller's lien for the purchase price. If this doctrine is followed, the risk of loss is on the city and it is not entitled to a deduction in the purchase price.

Some courts do not apply equitable conversion, and put the risk of loss on the seller by implying a condition in the contract that the contract is not binding if the building is destroyed. Others put risk of loss on the seller until the buyer takes possession. Under these views, the city's receiving an abatement in the purchase price is somewhat questionable. An abatement might be deemed inconsistent with the theory of implied condition (but granting specific performance without abatement to the buyer is also logically inconsistent with the implied condition, and surely the buyer has this option). More likely, an abatement would be granted if the damage is slight and easily ascertainable and rescission by the seller would be inequitable. It appears here that destruction of a small open bandstand is slight and damages are probably easily ascertainable, and that it would be inequitable to deprive the city of its bargain (*i.e.*, force it either to rescind or take specific performance without abatement). This gives specific relief to the buyer, with damages in the same suit for seller's failure to perform.

Delivery out of escrow: The city took title when the deed was delivered out of escrow with Leon's and the city's consent. By accepting the deed, the city has lost its right to rescind the contract, and the city's only claim now is for abatement in purchase price.

Termination of determinable fee: Upon the city's cessation of park use, the determinable fee will automatically terminate and Leon will have title. Was storage of city trucks cessation of park use? It may be that temporary storage of trucks will not be deemed indicative of intent to cease using the land for a park. The facts are not clear as to whether such use was temporary or as to the extent of land used for storage.

Leon's offer: Leon offered to return the purchase price to the city if the city reconveyed. This is an offer to purchase, which probably expired at Leon's death. Generally, offers cannot be accepted after the death of the offeror; however, since Leon's executor could easily perform, it is not clear that the rule ought to be applied.

Execution of deed from the city to Leon: After Leon's death, the city executed and recorded a deed to Leon. This deed is probably a nullity because Leon is dead and there is no grantee, or it may be invalid for want of delivery. Moreover, if the city's determinable fee has ended, the city has no title to convey. Assuming, however, that the determinable fee has not ended, and that the deed is not a nullity, the city can bring an action to cancel the deed on the ground of failure of consideration (inability of executor to be bound by Leon's offer).

Conclusion

A. **Escrowed funds:** Whether the city is entitled to a portion of the escrowed funds as damages (abatement in purchase price) depends upon whether the risk of loss is on the seller or the buyer in the particular jurisdiction.

The executor should not agree to release the funds because Leon owned the funds (perhaps minus partial abatement). Leon's offer to buy the land ceased at Leon's death.

B. **Land:** Leon's estate owns the land if the city's determinable fee has ended. It looks as if it has, but further development of the facts might indicate there has been no real cessation of park use.

ANSWER TO SAMPLE EXAM QUESTION V

A. **Nell vs. Olga**

This situation is the situation:
Moe to Nell, who does not record.
Moe to Olga, for valuable consideration,
    without actual notice of Moe-Nell deed;
    deed not then recorded.
Nell records her deed.
Olga records her deed.

Who prevails in a quiet title action depends upon whether the jurisdiction has a race, notice, or race-notice statute.

Race statute: If the jurisdiction has a race statute, the person who records first, wins. Nell recorded first. Nell wins.

Notice statute: Under a notice statute, a subsequent purchaser for a valuable consideration without notice prevails over a prior unrecorded instrument. In this case, Olga is a purchaser for value subsequent in time and prevails over Nell if Olga has no notice of the deed to Nell.

Olga has no record notice because the Moe-Nell deed is not recorded. Nor does she have actual knowledge. The only question is: Does she have inquiry notice? She does not have inquiry notice from Nell's possession because Nell is not in possession; the record owner, Moe, is in possession. However, the facts do not state what kind of deed this is from Moe to Olga. It looks like a quitclaim because it says "all my right, title and interest," and nothing is said about warranties. If the deed is a quitclaim, some courts hold it does not put the grantee on inquiry notice; others hold it does put the grantee on inquiry notice. A few courts hold that the grantee under a quitclaim deed cannot be a bona fide purchaser because the grantee takes only the title the grantor had, and in this case the grantor has no title.

If Olga is put on inquiry by the quitclaim, she still prevails, since nothing could be learned from a reasonable inquiry. The conveyance from Moe to Nell is a secret conveyance, and Olga has no reason to suspect Nell has an interest.

Only if this case is in one of those few jurisdictions where a quitclaim grantee cannot be a BFP will Olga lose, assuming a notice statute. Otherwise, Olga wins.

Race-notice: Under a race-notice statute, a subsequent BFP is protected only if she records before the previous instrument is recorded. Olga is protected only if she records before Nell. She did not. Therefore, Nell, prior in time, wins.

Note: It is irrelevant whether Nell pays valuable consideration or not. She is prior in time. It is the subsequent purchaser (Olga) who must pay valuable consideration to be protected. Therefore, the fact that the deed to Nell was to satisfy an antecedent debt is a red herring; Nell would win even if the deed were a gift.

B. Operation of tavern

Moe operated a tavern long before the zoning ordinance took effect, and it was a nonconforming use when the ordinance took effect. It could be argued that it was not a nonconforming use on July 1, 1981, because it was not in use on that day as a tavern. But this argument is very weak. A use is not abandoned unless there is intent to abandon it. A temporary closing while Moe's leg was mending shows no intent to abandon. Similarly, if Moe had closed the tavern for a summer vacation in 1981 there would be no intent to abandon the use. Moreover, even under the ordinance definition of abandonment, which does not mention intent, there has been no abandonment because use did not cease for six months. Therefore, the use was a nonconforming use on July 1, 1981.

Even if by some stretch of reasoning, the use was not nonconforming on July 1, 1981, laches would be a good equitable defense against the city. It brought no action to close down the tavern, which was bought by Olga in 1983. She relied on the existing use and would be greatly harmed by the delayed enforcement by the city.

Nonconforming uses can continue in existence after the zoning ordinance is enacted, unless abandoned. The issue is whether Olga abandoned the use when her liquor license was suspended for six months. This could go either way. Olga would argue that she did not ***intend*** to abandon, and that an "intent" requirement should be read into the ordinance. She will argue that if the intent requirement is not read in the ordinance it is of dubious constitutionality; it may be a taking of her property without compensation. She will argue that she is in the same situation as a person who closed the tavern because of illness for six months, or because a windstorm took the roof off which could not be replaced for six months.

The city will argue that intention is irrelevant, only objective acts count under the ordinance, and that the ordinance is constitutional without an intention requirement. Even if the ordinance would be unconstitutional as applied to persons who had to close involuntarily, the ordinance is not unconstitutional as applied to Olga because the suspension and resulting closure were self-inflicted.

The court may be influenced by the degree of wrongdoing by Olga and the reason for the suspension. If the city's arguments are accepted, the state liquor board has the power to put a tavern owner out of business by suspending the license for six months. The legislature may not have intended to give the board that power, but only the power of temporary suspension. Thus the zoning ordinance might be interpreted in such a manner as to withhold that power from the board. On the other hand, nonconforming uses are not favored and ordinances continuing them are strictly construed. It is difficult to predict the outcome of this case.

ANSWER TO SAMPLE EXAM QUESTION VI

Title to Blackacre: If Peter had a fee simple title at his death, he devised this to Sue. If he only had a life estate, he could not devise this to Sue. The first issue, then, is who had title to Blackacre at Peter's death. The conveyance from Peter to Quincy gave Quincy a fee simple, and the conveyance from Quincy to Peter gave Peter only a life estate unless the Rule in Shelley's Case or the Doctrine of Worthier Title applies. The Rule in Shelley's Case says a conveyance to Peter for life, remainder to Peter's heirs results in Peter, not Peter's heirs, getting the remainder. The remainder merges with Peter's life estate, giving Peter a fee simple. If the Rule is alive in the jurisdiction, Peter had a fee simple, which he devised to Sue. However, the Rule in Shelley's Case has been abolished in a large majority of states, and in those states, Sue would have to pursue other routes.

The Doctrine of Worthier Title is still alive in most states. It provides that a remainder to the grantor's heirs is void, and the grantor has a reversion. If this were applied, Peter would have a life estate and a reversion, which would merge, giving him a fee simple (which he devised to Sue). However, there are two problems here: First, the Doctrine only presumes a reversion, and this presumption can be rebutted by evidence of a contrary intent. Here the evidence shows that Peter wanted to avoid probate of Blackacre. The only way probate could be avoided would be to give Peter's heirs an interest (a remainder) during Peter's life. Therefore, the evidence shows that Peter intended to create a remainder. Second, Peter is not the grantor; Quincy is. However, this problem probably could be circumvented by a court of equity treating Peter as the grantor. Clearly Quincy was only a straw person, not intended to have a beneficial interest. The real grantor was Peter. Sue has a chance of winning on this Doctrine.

A third doctrine, destructibility of contingent remainders, may help Sue. After Quincy conveyed a life estate to Peter with a contingent remainder to Peter's heirs, Quincy had a reversion. By quitclaim, he conveyed this reversion to Peter. The life estate merges into the reversion, destroying the contingent remainder in Peter's heirs, and leaving Peter with a fee simple. Unhappily for Sue, however, destructibility of contingent remainders has been abolished in a large majority of states.

Thus, it is possible that Sue has a fee simple if Shelley's Case or destructibility of contingent remainders is alive. If Worthier Title is still alive, there is also a chance that Sue has a fee simple.

Rights against Rosie: If Peter had only a life estate, he could not lease beyond his death, but of course Sue is not interested if Peter had only a life estate. So assume here that Sue has a fee simple subject to the lease to Rosie.

Destruction of building: The lease contained a covenant that the tenant would repair the premises. The common law rule was that this covenant requires the tenant to rebuild, even if the building is destroyed without fault of the tenant. This is a harsh result, and statutes in several states have changed the rule. Similarly, the majority rule is that destruction of a building without fault of the tenant does not relieve tenant of liability for rent; the tenant has purchased a "leasehold," which has not been destroyed. Statutes in many states have changed this rule too. However, these statutes do not relieve the tenant from liability where the building is destroyed through the tenant's own negligence, and clearly Rosie was negligent here. Therefore, Rosie must rebuild the building and is liable for the rent.

Rosie might be relieved of liability for rebuilding if the word "repair" in the lease were construed not to include "rebuilding," but the majority of courts have rejected this construction.

Upon Rosie's abandonment of the premises, the landlord, Sue, has several remedies: (1) The landlord can **terminate** the lease. In most states, she cannot terminate the lease and receive damages for anticipatory breach, but in some states, she can. (2) The landlord can affirm the lease and **sue for rent** as it comes due. In many states, she has a duty to mitigate damages by finding another tenant and reletting, but it is not clear here that Sue would have a duty to mitigate by finding another tenant for a destroyed building which Rosie has a duty to rebuild, so the duty to mitigate damages, if it exists, may not help Rosie much. (3) The landlord can **repossess and relet** for the tenant's benefit if she gives the tenant notice, though under these facts, there is no building to relet, so this remedy seems inapplicable. In some states if landlord repossesses, she may effect a surrender and termination of the lease, excusing the tenant from further rent liability, if the court finds the landlord so intended. It would be dangerous for Sue to repossess in those states.

Conclusion: If Peter owned a fee simple at death, it passed to Sue by will. Sue has substantial rights against Rosie. Rosie has the duty to rebuild and pay rent for the remainder of the term. It would probably be in Sue's best interest to come to a settlement with Rosie, whereby the lease is terminated and Sue receives damages for anticipatory breach, so Sue can rebuild and make the property productive again.

ANSWER TO SAMPLE EXAM QUESTION VII

1. **Use Restriction**

   What is it? Can the residential use restriction be enforced against Ugo? First, did the deeds to lots 1-5 create a condition with a right of entry in Terry, or a covenant? The language is ambiguous; it speaks of "condition," and says "shall be cause for forfeiture," indicating a right of entry, but also says "may be enjoined," indicating a covenant. A right of entry is not expressly retained, but it will be implied if the language of condition is clear enough. If a right of entry is retained, Terry has the right to enforce the right of entry, not the neighbors. Where there is an ambiguity, the court prefers a covenant construction, to avoid forfeiture, and the neighbors will urge that this is a covenant.

   Creation of covenant: Nowhere is there in writing a restriction imposed on lot 6; the restrictions are imposed on lots 1-5. Therefore, the Statute of Frauds is not complied with, and a real covenant is not created on lot 6. However, in equity, in many but not all states a covenant (equitable servitude) will be implied on lot 6 if the common grantor showed by a scheme an intent to restrict all six lots. Here it looks like a scheme: The first 5 lots sold were restricted. If so, lot 6 is bound by an implied negative reciprocal servitude.

   Does the burden run to Ugo? If a court will imply a negative restriction on lot 6, it will be enforced in equity against Ugo if the parties so intend, if the burden touches and concerns the land, and if Ugo had notice (privity is irrelevant because the case is in equity, and cannot go into law because of the Statute of Frauds). As for intent, the parties did not say it runs to "assigns," but no technical words are necessary; the court will probably infer intent because of the nature of the covenant (to preserve high quality residential use). The restriction touches and concerns the use of the burdened tract. The real problem is ***notice.*** If Ugo had no notice, he is not bound by the servitude.

Ugo would have record notice if in the jurisdiction all deeds out from a common grantor (Terry) are in Ugo's chain of title (*i.e.*, give constructive notice to purchasers of other lots in the subdivision). Courts are split on this issue.

Ugo might be put on inquiry in some jurisdictions by the lay of the land, seeing residences on lots 1-4 (but lot 5 was vacant). If Ugo should reasonably be put on inquiry, he would have to read the deeds of lots 1-4, and would be held to know of the implied reciprocal negative servitude.

Does benefit run to Victor? Victor purchased his land after Ugo. Assuming Ugo's land is bound for benefit of lot 5 at the time Victor purchased, does the benefit run to him? The requirements of intent and touch and concern are met with respect to the benefit end if they are met with respect to the burden end (above).

Is servitude enforceable by owners of lots 1-4? Yes, in most states, either as third party beneficiaries of the implied promise Ugo made at the time of purchase or as beneficiaries of a restriction implied on lot 6 at the time of sale of lots 1-4. Courts are hard put to figure out the theory, but prior purchasers in a subdivision can almost always enforce an implied servitude. The scheme shows the intent of the subdivider to give them this right.

Defenses: Ugo might have the defense of laches, since his discotheque has been going for some time and no one has objected. Or he may argue that conditions have so changed in the neighborhood that the purpose of the restriction cannot be carried out and it would be inequitable to enforce it. The zoning change to commercial is some evidence that conditions have changed with respect to lot 6, but most courts will not allow this defense unless the conditions have changed in the whole restricted area, and lots 1-5 are still zoned residential, indicating residential purposes can still be achieved there. Therefore this defense probably will not help Ugo.

If the zoning ordinance is cumulative, it does not conflict with the private covenant, and the most restrictive use (private covenant) controls. If residences are prohibited in a commercial zone, Ugo has a nonconforming use and can stay. Therefore Ugo has small chance of succeeding in an argument that the rezoning lifted the private restrictions.

2. **Easement**

Ugo can use the easement for access to any development reasonably to be expected by the parties. The neighbors will argue that since lot 6 is restricted to residential use (above), the easement cannot be used for access to a commercial establishment. That is beyond the scope intended by the parties. This issue involves a weighing of the benefit to lot 6 against the burdens to lots 1-5. If the court finds lot 6 is not burdened by a restrictive covenant, then it is not likely to find excessive use of the easement here. But the court might find that lot 6 was burdened, though the burden does not run to Ugo for some reason (probably lack of notice), in which case, the court might find excessive use beyond the intent of the parties (road was to service residences). If this is excessive use, Ugo can be enjoined from using the easement for access by commercial customers.

Ugo has also extended the benefit of the easement to a nondominant parcel, the one-acre parking lot. This is not permitted, and can be enjoined. If the use of the easement to reach lot 6 cannot be separated from its use to reach the nondominant parking lot, the easement will be extinguished. However, if the express easement is extinguished, Ugo has a way of necessity over the same fifteen feet, as he cannot be left landlocked by Terry, the common grantor. Very likely a court would enjoin Ugo from using the easement to permit customers to reach the parking lot.

If Ugo cannot get access to the parking lot by way of the easement, the one-acre parking lot has an easement by necessity over Wayne's sixty acres to reach a public road. It was land-locked by the conveyance from Wayne, so Wayne's land is burdened by the easement. There can be no easement by necessity over the fifteen-foot strip to reach the parking lot since Terry did not landlock the one-acre tract.

3. Nuisance

Mortuaries are very often held to be nuisances in residential areas, and the mortuary use could probably be enjoined by the neighbors. Ugo's defense is that it is permitted by the zoning ordinance. This action might make the use presumptively not a nuisance, but is not conclusive.

The neighbors may also sue in nuisance against the discotheque. The court will weigh the gravity of the harm against the social utility. An important factor is that Ugo came into an established residential area and began his discotheque; his action is harming prior uses. There are not enough facts (amount of noise, traffic, etc.) to make a final determination.

4. Zoning change

The neighbors might attack the commercial rezoning as spot zoning, not in accordance with a comprehensive plan. This depends upon evidence not available here—principally, how much land was rezoned, and what evidence there is of a comprehensive plan. The plan does not have to be in writing, but can consist of policies adhered to by the planning commission. If the neighbors succeeded, this would hurt Ugo's defense to the nuisance action, and prevent mortuary use, not permitted in a residential zone. The discotheque would not violate the zoning ordinance, however, as it was a nonconforming use established before passage of the zoning ordinance.

5. Conclusion

In most states the neighbors can get the discotheque enjoined for violation of the restrictive covenant, but in some a strict view of the Statute of Frauds or a narrow view of what gives notice would bar the neighbors.

The neighbors can enjoin use of the easement to reach the parking lot.

The neighbors can prevent mortuary use either by suing for nuisance or by setting aside the rezoning. They might get an injunction against the discotheque as well, on grounds of nuisance.

TABLE OF CASES

Cox, State v. - §71
Crane Neck Association v. New York City/
    Long Island County Services Group - §1519
Crechale & Polles, Inc. v. Smith - §951
Crimmins v. Gould - §1389
Crosdale v. Lanigan - §1326
Crowell v. McCaffrey - §§1107, 1113
Crowley v. Knapp - §1519
Cushman v. Davis - §1387
Cushman Virginia Corp. v. Barnes - §1388

Darling Shops Delaware Corp. v. Baltimore
    Center Corp. - §946
Dartnell v. Bidwell - §1372
Daugharthy v. Monritt Associates - §1848
Davis v. Smith - §1966
Davis v. Vidal - §1245
Dawley, *In re* Marriage of - §780
DeCicco v. Barker - §216
Dennan v. Searle - §298
Dennison v. State - §1761
D'Ercole v. D'Ercole - §706
Devereux Foundation, Inc., Application of
    - §1699
Dick v. Sears Roebuck & Co. - §1490
Dickhut v. Norton - §1079
Dickson v. Alexandria Hospital, Inc. - §379
Dieffenbach v. McIntyre - §983
Doctor v. Hughes - §546
Doctorman v. Schroder - §1784
Donnelly Advertising Co. v. Flaccomio - §948
Dorsey v. Speelman - §386
Douglass v. Ransom - §1787
Dress Shirt Sales Inc. v. Hotel Martinique
    Associates - §1285
Duke of Norfolk's Case - §605
Dumont v. Kellogg - §1597
Dumpor's Case - §1289
Duncan v. Vassaur - §690
Duncan & Hill Realty, Inc. v. Department of
    State - §1766
Dunn Bros., Inc. v. Lesnewsky - §1315
Durant v. Town of Dunbarton - §1710
Durst v. Daugherty - §2042
Dutcher v. Owens - §856
Dyett v. Pendleton - §1015
Dyste v. Farmers & Mechanics Savings Bank
    - §227

E. A. Stephens & Co. v. Albers - §13
Eads v. Brazelton - §19
Eagle Enterprises, Inc. v. Gross - §1493
Earle v. Fiske - §2008
East Haven Associates v. Gurian - §1002
Eastwood v. Shedd - §2020
Echols v. Olsen - §2085
Eddington v. Turner - §1825
Edwards v. Habib - §§1078, 1082

Eells v. Morse - §990
Eidelman v. Walker & Dunlop, Inc. - §1235
Eliason v. Wilborn - §2082
Elliott v. Joseph - §1169
Elwes v. Brigg Gas Co. - §25
Emery, People v. - §535
Empire State Federal Savings & Loan
    Association v. Wukowitz - §715
Erbach v. Brauer - §1901
Ernst v. Conditt - §1248
Escalera v. New York City Housing Authority -
    §1300
Estancias Dallas Corp. v. Schultz - §1570
Evans v. Abney - §446
Evans, Estate of - §202
Evans v. Holloway Sand & Gravel, Inc. - §1318
Ewing v. Burnet - §§112, 158

Faber v. Creswick - §1110
Failoni v. Chicago & North Western Railway
    - §115
Farkas v. Williams - §§809, 820
Farmers Investment Co. v. Bettwy - §1609
Farnes v. Lane - §1380
Fasano v. Board of County Commissioners
    - §§1641, 1697
Favorite v. Miller - §22
Federated Mortgage Investors v. American
    Savings & Loan Association - §1279
Ferguson v. City of Keene - §§1622, 1623
Ferrell v. Stinson - §1901
Fetting Manufacturing Jewelry Co. v. Waltz -
    §951
Fifty States Management Corp. v. Pioneer
    Auto Parts, Inc. - §1193
Finley v. Teeter Stone, Inc. - §1586
Finn v. Williams - §1352
First National Bank & Trust Co. v. Scott -
    §1925
First National Bank of Oregon v. Townsend -
    §1873
First National Trust & Savings Bank v.
    Raphael - §1412
First Universalist Society v. Boland - §620
First Wisconsin Trust Co. v. L. Wiemann Co. -
    §1236
Fitzstephens v. Watson - §1484
564.54 Acres of Land, United States v. - §1751
Flanagan v. San Marcos Silk Co. - §1410
Fletcher v. Hurdle - §484
Flynn v. City of Cambridge - §864
Foisy v. Wyman - §1037
Foley v. Gamester - §931
Foley v. Smith - §1959
Fontainebleau Hotel Corp. v. Forty-Five
    Twenty-Five, Inc. - §§1544, 1627
Forbis v. Honeycutt - §1764
Foster v. Reiss - §197

Howard D. Johnson Co. v. Parkside
 Development Corp. - §2036
Hudgens v. NLRB - §185
Hudson View Properties v. Weiss - §978
Humber v. Morton - §1977
Hunt Land Holding Co. v. Schramm - §1361
Hunter v. Hunter - §673
Hurd v. Bickford - §247
Hurley v. City of Niagara Falls - §36

Illinois & St. Louis Railroad & Coal Co. v.
 Cobb - §55
In re - *see* name of party
Ingalls v. Hobbs - §1021
Innes v. Potter - §206
Irons v. Smallpiece - §193
Isle Royale Mining Co. v. Hertin - §90

Jaber v. Miller - §1248
Jackson v. O'Connell - §679
Jack Spring, Inc. v. Little - §1211
Jacobs v. Klawans - §1285
Jacobs v. Morand - §1003
Jamaica Builders Supply Corp. v. Buttelman
 - §1202
James v. Valtierra - §1295
Jasperson v. Scharnikow - §120
Javins v. First National Realty Corp. - §§1033,
 1044, 1049, 1062
Jee v. Audley - §627
Jeffries v. Great Western Railway - §51
Jenad, Inc. v. Village of Scarsdale - §1714
Joaquin v. Shiloh Orchards - §135
Johnson v. City of Wheat Ridge - §336
Johnson v. Hendrickson - §754
Johnson v. Johnson - §1915
Johnson v. O'Brien - §§1095, 1098
Johnson v. Whiton - §288
Johnson, State v. - §1671
Johnson, State v. - §2073
Johnston v. Michigan Consolidated Gas Co. -
 §1399
Joiner v. Janssen - §129
Jolliff v. Hardin Cable Television Co. - §1395
Jones v. Mayer - §§958, 976
Jones v. Northwest Real Estate Co. - §1521
Jones v. Taylor - §956
Jordan v. Savage - §1105
Jordan v. Talbot - §§1184, 1223
Joseph H. Reinfeld, Inc. v. Griswold &
 Bateman - §83
Joslin v. Pine River Development Corp. - §1520
Joy v. Daniels - §1301
Just v. Marinette County - §§1671, 1730
Justice Court Mutual Housing Cooperative v.
 Sandow - §876

Kaiser-Aetna v. United States - §1720

Kanefsky v. Dratch Construction Co. - §1389
Kanelos v. Kettler - §1115
Kasten Construction Co. v. Maple Ridge
 Construction Co. - §1783
Keeble v. Hickeringill - §10
Kell v. Bella Vista Village Property Owners
 Association - §1495
Kelly v. Schmelz - §1383
Kemery v. Mylroie - §1309
Kennedy v. Kidd - §1135
Kenney v. Morgan - §1523
Kentucky Department of Highways v. Sherrod -
 §1171
Keppell v. Bailey - §1446
Kergald v. Armstrong Transfer Express Co. -
 §88
Kern, Estate of - §545
Kerwin v. Donaghy - §832
Killam v. March - §2083
Kindred v. Crosby - §2038
King v. Cooney-Eckstein Co. - §1136
King v. Dunham - §552
King v. Greene - §710
King v. Moorehead - §§1040, 1055
King v. Wenger - §1769
Kleinberg v. Heller - §677
Kline v. 1500 Massachusetts Avenue
 Apartment Corp. - §1108
Knight v. Knight - §699
Knowles v. Gilchrist Co. - §83
Knudson v. Weeks - §1970
Koenig v. Van Reken - §1841
Kohn, Estate of - §677
Kohn, *In re* Estate of - §233
Konantz v. Stein - §2080
Kost v. Foster - §§483, 487, 492
Kotrich v. County of DuPage - §1702
Kramer v. Mobley - §1804
Krieger v. Pacific Gas & Electric Co. - §1384
Krzewinski v. Eaton Homes, Inc. - §1349
Kuehne v. City of East Hartford - §1694
Kulawitz v. Pacific Woodenware & Paper Co.
 - §1017

Laguna Royale Owners Association v. Darger
 - §860
Lake Country Estates, Inc. v. Tahoe Regional
 Planning Agency - §1726
Langer v. Planning and Zoning Commission
 - §1694
Larkins v. Howard - §2038
LaSalle County Carbon Coal Co. v. Sanitary
 District of Chicago - §55
Lauderbaugh v. Williams - §404
Laura v. Christian - §750
Lawrence v. Fox - §1508
Lawyers Title Insurance Corp. v. McKee -
 §2098

Miller v. Lutheran Conference & Camp
Association - §1395
Miller v. Race - §238
Miller v. Riegler - §§659, 676
Miller v. Schoene - §1731
Miller, State v. - §1664
Miller, State *ex rel.* v. Manders - §1715
Mills v. Damson Oil Corp. - §2016
Mills, Matter of - §§200, 211
Millwright v. Romer - §638
Minneapolis Athletic Club v. Cohler - §1333
Minonk State Bank v. Grassman - §681
Mister Donut of America, Inc. v. Kemp - §2036
Mitchell v. Castellaw - §§1315, 1351
Mitchell v. W. T. Grant Co. - §1182
Monroe v. Rawlings - §§111, 145
Moore v. City of East Cleveland - §§1643, 1674
Moore v. Phillips - §387
Morgan v. High Penn Oil Co. - §1543
Morris v. Austraw - §1152
Morris v. Nease - §1526
Morris v. Ulbright - §365
Morrison, United States v. - §35
Morse v. Aldrich - §1447
Morse v. Curtis - §2052
Mortensen v. Lingo - §2013
Moses Bros. v. Johnson - §1815
Mountain Brow Lodge No. 82 v. Toscano - §410
Mowatt v. 1540 Lake Shore Drive - §872
Mugaas v. Smith - §2006

National Audubon Society v. Superior Court -
§1593
National Land & Investment Co. v. Kohn
(Easttown Township Board) - §1676
Nectow v. City of Cambridge - §1639
Neponsit Property Owners Association v.
Emigrant Industrial Savings Bank -
§§1455, 1469, 1495, 1499
Newell v. National Bank of Norwich - §190
Newells v. Carter - §§120, 139
Newman v. Bost - §202
Newman v. Chase - §711
Newman v. Dore - §835
New York-Kentucky Oil & Gas Co. v. Miller -
§165
Nicholson v. Connecticut Half-Way House -
§1546
Nicholson v. 300 Broadway Realty Corp. -
§1493
Niernberg v. Feld - §1782
Nisbett & Potts' Contract, *In re* (1905) - §178
Nisbett & Potts' Contract, *In re* (1960) - §1486
Nogarr, People v. - §684
Nols' Estate, *In re* - §188
Noone v. Price - §§1582, 1583
North Shore Steak House, Inc. v. Board of
Appeals of Thomaston - §1702

Northwest Real Estate Co. v. Serio - §403
Northwest Realty Co. v. Jacobs - §1333

O'Callaghan v. Waller & Beckwith Realty Co.
- §1119
O'Conner v. Clark - §243
O'Connor v. Village Green Owners Association
- §977
O'Keeffe v. Snyder - §182
Oak's Oil Service, Inc. v. Massachusetts Bay
Transportation Authority - §442
Oldfield v. Stoeco Homes, Inc. - §§333, 335
Old Line Life Insurance Co. v. Hawn - §1176
Oliver v. Hewitt - §1490
165 Broadway Building, Inc. v. City Investing
Co. - §1451
Opinion of the Justices - §773
Orange & Rockland Utilities, Inc. v. Philwold
Estates - §1449
Orange County Taxpayers Council, Inc. v. City
of Orange - §1132
Osborne v. Hewitt - §1529
Osin v. Johnson - §2023
Othen v. Rosier - §1353
Ottavia v. Savarese - §118
Overton Farms, Ltd., Attorney General v. - §26
Owen v. City of Independence - §1726
Owens v. Sun Oil Co. - §203

Pace v. Culpepper - §631
Packard-Bamberger & Co. v. Maloof - §1261
Pai, State *ex rel.* v. Thom - §1909
Paine v. Meller - §1817
Pakenham's Case - §1451
Palmer v. Flint - §673
Palmer v. Palmer - §§1355, 1357
Paradine v. Jane - §1156
Park Enterprises, Inc. v. Trach - §234
Parker & Edgarton v. Foote - §1373
Parking Management, Inc. v. Gilder - §65
Parr v. Worley - §1894
Paset v. Old Orchard Bank & Trust Co - §34
Patterson v. Bryant - §2009
Patterson v. Reigle - §118
Patton v. United States - §1141
Pearson v. Gardner - §1778
Peet v. Roth Hotel Co. - §§72, 79
Pendergast v. Aiken - §1615
Pendoley v. Ferreira - §1538
Penfield v. Jarvis - §757
Penn Bowling Recreation Center, Inc. v. Hot
Shoppes, Inc. - §1389
Penn Central Transportation Co. v. City of New
York - §§1669, 1735, 1736, 1737
Pennsylvania Coal Co. v. Mahon - §§1732,
1733, 1734, 1735, 1737, 1738, 1739
Pennsylvania Natural Weather Association
v. Blue Ridge Weather Modification
Association - §1629

Sechrest v. Safiol - §1773
Sellers v. Contino - §1183
Shamrock Hilton Hotel v. Caranas - §§82, 86
Shanks v. Floom - §1363
Shaughnessy v. Eidsmo - §1775
Shaw, State v. - §9
Shay v. Penrose - §1814
Shelley v. Kraemer - §§407, 444, 863, 1082
Shelley v. Shelley - §829
Sheridan Suzuki, Inc. v. Caruso Auto Sales - §239
Shirokow, People v. - §1604
Shotwell v. Transamerica Title Insurance Co. - §2093
Shroyer v. Shroyer - §1901
Siferd v. Stambor - §1315
Sigrol Realty Corp. v. Valcich - §1175
Sigsbee Holding Corp. v. Canavan - §1139
Simis v. McElroy - §§97, 1790
Skelly Oil Co. v. Ashmore - §1822
Skendzel v. Marshall - §§1810, 1839
Slate v. Boone County Abstract Co. - §1998
Smith v. Fay - §1912
Smith v. Hadad - §1894
Smith v. Lewis - §792
Smith v. McEnany - §995
Smith v. Stanolind Oil & Gas Co. - §1600
Smith v. Warr - §1803
Smith's Estate - §219
Snow v. Van Dam - §§1499, 1510
Solberg v. Robinson - §1964
Somerville v. Jacobs - §92
Sommer v. Kridel - §1230
South Staffordshire Water Co. v. Sharman - §§20, 24
Southern Burlington County NAACP v. Township of Mount Laurel (Mount Laurel I) - §1678
Southern Burlington County NAACP v. Township of Mount Laurel (Mount Laurel II) - §1678
Southern California Edison Co. v. Bourgerie - §1531
Southern Title Guaranty Co. v. Prendergast - §2102
Southwest Weather Research, Inc. v. Rounsaville - §1629
Spencer's Case - §§1443, 1445, 1447
Sprague v. Kimball - §1480
Spring Valley Development, In re - §1671
Spur Industries, Inc. v. Del E. Webb Development Co. - §§1565, 1574
St. Louis County National Bank v. Fielder - §1907
Stadium Apartments, Inc., United States v. - §1842
Standard Oil Co. v. Buchi - §1313
State v. - see name of party

State Street Bank & Trust Co. v. Beale - §2081
Stein-Sapir v. Stein-Sapir - §777
Stevenson's Estate, In re - §202
Stewart v. Childs Co. - §1013
Stewart v. Lawson - §1014
Stockdale v. Yerden - §1399
Stoller v. Doyle - §§505, 589
Stone v. Duvall - §1912
Stone v. French - §2004
Stoner v. Zucker - §1324
Storke v. Penn Mutual Insurance Co. - §§331, 332
Stover, People v. - §1661
Stoyanoff, State ex rel. v. Berkeley - §1662
Stratton v. Mt. Hermon Boy's School - §1590
Stroh & Sons, Inc. v. Batavia Homes & Development Corp. - §2035
Strong v. Whybark - §2039
Strong v. Wood - §785
Stroup v. Conant - §1155
Sullivan v. Burkin - §832
Sullivan v. Little Hunting Park - §961
Sun Oil Co. v. Trent Auto Wash, Inc. - §1483
Suttle v. Bailey - §1513
Suydam v. Jackson - §§387, 1134
Svoboda v. Johnson - §1376
Swann v. Gastonia Housing Authority - §1300
Swartzbaugh v. Sampson - §685
Sweeney v. Sweeney - §1909
Sweney Gasoline & Oil Co. v. Toledo, Peoria & Western Railroad - §1119
Sybert v. Sybert - §534
Sylvania Electric Products, Inc. v. City of Newton - §1705
Symson v. Turner - §601

Takacs v. Takacs - §1909
Taltarum's Case - §361
Tapscott v. Cobbs - §50
Taylor v. Wallace - §1973
Tenhet v. Boswell - §687
Teodori v. Warner - §§1018, 1057
Theobald v. Satterthwaite - §66
Thomas v. Williams - §1906
Thompson v. Baxter - §932
Thompson, In re Estate of - §235
Thompson v. Shoemaker - §1007
Thornburg v. Port of Portland - §1622
Thornton, State ex rel. v. Hay - §1378
Thorpe v. Housing Authority - §1299
Threatt v. Rushing - §736
Thruston v. Minke - §1269
Tillman v. Wheaton-Haven Recreation Association - §968
Titusville Trust Co. v. Johnson - §188
Todd v. Krolick - §1321
Toland v. Corey - §2032
Totten, Matter of - §225

INDEX

note, §1828
purchase money, §1834
severance of joint tenancy, §§682-684
title theory, §§1843-1844
transfer by mortgagee, §§1851-1853
transfer of mortgagor's interest, §§1845-1850
  assumption of mortgage, §§1847-1848
  subject to mortgage, §§1845-1846

N

NAVIGATIONAL SERVITUDE, §1618
NUISANCE, §§1533-1579
coming to the nuisance, §1550
economic analysis, §§1553-1568. *See also* Economic
    analysis
  coase theorem, §§1557-1558
  externalities, §1556
  free ride problem, §1560
  holdout problem, §1559
  strategic behavior, §1561
  taking, §1573
overflights, §§1623-1626
private, §§1534-1575
public, §§1576-1579
remedies, §§1569-1575
trespass, distinguished from, §§1551-1552
utility of conduct, §1537
value of conflicting uses, §1549
zoning, §§1548, 1579

O

OFFICIAL MAPS, §§1715-1716
OIL AND GAS LEASES, §896
OUSTER, §§725-729
OVERFLIGHTS
See Airspace
OWELTY, §753

P

PART PERFORMANCE, §§1774-1780
PARTITION
See Co-tenancies
PERIODIC TENANCIES
See Landlord and tenant
PERPETUITIES
See Rule Against Perpetuities
POLICE POWER
See Eminent domain; Zoning
POSSESSION
See also Adverse possession
constructive, §4
defined, §§1-3
finders, §§15-36
remedies, §§37-61
wild animals, §§6-13
POSSIBILITY OF REVERTER, §§324, 434-439
alienability, §§436-438
creation, §435
PRESCRIPTION
easements, §§1358-1378, 1387
PRIOR APPROPRIATION DOCTRINE, §§1602-1604,
    1611
PROFITS
divisibility, §1396
easements, distinguished from, §§1317, 1396
minerals in place, §1317
PUBLIC HOUSING, §§1083, 1293-1302

PUBLIC USE
See Eminent domain

Q

QUANTUM OF ESTATES, §287
QUASI-EASEMENT
See Easements
QUIA EMPTORES, STATUTE, §261
QUITCLAIM DEED, §1239

R

RACIAL RESTRICTIONS
Civil Rights Act of 1866, §§958-961
covenants, enforceability, §§407, 444, 862-863
Fair Housing Act of 1968, §§862, 962-965, 1681, 1683
REAL COVENANTS
affirmative and negative, §1418
benefit runs without privity, §§1437-1441
burden running requirements, §§1432-1436
change in neighborhood, §1529
compete, covenant not to, §§1490-1492
condemnation, effect on, §§1531-1532
conditions, distinguished from, §§1426-1427
creation, §§1429-1430
defined, §1420
easements, distinguished from, §1425
equitable servitudes, distinguished from, §1424
liability of promisor after assignment, §§1458-1460
privity of estate, §§1444-1455
  horizontal privity, §§1445, 1451
  vertical privity, §1452
real covenant, §§1420-1421
record notice, §2027
remedies for breach, §1419
running with the land, §§1423, 1432-1441
  intention of parties, §1442
  necessity of "assigns," §1443
  privity of estate, §§1444-1455
  Spencer's Case, Rule in, §1443
  Statute of Frauds, §1429
  third party beneficiary, §1516
termination, §§1524-1532
touch and concern requirements, §1456
RECORDING SYSTEM, §§1984-2069
acknowledgment requirement, §§1863-1865, 2011,
    2015-2016
adverse possession, §176
bona fide purchaser, §§2017-2019
  consideration, §§2037-2042
chain of title, §§2043-2054
constructive notice, §§2027-2036
  inquiry notice, §§2028-2037
  record notice, §2027
creditors, protection of, §§2021-2024
defects in, §§2055-2069
estoppel by deed, §§2048-2051
failure to record, §§2007-2009
grantor-grantee index, §§1990, 1994-1998
how to search title, §§1992-1998
index, failure to, §2013
inquiry notice, §§2028-2037
quitclaim deed, §2029
shelter rule, §2019
tract index, §§1991, 1993
types of recording statutes, §§1999-2002
  notice, §2001
  race, §2000

Z